HOW TO DRAW AND PAINT

ANATOMY

ALL NEW 2ND EDITION

CREATING LIFELIKE HUMANS
AND REALISTIC ANIMALS

The Editors of
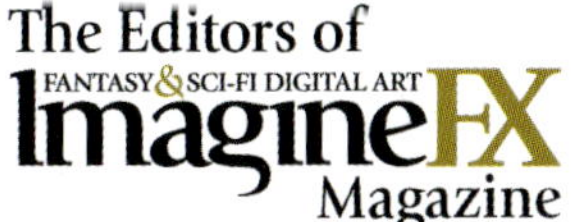

Magazine

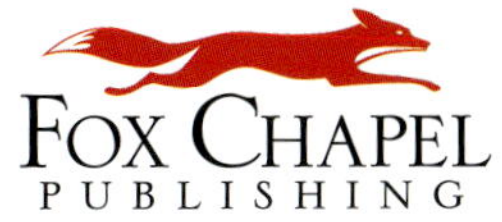

Published by Fox Chapel Publishing, 903 Square Street, Mt. Joy, PA, 17552

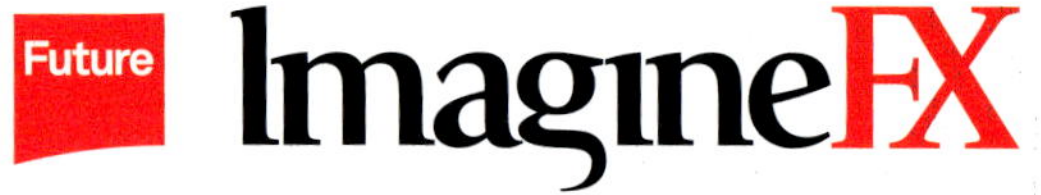

For more information about this and other Bookazines published by the Future plc group, go to *http://www.futureplc.com*.

ISBN 978-1-56523-966-1

The Cataloging-in-Publication Data is on file with the Library of Congress.

To learn more about the other great books from Fox Chapel Publishing, or to find a retailer near you, call toll-free 800-457-9112 or visit us at *www.FoxChapelPublishing.com*.

We are always looking for talented authors. To submit an idea, please send a brief inquiry to acquisitions@foxchapelpublishing.com.

Printed in China
Second printing

Welcome to

HOW TO DRAW AND PAINT ANATOMY

Art has taken many forms over the years, but nothing quite compares to holding a pencil in your hand and drawing the different aspects of arguably one of the greatest pieces of art in the world – the human body. From the muscles that make up our anatomy, to the very hands that we create art with, we aim to teach and inspire you with a plethora of imaginative tutorials. In this new edition of *How to Draw and Paint Anatomy*, you'll find plenty of creative projects to help you get to grips with your artistic capabilities, plus wealth of information contained within these pages. Not to mention the free online resources, including workshops, brushes, and more!

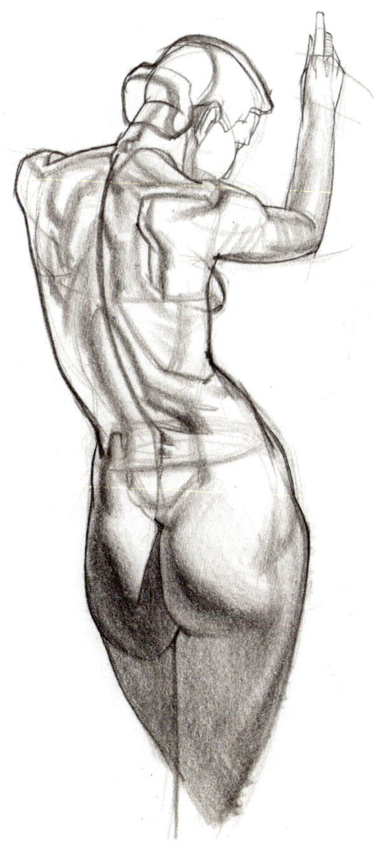

Contents

Learn to draw human and animal anatomy

Drawing anatomy

Muscle anatomy

Movement anatomy

Animal anatomy

Digital art

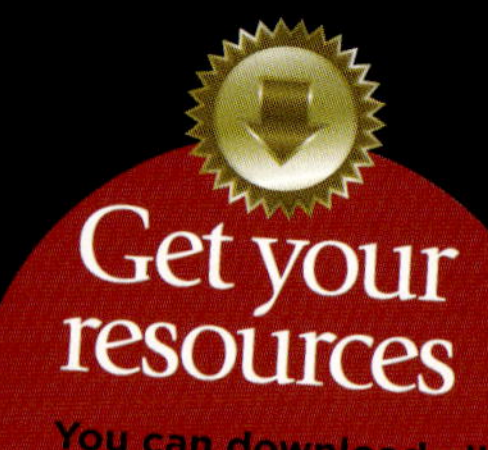

Get your resources

You can download all the workshop images and video files from this special book.

Contents

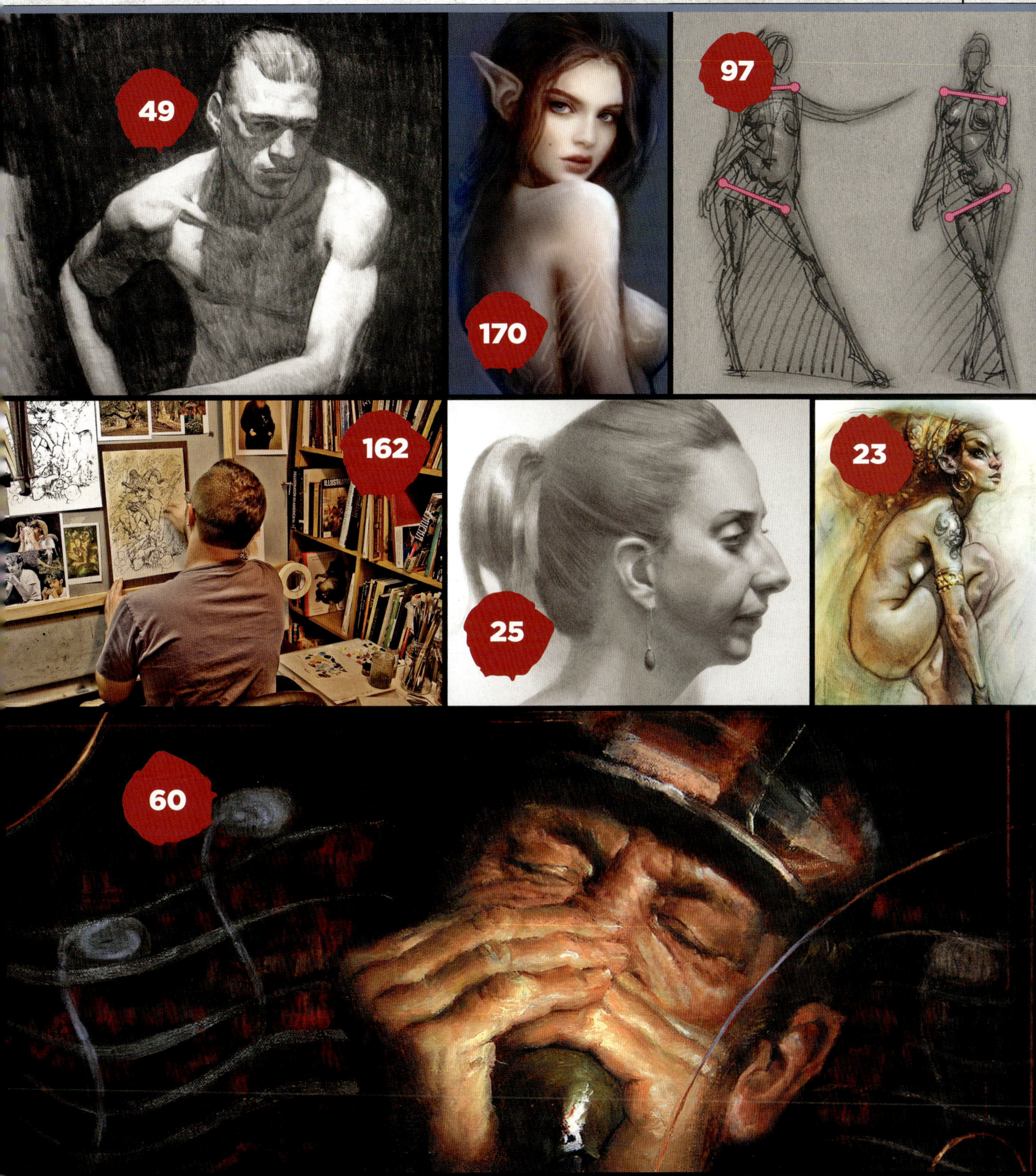

Drawing anatomy

Learn the simple shapes, forms, and structures to understand how to draw the human figure

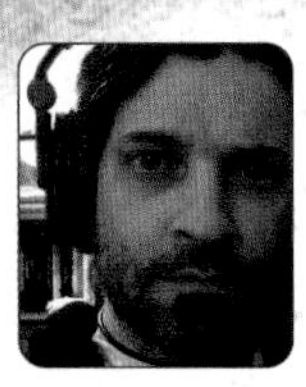

"It's important to understand how to draw the human figure, both in a static pose and in action."
(Ron Lemen, page 8)

Workshops

How to draw the human anatomy

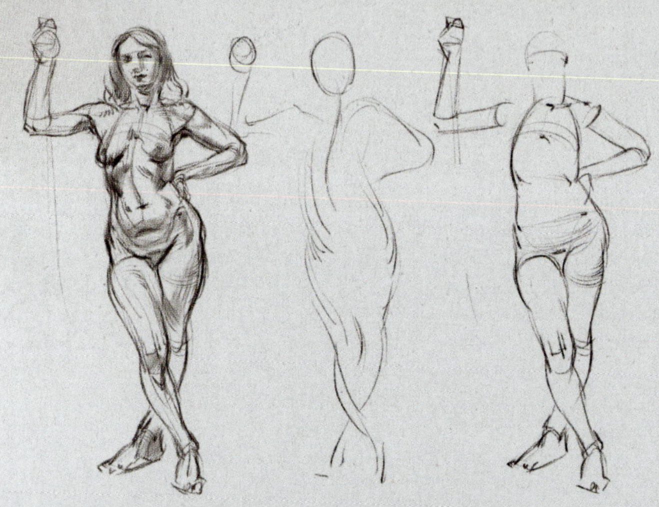

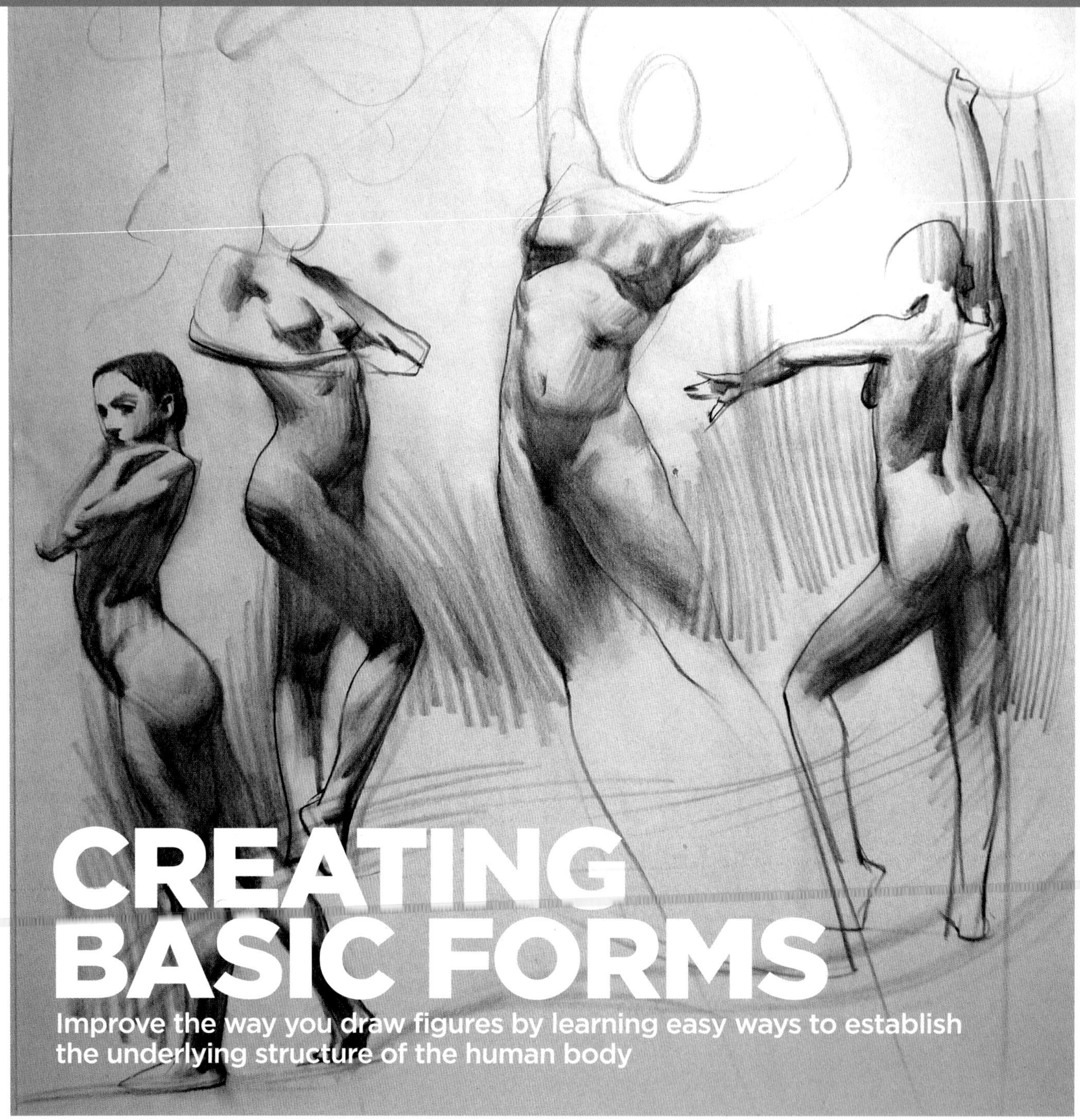

CREATING BASIC FORMS

Improve the way you draw figures by learning easy ways to establish the underlying structure of the human body

If you want to illustrate stories or book covers, design conceptually for games, or draw storyboards, it's vital to grasp the foundations of representational art. With most stories you'll want to involve people; it's key to understand how to draw the human figure, in a static pose and in action.

There are several techniques for drawing the human body, all leading to a similar goal: a three-dimensional, realistic figure. While it's not necessary to be an expert on anatomy to produce illustrations, the more knowledge you have, the easier it will be to solve problems and reach clear-cut solutions for any drawing you make.

What you lack in the foundations of your knowledge will show up in your work – in other words, the lack of understanding of certain key principles will be all too apparent in your finished piece. An artist's style can be reflective of a lack of understanding just as much as it can be a showcase for the total sum of his or her knowledge. Avoid that trap.

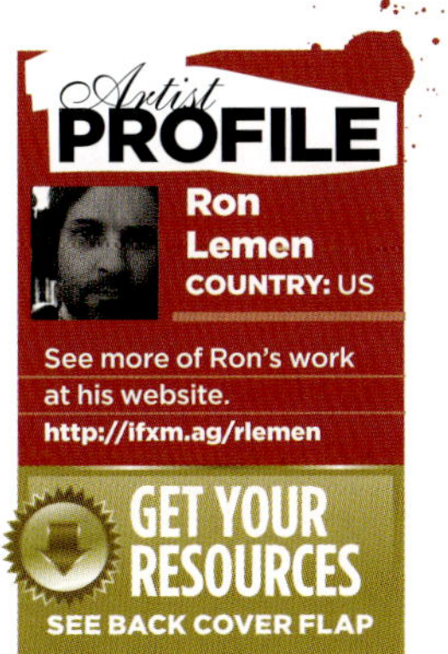

Figuring it out: two ways to draw

There are two distinct approaches to figure drawing: observational and formulaic. It pays to master both...

Learning to draw the human form can be a daunting prospect for any fledgling artist. Therefore, it's important to know what methods are available to you. The two approaches to figure drawing that I feel to be distinct are the observational approach and the formulaic approach.

Observational drawing has its origins in the sight-size methodology, which trains the eye to view a subject with accuracy, placing the object and the drawing side by side for comparative analysis. Plumb lines, levels, a fixed point, and a measuring line are used to help the artist in understanding dimensional and spatial measuring.

Observational drawing is a complex process that requires a great deal of reference material to accompany the words to be fully explained. In this part of our anatomy workshop, I'm going to take a detailed look at two of my favored methods of formulaic drawing.

Formulaic figure drawing uses abstract rhythms or interlocking shapes – basically design concepts – to build on. Once these formulas are memorized by drawing from life, you have a set of tools to recall, enabling you to design from your imagination if you wish.

It's important to have a solid understanding of both approaches if you truly want to be free as an artist. Observational drawing sharpens the eye and mind to capturing a likeness without using abstract concepts; formulaic drawing gives you a set of tools to develop both from life and, more importantly, from your mind's eye.

Observational drawing in practice: using a pencil to measure the body's dimensions.

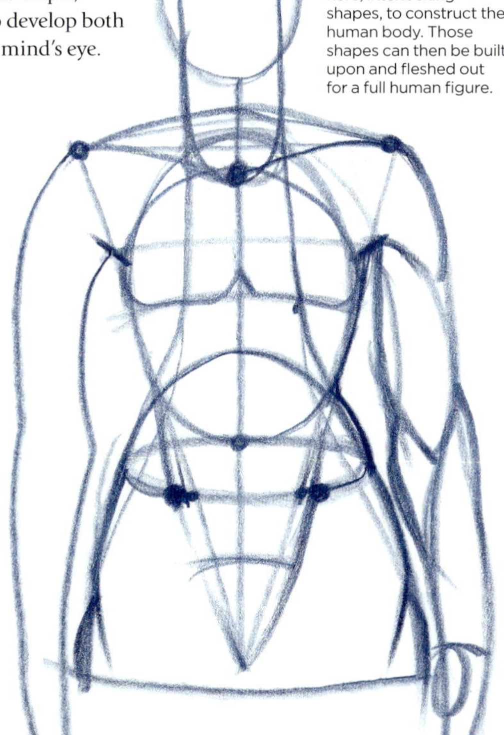

Formulaic figure drawing systems involve using abstract rhythms or, as shown here, interlocking shapes, to construct the human body. Those shapes can then be built upon and fleshed out for a full human figure.

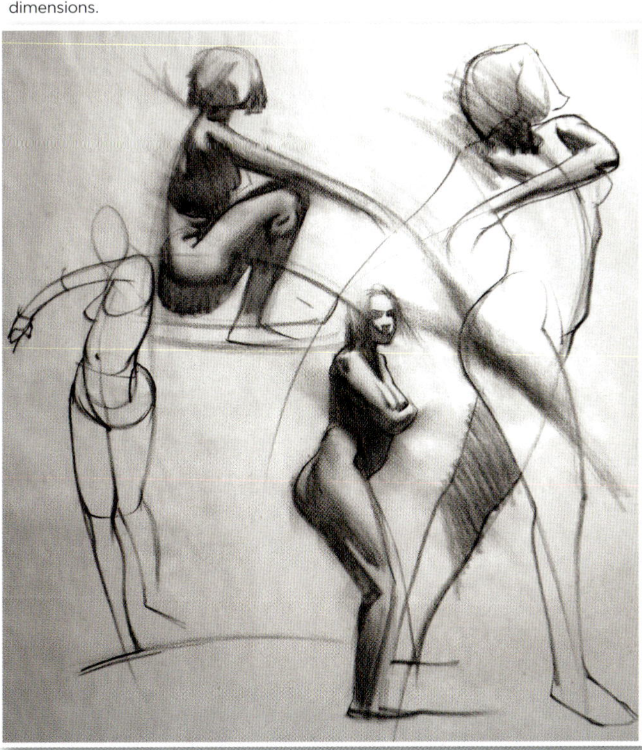

1. REILLY'S SIX LINES TO THE TORSO

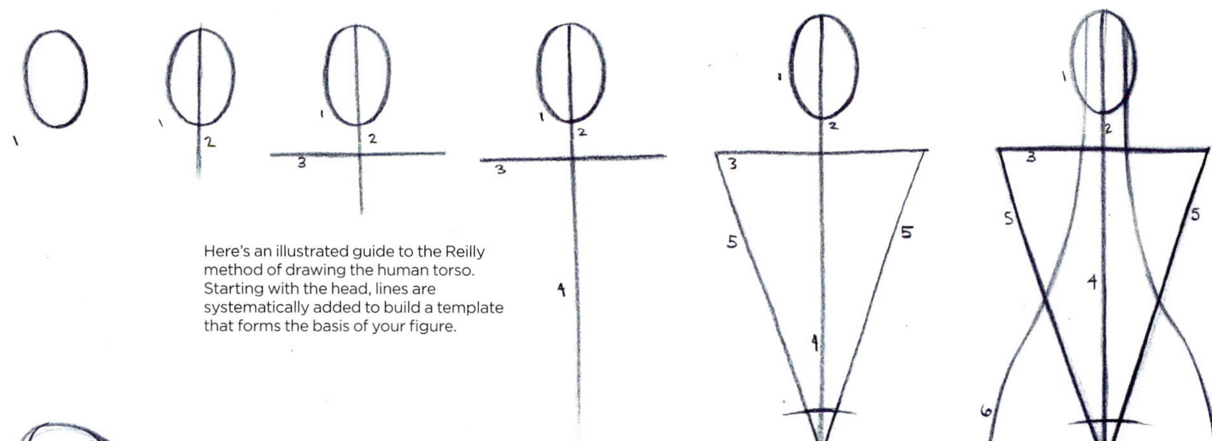

Here's an illustrated guide to the Reilly method of drawing the human torso. Starting with the head, lines are systematically added to build a template that forms the basis of your figure.

Exploring the Reilly method for figures

In this drawing system, you build a framework of overlapping lines to create the basis of your figure

There are as many ways to construct a human figure as there are artists, but two systems in particular form the basis of many artists' working practices. On pages 12 and 13, you'll explore the Industrial Design method; but first, let's look at the Reilly method.

Frank Reilly was an illustrator and instructor in the early and mid-20th century. He created a system of teaching that enabled students to quickly and easily digest the problems of drawing and painting, giving abstract concepts labels and definable schematics, and building a noteworthy step-by-step course of action to create figure drawings.

His system came from several sources, starting with Dean Cornwell and Frank Brangwyn, as well as George Bridgeman (one of Reilly's teachers) and Frank Vincent DuMond. Frank Reilly's system became a fashionable method in most of the American art schools of his day. His figure drawing approach is a linear one, starting with the structure of the figure before advancing on to the anatomy, then shading and finally detailing. His approach started with the core of the figure: the torso.

Capturing the action of the pose is probably the most important concern. The action begins with the head and radiates through the spine into the limbs.

To start the drawing, you need to make six lines: the head; the center of the head and neck; the shoulder line; the spine; the line relating the shoulders to the base of the pelvis; and, finally, the line showing the neck and hip relationship. These lines design and define the core of the pose.

Once you've learned the Reilly method, you can go on to create figures in a range of different poses. In this sketch of a kneeling woman, you can still see the construction lines, based on the sequence above.

"Frank Reilly's figure drawing approach is a linear one, starting with the structure of the figure and advancing on to the anatomy."

Arms and legs

Once the core of the pose is established, the arms and legs are attached to complete the action.

This simple construction creates the structure of the pose. The anatomy is then depicted within the structure you've created.

Muscles are woven like a fabric to the skeleton, connected to the bones with tendons

Capturing the action of the character's pose should be foremost in your mind. The action begins with the head and radiates from there.

– rope-like attachments. The point where the tendon attaches to the bone is defined as the insertion point. The figure abstraction helps place the major muscle groups into an organized and fluid pattern, making it quite simple to invent complex, realistic-looking figures.

The head has its own set of abstractions that requires a workshop of its own to fully understand. We look at techniques for drawing the head later in this book.

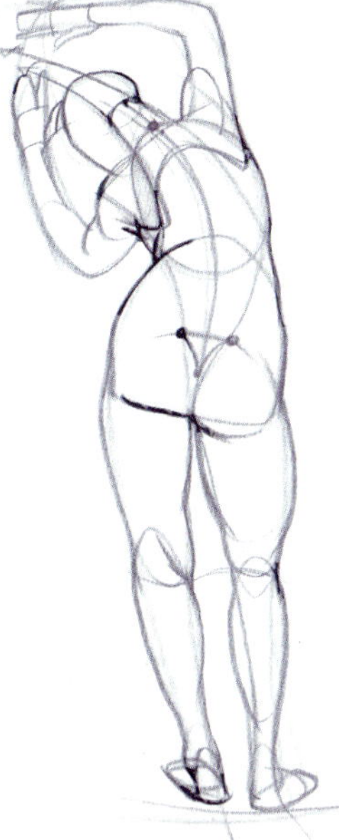

The body's anatomy is designed into the structure you create, weaving in muscles and tendons and gradually building up details.

Beyond Reilly

The fundamentals of the Reilly method are easy to grasp, but it's flexible enough to adapt as your drawing skills develop. Once you properly understand the figure abstraction underpinning the system, you'll find that you'll constantly change and rearrange lines to suit every pose and every situation. The standard set of lines you start with are charts for learning – they're just one set of possibilities, a stock vocabulary that will constantly flex, grow, and reinvent itself with each new image you create.

> "It's important to practice as much as possible, so that you can perform with clarity."

I cannot stress enough that this is just a system to learn from. All systems of drawing are designed for teaching and should be left behind as soon as they're mastered, like training wheels. Too many carefully followed rules can lead to pictorial sterility. It's very important that you train and practice as much as possible until the rules become background noise, so that when we perform, we can do so with total clarity and focus on the more important aspects of making a picture – the story content and the pictorial intent.

If you really do want to do some additional research on the Reilly method, then I recommend that you look up the work of Andrew Loomis, a famous mid-20th century American illustrator who covers some of these principles in his figure drawing manuals, and offers a great many useful techniques for other artists.

rhythm lines are a continuous thought! DON'T DRAW THE LEFT THEN THE RIGHT, DRAW IT ALL AT ONCE!

As you construct your figure, try to use long, flowing lines so that the drawing starts to feel alive, even at this early stage.

2. USE LANDMARKS TO FIND YOUR WAY AROUND THE HUMAN BODY

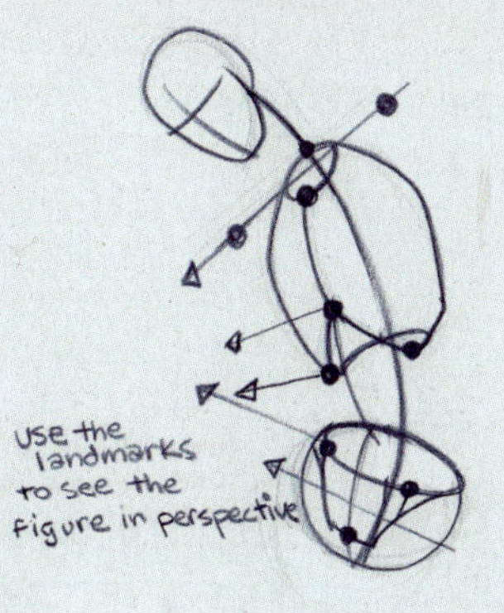

Once you've learned the Reilly method of creating a figure, you can move on to creating more flexible figures and poses from different angles. Here, I point out a few anatomical landmarks to help. Online are three videos, each on creating a figure from various viewpoints.

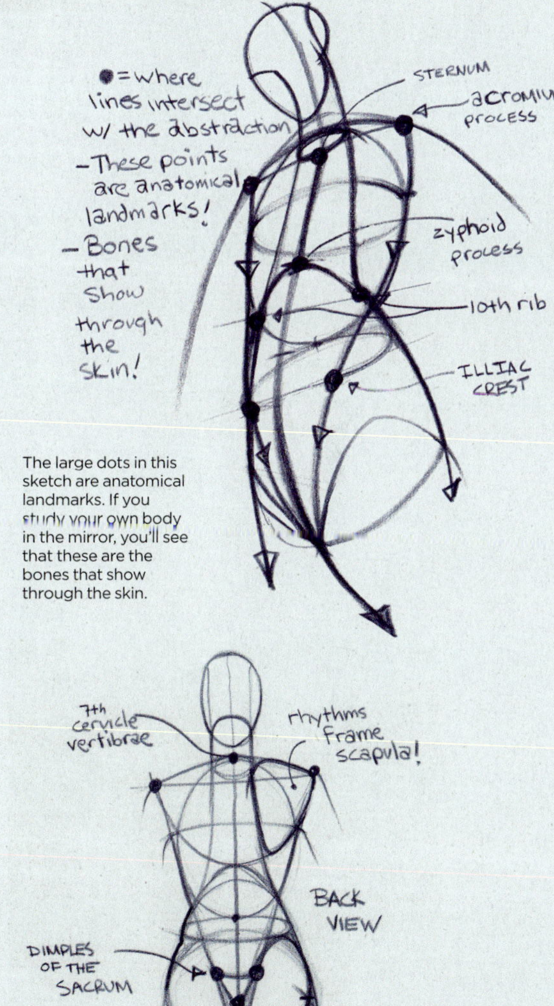

The large dots in this sketch are anatomical landmarks. If you study your own body in the mirror, you'll see that these are the bones that show through the skin.

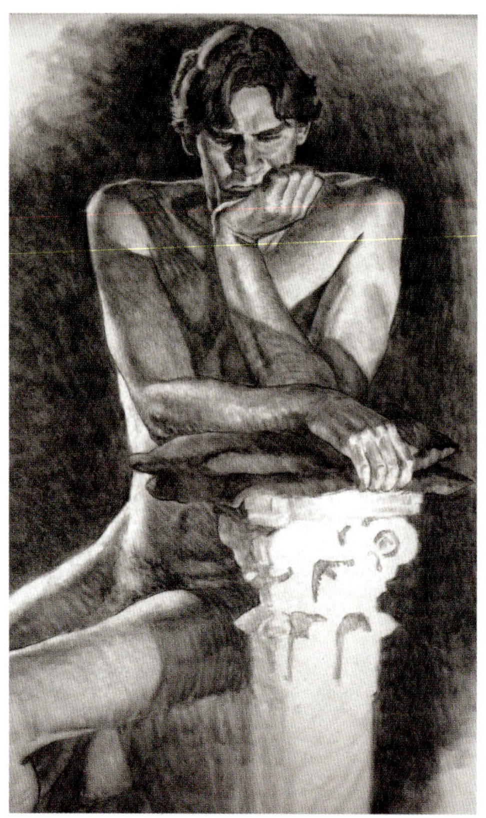

Exploring the Industrial Design drawing method

Use basic geometric shapes to make your figures feel solid and three-dimensional

3. DRAWING CYLINDER FIGURES IN GESTURE POSES

Here I'm going to look at a second abstract approach to figure drawing: the Industrial Design method. Its origins are age-old, but it was perfected at the Art Center of Pasadena in the 1950s.

I find Industrial Design the most practical technique to use when creating the figure for any purpose. It makes it easy to control the pose and achieve convincing foreshortening painlessly.

First, you need to sort the head, neck, and shoulders. These provide a starting point to build the figure gesture from. Viewed from the front, the head is an oval shape, while in profile or side view it's a bloated triangular form. The corners of the triangle depict the tilt of the head.

The panel below shows some examples of cylinder figures in gesture poses, which is what you have to find next. The gesture of the pose is a fluid, flowing line: it's the big sweeping movement that's made between the upper and the lower halves of the body. It should be graceful, and is ideally established in one or two curvy lines. Add to your first line a second line, which describes the width of the pose. This helps establish the overall volume of the figure – heavy or lean. These two lines should mirror each other, moving in relationship to one another. Line three is the centerline of the pose, attached to the pit of the neck.

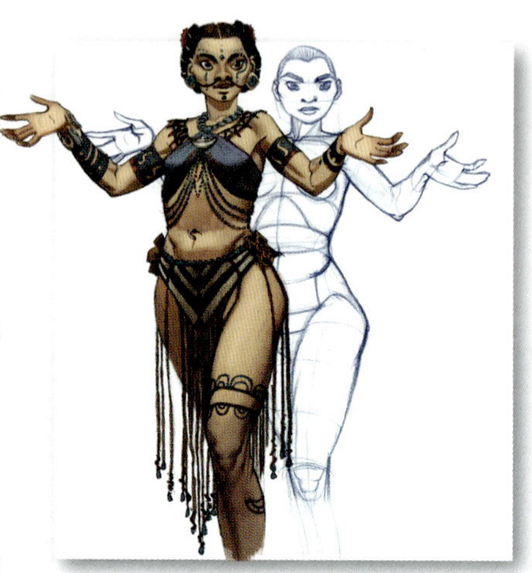

This cartoon character is fully realized using the shape design approach from life drawing. The technique can be used for any figure.

With a centerline drawn, you can now draw an ellipse or oval. This describes the depth of the form. The centerline gives you another point you can now convincingly attach the oval to, turning your three lines into an active cylindrical form.

Cylinders are easier to draw than a cube form, as you need to know perspective to make cubes look convincing. Cylinders, if drawn correctly in perspective, give the viewer a strong sense of position in space.

The shoulders are the top point of the cylinder, the pelvis its bottom. The pelvis varies in shape depending on what character you're drawing. It can be drawn as a soft, sphere-like shape – think of it as a marshmallow – or can be more defined.

The gender of your subject determines the shape of their pelvis. Female pelvises are more bell- or skirt-shaped, whereas male pelvises are much more box-shaped. The front of the pelvis terminates in a bullet-like shape. This is drawn inside of the body cylinder shape, cutting in in order to

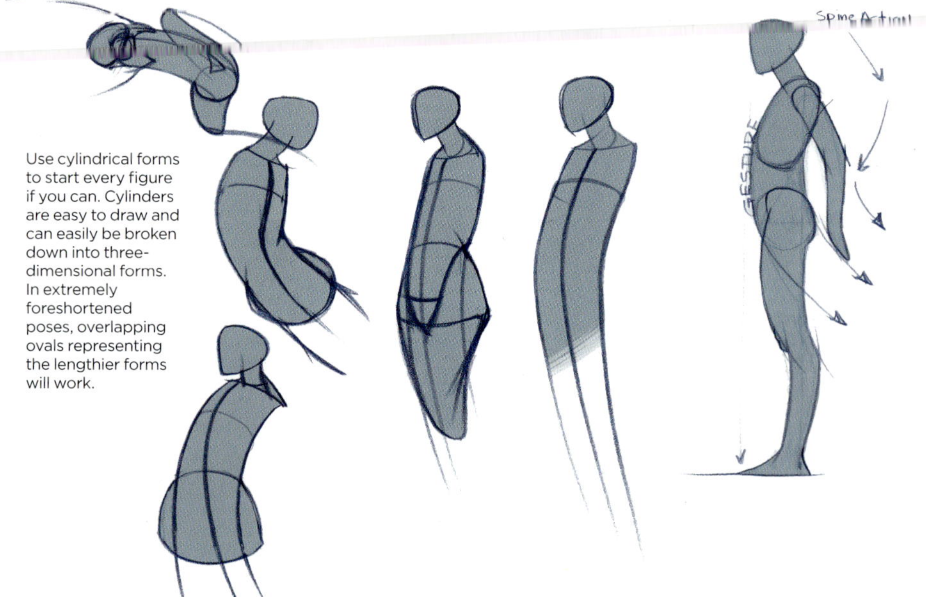

Use cylindrical forms to start every figure if you can. Cylinders are easy to draw and can easily be broken down into three-dimensional forms. In extremely foreshortened poses, overlapping ovals representing the lengthier forms will work.

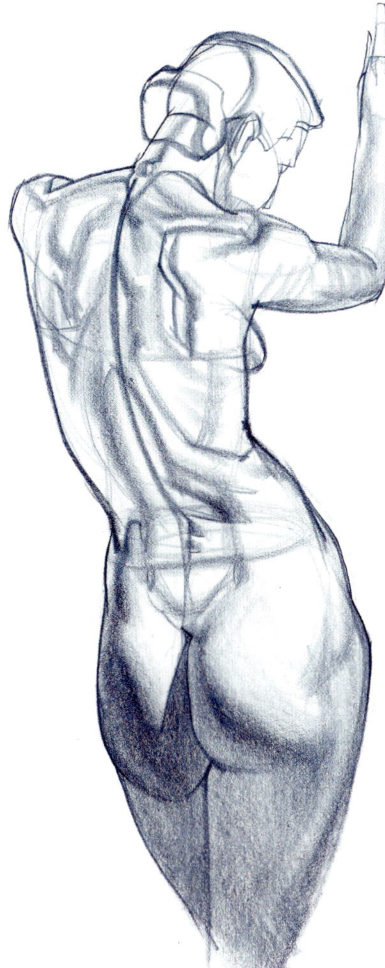

You can map shadows to the shapes you design on the scaffolding of the figure, with the patterns falling appropriately over the shapes you've drawn rather than drawing exactly what you see. The illusion of the drawing can suffer if you stick too rigidly to what you see without really thinking about how the forms are functioning in 3D space.

"If a figure is twisting or turning, you can easily depict this movement in the cylinder by pinching one side."

show the hip bones, the iliac crests.

Now draw an egg shape to indicate the rib cage, attaching it to the shoulder line and only breaching the cylinder form if the body is compressed or twisting. The rest of the torso is built up using ellipses or traversing lines across the centerline, to square up the two halves of the torso and pelvis.

The important landmarks to indicate are the nipples, the tenth ribs, the iliac crests, the navel, and the armpits. If your figure's back is visible, the scapulae, the dimples of the sacrum, the obliques, and the base of the pelvis are also helpful to use as landmarks.

If the figure is twisting or turning, you can easily depict this movement in the cylinder by pinching one side, or by creating an accordion-like relationship between the rib cage and pelvis masses.

The obliques play a role in shaping the cylinder: they are the third bulge on the compressed side of the cylinder. These bulges are described using S-curved lines (see the panel to the right), the only line type in drawing that can generate perspective in its own waviness. The S-curve starts against the outside of one shape, then swings over and completes its circuit below on the next succeeding shape. Each S-curve generates a more convincing illusion of overlapping forms.

You should switch often between gesture and structure to strike a balance of form and movement, hopefully in a similar dynamic to Michelangelo or Rubens – but with a modern flair, like that of Claire Wendling or Bruce Timm.

Once the structure has been defined, move back into gesture again, drawing the cylinders of the arms and the legs of the body. When your limbs are drawn in, move back into the structure and begin to define the muscles. Then, you should gesture again in order to describe the movement of the shadow patterns over the muscles, then structure to tighten them up.

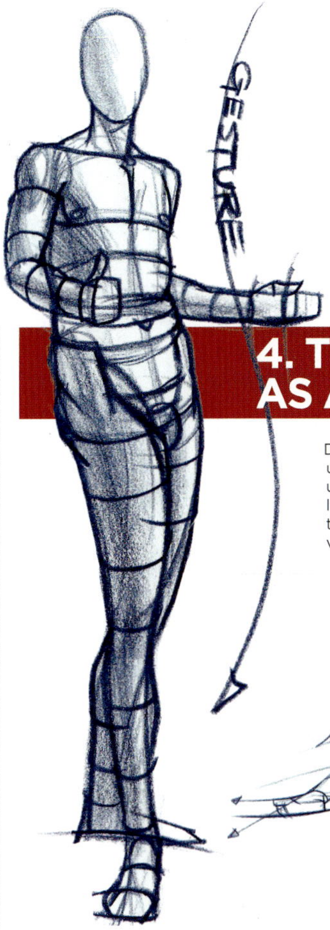

4. THE FIGURE AS AN S-SHAPE

Draw the rib cage as if looking up at it, with lines arching upward. Draw the pelvis with lines arching down. This keeps the forms tilted correctly to the viewer from straight on.

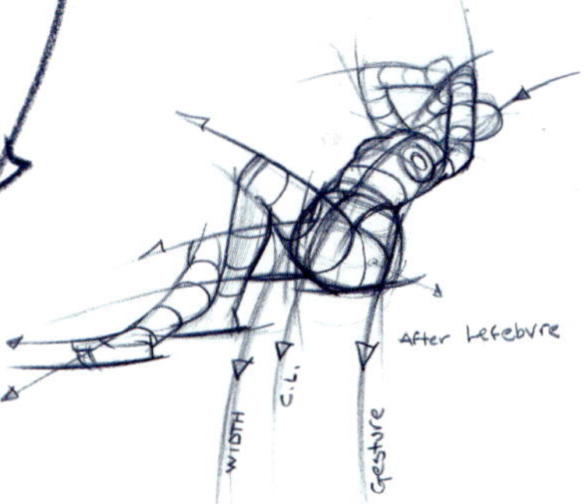

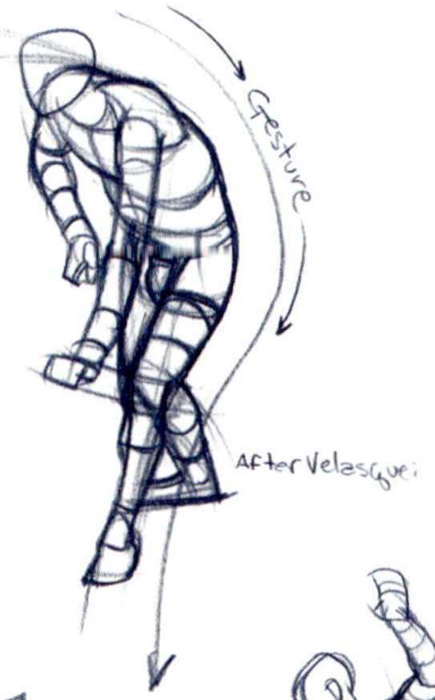

These drawings are fleshing out the dynamic movement in each pose. Using cylinders and dividing each segment of the cylinders into thirds, the scaffolding of the body is ready for muscles to be laid over them. The cross-contour lines help guide the muscles correctly around the form.

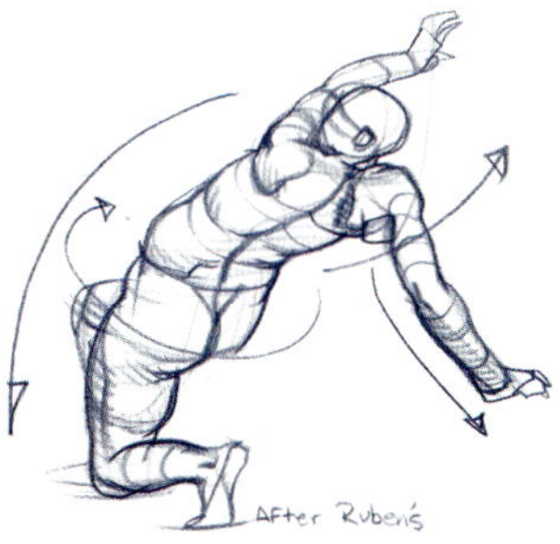

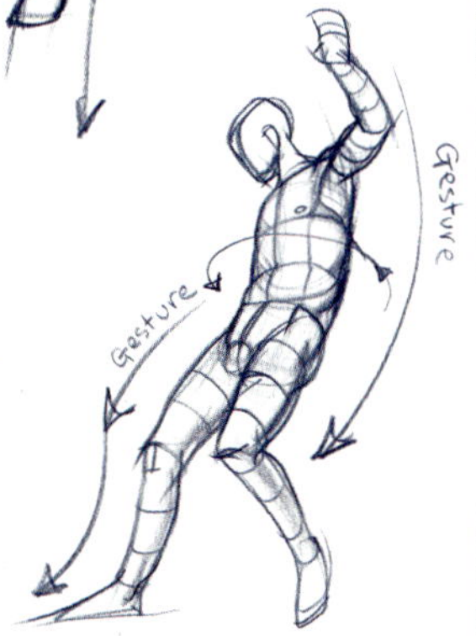

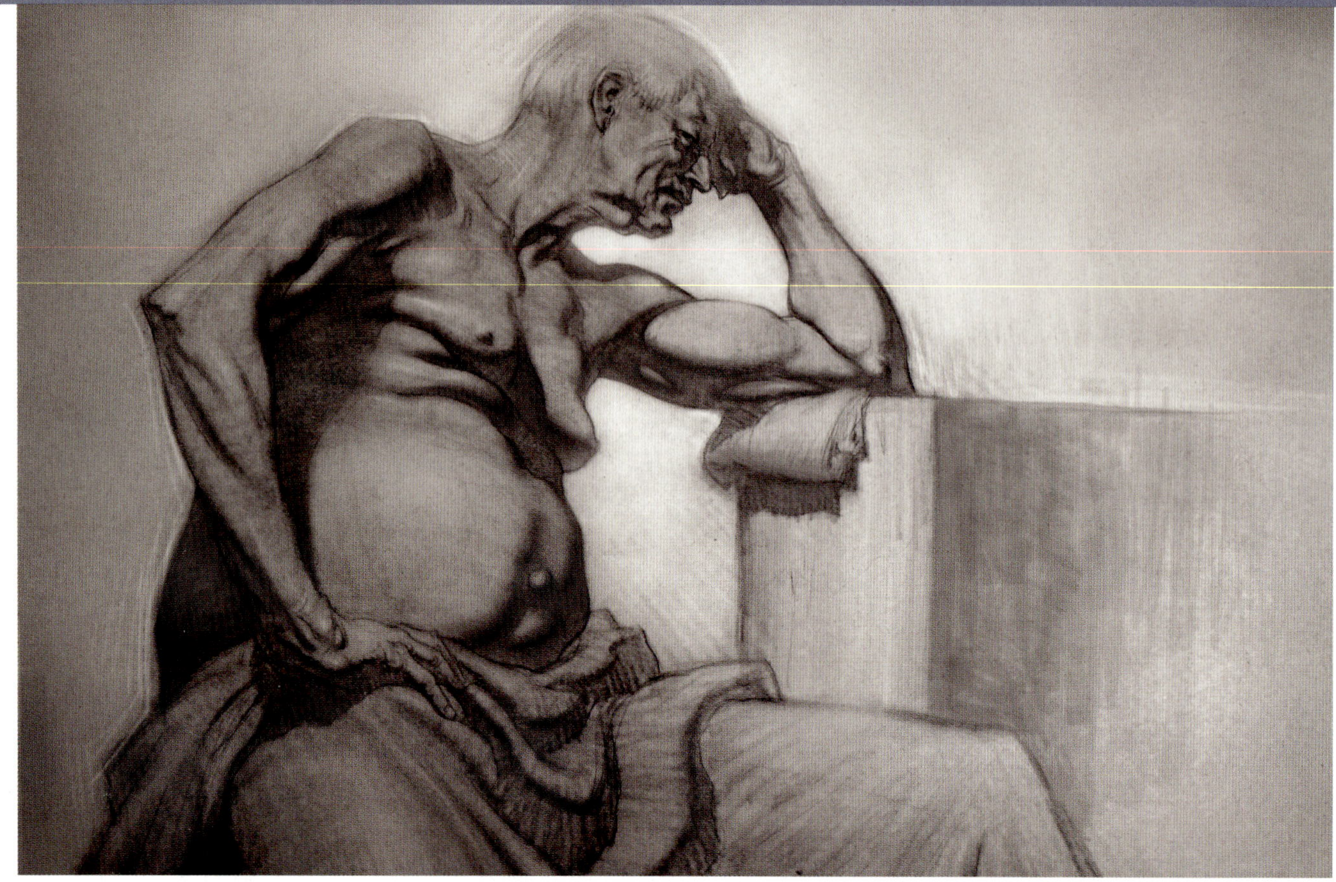

LIGHT AND FORM SKETCHING

Creating the illusion of light, shade, and form is a powerful tool. **Chris Legaspi** shares some strategies for creating beautiful and believable lighting

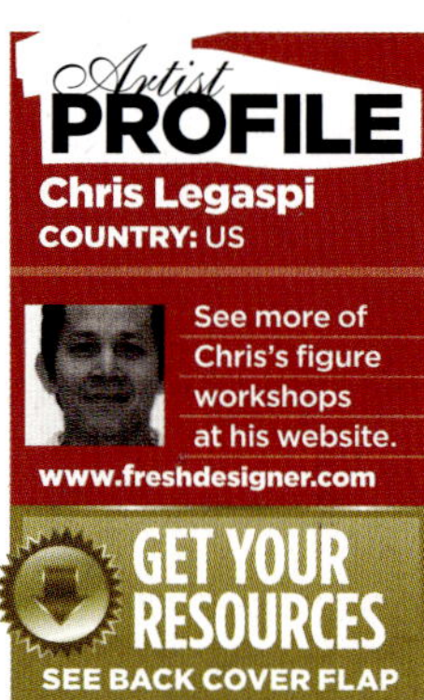

Light is how we see forms, and how we see our world; shadow is the absence of light. Where light and shadow meet is where the human mind interprets a form. Because this phenomenon resonates so deeply in the human mind, creating the feeling of light and shade, and doing it well, can have profound effect on the viewer.

In the natural world the effect of light and shadow is a very real, three-dimensional phenomenon. An artist can only create the illusion of light and shadow because of the limitations of our medium and materials. This is especially true when we are dealing with a flat, two-dimensional picture plane.

Because light is such a massive and important subject, I have attempted to highlight a few of the principles related to figure drawing. I will first attempt to show how light and shadow work, and then show some strategies that can be applied to figure drawing from life and drawing from imagination.

These principles and strategies will help to make your forms and figures feel solid, and three-dimensional, and add a layer of believability, so let's get started!

1. YOUR FIRST PRIORITY

When I begin the lighting process, my first priority is to separate light and shade. I ask myself, "What is in light, and what is in shadow?" as these are the important questions I want to answer for the viewer. I like to first observe the direction of the light and then squint to help find the border (or intersection). Then I like to lay down a light to medium tone on the shadows to give them clear separation.

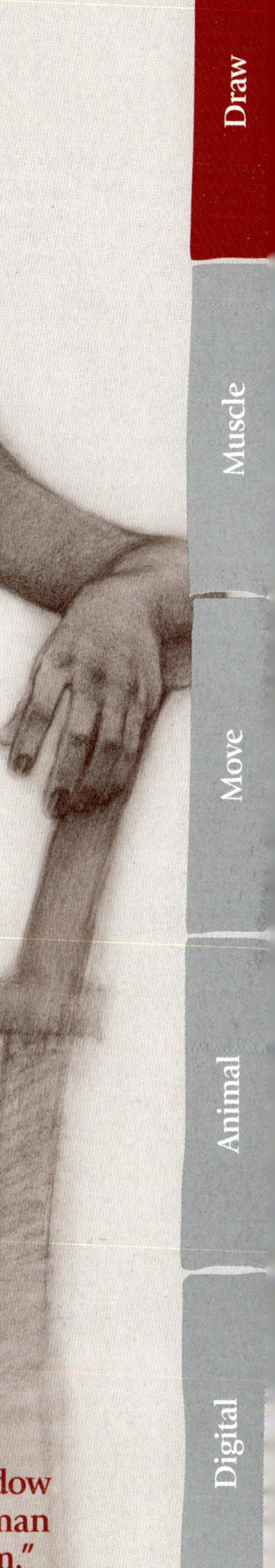

"Where light and shadow meet is where the human mind interprets a form."

2. THE POWER OF PLANES

Planes are a form principle that describes how the surface area of a form reacts to a light source. How much light an object or area receives depends on the varying degree to which planes face the light. Inversely, how dark an object or area is depends on the degree to which the planes turn away from light. In simpler terms, a change in value means a change in planes.

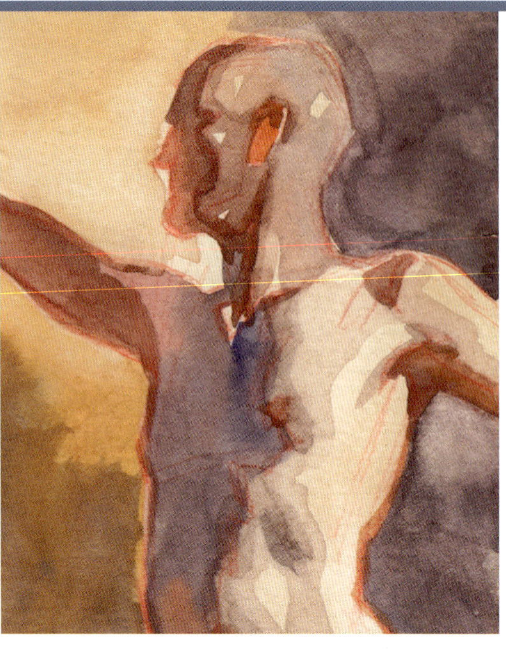

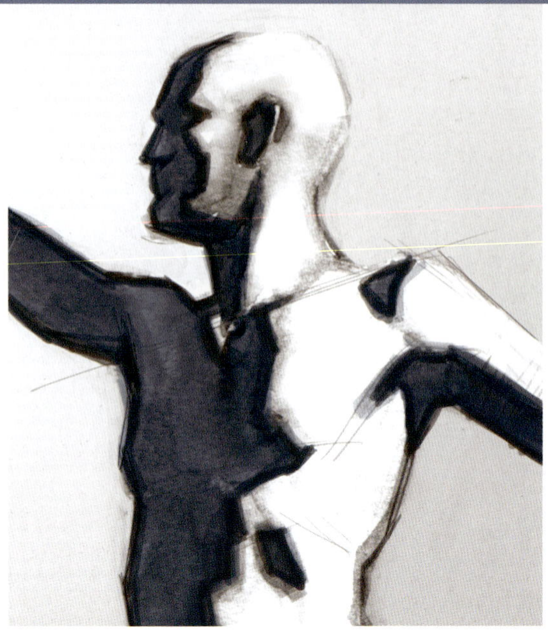

Using clearly defined light and shade shapes helps the viewer quickly identify form.

3. LIGHT AND SHADOW SHAPES

Just as the figure has a clearly defined shape or silhouette, light and shadow patterns also have their own shapes. The light and shadow shapes, and their relationships to each other, give the viewer a way to quickly identify form. In fact, I like to use shadow shapes as a design element. As we'll see later in this workshop, shadow shapes can help to define form and even add gesture and movement.

4. VALUES AND THE VALUE RANGE

Value refers to how light or dark something is, and is often measured on a scale numbered from 1–10 (or 0–10). In this model, the number 1 represents either pure white (or black), and number 10 represents the inverse (either pure black or white). In between these two there is an infinite range of values, especially when observing nature, but because of limitations of media and materials, it is not possible to have an infinite range of values as nature does.

> "In between pure black and pure white there is an infinite range of values."

PRO SECRETS

Shade under the spotlight

A good way to study light and shade is to draw from a subject lit by a single dominant light source that has little to no bounce light or environment lights. This setup is often referred to as "spotlighting." A strong spotlight makes for a clearly visible shadow pattern, and well-defined core shadows, cast shadows, and highlights. Whether working from life or a photo, this method helps me to focus on designing good shapes and refining edges.

5. PLACEMENT IS THE KEY

Because it is impossible (and impractical) to render an infinite value range, I focus on how values relate to each other. For example, a #5, mid-value tone on the value scale can look really dark next to pure white. The same #5 gray can also look really bright surrounded by pure black. Knowing what values to use, and where to place them, is how I create the illusion of a full value scale.

6. TWO-VALUE SYSTEM

Assigning one value for light and one value for shadow is the first value judgment I make. I often use the white of the paper as the value of the light shape and a medium tone as the value of the shadow shape. Simplifying things to only two values makes a clear and powerful statement that I always strive to maintain throughout the rendering process, even when adding more values. The key is to stay within the established value range.

"Edge describes how quickly the planes of a form turn away from the light."

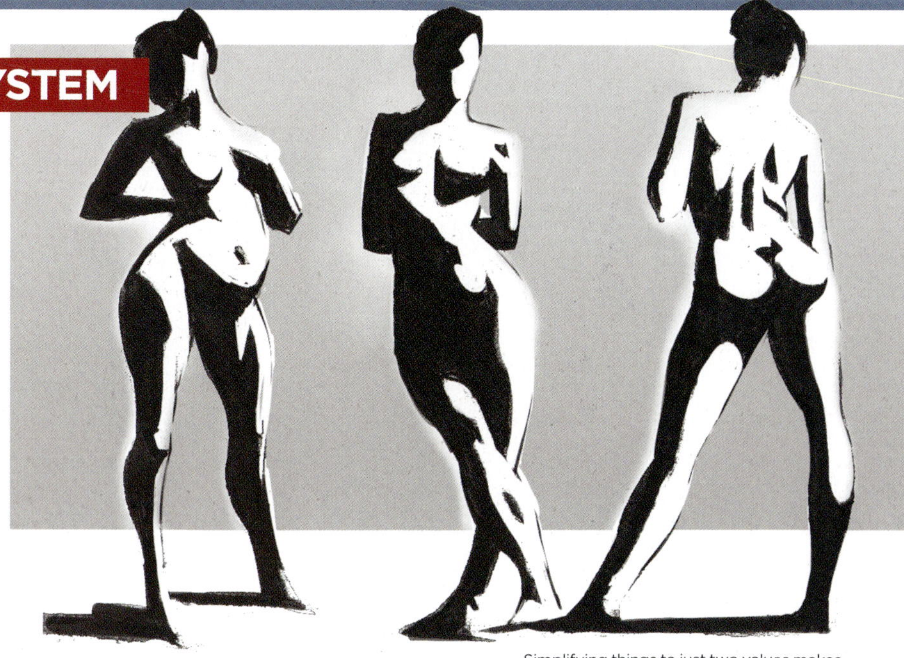

Simplifying things to just two values makes a clear and powerful statement about form.

7. EDGES DEFINED

Edge describes how quickly the planes of a form turn away from the light, and is defined using a range from soft, to firm, to hard. The human form has multiple edges, especially in the joints. An object's surface material and the intensity of the light can also affect the quality of the edge. In the same way that I limit my values, I like to limit my edges as well and focus on good relationships.

8. SOFT EDGES

Soft edges (aka "lost" edges) indicate a slow, gradual movement away from the light. Any round or egg-like form can be described perfectly with soft edges. For example, I like to use soft edges on round, fleshy parts of the body like the buttocks, the fat of the cheeks, or the meat of the thighs. Soft edges can also be used to blur an area to create the illusion of atmosphere and depth.

9. HARD EDGES

Hard edges (also known as "crisp" or "sharp" edges) indicate a rapid plane change. For example, the corner of a box or table can be described with a straight, hard edge. With the exception of cast shadows (see below), sharp edges generally don't exist in organic forms, so proceed with caution. I like to use hard edges for emphasis, or to add dramatic contrast to the shadow pattern.

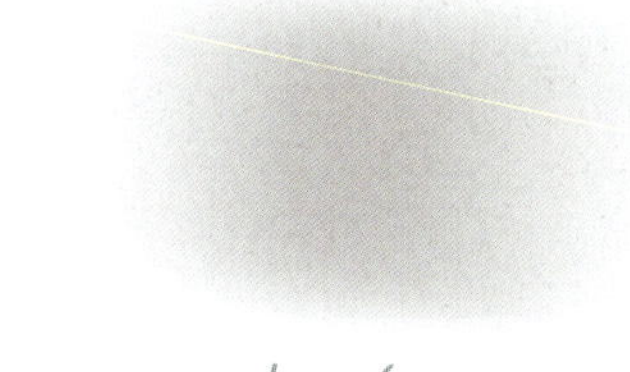

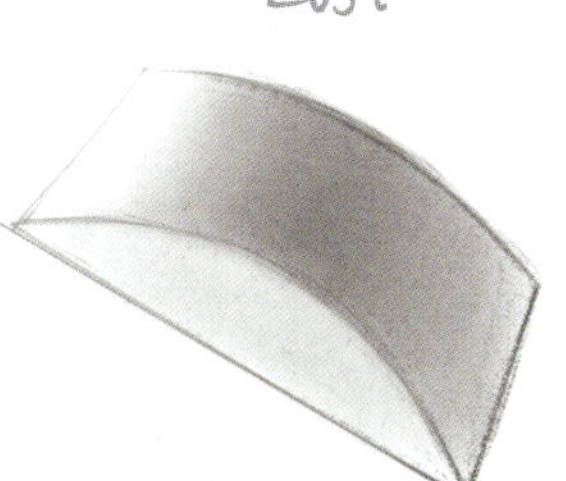

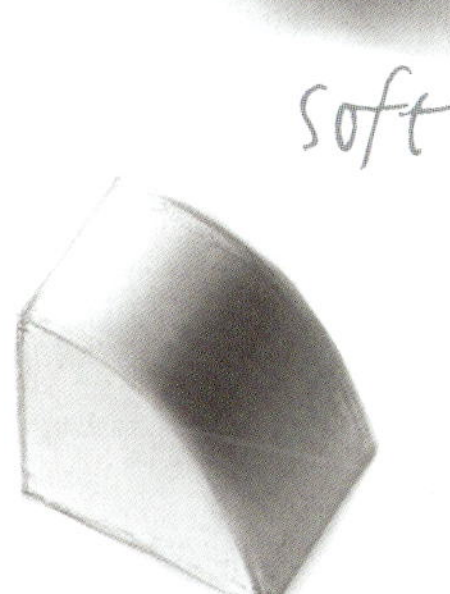

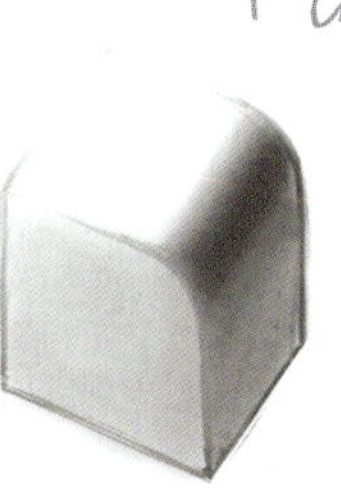

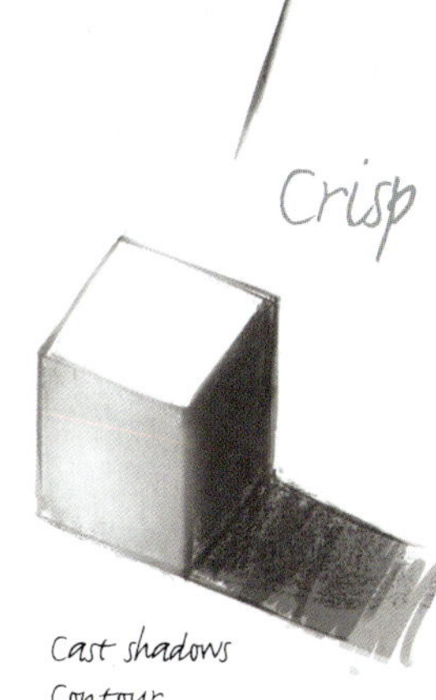

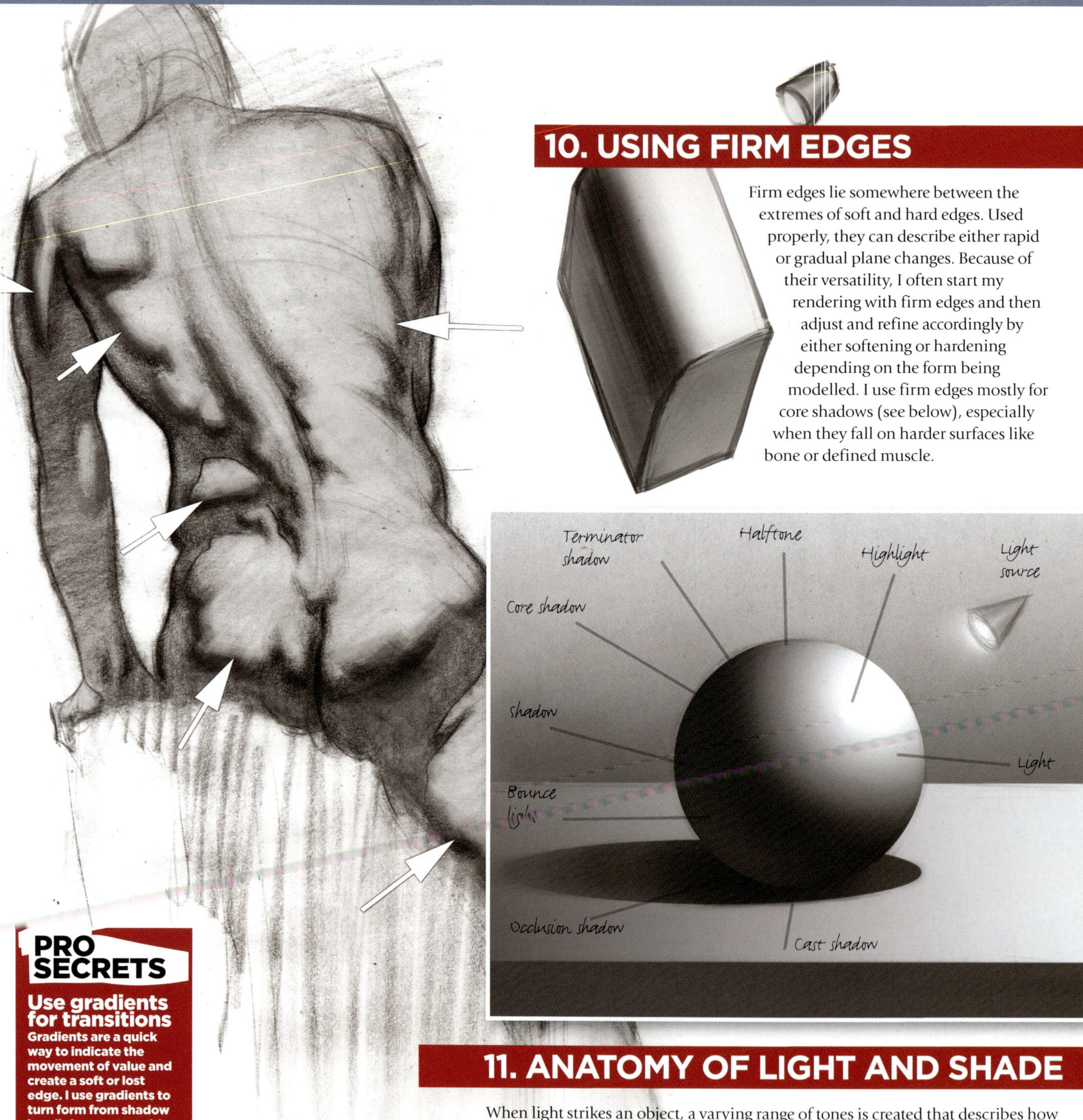

10. USING FIRM EDGES

Firm edges lie somewhere between the extremes of soft and hard edges. Used properly, they can describe either rapid or gradual plane changes. Because of their versatility, I often start my rendering with firm edges and then adjust and refine accordingly by either softening or hardening depending on the form being modelled. I use firm edges mostly for core shadows (see below), especially when they fall on harder surfaces like bone or defined muscle.

11. ANATOMY OF LIGHT AND SHADE

When light strikes an object, a varying range of tones is created that describes how light falls and transitions to shadow. These varying tones are often referred to as: highlight, light, halftone, terminator shadow, core shadow, reflected light (a.k.a. "bounce light"), occlusion shadow, and cast shadow. James Gurney referred to this as "the form principle," because identifying and understanding how these tones relate is vital to rendering a form.

PRO SECRETS

Use gradients for transitions

Gradients are a quick way to indicate the movement of value and create a soft or lost edge. I use gradients to turn form from shadow into light or to transition light to the halftones. Gradients can be done in many ways: I like to use either the flat side of my charcoal pencil or stick and, using a zigzag motion, I carefully lighten the pressure to lighten the tone as I move into the light side of the forms.

> "I use firm edges mostly for core shadows, especially when they fall on harder surfaces like bone or muscle."

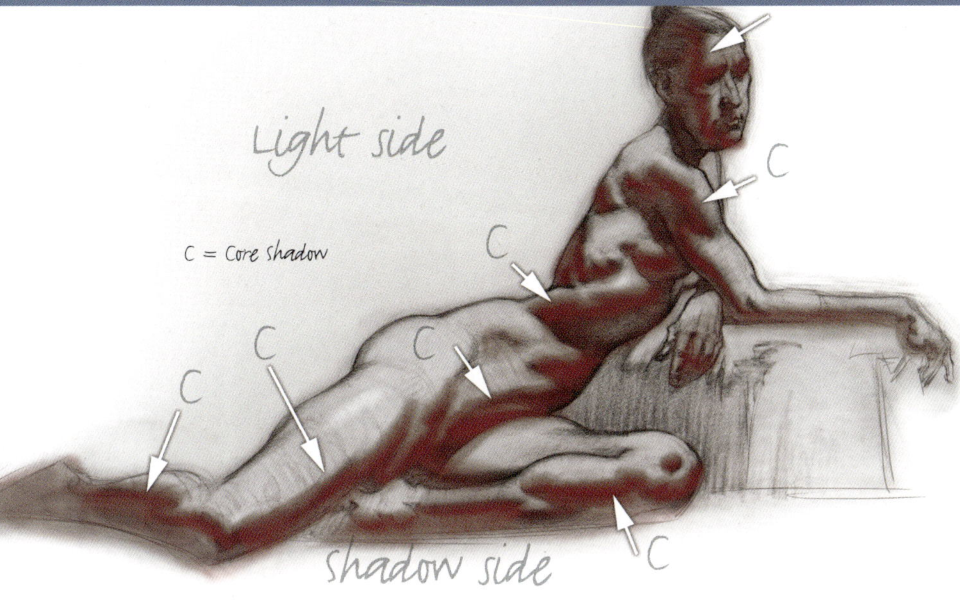

15. A NOTE ON BOUNCE LIGHT

Reflected light, or "bounce light," is created when light bounces off nearby surfaces and back into the shadow. Because bounce light appears relatively bright compared with the shadow, a common mistake is to make it brighter than it is – which kills the illusion of light, shadow, and form. I always use caution with bounce light to maintain the integrity of the value structure. When in doubt, keep it dark or leave it out.

12. THE CORE SHADOW

The core shadow lies at the border, or intersection, of light and shadow. Value-wise, the core tends to be much darker than the shadow because it is not affected by reflected light. I often begin the core with a firm edge and then soften as needed when transitioning to rounder, fleshier parts of anatomy. By simply darkening the core, I can quickly indicate reflected light and heighten the feeling of a three-dimensional form.

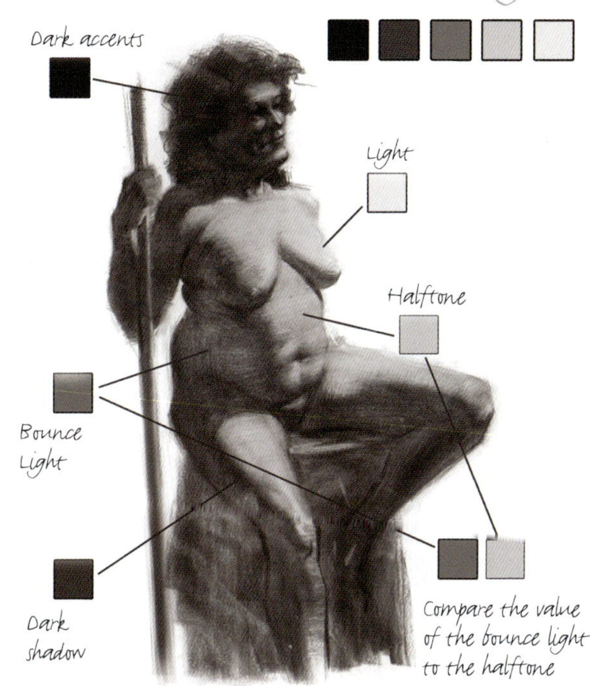

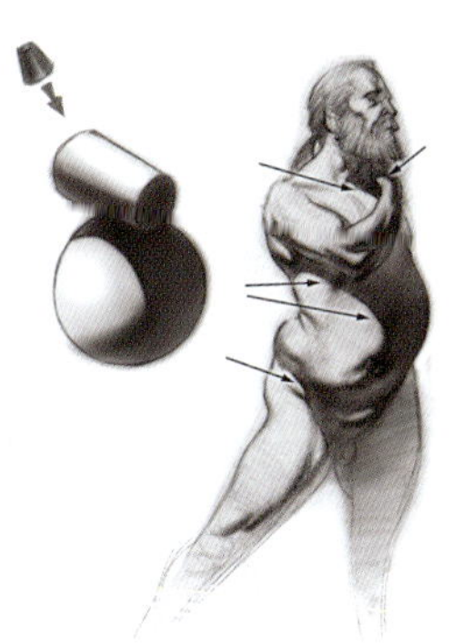

13. THE CAST SHADOW

A cast shadow is created when a form completely blocks direct light, which projects or casts a silhouette of shadow. As a general rule, hard, crisp edges are best for indicating cast shadows. The only exceptions are when light is diffused or is farther away. I like to use cast shadow as a design element. For example, I can intentionally curve the shadow cast by an arm over the torso to heighten the feeling of form and structure.

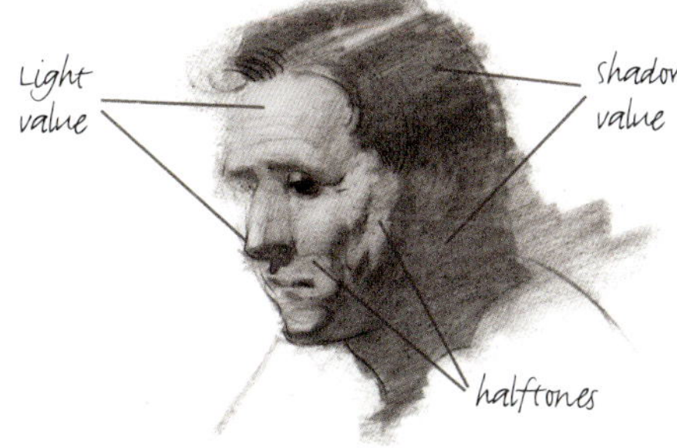

14. A NOTE ON HALFTONES

Halftones are between the value of the form in direct light and the value of the shadow, and indicate a light-facing plane that is slightly turned away from the light; it is within the values of the light, but a dark light. Because the difference between halftones and light values are so subtle, it takes a lot of skill, practice, and good observation to render them well.

16. A NOTE ON HIGHLIGHTS

Highlights occur when two or more light-facing planes intersect. As core shadows indicate plane changes, so do highlights. If I get lost in the light side of a figure, I'll look for the highlights to help locate hidden anatomy or plane changes. Highlights can also move in relation to the viewer's eye, so I always use caution and care when placing them.

GET BETTER AT FIGURE DRAWING

Peer over the shoulder of fantasy artist **Patrick J. Jones** as he draws live from his life-drawing workshop, without slavishly copying what he sees

When I got the great call from ImagineFX's editor to draw a life model for the cover illustration, I was beaming with energy and filled with notions of mighty gestural turns, curvaceous glutes, and hips a-sway, but the brief came with a hurdle: no nudity could grace the cover! A chaste nude can work, but usually at the sacrifice of the major curves that make the female figure so appealing and graceful. I decided then that it would be an artistic challenge!

Normally, I teach life drawing at a university, but for this commission I planned to record the stages live at my first private figure-drawing workshop, which was a big call, with every chance of me falling flat on my stupid face in full view of the class. It was also decided that an Asian model would be great too, and I agreed, but it would turn out to be my second challenge.

In this workshop I'll be working with classic butcher's paper (newsprint) and charcoal, while relating a tale of the wondrous unknown that greeted me as I walked into my first private life-drawing class with this exciting commission and cameras rolling…

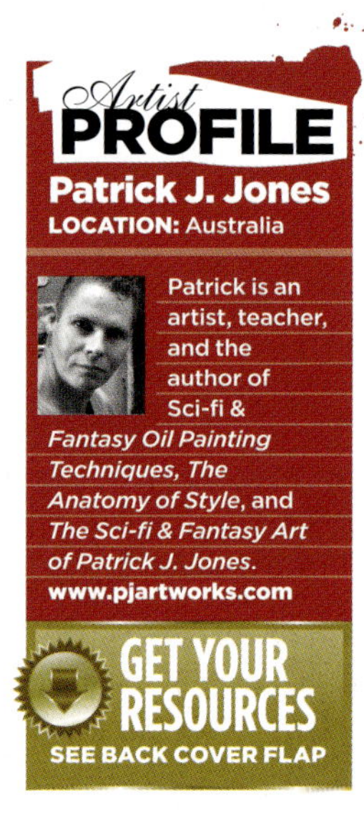

Patrick J. Jones
LOCATION: Australia

Patrick is an artist, teacher, and the author of Sci-fi & *Fantasy Oil Painting Techniques, The Anatomy of Style*, and *The Sci-fi & Fantasy Art of Patrick J. Jones*.
www.pjartworks.com

GET YOUR RESOURCES
SEE BACK COVER FLAP

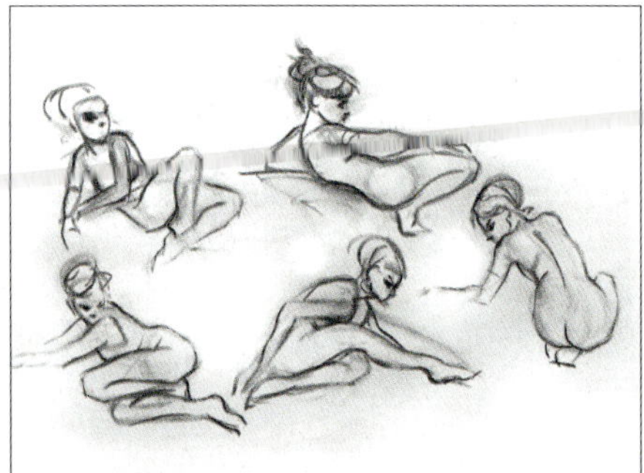

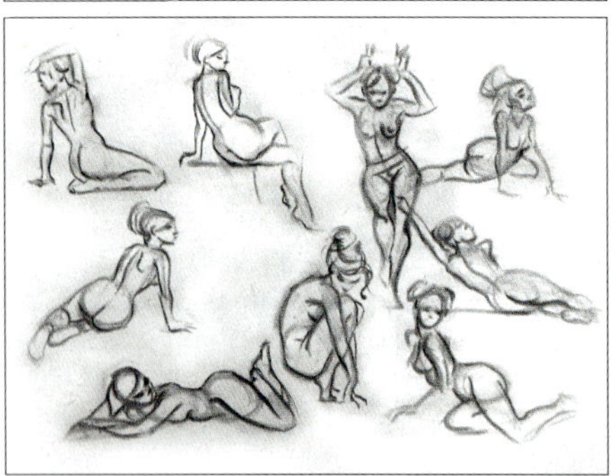

1 No time for the wicked

Time is already tight because I accepted the commission when I was in the US, so when I return home I get scribbling right away. Here's a sample of the 22 quick charcoal poses I come up with. I plan to add some ornaments to cover the full-breasted thumbnails, but they're still too risqué. Eventually, the central figure is chosen, with the request to lift the head up.

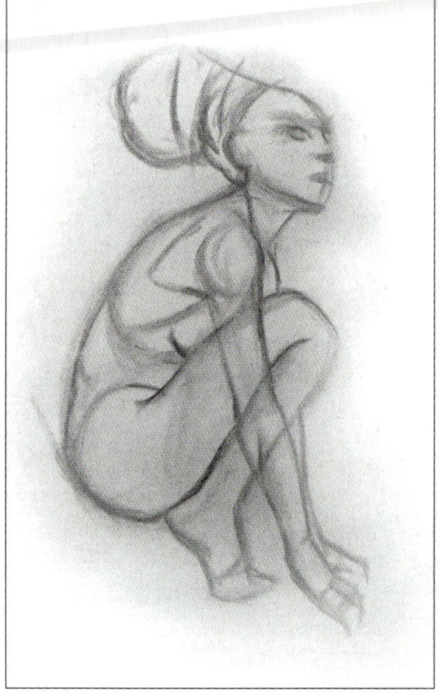

2 Rolling with the punches

Having hired my go-to model, Alana, I'm all set, but on the very day Alana falls sick and is replaced last-minute by a non-Asian model I've never worked with before! These are the times an artist must dig deep for inner strength. I show her the approved thumbnail, and she strikes the pose as I go to work blocking in the simple shapes with a willow charcoal stick.

3 Knowledge is freedom

During the class I'm also teaching the foundation of the figure to my students. Here's a study sheet drawn live during the same class, which not only helps the students understand my inner workings, but also keeps my internal anatomical knowledge fresh. My oft-said motto is, "Learn this stuff off by heart, then bury it in your subconscious."

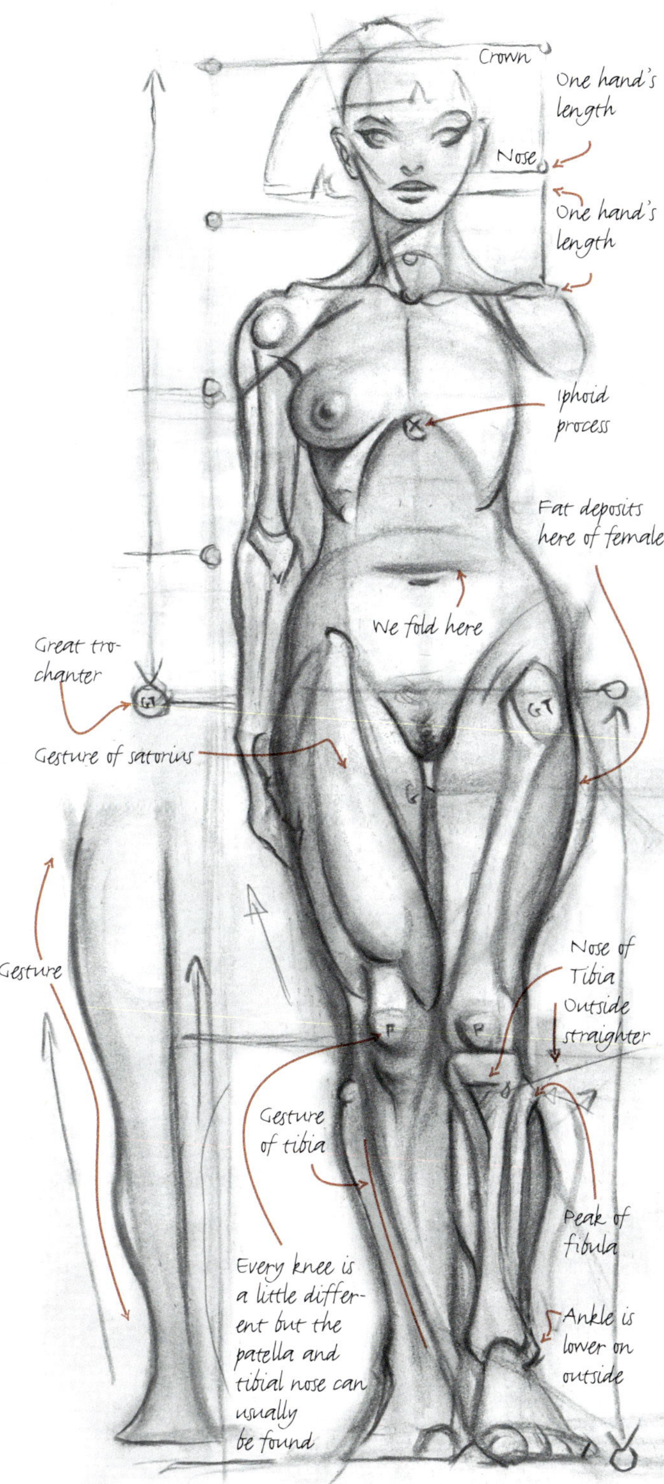

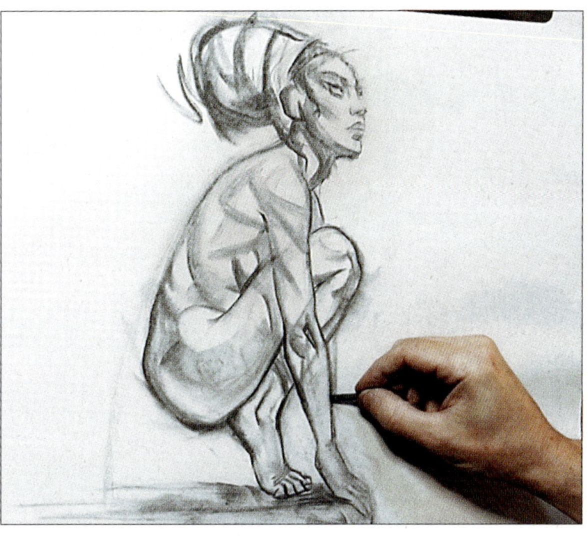

4 It's all in the gesture

Here I'm using my "gestural hand," which means I'm holding my sharpened willow charcoal stick underhanded rather than with the "detail hand," which we use for writing. This enables me to draw from the shoulder rather that the stiff confines of the wrist. At this point I'm refining the simple shapes and using the broad side of the charcoal for bigger tones.

5 The pencil with appeal

Having found my basic shapes and proportions, I begin to draw more solid lines. Here I'm using a charcoal pencil because it's the same material as the willow charcoal, just more dense. If I were to use a graphite pencil it would be too shiny and gray. This is a "peel-off" pencil that generally doesn't need sharpening if you work big. The way it works is: you peel the outer paper layer upward to reveal more point. Very handy and clean to use.

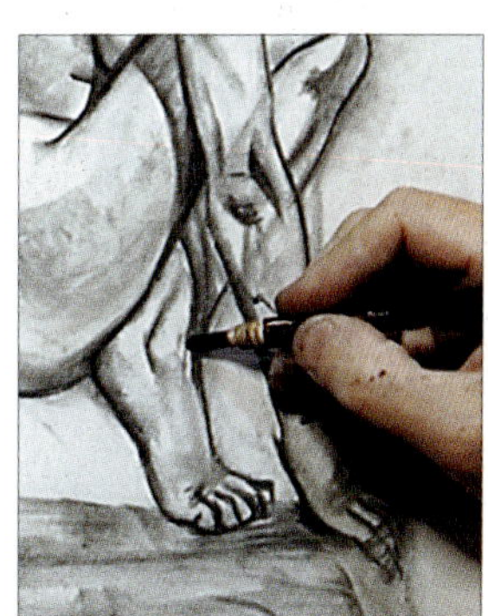

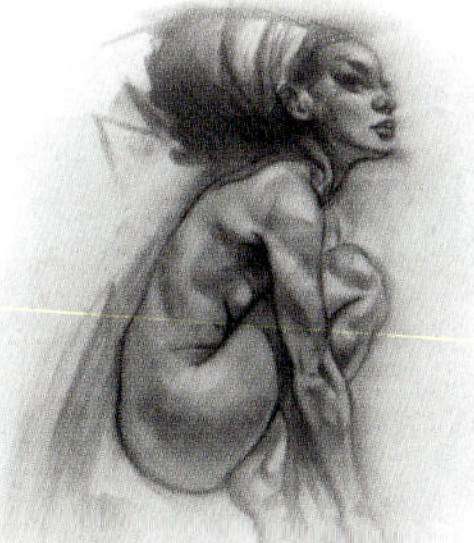

6 Drawing without copying

With the model on a break, I have the chance to work on the drawing without the distraction of that old trap of copying exactly what's in front of me. This gives me the chance to rub into the charcoal shapes with my fingers, thumbs, and tissue. It's also the perfect time to work some broad gestural shapes into the background, which adds movement to the figure. One last thing I do before the model returns is to work some Asian influence into the face.

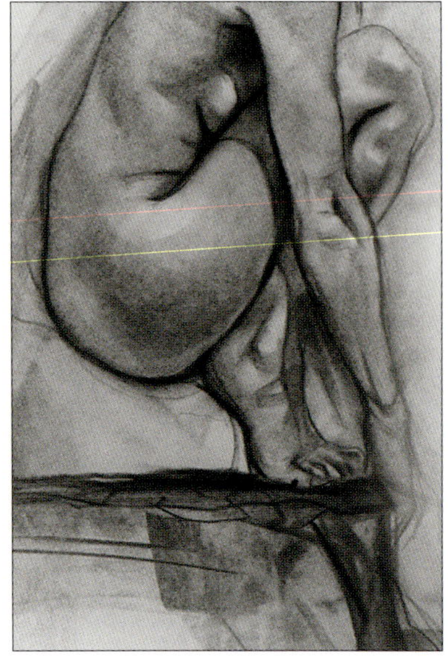

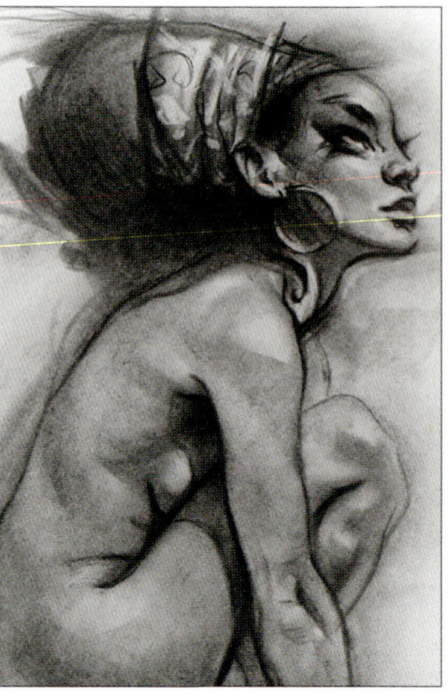

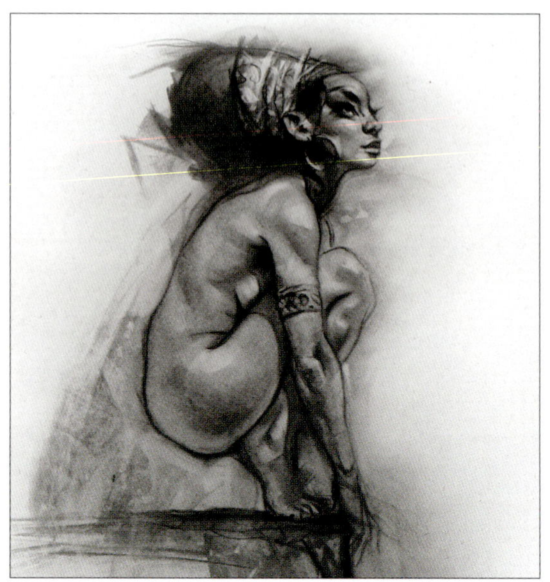

7 The thing with life drawing is...

When the model returns, she asks if she can change her hand position for better balance. This is no problem because I rarely work on parts in detail and had barely sketched the hands. The thing with life drawing is that the model will shift slightly here and there, which isn't entirely a bad thing, because it stops you from getting caught up in detail. With the drawing almost done, it gives me time to study and blend the connecting muscles. At this point I'm starting to consider style by making the lines more gestural.

8 A world of contrast

I add some texture to the background with crunched-up tissue, making the flesh appear softer by contrast. Contrast is something the eye always seeks, and we artists can add it as we please. The same goes for line: I place thicker lines on the shadow edge of the figure. At this point I use some imagination and chip off the sharp European chin for a more Asian turn of line.

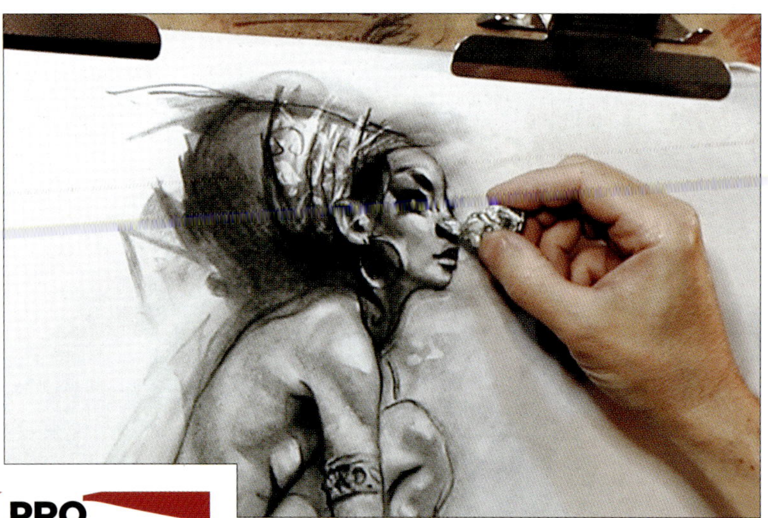

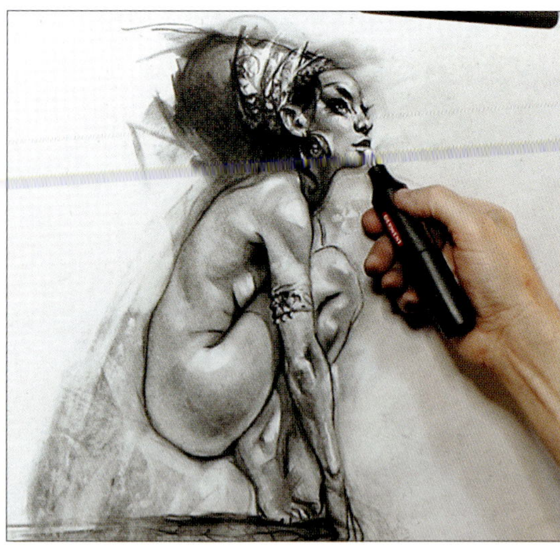

PRO SECRETS

Secret in the sand

Use a sanding pad to sharpen the end of your charcoal stick to a chisel point. That way you can produce a variety of marks from just one stick.

9 Love is all you knead

It's time now to give the drawing some love and added pop. I'm using a kneaded eraser here to pull out some highlights. Kneaded erasers are terrific because you can shape them like putty, hence they're sometimes sold as Putty Erasers. Using the kneaded eraser also gives me the chance to carve into the neck and face to achieve the exotic look I want. At this stage the face no longer resembles the original European life model at all.

10 The light touch

For those stubborn areas that forever hold the gray charcoal I use an electric eraser. It's important not to lean too hard, because you can easily tear butcher's paper. This tool is more commonly used on professional illustration board, which can take all kinds of punishment, but with a light touch it can also work well with butcher's paper.

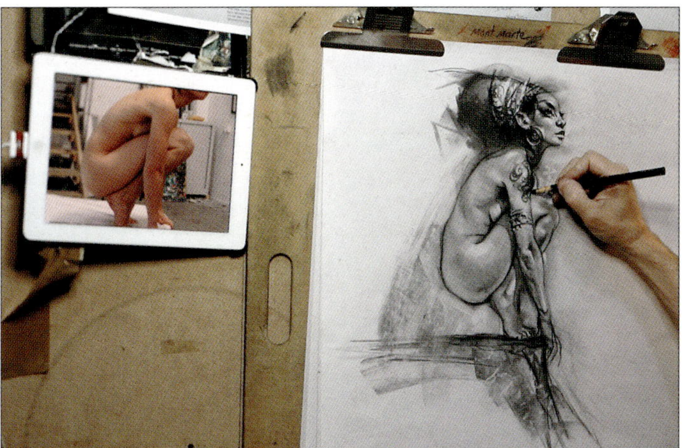

11 The exotic glamour

Because I'm teaching a class during this demo, I have no time to fuss around with detail, and so I pay the model some extra cash for a few reference photos during the next break, which also became an impromptu photography lesson for the class. Once the class finishes, I carry on drawing, adding more elements of style, such as the oriental tattoo. If you look in the background of the reference photo you can see the clutter of a painter's studio. My iPad is also hanging from my drawing board by parcel tape and bulldog clips. Ah, the glamour of it all.

12 A great notion

I take the drawing home and work on it the next day without reference interfering. Reference is an incredible tool, but it can stunt your artistic hand. Leaving the art out of sight for a while can also give your eye a rest. The notion of a fresh eye is all too true; I now see clearly what needs a tweak. The final touches of darks and lights, varying the thin and thick line, and it's done.

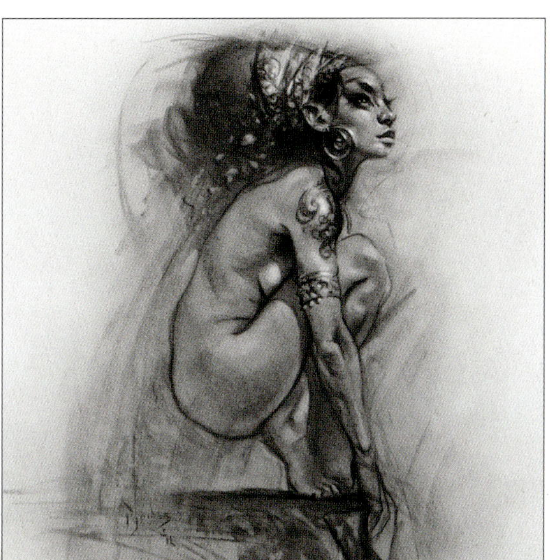

PRO SECRETS

Add texture

Charcoal is like a kind of monotone oil paint, in the sense that it's always "live" – so feel free to push the pigment around with your hands or lift some texture out with scrunched-up tissue, or anything you please.

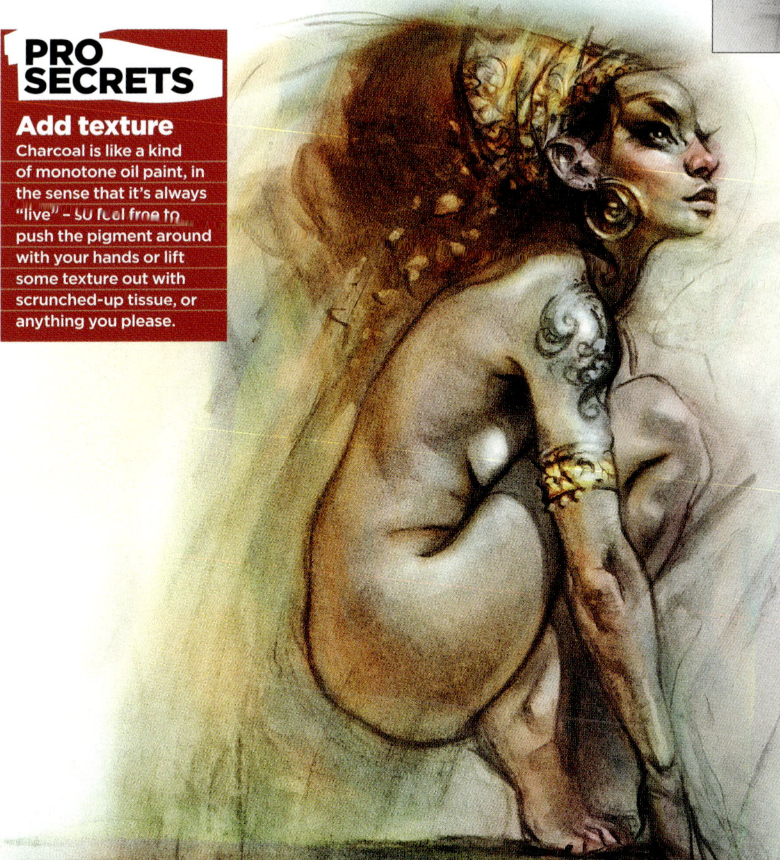

13 All awash

I'm not a big fan of bright color over line art, so with the request for a wash of color on top of my drawing I turn to Corel Painter's watercolor brushes. The default mode is Gel, which makes the colors a bit too garish for my taste, so I dial the Opacity settings down to 30 percent and change the mode to Overlay. This gives me the real-world feel of a traditional watercolor wash. The highlights on the metal edges are added with Painter's FX Glow brush.

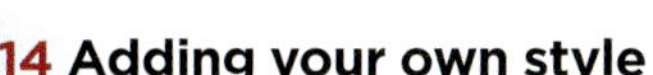

14 Adding your own style

So why bother with life drawing when we can simply trace photos? Well, the main reason is that we are artists who started out with the love of drawing, not rendering. Constantly drawing the figure frees us to be able to rekindle that flame and express movement within our oil and digital paintings.

HOW TO DRAW IMAGINED FIGURES

Ron Lemen explains how memorizing, observation, and structures of composition will help you take your anatomy knowledge a step further

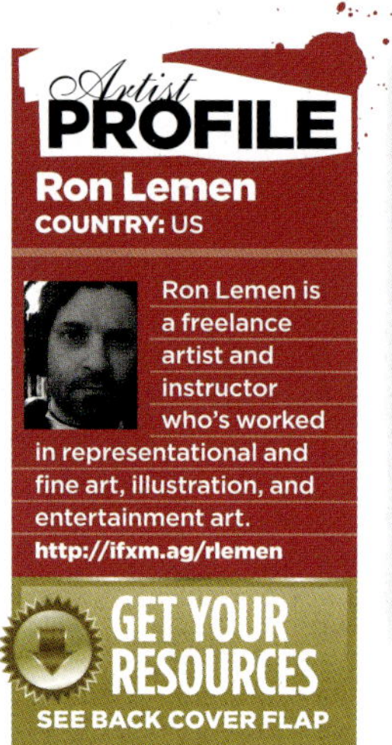

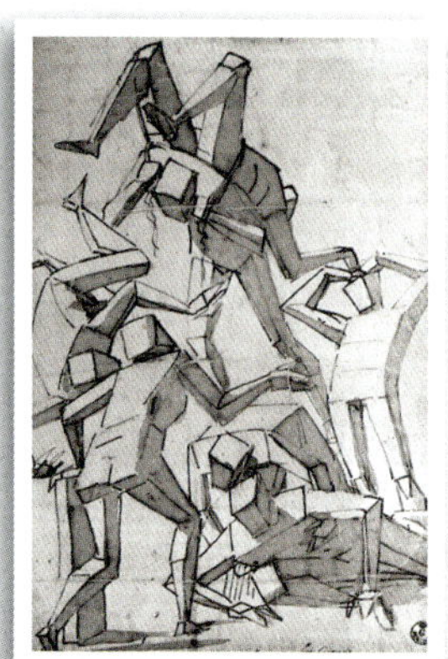

Understanding and communicating the structures that underpin everything will help you to communicate your ideas with your audience.

"Art is a visual language that can be understood by others with whom we do not share a common tongue."

Art is old, really old, we are tapping into a universal language. This is a visual language that can be understood by others with whom we do not share a common tongue. We take advantage of this language through signs, symbols, and other types of graphic communication, often subconsciously.

The systems of art are ancient. The Reilly method and the shape method, for instance, both date back to at least the fifteenth century, and two notable names in the history of art – Villard De Honnecourt and Luca Cambiaso – have used both of these concepts to great effect.

All the techniques used now by artists for drawing the figure will have their roots in old, time-tested concepts. Our shape-swapping method, for example – drawing a bowling pin for a forearm, a block for a hip, and so forth – is nothing new. While the symbols may be newer, these concepts are nothing more than a simplified means to convincingly achieve a difficult end result.

If you can master the methods that have stood the test of time and have been used by the great masters throughout the history of art, you will then be able to communicate with the clarity and verve that they did.

1. PROCESS FOR DRAWING

Let us look at a process for putting together a figure from life or from reference, such as a photo, then moving away from the original reference point. Finally I will explain how to draw a figure from memory and make it rhythmically animated.

I am structuring the process in this way because I often read about how to create an image, but not about how to make decisions on the processes of drawing and executing an image. Instead, the focus is usually on the journey from thumbnail to finished image. This tutorial will look at how to construct your drawings, and what skills to practice to strengthen your craft.

I consider the process of drawing to be similar to breathing – inhaling and exhaling, a back and forth effort. When drafting, the movement is from loose to tight, or gestural to analytical, and back again. The process of drawing evolves in several stages: the gesture (loose), construction (tight), contour (loose), notan (tight), gradation (loose), and accent/highlight (tight).

This process can then be broken down into more stages – starting with the construction and the notans/gradations per degree of scale, or the biggest shapes first, then working down into medium shapes and finally ending with the smallest shapes – what most would call details.

This is the process I use for studying from life or working from a photo. If you were to watch me work, you'd notice that I shift around between stages and methods as I draw, but that's because I am extremely comfortable with these processes now – and once you have totally mastered them too, you can choose the methods that work best for you.

So rather than labeling and finishing each step in a deliberate manner, I am more able to "react" – I am exploring more immediate methods that can eliminate all the steps once they have been mastered. Take as much time as you need to master the stages, make them as intuitive as possible, and then forget them in order to make great, responsive images.

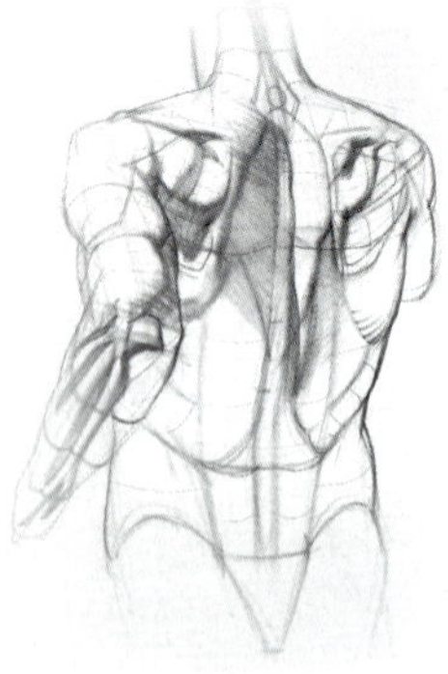

Use a loose, organic rhythm when drafting, similar to the breath, to keep your lines fluid.

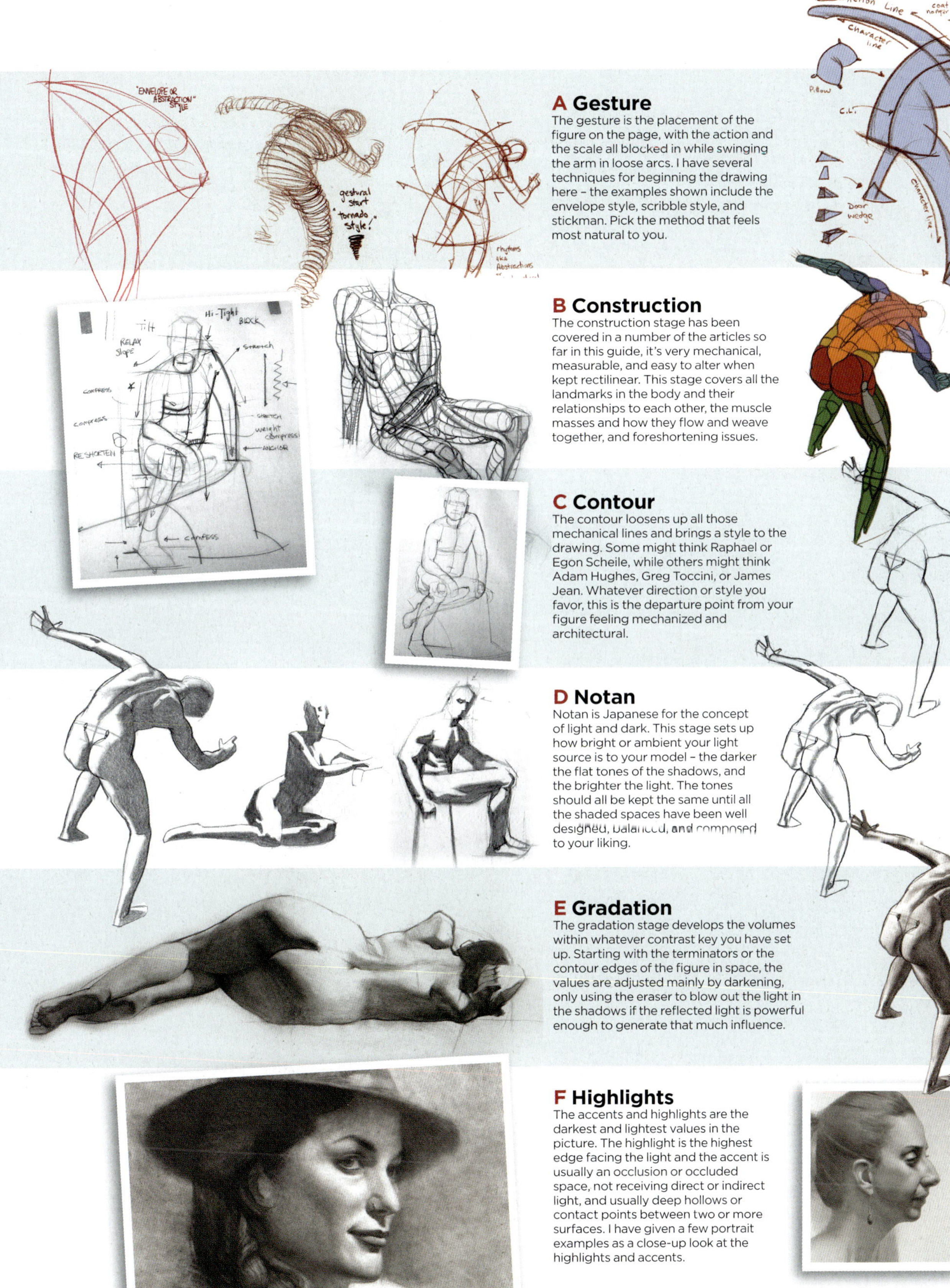

A Gesture

The gesture is the placement of the figure on the page, with the action and the scale all blocked in while swinging the arm in loose arcs. I have several techniques for beginning the drawing here – the examples shown include the envelope style, scribble style, and stickman. Pick the method that feels most natural to you.

B Construction

The construction stage has been covered in a number of the articles so far in this guide, it's very mechanical, measurable, and easy to alter when kept rectilinear. This stage covers all the landmarks in the body and their relationships to each other, the muscle masses and how they flow and weave together, and foreshortening issues.

C Contour

The contour loosens up all those mechanical lines and brings a style to the drawing. Some might think Raphael or Egon Scheile, while others might think Adam Hughes, Greg Toccini, or James Jean. Whatever direction or style you favor, this is the departure point from your figure feeling mechanized and architectural.

D Notan

Notan is Japanese for the concept of light and dark. This stage sets up how bright or ambient your light source is to your model – the darker the flat tones of the shadows, and the brighter the light. The tones should all be kept the same until all the shaded spaces have been well designed, balanced, and composed to your liking.

E Gradation

The gradation stage develops the volumes within whatever contrast key you have set up. Starting with the terminators or the contour edges of the figure in space, the values are adjusted mainly by darkening, only using the eraser to blow out the light in the shadows if the reflected light is powerful enough to generate that much influence.

F Highlights

The accents and highlights are the darkest and lightest values in the picture. The highlight is the highest edge facing the light and the accent is usually an occlusion or occluded space, not receiving direct or indirect light, and usually deep hollows or contact points between two or more surfaces. I have given a few portrait examples as a close-up look at the highlights and accents.

2. LEARN TO LOOK

To move away from references, we need exercises to help understand the scene you want to capture. As a portrait painter I prefer live reference, but I don't always get the luxury. As an illustrator I prefer not to use reference, because I am not capturing the same stillness in time. The practices are different but the results in the end should be similar: a living, breathing surface. It is all an attempt at suspension of disbelief, to take the viewer away and convince them this moment is real.

To do this, reference is only a part of the picture, the rest has to be "felt" – does it "feel" right when you look at it? The feeling is something deep inside that stirs your senses into believing what it sees is really happening. Rubens was one of the masters of this, as were Giambattista Tiepolo, Dean Cornwell, and Norman Rockwell, among many others. These artists "invented" their paintings while using living inspiration as the basis for their creations. This applies to both figures and to portraits, and I have provided several of each type as examples.

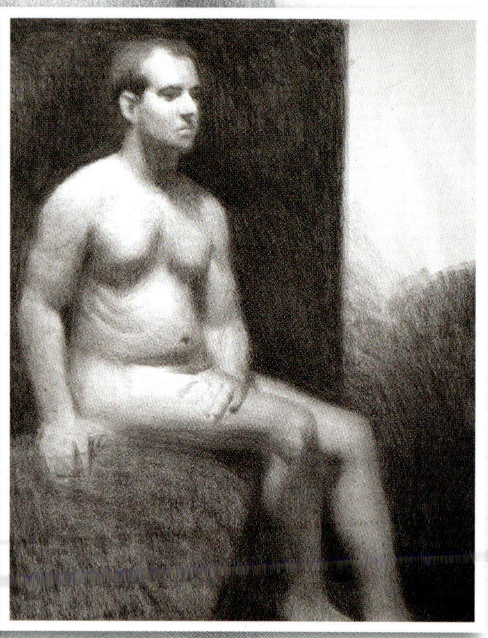

"To move away from references, we need exercises to understand the scene you want to capture."

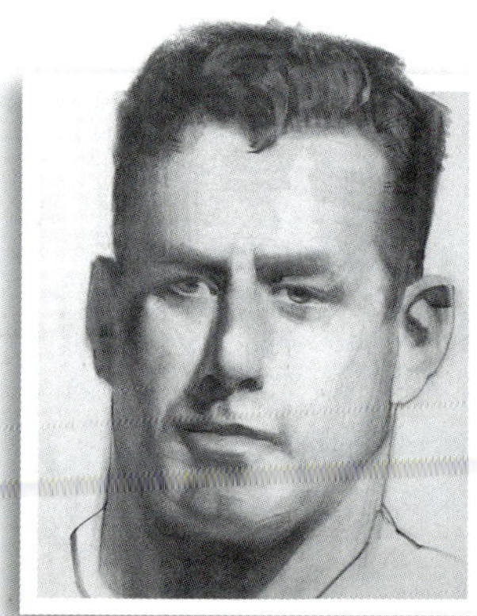

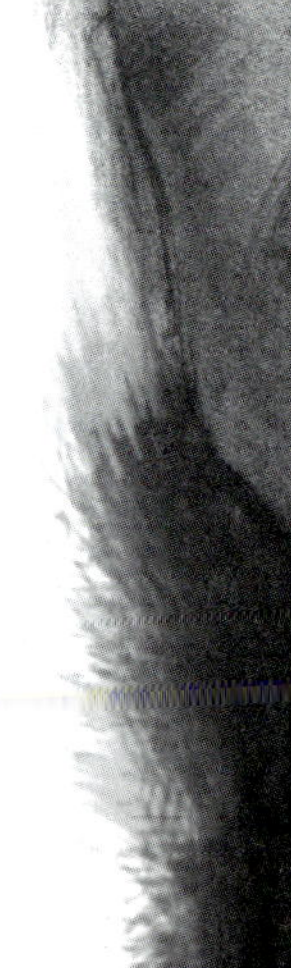

3. BREAKAWAY METHODS

To break away from using references, you need to understand drawing from life. You look up, you take in information, you look down, you remember, and you react (or output) what you thought you saw. This is memorization. You are already doing it, but it's just that the time between looking and outputting is so short that it goes unnoticed.

Now to test this, set your pad up in another part of the room from your model, or in another room. Find a spot in the room you favor as your view, take in what you can, then go and draw it. As you learn how to retain information for longer periods of time, distance yourself further and further from the reference to hold onto that data longer.

Once you have tried the method a few times, test yourself further: set up and draw from one position then, when you go home that night, start the drawing again, this time entirely from memory. Recall as much as you can from the image you created earlier. The more you do this, the more you will remember – this is a muscle you are activating, not a concept.

"A good memory exercise is to sketch from life and flip the image from what you see."

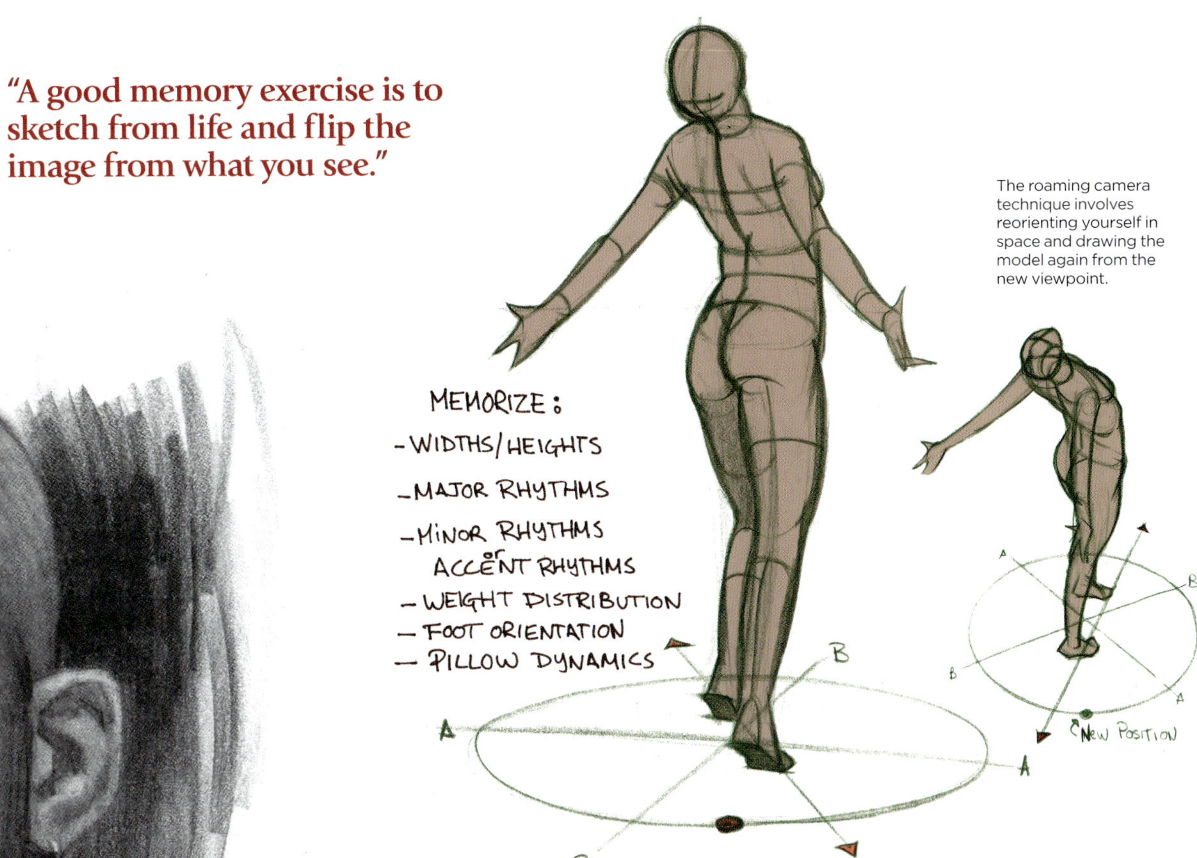

The roaming camera technique involves reorienting yourself in space and drawing the model again from the new viewpoint.

4. MEMORY EXERCISES

A good memory exercise is to sketch from life and flip the image from what you see. The reversed image can then be checked and corrected using a mirror. Any sketch done from memory that you can then compare with a reference is useful for correcting your judgment and sharpening your memory.

Another exercise that I like to give to my students is the roaming camera technique. Sit in a room in one position to the model. Now imagine a circle drawn around the model on the floor; this is the camera track. Make a note of where you are on that circle with a hash mark to indicate your location – it should be at the front center of the circle.

On that same circle, place a second mark in a different place on the circle – this will be where you sit for your second drawing. From the original position, set up a grid in the circle dividing it into four quadrants and then draw a line attaching both heels and another line attaching either big toes or little toes. Redraw the circle and mark your position on it, front and center, and redraw the interior information of the circle with regards to your new position. This will be the information rotated from where you first started.

Now, starting with rhythm and loose scribbles of some kind, gesture out the figure thinking of the pillow-shaped core and its bent and stretched sides. Think about the limbs and the cylinder forms they make when simplified. Gesture in the pose from this new position, and then compare the new drawing with the original one. Do they feel like they both belong to the same 360-degree view? Is the balance correct? Is the weighting correct? Are the limbs correct to the action, or did you reverse them?

"Compare a sketch done from memory with the initial reference to help correct your judgment."

"Draw an imaginary sphere around the subject, and just as with our pivot/rotation diagrams, you will use the model as the pivot."

5. THINK IN THREE DIMENSIONS

In addition to the circle on the floor, we can elevate or lower our view with a circle drawn all the way around the model, at any distance. This circle is really a sphere, and just as with our pivot/rotation diagrams, you will use the model as the pivot. Rotate the "camera" anywhere around the model, and project a cone from the virtual camera's lens to determine what you will be viewing. In addition to the camera, you can also do this with your light source: alter the position of the lighting on the model, and practice your lighting invention. In a way, we are constructing from memory a virtual 3D space in our brain. This is what it means to have an active imagination and a photographic memory. You are not just memorizing an instance, you are memorizing an entire moment, scene, or volumetric space all at once.

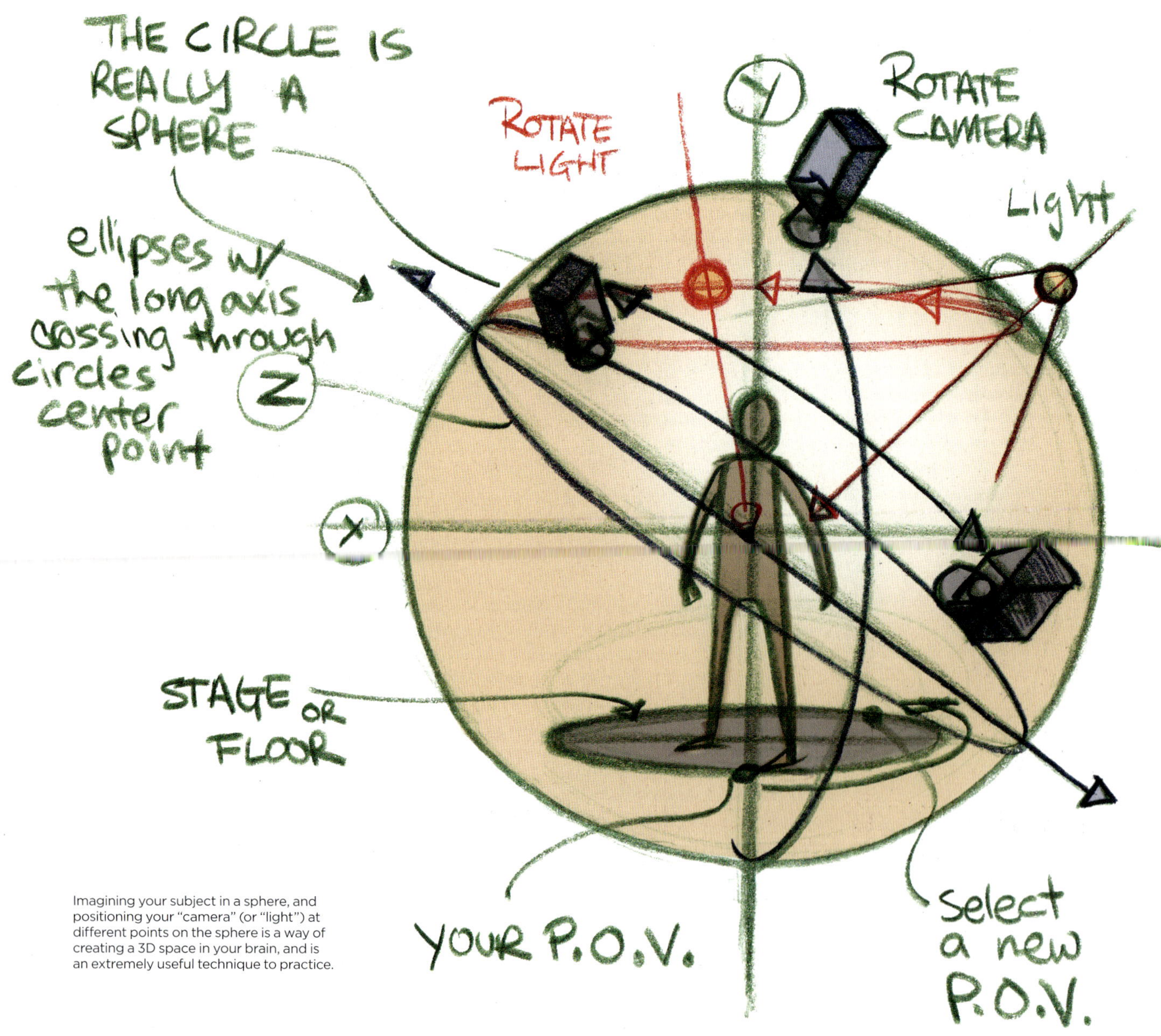

Imagining your subject in a sphere, and positioning your "camera" (or "light") at different points on the sphere is a way of creating a 3D space in your brain, and is an extremely useful technique to practice.

6. GRIDDING WITH ABSTRACTION

This last technique will be useful for those of you who are trying to tie your compositions together better.

The Reilly Abstraction, which we have discussed previously, is actually a part of a bigger concept. To construct or "abstract" an image through the use of implied rhythms that link to one another, weaving a larger tapestry of information together, is a process that comes from the ancient art of tapestries, an extremely technical artform tied together with hidden geometry and complex calculations. This artform was at its height in the Renaissance, and Peter Paul Rubens is a great example of this technique as he mastered all the grid structures, from musical to mathematical, and applied them all in some way or another.

Your canvas is a sacred square, designed in an ancient ratio that has ideal divisions built into it with regard to the corners and their distance to each other. The great Renaissance painters obsessed over these grids and structures; it is little wonder that we marvel over their paintings. Structure was so important that details such as the number of blades of grass, and their orientation in regard to other elements, would be carefully worked out.

The figure abstraction is a tipping point for your understanding of this great tool. It ties together the contours of exteriors to the interiors, from shadow patterns to anatomical relationships and back and forth between all of these elements.

The more you engage in this practice, the more you will see it in everything, everywhere. It is like a magical matrix, which is another name for the gridding process of painting.

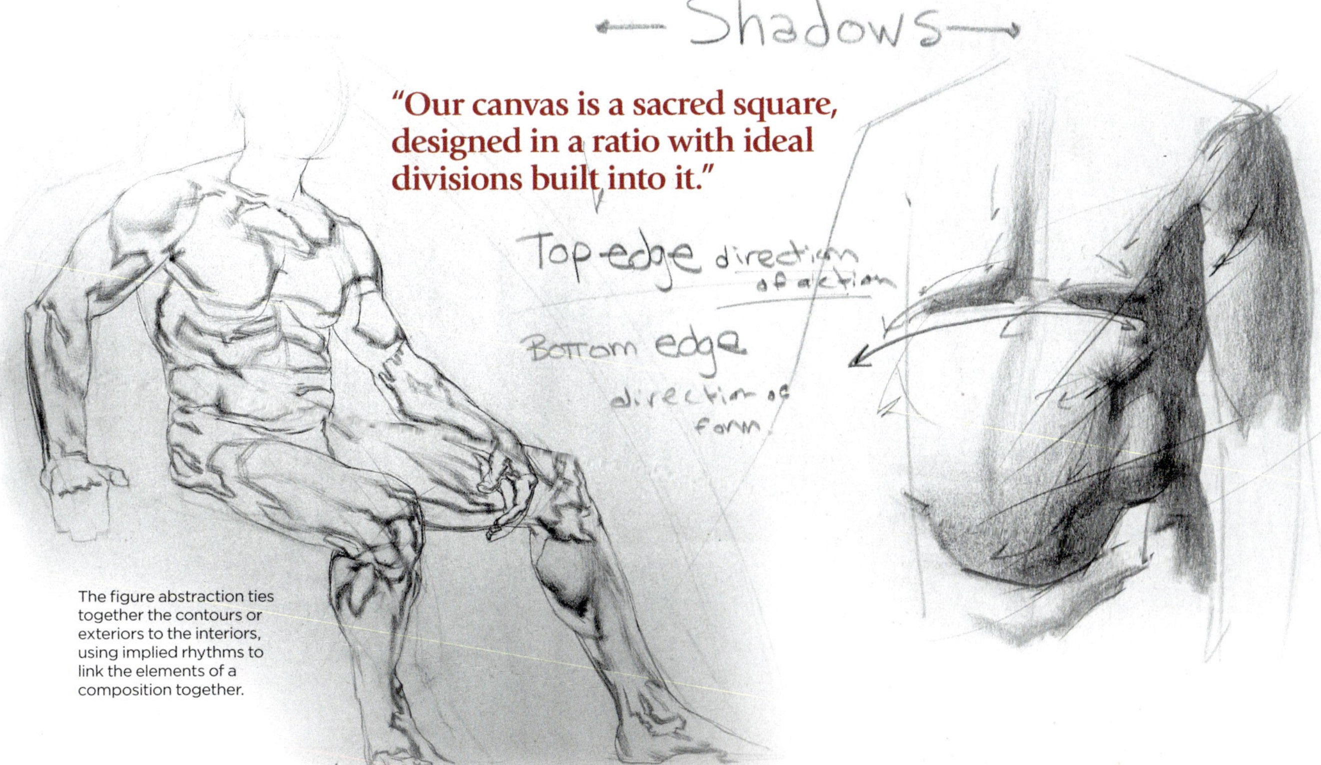

"Our canvas is a sacred square, designed in a ratio with ideal divisions built into it."

The figure abstraction ties together the contours or exteriors to the interiors, using implied rhythms to link the elements of a composition together.

7. CLOSING COMMENTS

My intention with this tutorial is to give you a little taste of the technique of drawing with abstractions – it would take a whole series of articles dedicated solely to this concept to get this abstract tool set to really mean something. I leave you with this because I want you to think harder about the pictures you make, and what they are really trying to say. I want to offer you a set of tools and then give you the chance to test them out, throw them against the wall, stomp on them, and prove them right or wrong. The fact is that making pictures is not easy. It is a science, and it requires a lot of learning and practice. It is part sport, part philosophy; but the more you are aware of what goes into your craft, the more you'll push yourself and the better your work will become as a result.

"The fact is that making pictures is not easy. It is a science, and it requires a lot of learning and practice."

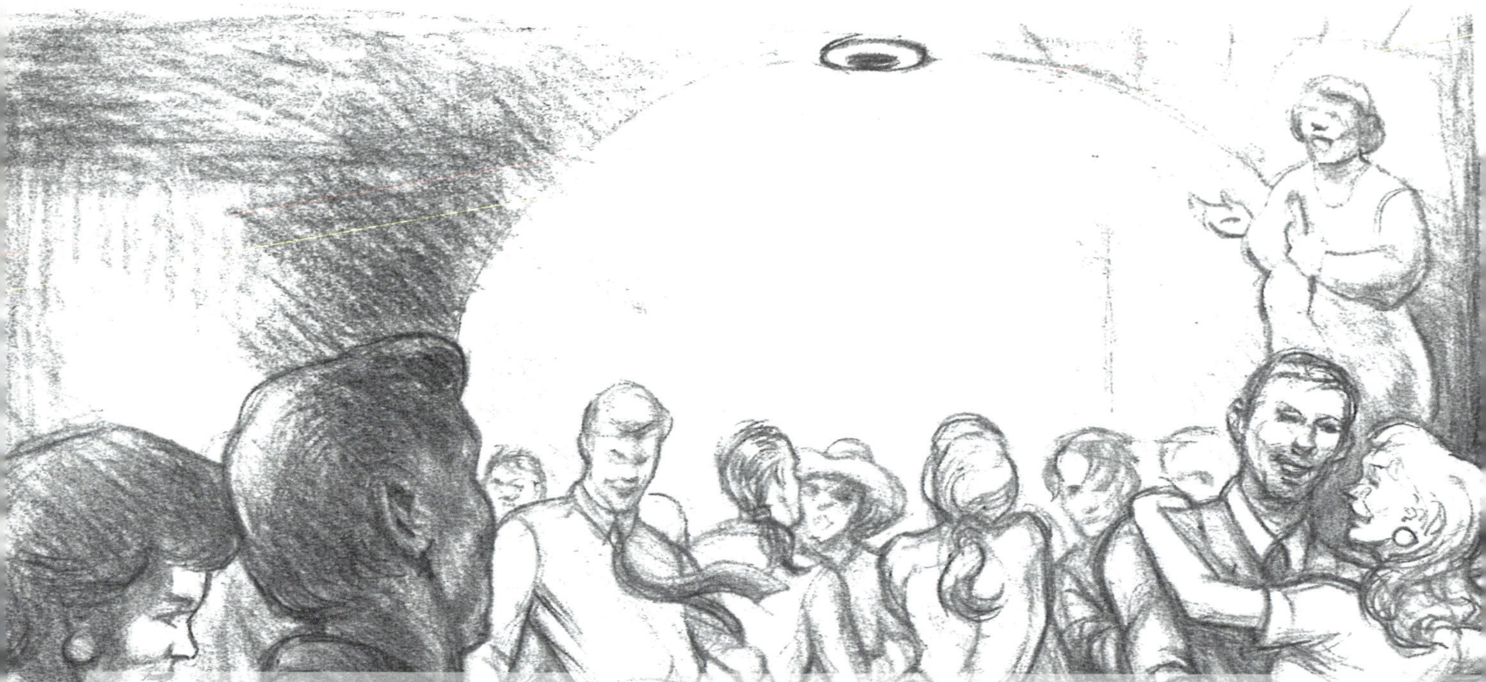

COMPOSE MULTIPLE FIGURES IN A SCENE

Jack Bosson puts together an engaging crowd scene involving two dancers as the main center of interest

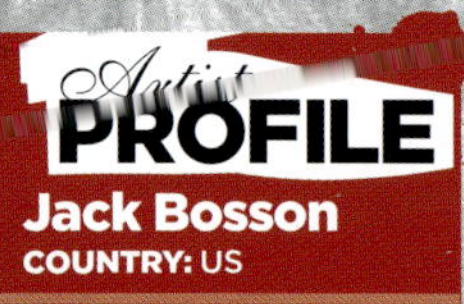

Artist PROFILE

Jack Bosson

COUNTRY: US

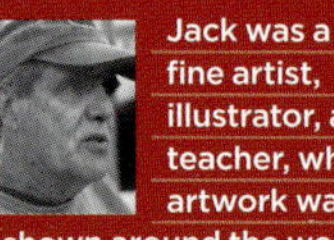

Jack was a fine artist, illustrator, and teacher, whose artwork was shown around the world. Sadly, he died in 2012.

www.jackbosson.com

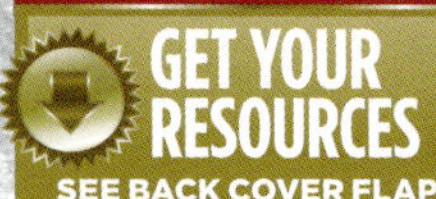

GET YOUR RESOURCES

SEE BACK COVER FLAP

This scene of dancers at a New York club with a jazz band is based on my own recollection of going to such a place, in the '50s, filled with great excitement and anticipation, when I was a kid in my late teens. I remember coming into the large room, seeing the spectacle, darkened forms, light, movement, hearing the music, then making out the undulating, moving bodies. Although it was a long time ago, I wanted to recreate the mood and sense of excitement I felt then.

Since this scene is entirely made up, it's important that it remain free, if possible, from clichés. As such, you have to return constantly to thumbnail sketches and observed figure studies. I did a lot of both.

When I first began work on this picture, I wasn't particularly conscious of working stages, from first concept to finished picture. I have to admit that it's only when facing the prospect of having to break it down for purposes of teaching it that the issue of procedure comes up. So what you get here is my own documenting of how I went about putting this together.

To go step by step into the construction of such a crowd scene, we have to recognize what's involved. I believe the success of such a picture depends largely on how well it's composed, perhaps even more so than on the individual figures and props within.

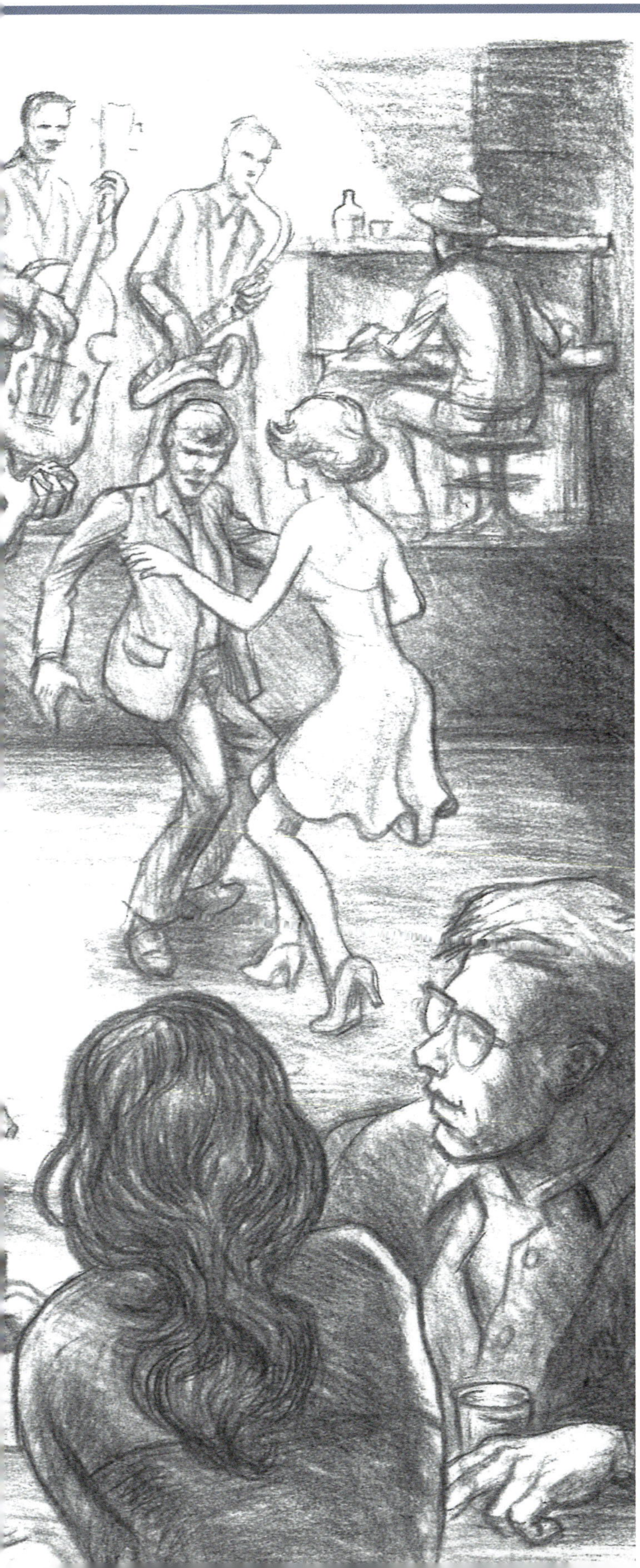

PRO SECRETS

Find your own sense of drama

Composition is personal, like any other facet of picture-making. There are no hard and fast rules. You choose the subject matter, make the choices regarding mood, distortion, expression, exaggeration, pace, and so on. An artist's style is the outcome and combination of his or her taste, inclinations, and skills in composition. Keep a sketchbook and a scrapbook of pictures that move you, excite you. You need to develop your opinions.

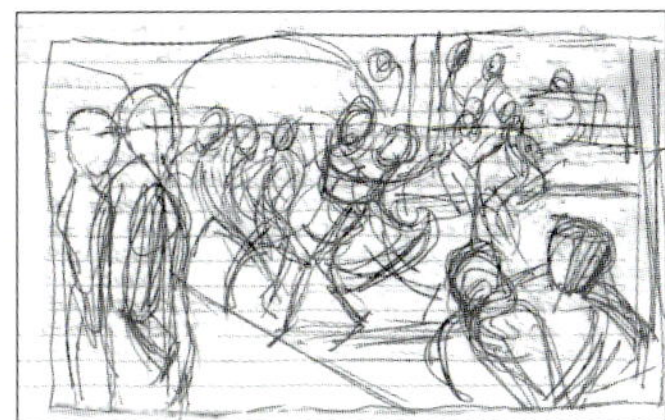

1 Composition is key

Composition shows us how a picture is constructed. It gives us the plan and the organization of shape, values, color, textures, and so on, all arranged according to principles of design: dominance, harmony, contrast, rhythm, and balance. Composition may be the biggest issue most artists have in their work. Their use of composition often weakens, clutters, or confuses the design, or renders it static and uninteresting. You just can't stick a bunch of figures together in a haphazard way and expect it to work.

2 Basic principles of composition

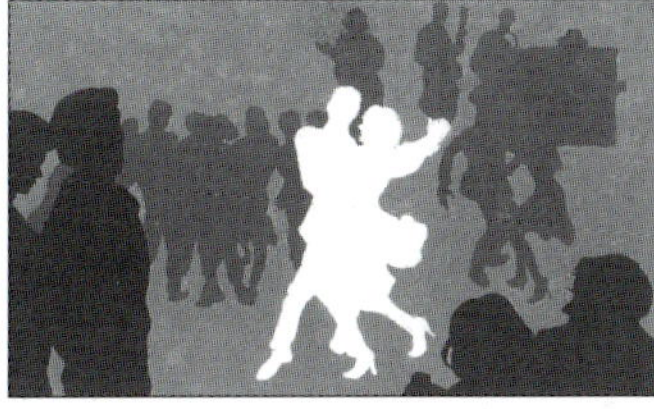

There are certain practical aspects of picture composition that must be considered. These involve balance and the placement of pictorial elements within the rectangle. I begin thinking about breaking my figure groups into foreground, middle ground and background groups, and about establishing a main center of interest.

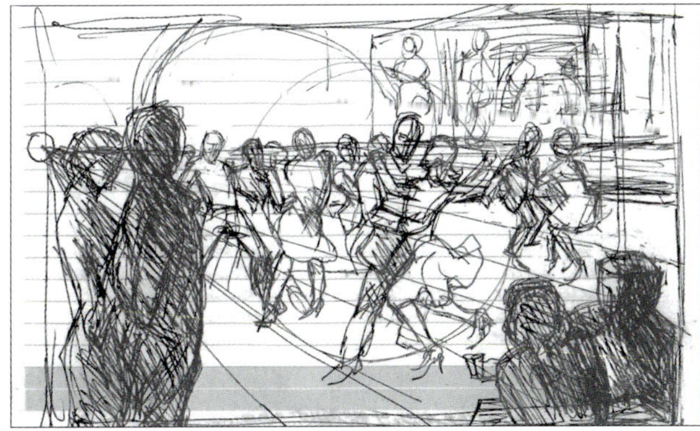

3 Framing and control

When determining the most effective composition, one must be aware of the borders one is working within. Composition is an arrangement of shapes that convey the subject with visually appealing clarity. Elements such as line, tone, gradation, color, or modelling of form and space can strengthen composition, but the flat contours of the shapes that comprise your picture are the strongest, most fundamentally effective means of controlling the impact of your images. Control is the basic requirement of composition. Good composition is intentional.

4 The Golden Section

The Golden Section is a mathematical ratio that's been cited as the ideal theorem for constructing composition. The theory – that a line divided in a way that the smaller part is to the larger part as the larger part is to the whole – would provide perfectly balanced proportions. However, I believe artists ultimately rely on their own intuition to create pictorial composition, not mathematics. I know I do. But it's a useful ratio that informs most of the world's great art and architecture, and I believe it's worth mentioning here.

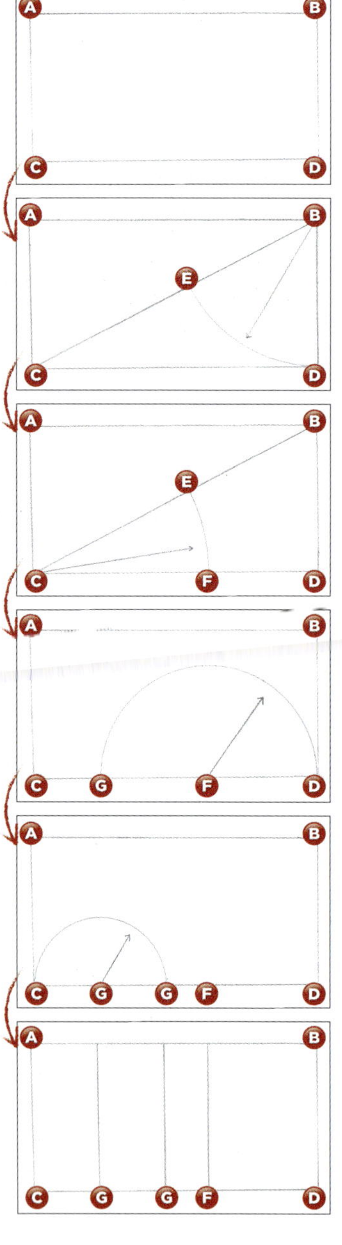

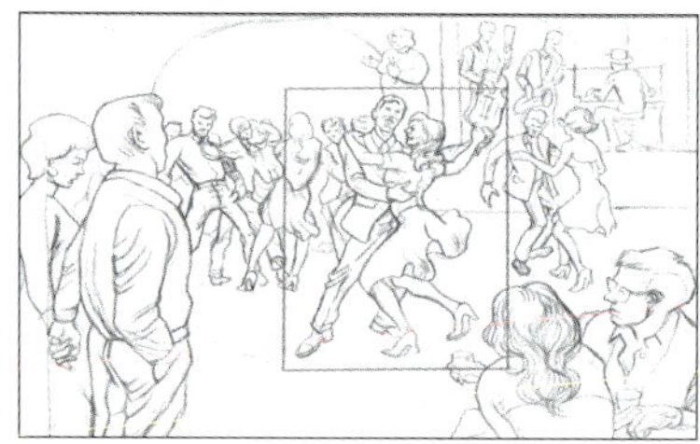

5 The center of interest

Start by determining your center of interest. In my picture it's the dancing couple who happen to be in the center of the image. It's not always necessary to place the main subject of interest at the picture's center. It could be to one side or the other, as the composition determines what the eye is naturally drawn to first. The composition assigns secondary roles to the less-important details.

6 Supporting the scene's focal point

Because there are several couples dancing, I need to differentiate one couple from the others. I do this in the following ways. First, the figures are organized into groups that occupy distinctive planes moving back toward the horizon (eye level). Second, I have the central couple of interest occupy their own level. They seem to be doing a different kind of dancing from the others, and their greater liveliness and contrast attracts our attention. Third, the main couple is highlighted. The use of tone and contrast not only helps to reinforce the pictorial design, but also draws the eye to the dancing forms in the center. Finally, several of the figures in the foreground and background are gazing toward the main couple. This reinforces the viewer's gaze toward the center.

7 Apply perspective

Of course, the quality of your work will be governed by your own experience and the extent to which you tap your own imagination and creativity. But at some point you need to set up a system for representing the images produced by your imagination in a coherent, three-dimensional world of spatial recession on a two-dimensional surface. For that you need to understand two types of perspective: linear and aerial.

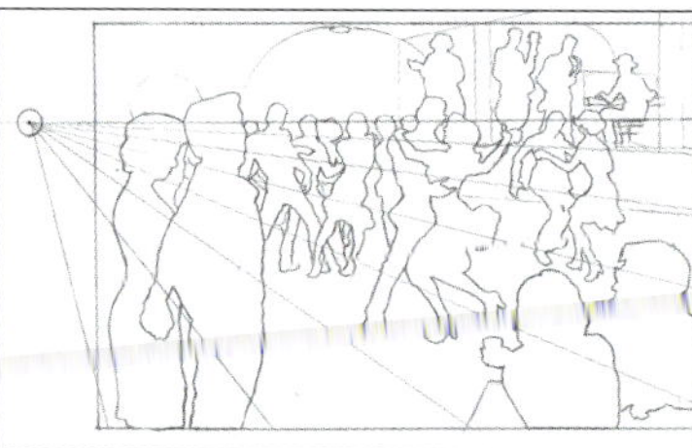

8 Linear perspective

This will give a picture apparent depth. First, establish a horizon. The term horizon line is synonymous with eye-level line. Everything in our picture is viewed from one vantage point, so our eye level is horizontal across the picture. Because the scene is an interior one, we can't see the horizon, but we need to establish it so we can refer everything we draw in the foreground, middle, and background to it, for consistency.

9 Establish eye level

If you're a man of average height, your eyes will be about 5ft. 8in. (1.7m) above the ground. So your eye-level will be roughly where it's shown in the outline sketch of the drawing. The position of the eye-level line governs everything in the picture. Everything and everyone taller than 5ft. 8in. will be above the line; anything lower than 5ft. 8in. will be below it – wherever in the picture it is.

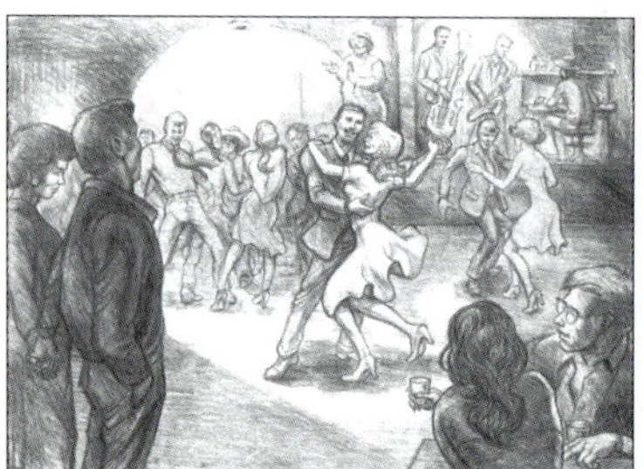

10 Aerial perspective

This deals with recession and depth in pictures. The technique, combined with overlap, renders some of the dancing figures and the band members in the background less distinct than the figures in the middle and foreground areas. Line weight also establishes depth. Notice that the middle and foreground figures are drawn with heavier lines. In painting, less strongly contrasting shades/colors are used to depict distant objects.

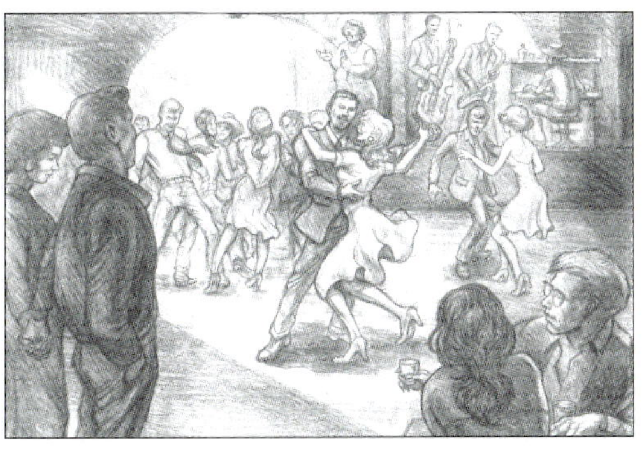

11 Contrast poses

Another way to highlight one part of the composition is to give that part greater liveliness and contrast. Note the two foreground couples. Their more static postures, in contrast to the dancers, immediately attracts the eye. This is reinforced by their closer proximity to our vantage point and their shadowy foreground presence. The main dancing couple is framed by these two elements, giving more importance to the center of interest. Also note how the standing male figure's boldly drawn head transitions into a darkened tone that forms an arch, directing our eye back to the dancers.

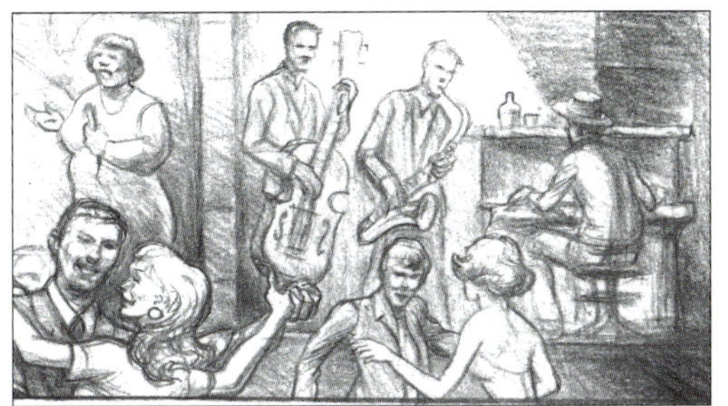

12 Introducing the band

In developing this scene, compositionally, I realize I have a problem: how to draw attention to the band and keep it as a part of the overall panorama without obscuring them behind the dancers. I consider putting them in the foreground and then building my center of interest with the other dancers back toward the horizon, but this doesn't work for me. I decide that they need to be in the background, but also able to command the viewer's attention. I put them on a stage above the eye-level of the dancers on the dance floor. In so doing, I'm able to give greater importance to the presence of the band, as the picture's purpose and meaning seem to demand.

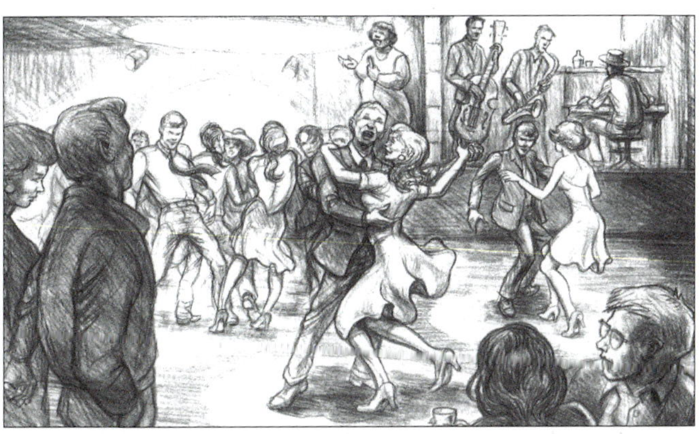

13 Reinforce composition and set the mood of the piece

I need to adjust the mood of my drawing, to create my sense of coming into a large room with muted lights and darkened areas, music, and dancing figures. In an otherwise darkened nightclub setting, I set up spots or fields of light shaped as arcs in the background to balance and tie in the groups of figures.

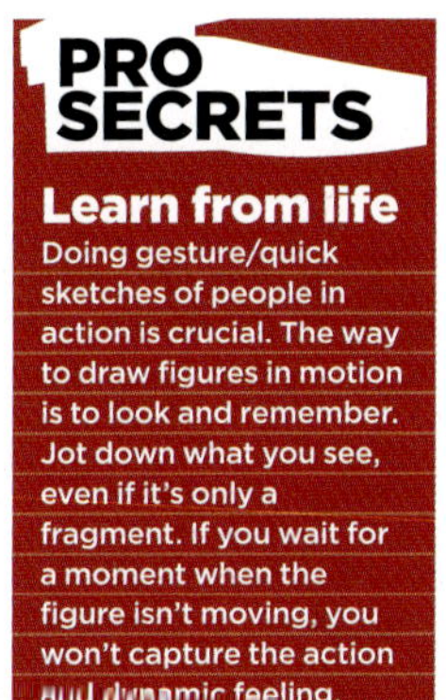

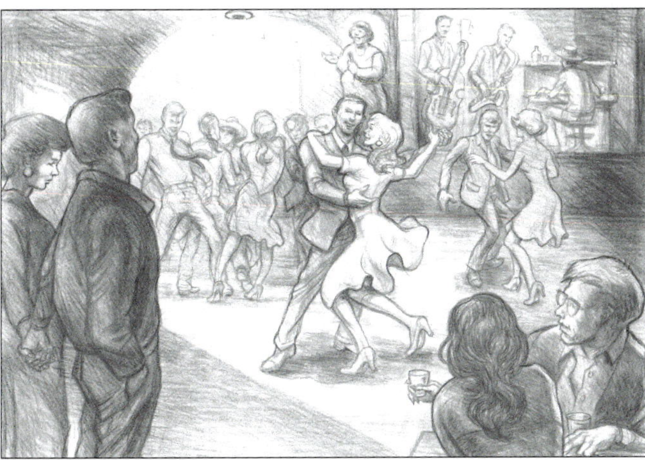

14 Light, shadow, and we're done...

There's a highlighted area next to the main dancing couple and a lighted area that stops as a diagonal shadow runs left to right between the two foreground couples. Light and shadow not only enhance the depiction of figural form, they also exist as a system of expression. They're the "what" and "how" of every drawing. It's by the mutual reinforcement of shapes and forms that our drawings come alive. Not only is the compositional structure reinforced, but the mood of the scene, at least for the storyteller, is also established.

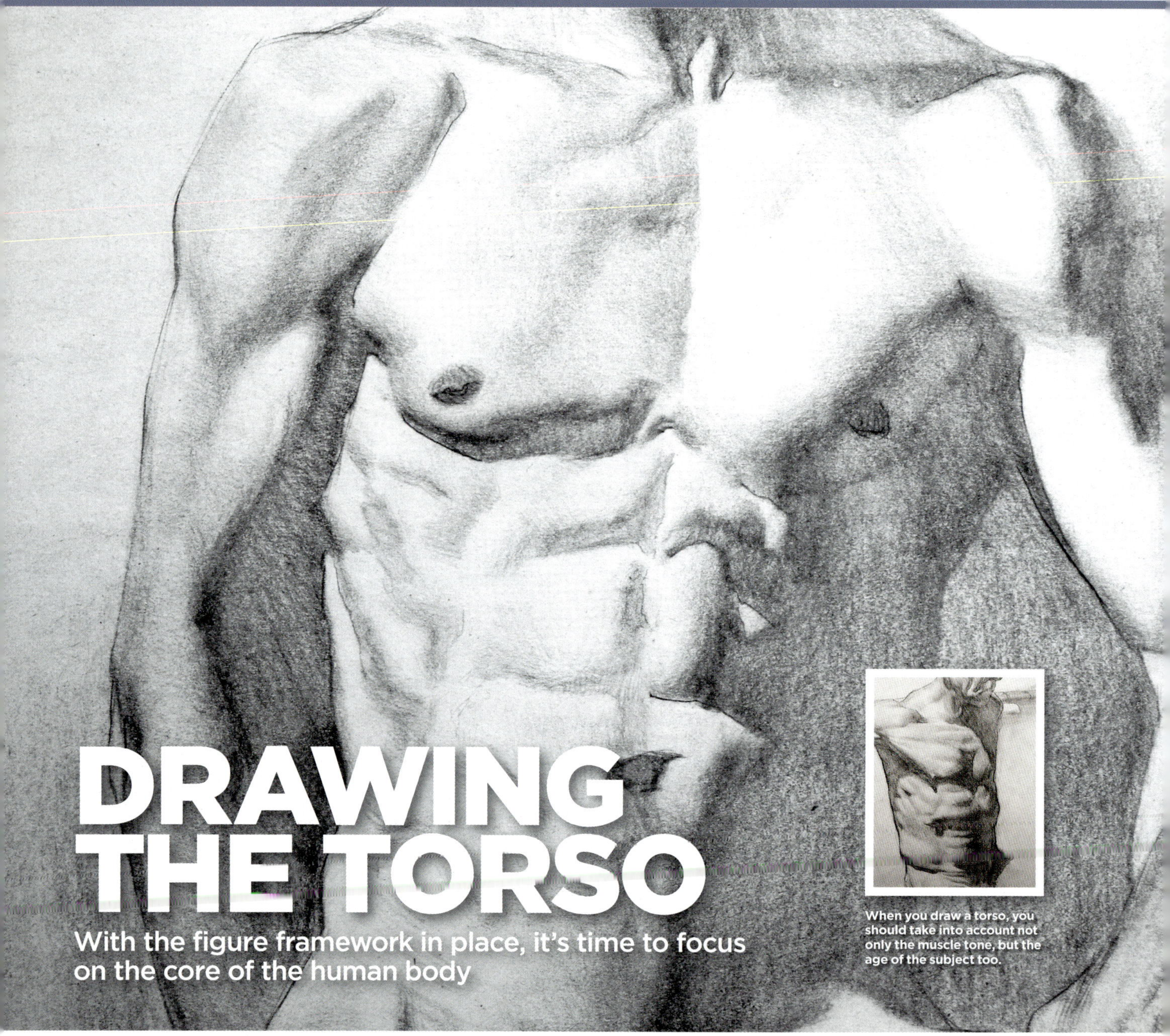

DRAWING THE TORSO

With the figure framework in place, it's time to focus on the core of the human body

When you draw a torso, you should take into account not only the muscle tone, but the age of the subject too.

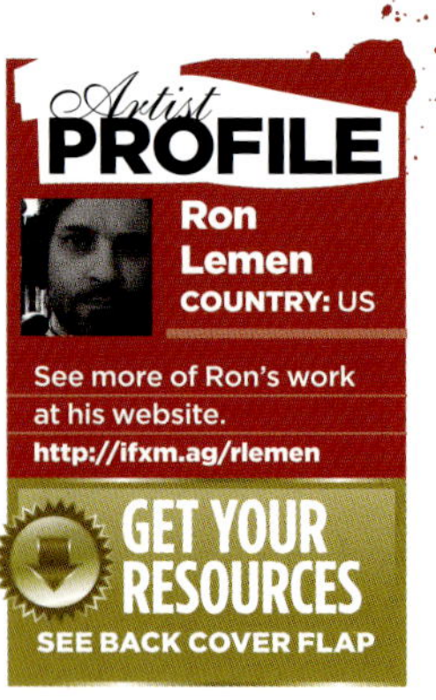
Artist PROFILE
Ron Lemen
COUNTRY: US
See more of Ron's work at his website.
http://ifxm.ag/rlemen

The torso is the core of the body: the complex center from which all our dangly parts originate. Our physical actions also originate from this core – therefore, you typically start with the torso in figure drawing to work out the dynamics of your pose.

The head is the ruler that you measure the body from; the body is the primary essence of the pose. Both are important to draw from the start, but the head can stiffen up quickly with no reference to the body. If you design the body first, the head has more chance of complementing the action of the body.

First, you need to find the action of the pose. This step is called the gesture. Using the Industrial Design method, as described on page 12, you can find this action in three lines: the gesture, the width, and the depth. Once the gesture or action of the pose has been established, the limbs are then attached to complement the twist, turn, or swivel of the torso. With the head attached, you can measure off the height and width of the torso more appropriately, or adjust the drawing to a more correct scale throughout the pose.

Next, draw a centerline through the middle of the torso. (Simply put, the centerline of the back is the spine.) The front of the body is divided through the center of the chest, or the sternum, and continues through the line that splits the abdominal muscles down to the pelvis.

The centerline is very important to draw. It finds the middle of the visible surface to match and align the forms on either side of it, and it's also an anchor and apex for matching rhythmical lines from either side of the body. Neglecting to draw the centerline in your structure is like forgetting to bring the manager along to the big game.

If you don't use boxes to design the pelvis and the rib cage, the next step is to find the three-quarter line of the figure, or where the figure turns from the frontal planes to the side of the body. In many poses, this landmark can be as important as the centerline: it's a major breaking point in form, critical to both the perspective and the alignment of the limbs from the left side to the right side of the figure.

Torso muscles

The front of the body is made up of six major visible muscle groups: the pectoralis muscles, the abdominal muscles, the obliques, the serratus muscles, the trapezius muscles, and the lattisimus muscles, which you can see if the arms are lifted. Unfortunately, two of these muscle groups have multiple heads to them, but are well organized, so rendering them is just a matter of finding the larger shape that keeps the smaller ones organized and harmonized.

The body wedges down from the acromium processes – the bumps at the shoulders – and tapers to the base of the crotch. The wedge forms the true front plane of the body; the masses on either side of the wedge taper at a sharp angle, and become a part of the side planes of the figure. The wedge form passes through the obliques, or what we usually

1. GETTING THE PECTORALIS MUSCLE RIGHT

The pectoralis muscle sits on the upper half of the rib cage, and inserts onto the upper arm bone, or humerus, around the upper third division of its length. The muscle wraps underneath the humerus toward the back of the arm, and is a five-sided shape.

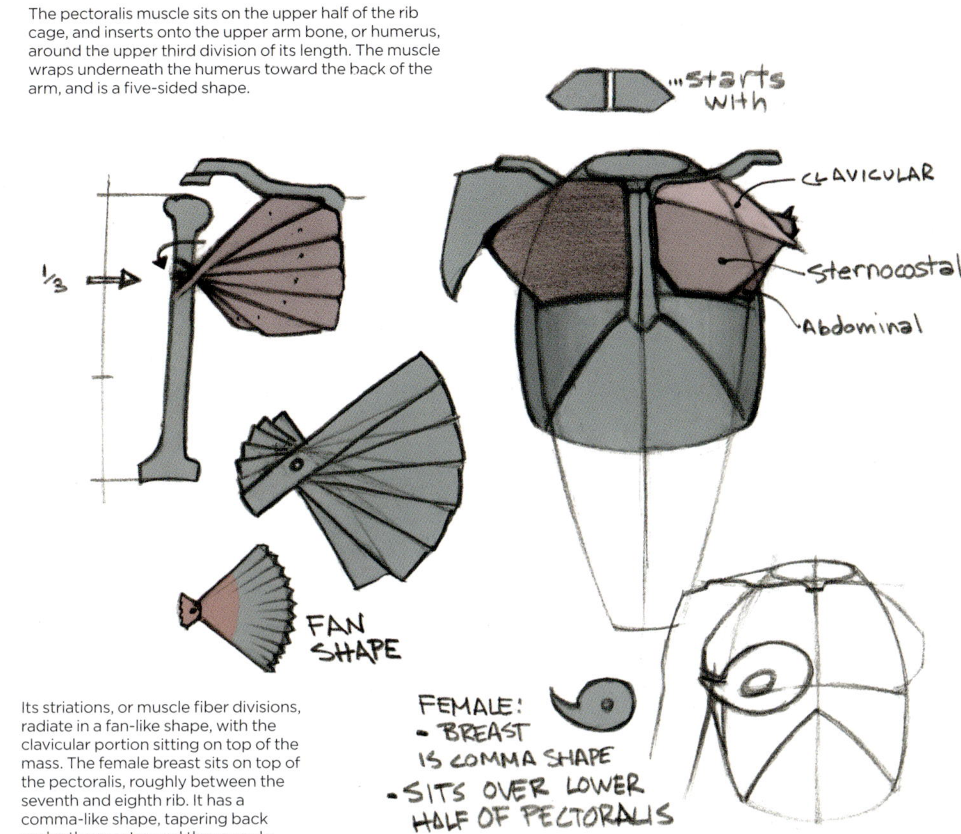

Its striations, or muscle fiber divisions, radiate in a fan-like shape, with the clavicular portion sitting on top of the mass. The female breast sits on top of the pectoralis, roughly between the seventh and eighth rib. It has a comma-like shape, tapering back under the arm toward the scapula.

2. THE COATHANGER METHOD

The trapezius muscle is a back muscle, but sits atop the shoulders and connects to the back of the neck. The visible portion on either side of the neck creates a coat hanger-like rhythm, which goes from the acromium processes at the shoulders to above the seventh cervical, vertebrae, along the clavicles and across the sternal notch. From three-quarter view to profile, the trapezius muscle is a ramp, taking up about half the space of the top plane of the torso. The ramp varies in height depending upon athletic build.

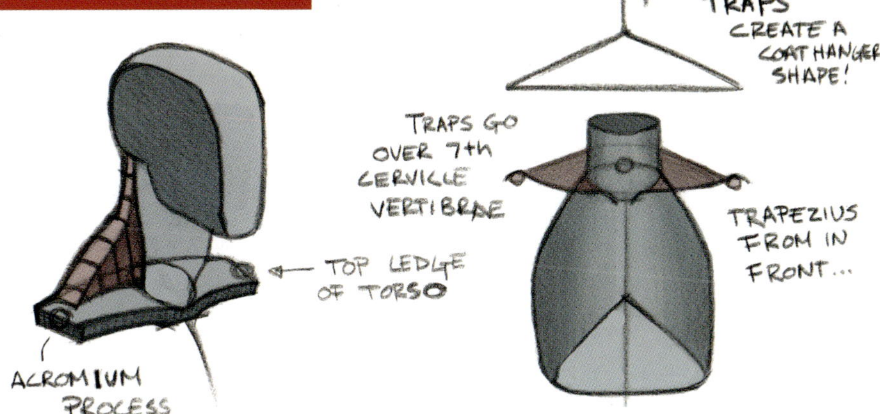

3. DRAWING THE HUMAN FIGURE: A FOUR-STEP GUIDE

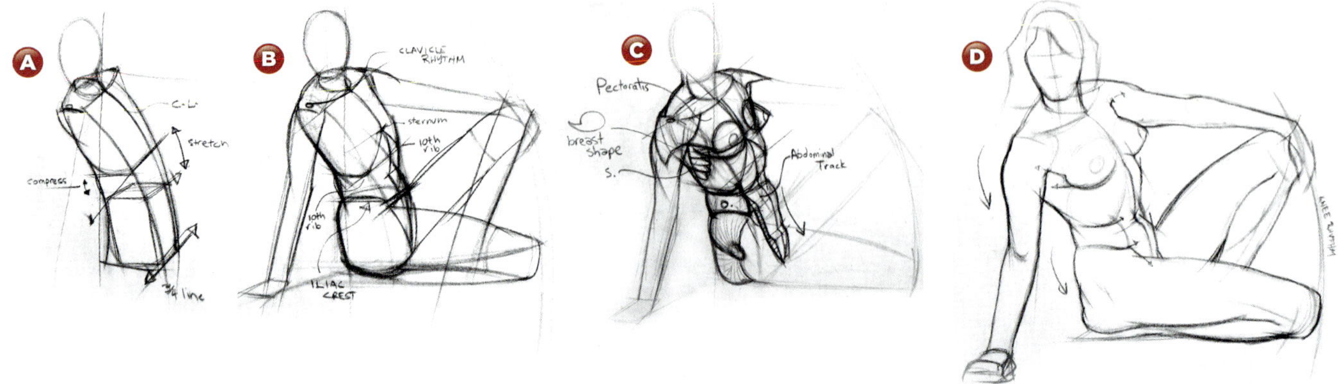

Here's how to build up a complete figure, starting with the core. Use a rhythmical cylinder form to start the pose (A), then find the rib cage and pelvis forms within the rhythm lines; look for key bony points to keep the shapes squared up from top to bottom, and to find the compression between them. Then the perspective is designed (B) with the three-quarter line drawn into the figure to help keep the muscle forms from drifting too close to the right arm. The muscle rhythm lines are then added to fill out the anatomy structure (C). All this should be done lightly so it can be easily removed when the final rendering takes form. When everything is finished, most of the anatomy will not be visible (D), but the bumps and little dark markings drawn in the pose will have a more visual believability and more accurate design to them.

call the spare tire muscles. These muscles are the soft mass between the rib cage and the pelvis. They taper in narrowly at the rib cage and widen at the hips, resting atop the iliac crest. This wedge can be linked to the two lines that form the neck in a rhythmical relationship that helps keep the oblique muscles from becoming too unusual in their shape design. The obliques form true side walls – perpendicular planes to the front and back planes of the body – and blend with the angular sides of the rib cage.

The torso is extremely pliable between the rib cage and pelvis. The further you push the rhythm between these two shapes, the more convincing the action design will feel. The muscles on the front of the body are very pliable and can be stretched and twisted as much as needed to help enhance the gesture of the pose.

It's very important to start the pose with the gesture first, to seize the moment and the action. Then you can proceed to the structure of the pose, and finally the design and articulation of the muscle groups in the body.

If the gesture is dynamic, the muscles must follow that dynamic. Don't stiffen up the design at this point in the drawing. Everything is pliable, no matter how geometrically you might draw your pictures, and the shapes you design for the muscles must not stiffen up in the dynamic gesture you've created. Many comic book images show this latter trait, especially comics from the '80s and '90s. If you can find a few examples, they serve as a good lesson in what not to do when anatomy meets gesture.

As always with anatomy, no matter how much you know, there's always more to learn. Remember: the key is to practice, practice, and practice some more – and to have fun doing it.

4. GETTING THE TORSO STARTED

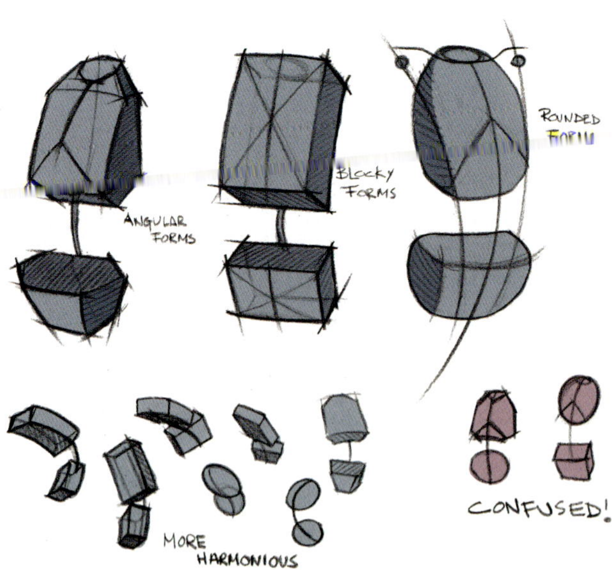

Here are a few ways to start the torso. The first is angular, the second box-like, the third spherical. There is no right or wrong set of shapes, but there may be confusion in the structural design if there are too many shapes to start with. A more harmonious way is to maintain a shape design consistency throughout. These shapes are flexible, bending on the spinal axis.

5. A PINCH HERE, A STRETCH THERE

Seen from profile, the abdominal muscles each have a different type of contour. The top two muscles are angular: the top heads predominantly face up over the rib cage and the second set of heads face downward. The middle heads face flat forward, and the lower abs bulge at the top in a rounded taper toward the base of the pelvis. The muscles have this structural design to help when the body leans forward. The figure on the far right has been drawn using construction forms to keep the anatomy geometric, planar and simple. The right side is pinching or bending in; as a result, the shapes on the right profile all take on a bulging appearance from compression. The left side of the figure is stretched out, and the shapes relate to this.

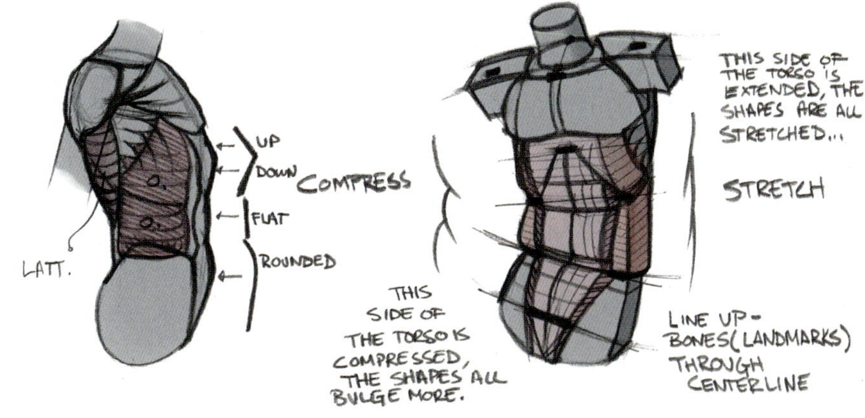

6. WORKING THE SIX-PACK

All the abs stacked up on each other have a rhythmical relationship to one another, as all the head divisions can be connected together at a point to the side of the body. This relationship keeps all the muscle heads organized in the architecture of the bones of the torso.

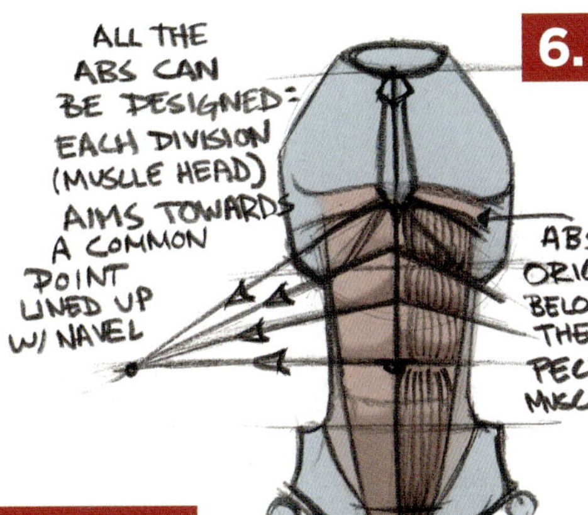

7. SORTING OUT THE CONNECTIONS

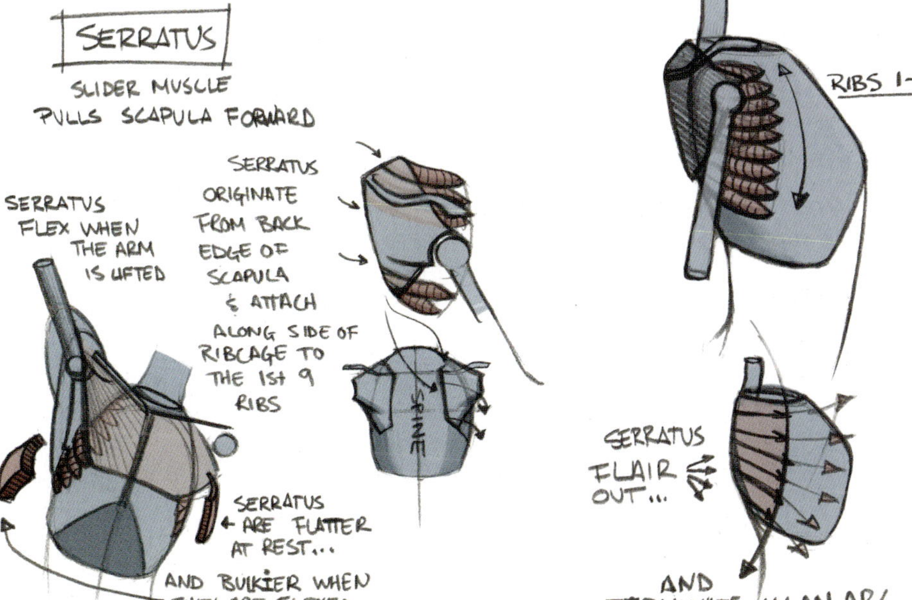

The serratus muscles connect the scapula to the rib cage from beneath the scapula. The muscle heads originate along the inside edge of the scapulae on the back, closest to the spine, and terminate halfway along the first nine ribs. These muscles insert snugly into the obliques, and radiate in an arc on the side of the body, with all the muscles fanning out from top to bottom.

8. HOW THE TORSO ROTATES

The obliques are the big muscles that bend and rotate the torso of the body. The flank portion of the muscle sits between the rib cage and pelvis on the sides of the body. The flank drapes over the iliac crest, giving the pelvis what looks like a downturn on the tops, rather than the upturn of the bones' design. They have three distinct visible planes from the side of the torso. The rest of the oblique travels up the rib cage and laces together with the serratus muscles, and blends to the abdominal appaneurosis.

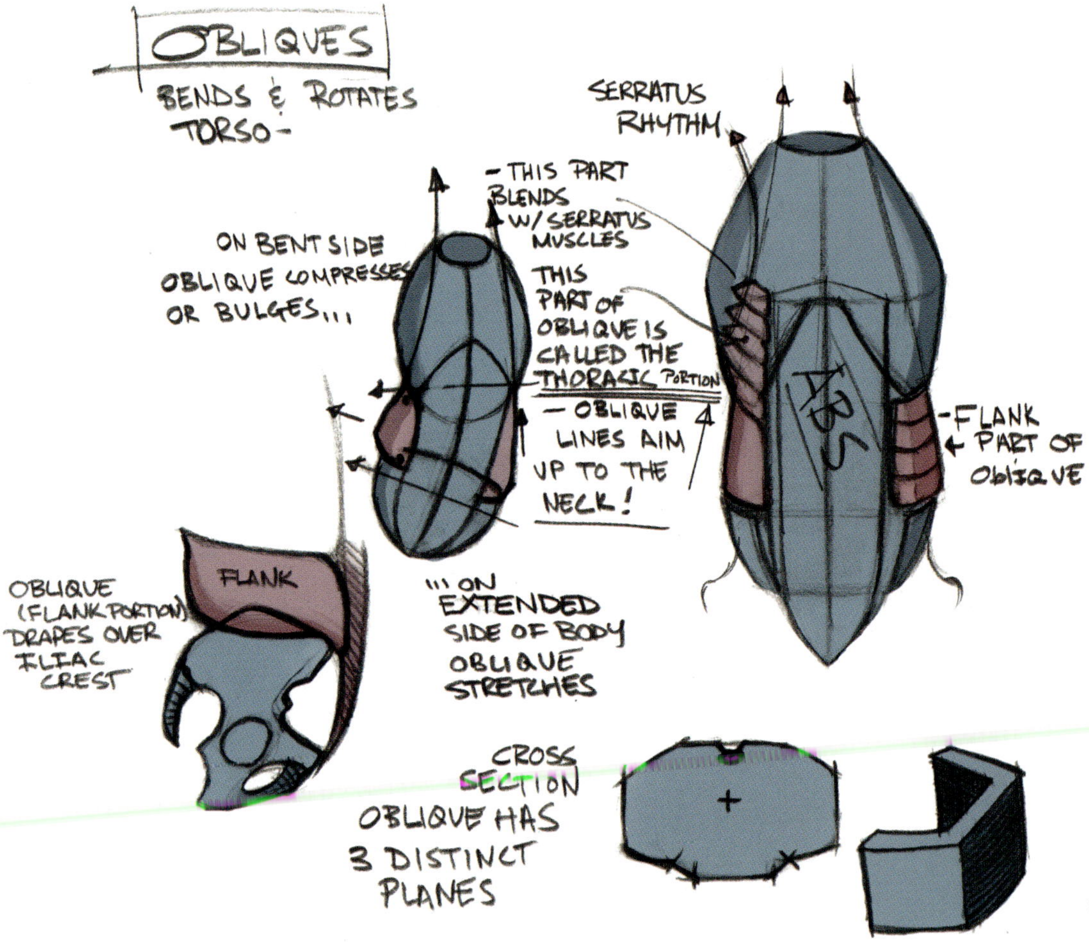

OBLIQUES
BENDS & ROTATES TORSO -
ON BENT SIDE OBLIQUE COMPRESSES OR BULGES...
- THIS PART BLENDS W/ SERRATUS MUSCLES
THIS PART OF OBLIQUE IS CALLED THE THORACIC PORTION
- OBLIQUE LINES AIM UP TO THE NECK!
SERRATUS RHYTHM
ABS
-FLANK ← PART OF OBLIQUE
FLANK
OBLIQUE (FLANK PORTION) DRAPES OVER ILIAC CREST
...ON EXTENDED SIDE OF BODY OBLIQUE STRETCHES
CROSS SECTION OBLIQUE HAS 3 DISTINCT PLANES

"The muscles on the front of the body are very pliable and can be stretched and twisted as much as needed to help enhance the pose."

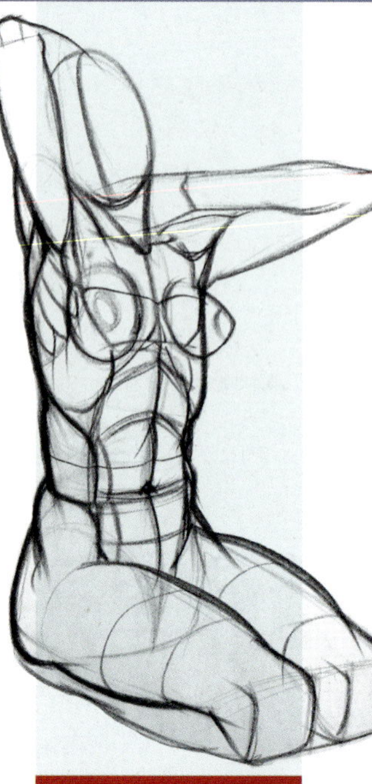

9. MAKE IT FIT

The drawing is never correct until the whole has been established. This means that to understand the relationships of the parts, you must see them all assembled together. Don't become critical of one drawn line; try to draw the entire pose quickly, then assess as a whole what can be fixed or altered to create a stronger, more convincing pose.

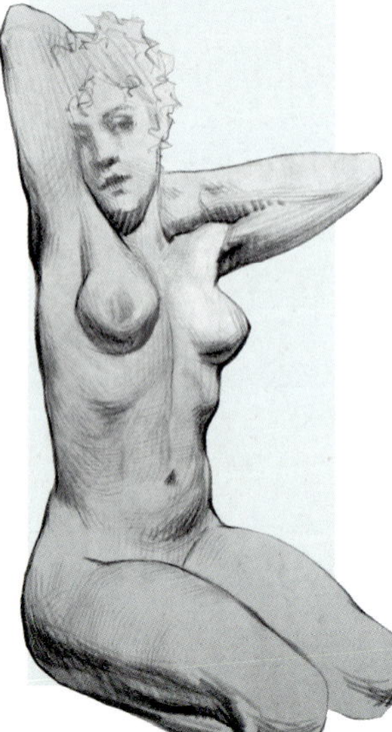

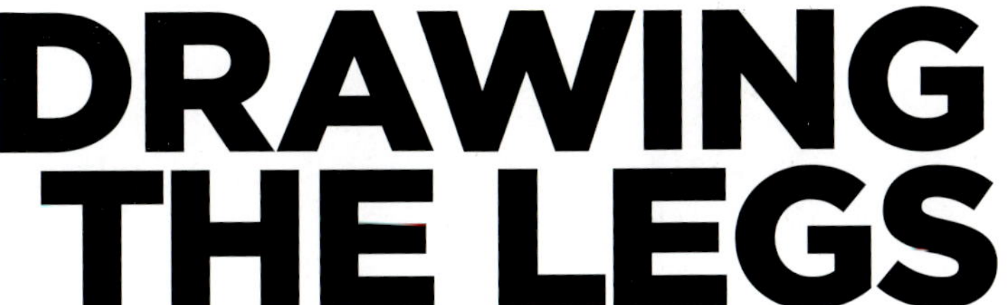

DRAWING THE LEGS

Master your depiction of the limbs that drive the rest of the body

Artist PROFILE

Ron Lemen
COUNTRY: US

See more of Ron's work at his website.
http://ifxm.ag/rlemen

GET YOUR RESOURCES
SEE BACK COVER FLAP

The legs provide support for the body and power much of its movement. Like the arm, the leg has groups of muscles that oppose one another in their action. For example, the quadriceps at the front of the body are used to extend the leg, with the bicep femoris, semi membranosis, and tendonosis acting as flexors. Both the arms and the legs start wide at the torso and taper to about half that width at the wrists and ankles. The biggest structural difference is the organization of muscles around the kneecap, which differs to the ridge or rotator muscles in the elbow.

Now, without getting too caught up in the names, let's get down to discussing the shapes and rhythms in a leg, breaking the drawing down into easy steps.

You should start with a simple gesture; a line connected to the hips will do. The hips are the pivot point for the legs and act as an axle. Remember that both sides of the hips are fused together, unlike the shoulders, which float independently of each other. The tilt of the hips opposes the angle of the shoulders, meaning that the action at the top of the body is counter-balanced by the position of the lower body, which creates stability. The hips can be drawn as one of several different masses, depending on your preferred drawing methodology, but they all serve the same function: volume and construction.

Leg bones and muscles

The pelvis is a narrow shape tunnellling inward toward its base. The wide point of the hips is created by the femur and the hip muscles, which are mostly responsible for connecting the leg to the body, and fill in the space between the pelvis and femur. These hip muscles flair out in an A shape and act in a broadly similar way to the shoulder muscles, which we look at in more detail later in the book.

Moving down the legs, the femurs both taper inward, forming a semi-V shape between them. The figure looks knock-kneed at this stage, but that's normal until we place muscles over the bones. In a standing position, the knees are almost directly below the iliac crests of the pelvis. The thigh is divided into three major masses: the front mass, which consists mostly of the quadriceps and sartorius muscles; the inside of the thigh, or adductor muscles; and the back of the thigh, or the bicep mass. All of these muscle groups start out large – the muscle heads account for about two thirds of the length of the leg and taper around the knee as the muscles terminate in tendons, exposing more bone than they cover.

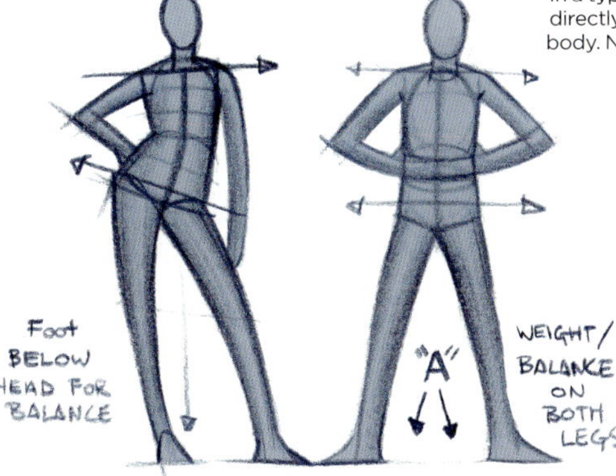

In a typical standing pose, unless the legs are spread, one foot always sits directly below the skull for balance at the two polar extremes of the body. Notice how the hips move to compensate for the tilt of the shoulders. If the legs are spread, they maintain an A-shape, distributing the weight of the figure evenly across the ground.

1. THE RELATIONSHIP BETWEEN HIPS AND SHOULDERS IN POSES

2. DRAW ARCS TO CONNECT KEY AREAS TOGETHER

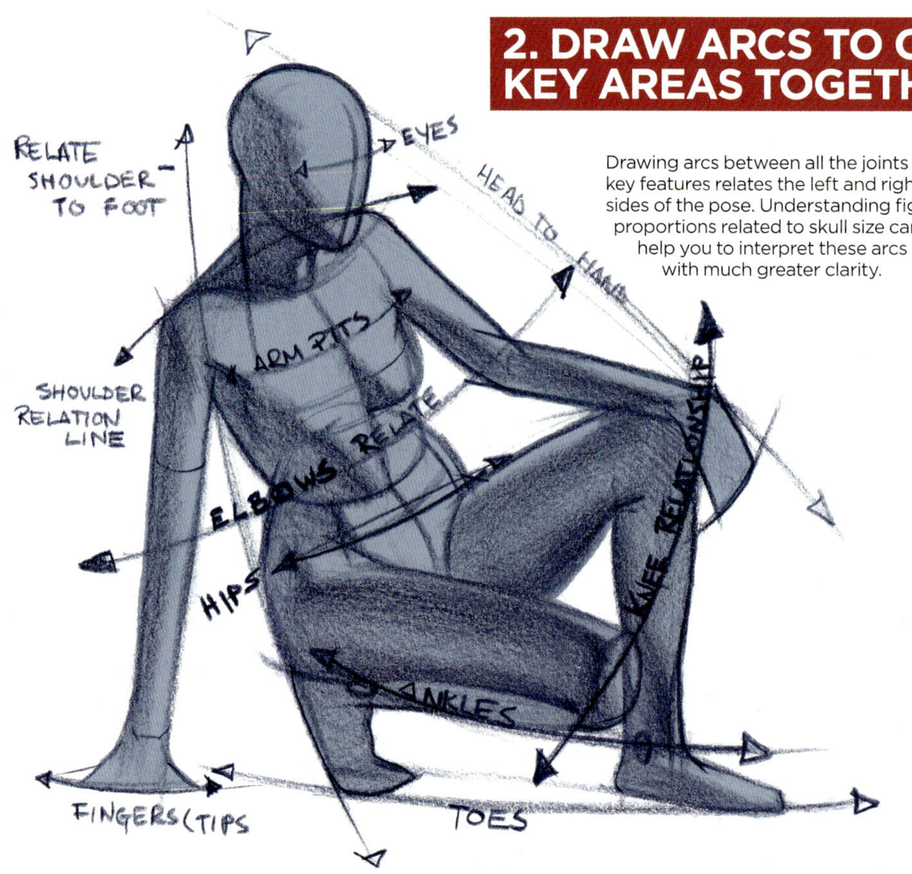

Drawing arcs between all the joints and key features relates the left and right sides of the pose. Understanding figure proportions related to skull size can help you to interpret these arcs with much greater clarity.

"Remember that both sides of the hips are fused together, unlike the shoulders, which float independently of each other."

3. FINDING THE BIG RELATIONAL SHAPES IN POSES WHERE THE FIGURE ISN'T STANDING

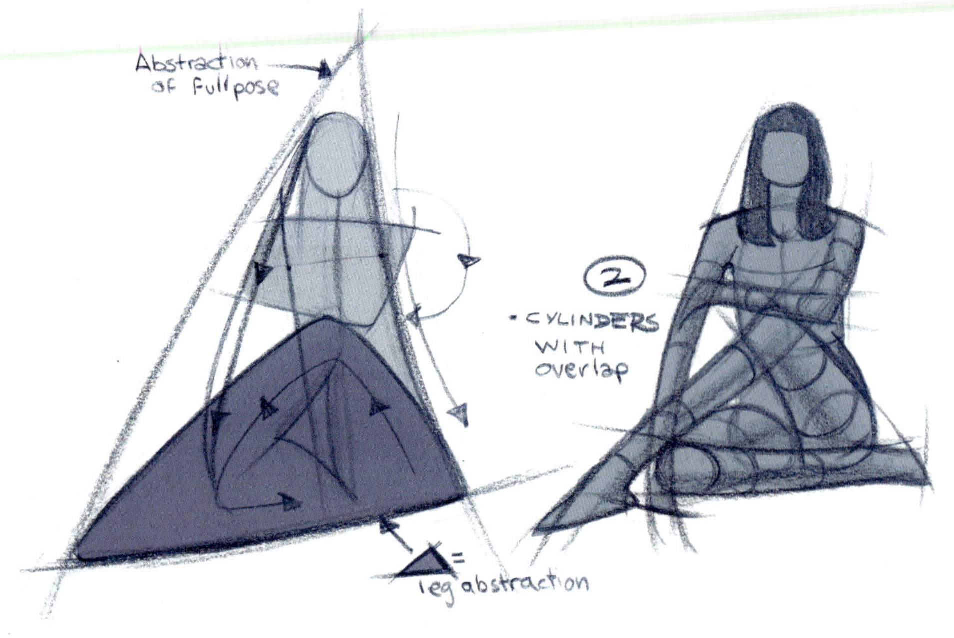

For compressed or seated poses, I like to start the gesture of the pose by finding the big shapes – or, in this case, the shape – that both legs create together. This abstraction helps to strengthen the relationship between the limbs, as well as keeping the legs relating to each other dynamically and proportionately.

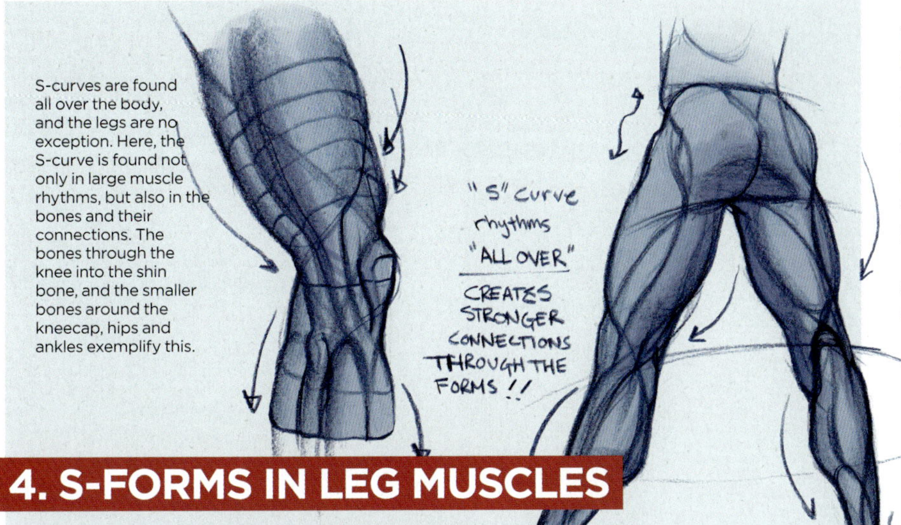

S-curves are found all over the body, and the legs are no exception. Here, the S-curve is found not only in large muscle rhythms, but also in the bones and their connections. The bones through the knee into the shin bone, and the smaller bones around the kneecap, hips and ankles exemplify this.

4. S-FORMS IN LEG MUSCLES

When drawing the leg, keep in mind that the muscles spiral over the form in an S-like rhythm. This rhythm is universal throughout the body, but it's particularly noticeable in the arm and leg muscles, so it's good to bear that in mind while drawing these areas. Rhythm keeps any form from getting too stiff in its design. One of these S-curves is the sartorius muscle, which is attached to the iliac crest and spirals down and around the inner wall of the leg. It acts as a major landmark, dividing muscle masses and surfaces like a fence between two gardens. The iliotibial band does the same thing on the outside of the leg. These divisions are usually where the strongest shadow patterns are formed on the legs, regardless of how active the pose is.

The kneecap itself is a small free-floating bone that hovers over the head of the femur and is attached to the leg by tendons coming from above and below the cap. The most prominent of these tendons is the large ropelike cord that extends below the kneecap to the forward protuberance of the tibia, or shin bone.

The kneecap or patella is shaped somewhat like a pentagon. When the knee is bent, the larger shape of the leg mass between the femur and the shin bones echoes the shape of the patella with a five-sided form. In this position, the side walls are more flat than angled. The lower leg is more triangular than cylindrical in its cross-section. The shin bones form a wedge, with the sharp edge facing forward and the wide side as the calf muscles. The lower half of the leg is about two thirds muscle mass, tapering to a block form at the ankles, with the inside of the ankle higher than the outside. The lower leg forms a bowling pin shape, similar to the forearm, and the foot fits in neatly at the base of the pin.

Notice how the leg and the arm are similar to one another in their physical structure. The biggest differences between them are at the joints.

The knee can be designed with three vertical planes and three horizontal planes, looking like the top of a diamond. Structuring the knee in this way makes it much easier to map the undulating furrows of the bones.

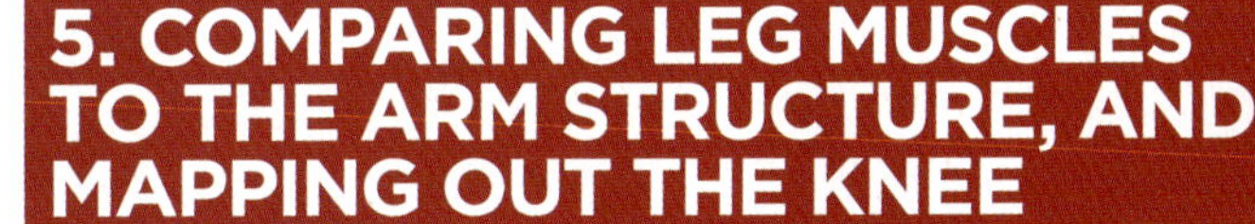

5. COMPARING LEG MUSCLES TO THE ARM STRUCTURE, AND MAPPING OUT THE KNEE

The arm and leg have quite similar proportions with regard to tendon mass versus muscle mass; even the upper and lower portions of the limbs have similar divisions. The upper two thirds of each segment is muscle mass, the upper third usually contains the largest bulk of muscle, and the lower third is mostly made up of bone and tendon. The upper part of each segment is rounded like a cylinder, and the lower parts (wrists and ankles) terminate with a block form.

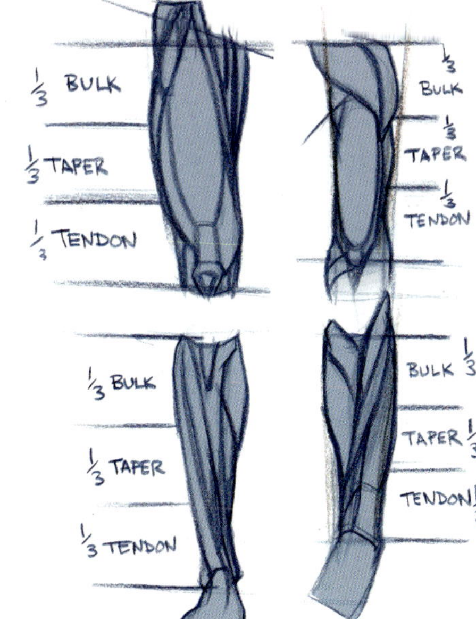

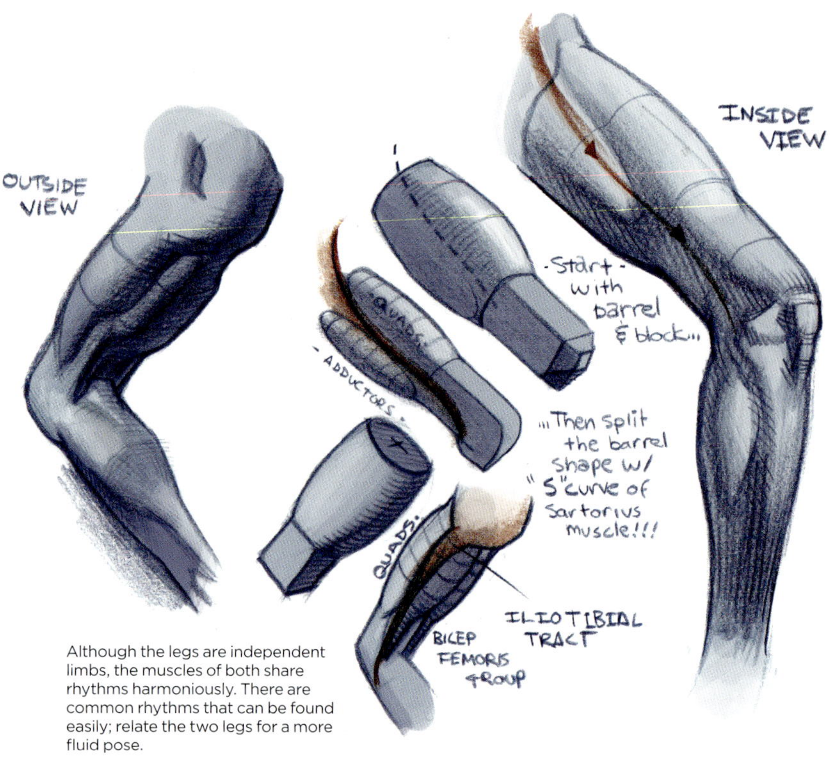

Although the legs are independent limbs, the muscles of both share rhythms harmoniously. There are common rhythms that can be found easily; relate the two legs for a more fluid pose.

Here you can see how the sartorius on the inside of the leg splits the barrel shape into two parts, while the iliotibial band on the outside of the leg divides the front from the back. These two prominent separations are usually visible, so don't ignore them.

6. USE PISTON SHAPES TO CAPTURE THE REGULARITY OF THE SHIN

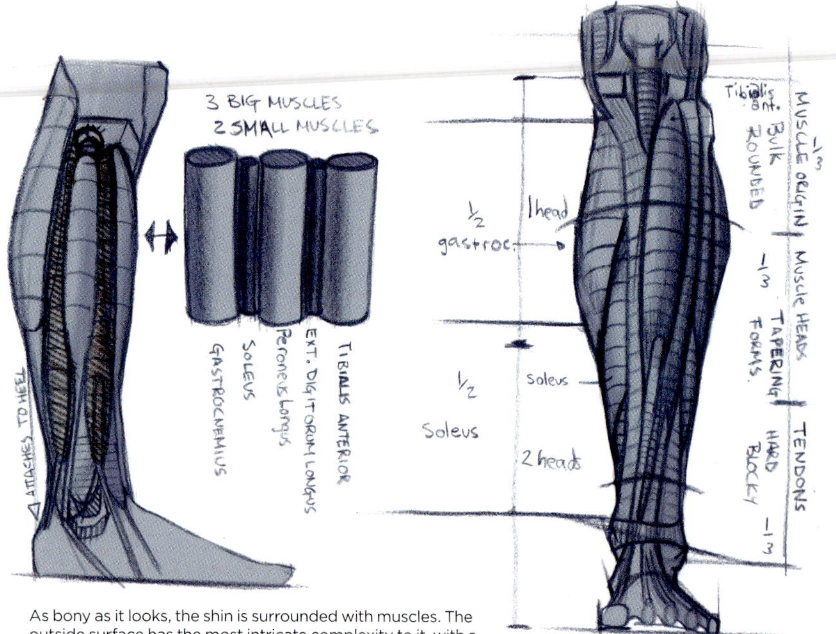

As bony as it looks, the shin is surrounded with muscles. The outside surface has the most intricate complexity to it, with a repetitious, organized pattern of piston-shaped muscles.

7. BUILD UP LEG MUSCULATURE IN THREE SIMPLE STAGES

Start the pose off with cylinders; they're simple enough for anyone to draw. Once the cylinders are placed and you've found their centers, divide them into planes. Beginning with simple surfaces is much easier than trying to start with the muscles, and the legs look more organized as a result.

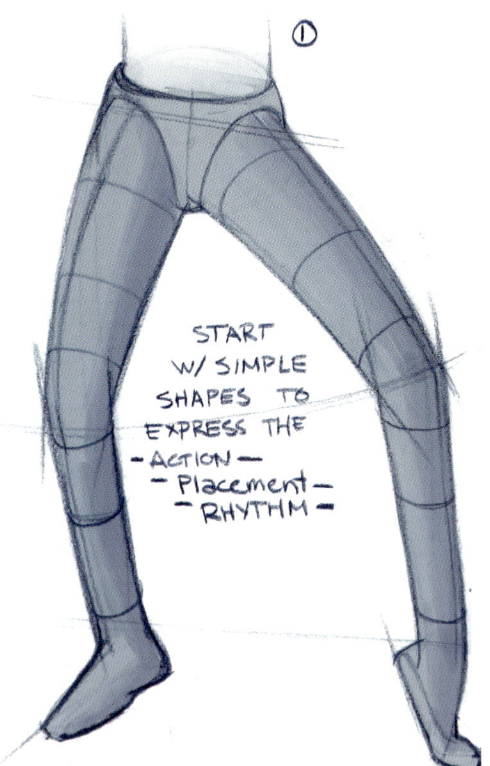

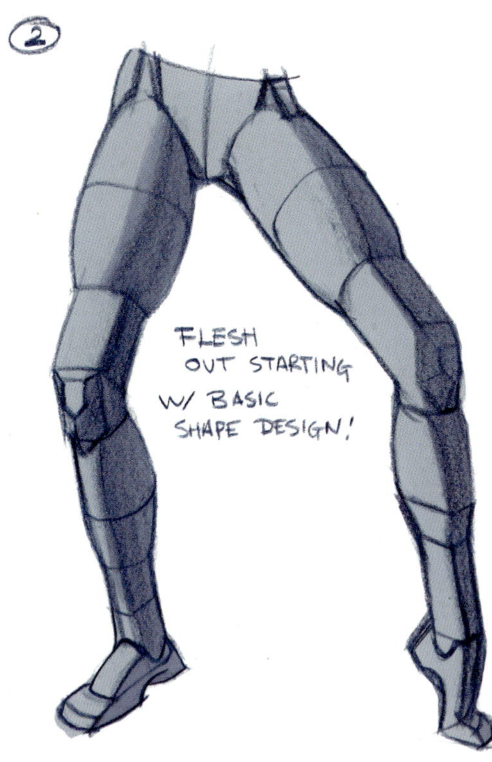

③

- THESE MUSCLES UNNATURALLY MEET THE CONTOUR (SKIN IS PRETTY THICK)
- BUT INSIDE THE SHAPES BUILT IN STEP ② ARE NOW DIVIDED INTO MUSCLE ABSTRACTIONS
- THIS ONE IS OVER THE TOP -

"Stick to muscle groups rather than individual muscles. Only the muscles that are being used show more detail, expanding as their fibers bunch."

When developing the legs, stick to the muscle groups rather than focusing in on individual muscles. Only the muscles that are being used should show more detail, expanding as their fibers bunch together. If unused or not fully taut, the muscles blend into their respective groups or, if really relaxed, back into their biggest basic shape.

One important point: remember that legs come in pairs. Be sure to relate the two legs to each other throughout the early stages of the drawing, making sure that the action doesn't destroy the proportions and balance of the pose. If the legs look off from each other, then the entire pose feels off. Balance starts from the bottom up, so if you start the drawing with simple forms and sound placement, the rest practically takes care of itself.

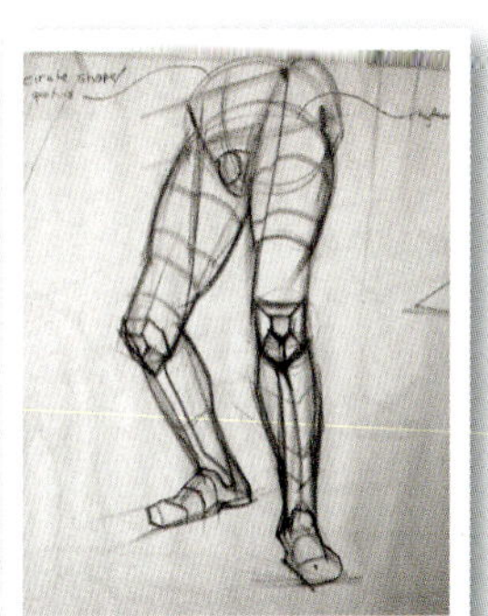

Using the simple rules of form and function, you should soon be able to work yourself up a pretty fine pair of legs. Just don't forget to take proportion and muscle use into account.

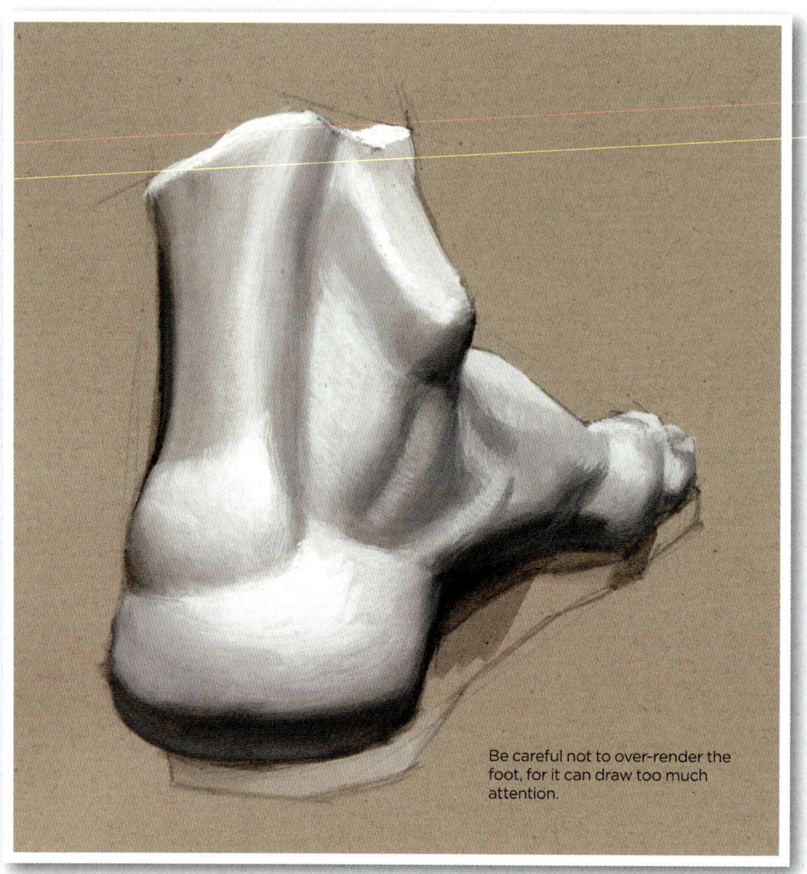

Be careful not to over-render the foot, for it can draw too much attention.

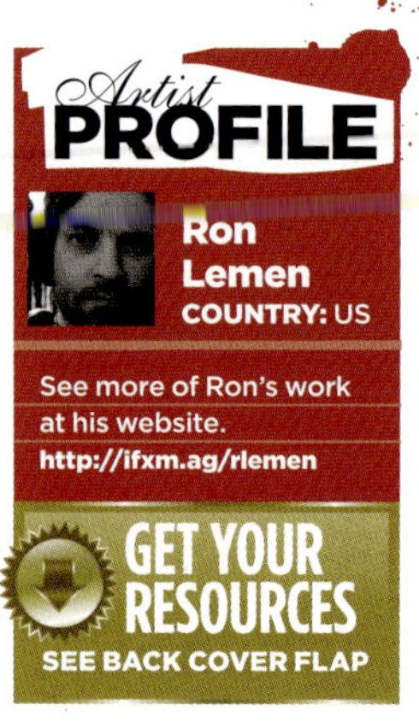

DRAWING FEET

Discover how to use form to create solid-looking feet – and why you shouldn't use too much detail when you draw them

Let's clear the air about feet – the ugly cousins to the hands and a part of the body that many artists dread to draw. They're bony, they're complex, and they're not the nicest things to look at. But anyone who's serious about figure drawing is going to have to tackle feet at some point. Even if you intend to only ever draw characters who have shoes on, your drawings will only be convincing if you have a good grasp of how to structure the feet inside the shoes.

Storyboards, pin-ups, covers, character designs, movie posters, comic books… all of these are instances when you might want to draw a full figure from head to toe. This means that you have to put feet on the legs. As painful as this can be to master, it is a must-do, must-learn situation. Here are some helpful hints and solutions to tackling these little beauties, helping you on your way to achieving the sweetest feet.

Get a foothold: drawing perfect feet

Put feet into perspective and start with footprints as the foundation for the correct overall pose

Let's start by looking at size. The typical foot is between ten and 12 inches in length. Roughly speaking, that's about as long as the entire skull from top to chin. The foot's width is a bit less than half the width of the head, or about the same width as the hand's four fingers (excluding the thumb). You can readily see these measures for yourself with your own hand and foot.

To start a full-figure drawing or even a three-quarter drawing of a figure, it would be wise to begin with the ground plane to work out the correct perspective in the shot, relating the figure to the rest of the environment so it feels truly planted in the world. The perspective will help keep the foot in correct scale to how you see the action, to the character's head, and to the viewer, as well as keeping it at the correct skew – if there is any – from camera distortion.

I begin by drawing footprints on the floor (or steps, or slope; wherever the foot is to be located). This can make it easier to draw the legs with the right foreshortened look to them and with the correct action to the pose.

Boots and shoes usually cover the feet, but I recommend that you start with the foot without a cover over it so there's a proper scale of foot size to the figure before any distortion created by the shoe design occurs. Feet are sometimes drawn oversized for weighting or stylistic reasons, but I would still draw the foot bare before covering it with a big shoe design so that the foot relates back to the scale of the rest of the character.

Toes are bulbous at the end, which means they're rounded like a bubble, but squish flat when pressed against a surface. When this happens, the toe mass spreads out a bit further than the toe's actual size, usually joining toes where they come together. If this is the case, don't draw lines in between each toe; this has the visual effect of spreading them apart from each other. Use simple tones or light gradations to join the mass and separate the toes.

Toes step downward like stairs from the metatarsal bone to the toe's tip. There are many little complex surfaces, from bone top to knuckles and nails, that can be rendered or shaded to give the feet more dimension and complexity.

Defining the toes

Be careful not to add too much detail to the toes if the foot is small in the illustration; too much rendering in such concentrated spaces can force the rest of the illustration toward a direction of over-rendering. It can also push the focus to the bottom of the picture in the same way as under-scaling the feet, unless you catch the mistake early enough.

The bottom of the foot has an arch on the inside and two separate pads that squish to whatever they press against, creating a straight line. The toes bend about a third of the way back behind the ball of the foot. When the toes spread, the biggest separation occurs between the big toe and the second toe. The little toe is usually drawn as a bulbous shape. It typically floats a bit more off the ground when the foot is arched up, but with the toes still making contact with the ground plane. The big toe points in toward the other four toes, and these toes bend toward the big toe.

Don't forget that the foot is a full shape with six sides, like a block, with corresponding

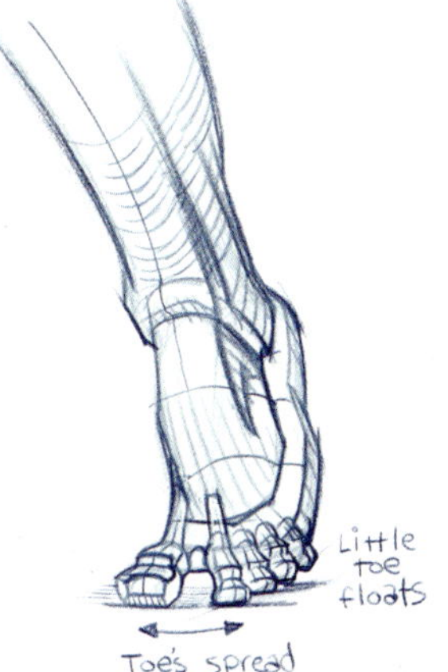

As the figure's leg lifts, the toes on the ground spread out – one of the few times they can be drawn separated.

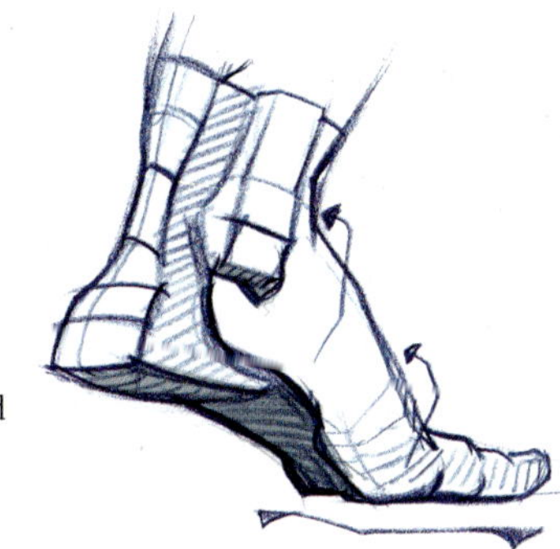
The toes bend behind the ball of the foot, not in front of it.

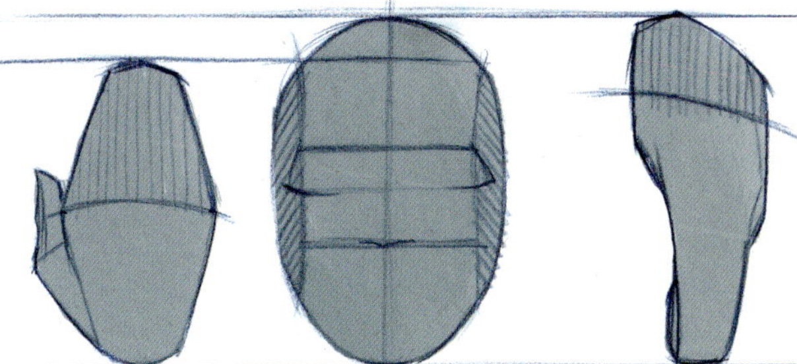
The footprint is as long as the entire skull from top to bottom – the same way the hand is the same length as the face from hairline to chin.

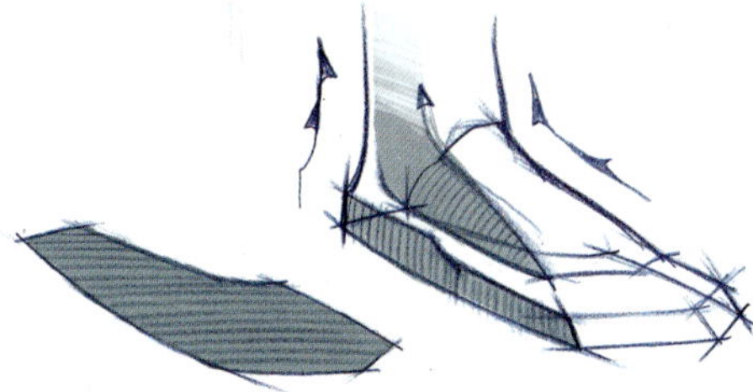
Drawing the footprint first helps you ground the foot to the surface it's connected with.

1. FEET FROM THE GROUND UP: USING FORM AND PERSPECTIVE

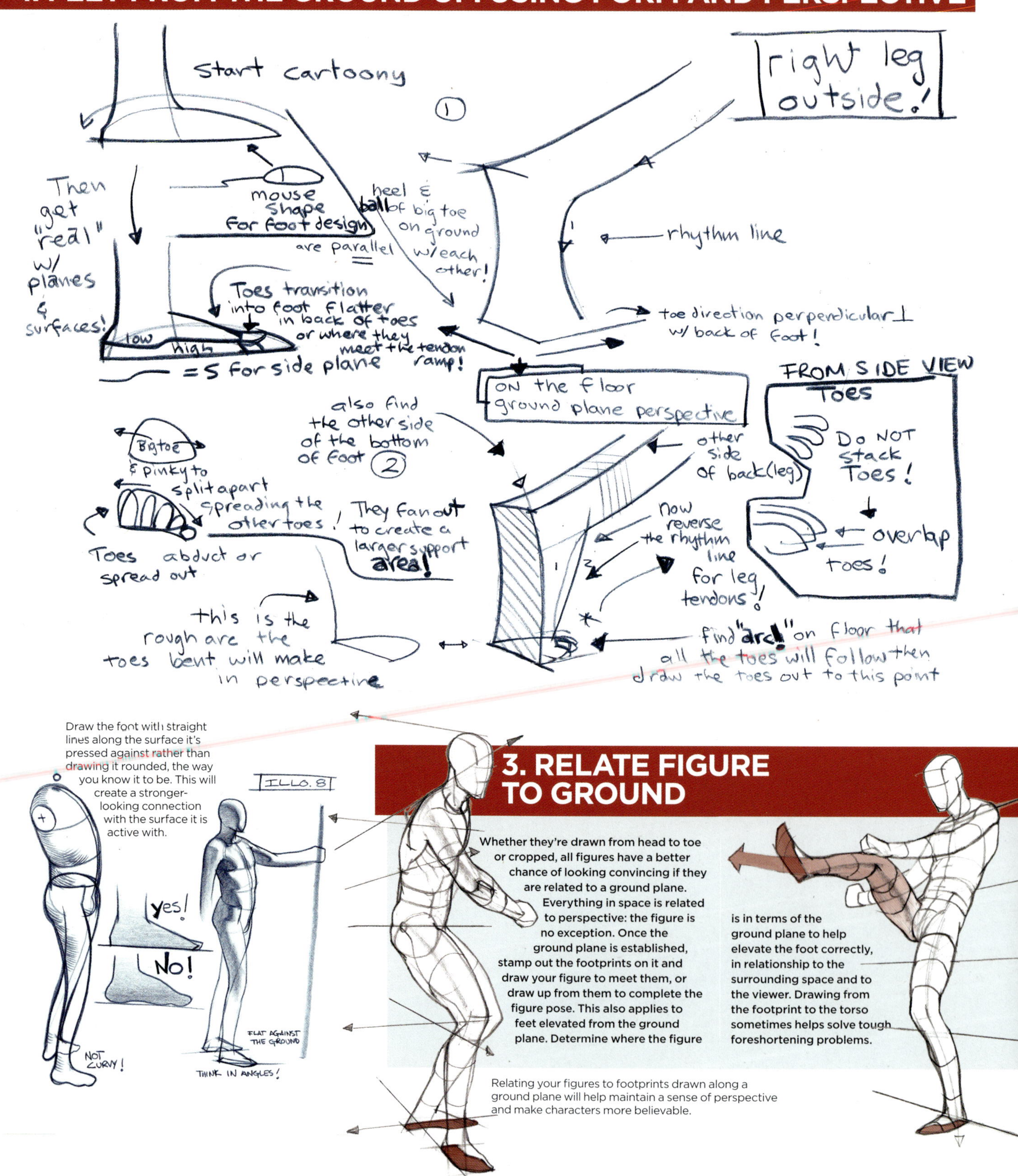

Draw the foot with straight lines along the surface it's pressed against rather than drawing it rounded, the way you know it to be. This will create a stronger-looking connection with the surface it is active with.

3. RELATE FIGURE TO GROUND

Whether they're drawn from head to toe or cropped, all figures have a better chance of looking convincing if they are related to a ground plane. Everything in space is related to perspective: the figure is no exception. Once the ground plane is established, stamp out the footprints on it and draw your figure to meet them, or draw up from them to complete the figure pose. This also applies to feet elevated from the ground plane. Determine where the figure is in terms of the ground plane to help elevate the foot correctly, in relationship to the surrounding space and to the viewer. Drawing from the footprint to the torso sometimes helps solve tough foreshortening problems.

Relating your figures to footprints drawn along a ground plane will help maintain a sense of perspective and make characters more believable.

2. CONNECTING THE FOOT TO THE LEGS OF YOUR CHARACTER

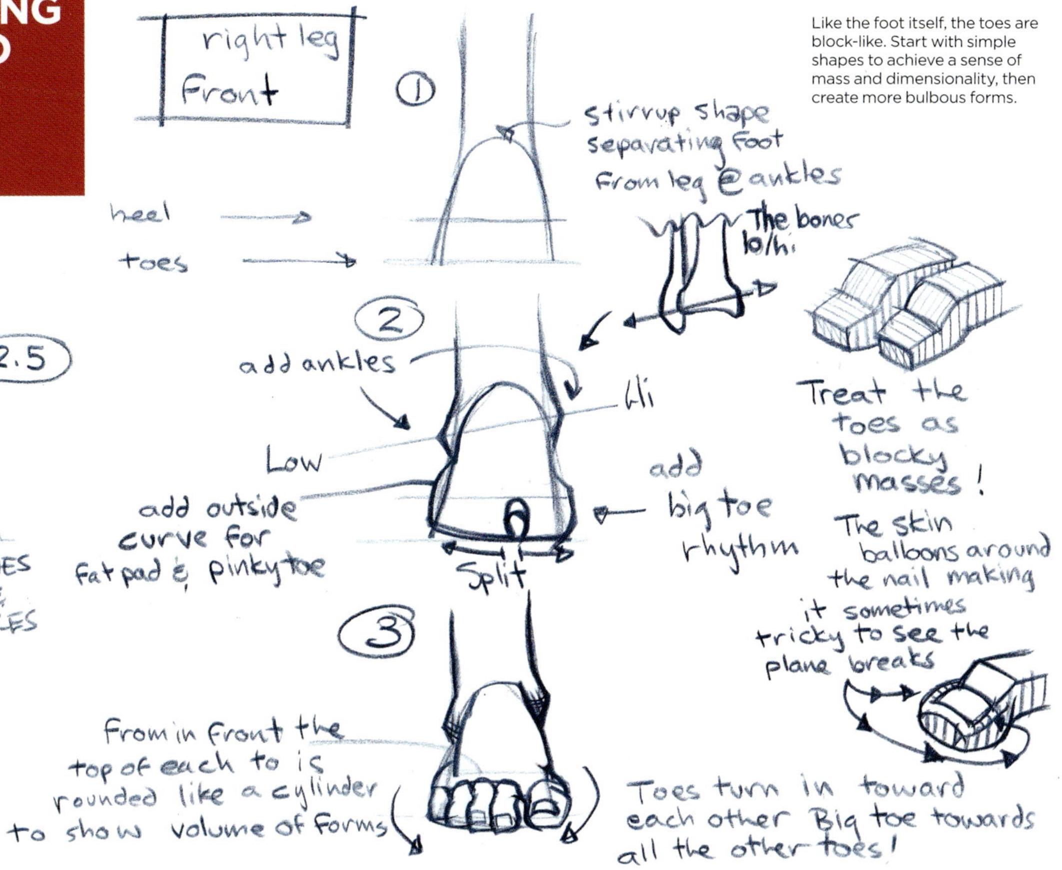

right leg
Front

①
stirrup shape separating foot from leg @ ankles
heel
toes
The bones lo/hi

②
add ankles
Hi
Low
add outside curve for fat pad & pinky toe
add big toe rhythm
Split

2.5
SHADING PLANES OF THE SIDES & FRONT SURFACES

Like the foot itself, the toes are block-like. Start with simple shapes to achieve a sense of mass and dimensionality, then create more bulbous forms.

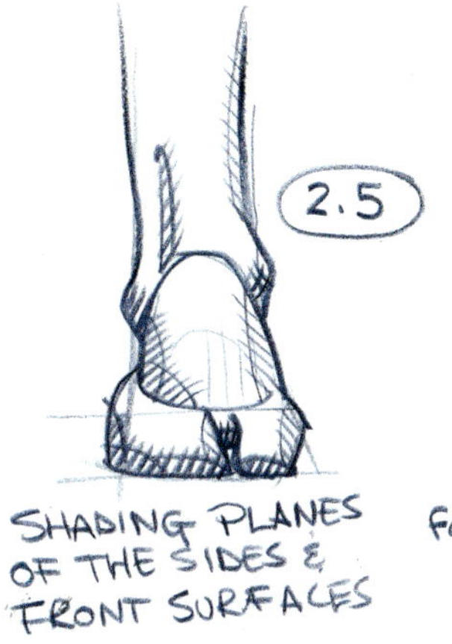

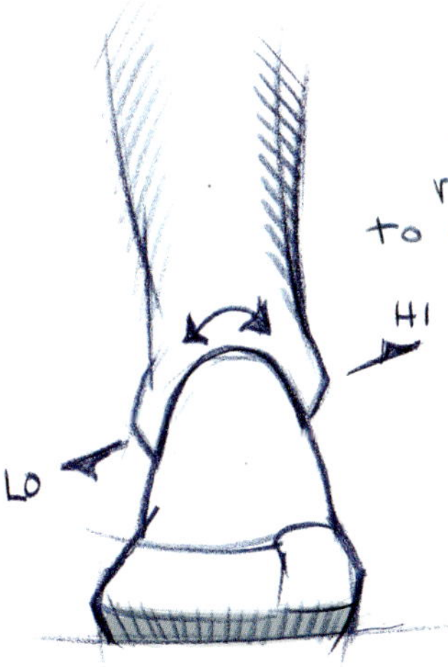

Treat the toes as blocky masses!

The skin balloons around the nail making it sometimes tricky to see the plane breaks

③
From in front the top of each to is rounded like a cylinder to show volume of forms
Toes turn in toward each other Big toe towards all the other toes!

HI
LO

The ankles can be thought of as a stirrup shape to help relate them to one another. The inside anklebone (maleolus) is higher in elevation than the outside ankle bone.

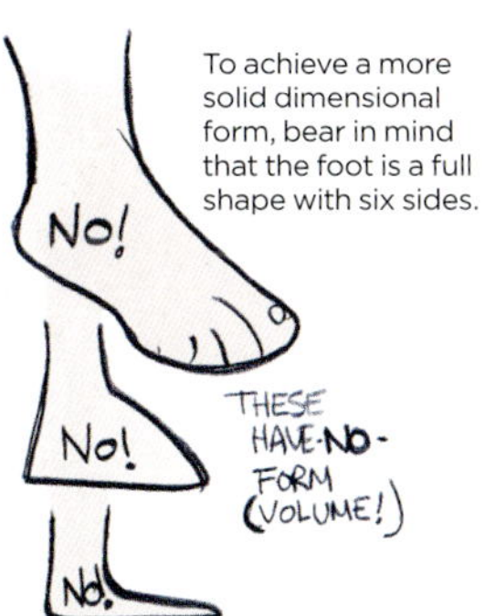

To achieve a more solid dimensional form, bear in mind that the foot is a full shape with six sides.

shading planes. Draw through the form to generate a more solid-looking and dimensional form.

When you've perfected your feet, you'll want to add them to the rest of the character. Now's the time to consider ankles and legs. See in my diagrams above how I've drawn the right foot and started to attach it to the right leg. I've shown the connection from a front perspective in these examples.

The ankles connect the feet to the legs. For easier ankle drawing, it helps to think of them as a stirrup-like shape. The inside anklebone is more elevated than the outside one.

Feet have typically been the bane of many artists. Some illustrators hide them with smoke, push them into silhouettes and shadows or even crop the image to avoid drawing them. But when an artist can draw them correctly, how much character they add to the image! The hands and feet can say just as much as a convincing facial expression.

Because of their complexity and gesture or action, feet usually become a secondary or tertiary focus in a figure drawing. It's a good idea to tackle these difficult issues early on and ideally make it second nature to design them convincingly. You would be surprised how many people will comment on how well feet are drawn if they really are; it's not every day that you find an artist with a real understanding of the ground they stand upon.

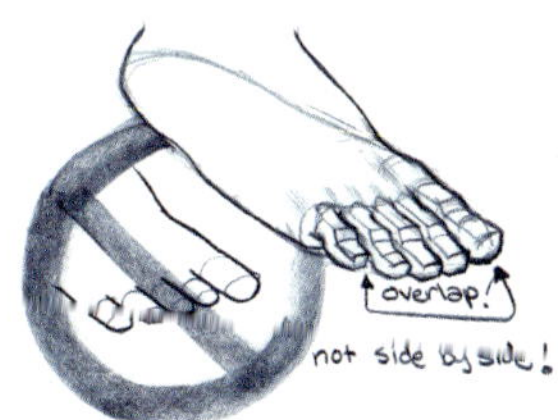

Overlap the toes when the foot is not drawn straight on. This will avoid the "clump of bananas" look, and help the foot look less cartoony.

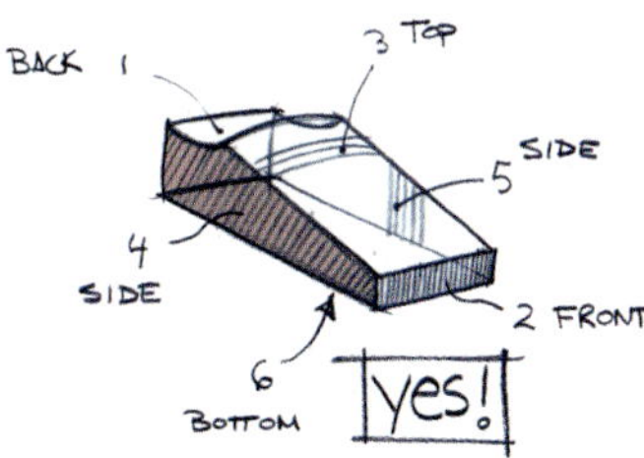

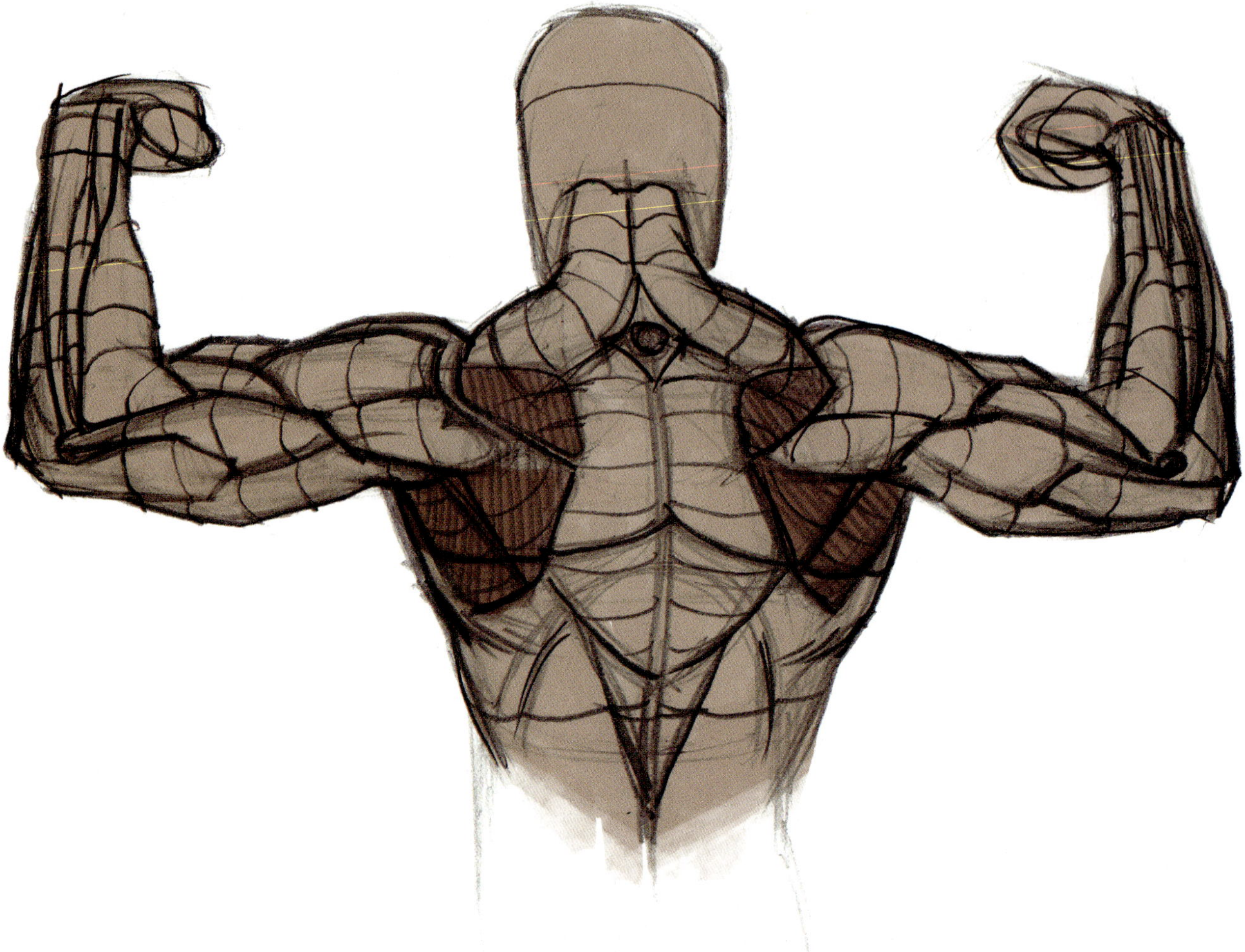

DRAWING THE SHOULDER AND UPPER ARM

Don't allow the complex interaction of muscles in this area to distract you from anatomy's guiding principles

So far we've seen how to define the armature of the figure and its underlying gesture, before starting to flesh our figure out with the torso and legs. We continue our journey with the upper part of the arms and the way they connect to the shoulder, one of the more complicated spots on the body to draw. The place to start is at the skeletal structure. Understand the shape of the scapula and humerus, especially the edges of the scapula and the ends of the humerus. Without knowing the bones and their shapes, the muscles have nowhere to start or terminate. Keep in mind that the diagrams I have drawn are mostly fleshed over, so the points where the muscles attach are covered – but the shapes are solid and directional because of where the muscles attach to the bones.

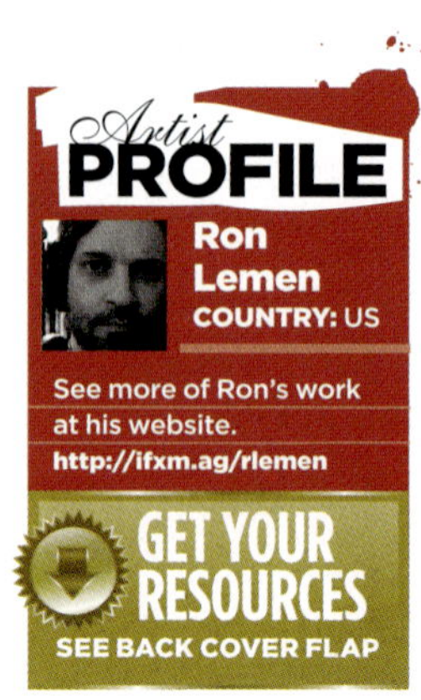

Learning the relationships between muscle and bone

Drawing the shoulders to complement the action of the upper arm muscles

Drawing this part of the body begins much like any other part. First, gesture in the pose, then accent the lines you feel good about using for the final pose before starting to define the body masses in more detail.

When drawing the figure, a clear understanding not just of the muscles but what the skeleton looks like beneath all the muscle masses is needed to draw muscles with any believable visual action to them. Without this understanding and observation, the muscles can end up drawn as bubble shapes that are lifeless, weightless, or competing against the action you want to depict.

Shoulder structure

The shoulder floats over the rib cage, with only the clavicle at the sternum on the rib cage acting as an anchor for the entire arm. This means that the arm has a lot of free motion over the rib cage.

When drawing the arm connected to the body, you need to first find the correct action of the shoulder to avoid a stiff-looking drawing. For example, if the arm is winding up to throw a ball, the shoulder will be toward the back of the

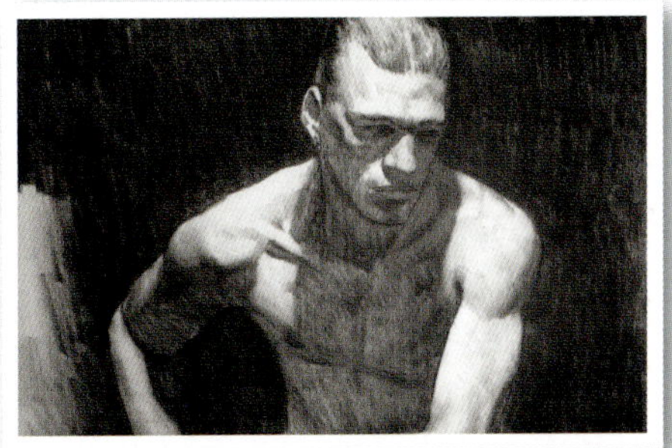

This drawing is all about the shoulders and the upper arms. Note how the shape and form of the forward-pointing left arm is entirely different from the right. Think about how the muscles and bones are moving and interacting with the skin and the light.

1. THE PRINCIPAL STAGES OF ARM MOVEMENT

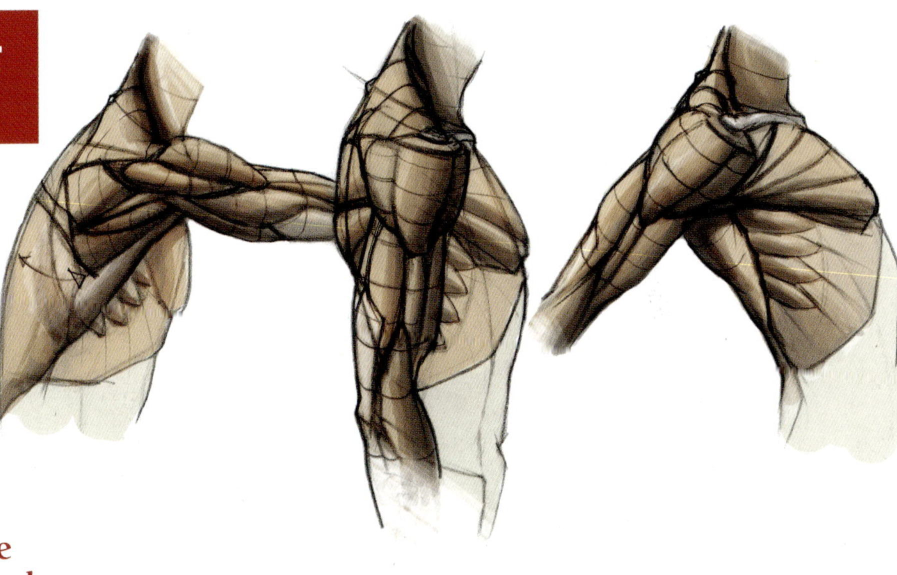

The shoulder has quite a bit of movement around the rib cage. Here you can see three positions of the arm. The first is forward, moving the attachment of the deltoid forward and stretching the shoulder muscles. The second is in a reference position, by the side of the rib cage. More of the back of the arm and shoulder show when the arm is relaxed in this position. Meanwhile, for the third position, the shoulder is pitched back behind the body. The shoulder is now behind the rib cage, stretching the pectoralis muscles and serratus muscles.

"Don't memorize the muscle chart. Memorize the muscle insertions and connections to the bones."

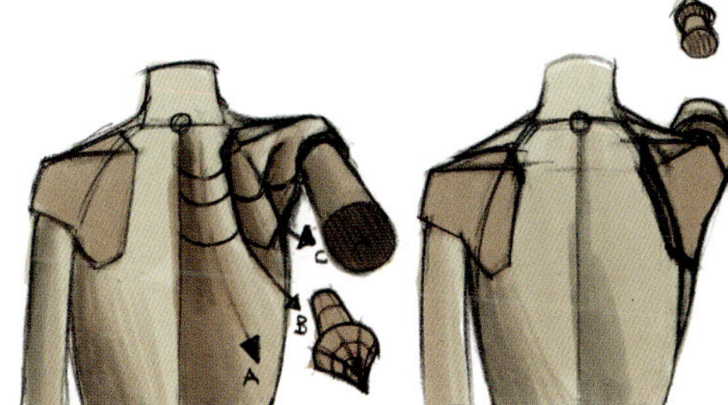

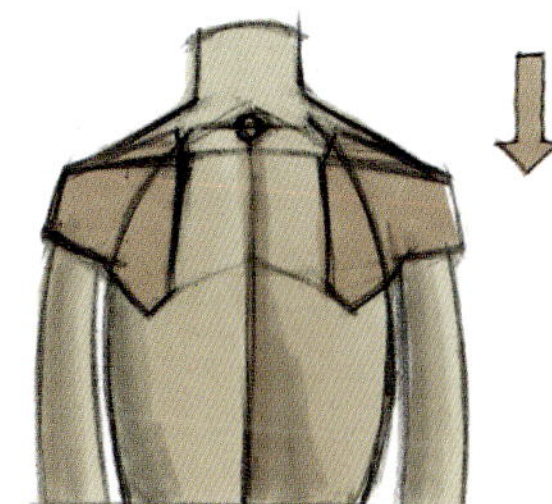

Here we see the shoulder from behind the rib cage. Line A of the first rib cage represents the rhomboid and trapezius muscles, bunched up between the spine and the spine of the scapula. Line B represents the crease under the scapula that follows the serratus muscles. Line C splits around halfway between the shoulder muscles perpendicularly.

2. PERSPECTIVE AND DYNAMISM IN MUSCLE DESIGN

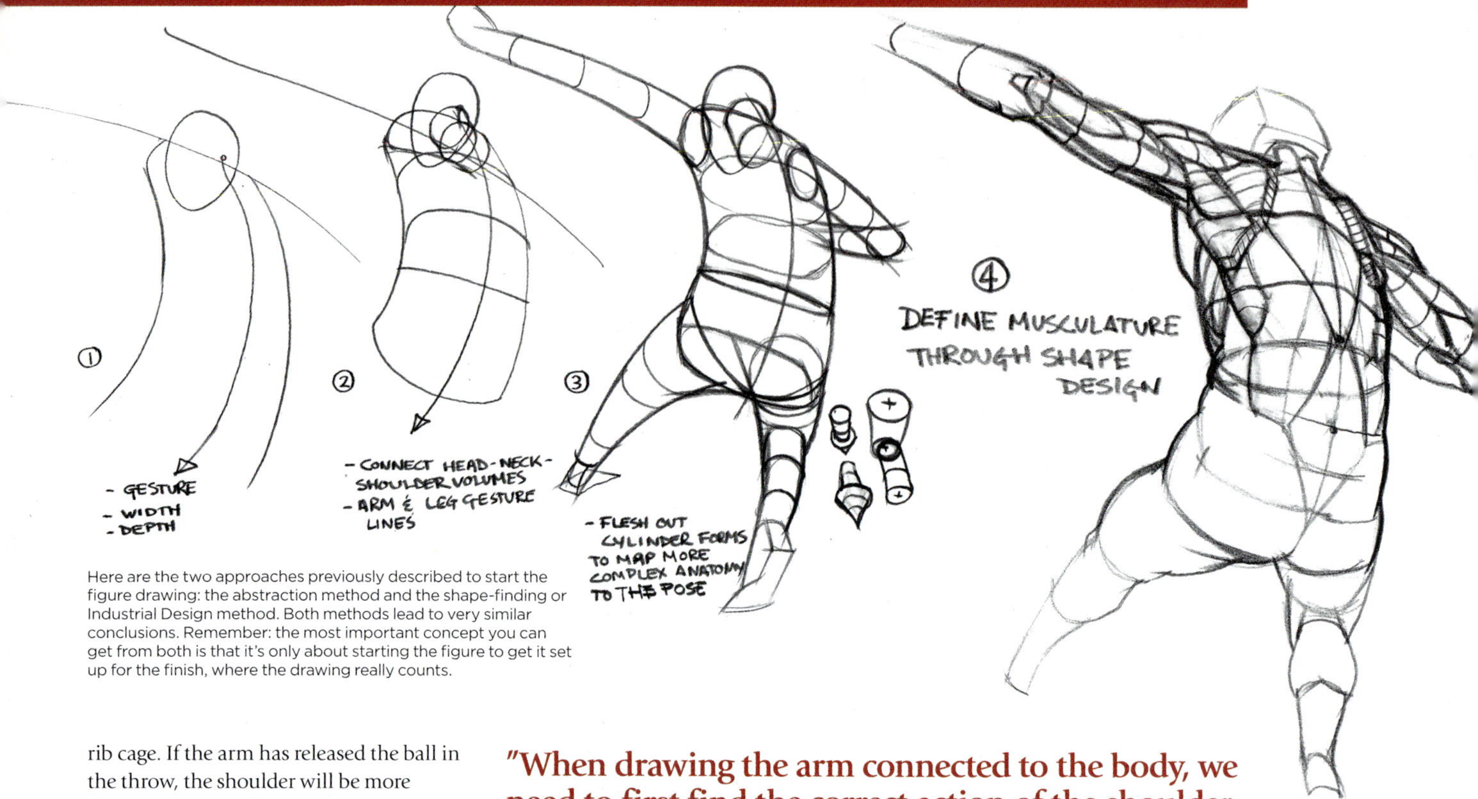

① - GESTURE
- WIDTH
- DEPTH

② - CONNECT HEAD-NECK-SHOULDER VOLUMES
- ARM & LEG GESTURE LINES

③ - FLESH OUT CYLINDER FORMS TO MAP MORE COMPLEX ANATOMY TO THE POSE

④ DEFINE MUSCULATURE THROUGH SHAPE DESIGN

Here are the two approaches previously described to start the figure drawing: the abstraction method and the shape-finding or Industrial Design method. Both methods lead to very similar conclusions. Remember: the most important concept you can get from both is that it's only about starting the figure to get it set up for the finish, where the drawing really counts.

rib cage. If the arm has released the ball in the throw, the shoulder will be more forward over the rib cage. If the hands are held high above the head, the shoulders are closer to the ears.

Each set of muscles crosses over from one bone to another. For example, the shoulder starts in the torso, connects to the clavicle and the scapula, and terminates at (or crosses over and inserts onto) the upper arm bone, known more formally as the humerus.

The muscles of the upper arm originate both on the humerus and on the scapula, and terminate on the two forearm bones, known as the ulna and the radius. The hands and feet are a few places on the body where the muscles are referred to as intrinsic: they stay within the bone mass. Otherwise, muscles connect two or more different bone groups together.

The scapula floats over the serratus muscles, which we see as little bump muscles on the rib cage under each arm, or the "superhero muscles." The shoulder muscles all start on the spine edge of the scapula, and cross over to the top or the upper third of the humerus. These four muscles help the upper arm rotate out and in from our body – when you hold both your arms out like a cross, for

> "When drawing the arm connected to the body, we need to first find the correct action of the shoulder in order to avoid a stiff-looking drawing."

3. FOLLOWING THE RHYTHM OF THE MUSCLES

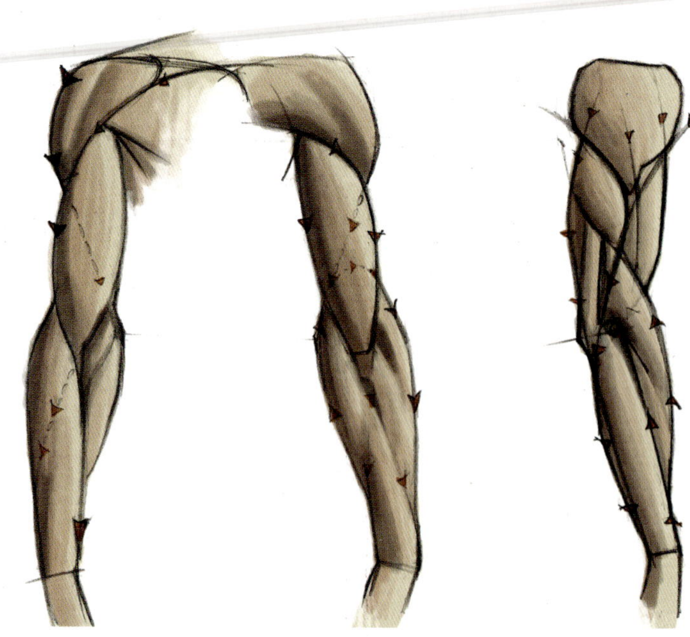

These lines represent the rhythm lines, or the abstraction lines that flow between the muscles once the architecture has been designed. These lines help harmonize the muscle forms to create a seamless rhythmical movement of muscles, bones, and ligaments.

4. THE GEOMETRY OF THE HUMAN FORM

Draw muscles with simple geometry to understand and memorize them, or to turn them into something that you can remember easily. Here are the four muscles inside the scapula. Each muscle is drawn individually to help you understand the shape, where it starts – or where it's connected – and where it goes to. This is important information to remember, because all the lumps, bumps, dark spots, and highlights you see on the back only show up when the arm is active.

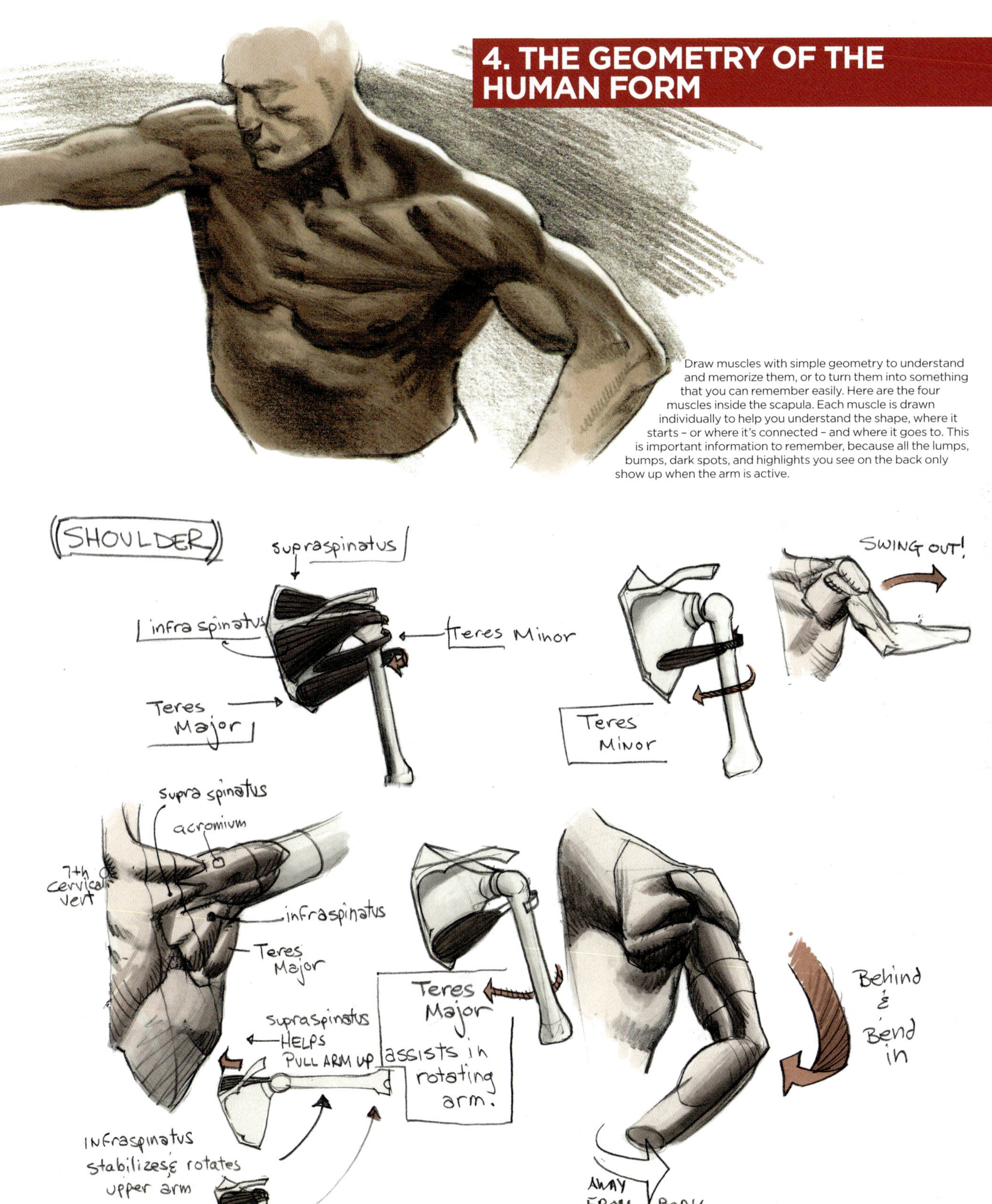

5. HOW MUSCLES CONNECT, MOVE AND INTERACT

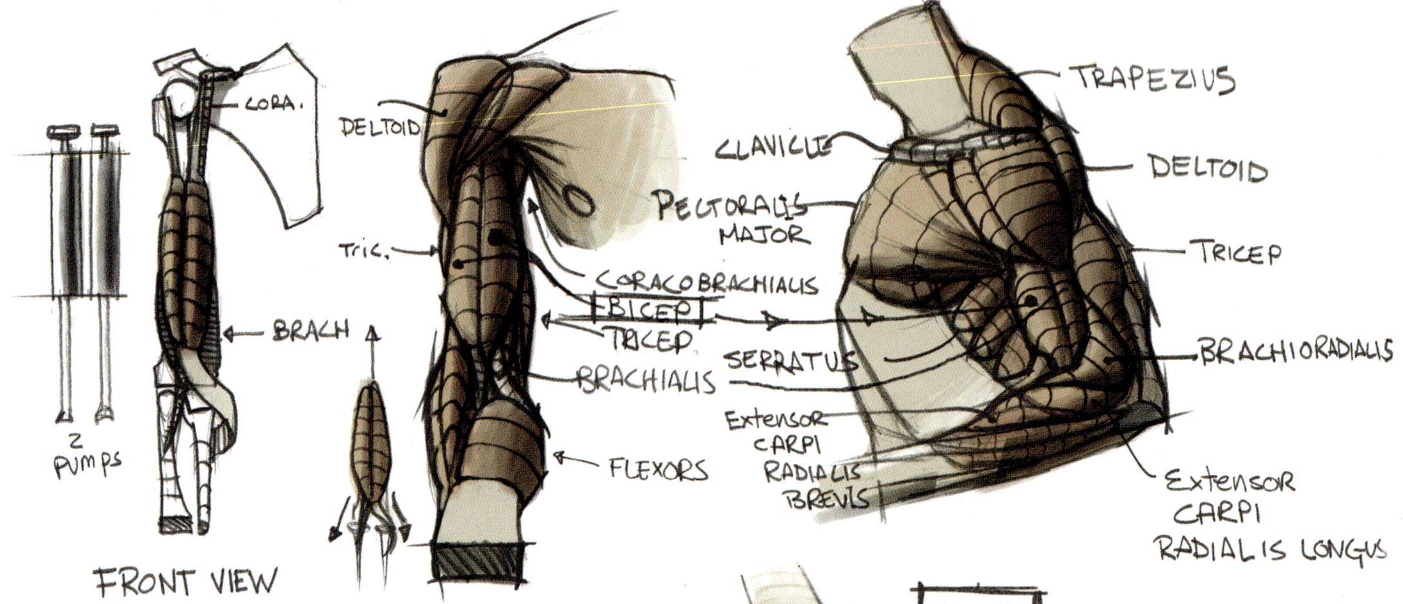

"The muscles should be drawn only when active, not charted and shaded like a muscle diagram."

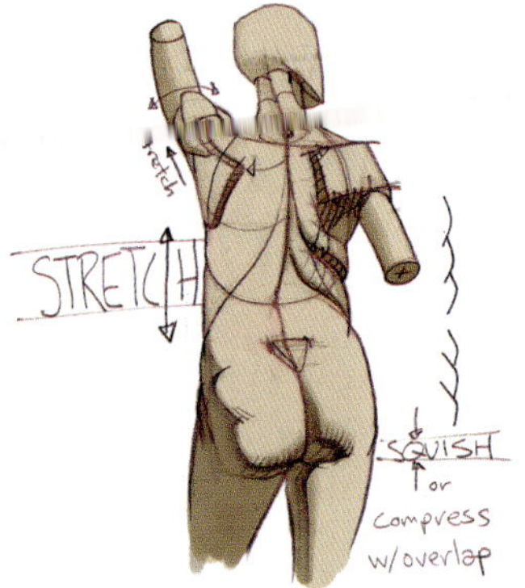

Here, the arm is pulled behind the body, causing several creases to occur. These creases run perpendicular to the muscle striations of the muscle heads. The three creases here are: along the base of the oblique; under the serratus muscles and through the lattisimus and the rhomboid; and under the scapula's base edge.

example, or when you put both hands behind your back, as if handcuffed.

The deltoid covers part of these muscles and wraps around the top of the arm. It functions as a swivel muscle, or the muscle that enables you to swing your arm around like a wheel. Then we have the biceps and triceps. These muscles cross over to the forearm bones at the top third of the humerus. The triceps extend or straighten out the arm; the biceps flex it or draw it into the body.

I urge caution in learning and drawing muscle distribution. Don't memorize a muscle chart. Memorize the muscle insertions and connections to the bones, or where the muscles originate from and where they end on the skeleton. Learn their function and action, and group them so you are not drawing every muscle.

Shoulder structure

Let's now have a look at the anatomy of the upper arm and shoulder. These muscles in particular should be drawn only when active, not charted and shaded like a muscle diagram; most humans don't normally look this way, even when well developed. Body builders create a Living Human Anatomy Chart with their bodies — and we should thank them to some degree – but keep in mind that these muscles are developed to their limits, and are not the shapes we easily identify with. The muscle charts you see in an anatomy book are based on medically ideal bodies. In reality, the size and scale of each muscle vary from person to person, based on their personal activity, diet, and other factors. The anatomy books start us at an ideal point of reference. To accommodate all possible body types, you will have to veer away from these and use your eye and guiding principles instead. Art rules are a starting point, only meant to be altered with care to enhance our individual ways of working, which are as unique as we are to one another.

By examining not only the limb, but each and every part of the limb, you will have a better understanding of what to draw and how to make the actions look

7. RELATIONSHIPS WITH THE SKIN

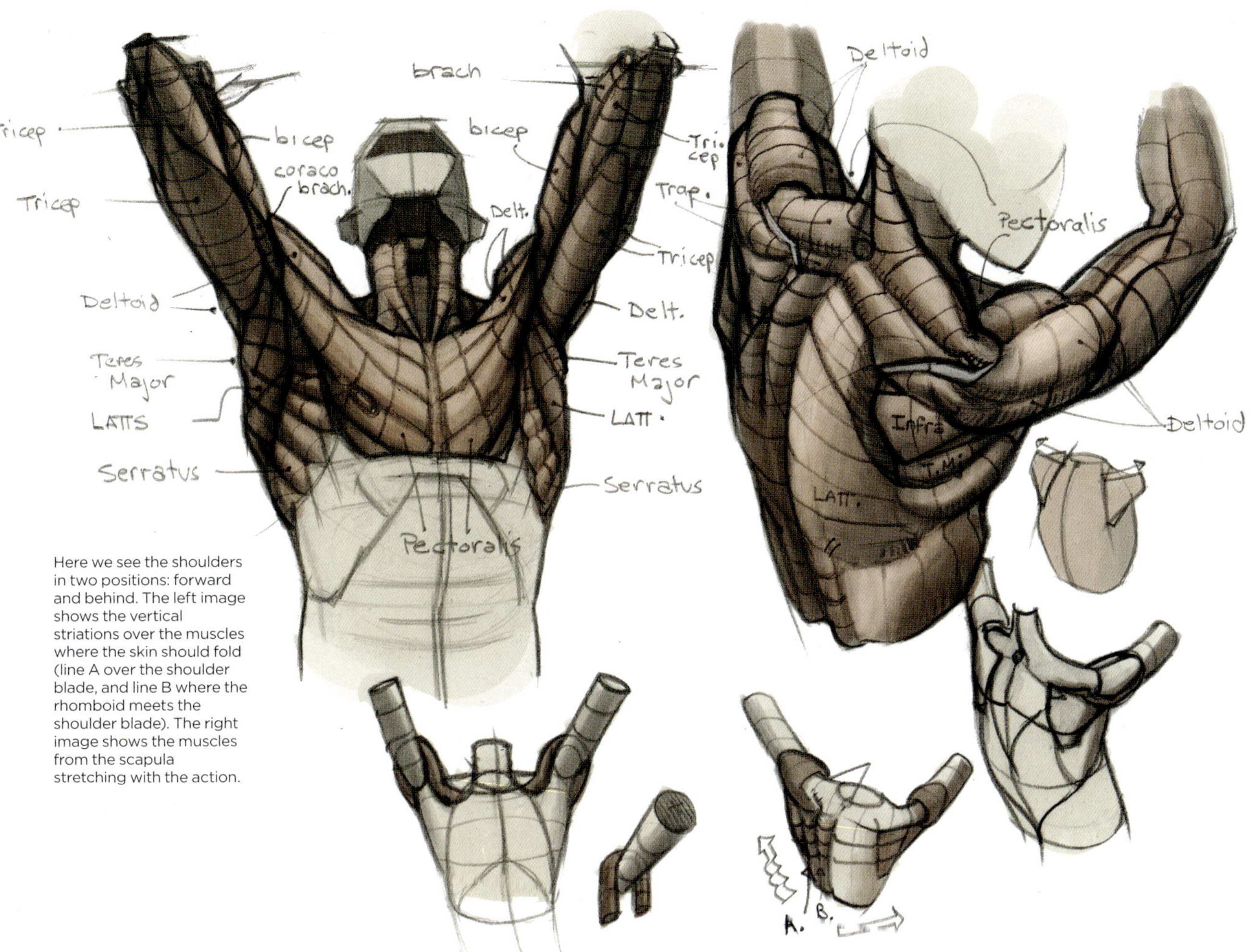

Here we see the shoulders in two positions: forward and behind. The left image shows the vertical striations over the muscles where the skin should fold (line A over the shoulder blade, and line B where the rhomboid meets the shoulder blade). The right image shows the muscles from the scapula stretching with the action.

6. SHEATHING OVER THE MUSCLE MASS

Anatomy books and live models are very different to look at. Here are a few points to help make studying easier. First, anatomy books have no skin. A quarter-inch of volume, if not more, needs to be added to the muscle mass. Think of it as a blanket resting on the muscles. This brings up the second point: skin is a cover. When the arm is pulled behind the body, the skin creases vertically through the shoulder instead of following the muscles horizontally across the back. The muscle fibers go one way; the skin creases perpendicular to them. This occurs everywhere on the body. Finally, more important than memorizing the muscles is knowing when to draw them. A chart shows you how the human machine works, but muscles are only clearly visible when active. At rest, the muscles blend into a more generic, simpler shape, similar to the visual metaphors you're using to decipher drawing the body.

convincing. Studying the limbs one section at a time makes learning and memorizing the information much easier to digest. Anatomy is a large subject to tackle, but it needn't be difficult once you conquer the basics. Breaking each limb down into sections not only helps you take in the information quicker, but also helps to isolate the importance of each part of the body and the important individual characteristics related to those regions. Practice 'til it hurts, then practice some more. Mileage is the key to artistic progress. Enjoy!

This version of the shoulders shows the arms from in front and below the figure. Note how the muscles of the deltoids, pectoralis, serratus, and, eventually, the abs and obliques all flow seamlessly together in their striations and radiate from the shoulders through to the pelvis on either side of the body, using the shoulder as the point of radiation. The deltoid muscles are draped over the arms, seen both from in front and behind. Think of the muscle draped like a towel over the shoulder.

DRAWING THE FOREARMS

It may seem like a simple area of the body, but the forearm is more sophisticated – and elegant – than you suspect

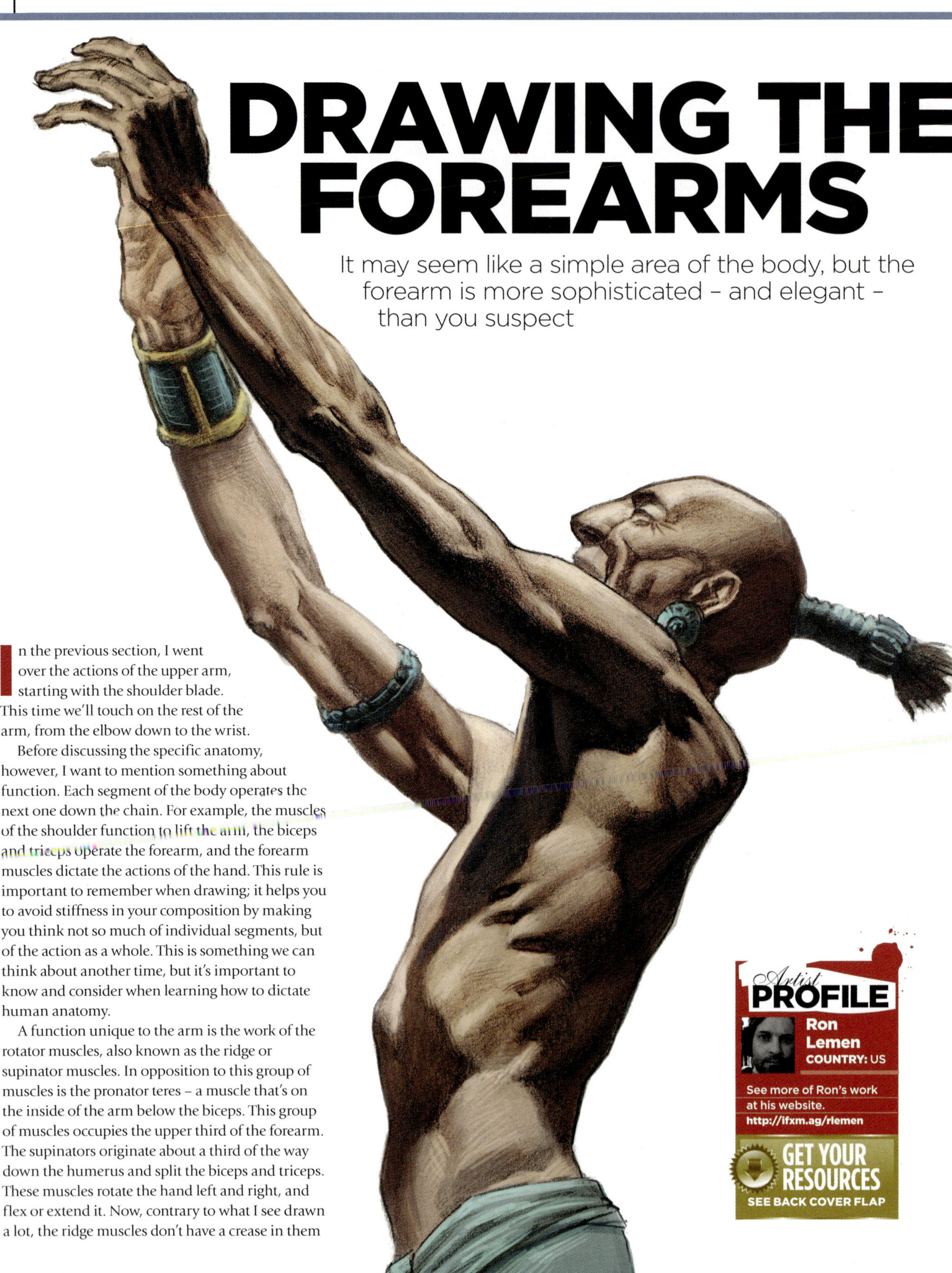

In the previous section, I went over the actions of the upper arm, starting with the shoulder blade. This time we'll touch on the rest of the arm, from the elbow down to the wrist.

Before discussing the specific anatomy, however, I want to mention something about function. Each segment of the body operates the next one down the chain. For example, the muscles of the shoulder function to lift the arm, the biceps and triceps operate the forearm, and the forearm muscles dictate the actions of the hand. This rule is important to remember when drawing; it helps you to avoid stiffness in your composition by making you think not so much of individual segments, but of the action as a whole. This is something we can think about another time, but it's important to know and consider when learning how to dictate human anatomy.

A function unique to the arm is the work of the rotator muscles, also known as the ridge or supinator muscles. In opposition to this group of muscles is the pronator teres – a muscle that's on the inside of the arm below the biceps. This group of muscles occupies the upper third of the forearm. The supinators originate about a third of the way down the humerus and split the biceps and triceps. These muscles rotate the hand left and right, and flex or extend it. Now, contrary to what I see drawn a lot, the ridge muscles don't have a crease in them

Artist PROFILE
Ron Lemen
COUNTRY: US
See more of Ron's work at his website.
http://ifxm.ag/rlemen

GET YOUR RESOURCES
SEE BACK COVER FLAP

1. MUSCLE MOVEMENT

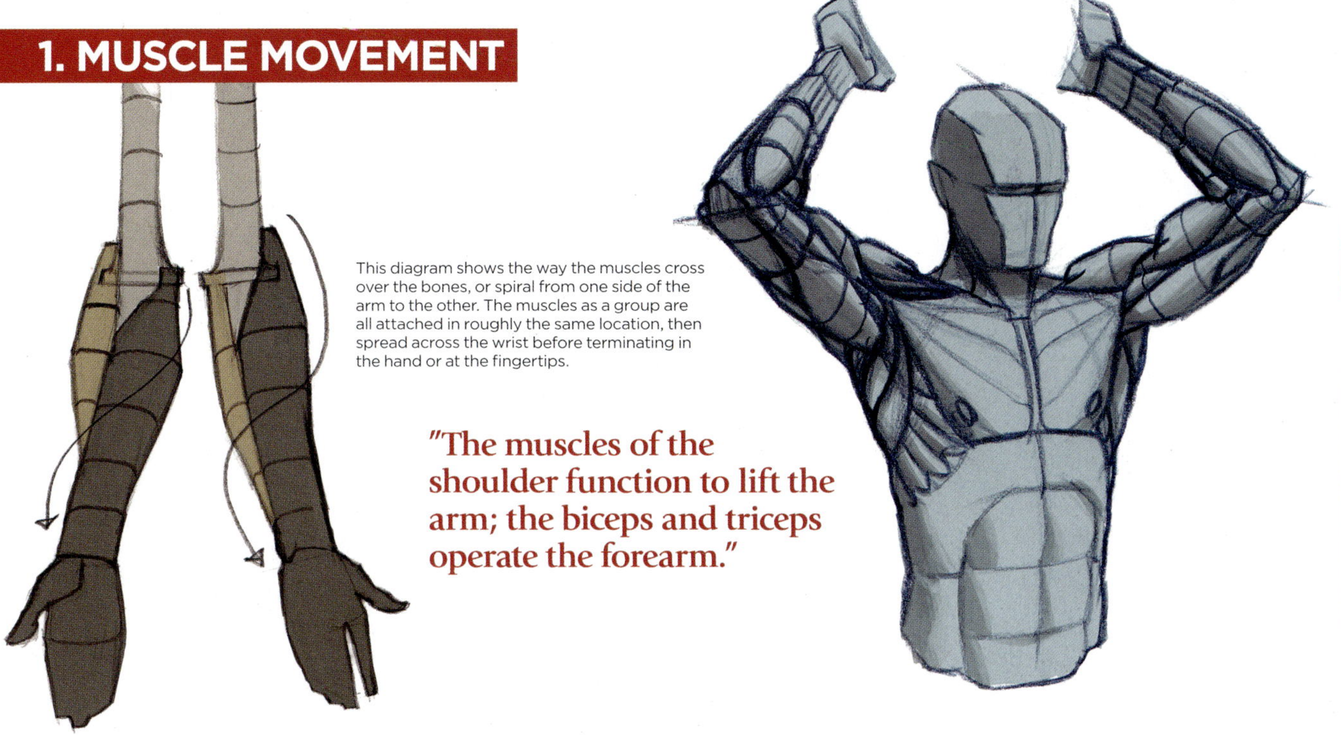

This diagram shows the way the muscles cross over the bones, or spiral from one side of the arm to the other. The muscles as a group are all attached in roughly the same location, then spread across the wrist before terminating in the hand or at the fingertips.

"The muscles of the shoulder function to lift the arm; the biceps and triceps operate the forearm."

2. MUSCLE SEGMENTS AS LINKS OF A CHAIN

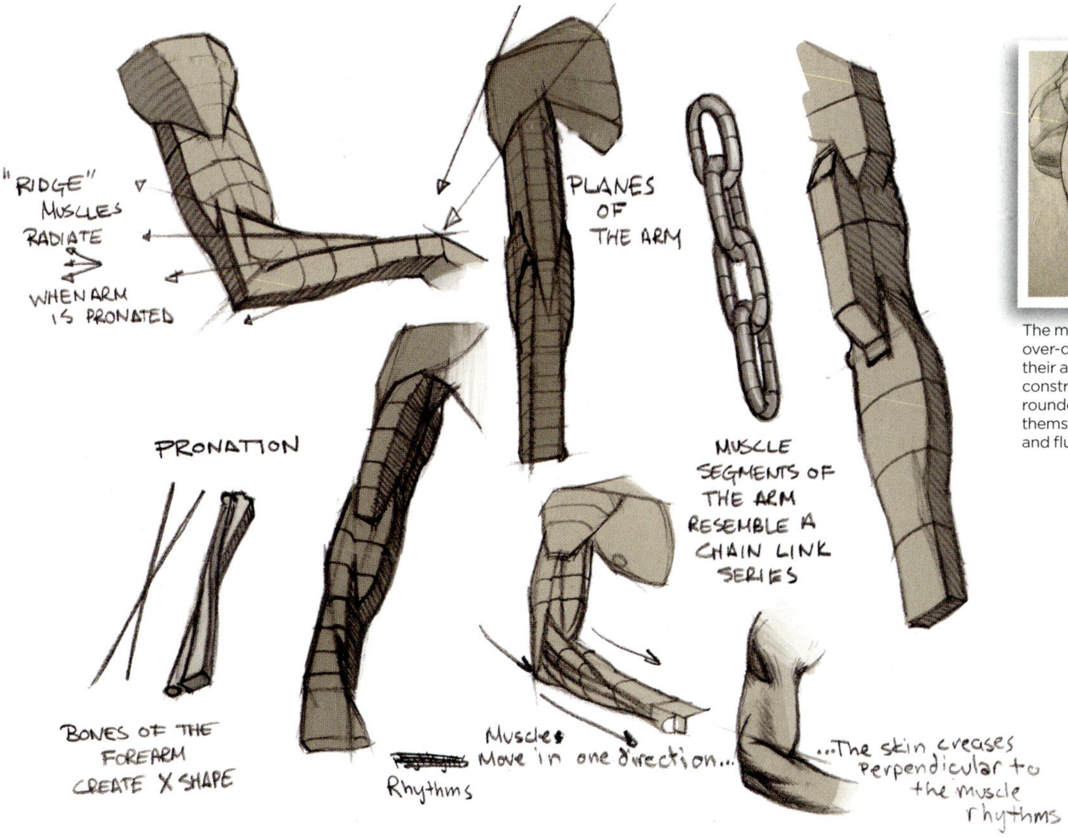

"RIDGE" MUSCLES RADIATE WHEN ARM IS PRONATED

PLANES OF THE ARM

MUSCLE SEGMENTS OF THE ARM RESEMBLE A CHAIN LINK SERIES

PRONATION

BONES OF THE FOREARM CREATE X SHAPE

Muscles Move in one direction... Rhythms

...The skin creases perpendicular to the muscle rhythms

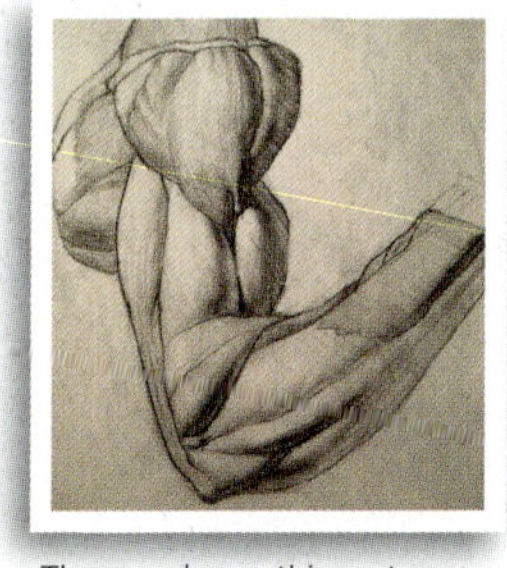

The muscles on this cast are over-developed to emphasize their artistic shape and construction. The slightly rounder forms also lend themselves to more dynamic and fluid rhythm lines.

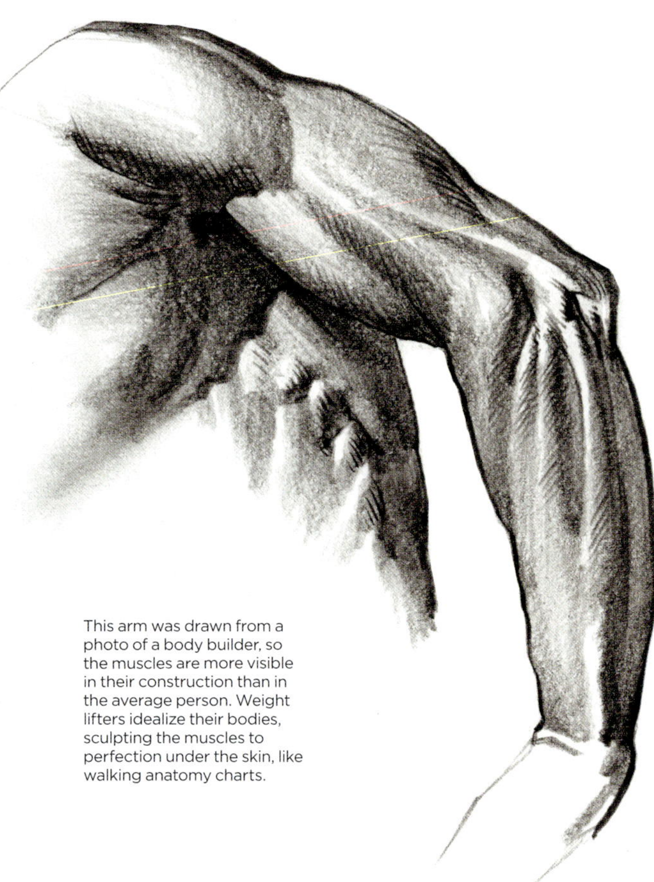

This arm was drawn from a photo of a body builder, so the muscles are more visible in their construction than in the average person. Weight lifters idealize their bodies, sculpting the muscles to perfection under the skin, like walking anatomy charts.

"Contrary to what I see drawn a lot, the ridge muscles do not have a crease in them. The crease you see is the skin folding, not the muscle."

3. NOTING HOW MUSCLES CHANGE WITH ACTIVITY

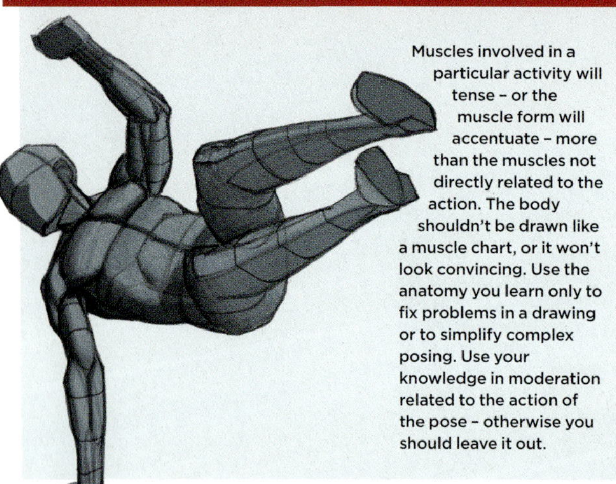

Muscles involved in a particular activity will tense – or the muscle form will accentuate – more than the muscles not directly related to the action. The body shouldn't be drawn like a muscle chart, or it won't look convincing. Use the anatomy you learn only to fix problems in a drawing or to simplify complex posing. Use your knowledge in moderation related to the action of the pose – otherwise you should leave it out.

4. EXAGGERATE THE BONE STRUCTURE

when the arm is bent. The crease you see is skin folding, not the muscle. Think of the muscle as a cable or a piston – neither of these objects fold over on themselves. Instead, they go slack. As a rule, skin folds perpendicular to muscle fibers, and this is what's taking place in this region. The skin folds, the muscle stays the same shape – just compressed a little bit more.

When the hand is pronated, the ridge muscles cross over from the outside to the inside edge of the arm. The ridge muscles attach just below the thumb so, as a rule of thumb (sorry, couldn't help it), wherever the thumb is, the ridge muscles are pointing to it. The ridge muscles break up the even symmetry between the arm's outside and inside edges.

One way to remember where and how all these muscles work together is to think of the arm as a series of chain links. Each link alternates direction, and that's what the arm does from shoulder to hand. For the arm to fold in on itself, or flex, the muscles have to be positioned to interlock with each other to prevent any conflict of space between all the mechanical parts within the arm mass.

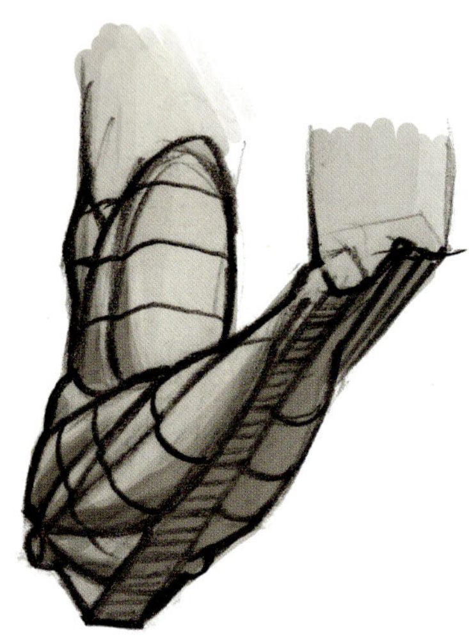

Here is an arm drawn from the underside, with the ulnar crest over-emphasized to show where it is and how it separates the flexor and extensor muscle groups. This bone ridge is over-emphasized to show how the bone travels from the elbow to the wrist.

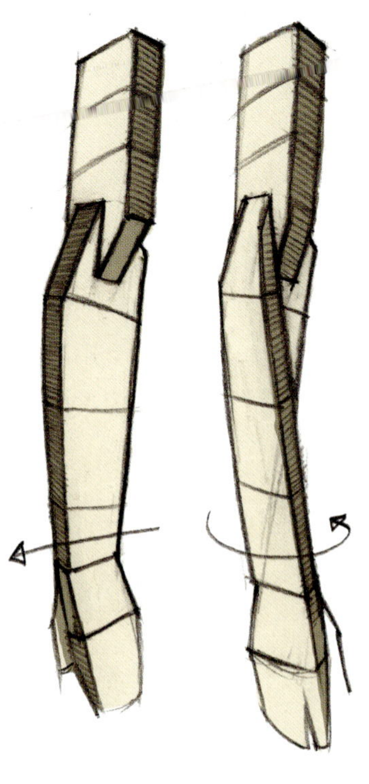

Ridge muscles

The ridge muscles share in the profile of the flexors and the extensors, blending into both sides in the upper third of the forearm. The inside of the arm seats the flexor group – the set of muscles that flexes the hand toward the body. The brachioradialis – the biggest muscle of the group – overlaps onto the inside surface of the arm, the opposing mass to the flexor group and pronator teres. Both of these sets of muscles funnel together in the body below the

5. FITTING THE MUSCLES TOGETHER

If the muscles are grouped together, they can all be paired to make drawing them easier to manage. The forearm is drawn foreshortened to show the relationship between the generic shape design and the significant anatomy underneath. The anatomy design is missing the pronator muscle to show how the flexors and extensors are separated by the bone structure.

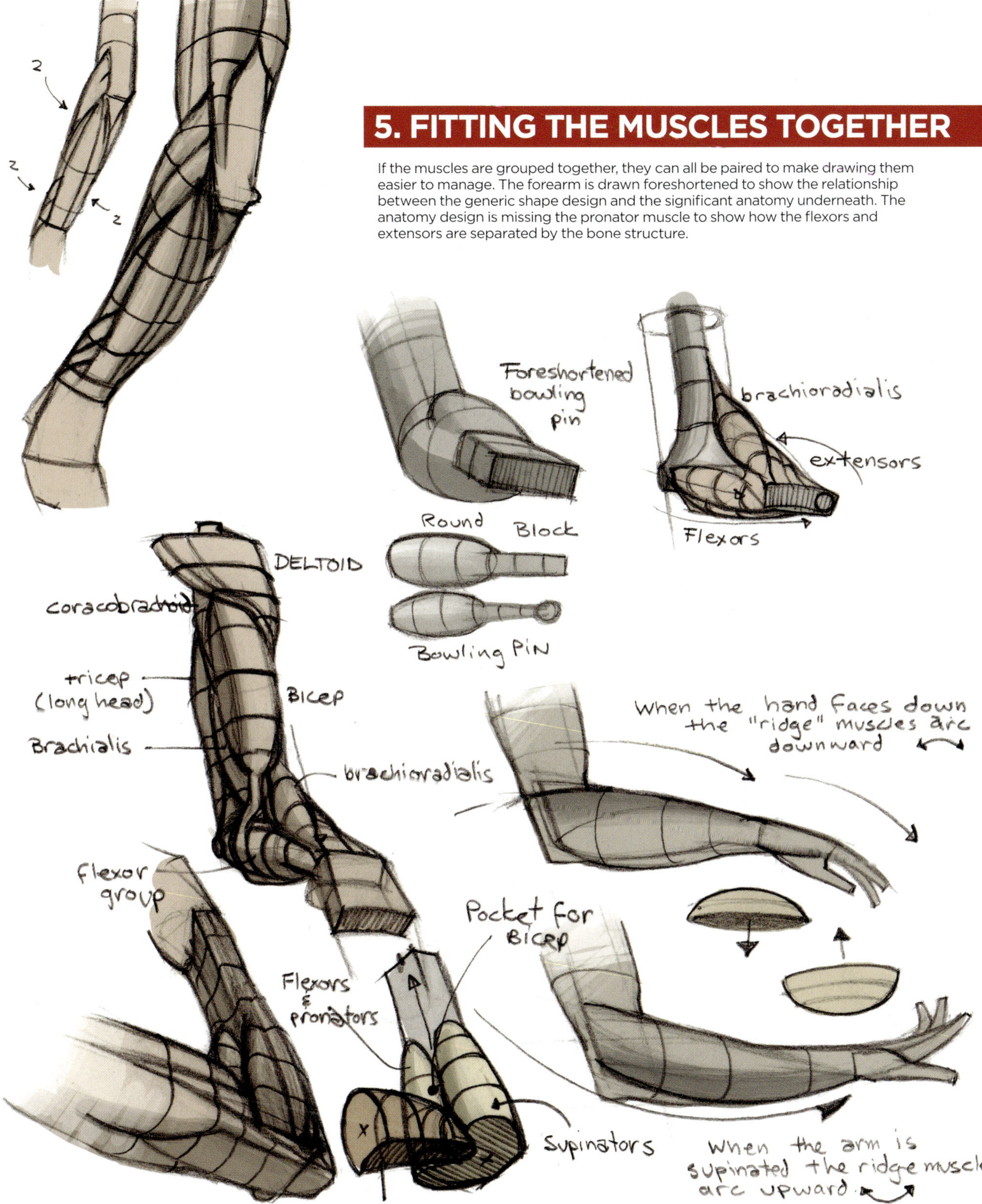

6. UNDERSTANDING HOW MUSCLES WORK BENEATH THE SKIN

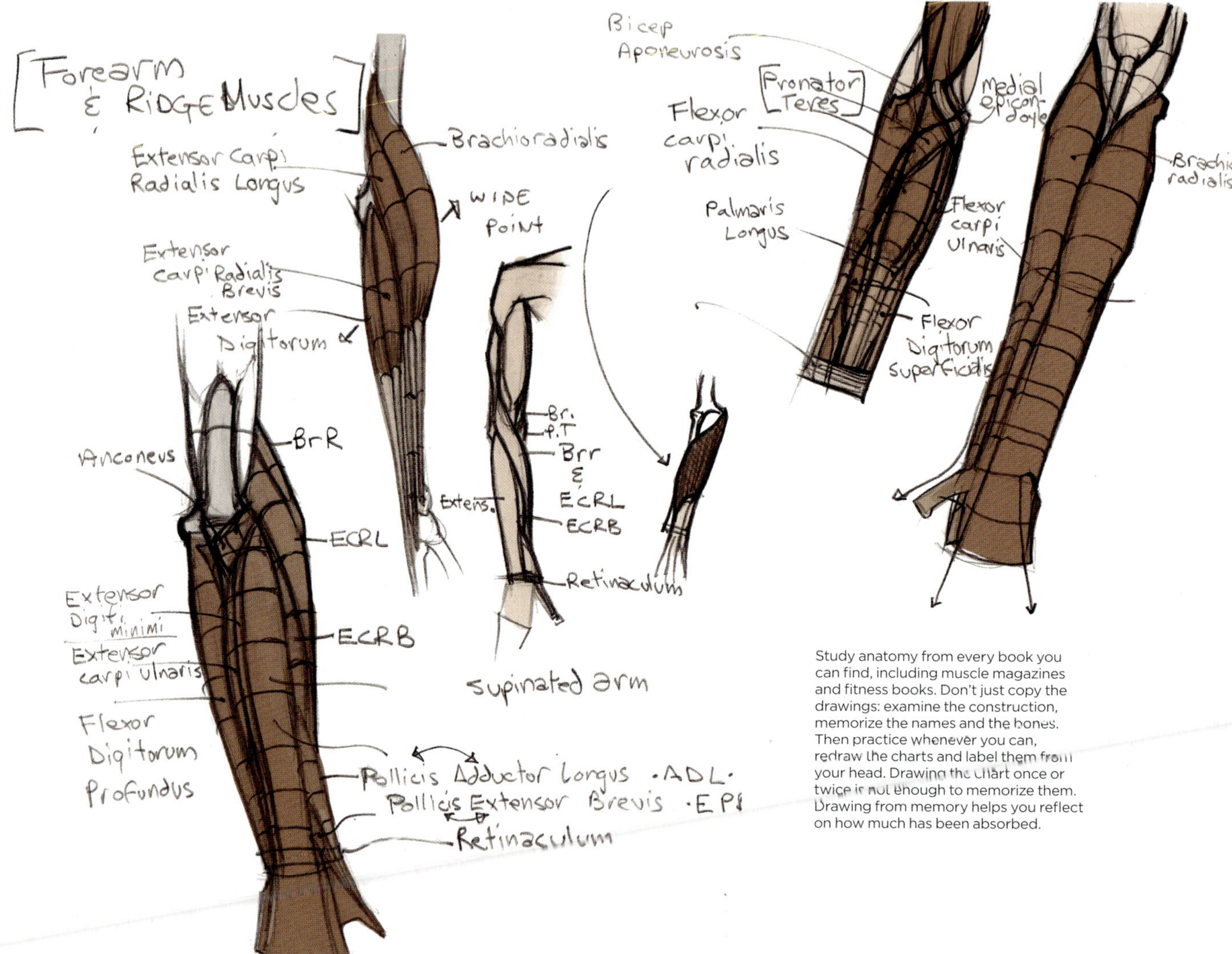

Study anatomy from every book you can find, including muscle magazines and fitness books. Don't just copy the drawings: examine the construction, memorize the names and the bones. Then practice whenever you can, redraw the charts and label them from your head. Drawing the chart once or twice is not enough to memorize them. Drawing from memory helps you reflect on how much has been absorbed.

bicep to form the pocket it sits inside of when the arm is bent. The extensor carpi muscles – two more muscles belonging to the ridge group – blend in with the extensors at the elbow and then across the top of the arm. On the other side of the arm, the extensors and flexors are separated by the ulna bone – a split in the muscles known as the ulna crest.

The flexors originate at the elbow on the inside bump (known as the medial epicondyle) of the humerus, the bone that connects the arm to the shoulder (also often known as the upper arm). The muscles cross over the two bones of the forearm – the ulna and radius. Most flexors terminate at the fingertips, while a few terminate in the palm of the hand. There are many layers of flexor muscles. Because the flexing of the hand – for gripping, holding, and so on – is its primary function, more muscles are assigned to assist in their actions.

"As flexing, gripping, holding, and so on are the primary functions of the hand, more muscles are attributed to assist in these actions."

The extensors originate from the outside bump of the arm (the lateral epicondyle) and cross over the two bones of the forearm, spreading out across the topside of the arm and terminating at the fingertips. These muscles are responsible for opening the hand and pulling back in a halt position – the opposing functions of the flexor group, in other words. The extensor group is the most active of the forearm muscles. If you're drawing superheroes or some other idealized body form, the inside of the arm (flexors) is a big ball-type shape, while the extensors are a series of pipes radiating from the elbow.

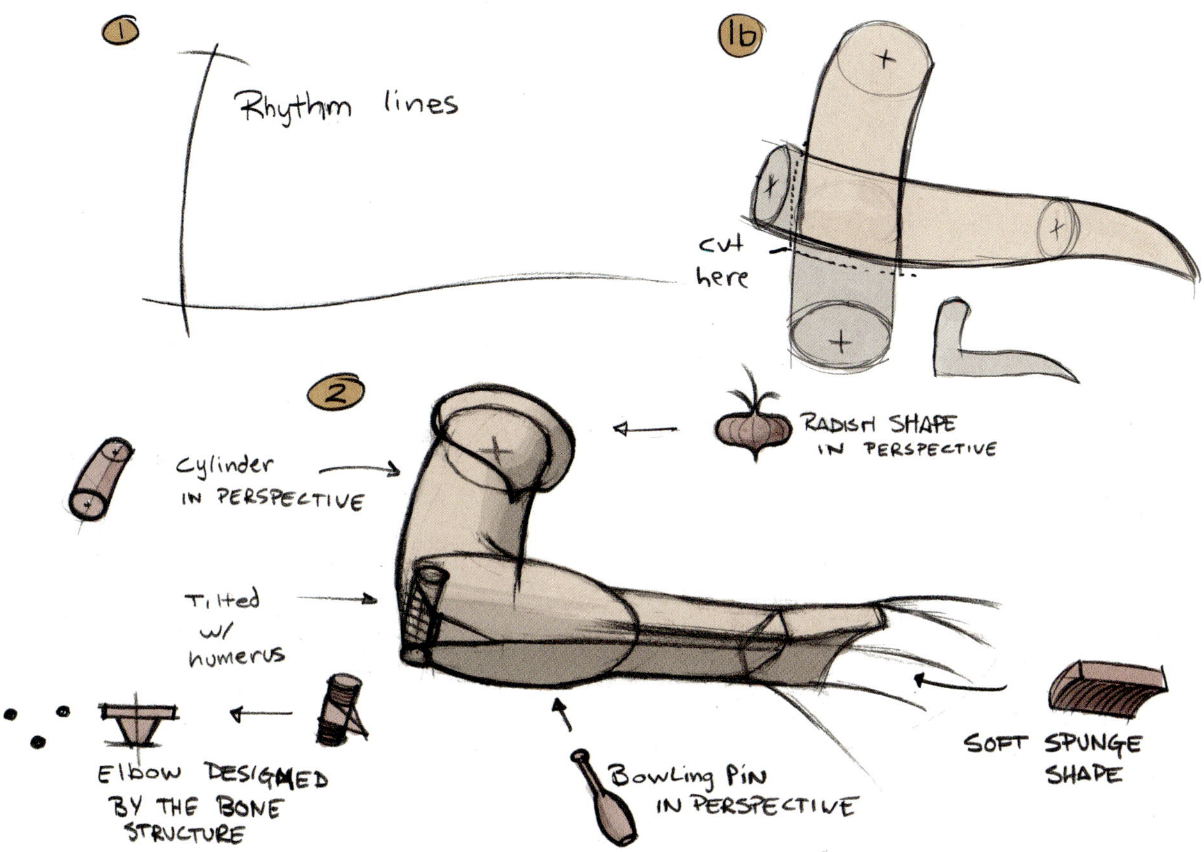

7. BUILDING UP THE ARM IN FOUR SIMPLE STAGES

Figure 1 locates the arm in space and its action. Figure 1b then describes the simple cylinder forms fleshed over the action lines. Figure 2 is a simple version of what the muscle shapes might look like as other shapes. Figure 3 is the anatomically fleshed out version of the arm. The next step (not shown here) would be to flesh out the rendering and lose most of the anatomy chart to light and shade.

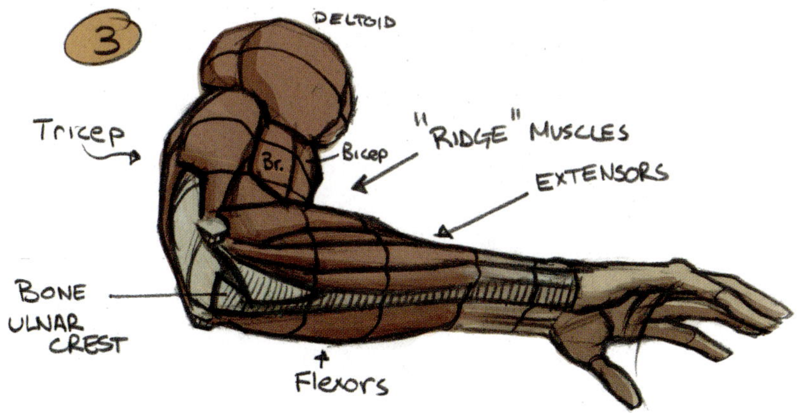

All of the forearm muscle tendons are protected as they pass over the wrist by the retinaculum. This might look like a wrist band, but it attaches separately to both the top and the bottom of the hand. This keeps the tendons from popping out any old way from the arm.

When drawing the arm, you should keep in mind that grouping the muscles together is a better way to begin than drawing the individual shapes. Drawing the figure one muscle at a time is painful and more than likely going to grow into its own unique shape – one that doesn't necessarily resemble a real figure. The visual symbols in the images here should help make some sense of what I mean by this. Study the muscles as one exercise, but learn to consolidate them into groups as another exercise – and as a mantra for your work.

Drawing is not about parts; drawing is about suspension of disbelief, fooling the eye into believing what is seen. We study parts to identify them as a function, only to throw them back into the pile of tools called intuition.

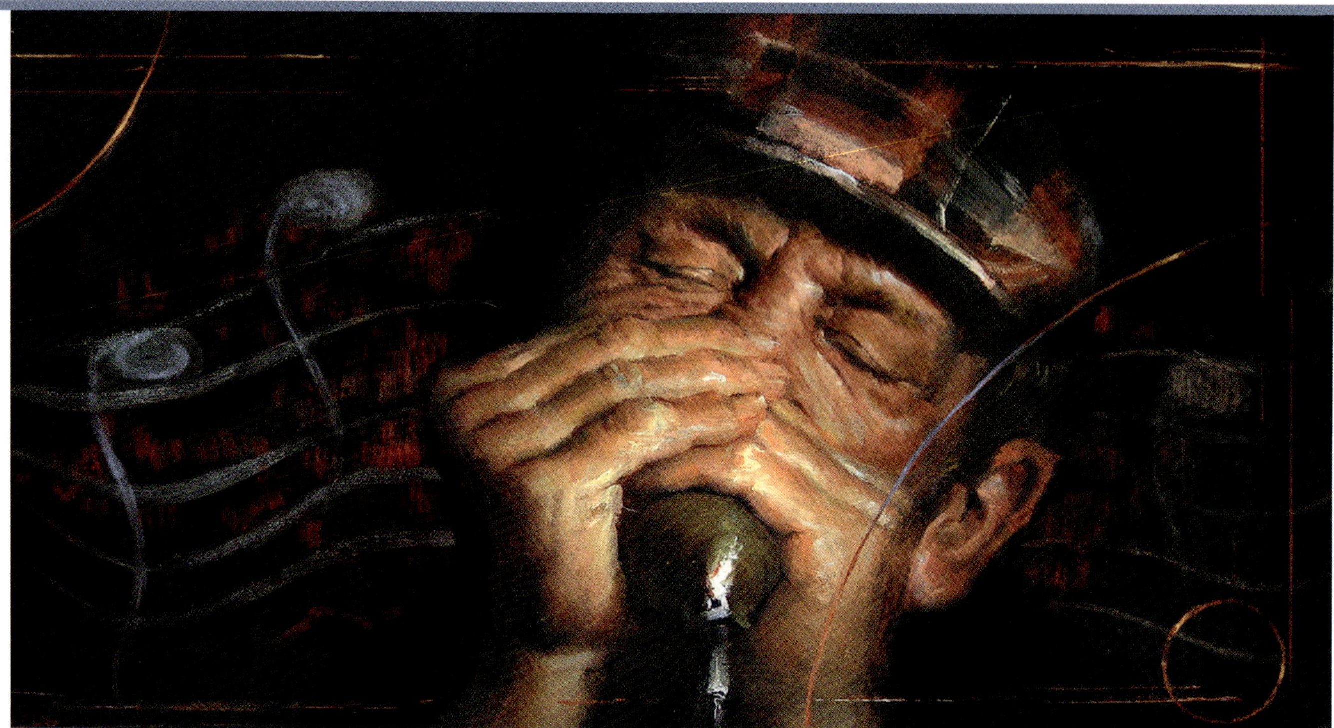

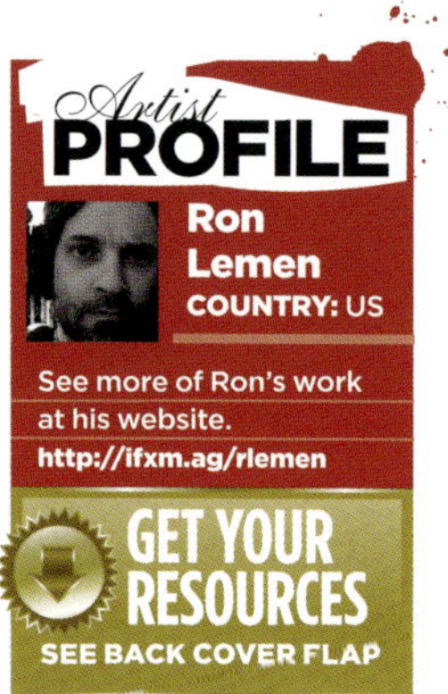

DRAWING THE HANDS

Many artists fear drawing this part of the body, but apply the principles you've learned and learn the anatomy, and you'll find the process much easier

Before diving into further drawing advice, let's think about a few concepts to help make the process of drawing a complex shape such as the hand easier. The hand actually has very few muscles in it: its mechanics are guided by the forearm, and its design is based mostly on bone and fatty tissue. The thumb is a distinct shape rooted to the hand mass and should be drawn into the image after the bigger mass has been designed. The four main fingers all radiate toward a common point: the index finger and the pinkie curve toward each other, and the other two fingers fit somewhere between them. The fingers are not parallel with each other, although some actions may make it seem that way. Fingernails and knuckles are details; leave them until last.

It's important to keep steps in their particular order while you absorb the process behind them. Whether the drawing you're making is simple or complex, if something falls apart, it's easier to detect where it went wrong in the process. Once you're confident and well-trained in your craft, it's up to you to find your own way of working, and you may well deviate from the academic or school-taught way. This is where you'll find your independent style – not in copying others, but in reassessing your working order. Learn it right, break the rules and tools if you choose, and find your own voice.

Hands can be convincingly drawn interacting with objects or surfaces. I can't stress enough that learning from life is the key to understanding everything you'll ever need to know in art. While art books might give a cool trick for getting a certain look or appearance, solving the problem dimensionally or from every angle will give so much more wisdom and insight. If you can't take an art class, use a mirror. You can use yourself to study from, and you don't have to pay a model fee.

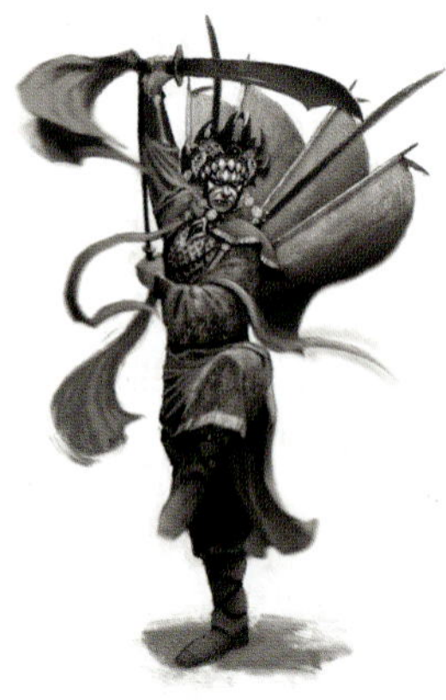

Starting with the overall gesture of a pose helps you design realistic hands.

Getting to grips with the anatomy of hands

Find out the best ways to approach drawing the human hand

Anatomy is important – but more so to a doctor than to an artist. The part of anatomy you should be first concerned with is the shape design, and how you can simplify your thinking and drawing down to the core essence of these shapes.

Finger bones have a particular design to them. The fingers are more than 60 percent visible bone shapes defining what we see, so understanding the finger bone or knuckle shapes is key in making a more convincing drawing. The finger joints are spool-shaped, depressed slightly in the middles for the tendons of the extensor muscles of the forearm. The metacarpal knuckle – the big one the finger is attached to – is barrel-shaped, not totally spherical, and the tendons that sit in the grooves of the spool shapes on our fingers sit on top of the barrel-shaped knuckle. As research, look at Norman Rockwell's hands in his paintings. He did it better than almost any other illustrator out there.

The hand has a squishy side and a firm side. The squishy side – the palm – is where the majority of muscles of the hand are located. The other visible soft spot is between the thumb and index finger on the hand's back, or dorsal, side. These soft areas are the points on the hand that flex and change shape when active with an object or surface. The hand then conforms to the shape of the object it holds. This last detail can really throw off the best of us at times – unless you remind yourself of a few basic concepts of construction that you can fall back on.

Mechanics of anatomy

Different hands can look like they are different shapes – babies' hands, for example, are chubbier than old people's. But we are built similarly, our hands included. The hand is blocky by nature; it has mass, a top, a bottom, sides, a front, and a back. The hand is also circular, as it swivels and pivots in the wrist.

When the fingers are pressed together, the hand looks like a spade. This is where you want to start drawing the hand. Imagining the hand as a soft, blocky form, something akin to a sponge in texture, helps you to remember what you're drawing is a physical object. If you can't

2. SOFT SPOTS

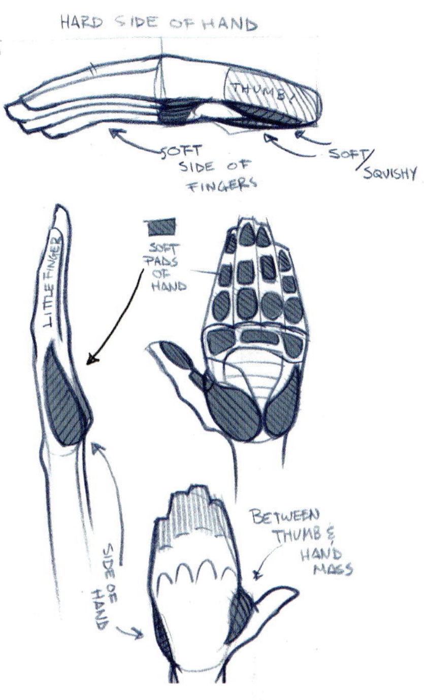

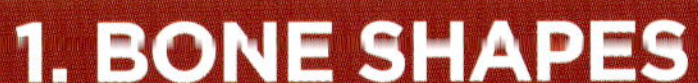

1. BONE SHAPES

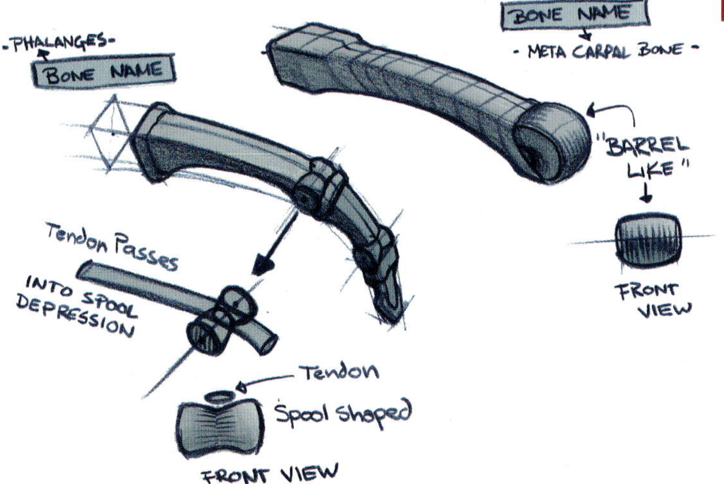

3. HAND HOLDING A BALL

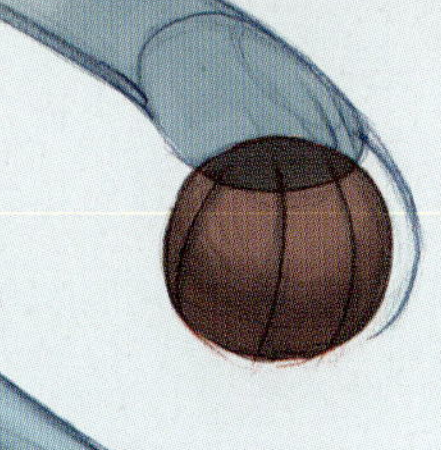

Start with the object to be held (the ball, top). Next, add the arm rhythms and the ball shape for the palm of the hand, then attach the finger wires to the ball mass, These wires should represent the absolute middle profile contour, the middle of the finger mass.

Now flesh out the forms. This means adding dimension to the shapes by giving them planes. To locate the finger segments, find the arcing lines: these segments arc more than 90 percent of the time. The arcs determine the relationship of each particular band of knuckles – proximal, middle or distal – from finger to finger. Knuckles are knobby; either round or blocky. However, you may find that stylizing will change this blocky appearance.

remember the anatomy, remember the concepts; they'll get you through any doubts you have about what you're drawing.

The fingers are roughly the same length as the hand mass. Remembering this is a good check-and-balance to make sure your drawing's proportions are right, even when the fingers are folded and the hand is foreshortened. Proportions have a way of being understood even when obscured.

The hand is attached to the arm, and the arm is an extension of the torso, so starting with an overall gesture of the pose ensures that the design you pick for the final hand is correct. The hand position is relative to the rotation of the arm (or its pronation or supination). The sketch hopefully solves the dilemma of how to start the design of the hand. I sometimes think of designing the hand in action by drawing the object first. Once I know where the object is, relative to the pose of my character, I can work out the rest of the action.

Interactive hands

Another way of establishing the hand's interaction with an object would be to draw the object, draw a hand print on the object so you know where to define the details, then build up off of the hand print all the formal shapes, the hand block, the finger masses, and so on.

The line that shows the connection with the object is the weld line. Press it firmly against the object, showing off the object's form more than the hand. No matter how much you see a little space between the joints, don't make them important. Make the weld line show off the action.

Draw details – fingernails, knuckles, wrinkles – last. They sit better on the fingers when they are well designed dimensionally. Before this, render the surfaces: find the shadow patterns, and use planes to chart values across the surfaces. This is what it means to render a form, making a stronger visible shape, not adding details.

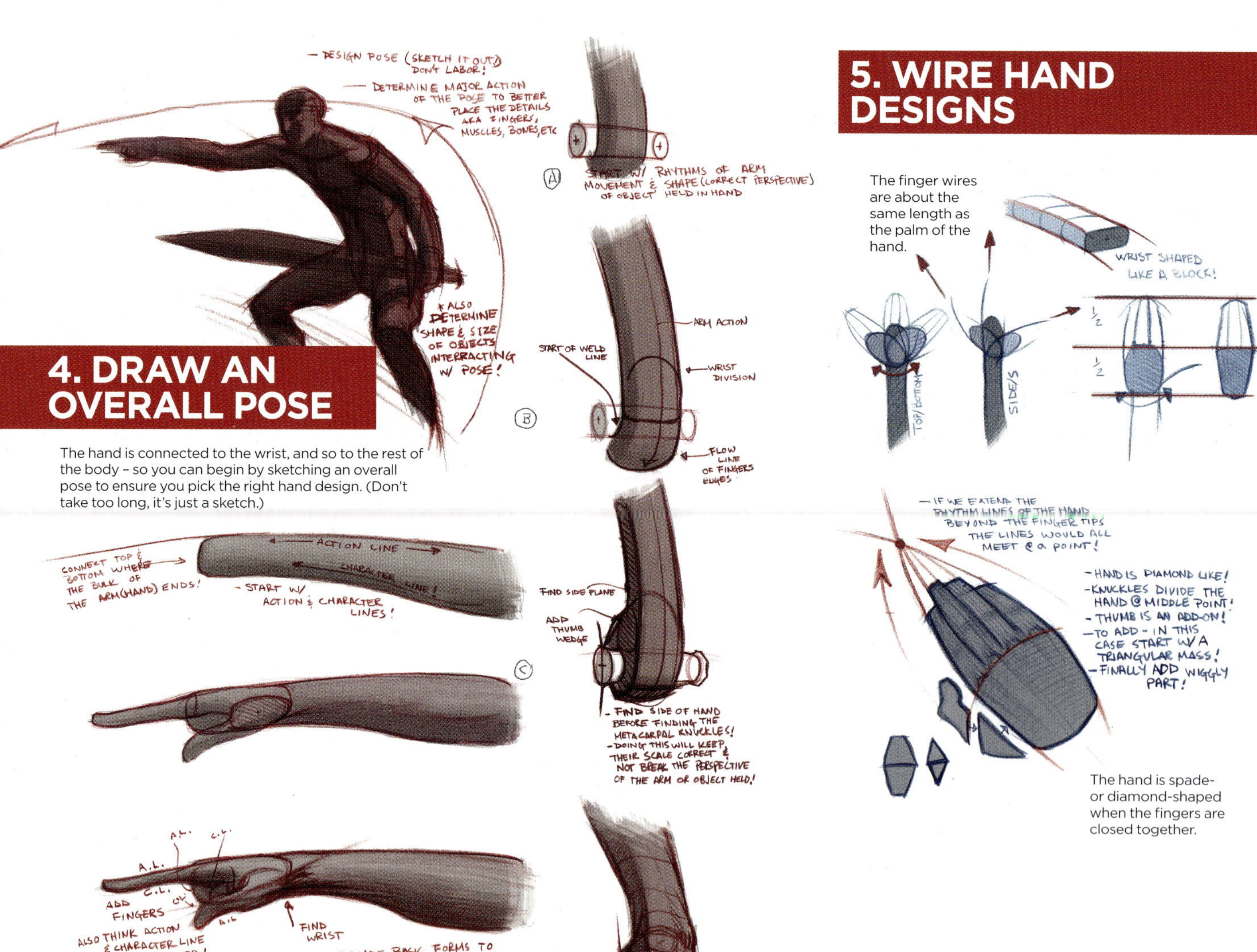

4. DRAW AN OVERALL POSE

The hand is connected to the wrist, and so to the rest of the body – so you can begin by sketching an overall pose to ensure you pick the right hand design. (Don't take too long, it's just a sketch.)

5. WIRE HAND DESIGNS

The finger wires are about the same length as the palm of the hand.

The hand is spade- or diamond-shaped when the fingers are closed together.

6. DRAWING GRIPPING HANDS

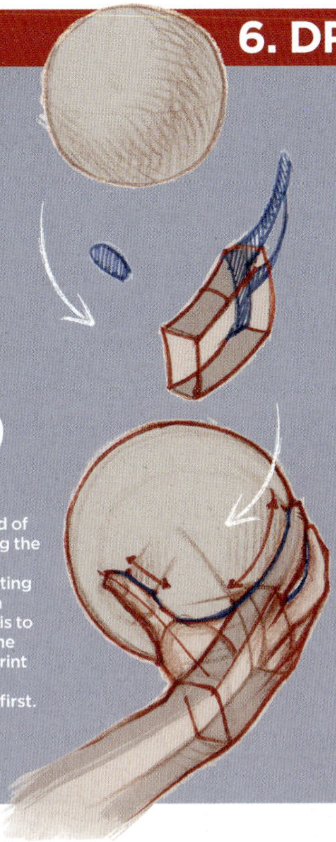

1

One method of drawing the hand interacting with an object is to draw the hand print on the object first.

2

Drawing the object first helps you when drawing the hand in action. Here, I've begun with the object before using the weld line (shown in blue) to connect the hand and object correctly.

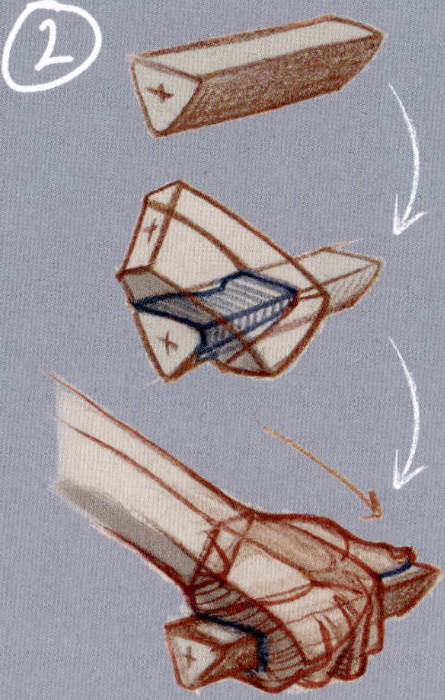

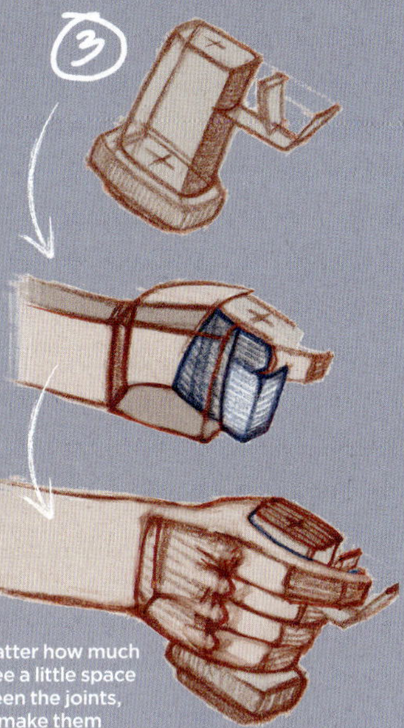

3

No matter how much you see a little space between the joints, don't make them important. Use the weld lines.

7. CONSTRUCTING A HAND

Begin with the central part of the hand. The lines indicate movement and thumb position.

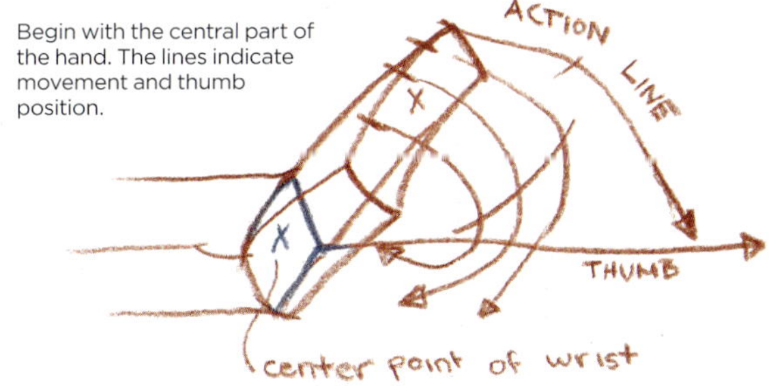

The different-colored lines here indicate the gesture of the hand and the character, showing how the object sits in relation to the character.

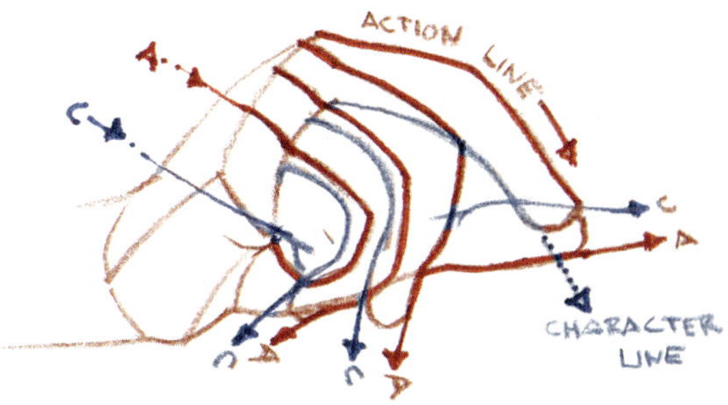

Next, it's time to subdivide surfaces. Here, I'm using the plane structure method to chart values and tones across the surfaces, working up from flat values.

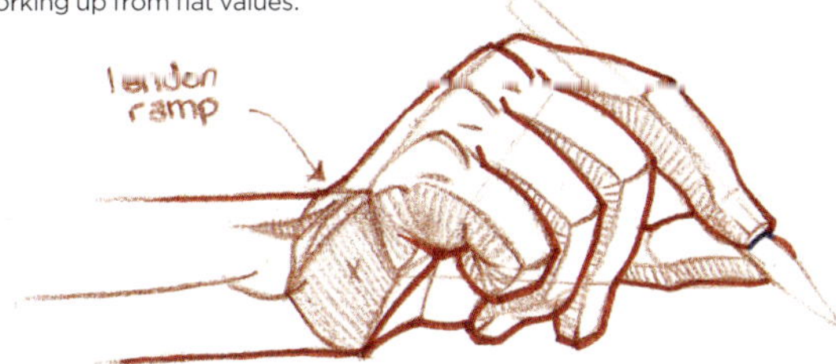

Only when all of this is done do I begin to shade and detail the hand. Once I have the hand shape rendered, I can then add details such as creases, fingernails, and knuckles to make it look realistic.

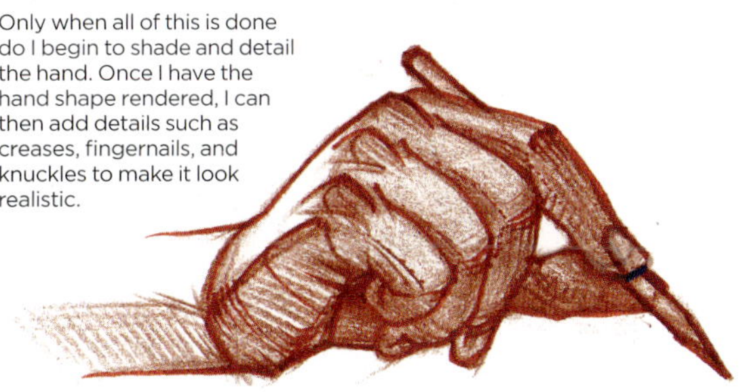

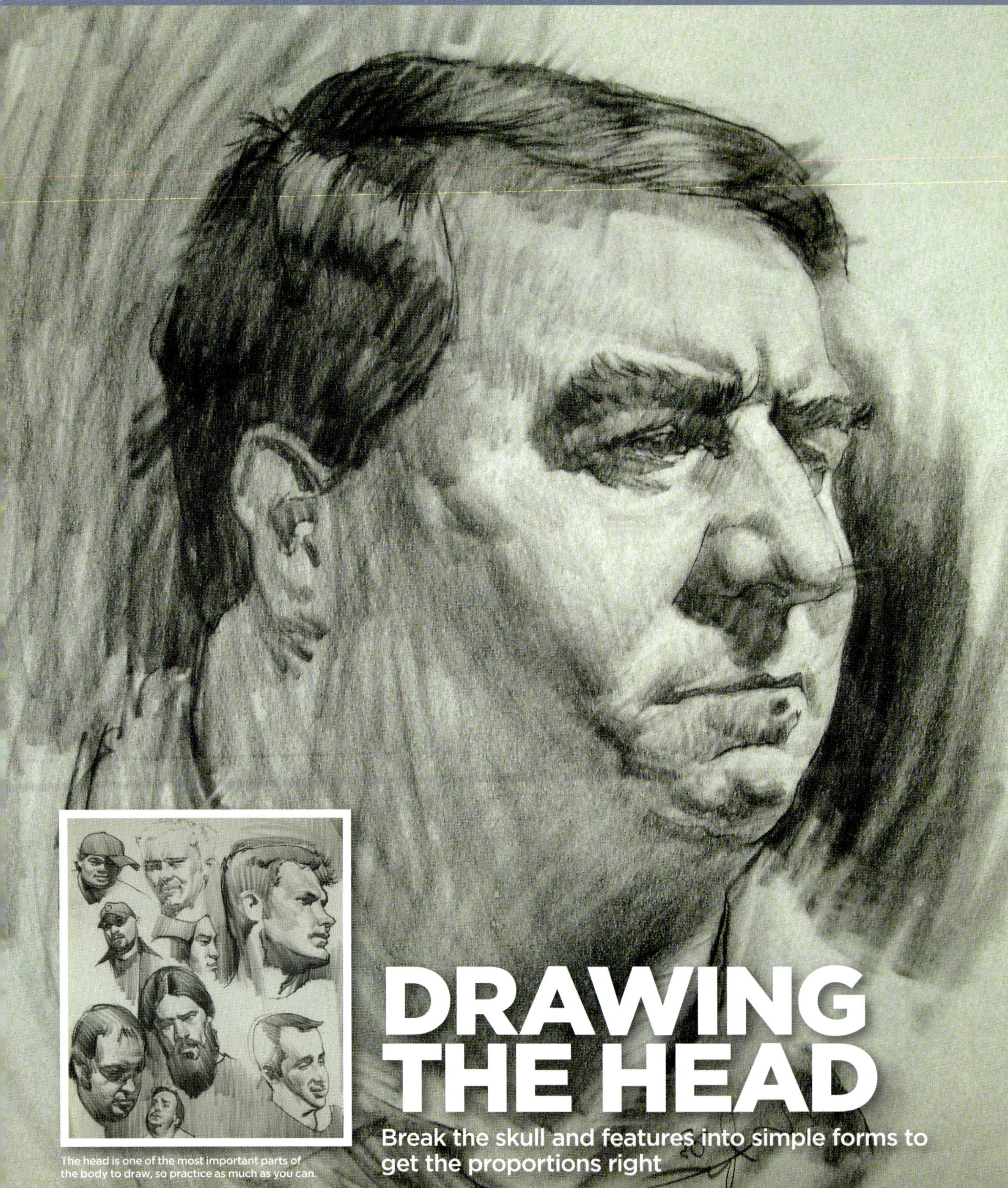

The head is one of the most important parts of the body to draw, so practice as much as you can.

DRAWING THE HEAD

Break the skull and features into simple forms to get the proportions right

When drawing the human body, one thing that's essential to perfect is your method for drawing the head. The skull is the traditional academic measuring stick of the human form: formulae have been created that enable artists to use the skull as a tool to draw the rest of the figure with, helping you to maintain correct proportions and scale for the figure.

Here, I'm going to talk you through my basic process for creating well-drawn heads. The theory is important and can offer a certain degree of freedom from reference – but, as I've said before, nothing beats hands-on practice.

Get a friend or family member to model for you at every opportunity, hire a model, or with the help of a mirror or photos, draw yourself. Theory alone cannot give you enough experience as an artist to work through every problem you'll encounter in your career.

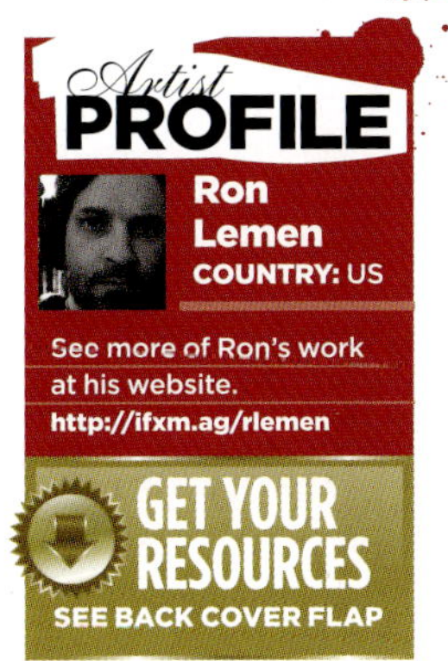

Shape up: basic head forms

Put your head in a box to ensure that you've got the correct dimensions

Below is my sketch of a head in front and side profiles, split into three roughly even sections. Measuring the skull from the side (including the nose), it fits roughly into a square box (as you can see to the right). From the front but excluding the ears, it's about two-thirds the width of that box at its widest point.

When children draw a head, they usually start with a vaguely oval or "egg" shape. The head is really neither an oval nor a block, of course, but thinking about both while designing the skull will help you achieve realistic dimensions.

So, like a child, begin with an oval. Draw a line to find the inside corner of the face, or the change of plane from the front to the side. This is usually where portraits fall apart: without a three-quarter line, the features drift from the front to the side of the head, and proportion, direction of gaze, and symmetry all fall out of alignment.

Now draw a centerline. This helps keep the features squared up on the face plane and is especially necessary when the head is tipped or tilted.

Draw perpendicular lines attached to the top and bottom of the centerline to forehead and chin. The skull shape should now be

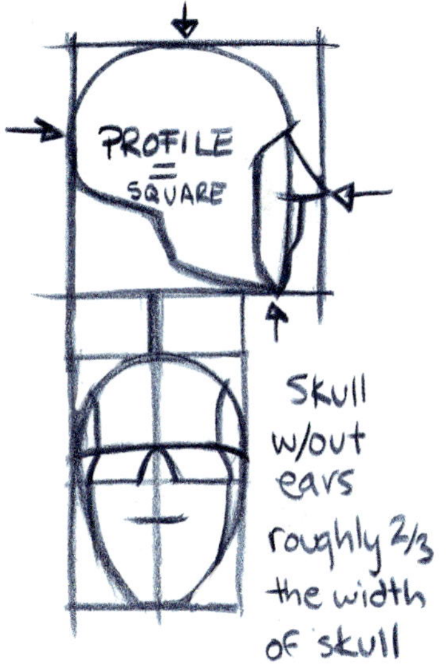

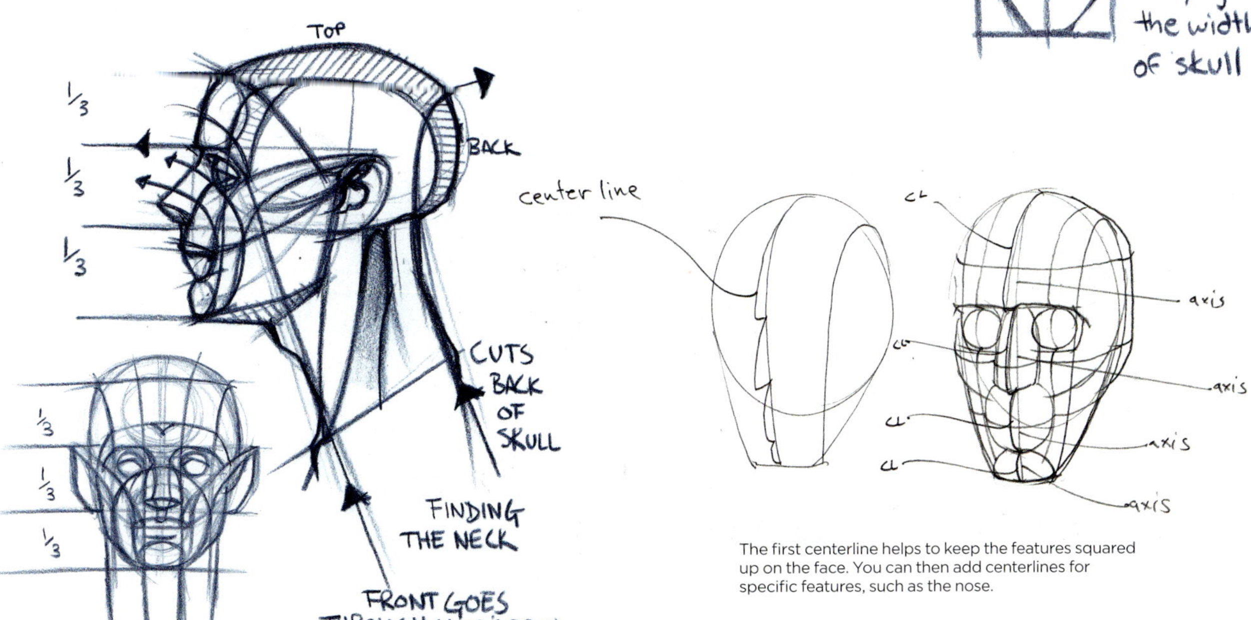

The first centerline helps to keep the features squared up on the face. You can then add centerlines for specific features, such as the nose.

divided into three visible surfaces; this will help get the proportions more accurate for the smaller shapes. Draw a second, more organic, centerline to define the centers of the extruded features – the lifted brow, nose, tooth cylinder, and chin.

The first feature to start with is the split between the eyes; this is known as the glabella. Typically, it's a wedge shape between the eyebrows, just above the bridge of the nose. I choose to begin here because the glabella establishes an overall width for all the rest of the features. Next, attach a horizontal line to the top of the glabella wedge to establish the tilt of the eye sockets in relation to the centerline (a perpendicular relationship).

Drawing the nose

Drawing the nose is tricky, but good organization will make it a whole lot easier. Start with a tall triangle, flat against the face plane as though you've shaved off the nose. The top of the triangle overlaps the glabella and creates the interior line of the eye sockets. Knowing the perspective of the head makes it easy to draw the perspective of the nose. Extrude the bridge in the same direction as the side plane of the head. This ensures that the nose stays centered between the eyes correctly.

The bottoms of the eye sockets are next to draw. Make these parallel to the top line, intersecting the nose about halfway down its length. Extend the top line around to the side planes, keeping it at the same elevation to the top of the head.

The eye sockets should look somewhat like sunglasses in their design. Take the bottom line and do the same thing you did with the top one. Both of these lines frame where the ear should be placed on the side plane in correct elevation to the top and bottom of the head.

Cheeks and teeth

The cheeks and tooth cylinder can be drawn together in a rhythm, starting with an arc that crosses through the face plane from cheek to cheek. From directly in front, this rhythm can be drawn as a circle; more work is needed from the side view, since the cheek shares its rhythm with both the front and side planes. The ears are used to help design the cheeks (see the diagram to the right).

The tooth cylinder is connected to this cheek and drops down

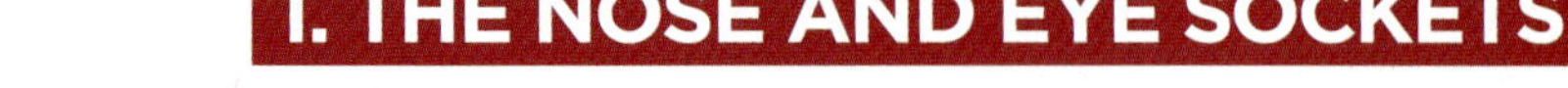

1. THE NOSE AND EYE SOCKETS

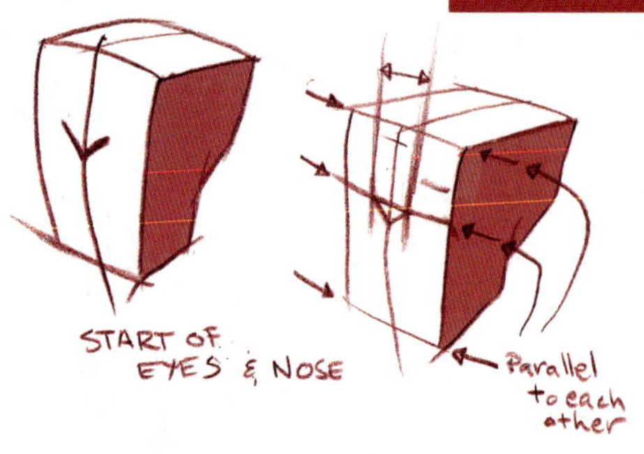

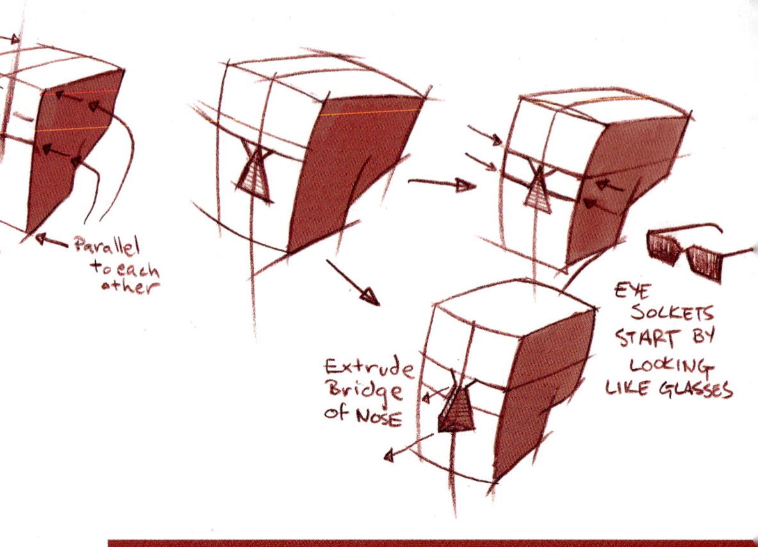

2. CHEEKS AND EARS

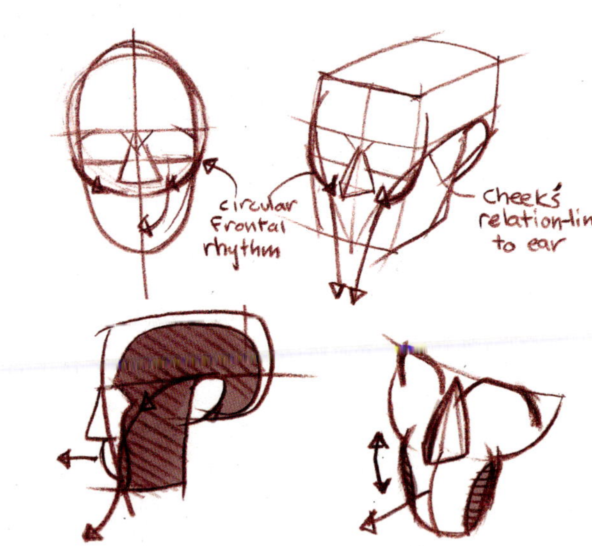

3. THE TOOTH CYLINDER RELATIVE TO THE NOSE

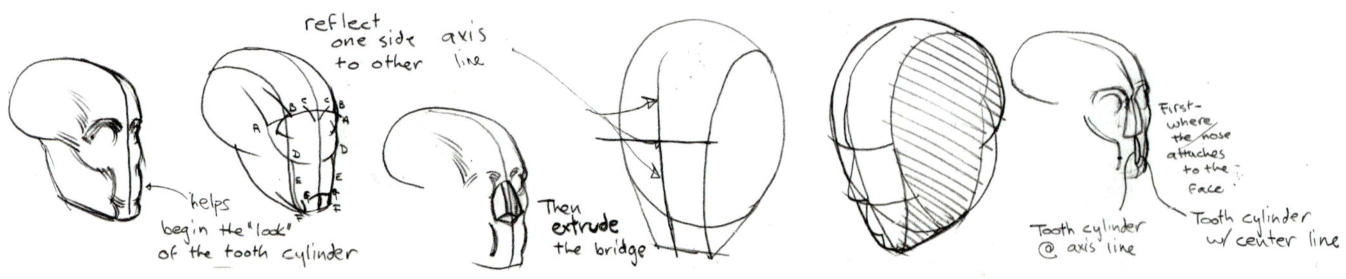

toward the chin, arcing across the centerline and up the other side, leaving enough space for the ball of the chin.

The mouth extends from the face like a mound. Often, it is more cylindrical than rounded, which is why it's commonly known as the tooth cylinder in life-drawing manuals.

The top of the skull, while rounded, can actually be drawn as a block. When drawing the hair onto the head, thinking about the skull as a block can add extra dimension to the hair mass.

The best way to draw the hair is to start with the hairline. I do this as follows (refer to my sketch below to help): draw the head as a basic shape, and attach the face like a mask, with the hairline framing the upper half of the mask shape.

It's just as important to see the hairline as a geometric shape as it is any of the other features. Visualising the hairline as part of the face mask can help attach the hair correctly to the skull and keep everything lined up around the head.

When drawing anything organic, think about the shapes with edges and corners first. The perspective of a form is found much more easily if there are points to use as landmarks, and a straightish line connecting them.

4. ADDING THE HAIRLINE, USING BLOCK SHAPES FOR DIMENSION

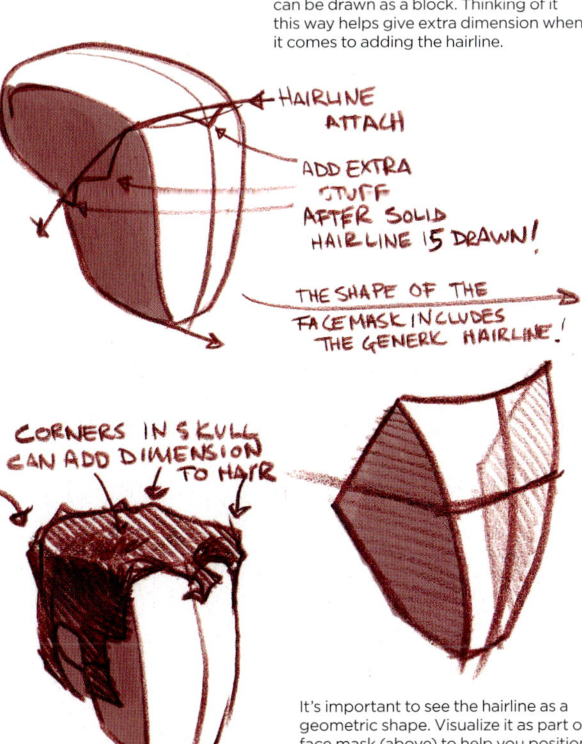

While the top of the skull is rounded, it can be drawn as a block. Thinking of it this way helps give extra dimension when it comes to adding the hairline.

It's important to see the hairline as a geometric shape. Visualize it as part of the face mask (above) to help you position it correctly on the skull.

5. HEAD AND SHOULDERS

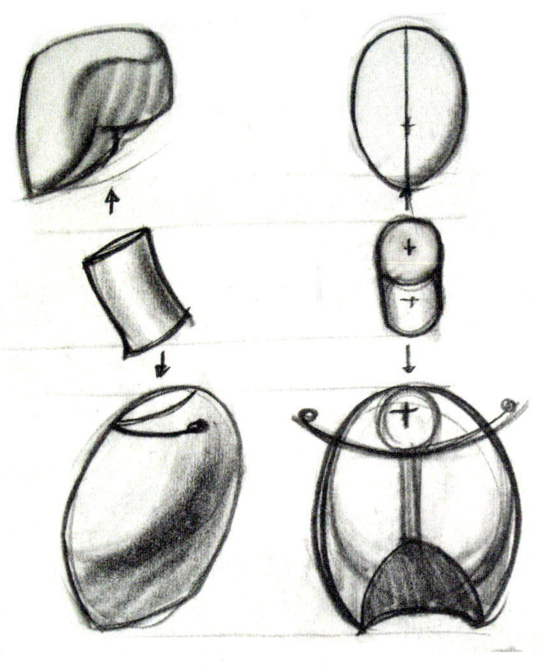

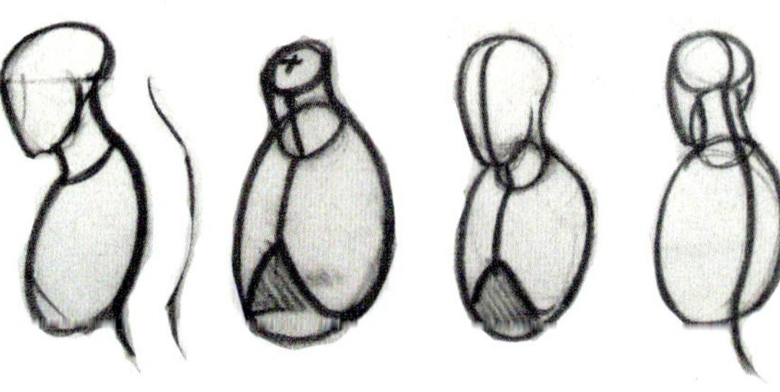

Unless you're drawing a disembodied head, there will come a time when you'll want to attach it to the rest of the body, which means adding the neck, rib cage and shoulders.

Attaching the neck and shoulders to the head can be a tricky business. If you're drawing the head first, it's at this point that the rest of the pose is about to be drawn. This connection will help you to develop and define the shapes of that pose, ensuring that it fits correctly with the head you've already got.

Attach the head (ball) to the neck (cylinder), then attach the cylinder to the rib cage (ball). The shoulders float over the rib cage. The only point where two bones connect together is at the pit of the neck, where the clavicle connects to the rib cage. Therefore, the rib cage is the most important structure after the head and neck.

TAKE AN ANATOMY MASTER CLASS

Glenn Vilppu shows how focusing on action and making use of the "icons" of basic rendering are the keys to creating expressive anatomy

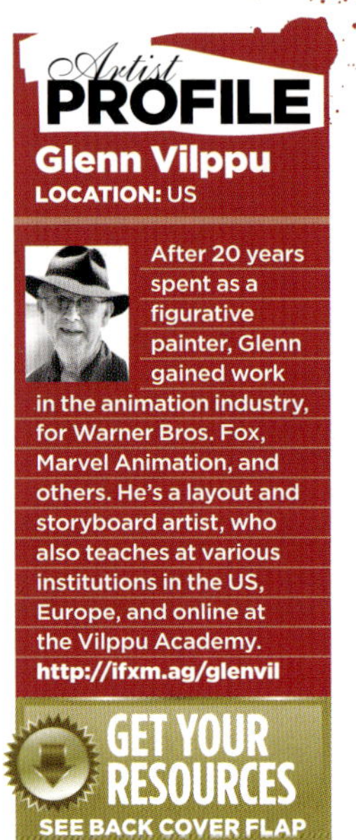

Over the next few pages, I'll reveal the basic steps I use in my lectures and how they're related. I'll start with the first conception or inkling and take you through to the final presentation.

Each step has an accompanying video instruction and involves applying core visual tools, like selecting icons for a particular program, that you need to know how to use, to develop your concept. Continuing the computer analogy, drawing is the graphical interface to your imagination. These tools enable you to relate your idea to yourself and the world.

I've organized these tools into a series of logical steps that can be applied to any visual presentation.

All of us know a lot more than we think we do, and much of what I teach is simply making this knowledge accessible. My desire is to bring a feeling of life to the drawing, based upon movement. In this workshop I'll focus upon the action – otherwise known as gesture – and the primary rendering steps involved in drawing the figure from imagination.

1 Tools, not rules

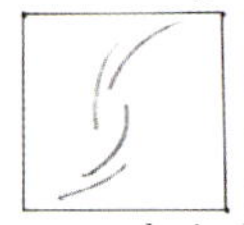

When drawing from life and from imagination, the key is to understand the action that you're trying to depict. This is an analytical process. In this example, the lines lead you through the figure – they're not copies of shapes, outlines, or stick figures. Each fragment leads you to the next, as if you were animating a trip through the figure, moving from one side to the other. No dead drawings like CSI. It's all about transition. Make the viewer's eye move.

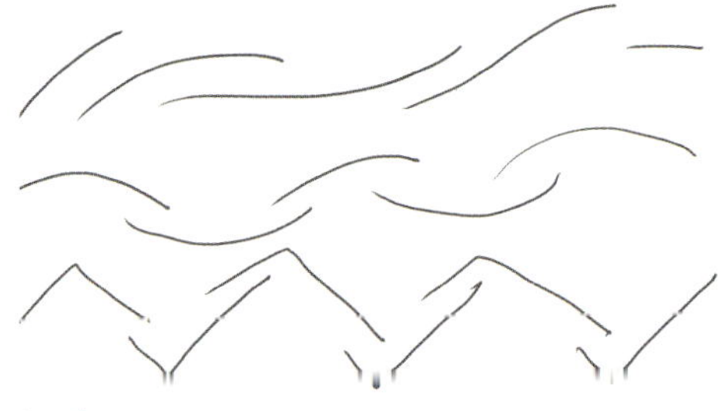

Artist TIP:
Think of each of the tools as icons on a computer that you access to create a drawing.

2 Go across the form

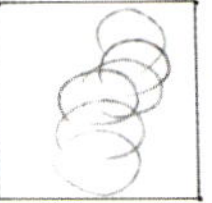

The next primary tool is using lines going across and around the form, similar to a basic wire frame. Notice how it gives the first step a clear understanding of the forms in space. Focus on 3D, not shape or tone.

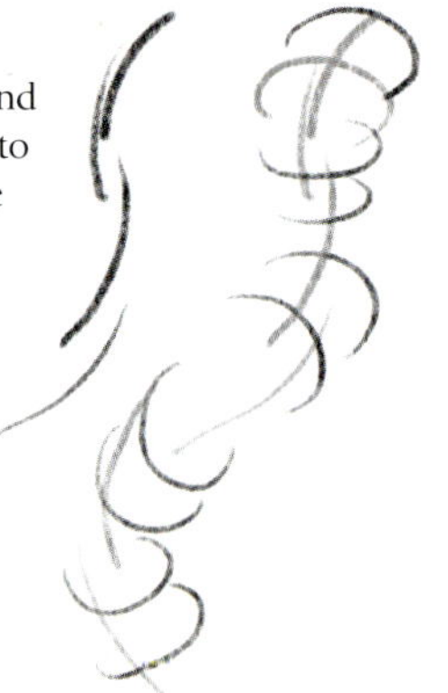

Artist TIP:
Follow through, and take the line across and around the form. Imagine your pencil on the forms going over the contours.

3 Build up the figure

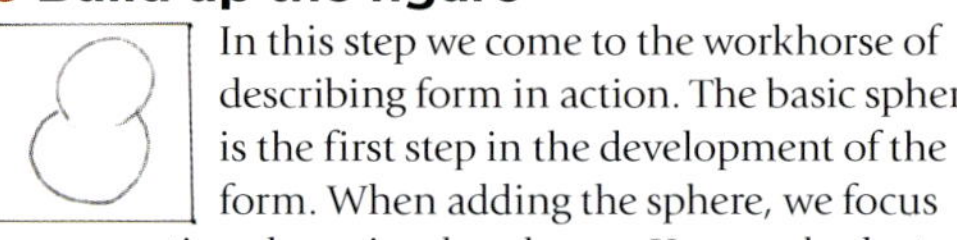

In this step we come to the workhorse of describing form in action. The basic sphere is the first step in the development of the form. When adding the sphere, we focus upon creating clear, simple volumes. You can look at these as prototype anatomical structures, but don't get obsessed about having to make them perfect for now. These are general forms that will be adjusted as we go along. But for now, pay particular attention to how they overlap.

Artist TIP:
Draw very lightly so that you can change without erasing. Rehearse the strokes: three looks, two thinks, one application.

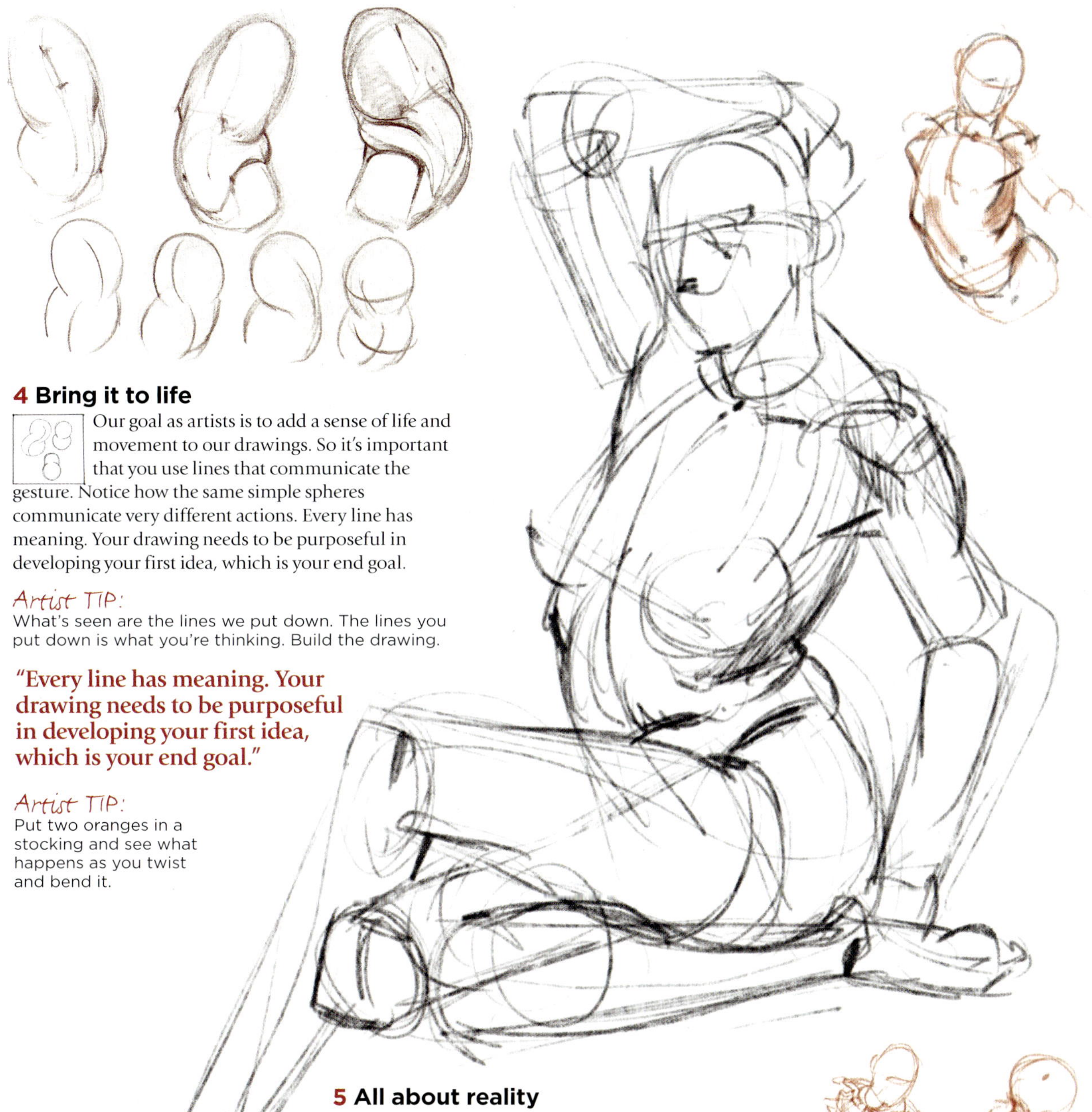

4 Bring it to life

Our goal as artists is to add a sense of life and movement to our drawings. So it's important that you use lines that communicate the gesture. Notice how the same simple spheres communicate very different actions. Every line has meaning. Your drawing needs to be purposeful in developing your first idea, which is your end goal.

Artist TIP:
What's seen are the lines we put down. The lines you put down is what you're thinking. Build the drawing.

"Every line has meaning. Your drawing needs to be purposeful in developing your first idea, which is your end goal."

Artist TIP:
Put two oranges in a stocking and see what happens as you twist and bend it.

5 All about reality

How your drawing communicates a sense of physical reality is key to your drawing having a sense of life. The first exercise in studying animation is the bouncing ball and the primary elements of how the ball changes shape on hitting the ground and regains its shape in rebounding. Squash and stretch are fundamental drawing terms. I first heard these in discussions of the works of Michelangelo and Pontormo. Look at the Belvedere torso, copied by artists since Roman times. Note how I'm applying this basic concept to the simple forms of the figure.

6 Use the cylinder

As we drew the simple cross contours back in step 2, each showed a section of a cylinder. The cylinder becomes our next basic tool for the figure and a building foundation for anatomical information. Where you place the ends of the cylinders and how you draw the ellipse are the main points in showing direction and foreshortening. The cylinder becomes part of a visual structure we build anatomical structure on.

Artist TIP:
This approach also works for anything that's coming forward or back, from snakes to branches.

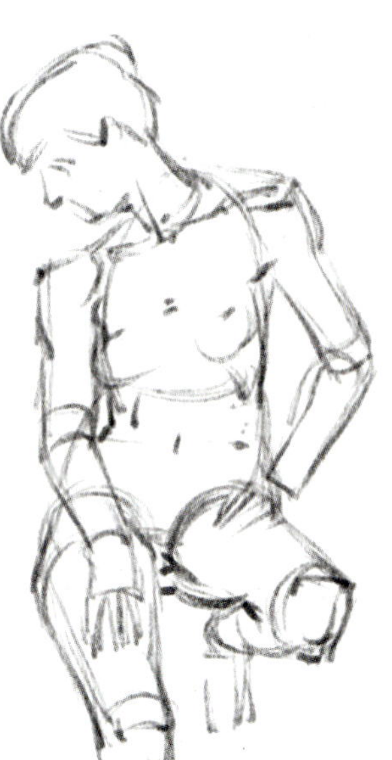

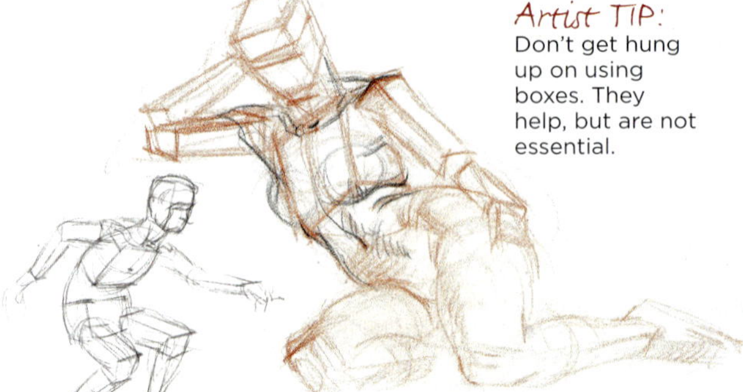

Artist TIP:
Don't get hung up on using boxes. They help, but are not essential.

7 Symmetry awareness

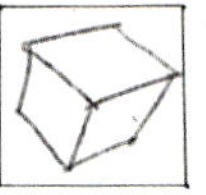

Analysis of the pose is key when drawing from a model. In doing the drawings so far I've been building on an idea in my head, but in drawing from a model it's not often clear what the action is. Our next tool is the box, which works to both clarify our understanding of the live model and our conceptual intent. This is because it introduces critical anatomical landmarks that show us symmetry – a key element in revealing action.

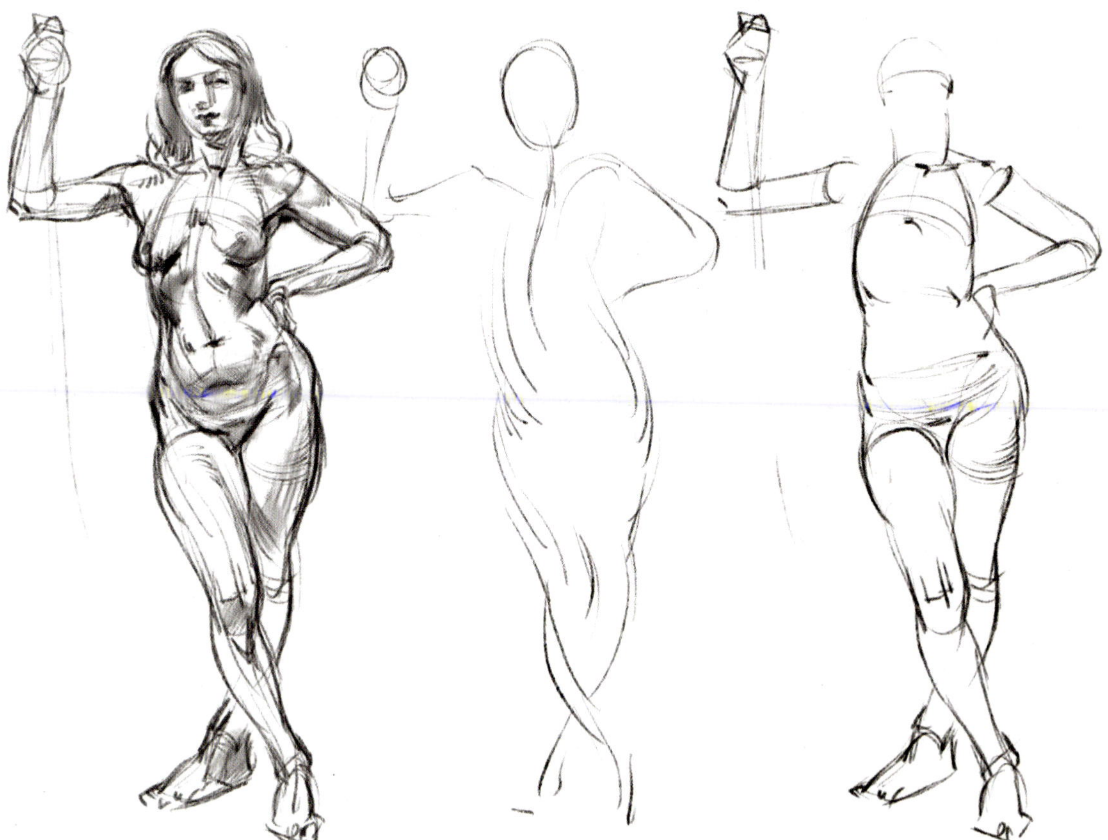

8 Make it move!

At this point in the drawing we get a merging of fundamental construction and anatomy in action. All the muscles are connected at two points and some at more. How the basic underlying structure moves and interacts is giving visual expressions to how they affect the surface anatomy. So now is the perfect time to focus on not only the muscles but the fabric of skin and fat on top of the muscles and their interaction. Remember that everything goes over, around, compresses, and stretches.

Artist TIP:
Make the pose yourself to feel the action.

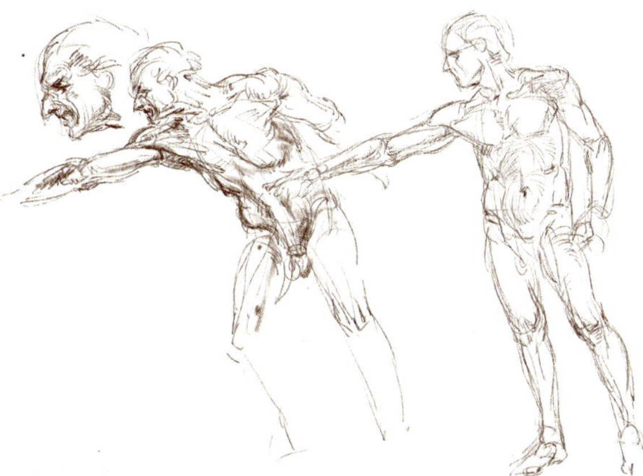

9 Keep the movement

It's important to focus on how our original gesture sketch is applied in the development and rendering of the anatomy. We're drawing figures in action, not anatomy book illustrations. Each of the lines leading through the figure are transitions from one point to the next. In using these lines as guides, I compose the anatomy to communicate the action.

Artist TIP:
Feel the pencil as it goes over the form. Focus on the total, not the parts.

"Diagrams only show what anatomy looks like. You have to bring it to life."

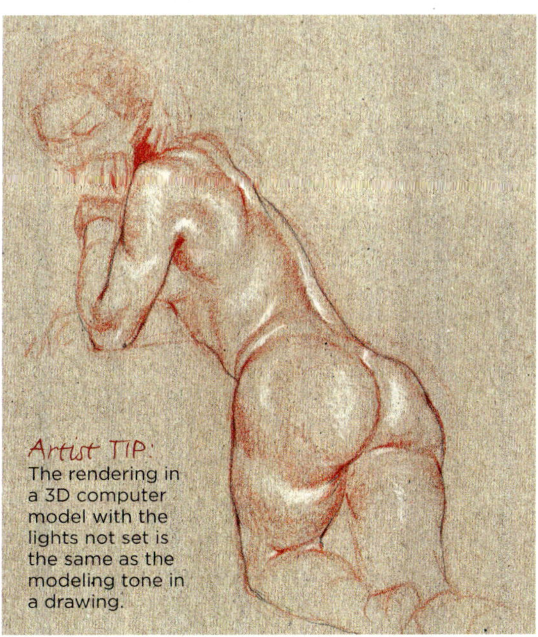

Artist TIP:
The rendering in a 3D computer model with the lights not set is the same as the modeling tone in a drawing.

10 Use the tone

The first tonal rendering tool is the modeling tone. Push the sides back, and what faces you is in light. As the form turns away it goes into tone. The tones move the eye in the same way lines do. They have to direct and describe the form. Don't copy tones, but use them to describe form.

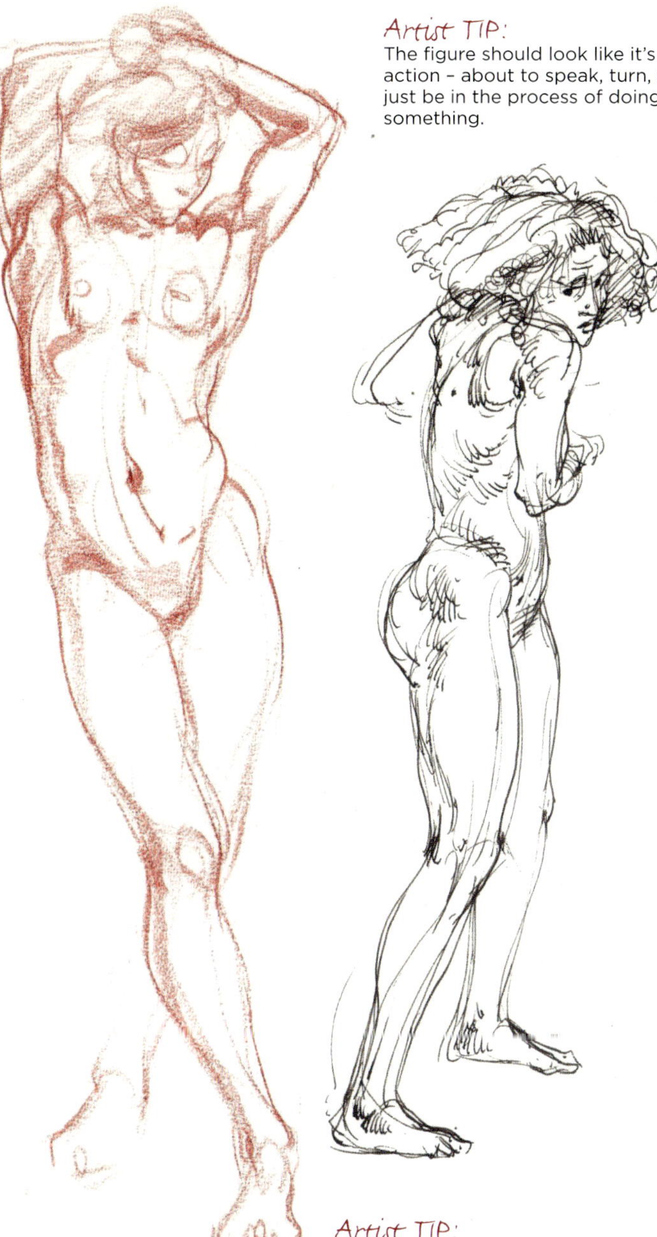

Artist TIP:
The figure should look like it's in action – about to speak, turn, or just be in the process of doing something.

11 Bring it to life

A major element in the drawing that's often overlooked is the subjective content of the subject. In this example, notice how the look of the eyes and expression change the feeling of the drawing. Make the action and body language obvious, or no one will understand your intentions for the piece.

Artist TIP:
It's about stretch, compression, and how to describe form. Anatomy diagrams only show what it looks like. You have to bring it to life.

12 Use the photo, don't copy it!

When working from photographs, it's important to keep in mind that a copy of a figure in action doesn't mean the drawing will show action. You must create it. I tell my students, we never copy, we analyze and construct. Compose the anatomy to show the action.

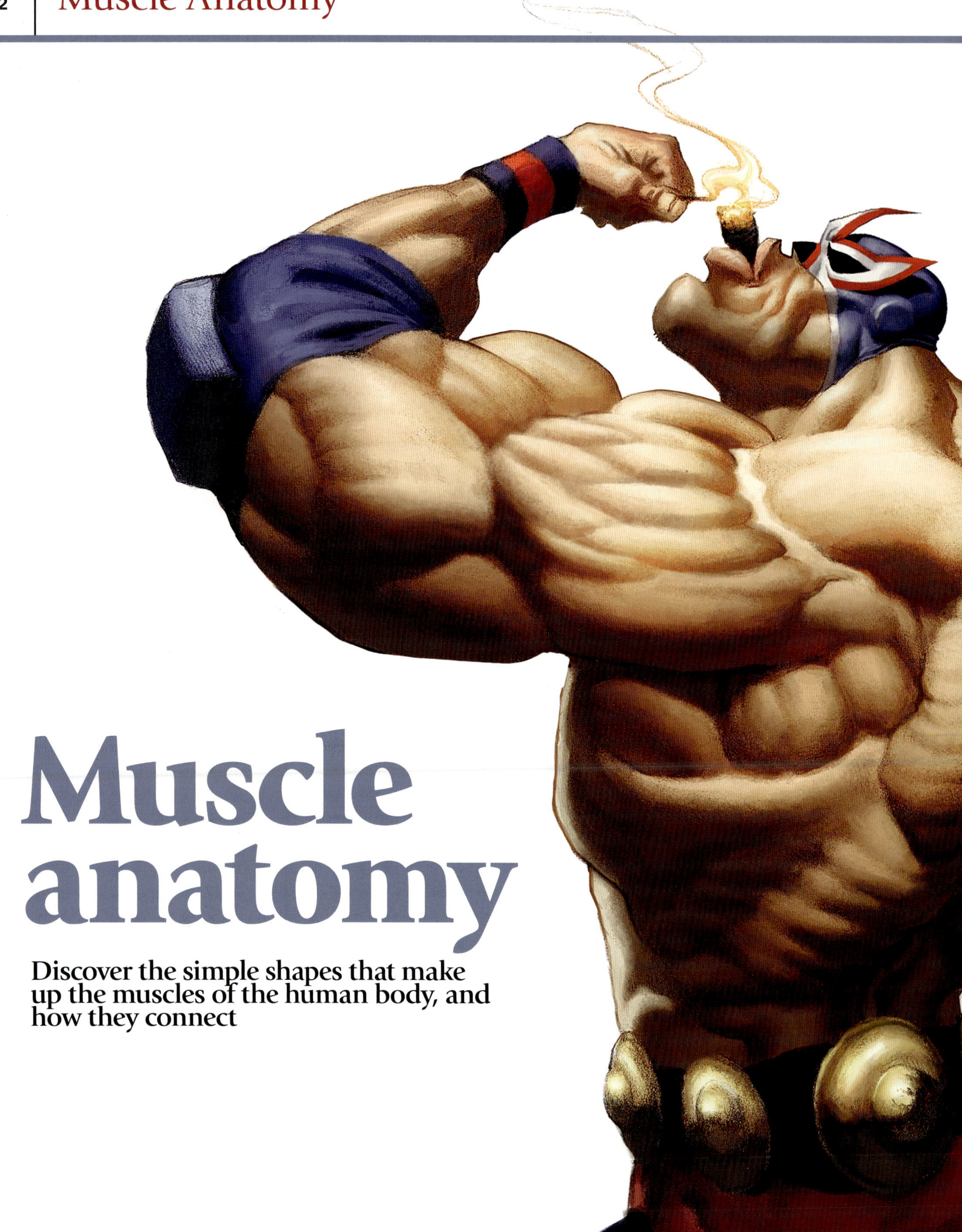

Muscle anatomy

Discover the simple shapes that make up the muscles of the human body, and how they connect

Workshops

How to draw the muscles of the body

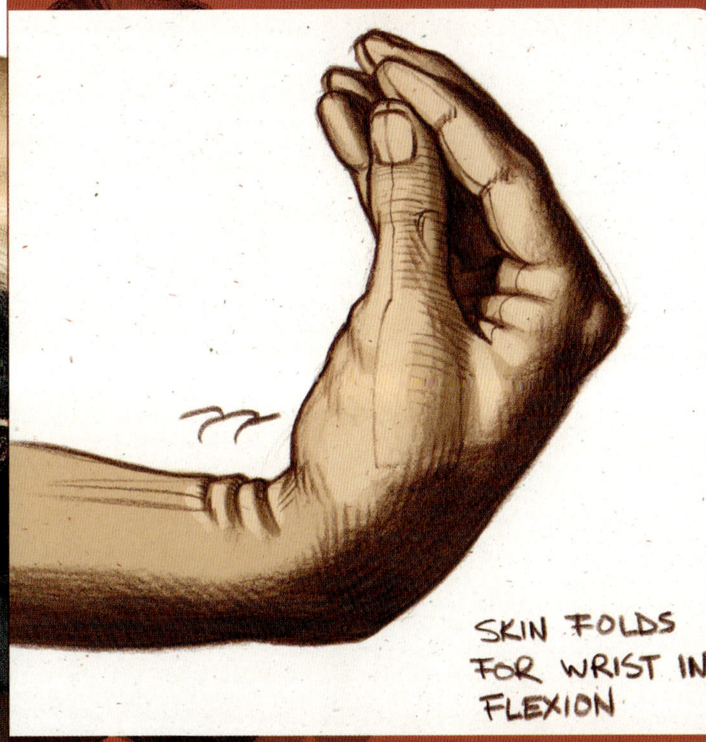

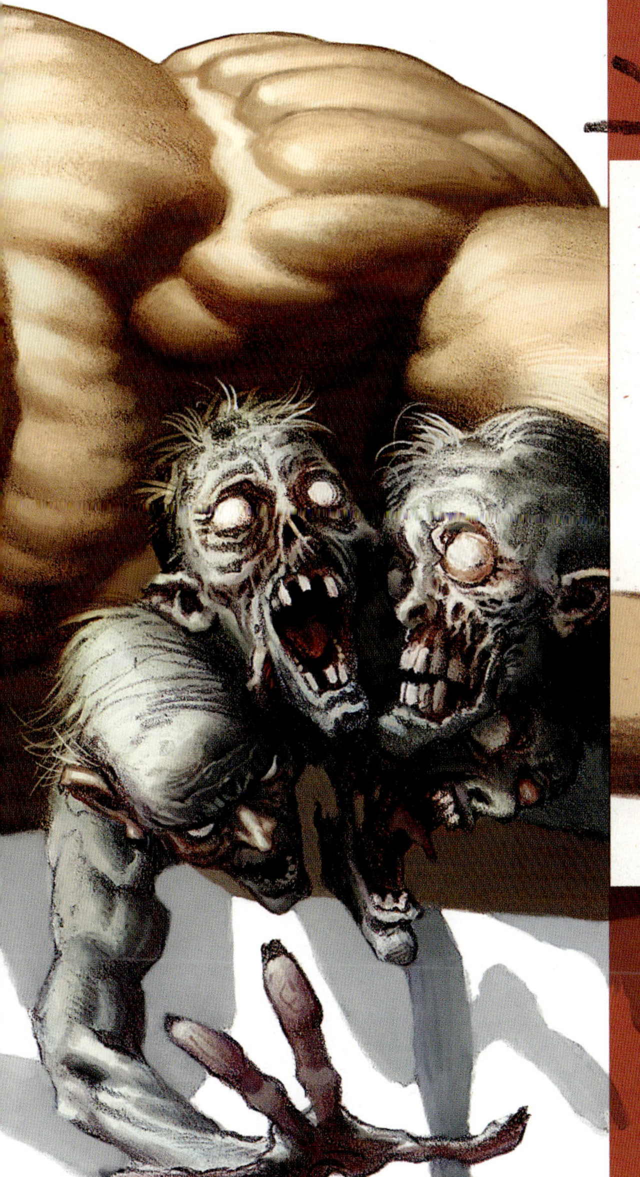

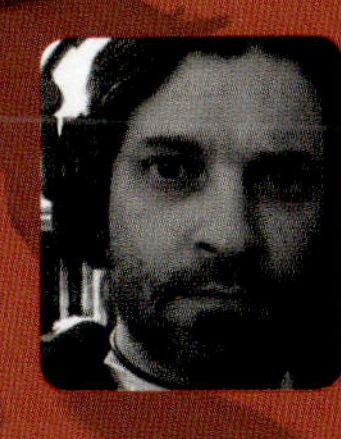

"To understand the wrist, you must first look at the lower arm – its rhythms and connections."
(Ron Lemen, page 86)

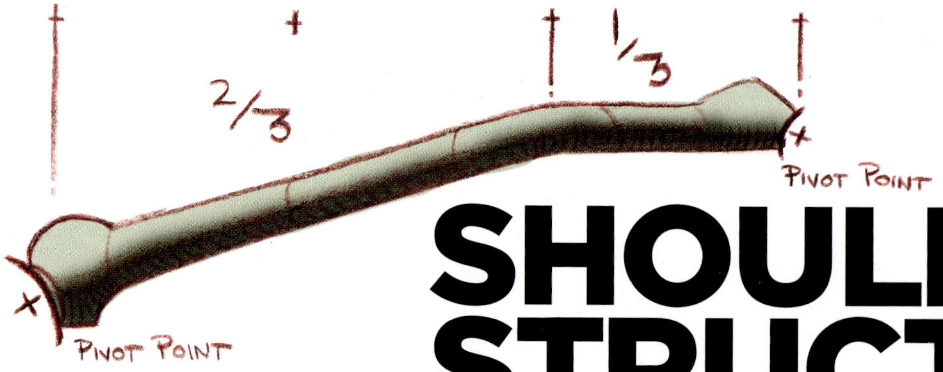

SHOULDER STRUCTURE

Learn how to make one of the more difficult areas of the human form easy to decipher and to draw, with **Ron Lemen**

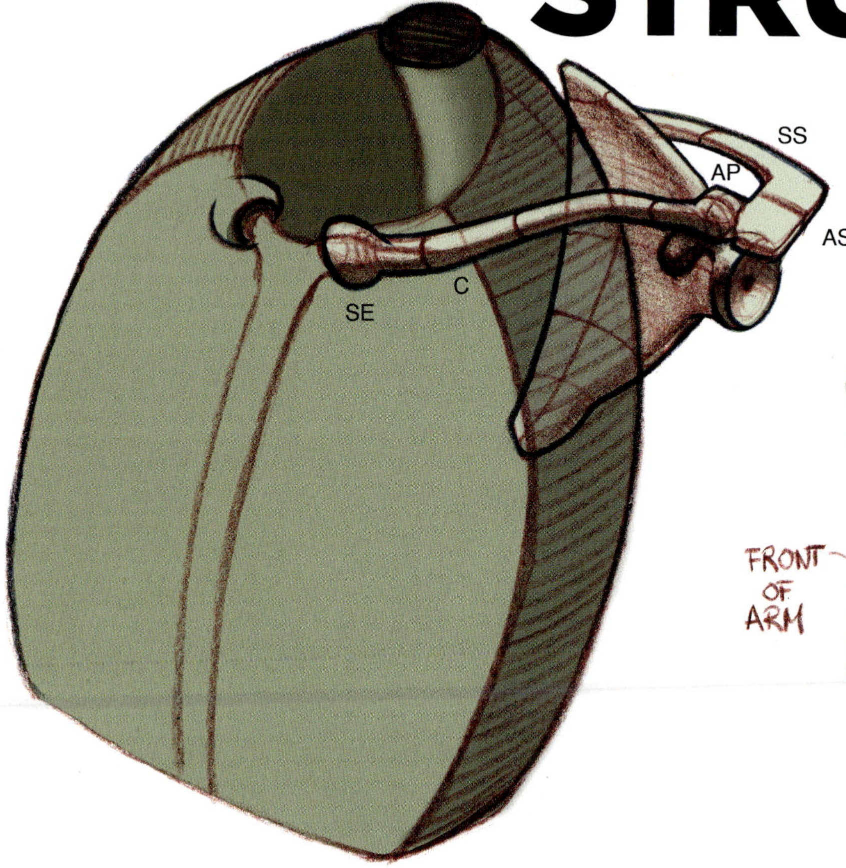

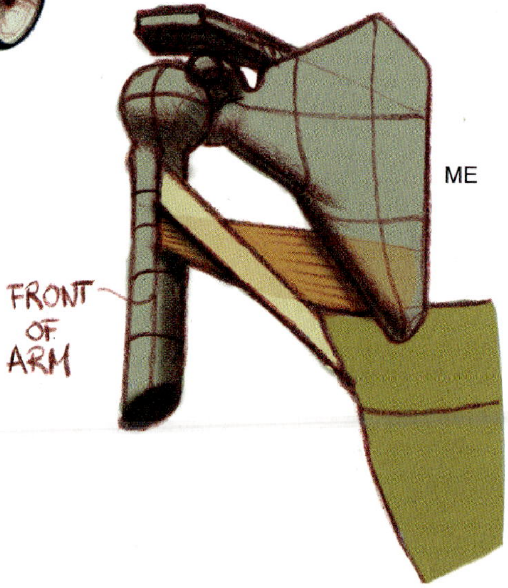

"Once these positions have been observed we can see the places to connect other shapes together."

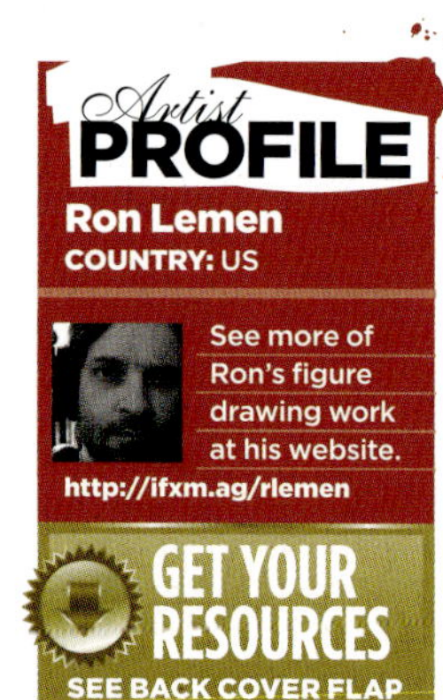

1. SHOULDER SKELETON

The skeleton is the key component for getting this invention method to work. Knowing how the bones are shaped and in what position they're in, based upon their shape and the action taken, is invaluable. Once these positions have been observed, the "landmark" shapes identified, we can see the places to connect many other shapes together. These landmarks of the shoulders are the acromial shelves or edges (AS), the spines of the scapula (SS), their medial edges (ME), the clavicles (C), their sternal end (SE), and the acromion process (AP).

These landmarks do not always appear, because of body weight and physique, the activity and pose taken, as well as viewer's position. Regardless of whether they are seen or not, they exist and have a place in space. We want to find these landmarks so we can put the rest of the body together with ease and speed.

2. MEASURING THE SHOULDERS

We can estimate and find measurements from ideal proportions as a starting point to any pose. There are several different approaches to measuring, but all of them involve order and memory. Idealizing has a set of tools that can be memorized, although you have to learn and memorize this by drawing from life and not just learning formulas. The figures will always end up stiff and formulaic if you don't relate them to reality and learn how to distort and push the ideal into a solid likeness.

The head is two-thirds the height of the rib cage. From our ideal of the skull as a 2:3 ratio, we can establish a height and width of the skull. The width of the widest part of the skull is roughly the same width as the distance between the scapulas. The height of the scapulas is roughly half the height of the rib cage. This makes the space between the scapulas and the size of the scapula roughly a square unit of measure. This equals three units of measure across from acromion process to acromion process. From this ideal you can then tweak the width of the shoulders to accommodate a male or female, a god or goddess, hero or fool, weak or powerful. The pectorialis is connected to two-thirds the length of the clavicle and the deltoid is connected to the furthest one-third of its own length, reaching out to its acromion process.

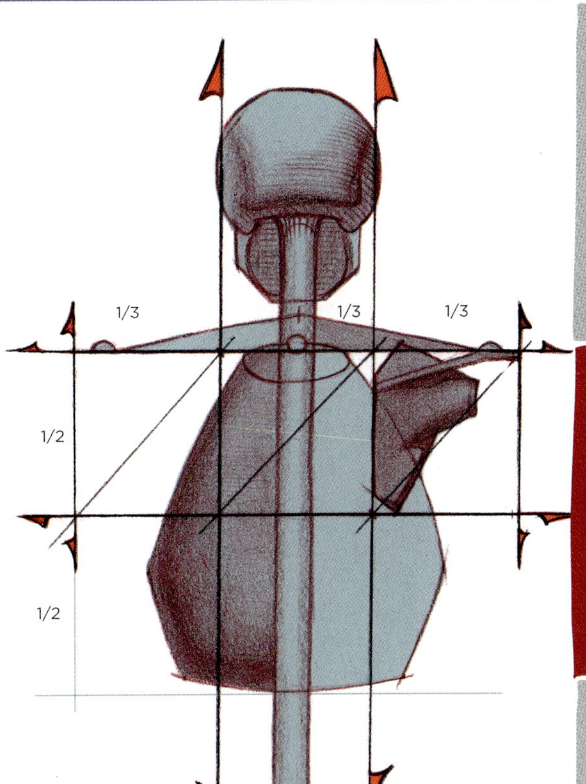

3. MEASURING THE SCAPULA

From the square unit of measure established above, we can divide this square diagonally in half, and this is our ideal shape and space for the scapula. From acromial shelf to medial edge, top to bottom. Now, the scapula is not a perfect square unit of measure; to confidently draw such a complex space we need a starting point. This diagram to the right shows the process for designing a scapula from a square.

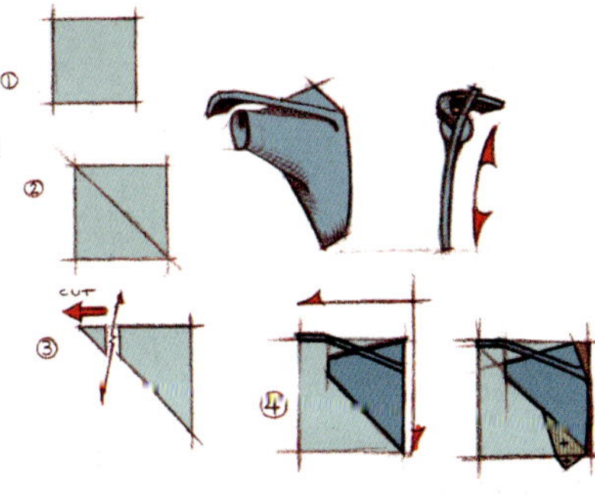

SPINE OF SCAPULA RHYTHM
TRAPEZIUS RHYTHM
BASE OF SCAPULA RHYTHM
SHOULDER TO PELVIS RHYTHMS
HIP TO NECK RHYTHMS
RHYTHMS/ABSTRACTIONS

4. RHTHYMS OF THE SHOULDERS

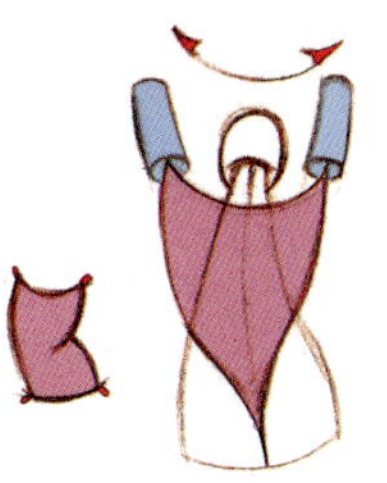

Rhythms occur in every way within our process of drawing, from rhythmical starting abstractions to the rhythms we design for the folds in the skin. Everything we draw relating the human form will have some rhythmical association between the parts in every action we consciously take. Movement is fluid; finding the linking rhythmic lines can make constructing the human form from memory easier.

A Find the scapulas

Start with the figure abstraction to find the torso, then the rhythms from the shoulders to the pelvis and the neck to the hips. Where they cross over each other, block out the space the scapulas sit within. There are also two other sub-rhythms that can be found crossing the back to relate the spines of the scapulas as well as their bases. There is another rhythm line across the back to design out the trapezius muscles, too.

B Rhythms change

Depending upon the arms' movements, the trapezius rhythm can change from an arc to a straight line to an S-curve to a mix. The set of rhythms here are a starting point, and every action the model takes will dictate a new set of individual rhythms for you to discover and design in your art.

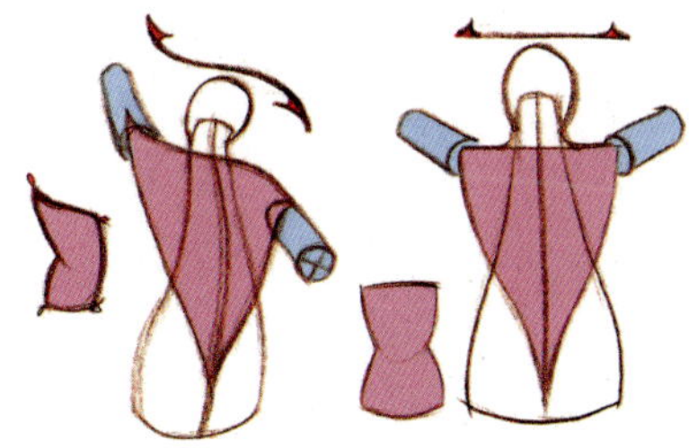

C Strong center

Here is another simple geometric rhythm we can use when the figure is in profile. The neck and the arm flow together both at the back and the front. This rhythm can help visually connect these elements together for a stronger harmony among all the separate pieces of the neck and arm.

5. SHOULDER MOVEMENT SIMPLIFIED

The scapula is a very fluid area of the body and affects how other parts move, for example the arms. Knowing how the scapula moves and interacts, learning its patterns and motions, will enable you to draw other body sections, such as arms, more easily. This can even offer more insight into foreshortening.

A Scapula movement

First let's look at how the scapula moves. Here are a few drawings showing the scapulas in simple squares and some designed in triangles, the arrows describe the directions the scapulas can travel in.

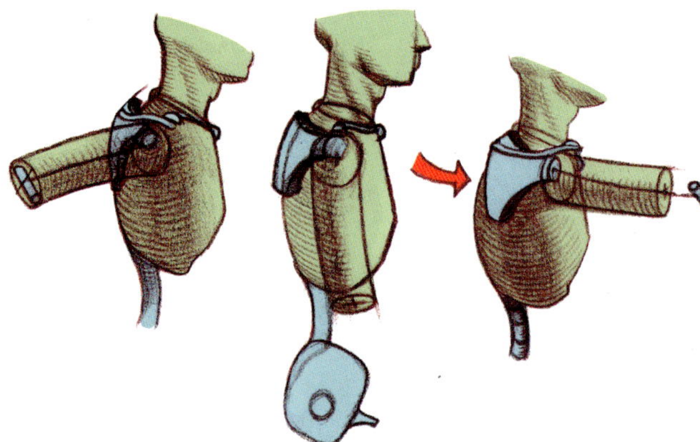

B Scapula diagram

Scapulas can move all over because they are not attached to any surface other than at the acromion shelf and process. This is the only anchor for the scapula, and because the arm is only attached at the sternum by the clavicle, this gives the arm quite a bit of freedom to move about the side of the body. It allows the arm to cross over the front and back of the torso with ease and less obstruction from the rib cage. It is easier to see this connection in the cross-section drawing.

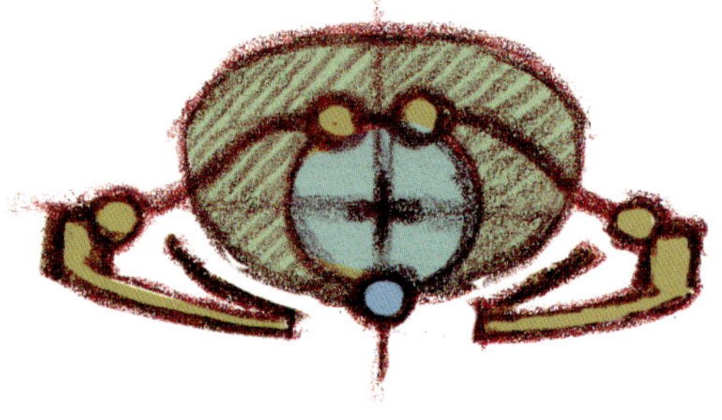

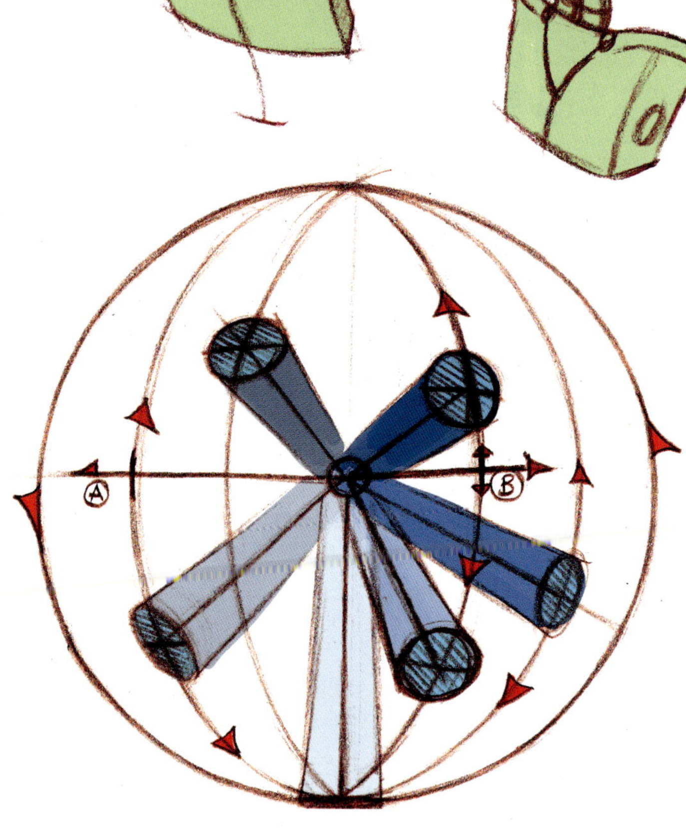

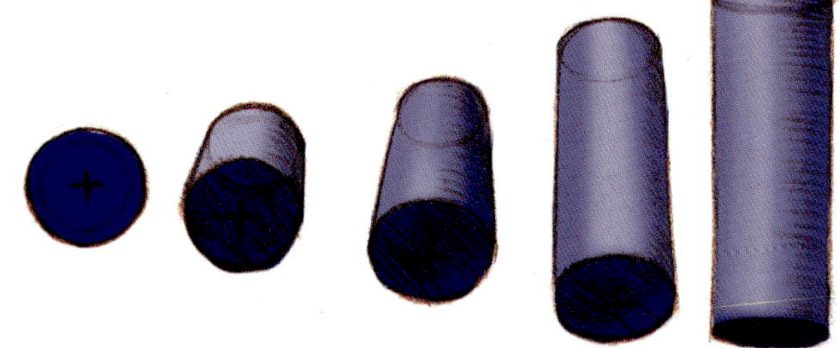

C The shoulder and foreshortening

The arm circumducts, or circles, around a pivot point like a wobbly prop on an airplane. We can get a fluid motion but the arm does not easily rotate a full 360 degrees. To draw this movement we need to learn foreshortening. Knowing that the upper arm is the length of the rib cage, we can start where the shoulder and elbow are in a neutral position (called "reference") to take a measurement of the upper arm's length. Now from the pivot point of where the shoulder will be positioned we can rotate that length elliptically until we find what we are looking for, and then solidify the mass around that line as a cylinder.

The chart above might look confusing at first, but keep in mind that all of the arcs drawn are the pathways the arm might follow along that elliptical track. Start with a line projecting from the head of the humerus, and let it cross the path of the elliptical movement (A). Then draw the crosshairs or the minor to the major axis of the ellipse that we use as the volume of the arm (B). Then draw the ellipse that represents the pitch of the arm cylinder and continue drawing out your muscle forms on the cylinder form.

6. SHAPES AND SYMBOLS

A key way to make drawing the body and its anatomy easier, particularly when drawing from memory, is to break the forms down into simple shapes and symbols. Drawing the shoulders is no different.

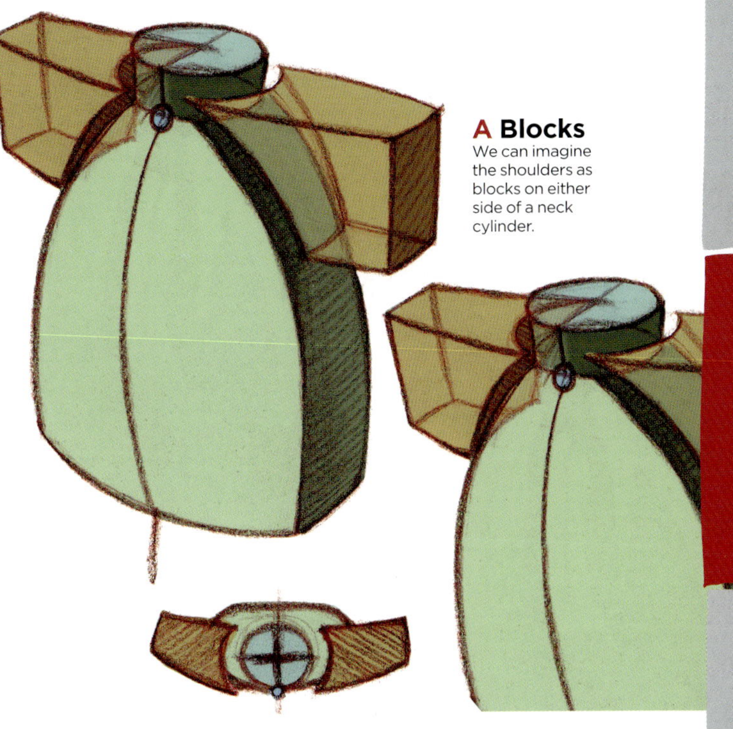

A Blocks
We can imagine the shoulders as blocks on either side of a neck cylinder.

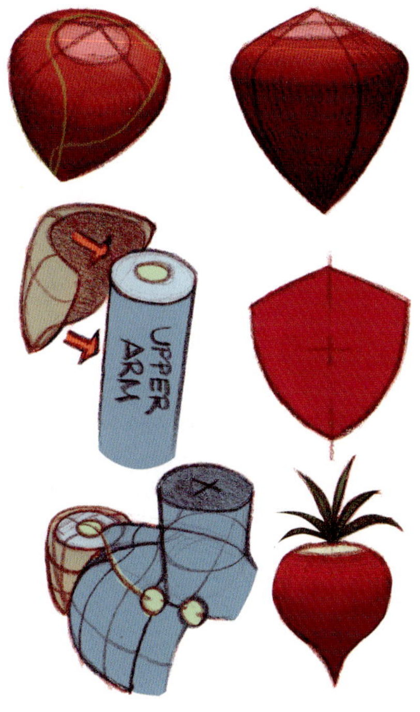

B Triangles
This shape blocks out the clavicle to scapula, around the corner across the acromial shelf-line, and it also roughly blocks out the space of the deltoid mass. This mass is about one-third of the height of the rib cage, and both blocks merge together to make the top plane of the torso. And it just so happens that the deltoid attaches one-third of the way down the humerus – your upper arm bone! The deltoid can be seen as an inverted soft triangle, a radish, or a spinning top.

"The deltoid can be seen as an inverted soft triangle."

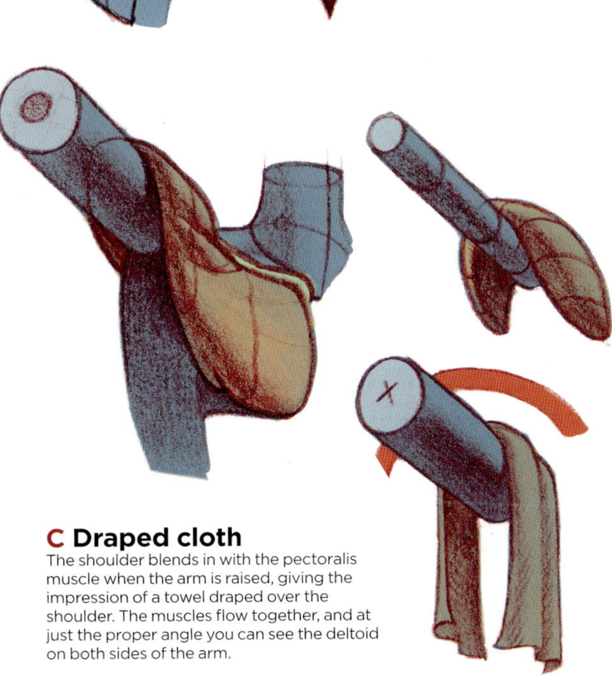

C Draped cloth
The shoulder blends in with the pectoralis muscle when the arm is raised, giving the impression of a towel draped over the shoulder. The muscles flow together, and at just the proper angle you can see the deltoid on both sides of the arm.

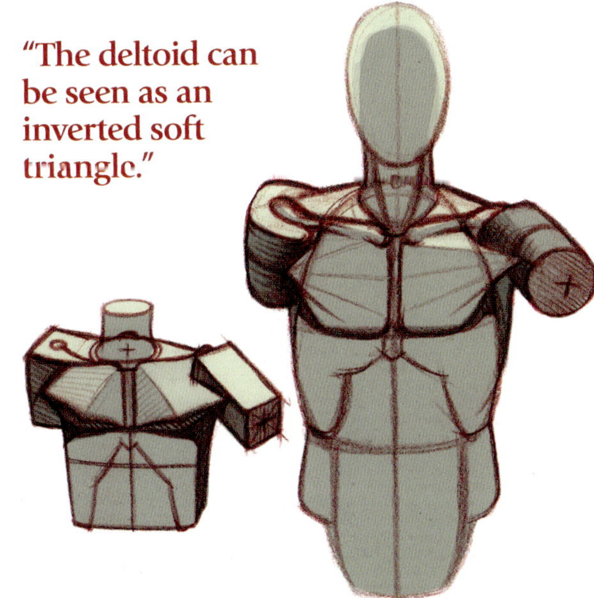

D Cylinders
The arms can be designed in cylinder or block-like forms. This shape design starts in the shoulders and travels down into the hand. In either case, the acromion process sits in the middle of the shape. Simple shapes are easier to remember!

7. ANATOMY

The muscles of the shoulder are: the deltoid, the supraspinatus, the infraspinatus, the teres major and the teres minor. These muscles weave, along with the lattisimus, around the coracobrachialis and the tricep, complicating matters in designing the space when drawing the figure.

On this page are some images to help simplify a complex area. When the arm is fully extended to the side of the body, the angle that bridges the arm to the body is made up of both the lattisimus and the teres major. The teres major is the tail end extending out onto the arm, and the lattisimus is the tail end extending onto the rib cage.

Below is also a diagram to show the idealized stretching movements of the deltoid. These are for drawing big, buffed hero types; always keep the anatomy correct when drawing superheroes.

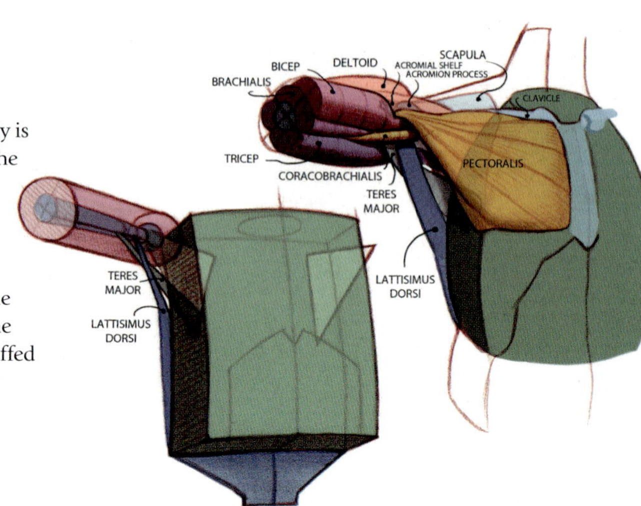

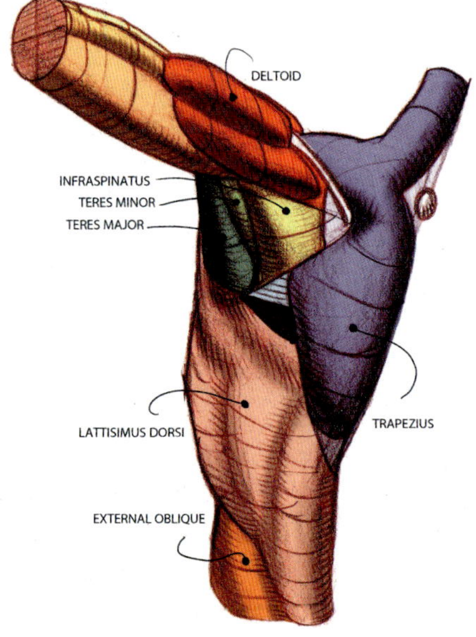

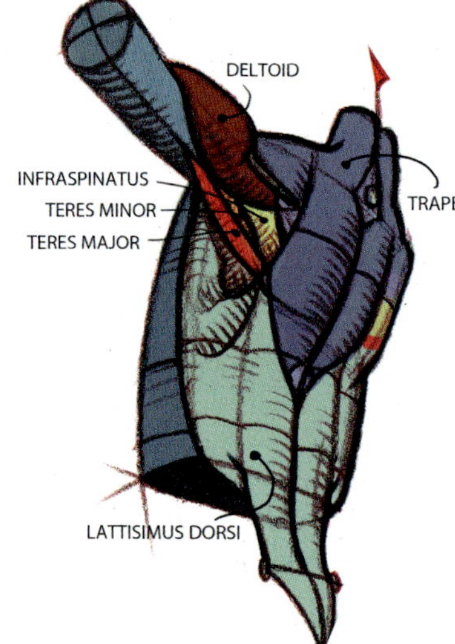

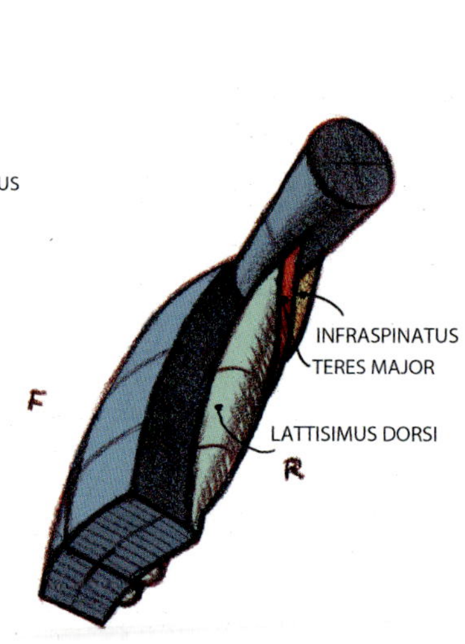

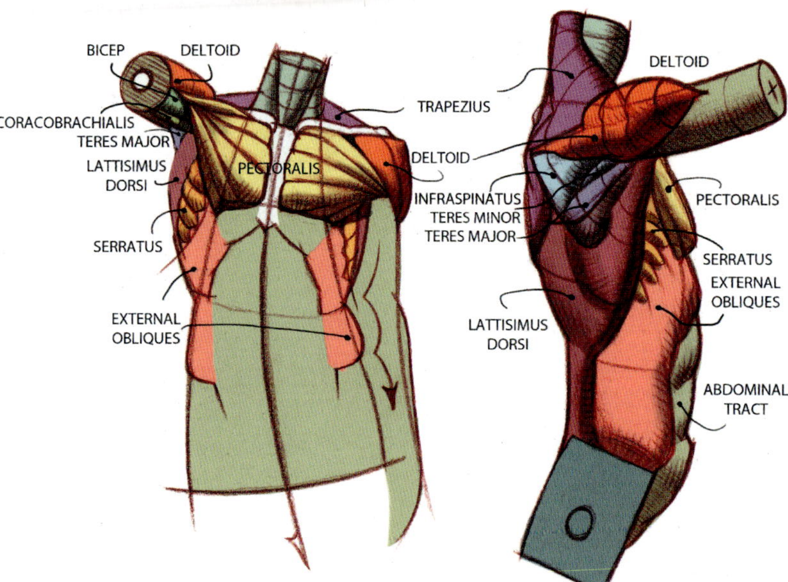

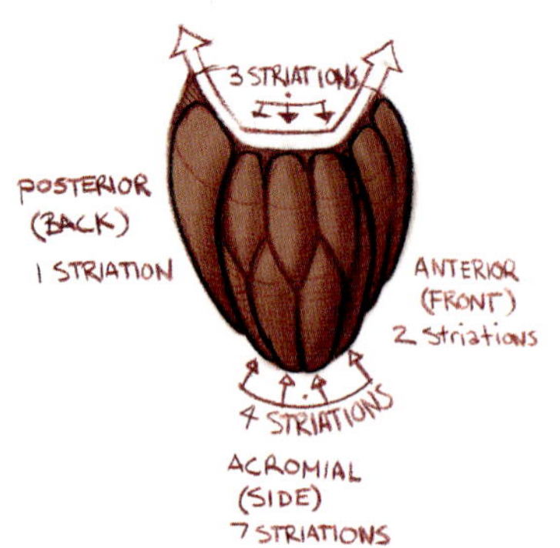

"Keep the anatomy correct when drawing superheroes."

8. HOW THE MUSCLES WORK

The deltoid rotates and raises the arm. The front head pulls the arm forward and rotates it inward, while the back head pulls the arm backward and rotates it outward. The supraspinatus lifts the arm laterally and helps with the outward rotation. This muscle is also buried under the trapezius and attached to the top of the humerus. The infraspinatus rotates the arm laterally and extends the raised arm. This is attached to the top of the humerus. The teres minor pulls the arm in and rotates it outward, while the teres major pulls the arm toward the body and rotates it inward, lowering the raised arm.

PRO TIPS

It's connected

Start from the core of the pose, the torso, and then build the legs, arms, neck, and head. It will save you so much trouble in the end of getting the pose to feel active. That pillow shape is key. It tweaks how we draw the shoulders, sometimes pushing the expression even further because the rib cage is turned harder away from the line of action. Thinking about the rib cage and pelvis together, understanding everything is connected, really does make for a stronger shoulder action.

9. PLANES AND SURFACES

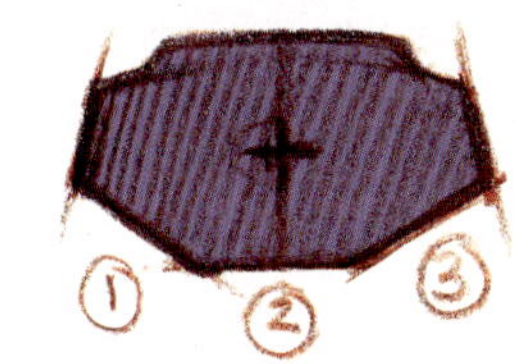

The back can be broken down into a series of three larger planes in both horizontal and vertical directions. The middle of the back will not have the angles that the muscles take when first sketched, just three simple flat planes to help visualize the bigger facets for stronger relatable proportions, before the details disguise them. Once these planes are built out, we then subdivide the surface into smaller facets. The scapulas, the spinal muscles, and the spine all get their own surfaces, as we can see in this diagram. The line drawings are cross-section drawings of the planes to better visualize their dimension and depth.

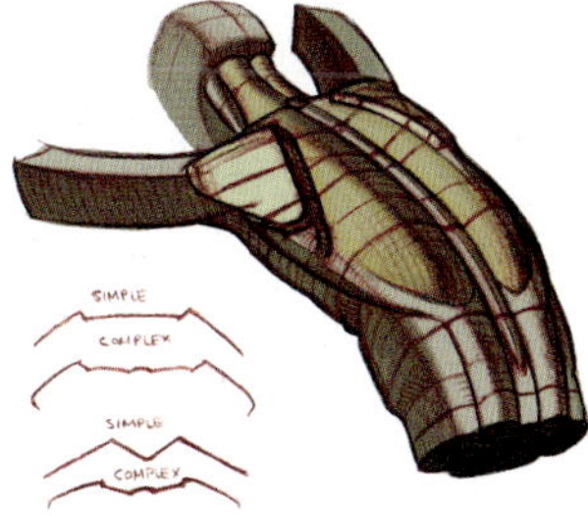

10. THE SKIN AND SURFACE

The skin loosely slides over the muscles, bones, and tendons. It is attached by a fascia or an under layer that is connected to the surfaces of the bones, muscles, and tendons.

When the arms are active, the skin on the shoulders stresses depending upon the action and its direction. The skin folds perpendicular to the muscle fibers. If the arm is drawn back, the shoulders will stress and folds will form. These folds can be drawn using a spiral, the more intense the spiral, the more drawn back the arm will look.

When the arm is lifted above the shoulder line, the skin folds over the acromial shelf and the acromion process. This creates a crease that softly squares out, generating a box-like insertion into the deltoid muscle.

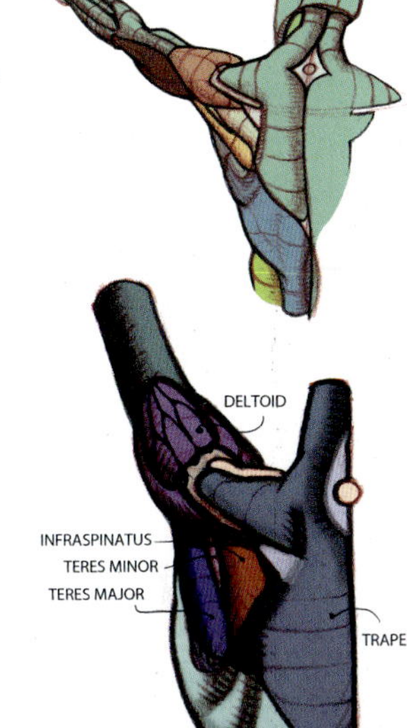

SKIN
MUSCLE HEAD
PERPENDICULAR CREASE

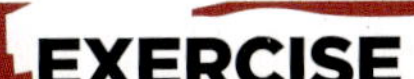

EXERCISE

When drawing the back, sketch several pillow shapes and then find the rib cage shape within the pillow. Divide this shape in half. This is the height of the scapulas in the back. Now divide your pillow shape into thirds from shoulder to shoulder. You will see the spaces for the scapulas if the arms are at the sides of the body. Inside the shoulder squares, divide the space into two halves using the diagonal from corner to corner; the pointy end should be toward where the arm goes. Draw a line next to the body attached to the pointy end of the triangle, and then place a little line at the end of this, perpendicular to its length, making an upside down T. Divide the length of the arm line into thirds. Put the shoulder muscles on the body according to the divisions given. Practice until you think you can do it by memory, then draw another page of pillows, rib cages, and arms.

SIDE VIEW

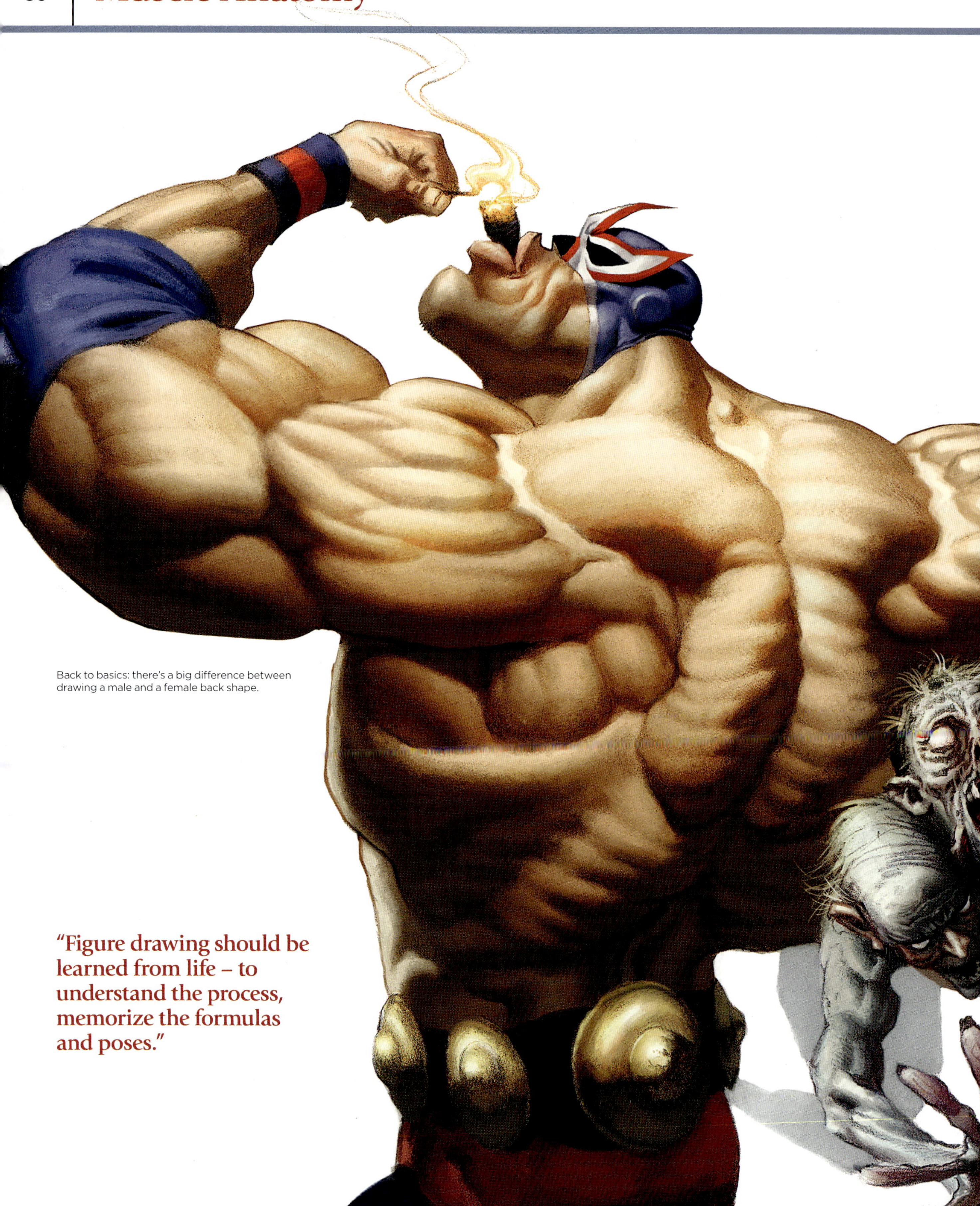

Back to basics: there's a big difference between drawing a male and a female back shape.

"Figure drawing should be learned from life – to understand the process, memorize the formulas and poses."

DRAWING AND POSING THE BACK

The back is a complex space, so **Ron Lemen** breaks it down into conceptual formulas to make drawing and posing it easier

Artist PROFILE
Ron Lemen
COUNTRY: US
Ron Lemen is a freelance artist and instructor who's worked in fine art, illustration and the entertainment industry.
http://ifxm.ag/rlemen

GET YOUR RESOURCES
SEE BACK COVER FLAP

In this workshop I'm aiming to help clear up all the confusion the back, a complex area of the body, can sometimes cause us artists. I've also included a step process and some exercises that I hope you'll try. I'm going to go over two different techniques that I find are identical in so many ways, and yet each finds something very important in figure drawing that I think you'll find interesting.

After reading this tutorial – along with the shoulders workshop – I hope you understand where I'm going with all of this and can use new techniques and thought processes to your advantage. Remember that figure drawing should be learned from life. To better understand this process, memorize the formulas and poses, and work through a rigorous repetitious process in order to fully develop our skills.

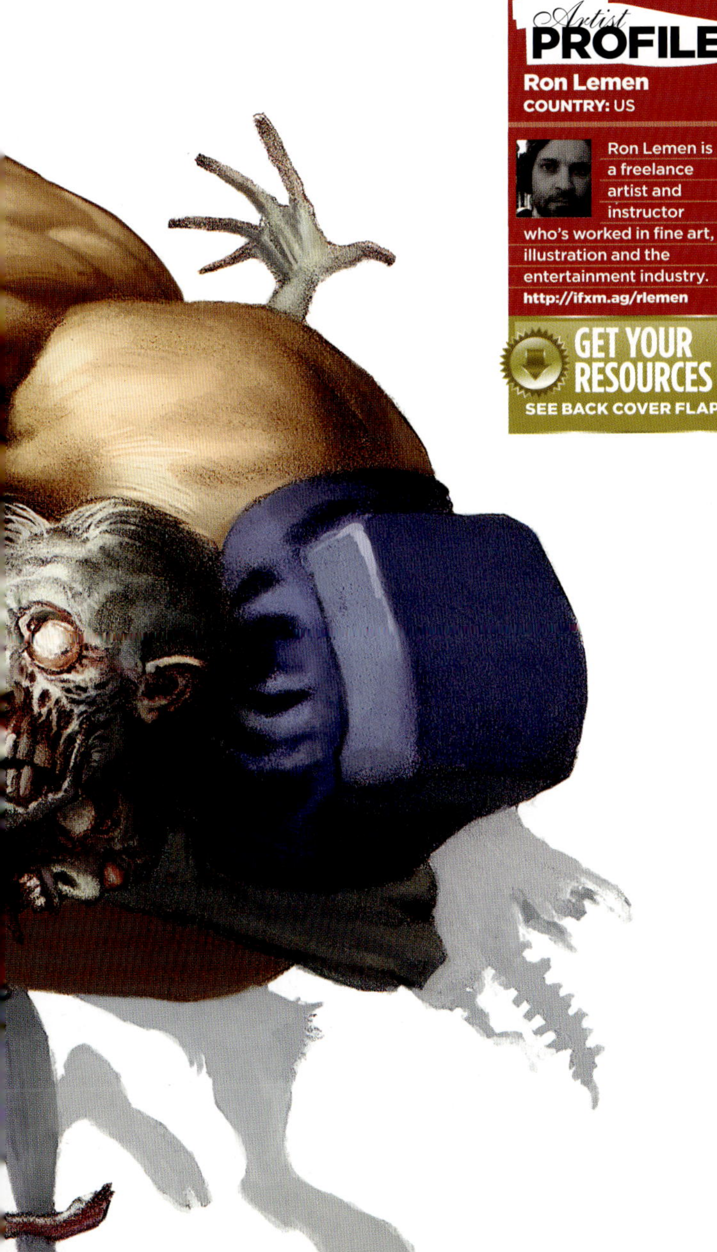

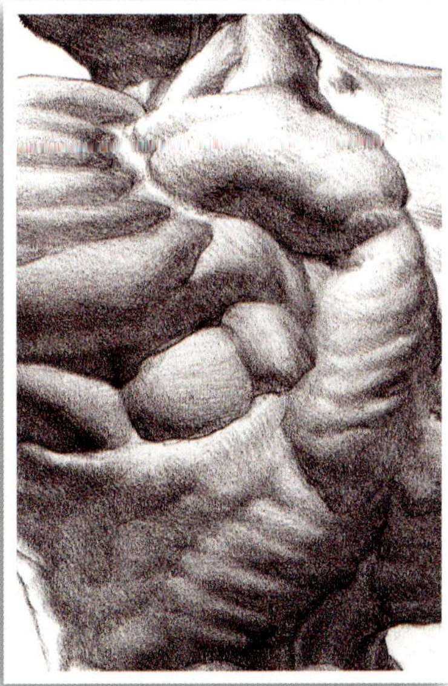

Rhomboid, trapezius, latissimus dorsi, external obliques, the sacrospinalis group... the back is one of the most – if not *the* most – complex parts of the anatomy. But you won't need to learn Latin or have a biology degree to be able to paint it well.

1. BACK MUSCLE GROUPS

First off, let's look at the muscles and come up with some simple shapes to help remember what they look like and how they fit together. The back muscles or groups of muscles we artists are interested in are the rhomboid, trapezius, latissimus dorsi, external obliques, and the sacrospinalis group.

The muscles of the back are broken up into groups. Combine the left and the right side of the body together to create the shapes we will be using to design the back with. These are the basic shapes of our figure construction. The points of origin and insertion points are painted with red on the charts provided.

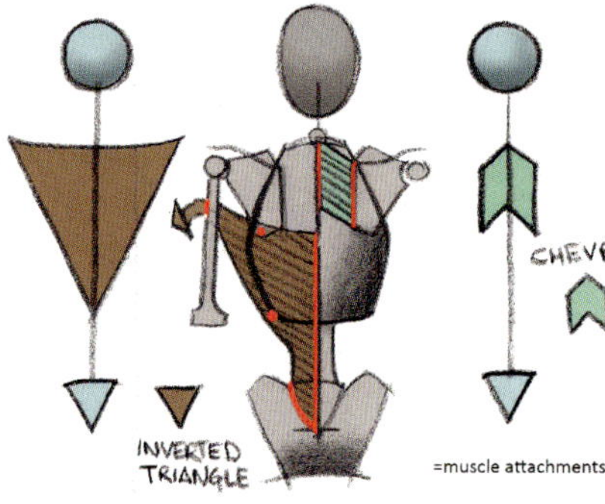

A Rhomboids

The rhomboids (above) sit under the trapezius muscle and connect the scapulas to the spine. They are slider muscles and they draw the scapulas in toward the spine. Here we use a chevron-like shape for the basic construction.

B Sacrospinalis

The long sacrospinalis muscles (right) are column-like muscles, although they terminate in more of an arch and sit on either side of the spine – they are responsible for pulling the body up and straightening it out. The basic shape looks a bit like a stretched-out doughnut.

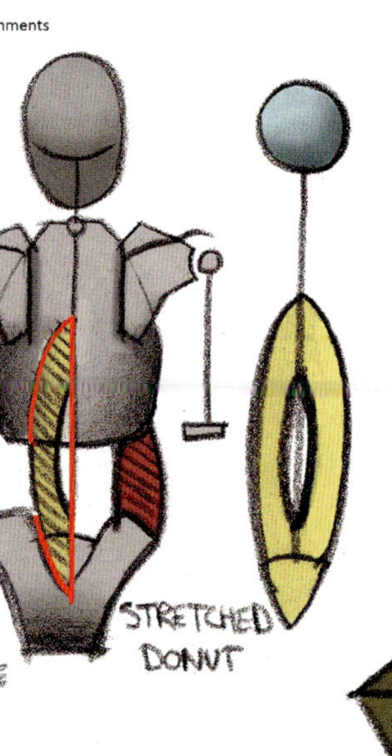

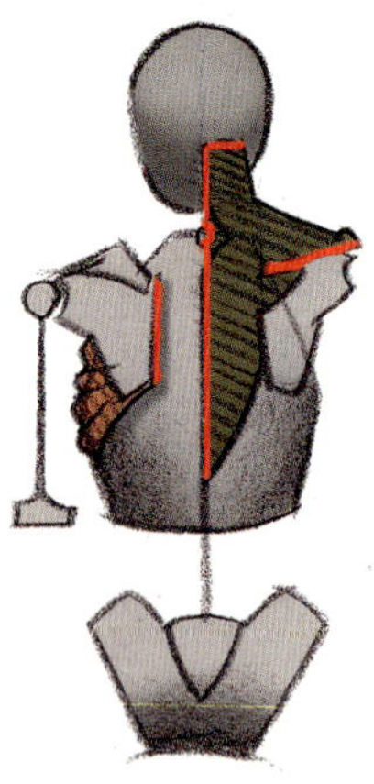

C Latissimus dorsi

The latissimus dorsi muscles (left) are the cape muscles on the back. They start at the spine, connect to the bottom of the scapula and the bottom of the rib cage, and end on the front of the humerus (arm). These are extender muscles, which pull the arms behind the body. Their basic shape is an inverted triangle.

Our scapulas are also connected to the rib cage by the serratus muscles. The serratus muscles start on the inside edge of the scapulas and connect to the first nine ribs of the rib cage. This slider muscle group pulls the arm forward. The shapes we can design to more easily explain these muscles are a fan-like shape, or a nine-fingered hand grasping the side of our body, the fingers extended around the form.

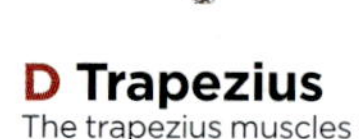

D Trapezius

The trapezius muscles sit on top of all the other back muscles and connect the scapulas to the spine and the skull. They are slider muscles and they pull the scapulas toward the spine. This muscle can be started as a kite-like shape, the top of the kite connected to the base of the skull.

2. BASIC SHAPES

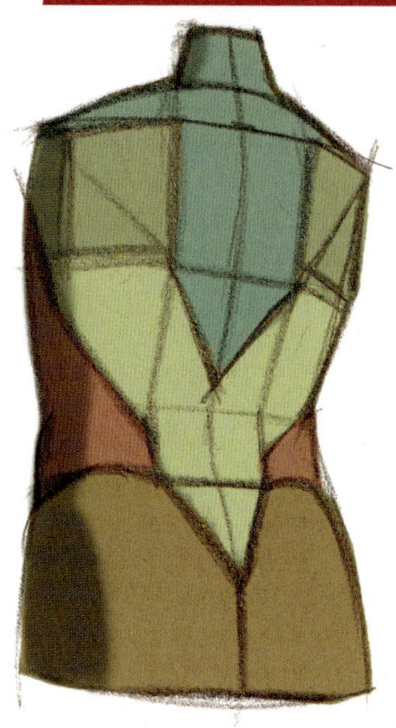

Everything can be broken down into basic shapes, and the body is no exception. Once we learn how to control these shapes, shade them, draw them in perspective, and overlap them with each other, we can apply them to any figure we see or imagine – the ultimate goal is to draw upon ideas from the imaginative process. If we stick with basic construction concepts, the most complex of designs can be simply drawn again and again. But this is a process, and each stage must be completed before the next can successfully be applied. Once you have practiced the process enough, then hopefully you'll find a way to make the process intuitive and your own – or, rather than sticking to every step, you'll find a creative way to over-step or combine the steps and make the process your own that way.

"Everything can be broken down into basic shapes and the body is no exception."

3. GESTURE DRAWING

The first step in this drawing process is to start with a gesture drawing, loose and rhythmical. This is a rough rendition of the pose, allowing us to play with the action and the gravity before investing time in measuring and shading. The gesture should resemble the finished drawing, using all the tools we will be discussing, but with no deliberate intention of making anything solid and dimensional.

PRO TIPS

Messy lines
Start with simple shapes. First, simple shapes are easier to move (or what I call "animate") to correct the gesture, which means you are moving the body parts to a better position for either a more convincing action or for more clarity of the silhouette. Second, we invest time in our work. Erasing something that took time to render is not something we easily do and can stubbornly refuse to, at the loss of a good drawing.

Simple shapes
The ellipses I draw around the body and limbs help me see the volumes of the body with greater clarity. Drawing is all 2D, so any tool that helps me visualize or see the dimensions I'm designing to, will make my drawing feel more convincing and I don't stress out as much. Simplifying the body into simple geometry and/or drawing cross contours and centerlines on the shapes I make are just a few ways to help me visualize the dimensions and volumes.

4. TORSO DRAWING

The torso can be gestured in using a shape resembling a pillow. The top two corners represent the acromion processes, or the little bumps on the shoulders. The bottom two corners represent the greater trochanters, or the bumps that stick out on our thigh bones. The crease in the pillow indicates which direction the body is bending, and also represents the bottom of the rib cage. When drawing this shape, make both halves of the bent side equal in length. The figure abstraction is similar, in that it finds the top and the bottom of the torso, using triangles to connect the same points of anatomy. The neck is a part of this abstraction, and from the front the nipples are mapped into the lines; from the back, the scapulas. The key to either of these torso concepts working well is animation.

A Legs and arms

The legs and arms are drawn in with two tapering lines; the first line describes the action of the pose, the second the character of the model, or how heavy or skinny the figure is. The head is drawn with an oval, or a plump triangle for the side and three-quarter views. And don't forget a neck, a small cylinder.

B Construction shapes

These loose gesture lines are used as a guide to place more deliberate shapes that represent segments of the body, now in a more dimensional and geometric form. The torso is converted into blocks or spheres, the arms and legs into blocks or cylinders, and they all should have cross contours drawn over them to indicate their axis. These geometric shapes can then be divided for more specific muscle shapes, drawn over top of them.

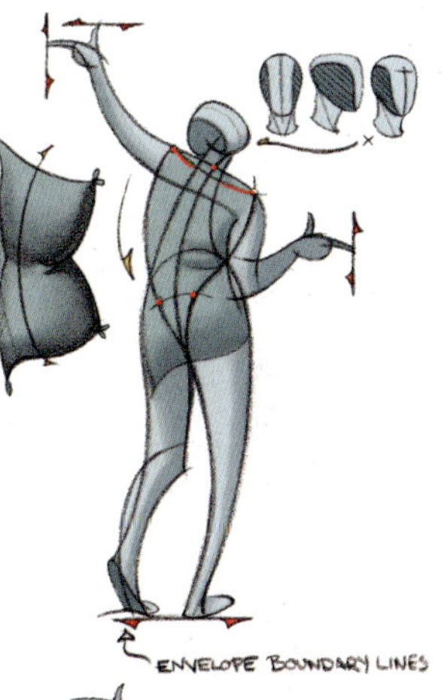

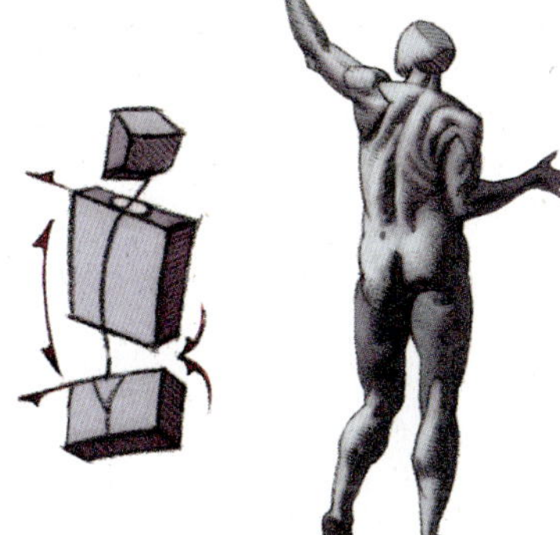

C Shading form

The muscle groups can be drawn in using the basic shape designs we are simplifying the muscles into, for quick placement and sense of scale. Don't forget centerlines for anything symmetrical, to help establish balance and proportion.

5. BACK MEASUREMENTS

Focusing on the back, let's take some measurements that will help assist in building this space. First, the back of the skull, or the cranial mass, is roughly the same width as the separation between the scapulas. Each scapula can fit into a perfect square and, including the space between the scapulas, the back is three of these squares from shoulder to shoulder. The scapulas are roughly one half the height of the rib cage from the C7 (where the bottom of the neck meets the shoulder) to the 10th rib. When attaching the lower back muscles directly from behind, to the sacrum and iliac crest, the divisions between these spaces are roughly three-quarter between side (oblique), sacrum, and other side (oblique).

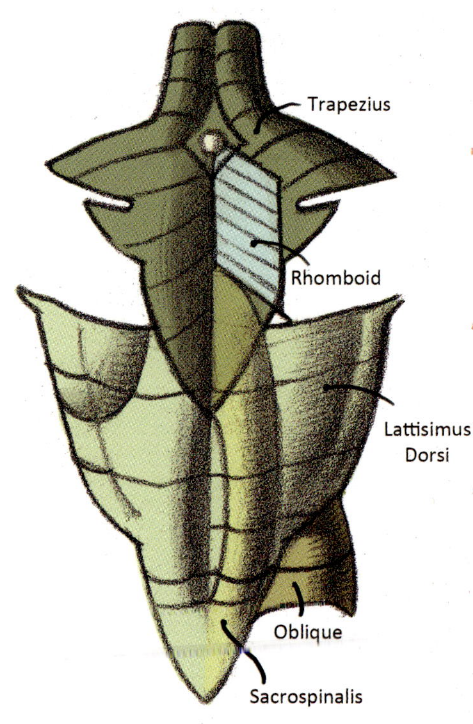

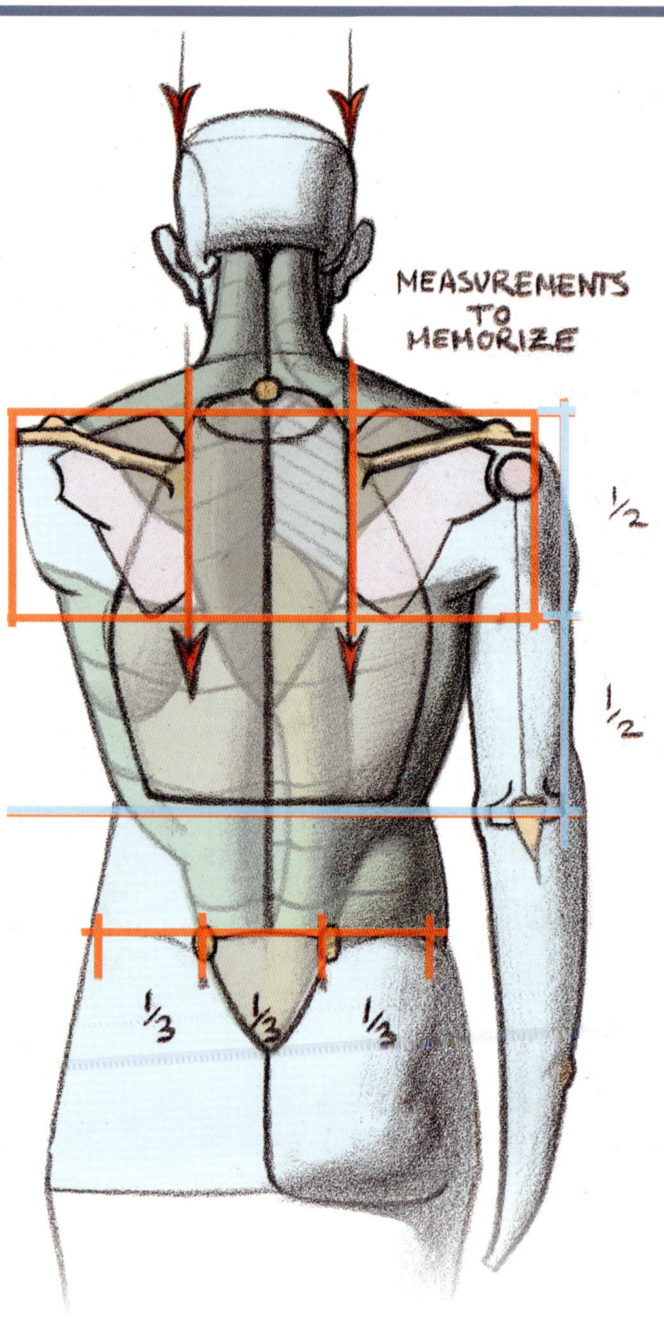

6. SET MARKERS

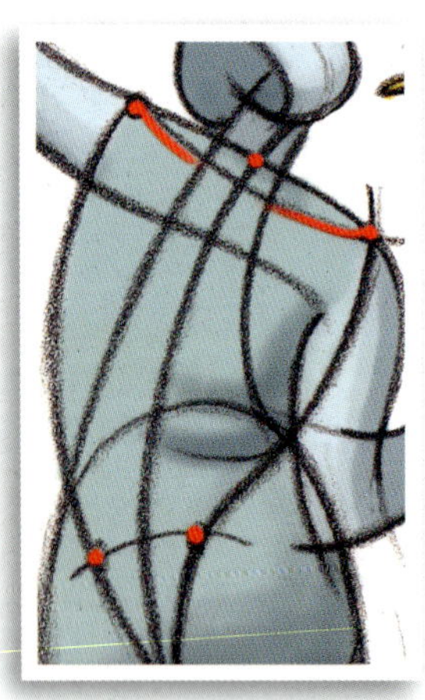

In addition to the measuring, we also want to place a few points where the bones are most visible under the skin – we call these subcutaneous landmarks. From the back these points are the C7 of the spine, the acromion processes, the spines or wings of the scapulas, the inside edges of the scapulas, and the dimples of the sacrum. In addition to these being used as landmarks to attach muscles, they are also useful to help you measure, especially across the figure, for symmetrical evaluation, too.

> "We also place a few points where the bones are most visible under the skin – subcutaneous landmarks."

7. DRAWING BACK POSES

Following the construction stages, it's now time for the tonal stage. Now our focus is to construct and assemble any pose, simplifying it down into the most basic abstracts that can easily be interpreted visually.

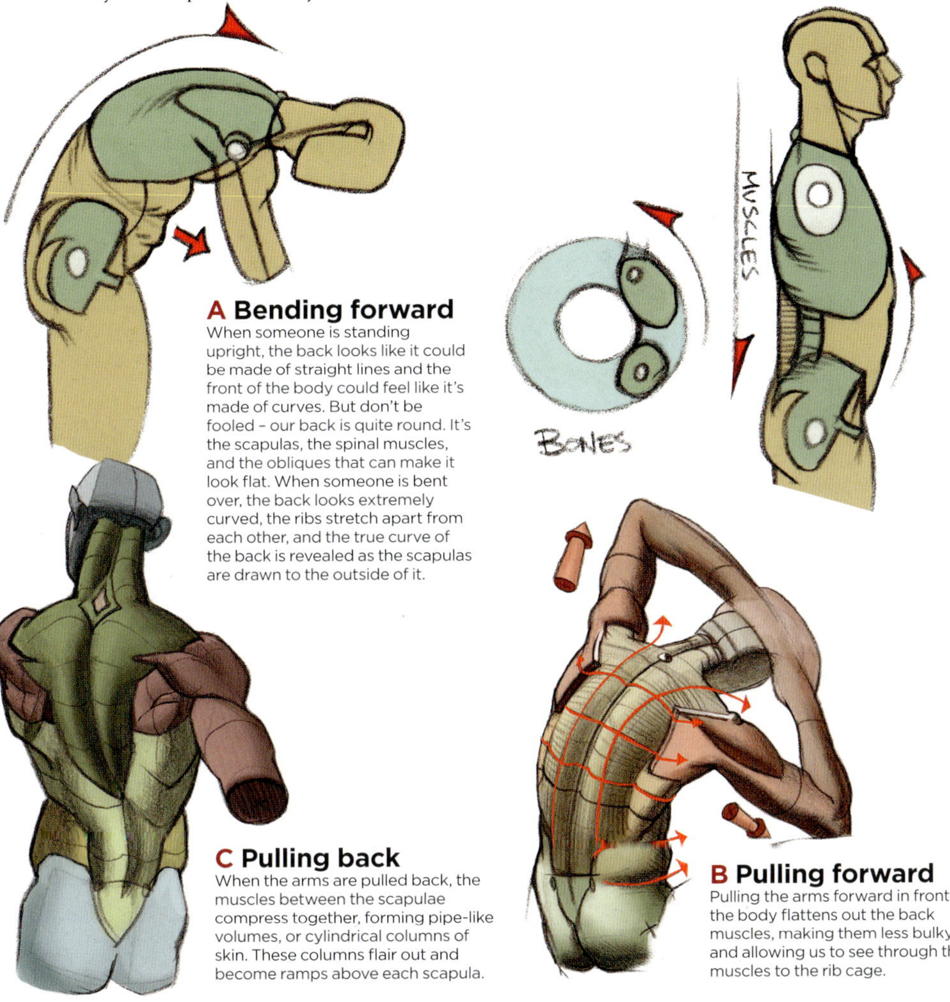

A Bending forward

When someone is standing upright, the back looks like it could be made of straight lines and the front of the body could feel like it's made of curves. But don't be fooled - our back is quite round. It's the scapulas, the spinal muscles, and the obliques that can make it look flat. When someone is bent over, the back looks extremely curved, the ribs stretch apart from each other, and the true curve of the back is revealed as the scapulas are drawn to the outside of it.

C Pulling back

When the arms are pulled back, the muscles between the scapulae compress together, forming pipe-like volumes, or cylindrical columns of skin. These columns flair out and become ramps above each scapula.

B Pulling forward

Pulling the arms forward in front of the body flattens out the back muscles, making them less bulky, and allowing us to see through the muscles to the rib cage.

8. MALE AND FEMALE BACKS

Drawing the difference between genders comes down to the choice of design triangle (abstraction) you enhance. The upright triangle is enhanced when drawing the female form, from the gluteus muscles into the sacrospinalis group. For males, the downward pointing triangle is the most appropriate. It starts at the acromion processes and ends in the tailbone or sacral point.

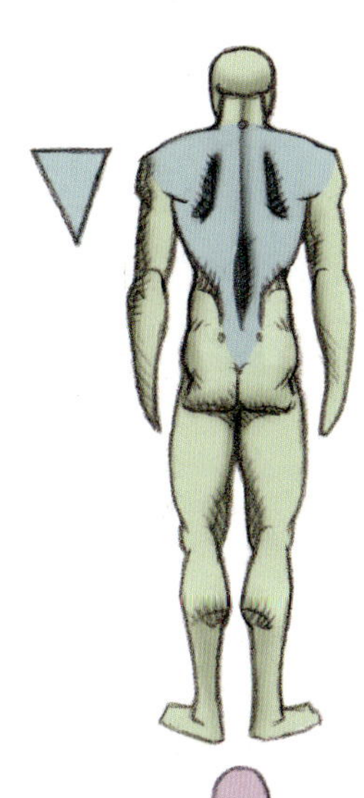

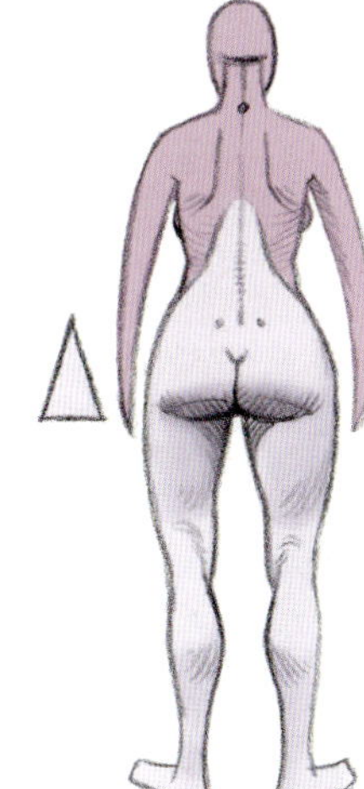

EXERCISES

1 Draw the pillow shape of the torso at every pitch, tilt, and turn without limbs attached. Next, pull a few of the more interesting drawings from the bunch and attach legs and arms. Do the poses feel weighted correctly? Can they be pushed more? If so, animate the next one over the existing drawing and reattach exoskeleton.

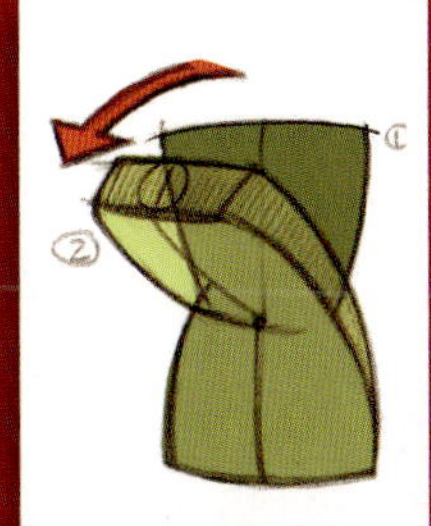

2 Draw the figure abstraction using the two rhythms just explained, making sure the lines used to find the neck also find the scapulas. When both sets cross each other, they should land where the rib cage ends. Think how similar these techniques are and how they might be combined. Now do more of each.

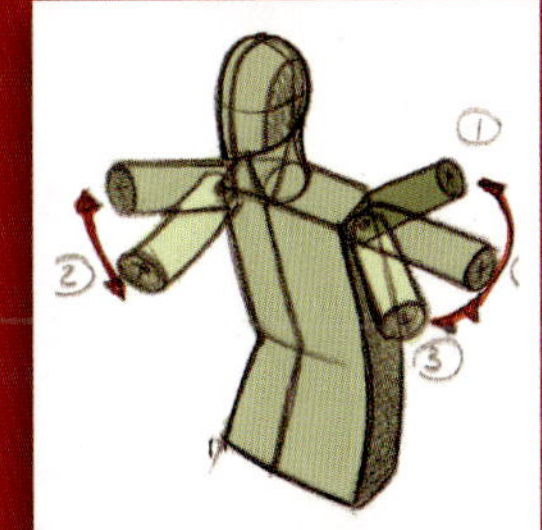

DRAWING THE WRIST IN MOTION

Drawing the wrist can be surprisingly hard to get right. Get under the skin of this tricky body part as **Ron Lemen** shows how to draw it in motion

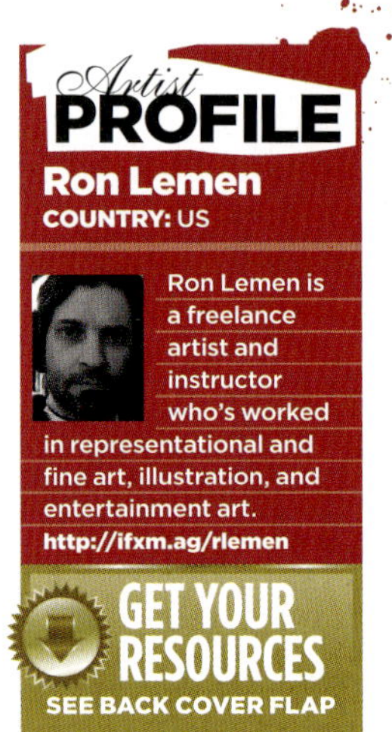

The wrist may be a small part of the body but it can cause some big problems for artists. It joins the lower arm and hand, and can move in all manner of ways and formations that effect how the arm and hand behave and look. To understand the wrist, you need to first look at the lower arm – its rhythms and how it connects with the wrist. Here I'll explain the make-up of this part of the body and how it interconnects with other parts, and, break it up into simple shapes, connections, and movements.

1. THE SKELETON

The forearm is made up of two bones, the radius and the ulna. The ulna is fixed while the radius rotates around it, as the name suggests. The wrist itself is made up of eight carpal bones plus the scaphoid and lunate bones, which articulate with the radius and ulna to form the wrist joint.

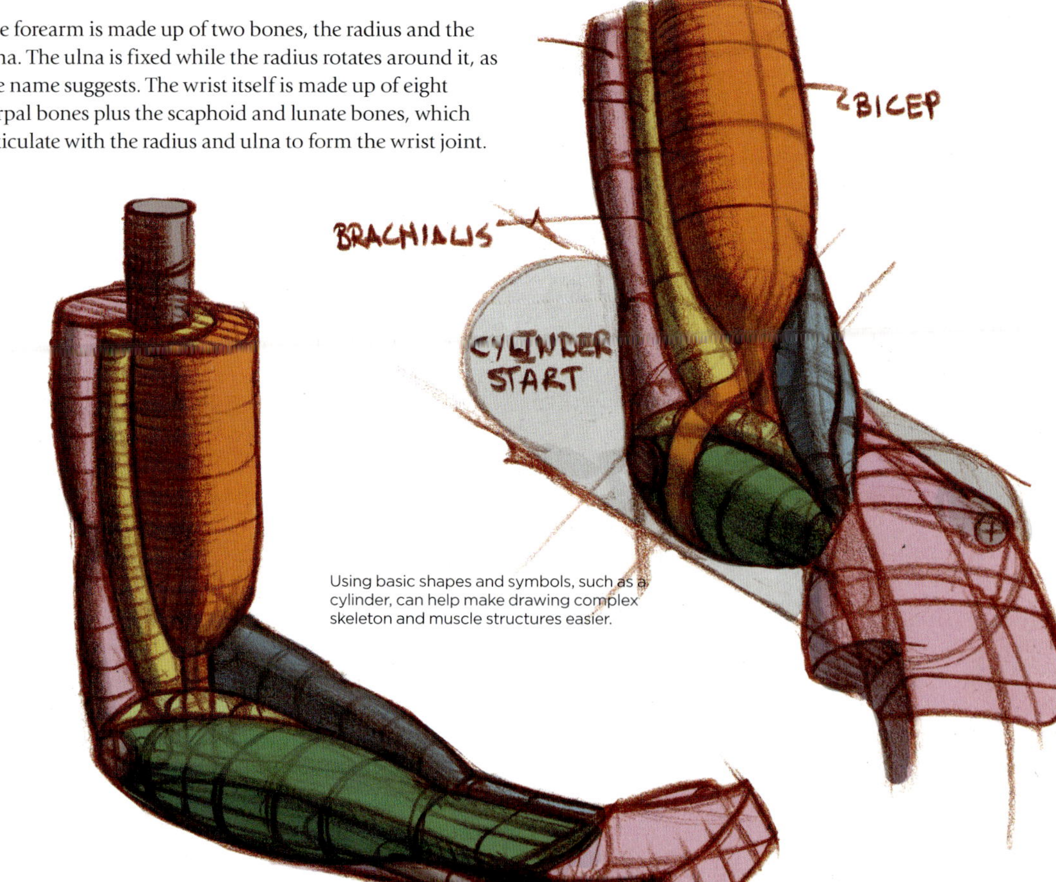

Using basic shapes and symbols, such as a cylinder, can help make drawing complex skeleton and muscle structures easier.

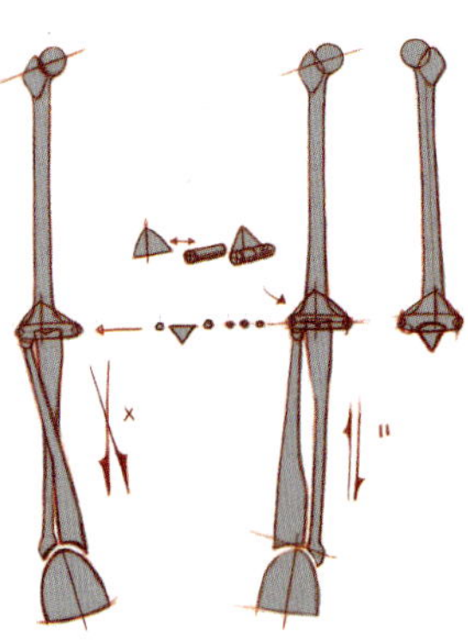

The bones of the body can be turned into simple shapes, such as triangles for joints.

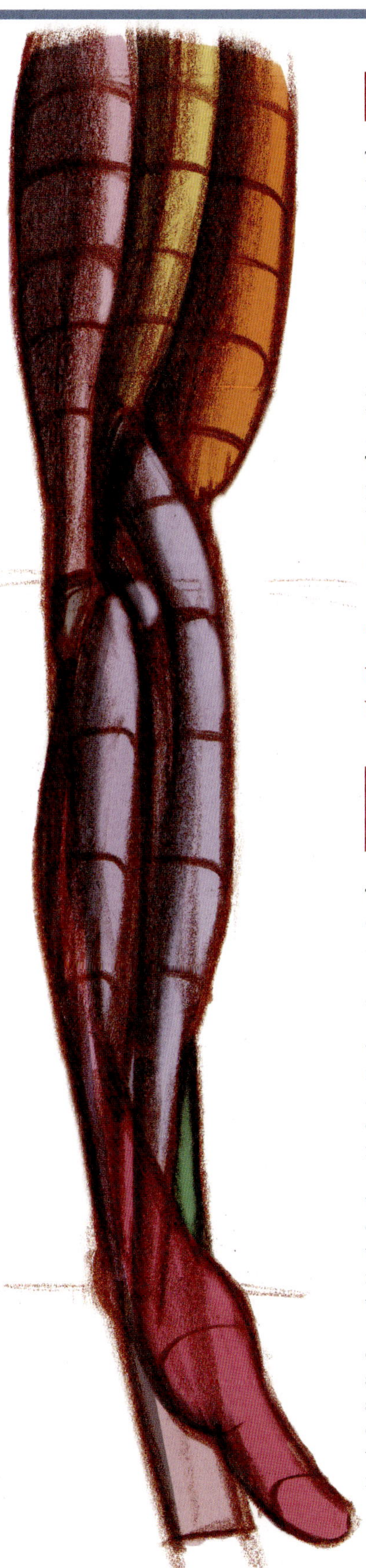

2. SCALE AND MEASURING TRICKS

There are tricks that can help you when drawing the arm. For example, the hand is the length of the face plane from the hairline to the chin. The forearm (with the hand closed in a fist) is the same length as the upper arm, which in turn is the same length as the rib cage. When the arm is resting at the side of the body, the wrist will sit upon the greater trochanter of the femur.

Another handy trick to remember is the golden ratio: the lower arm is about two-thirds of the length of the upper arm, and the hand is about two-thirds of the length of the lower arm. The fingers are two-thirds of the length of the palm, and each phalanx (section) of the finger is two-thirds of the length of the previous phalanx. Remembering these simple ratios will save you a lot of grief when drawing figures.

"There are handy tricks, like the golden ratio, that help you when drawing the arm."

3. FIND THE ARM'S RHYTHMS

The rhythms of the forearm are connected to the muscles in the upper arm. To begin tracking the rhythms, the arm has to be designed. Start with the action line, which comes from the torso – this is the largest movement and needs to be found first because it links the movement to the torso, and will take away the "hard corners" that can otherwise develop when building the figure piece by piece.

Once the action has been found and the character line is established, the width of the limb and then its rhythms are traced over these two edges. Typically, the rhythms traverse the limb, crossing from the outside to the inside.

Rhythms should not be isolated to tiny channels of information – a rhythm should tie everything together by swinging through it and adapting a part of each section to the "implied pathways" that the artist establishes to help read the image and find its focus.

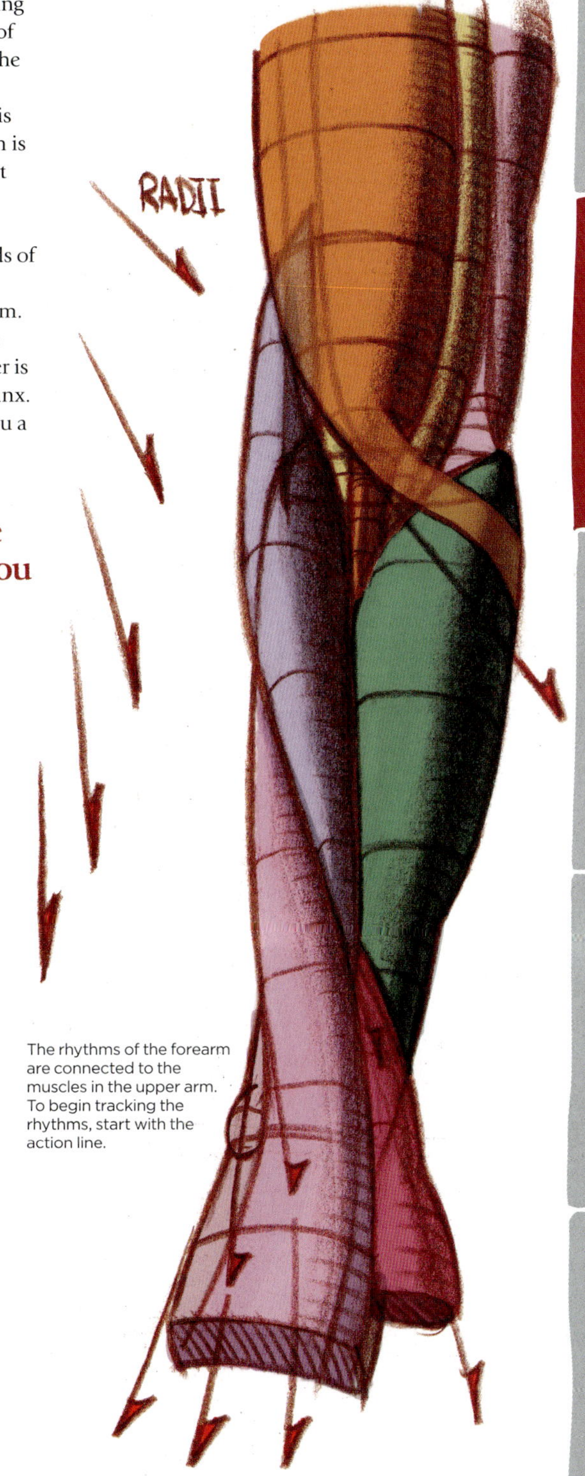

The rhythms of the forearm are connected to the muscles in the upper arm. To begin tracking the rhythms, start with the action line.

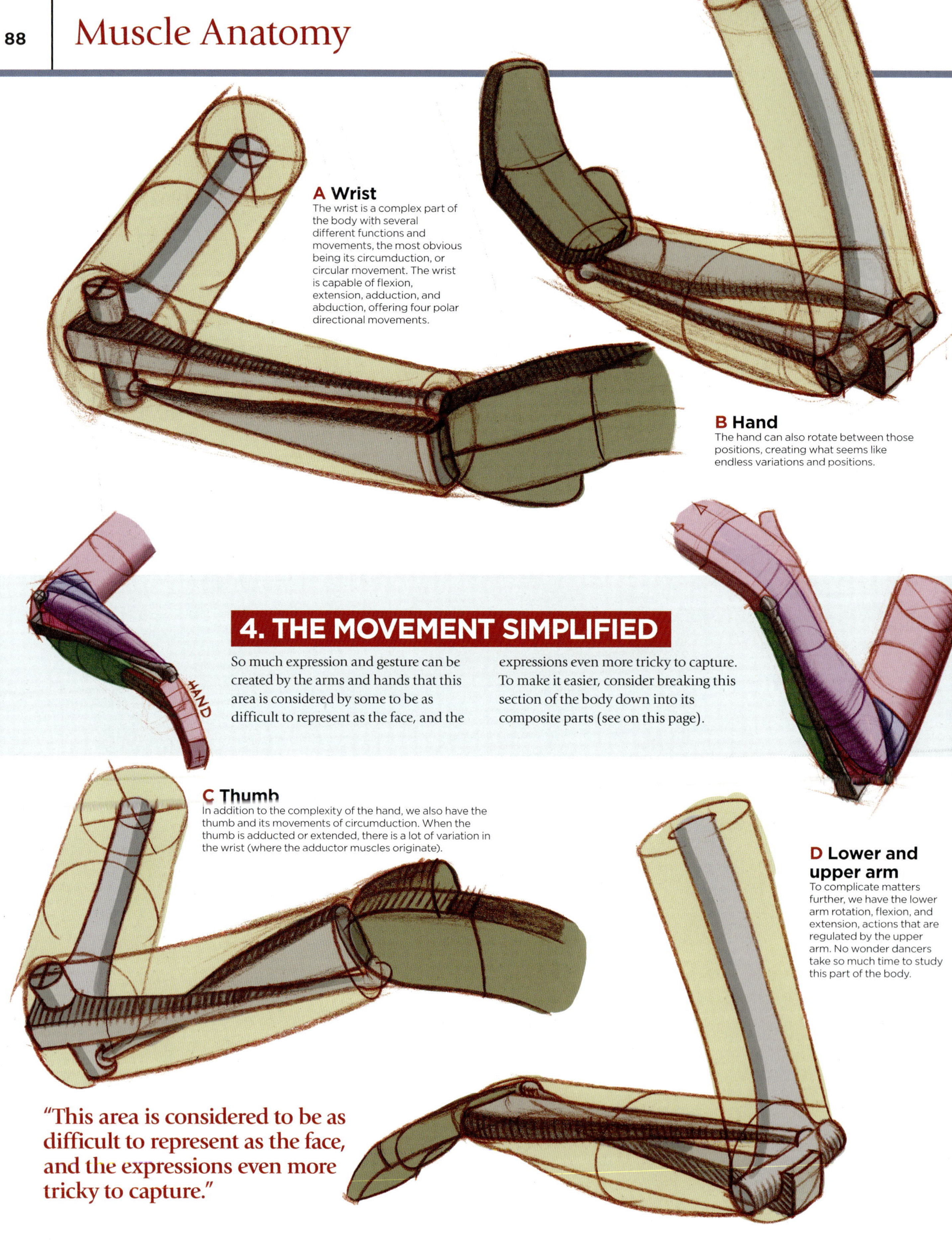

A Wrist
The wrist is a complex part of the body with several different functions and movements, the most obvious being its circumduction, or circular movement. The wrist is capable of flexion, extension, adduction, and abduction, offering four polar directional movements.

B Hand
The hand can also rotate between those positions, creating what seems like endless variations and positions.

4. THE MOVEMENT SIMPLIFIED

So much expression and gesture can be created by the arms and hands that this area is considered by some to be as difficult to represent as the face, and the expressions even more tricky to capture. To make it easier, consider breaking this section of the body down into its composite parts (see on this page).

C Thumb
In addition to the complexity of the hand, we also have the thumb and its movements of circumduction. When the thumb is adducted or extended, there is a lot of variation in the wrist (where the adductor muscles originate).

D Lower and upper arm
To complicate matters further, we have the lower arm rotation, flexion, and extension, actions that are regulated by the upper arm. No wonder dancers take so much time to study this part of the body.

"This area is considered to be as difficult to represent as the face, and the expressions even more tricky to capture."

5. SYMBOLS WE CAN DRAW EASILY

When I design the bones of the wrist, I think of them as a pliable plank of wood that merges into a cylinder, or I use a bowling pin or drumstick-like shape to start with. This bowling pin–like shape groups together all the complex anatomy of the forearm but gives no indication of surface direction. We need to draw the four polar axis points on an ellipse to assist in finding the surfaces, using a perpendicular "+" shape to represent the ellipse's major and minor axes.

Where it joins to the hand the wrist is an ellipsoid joint, similar to a ball-and-socket joint such as the shoulder, and allowing the same type of movement to a lesser magnitude.

> **"We need to draw the four polar axis points on an ellipse to assist in finding the surfaces."**

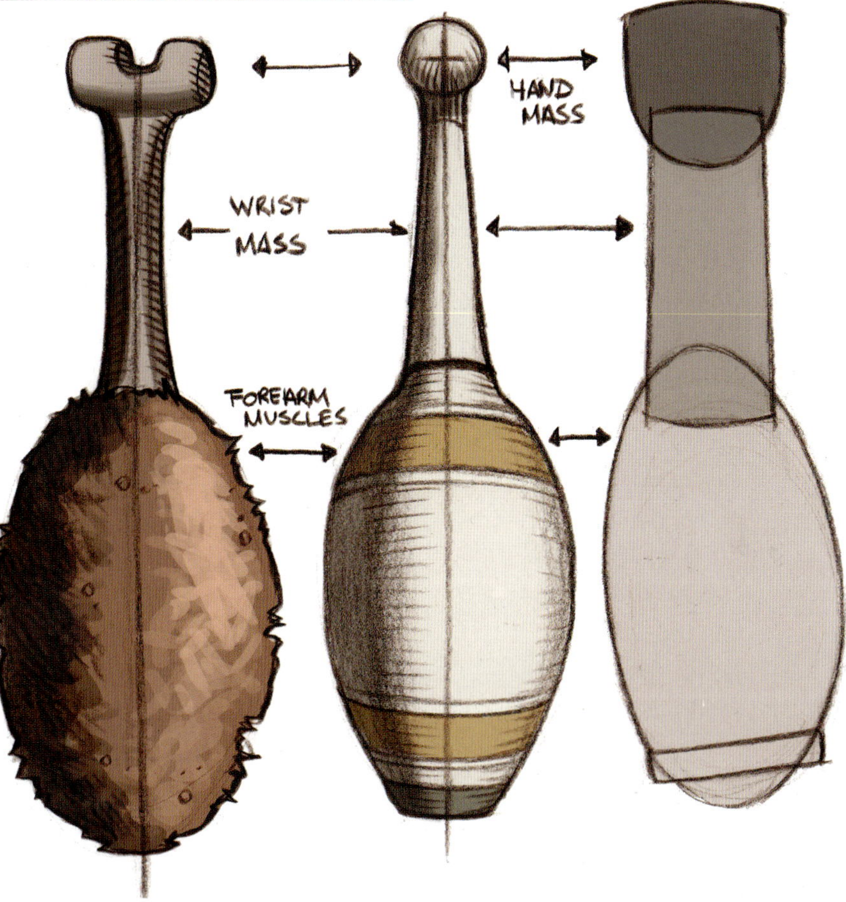

Using abstract shapes and symbols in simple stages can make complex drawing easy to manage.

6. MUSCLES OF THE FOREARM AND THEIR FUNCTIONS

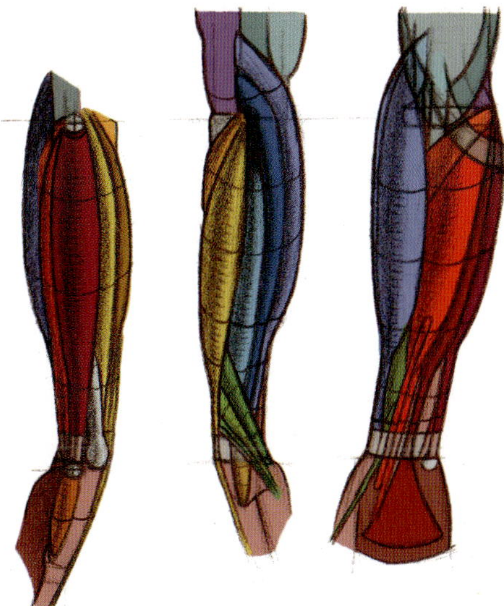

The anatomy of the forearm is very complex, but here we shall look at a basic list and some rough illustrations to help you remember the placement and function of the muscles.

In its most simplified form, the forearm has four groups of muscles, with each group performing a specific function and assisting in stabilizing the opposite motion. They fall into two main groups – a flexor/pronator group and an extensor/supinator group – plus the thumb adductor group.

The flexors flex the fingers, the extensors extend the fingers, and the adductor muscles of the thumb extend the thumb or draw it away from the hand.

PRO TIPS

Understand your lines

When drawing limbs it is essential to start with two lines, the action and the character lines. These two lines will have a great impact on how you organize the spaces and connect the two sides together through rhythmical means. The action line denotes the activity of the arm or leg, and the character line describes the physical body type of your subject, and will help you flesh out the body. The lines are not necessarily parallel, though – limbs are tapered and are wider where they connect to the body.

7. PLANES AND SURFACES OF THE HAND AND WRIST

To plane out the arm, we have to transform our cylinders to blocks. Find the center of the cylinder and, at the wrist end, draw a line from one edge of the cylinder to the other, through the center. Think of this line like an airplane propeller; spin the prop until it is in position, then box it into the block shape, making it the centerline of the long axis. Label the thumb side to avoid confusion.

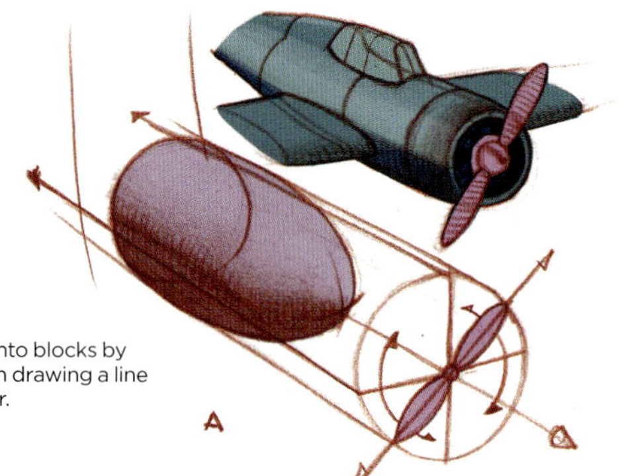

Transform your cylinders into blocks by finding the center and then drawing a line from one edge to the other.

PRO TIPS

Line expression

Start simple and keep your image uncluttered – it is easier to solve the activity of a pose without extra lines everywhere. A loose gesture will give more life to a drawing than building it bit by bit. To keep gestures loose, find a place to attach them – think of the bones and tendons or the straighter lines in the arms and legs and torso as the gesture lines. Restrain your urges to start with the lumpy, bumpy bits – these elements can wait until you are ready to decorate the movement.

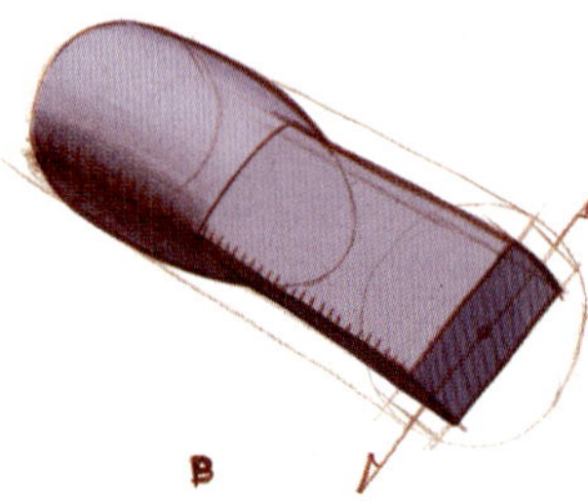

Once you have boxed your cylinders into block shapes, label the thumb side to avoid confusion.

A Forearm and elbow shapes

The ulna bone has the "ulnar furrow" along the length of the forearm, which separates the flexors from the extensors. The back of the elbow is another landmark to take note of. When the arm is extended, the ulna, humerus, and the bones of the elbow line up perfectly. When the elbow is bent, these three landmark points form a triangle and change the shape of the elbow to a triangular-like space that can be encapsulated in the cylinder.

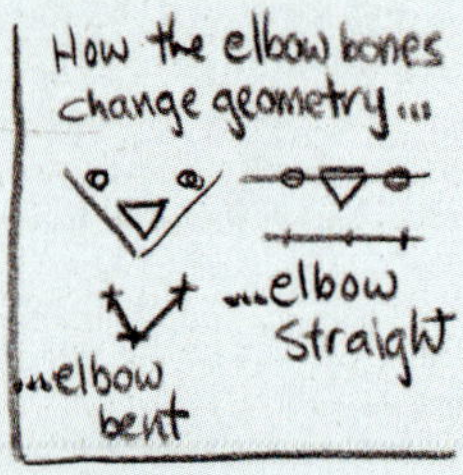

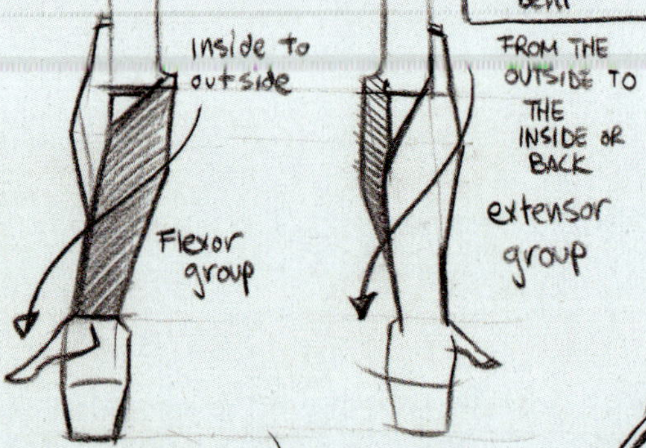

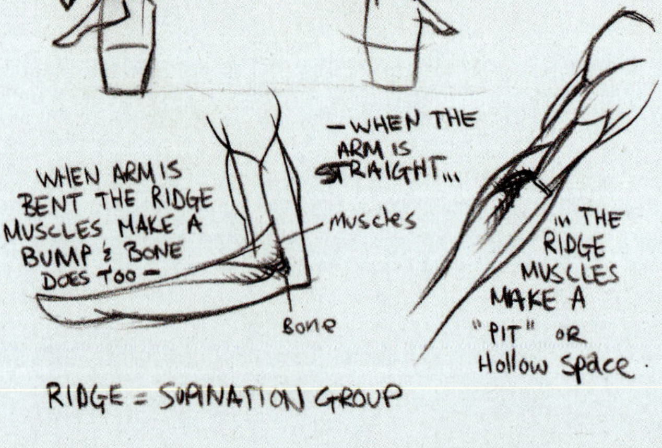

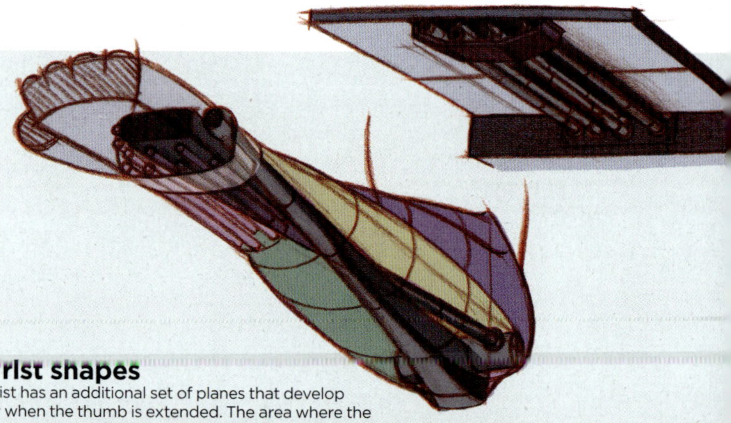

B Wrist shapes

The wrist has an additional set of planes that develop slightly when the thumb is extended. The area where the hand and wrist meet changes shape with the movement of the tendons connecting the thumb to the wrist, bridging the shapes rather than traveling in the direction of the bones. These additional planes form a space referred to as the "snuff box" – a triangular deepening on the radial, dorsal side of the hand where it connects with the thumb.

C Hand shapes

When the hand is flexed or extended, the bent side forms a ramp with ripples of skin crossing it and the stretched side turns into an angle because of the tendons stretching around it. Understanding the basic shapes of the hand as it bends with the wrist will enable you to judge the surface correctly.

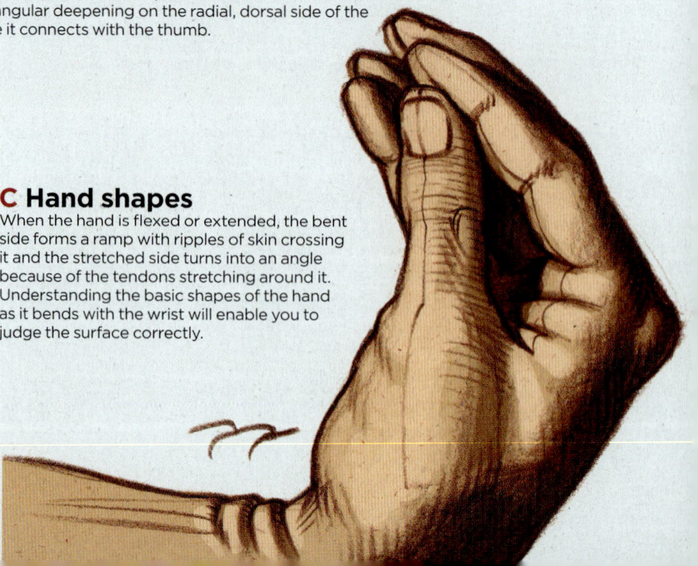

8. THE SKIN AND SURFACE

The flexor muscles move the fingers through cord-like extensions called tendons, and the skin will crease across the tendons in a perpendicular direction.

When the wrist is bent in either direction, the skin across it will crease in several places to alleviate the pressure of the stressing taking place. These creases have a major fold that emanates from either bone in the wrist, creating several ridges of skin (like stairs). When the thumb is extended, the two tendons above and below the thumb create the triangular "snuff box."

> "When the wrist is bent, the skin will crease to alleviate the pressure of the stressing."

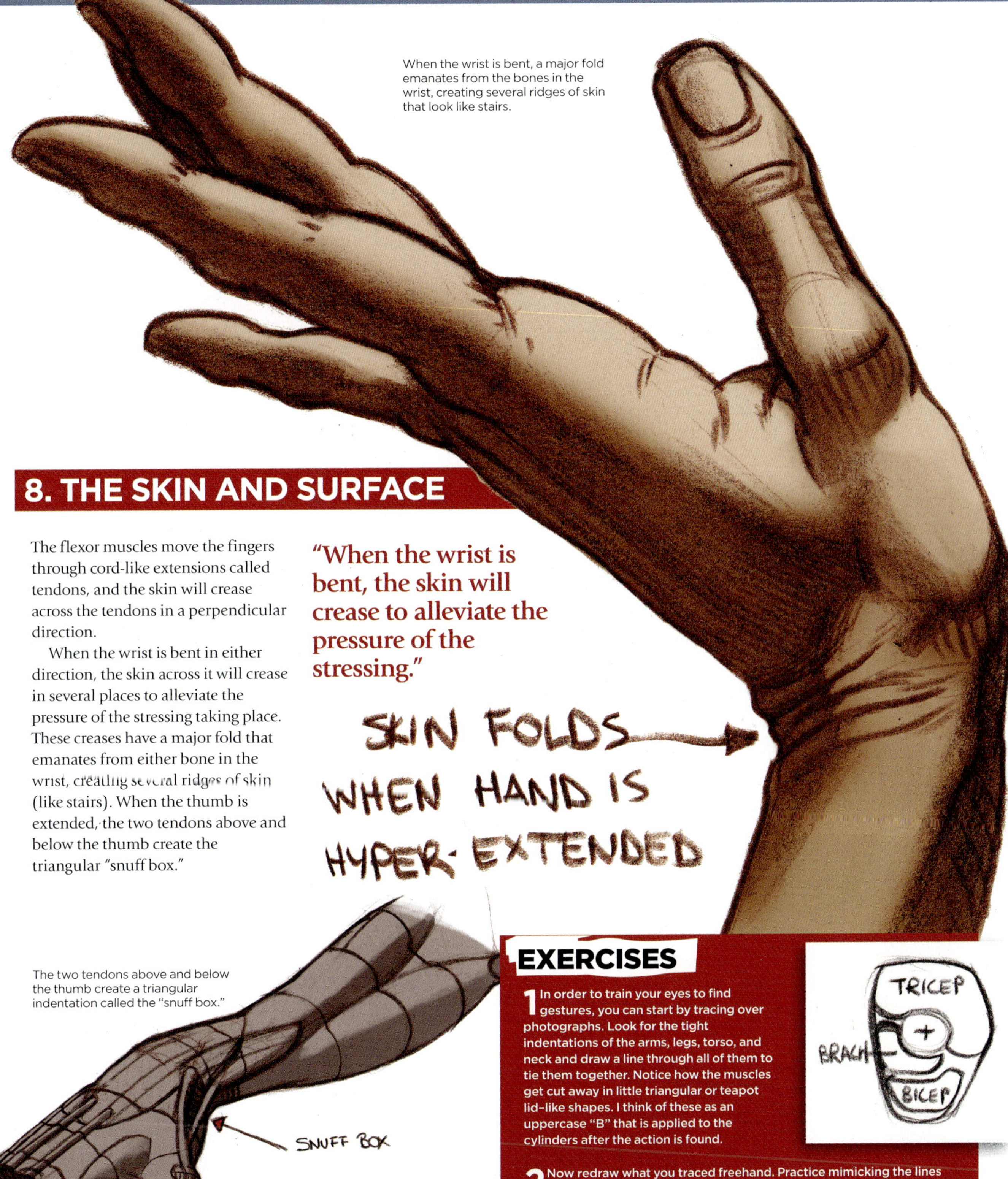

When the wrist is bent, a major fold emanates from the bones in the wrist, creating several ridges of skin that look like stairs.

The two tendons above and below the thumb create a triangular indentation called the "snuff box."

EXERCISES

1 In order to train your eyes to find gestures, you can start by tracing over photographs. Look for the tight indentations of the arms, legs, torso, and neck and draw a line through all of them to tie them together. Notice how the muscles get cut away in little triangular or teapot lid-like shapes. I think of these as an uppercase "B" that is applied to the cylinders after the action is found.

2 Now redraw what you traced freehand. Practice mimicking the lines you generated and learn to move your arm in a fluid fashion, from the shoulder to the wrist, holding the pencil on its side to stop your hand from acting as an anchor (as it does when you hold a pencil to write). Keep your movements large, loose, and sweeping. Finally, memorizing is key to becoming an artist, so every time you copy or trace something, draw it a number of times from memory to practice this skill.

Movement anatomy

Learn how the core parts of the human body move to draw dynamic figures from your imagination

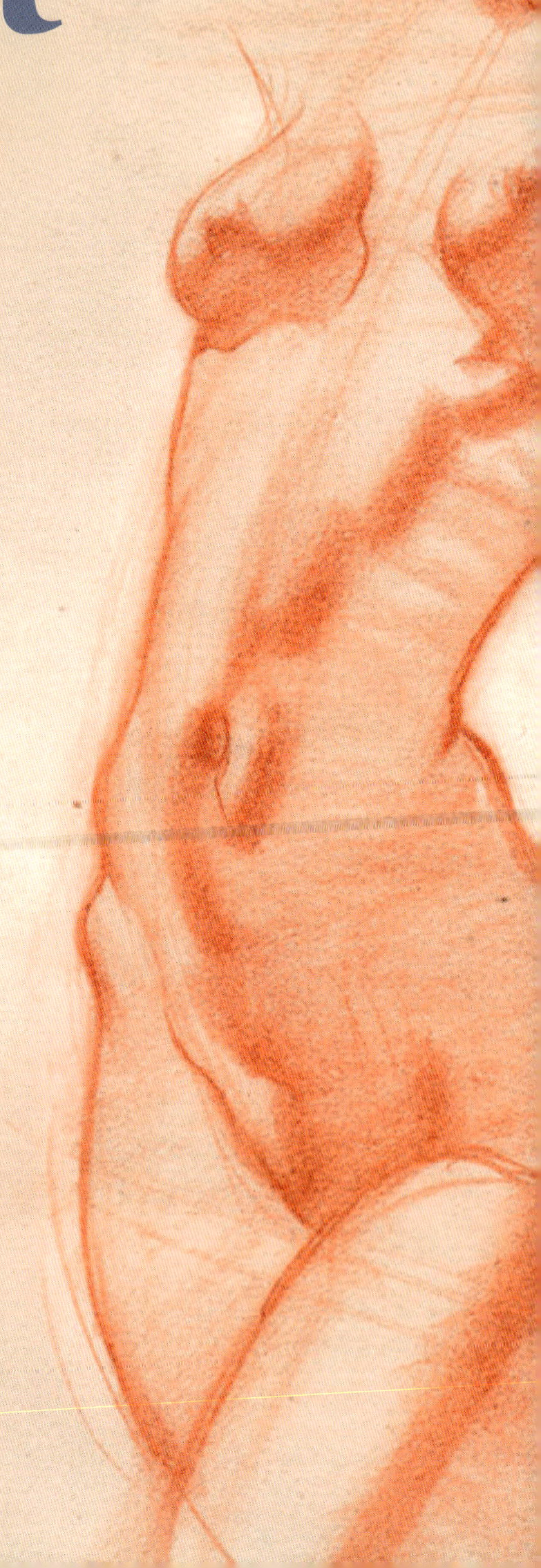

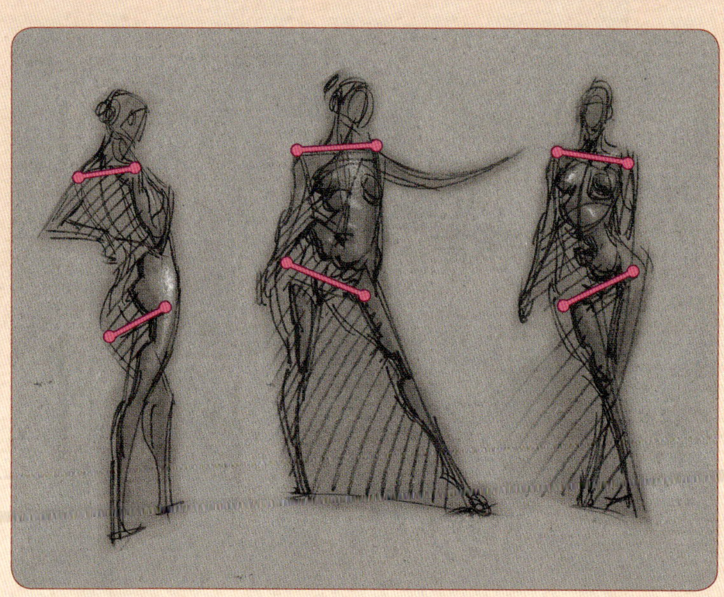

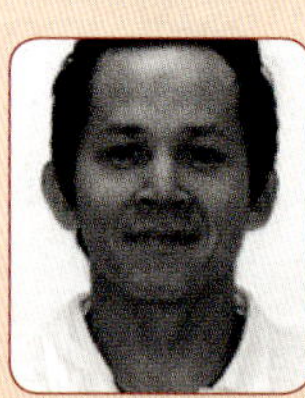

"Gesture is the cornerstone by which an artist can build their image."
(Chris Legaspi, page 94)

Workshops

How to draw the body in motion

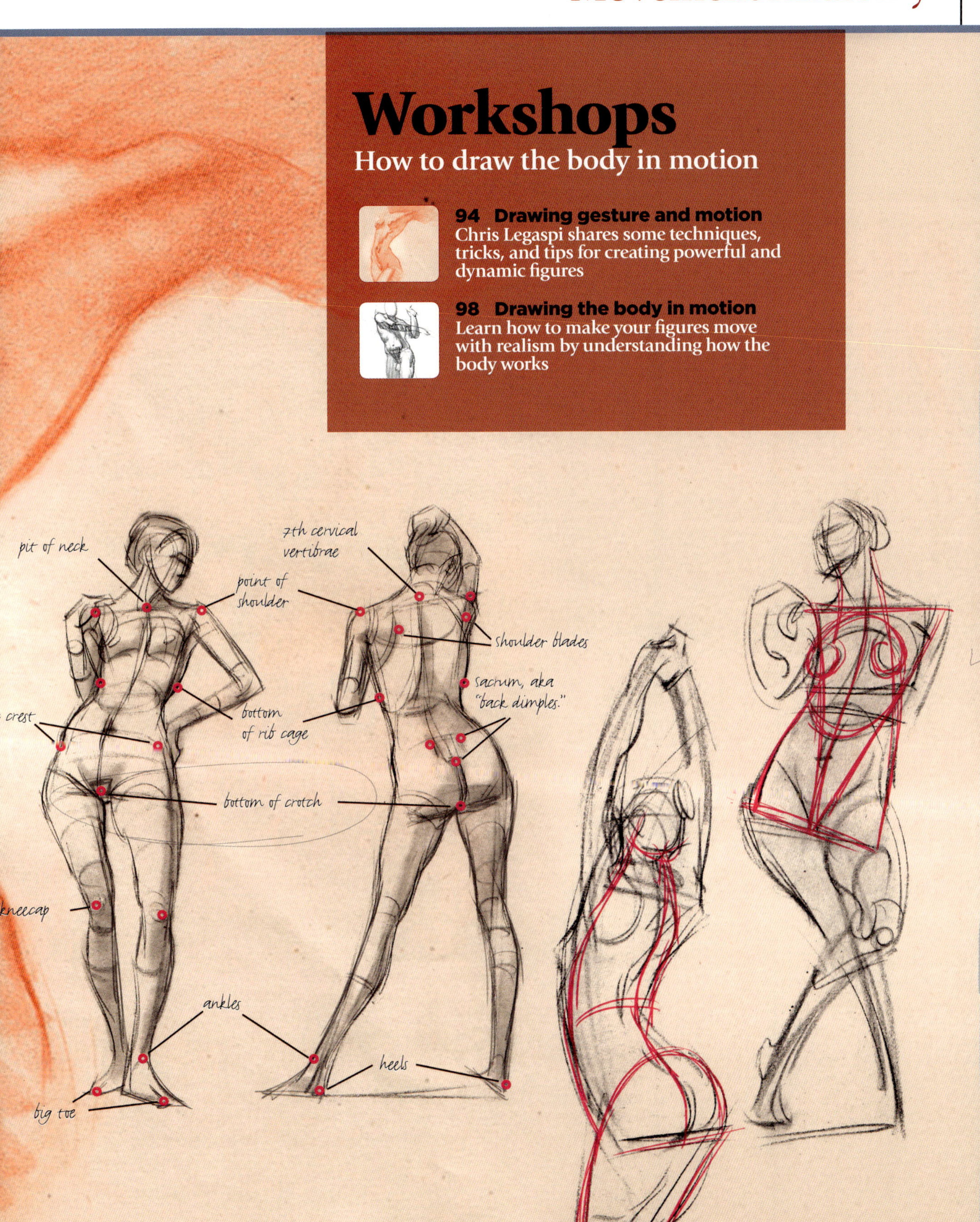

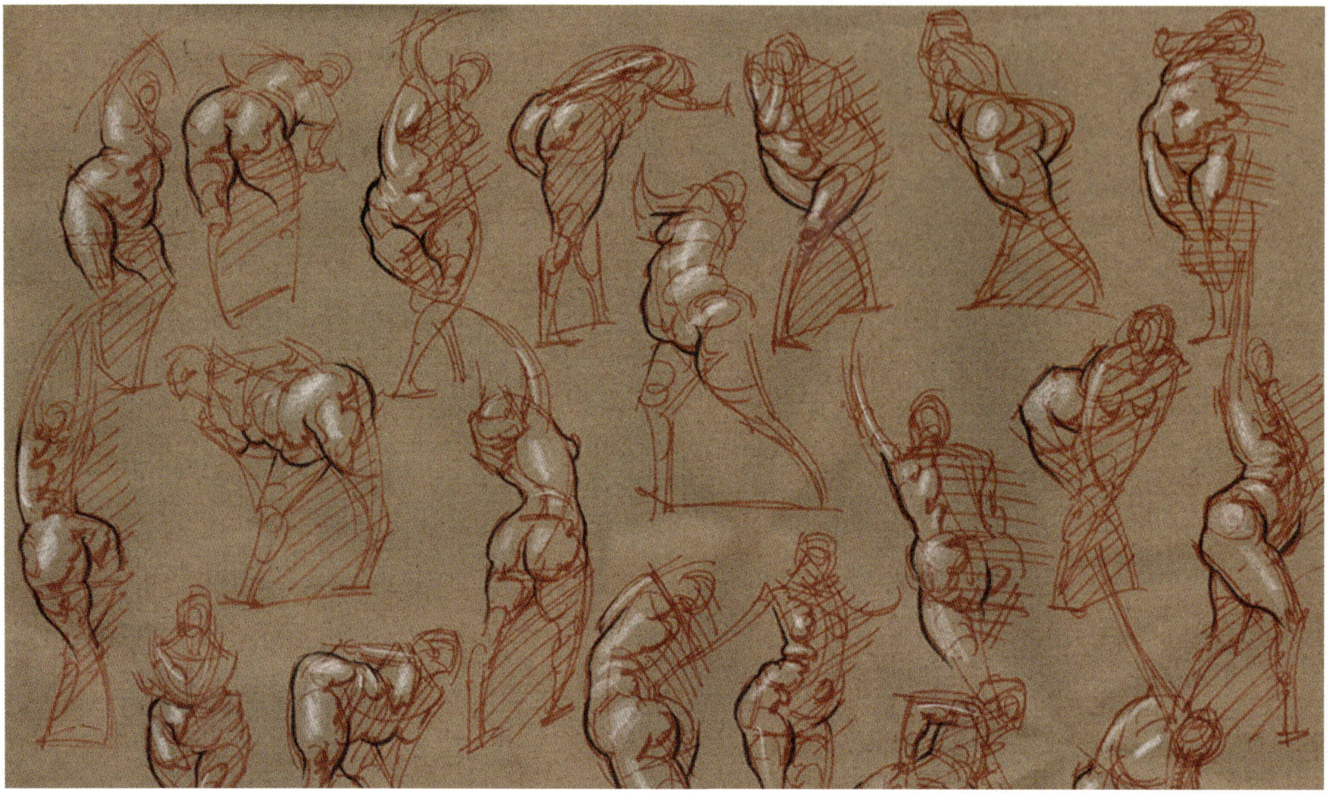

DRAWING GESTURE AND MOTION

Excellent figure drawing is a vital skill for any artist. **Chris Legaspi** shares some techniques and tips for creating powerful and dynamic figures

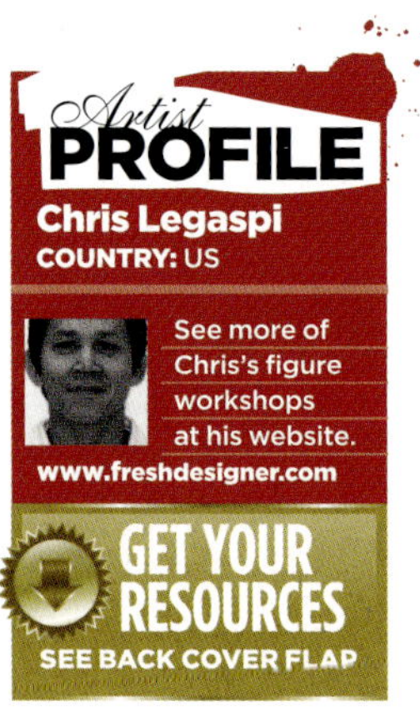

Gesture can be defined as the thrust, action, intent, or life force that drives the pose of the figure. In other words, gesture is the action of the pose. "What is the figure doing?" is the key question the artist must answer for the viewer.

In figure drawing, gestures serves to give our figures life and movement, even in a still, two-dimensional drawing. Because of this, we must give gesture primary consideration if we want our figures to come alive.

Gesture is not only the first concept or idea to consider in figure drawing, but it is also the initial step – the cornerstone from which an artist can build their image. Therefore, the foundation of all great figure drawings is gesture!

In this workshop, I will share some simple and elegant strategies for understanding and mastering this critical first step in figure drawing. These will not only add movement and flair to your figures but will also bring your drawings to life. Let's get started!

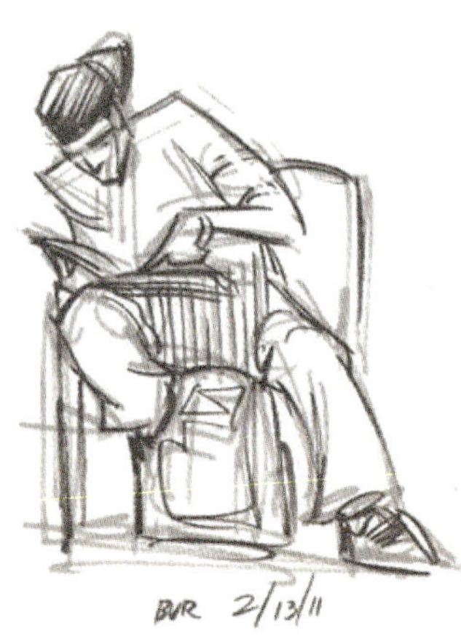

Draw Muscle Move Animal Digital

1. HOW TO OBSERVE

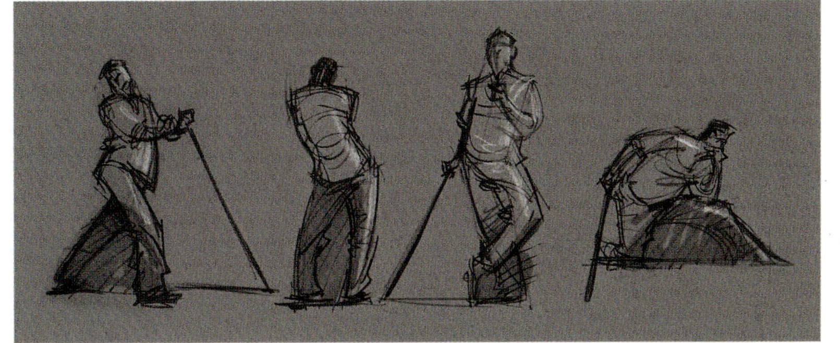

First, pause and take a few moments to simply observe. Observe the head and torso. Note the curvature of the spine, the direction of the model's gaze, the distribution of weight, and the direction the limbs are pointing in. Since gesture is the thrust or action of the pose, the key question to ask yourself is: "What is the model doing?" Learning how to see properly is key to unlocking the complexities of figure drawing.

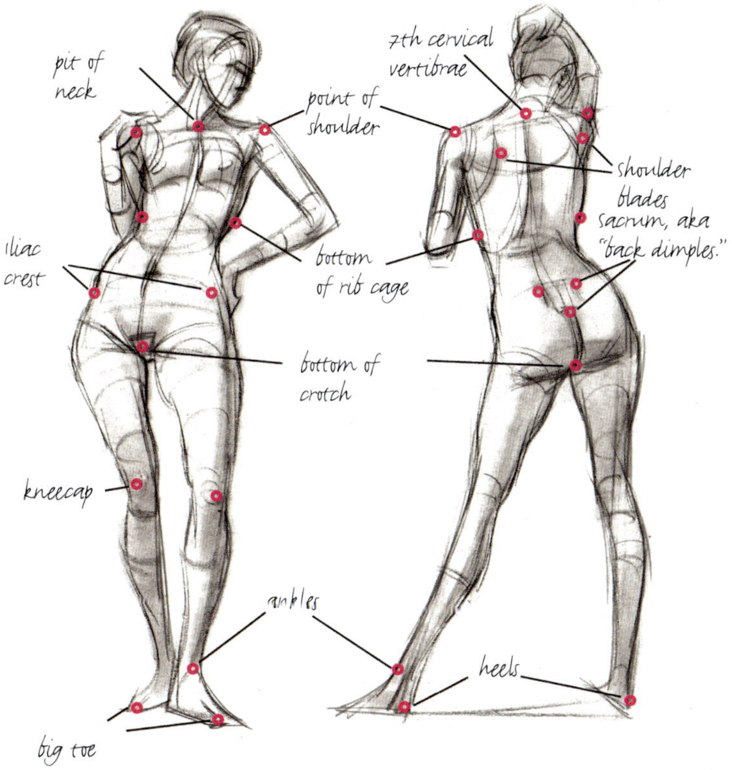

pit of neck
point of shoulder
7th cervical vertibrae
shoulder blades
sacrum, aka "back dimples."
bottom of rib cage
iliac crest
bottom of crotch
kneecap
ankles
heels
big toe

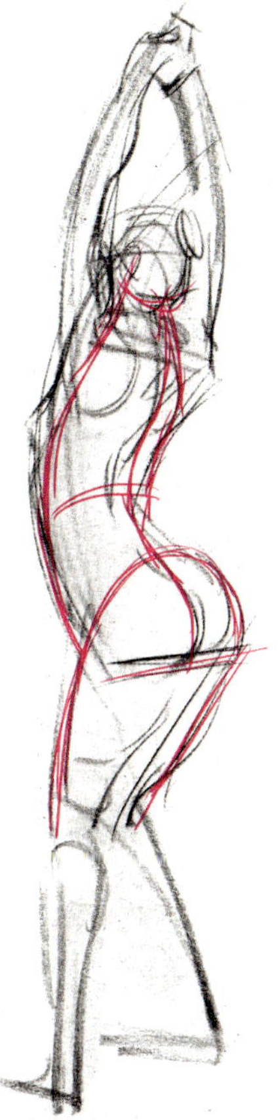

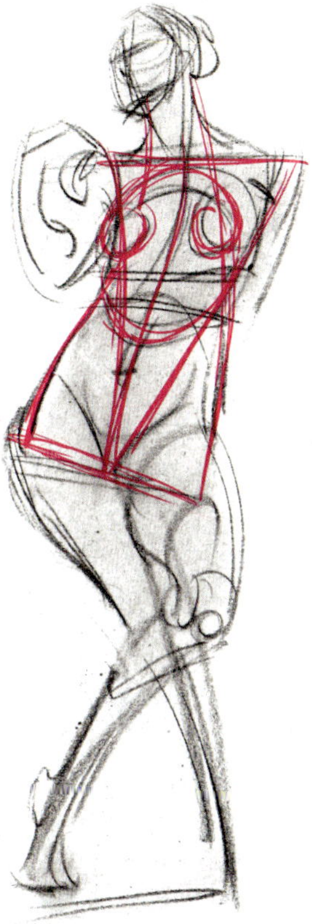

2. KNOW THE LANDMARKS

Landmarks are key points on the body that I use to measure, construct, or locate other key points of anatomy. Some of the key landmarks I use are: the pit of the neck, the points of the shoulder bones, the bottom of the rib cage, the iliac crest (peaks of hip bone), the bottom of the crotch, the kneecaps, ankles, and big toes, the seventh cervical vertebrae (upper back), the scapulae (shoulder blades), and the sacrum (often seen from behind as two back dimples).

3. THE LONG AXIS ACTION LINE

The Reilly Method breaks down figure drawing into lines, gestures, and forms, and uses lines to represent the axis or direction of the major forms and express the action of the figure. To draw the action of the pose, first I locate the long axis. The long axis, or action line, is the longest uninterrupted line that runs either through the form or at the edge of it. I like to make the long axis or action line as long and fluid as possible. Every form, even the smallest, has a long axis.

4. RHYTHMS OF THE BODY

Rhythms are the natural flow of anatomy that runs through the body. For example, a line drawn from the pit of the neck to the crotch is the centerline rhythm. There are also rhythms that run from the neck to the hip. Just like knowing how to look for key landmarks, I use rhythms as another tool to locate key anatomy, emphasize the gesture, and lengthen the action line, which adds a sense of movement and believability.

5. GESTURE VS. STRUCTURE

Gesture is defined as movement along the form. For example, a line drawn from the chin down to the pelvis is gesture. Structure is also gesture or movement, but it is movement across or over forms. For example, a line drawn from the right armpit to left side of the ribs is structure. Because gesture is fluid and moves, structure gives us solidity, form, and balance by creating a container for the fluid nature of the body and that of any living form.

"Exaggerate the areas that bulge out when resting on a ground plane."

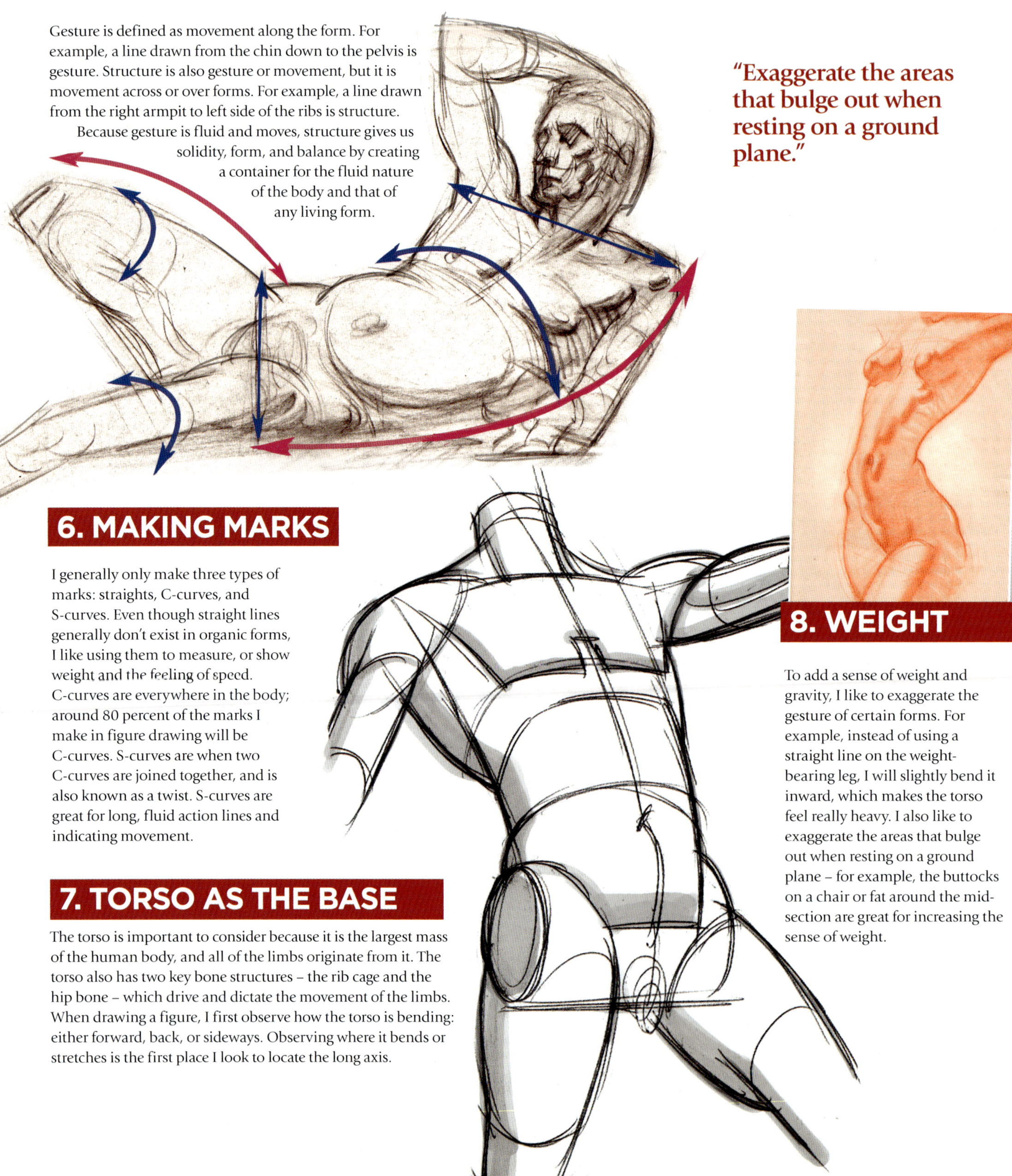

6. MAKING MARKS

I generally only make three types of marks: straights, C-curves, and S-curves. Even though straight lines generally don't exist in organic forms, I like using them to measure, or show weight and the feeling of speed. C-curves are everywhere in the body; around 80 percent of the marks I make in figure drawing will be C-curves. S-curves are when two C-curves are joined together, and is also known as a twist. S-curves are great for long, fluid action lines and indicating movement.

7. TORSO AS THE BASE

The torso is important to consider because it is the largest mass of the human body, and all of the limbs originate from it. The torso also has two key bone structures – the rib cage and the hip bone – which drive and dictate the movement of the limbs. When drawing a figure, I first observe how the torso is bending: either forward, back, or sideways. Observing where it bends or stretches is the first place I look to locate the long axis.

8. WEIGHT

To add a sense of weight and gravity, I like to exaggerate the gesture of certain forms. For example, instead of using a straight line on the weight-bearing leg, I will slightly bend it inward, which makes the torso feel really heavy. I also like to exaggerate the areas that bulge out when resting on a ground plane – for example, the buttocks on a chair or fat around the mid-section are great for increasing the sense of weight.

9. CONTRAPPOSTO

Contrapposto is an Italian word that means "opposite" or "counterpose." It is caused when body weight is distributed unevenly, which causes the angle of the hips to oppose or "counter" the angle of the shoulders. I use contrapposto to add a dynamic tension or a relaxed, realistic feeling. I also use contrapposto as a tool to locate either the angle of the hips or the shoulders when one or the other is hidden from view.

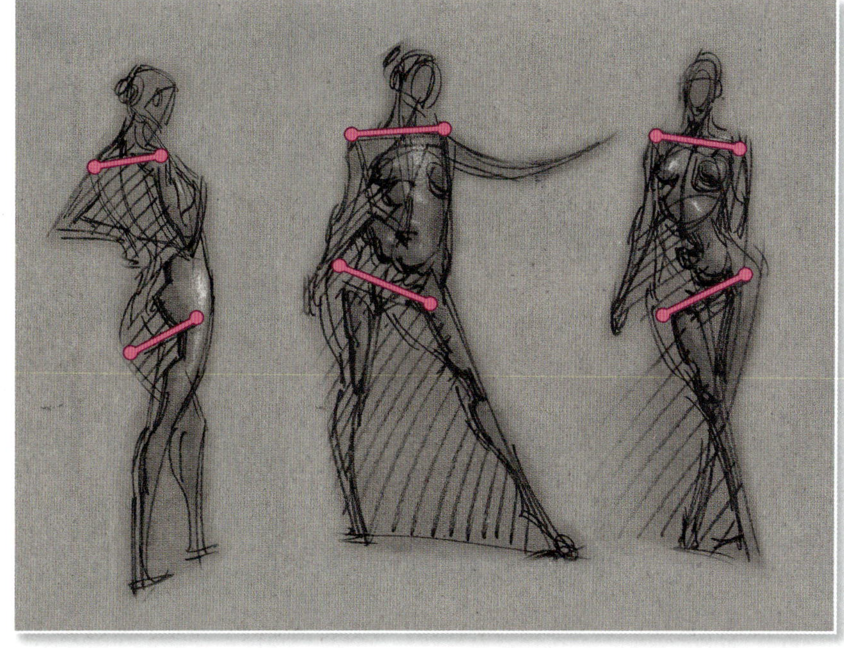

"Use silhouettes to design the big shapes that emphasize the pose's action."

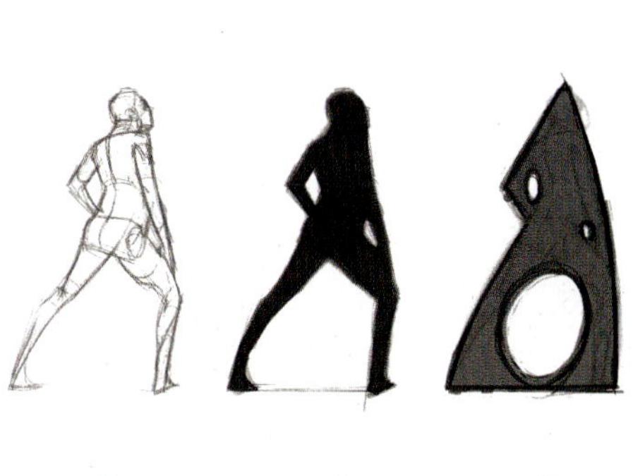

11. SILHOUETTE

Silhouette is the outer edge of the figure or form. It is the visual space that a figure takes up in a picture plane. I use silhouette to design big shapes that emphasize the action of the pose. For example, a triangular shape can add stability, weight, or a powerful upward thrust. I also use silhouette to give the viewer an instant "read" as to what the figure is doing.

12. MANY WAYS TO DRAW

There are many ways to draw gestures and figures. I was trained in and use the Reilly Method, which uses a lot of rhythmic lines and abstract shapes to design and construct the figure. Some artists like squiggly, calligraphic lines. Some artists like to use tone. There is no right or wrong way to draw the human body – I say learn all the methods and choose what works best for you and the pose.

10. RELATE TO THE HEAD

The Reilly Method suggests starting with known quantities, such as where the head is in relation to the rest of the body. I don't just relate to the head with the long axis, but also try to relate every part or action back to the head. I connect everything, from the hips and arms to fingers and toes. Since thought precedes action, this is a great tool for adding an extra layer of life and believability. I also use this concept to measure and design simpler, bolder shapes.

PRO TIPS

Life drawing

Draw from life as much as possible. The most ideal setting for this is a figure drawing workshop with a live model. If sketching a live model is not possible, take a sketchbook to your favorite cafe, bookstore, or even restaurant – any public place is great for capturing studies and quick gestures of the people around you in your environment. There is absolutely no excuse not to draw from life.

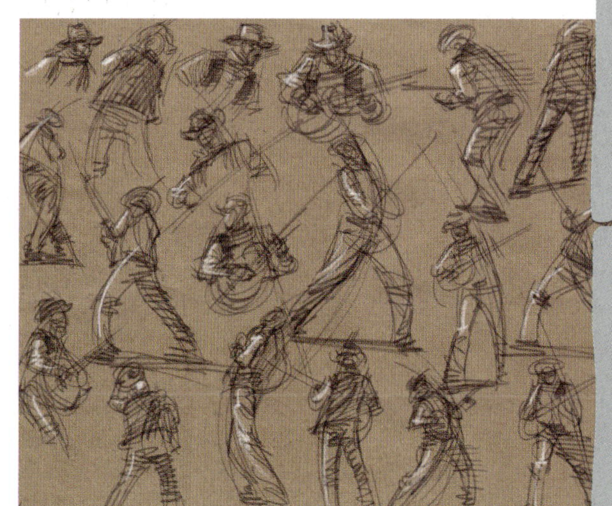

DRAWING THE BODY IN MOTION

Make your figures move with realism by understanding how the body works; **Ron Lemen** explains the ins and outs of movement...

Every artist has his or her own version of 3D rendering software in their head, but, without the correct training, that program will lie dormant.

Work on your 3D "muscle" by doing repeated exercises in your mental gym – these muscles will build up and the camera, the artist's inner vision, will come to life. Life drawing demands a rich visual library, which should be memorized by drawing the same exercises and muscle forms and rhythms over and over again.

These kinds of mental exercise will assist in turning your mental "camera" on and helping you interpret how the human machine works and appears. Read my words in this workshop carefully, over and over – they describe specific motions and will help the information to "stick" the more you revise it.

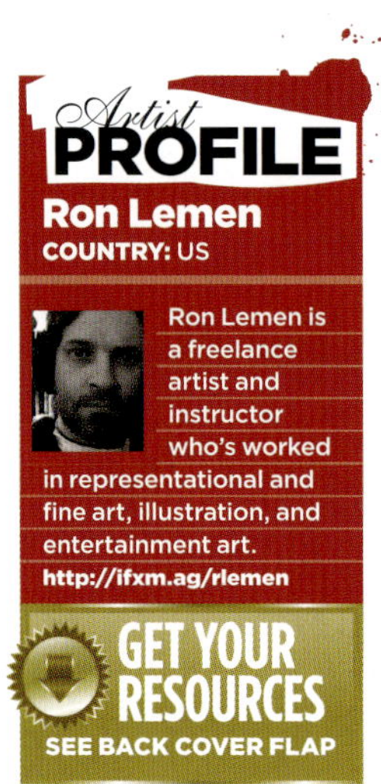

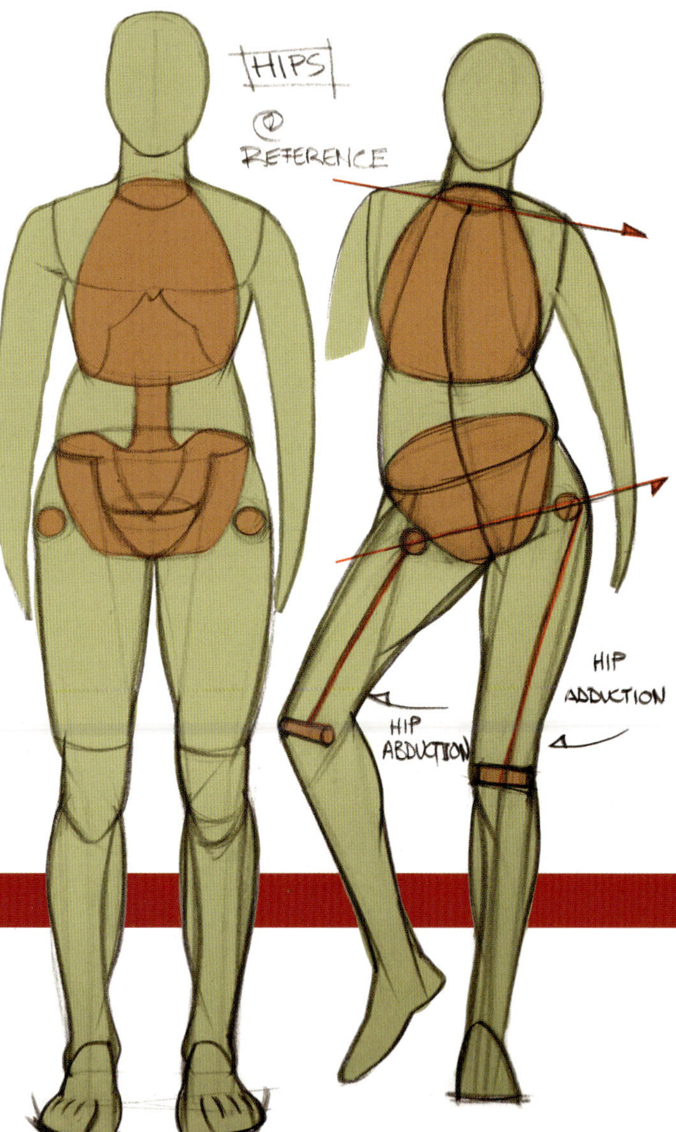

1. BODY MOVEMENTS

To start with, let's look at how different sections of the body move and bend. Dividing the body into parts like this offers a detailed understanding of how we move; then we can put it all together...

A Shoulders, ankles, and fingers...

Circumduction is a circular motion combining flexion, extension, adduction, and abduction, and is attributed to parts of the body that are round in design like the ball joints. The shoulders and hips are the largest areas, and other areas include the wrists and ankles, fingers and toes, and the head. We use circumduction when winding up for something like a softball pitch or swinging a tennis racket.

"Circumduction is a circular motion attributed to parts of the body that are round in design."

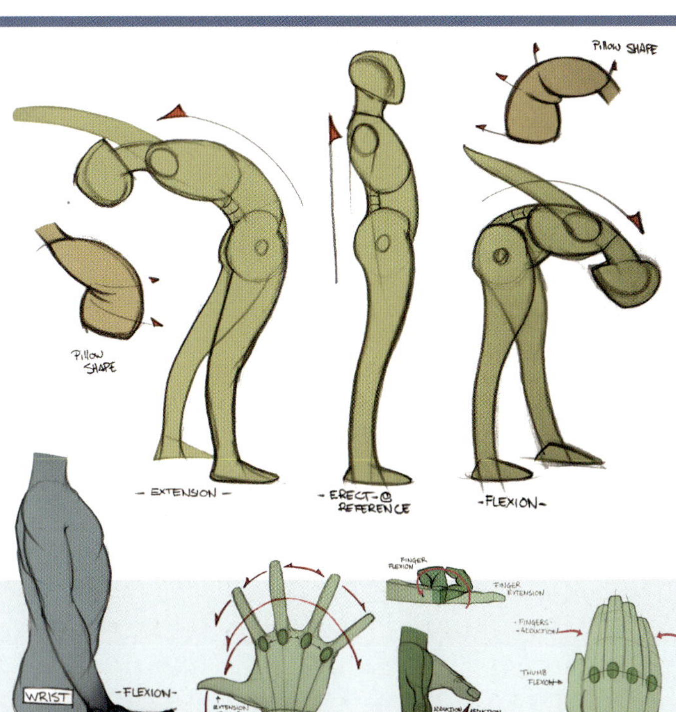

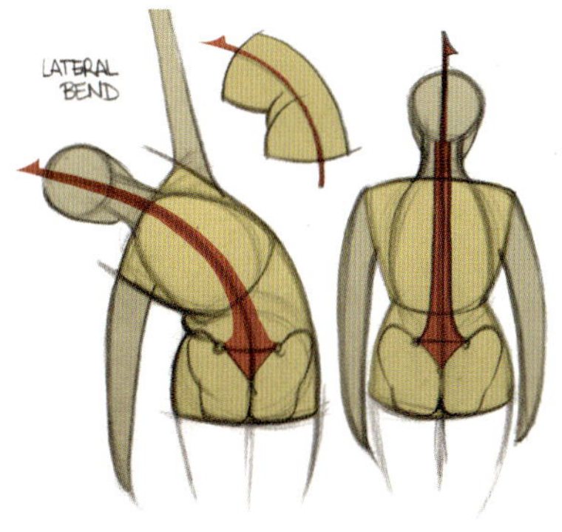

B Torso and core

The trunk or core of the body flexes, extends, and bends to the side. The combination is called rotation or circumduction, which is usually applied to ball joints, but also to the core as each vertebra is a swivel and pivot point.

C Arms, hands, and feet...

The arms, hands, fingers, legs, feet, and toes all have a number of movements available to them: abduction (flexing), adduction (drawing together), flexion (moving toward you), extension (moving away from you), and reference, the natural resting point for the limbs.

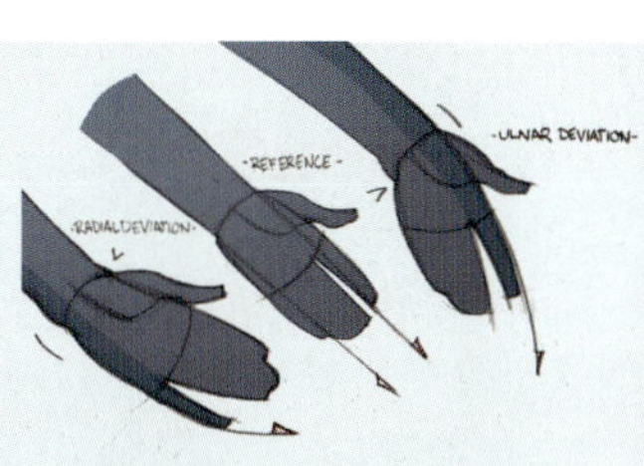

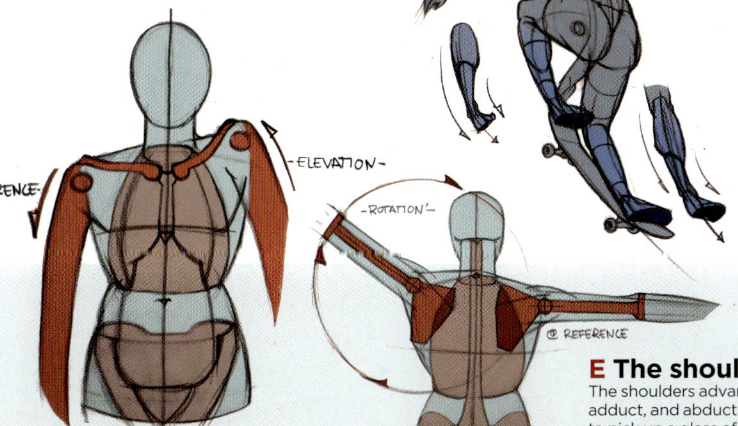

D The foot

The foot inverts and everts. If you skateboard, then you will invert the foot to do an "ollie" while the everting fool brings the rider back to a normal stance. The foot performs dorsiflexion to lift the toes toward the shin, and plantar flexion to point the toes to the floor.

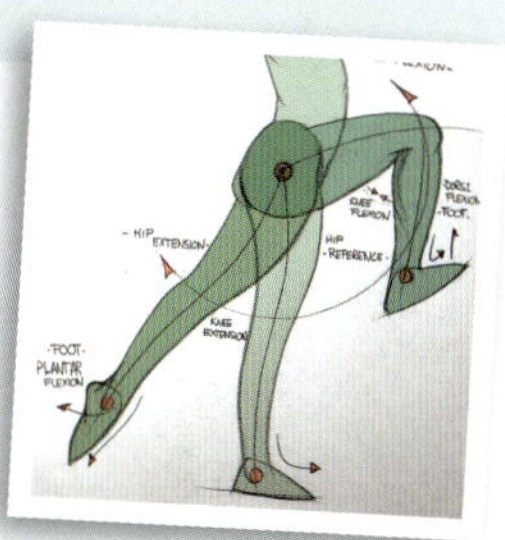

E The shoulders

The shoulders advance, retract, elevate, adduct, and abduct. When the arm is extended to pick up a glass of water, that is advancing. The arm is pulled back to yawn and stretch, and is pulled back and up over the head in a stretch. These actions are retracting. The arms advance and retract according to their forward or backward motion.

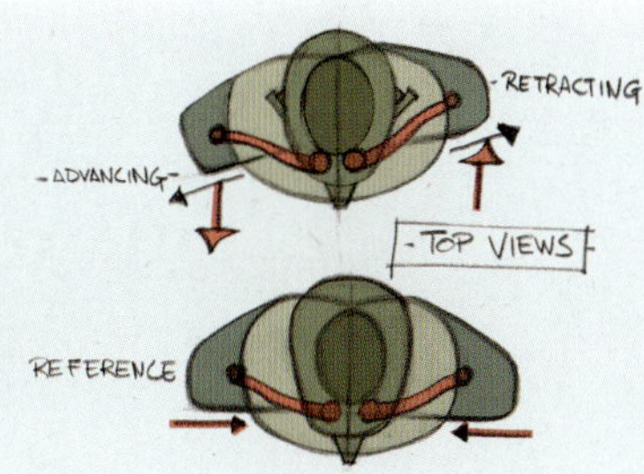

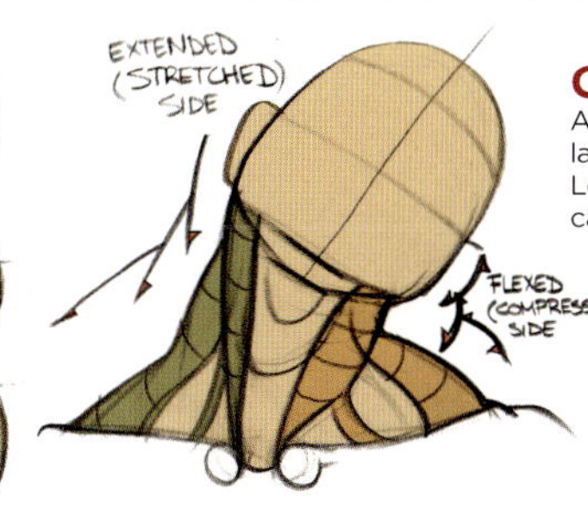

G The neck

Another incredibly flexible part of the body, the neck laterally bends, rotates, flexes, extends, and circumducts. Learning to control the movement of your figure's neck can help convey all manner of emotions.

F Forearms

The forearm's specialized movements are pronation and supination, and rotation of the wrist. The forearm and wrist are flexible parts of the body that can be difficult to capture accurately.

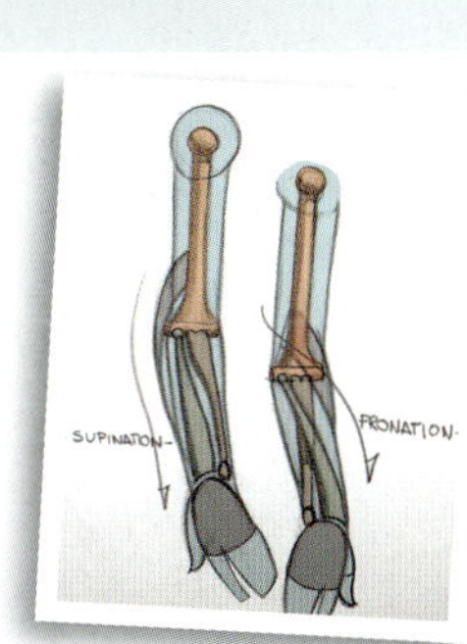

2. UNDERSTANDING ACTION

As with anything that we create from imagination, it is important to first practice it from life. Looking at reality in the first instance helps make a connection with the imagined images we have in our minds. We are attempting to mimic the human machine and its activities driven by emotions, so it is good practice to start with reality as your guide.

There are some useful concepts I keep in mind when inventing figures in action. First, the entire body reacts to the action; there is no part of the body that does not contribute in some way. Since all the different parts of the body are attached to the movement, there should be some rhythm or parallel relationship to the direction of the primary action.

The rhythm lines and points of radiation tie the entire body together through abstraction and implied line design, thus making a much stronger overall pose.

The muscles of the body are woven together rather like a rope, so they will react together to an action, and will also have a spiraling or winding relationship to each other.

"The muscles of the body are woven together rather like a rope, so they will react together to an action."

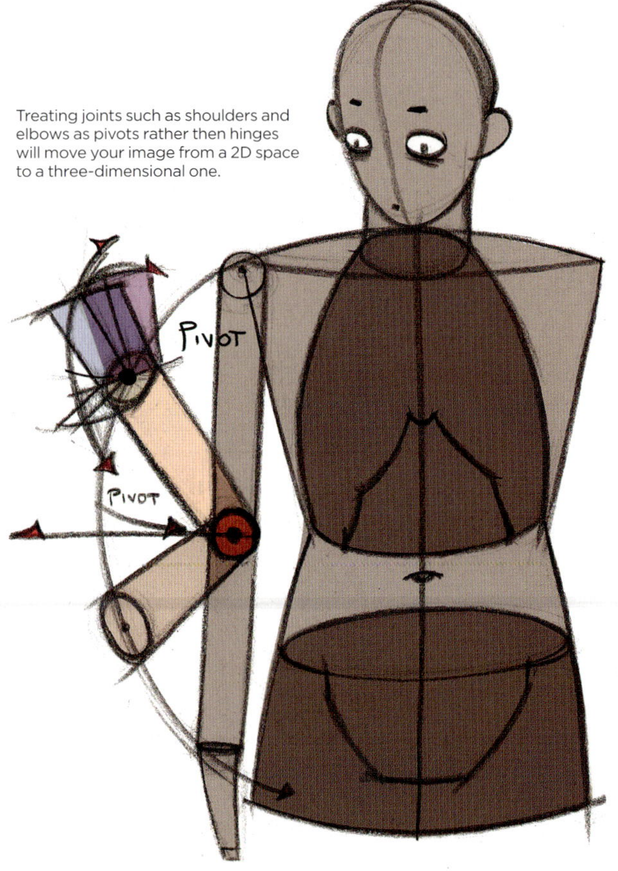

Treating joints such as shoulders and elbows as pivots rather then hinges will move your image from a 2D space to a three-dimensional one.

3. ANIMATION TECHNIQUES

Animation techniques are favored in an attempt to free the mind of the need for reference. Starting with simple shapes helps disconnect the artist from the need to commit to details. Animation practice should be simple and loose, and if you call it animation it will no longer be sketching but something more dynamic in the mind. Change the word and it can change our perception of the task.

PIVOT

4. ANIMATE YOUR FIGURE

Since circumduction is circular, we can use the shoulders, wrists, hips, neck, and spine as pivot points for our animations. Treating them like a hinge inhibits most of the circumduction, and treating them like a swivel allows us a three-dimensional space to move around in. All of these concepts are controlled by drawing arcs from the outermost point of the limb that we are animating around the pivot point. Draw a perfect ellipse, which controls the action very specifically. A perspective exercise will help with this: move a shape in space and observe how the planes relate to each other by volume, distance, and overlap.

"Circumduction is circular, so the shoulders, wrists, hips, neck, and spine can all act as pivot points."

5. GESTURE DRAWING

After trying to animate something mechanically, discard the ellipses and pivots and try to animate using gestural lines and swift C- and S-curves to convey movement. Also consider the options of compression and stretching, or squash and stretch as it is known in animation. This means thinking about how an object can stretch out to support a convincing motion, or squish up into itself to show anticipation or cowardice. All of these devices were used by Rubens, Tiepolo, Michelangelo, and other great masters, and Norman Rockwell is a great contemporary example of how to exaggerate the human expression.

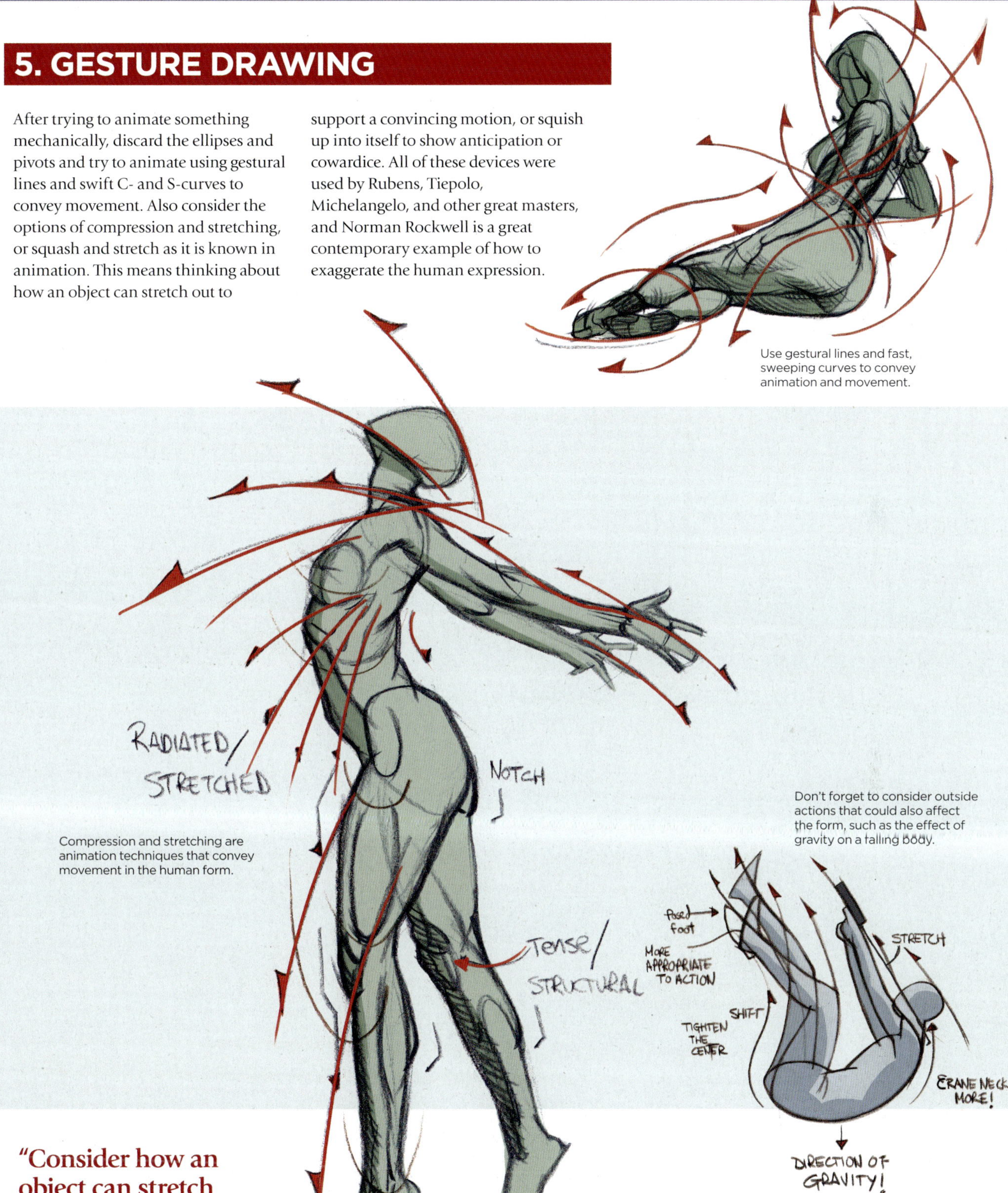

Use gestural lines and fast, sweeping curves to convey animation and movement.

Compression and stretching are animation techniques that convey movement in the human form.

Don't forget to consider outside actions that could also affect the form, such as the effect of gravity on a falling body.

"Consider how an object can stretch out to support a motion, or squish up into itself."

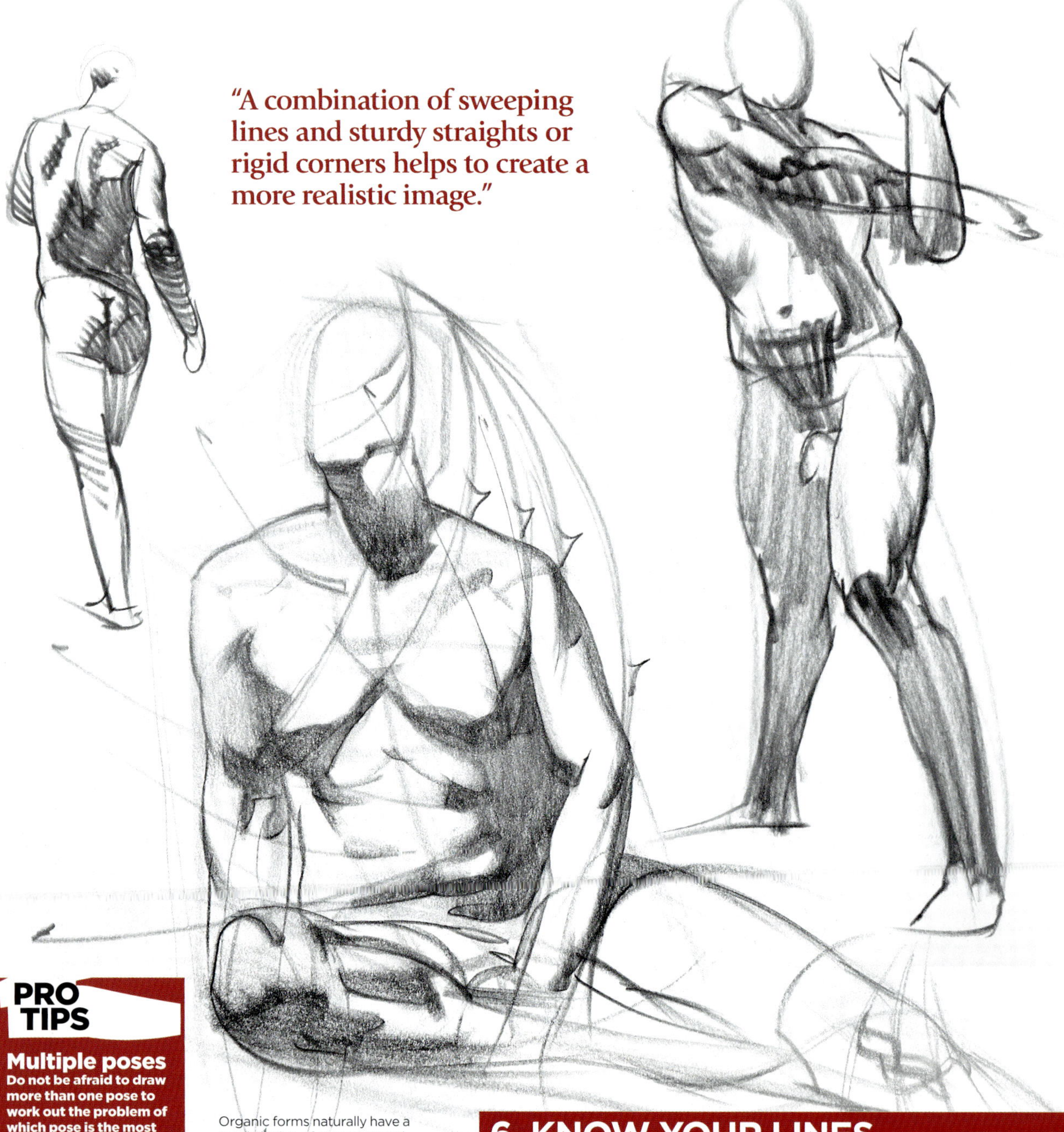

"A combination of sweeping lines and sturdy straights or rigid corners helps to create a more realistic image."

Organic forms naturally have a combination of sweeping and straight lines, and a mix of hard edges and soft, rounded shapes.

PRO TIPS

Multiple poses

Do not be afraid to draw more than one pose to work out the problem of which pose is the most effective for your art. Iterations are important. It's too easy to add more detail than we need to. Think about changing the word "sketch" into "animate" to grasp the idea of movement. You might not want to be an animator, but doesn't the idea of "animating" a pose sound better than drawing it 20 times until you get it right?

6. KNOW YOUR LINES

A combination of sweeping lines and sturdy straights or rigid corners helps to create a more realized, realistic image. In Photoshop, import a Rubens or Michelangelo image and paint over the straights. The image gets very rubbery, very animated, not so realistic looking.

These artists understood how to bring something to life using color, with believable forms, convincing textures, optically correct perspective, and with animation and movement. In fact, these artists can be considered the first animators. If you are wondering how to bring a realistic picture to life and make it animated without lessening the quality of the work, the artists I have mentioned here are worth investigating.

7. ADD MOTION WITH LINES

Another type of rhythm and movement is line movement over and around the forms. I have included many examples here done in charcoal, all five-minute sketches. Each is a different attempt at getting a pose that can often feel static and bringing it to life, or adding excitement to something that we do not see as active. These images are not made up, they are inspired by live models.

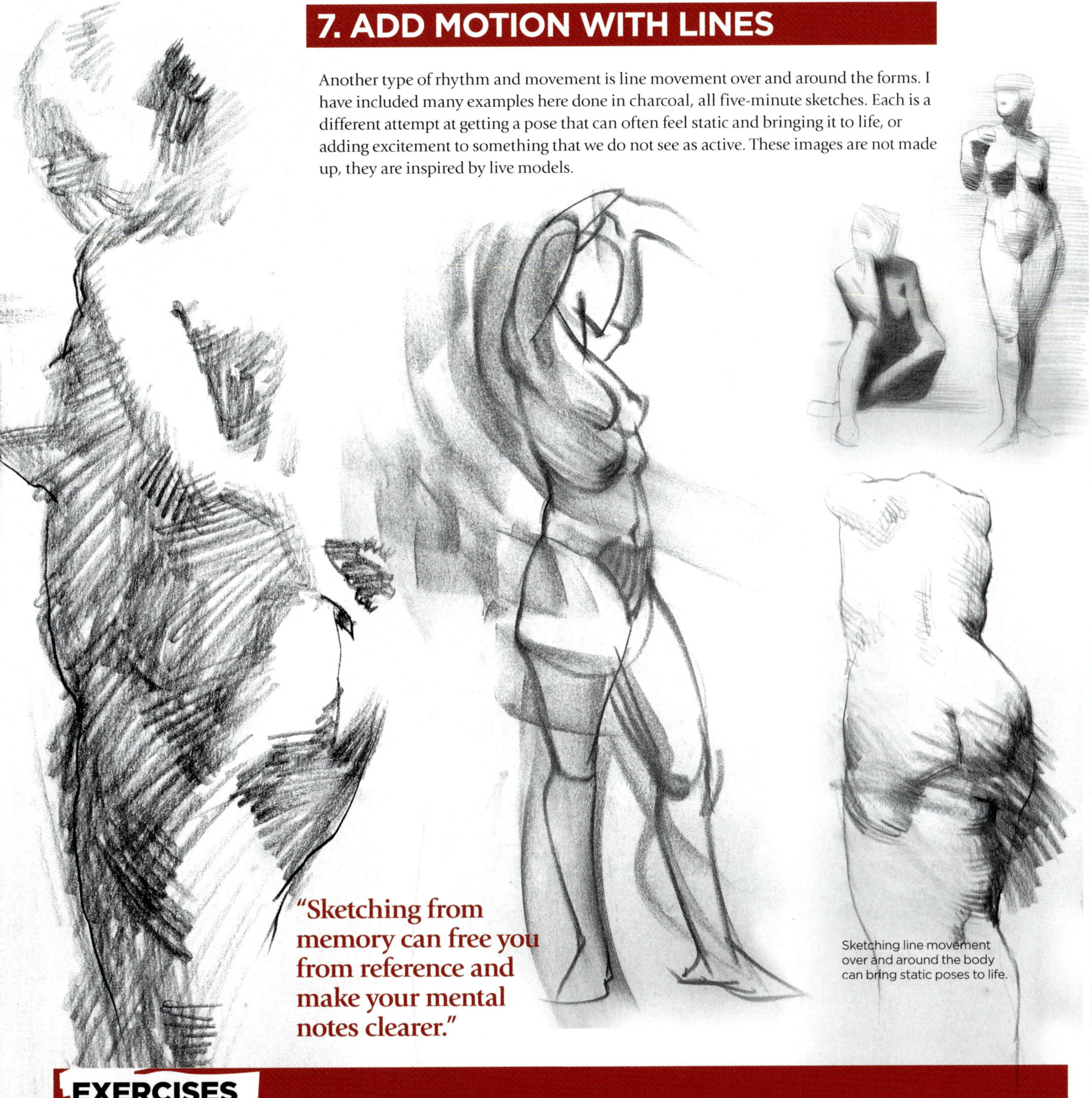

"Sketching from memory can free you from reference and make your mental notes clearer."

Sketching line movement over and around the body can bring static poses to life.

EXERCISES

1 Stretch your mental muscles. Watching a video, capture a pose in your mind then look down and draw it. To check the pose, rewind the video and watch again, freezing it on the moment you were attempting to capture. This is a form of memory sketching. By doing this from active motion, we can confidently go out into the real world and do the same thing with the people around us. Mental sketching can free you up from reference; it can also make your mental notes so much clearer, and make them available for future projects – not just the one you are working on now.

2 If you have access to a life drawing class, try these exercises. Set up your easel so you are standing with your back to the model; or you can set up your pad in another room entirely. Take in as much information as you can, then go and draw without looking back. This is another way of exercising memory. The time between viewing and drawing when facing the model is very short, and we do not notice that we are working from memory. When you stretch out that time, you are flexing your mental muscles, which will sharpen your photographic memory. This is an extremely valuable exercise.

Animal anatomy

How to draw animal forms and structures and then apply it to imaginary creatures

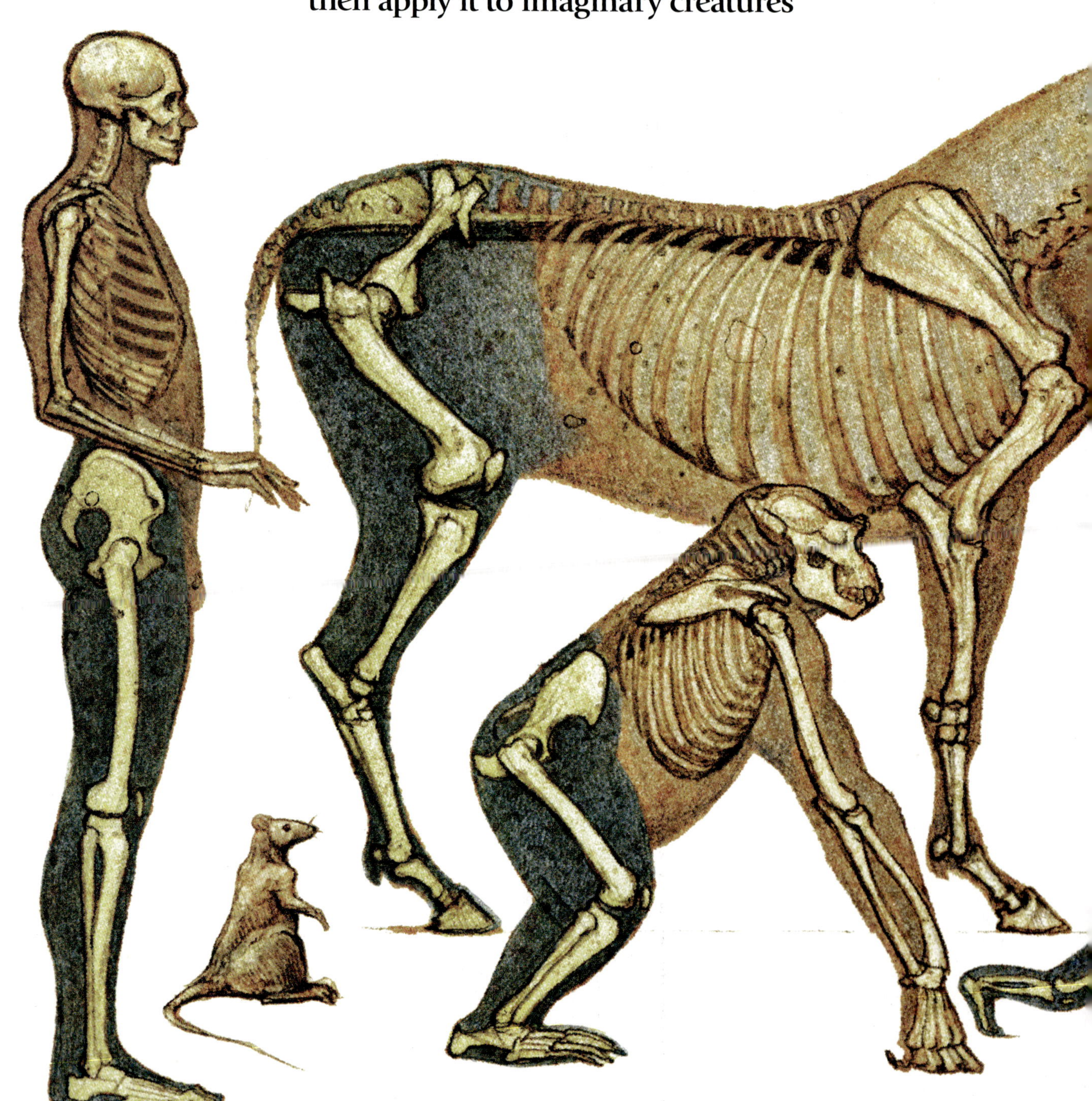

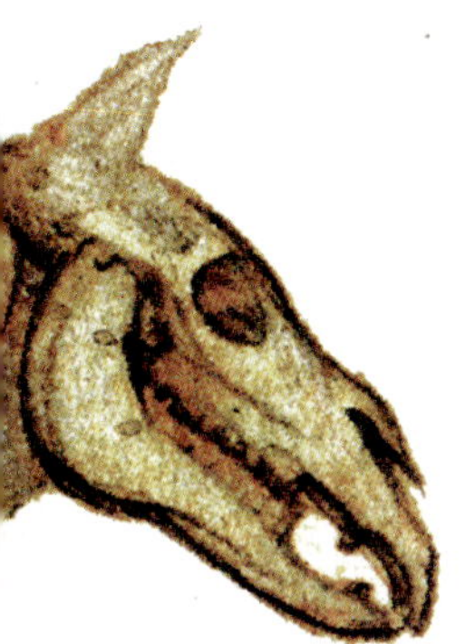

Workshops

How to draw the anatomy of animals

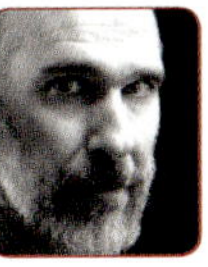

"Sometimes a human face inspires an animal – a monkey, mouse, or a kitten… after all, what is a child but a talking animal."
(Marshall Vandruff, page 140)

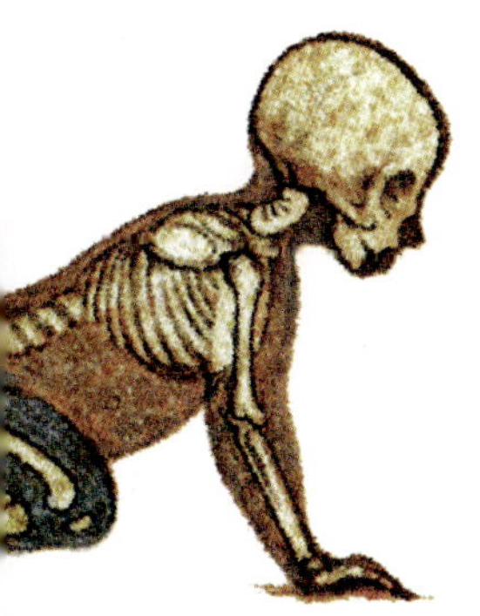

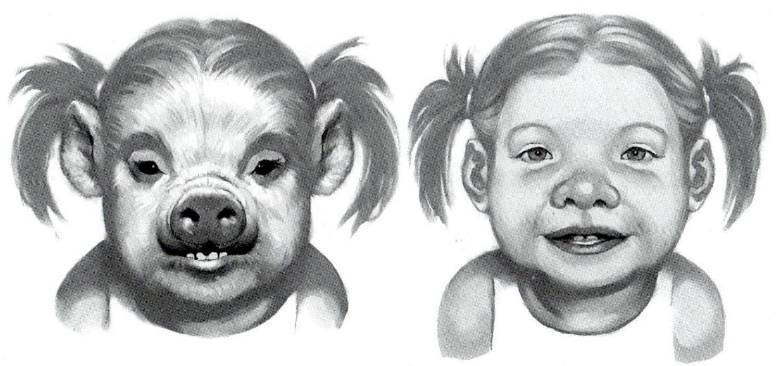

BASIC FORMS

Begin your exploration of creature anatomy by seeing the shapes beneath the skin and fur

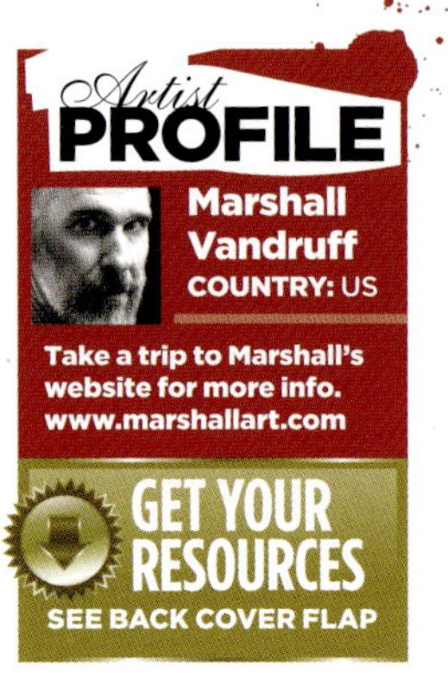

Animals are something I love to draw, especially from imagination. For years I had no idea how animators, comic-book artists, and old masters could not only draw animals without copying what they saw, but actually make animals look thicker, stronger, funnier, and more alive than anything they could see. Then I learned that there are secrets to animal anatomy – old secrets, well-known to a few. These workshops reveal the secrets of inventing animals. Whether you draw, paint, sculpt, model, or animate, basic knowledge of anatomy and form will enable you to get your ideas into images. When you can create any animal you see in your mind's eye, that's mastery.

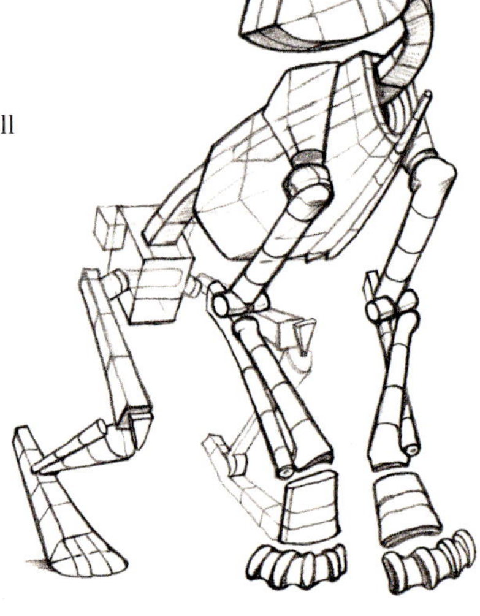

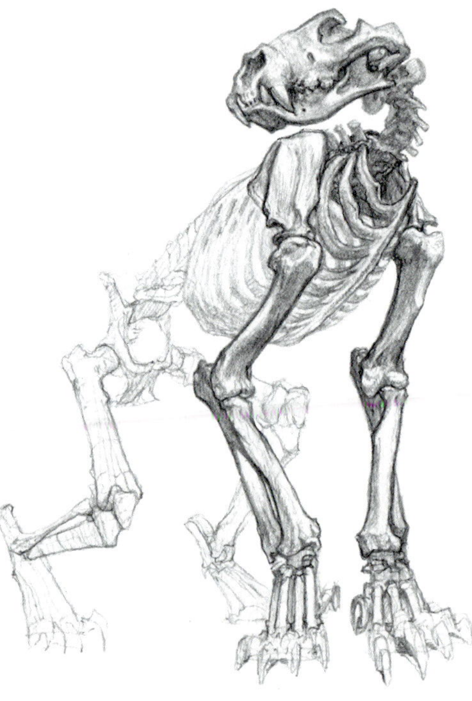

I drew the skeleton from real American Lion bones at the Page Museum in Los Angeles. The form analysis (right) is an exercise in applying perspective to anatomy. The pencil rendering of the head is a speculation of how the fleshed creature may have looked.

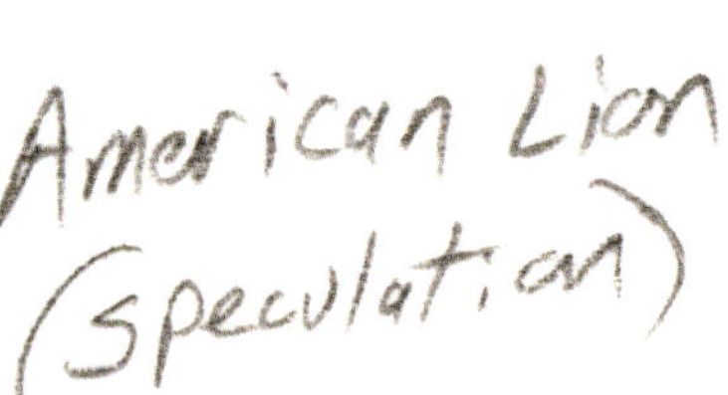

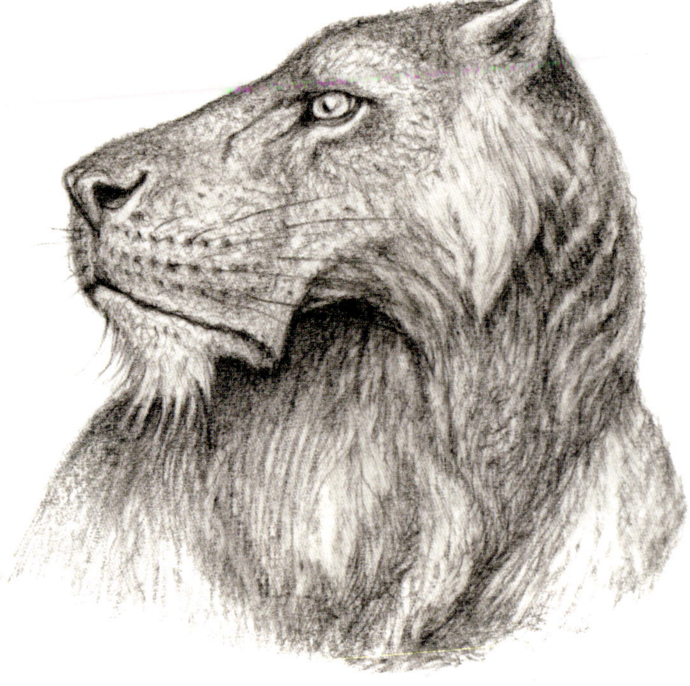

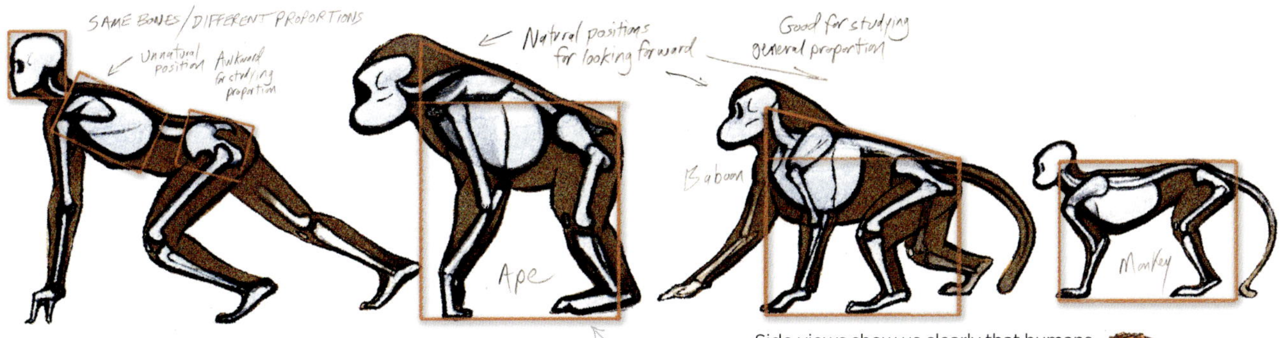

Side views show us clearly that humans aren't made to crouch. Apes can rest on their knuckles and look forward.

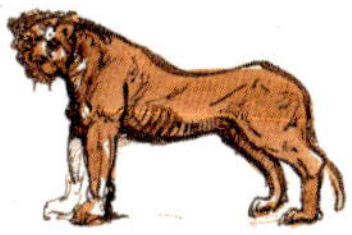

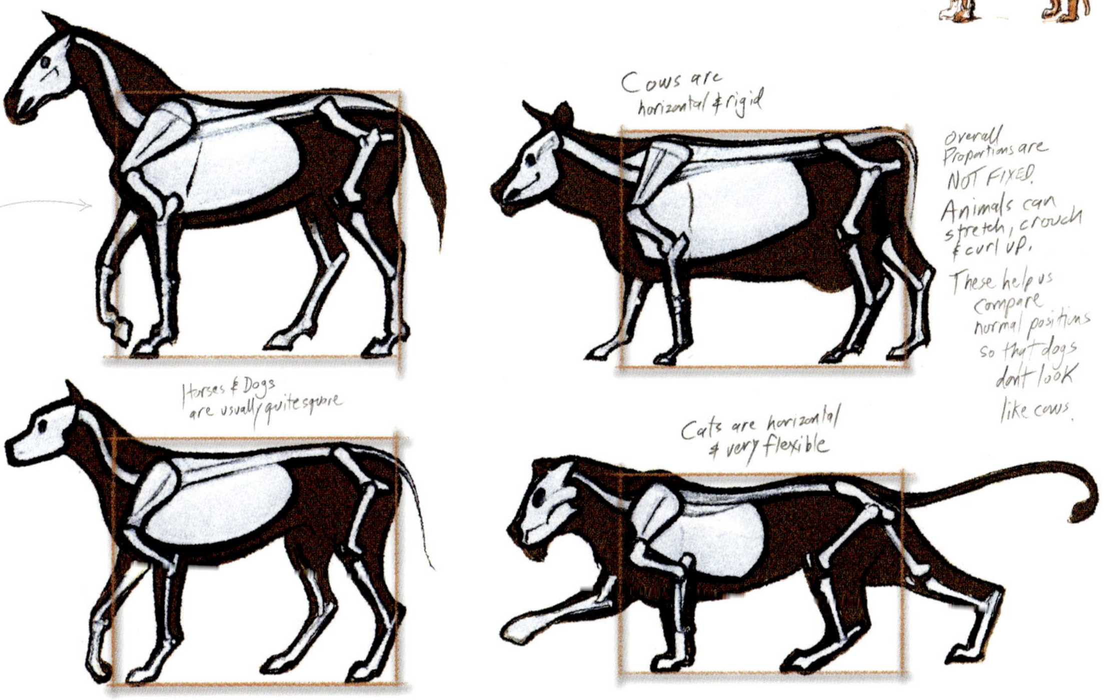

Boxes simplify the whole beast – a good way to study proportions. Compare the boxes, and you can see that some animals, like horses and dogs, are quite similar. When we see basic shapes, we see subtle differences.

1. PROPORTIONS

UNDERSTANDING THE SIMILARITIES AND DIFFERENCES WITHIN BONE GROUPS CAN LEAD TO GREATER ANATOMICAL AWARENESS...

Mammals, reptiles, and birds share most of the same bones and muscles, but at different sizes and ratios. That's why you should study proportion. When you look at two-legged beasts (bipeds) like humans, or other plantigrades that plant feet on the ground, you can begin with front views. But creatures who run around on four legs (quadrupeds) don't take to being studied from the front. It's like trying to judge the length of a ship by looking down one end.

Proportions reveal what an animal does. Our bones show that people are designed to stand up: we have long legs, shallow rib cages, shoulder blades on our backs, and arms that are good for playing instruments, drawing, and hugging, but not made to support our weight. Four-legged animals have deep rib cages with shoulder blades on the sides, and arms that act as legs. Different functions, different forms.

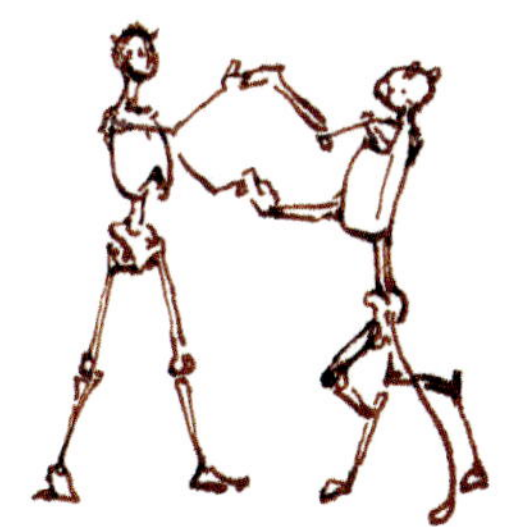

HOMEWORK ASSIGNMENT

Master proportion

Diagram an animal from the side. Measure a box that fits the big parts of the torso: this trains you to see big things first. By reducing heads, hind legs, and rib cages into boxes, triangles, and eggs, you learn to see complex components as simple shapes. That's the underlying secret to mastering proportion.

2. BONES AS FOUNDATION

BONES DON'T BEND OR STRETCH – THEY STAY AS CONSTANT AS ROCK, SO STUDY THEM FIRST...

Overcomplicated anatomical charts full of ribs and gnarls can confuse the more delicate learner students. The diagrams below leave out the more exacting details and hidden bumps, and simplify the hard-surface architecture that artists can use.

There's plenty of time to get into the details later.

For now, compare the color coding on the diagrams to see the analogies between human and animal bones. They are often quite striking.

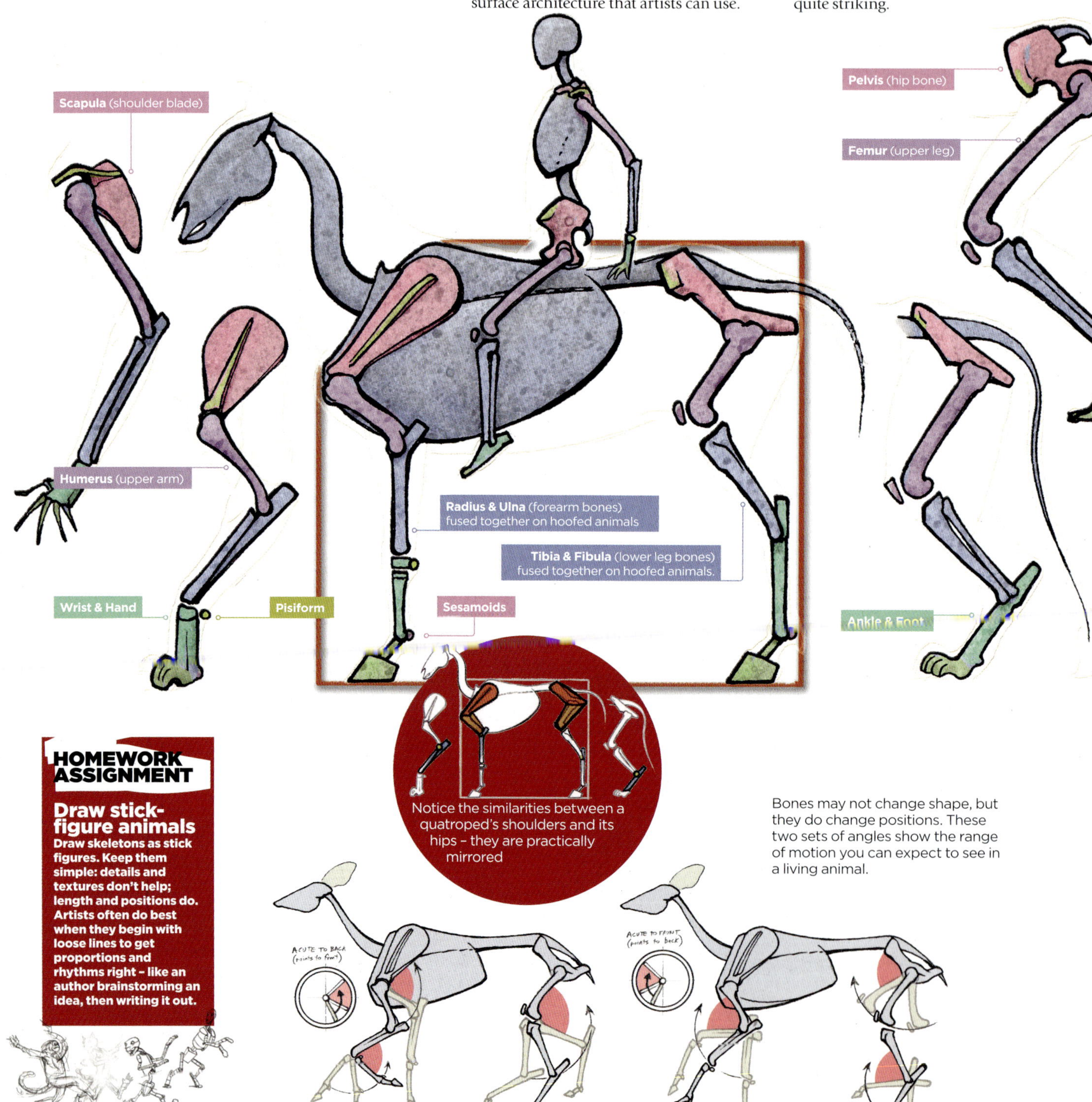

Notice the similarities between a quatroped's shoulders and its hips – they are practically mirrored

Bones may not change shape, but they do change positions. These two sets of angles show the range of motion you can expect to see in a living animal.

HOMEWORK ASSIGNMENT

Draw stick-figure animals

Draw skeletons as stick figures. Keep them simple: details and textures don't help; length and positions do. Artists often do best when they begin with loose lines to get proportions and rhythms right – like an author brainstorming an idea, then writing it out.

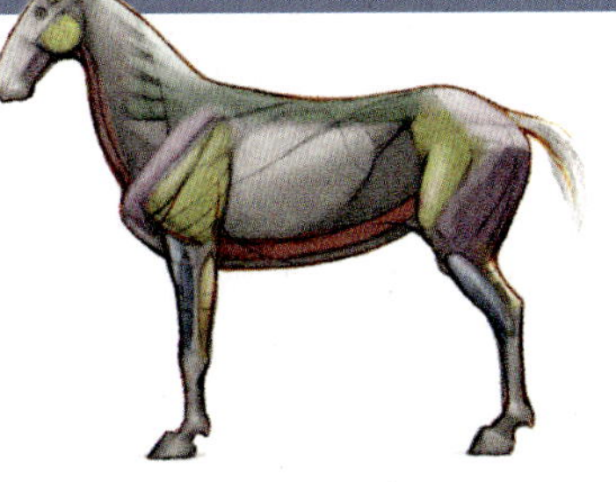

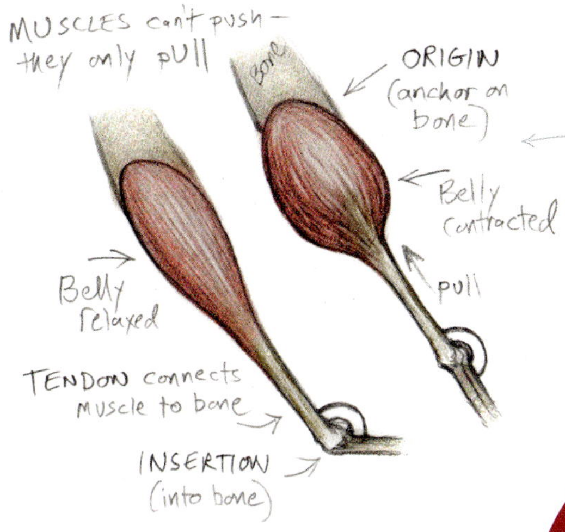

MUSCLES can't push – they only pull

ORIGIN (anchor on bone)

Belly contracted

Muscles change shape, like rubber bands. They pull on the bones.

Belly relaxed

TENDON connects muscle to bone

INSERTION (into bone)

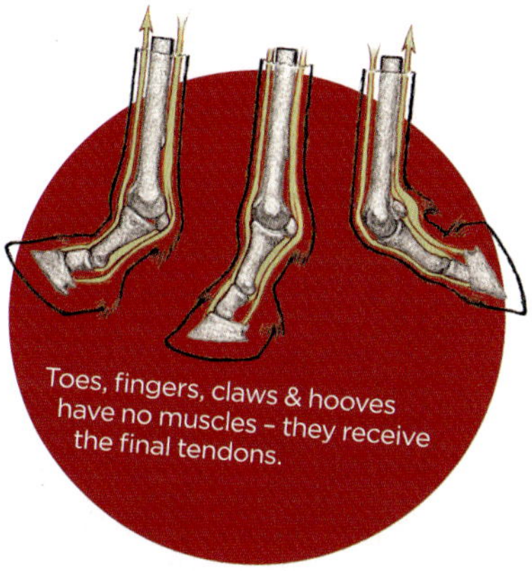

Toes, fingers, claws & hooves have no muscles – they receive the final tendons.

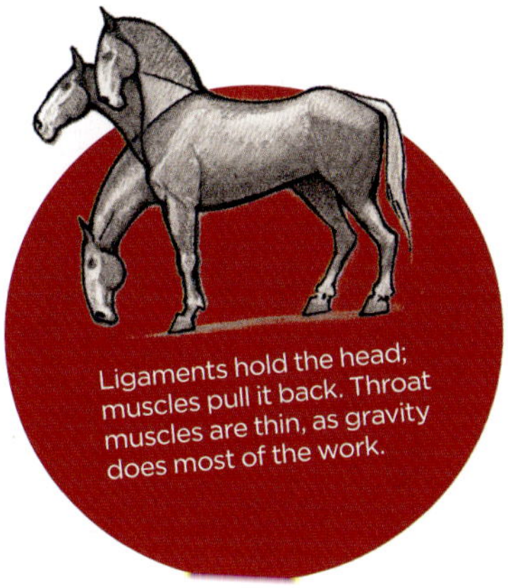

Ligaments hold the head; muscles pull it back. Throat muscles are thin, as gravity does most of the work.

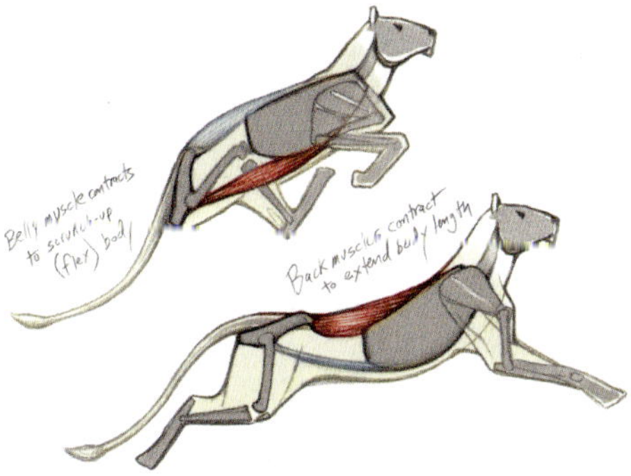

Belly muscle contracts to scrunch-up (flex) body

Back muscles contract to extend body length

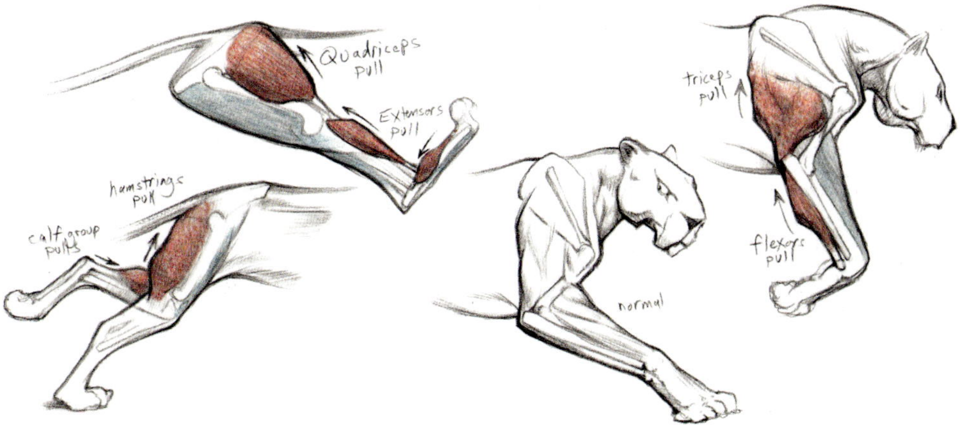

Quadriceps pull

Extensors pull

hamstrings pull

calf group pulls

triceps pull

flexors pull

normal

3. MUSCLES & TENDONS

HOW THEY ATTACH, AND HOW THEY RELATE TO EACH OTHER...

Muscle charts are more confusing than bone charts – not just because there are more muscles, but because muscles are layered. Surface muscles can be so thin that they disappear on a fleshed creature, while buried-deep muscles can show as large bumps on the surface.

Let's start proceedings with some general observations:

- Muscles anchor close to the trunk (proximally), and insert distant from the trunk (distally) to move the limbs.
- Muscles are thick near the trunk, lean as they move away. On hoofed animals, the distal limbs look like shrink-wrapped bones.
- Muscles can be simplified by grouping them. Several extensors with hard-to-remember Latin names can make a single easy-to-remember egg shape.
- Muscles work in pairs that pull against each other, shown in the illustrations using complementary colors.

We'll study specifics later. First, look at these images to see how they work.

4. FORESHORTENING

HOW TO KEEP PROPORTIONS CORRECT WHEN DRAWING ANIMALS FROM DIFFERENT ANGLES...

The longest measurement of anything – a bone, a limb, or an entire animal – is its major axis. When you look along something, its length appears to collapse until you can't tell how long it is. Artists keep track of this so that they can tip, swivel, and roll objects around yet keep them looking true.

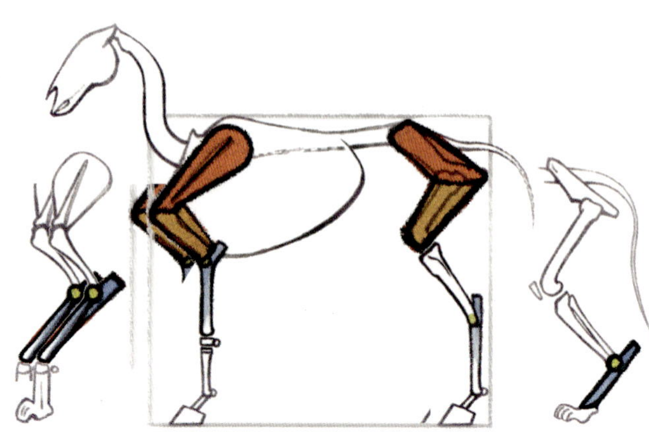

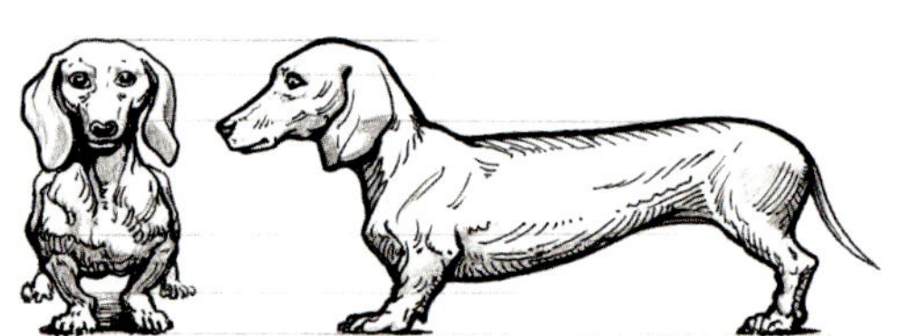

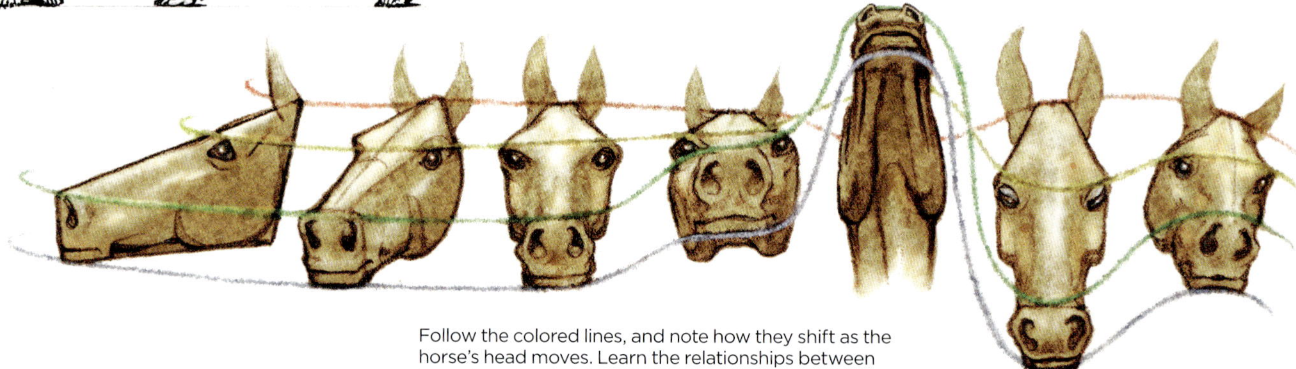

Follow the colored lines, and note how they shift as the horse's head moves. Learn the relationships between these lines, and proportions will come easier to you.

The secret to foreshortening is to reduce complex forms to simple ones, like blocks and cylinders.

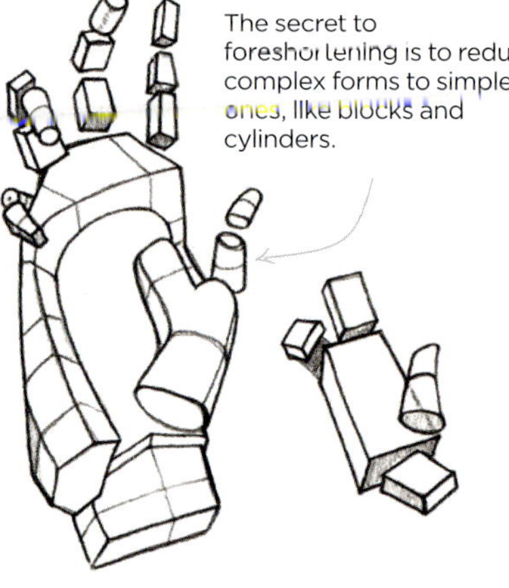

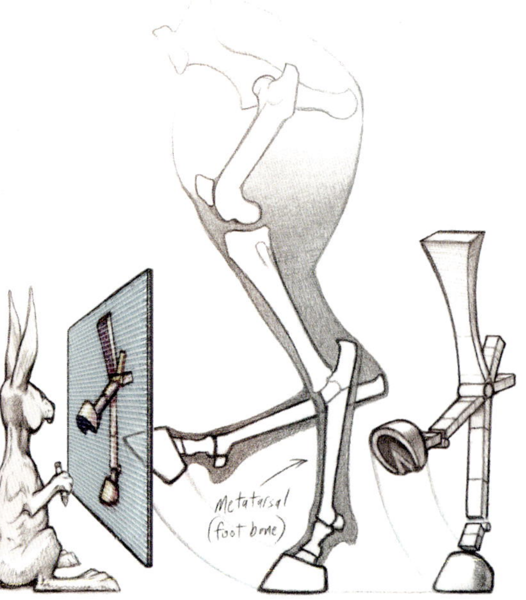

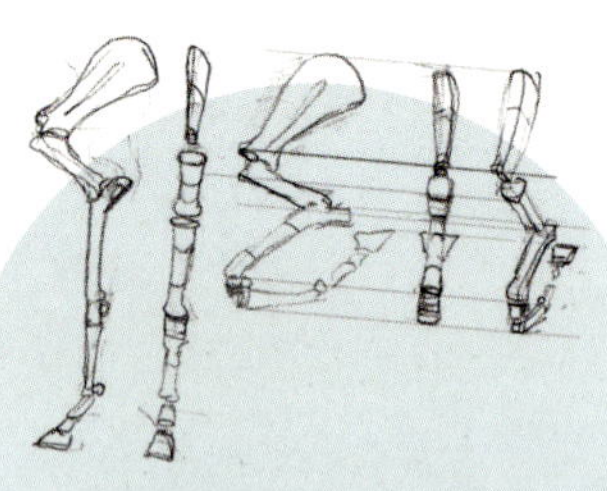

Learning the fundamentals of foreshortenening is vital to creating dynamic animal images.

The length of the metatarsal appears to shorten when it comes forward. That's foreshortening. Beginners fear it. Serious students work on it. Masters practice it to ease.

HOMEWORK ASSIGNMENT

Learn from the rabbit

Look at a side view of an animal. Now draw it as if swivelled into a three-quarter foreshortened position. It's difficult, but not impossible. Remember to reduce complex forms to simple ones to help you visualize the perspective.

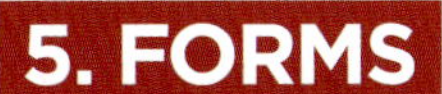

5. FORMS

SIMPLIFY ANIMAL ANATOMY INTO BASIC STRUCTURES…

Mastering classic animal drawing enables you to invent as well as observe. The secret is to learn simple forms – cylinders, blocks, and spheres that are based on anatomy – then assemble them into complex beasts. After all, what are animals but 3D creatures in a 3D world? You can build them from 3D forms – any way you like!

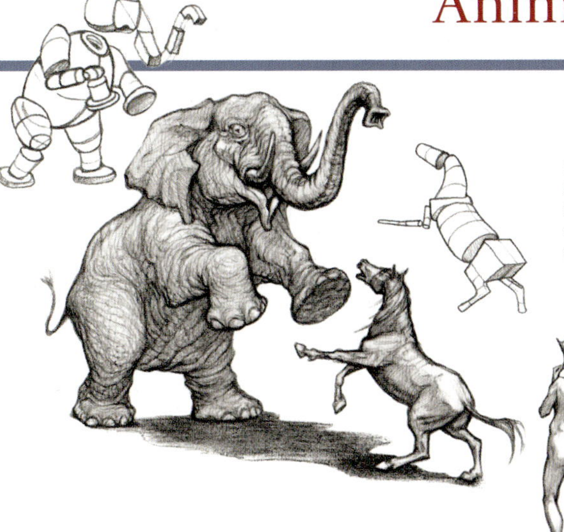

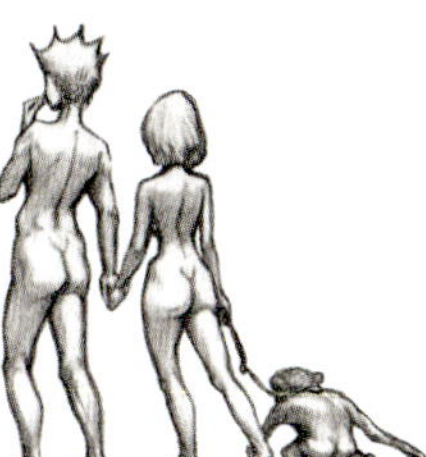

Once you understand the relationship between the shapes and proportions of an animal, you can begin to flesh them out into dynamic and realistic creatures.

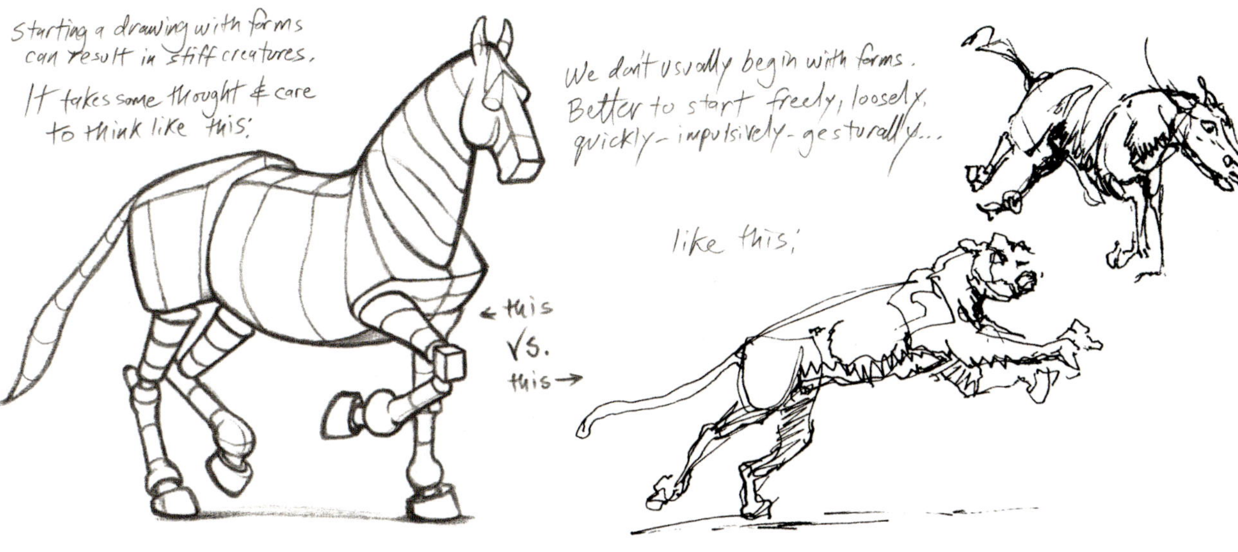

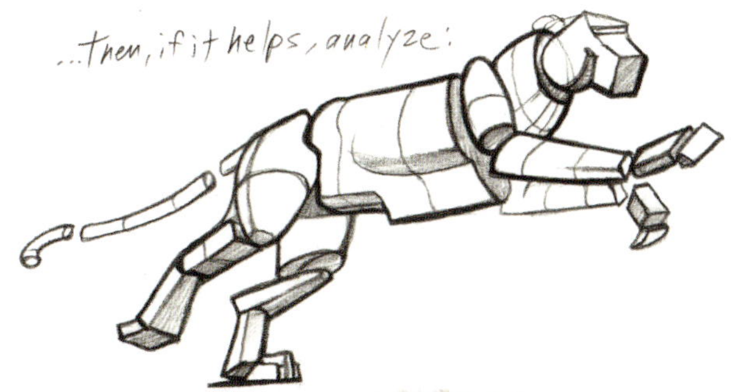

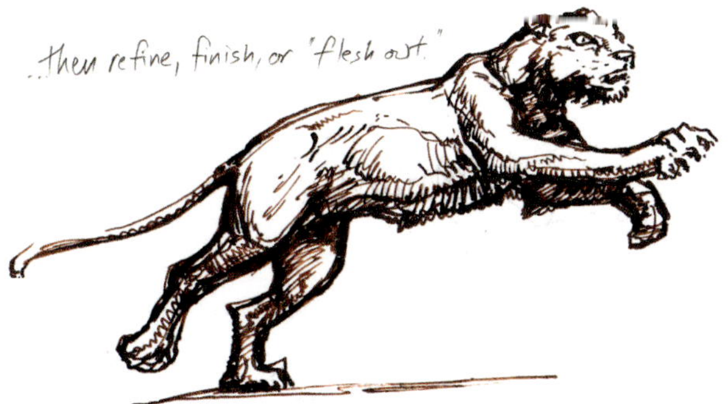

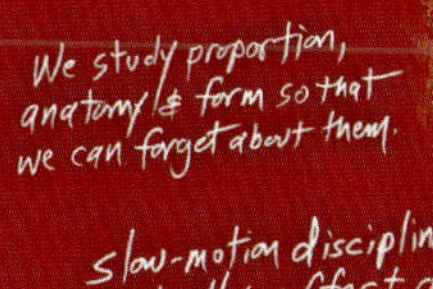

Slow-motion disciplines eventually affect our fastest scribbles.

Artists arrange couplings.

Chaos & Order
Energy & Skill
Wildness & Control

FUSION TOWARD MASTERY

THE ANIMAL TORSO

Find out how the core of the animal body operates and how you can use it to bring life to your animal artwork

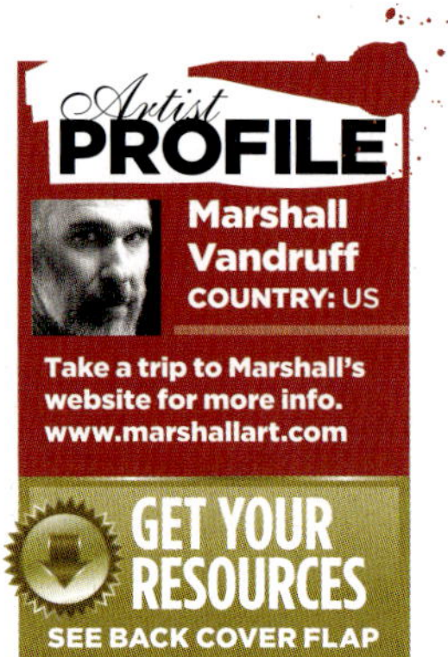
Artist PROFILE
Marshall Vandruff
COUNTRY: US
Take a trip to Marshall's website for more info.
www.marshallart.com

GET YOUR RESOURCES
SEE BACK COVER FLAP

When I first saw a famous art teacher's approach to figure drawing – human torsos with no limbs, strange-looking bean-bodies twisted and floating – it baffled me. It took me years to understand the value of that approach.

There are several sound ways to draw the figure, but beginning with a solid torso is a good one that's shared by Michelangelo, Rubens, Tintoretto and scores of other masters. It puts the big parts of anatomy first – which is the best place to start. This approach should be applied not only to human figures, but to animals. They have torsos much like ours, but are different in ways that enable them to run faster, jump higher, kick harder, and have trouble standing up or sitting in chairs. Here, I approach them simply, naming the basic parts, helping you to learn their structure and understand their functions. In later lessons, I'll get to the limbs, but let's begin with the big parts.

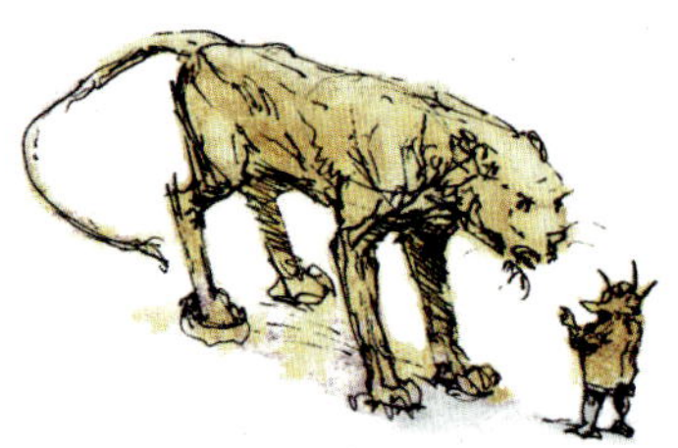

Just as 3D programs need three views to invent, so do artists. You'll understand anatomy best by drawing from different views, looking along, up, and down at an animal.

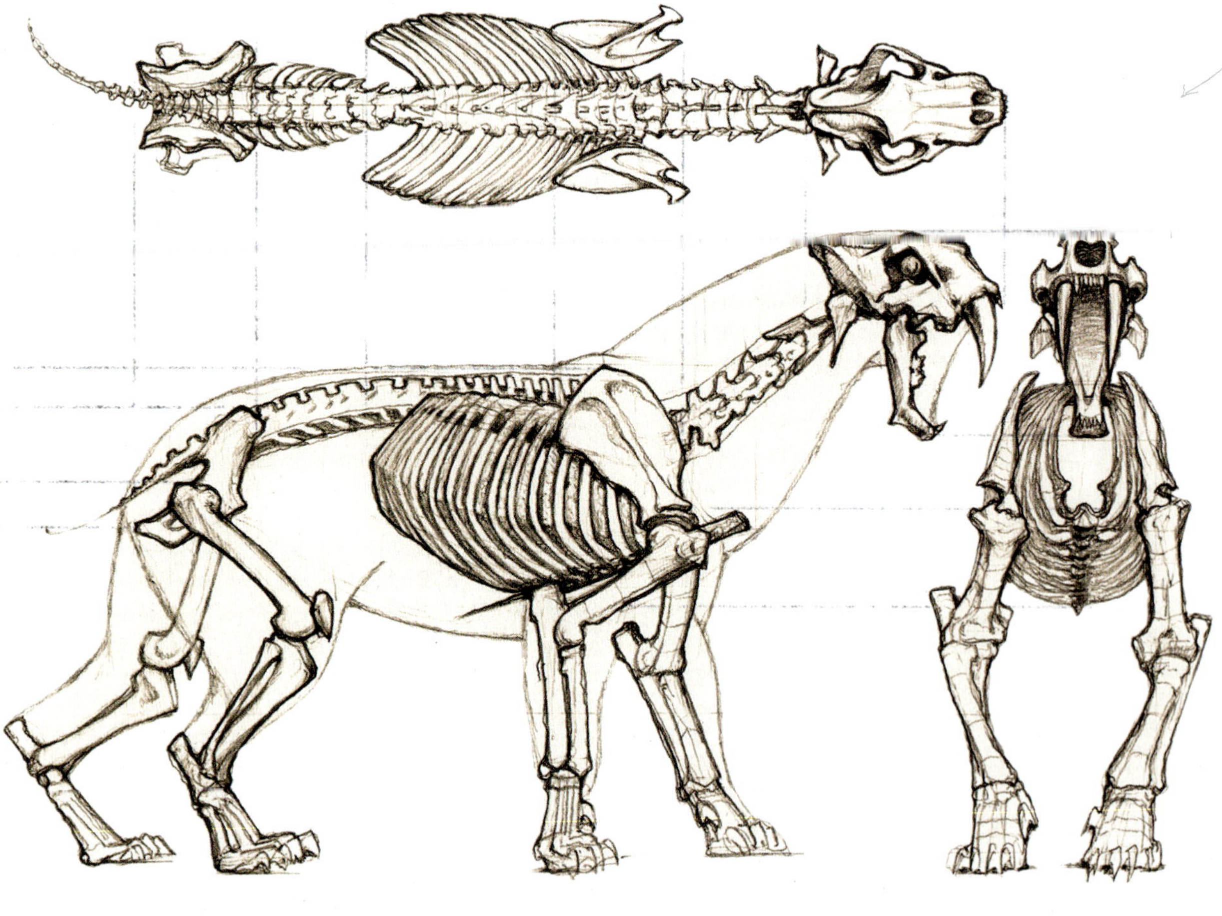

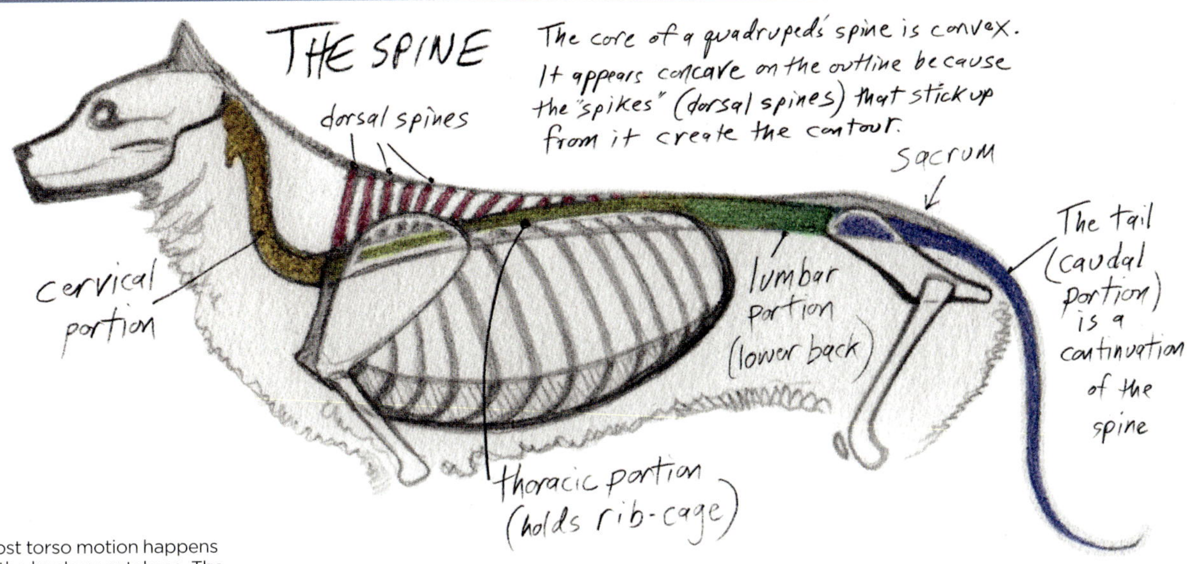

Most torso motion happens in the lumbar vertebrae. The pelvis is a solid form, the rib cage almost so, but it expands for breathing.

1. TORSO BONES

START WITH THE CORE OF THE BODY: THE RIB CAGE AND PELVIS, AND THE SPINE THAT CONNECTS THEM...

Vertebrate animals grow out from the spine, which runs from the base of the head to the tail, connecting the rib cage (thorax) and pelvis (hip bone). Study these parts generally: ignore the little bumps on the pelvis that are mostly hidden and the individual ribs that do you no good until you've established the simplified rib cage. Here are some observations about animal torsos to set you off.

Human thoraxes are proportionally wider than other animals

Sternum on chest is flat unless an animal needs to anchor large pectoral muscles to pull down its arms

Horse has a "Keel" sternum like a boat

Birds have huge sternums for pectorals big enough to pull wings down and propel bird up.

HOMEWORK ASSIGNMENT

See the spine

Draw a series of animals with a single line – the spine. It's easiest from the side view, but don't forget to see the convexity of the curve – and don't expect it to impress anyone. It's an exercise to develop the X-ray vision of artists who know anatomy. When it gets easy, make it tougher by adding the rib cage and pelvis.

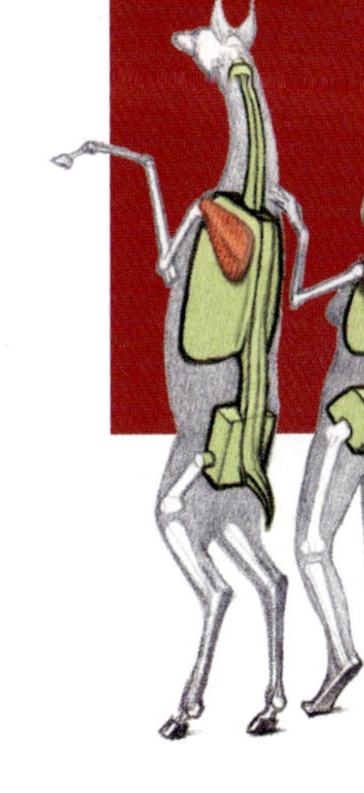

2. TORSO MUSCLES

BONES DON'T MOVE UNDER THEIR OWN POWER – THEY MOVE BY THE TENSION OF HIDDEN CORDS...

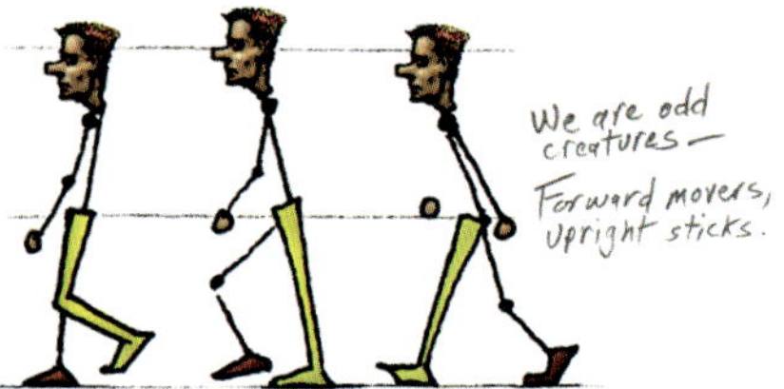

We have muscles in our backs, bellies, and haunches to hold us upright. Four-legged animals have the same muscles, but in different proportions and for different reasons. They are made to move forward more efficiently than we are.

Torso muscles include thin layers that don't show on the surface. I'll focus here on the core functional set of three.

Straight muscles, like those on the back and belly, simply pull to straighten or bend the torso. But spiral or oblique muscles, like those on the side, pull to spin or twist the torso, allowing it to lean and turn. These muscles can barely be seen on a fleshed animal, but study them to know what goes on under the surface, so you can exaggerate convincingly.

Unlike bones, muscles change shape. Think of them as rubber straps. They either stretch and get thinner, or squash and get thicker.

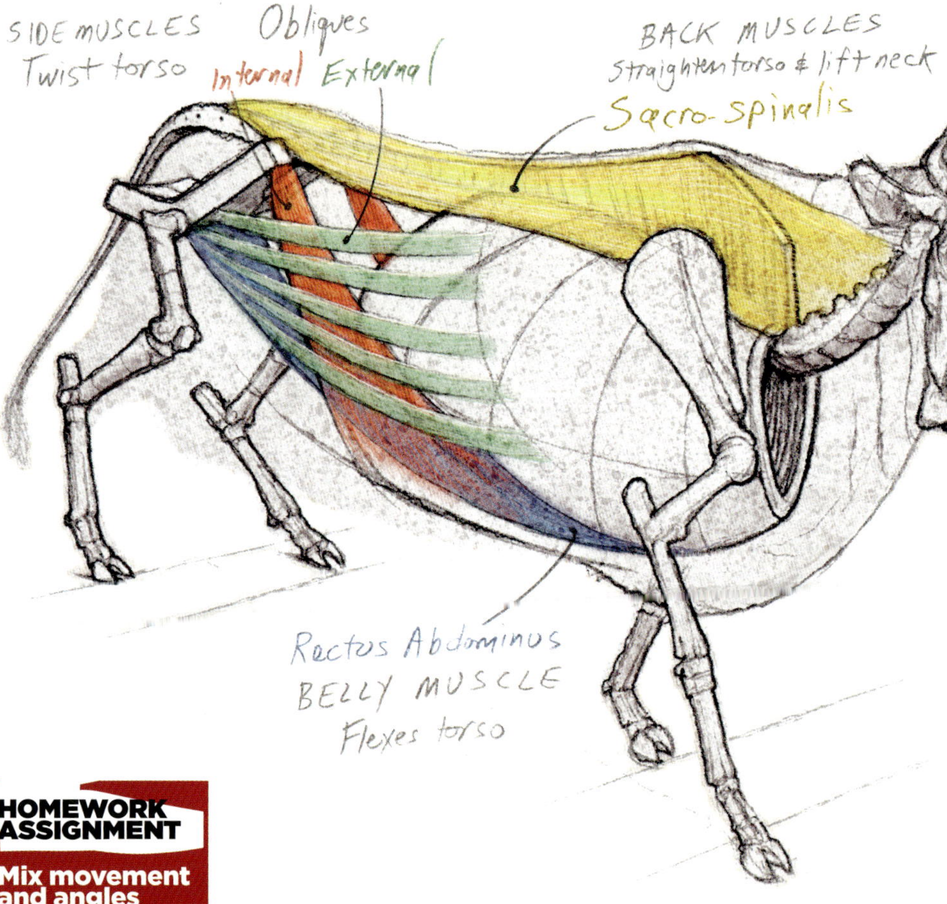

SIDE MUSCLES
Twist torso
Obliques
Internal External
BACK MUSCLES
Straighten torso & lift neck
Sacro-spinalis
Rectus Abdominus
BELLY MUSCLE
Flexes torso

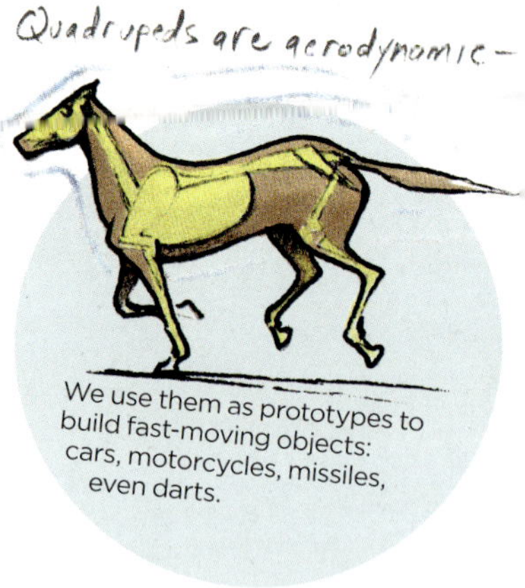

Quadrupeds are aerodynamic –

We use them as prototypes to build fast-moving objects: cars, motorcycles, missiles, even darts.

HOMEWORK ASSIGNMENT

Mix movement and angles

Try drawing variations of the pitch, yaw, and roll motion diagrams from different angles: above, at eye-level, below, and in various foreshortened positions. If you use photo reference, see if you can catch glimpses of the torso muscles at work. They're subtle andusually covered with fur, but they ccasionally show up in extremely well-cut short-haired animals, like racehorses.

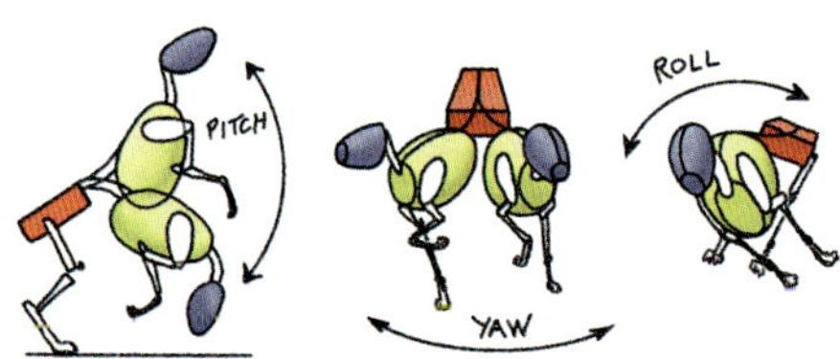

PITCH, YAW & ROLL

As animals travel, they adjust their movement in the same three ways as airplanes. Pitching describes the forward and back movement – the back and belly muscles are at work. Yaw means heading to the left or right — muscles on one side pull the torso toward that side. Rolling occurs when muscles on each side pull to twist the rib cage.

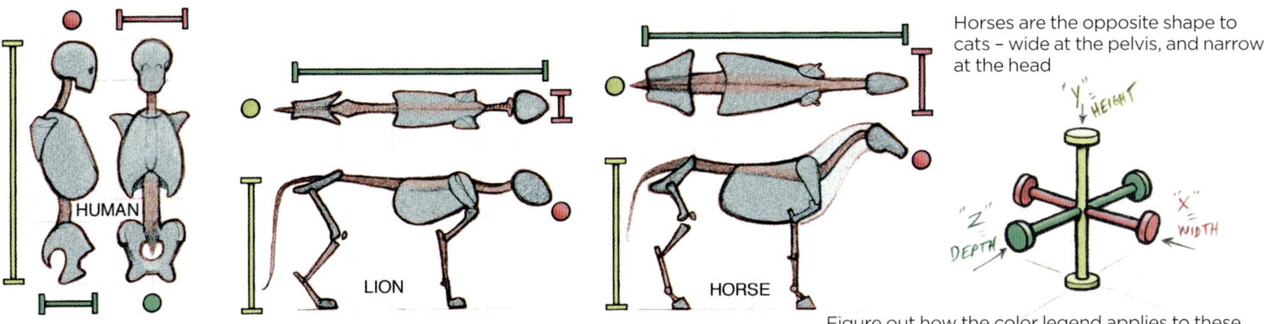

Horses are the opposite shape to cats – wide at the pelvis, and narrow at the head

Figure out how the color legend applies to these illustrations and you'll understand the foundation for making anatomy three-dimensional.

3. TORSO FORMS

UNDERSTANDING MULTIPLE VIEWS AND BUILDING FROM SIMPLE COMPONENTS...

Studying side views isn't enough – they only give us two dimensions of a three-dimensional animal. We need another view to see width measurements, as witnessed in the examples above.

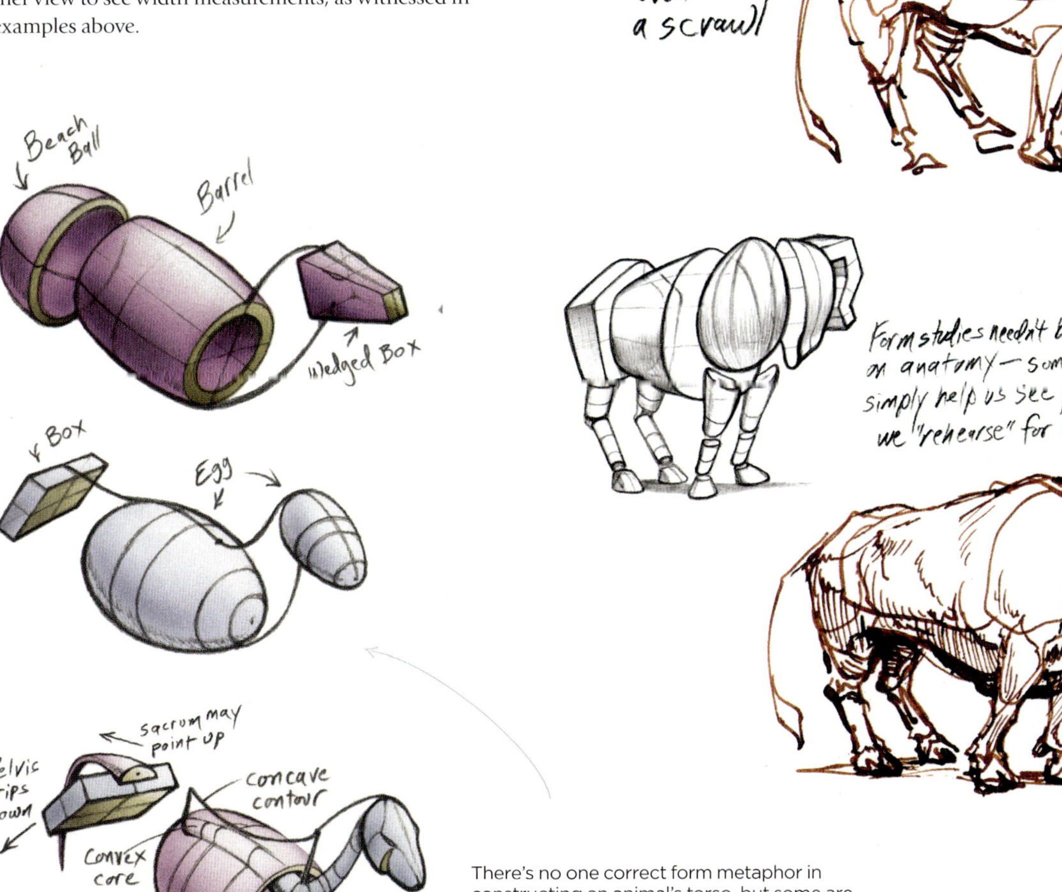

There's no one correct form metaphor in constructing an animal's torso, but some are more useful than others. Use whatever forms you need to create their structures and place our points-of-view. Choose what works for you, however strange it may appear.

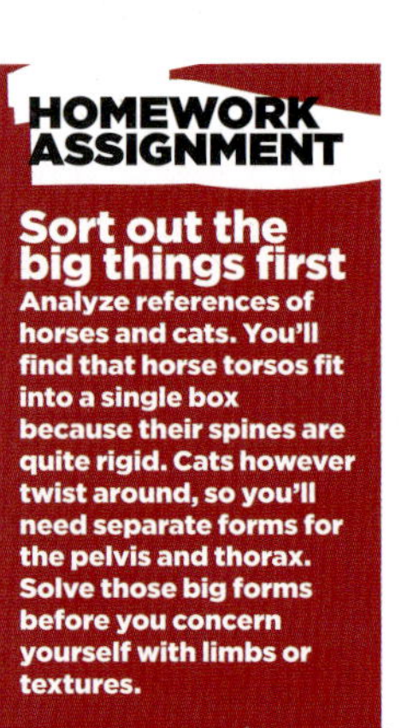

HOMEWORK ASSIGNMENT

Sort out the big things first

Analyze references of horses and cats. You'll find that horse torsos fit into a single box because their spines are quite rigid. Cats however twist around, so you'll need separate forms for the pelvis and thorax. Solve those big forms before you concern yourself with limbs or textures.

4. MORE TORSO FORMS TO TRY

LEARN TO DRAW THE COMPLICATED THINGS BY MAKING THEM SIMPLE...

Look for the basic structure that simplifies bone and muscle into a single form. It can be a big bean from which appendages emerge, or any invented form that helps you twist or add body to the spine.

The important thing to remember is that torsos are complex, so you must simplify them enough so that they can be drawn in any position you care to choose.

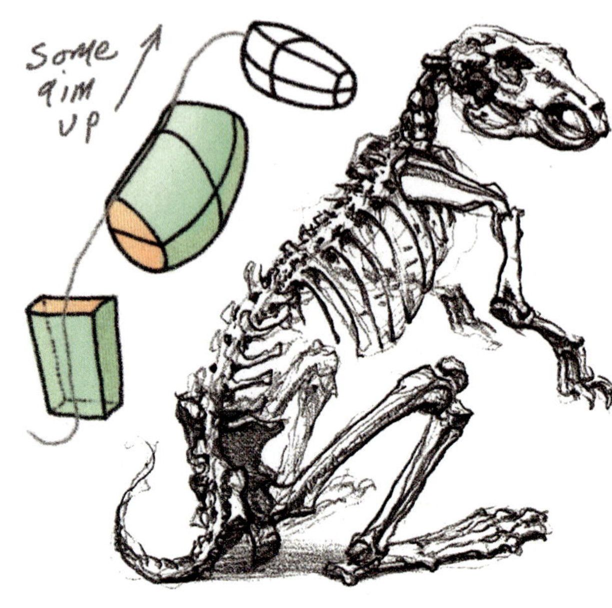

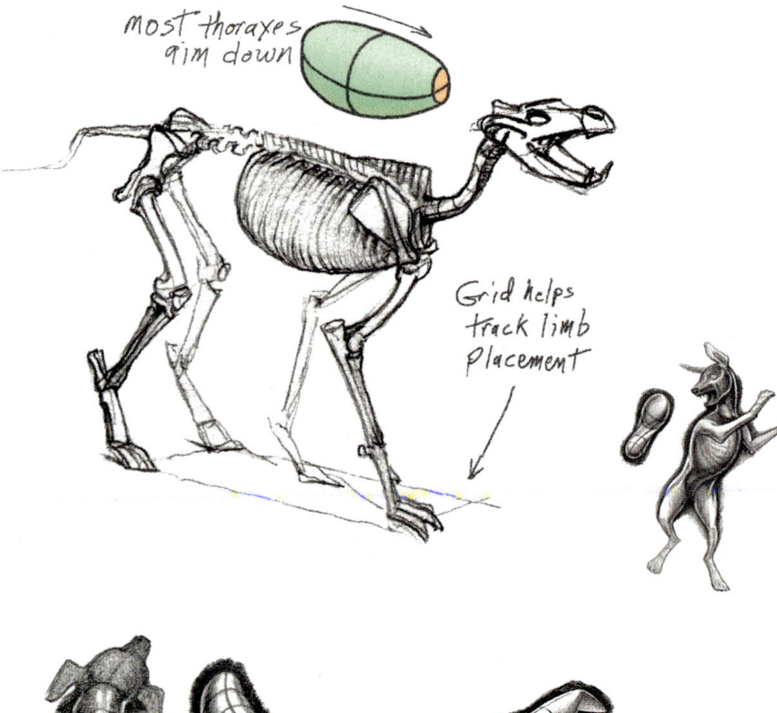

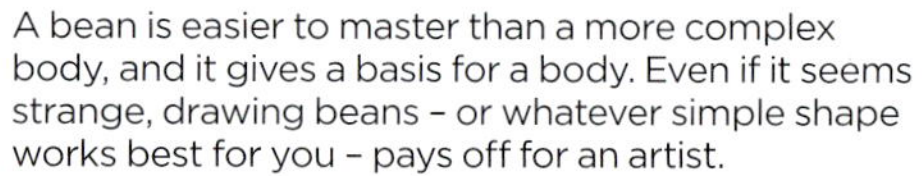

A bean is easier to master than a more complex body, and it gives a basis for a body. Even if it seems strange, drawing beans – or whatever simple shape works best for you – pays off for an artist.

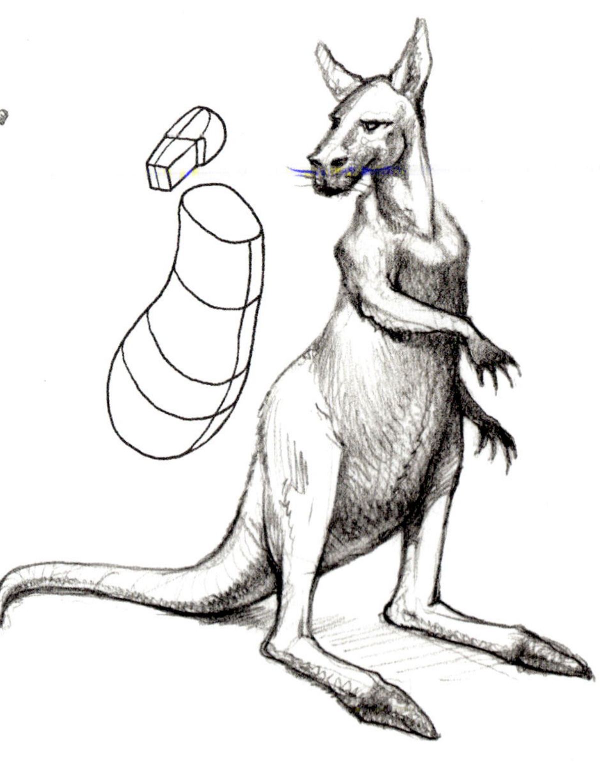

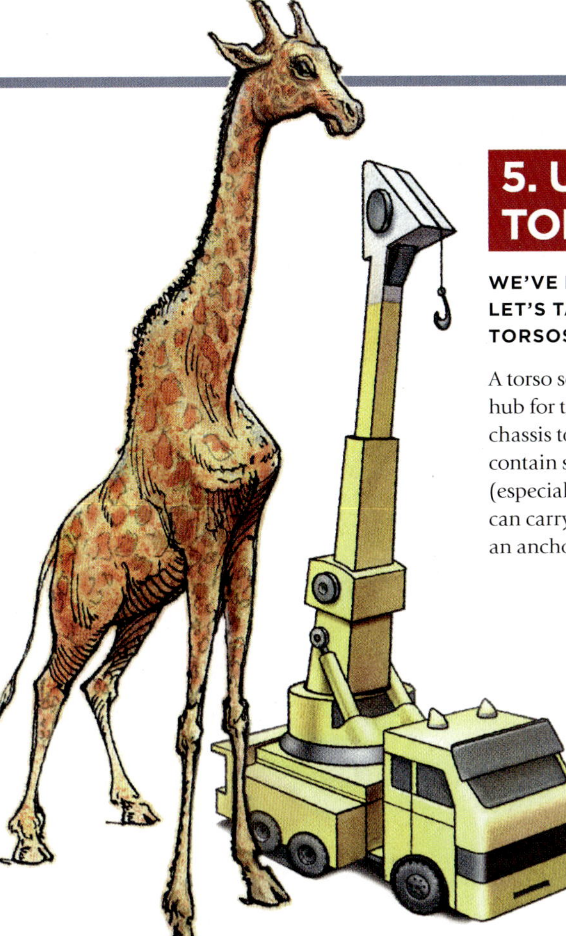

5. UNDERSTANDING TORSO FUNCTIONS

WE'VE DONE OUR TECHNICAL HOMEWORK – NOW LET'S TAKE A FRESH LOOK AT WHY WE STUDY TORSOS FIRST...

A torso serves several functions: as a core for the body; a hub for the limbs; a trunk from which branches emerge; a chassis to support a craning neck. A rib cage is a cage to contain soft parts and protect them. A spine is a spring (especially with cats), or a bridge, or a flatbed truck that can carry a load. A bird's sternum is both a boat's keel and an anchor for muscles...

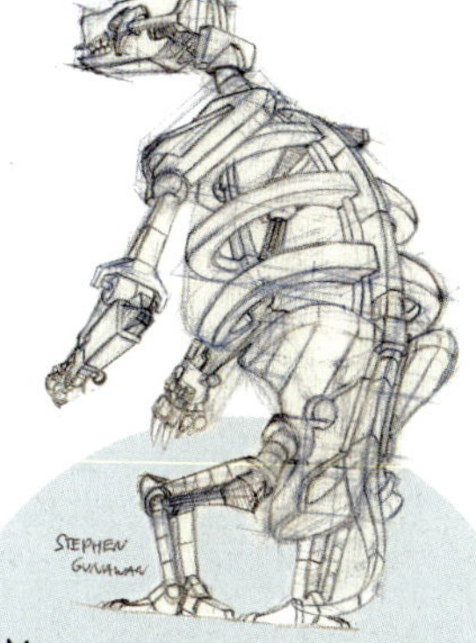

My student Stephen Gunawan did this exaggerated analysis of a sloth skeleton, treating bones as robot parts, and understanding their mechanical functions – a great way to learn.

Find your own comparisons for fun and insight. The foundation of creativity is making connections. Anatomy and form are technical skills, whereas analogies are creative.

Seeing the relationship between a horse and a rocket, or a cat and a slinky, helps us exaggerate.

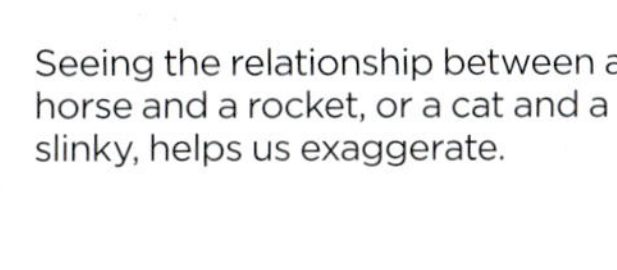

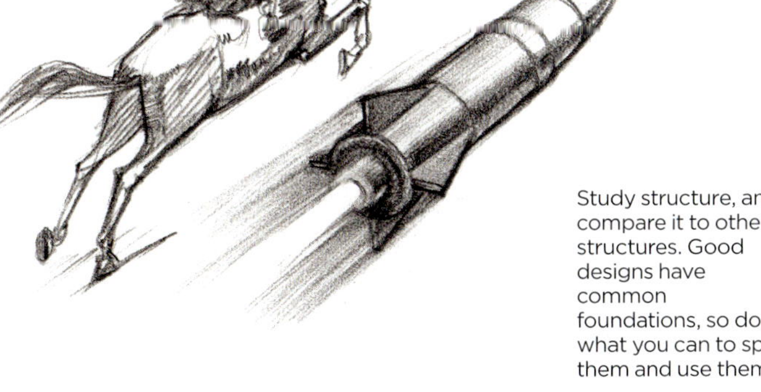

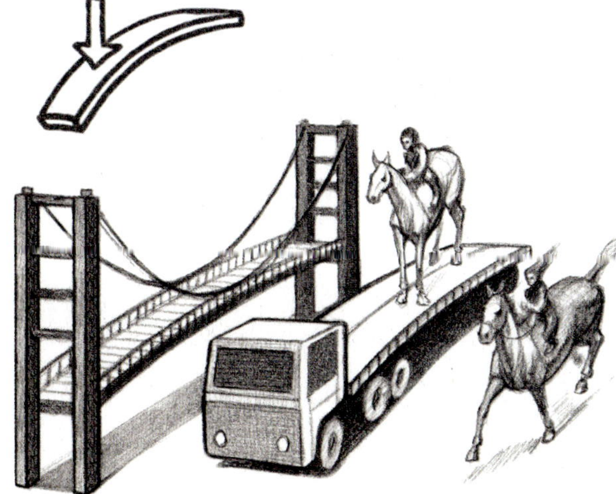

Study structure, and compare it to other structures. Good designs have common foundations, so do what you can to spot them and use them.

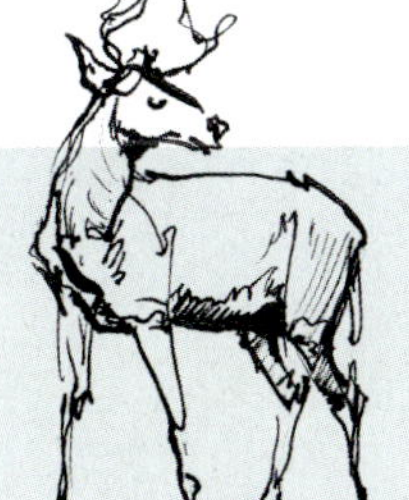

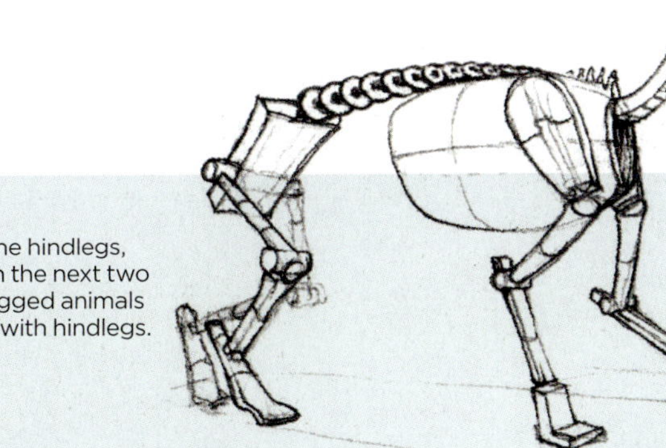

Torsos are the source of the other parts. The hindlegs, forelegs, neck, and head emerge from it. In the next two workshops, we'll study the limbs of four-legged animals and compare them to our own, beginning with hindlegs.

THE HIND LEGS

Explore the rear-wheel drive of animals, and how you can use this part of the body to propel your artwork forward

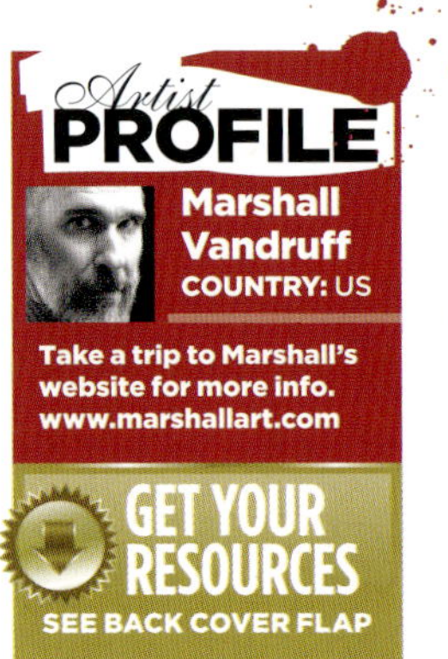

When the first artists drew animals, they drew the way all children still draw, with outlines around the shapes they could see. That's the foundation of drawing: charming and primitive. As drawing evolved, artists worked to make their illusions seem real, as if the picture were a window into a world of animals with meat on their bones.

Look at an animal's hind leg and you'll see a shape. Cartoonists capitalize on that. You'll also see a surface with color and texture: short hair, long hair, rough skin, smooth skin, mottled, groomed, light, dark… Painters and photographers care deeply about such surfaces.

However, I'll begin with bones and muscles. I'll explain how these affect the living animal's rear-wheel drive system: its hind legs.

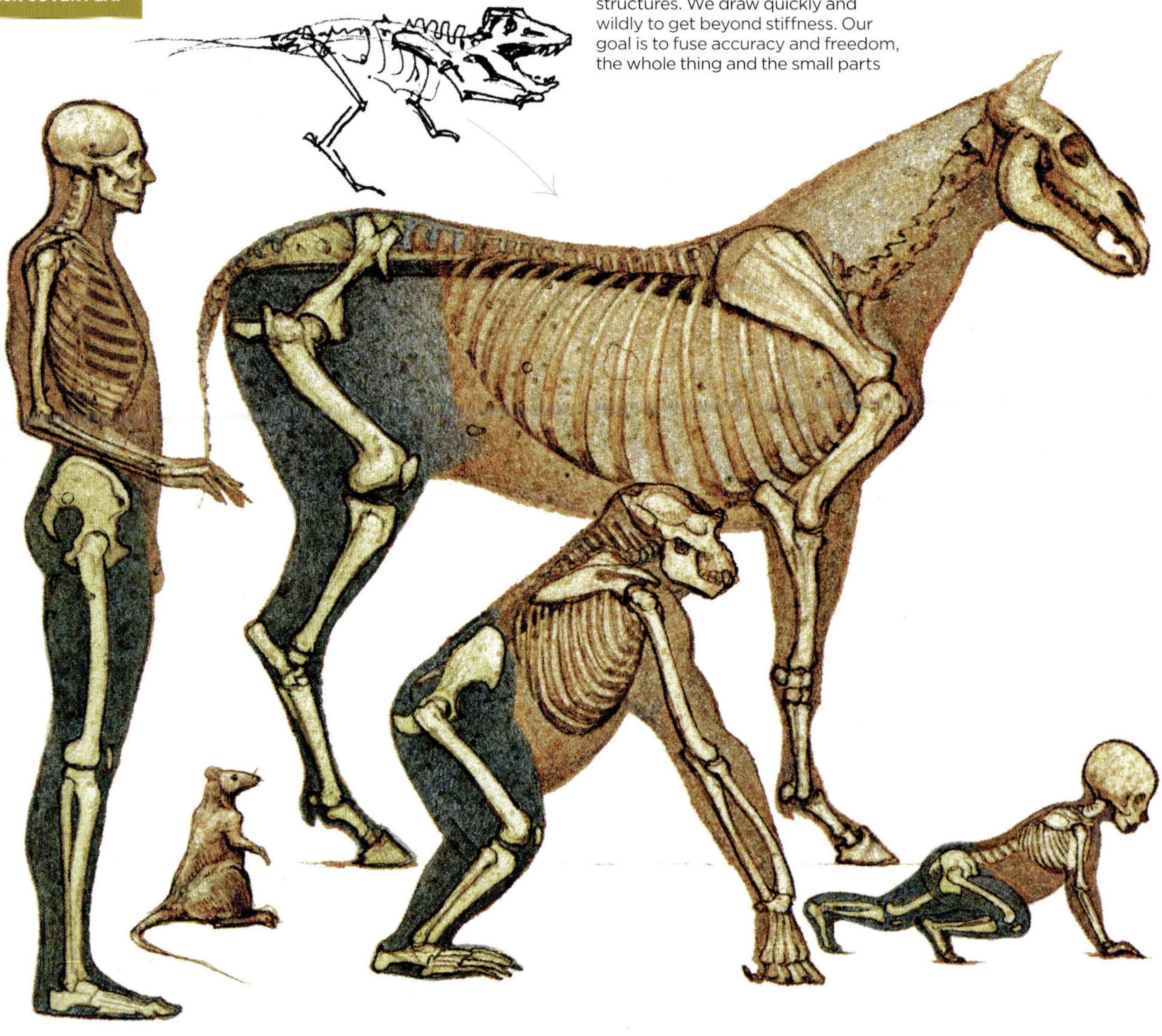

Drawing, like any artistic discipline, requires contradictory skills. We draw slowly and carefully to learn the structures. We draw quickly and wildly to get beyond stiffness. Our goal is to fuse accuracy and freedom, the whole thing and the small parts

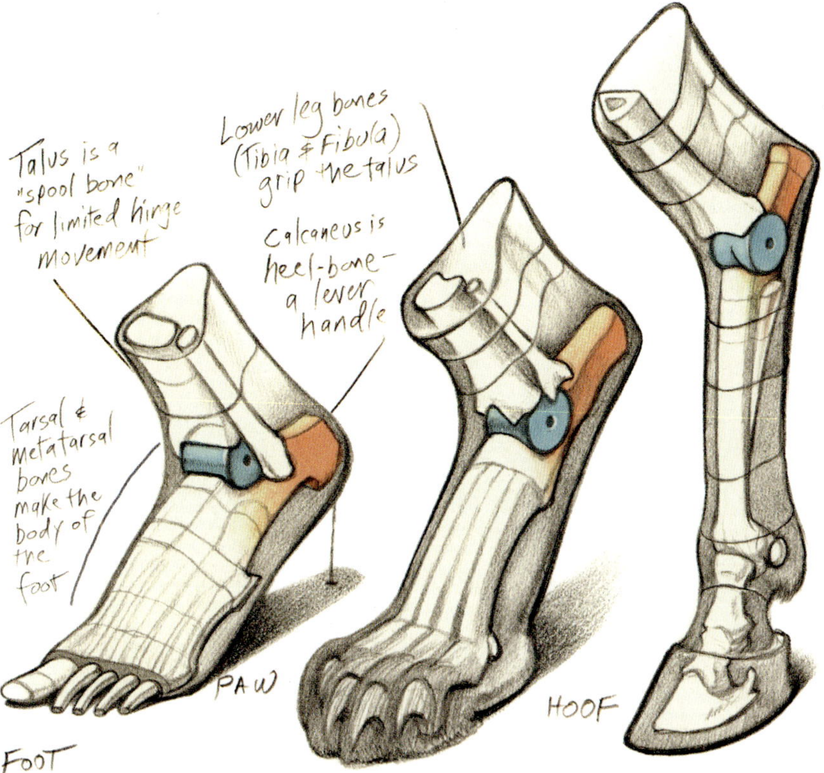

Foot bones

You can study between 10 and 20 bones in a foot, but it's easier to group them. The most important are the heel (calcaneus) and ankle (talus) bones, colored here to show their placement and function.

Plantigrades plant their feet on the ground. We call their feet, feet. Digitigrades walk on their digits; we call their feet paws. Ungulates walk on a toenail or two, which we call hooves.

Leg mechanics

The best way to understand bones is by their function. Try to see them as perfectly designed mechanical assemblies.

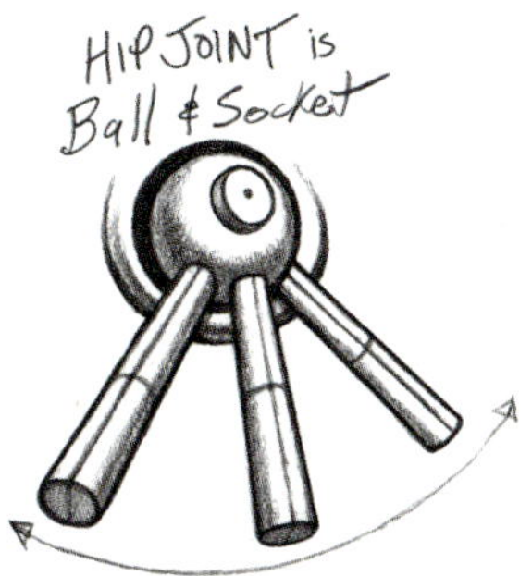

The femur has a ball at its top. The pelvis has a socket. These form a perfect union for getting around.

The ball-and-socket joint of the hip enables the upper leg to swing and swivel, kicking out to the side.

1. HIND LEG BONES

BONE MACHINERY: UNDER ALL THAT FLESH IS A MECHANISM OF SOCKETS, HINGES, LEVERS, AND SPOOLS...

Whichever names you choose to use to refer to the bones in the leg – femur, fibula, tibia, tarsal mass, or others – they still have the same job: to support and propel the animal, and, occasionally, to enable it to kick out at an aggressor.

In most animals, there are two bones in the lower leg. The bigger one is the tibia; the smaller one is the fibula. This is different in hooved animals, however. A horse's fibula fuses right into the tibia, and so it can hardly be thought of as a separate bone. Artistically, however, you are less concerned with the number of bones in the lower leg, and more concerned with the fact that hooved animals don't wiggle their toes or retract their claws. This means that they don't need a wide lower leg to anchor those extra muscles.

Knee bones

The knee is a hinge joint, but it isn't fixed like a door hinge. The kneecap (patella) pulls on a strap to lift the lower leg.

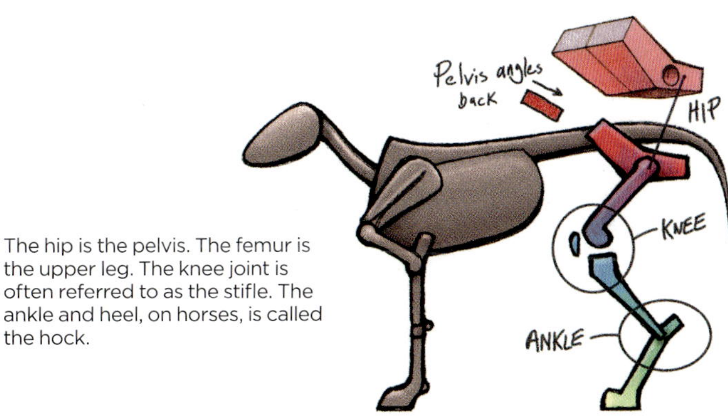

The hip is the pelvis. The femur is the upper leg. The knee joint is often referred to as the stifle. The ankle and heel, on horses, is called the hock.

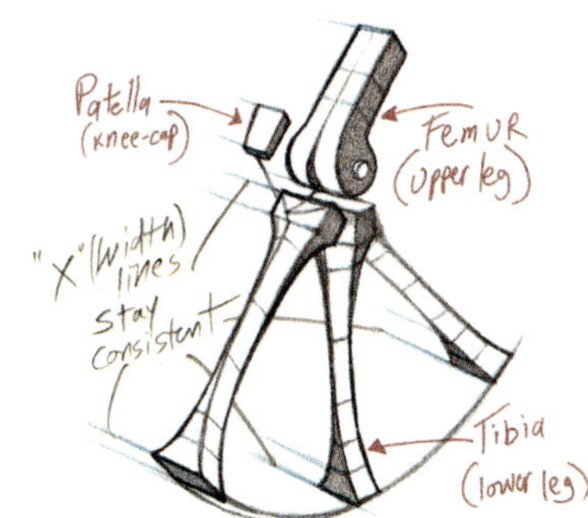

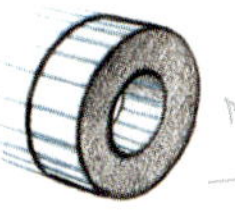

As with all hinges, when the limb swings, the X lines stay consistent throughout the arc.

2. MUSCLE GROUPS

HUMAN AND ANIMAL LEGS BOTH MOVE BY THE SAME SOURCE – THE PULL OF MUSCLES...

There are over 16 muscles in the hind leg that artists can study – but even if you came to know every one of them, it would help you less than knowledge of their groups and functions. Here are the simplified structures for understanding hind legs.

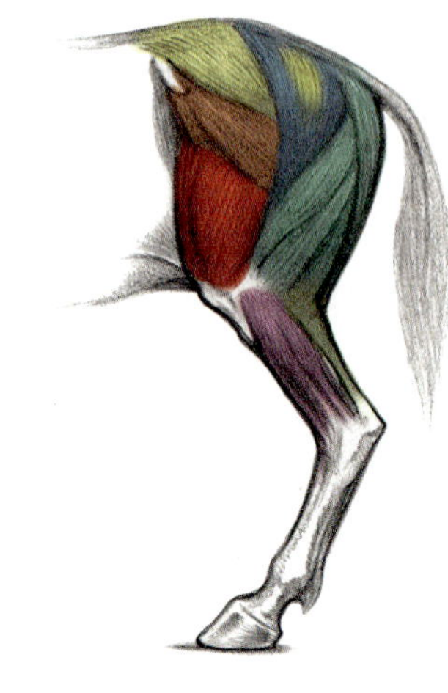

Quadruped muscle charts use different names for the variations, but there are two consistent groups: the big pair on the upper leg, and the smaller pair on the lower leg

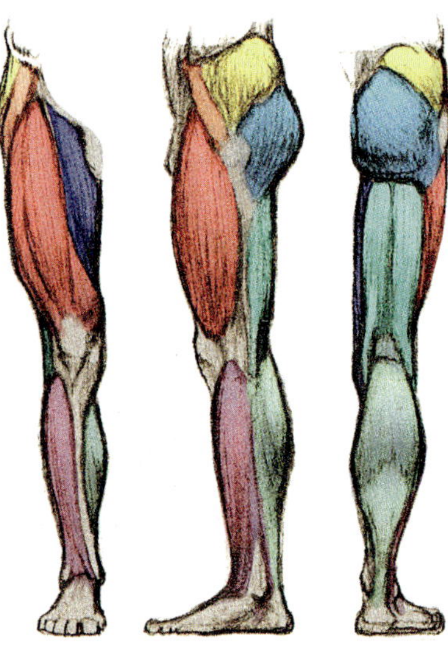

A big pair

Quadriceps and hamstrings are the main group of the upper leg. The quadriceps (red) on the front of the thigh pull on the kneecap to straighten the lower leg. The hamstrings (green) on the back of the thigh pull on the lower leg bones to bend the leg.

Compare the color maps of the human muscle groups to those of the horse and the bear.

A bear's hind leg is remarkably similar to a human's, mainly because bears also plant their feet on the ground.

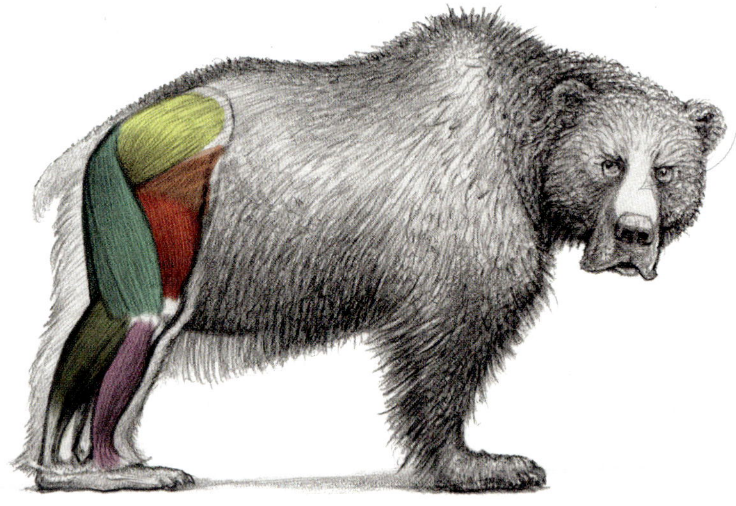

HOMEWORK ASSIGNMENT

Target the muscles

Once you understand the basic groups, you can separate them into individual muscles. For example, the hamstrings are divided into two parts: the medial (inner) and lateral (outer) sets. The medial set actually divides into two more: the semitendinosus and semimembranosus. Names like that can put off delicate learners, but note that, on a horse, the semimembranosus muscle alone is larger than a human's entire upper leg.

A smaller pair

The calf and extensor groups insert into the feet. They are leaner than the thigh muscles because they have less mass to move.

The heel of the horse, like any hooved animal, is high in the air. The proportion is very different from a human leg, but it has many analogous parts. Remember that muscles are bulkier near the torso and leaner as they move down the limbs.

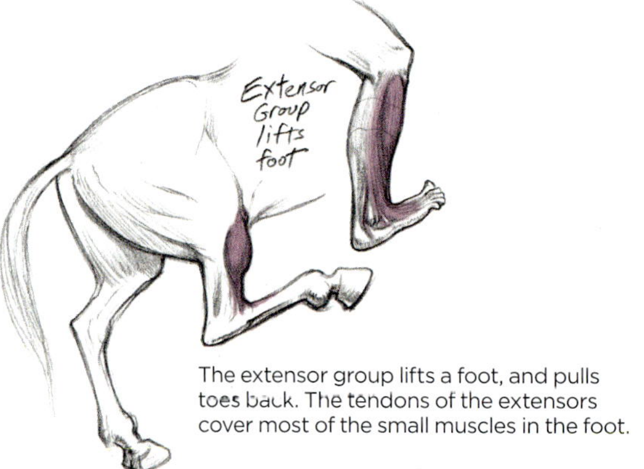

The extensor group lifts a foot, and pulls toes back. The tendons of the extensors cover most of the small muscles in the foot.

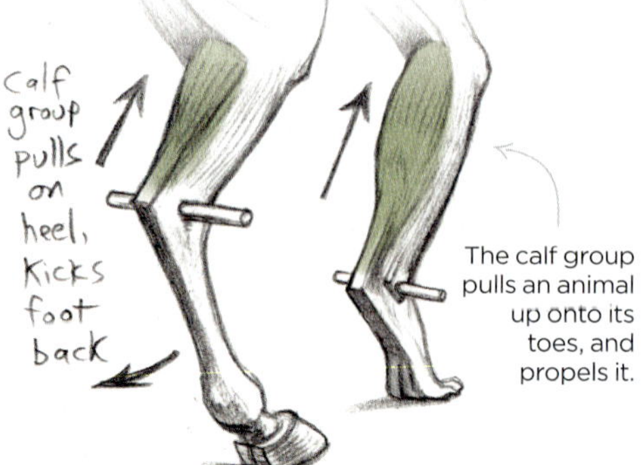

The calf group pulls an animal up onto its toes, and propels it.

Naming parts
Every detail gets a name. Names let us point things out and talk about them.

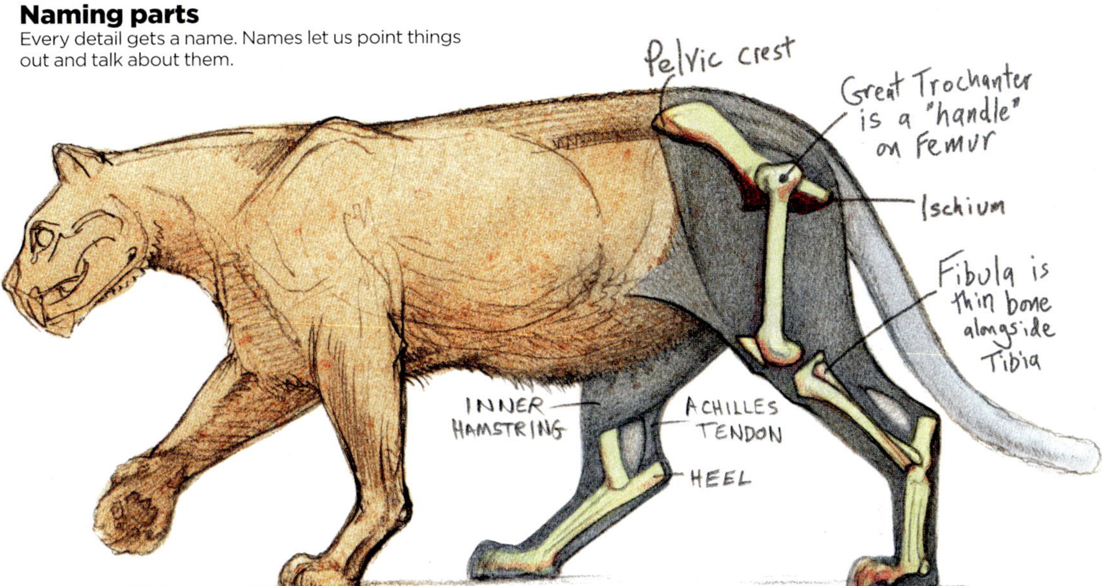

3. INTERNAL STRUCTURE

THE SURFACE OF AN ANIMAL IS DETERMINED BY THE SUBSTANCE INSIDE, SO DEVELOP X-RAY VISION TO DRAW WITH AUTHORITY...

Study animal anatomy from books, and you'll find that four books may use four names for the same part. The part that I've labelled pelvic crest on this cat can be found in any book – but it may be called the pelvic point, the tuberosity of the iliac crest, the tuber coxae, or the anterior superior iliac spine. If you're trying to impress people, you should learn all the names. But if you're trying to master drawing, any name will do. Your concern isn't the name, but that it's the wide point of an animal's haunch. Pelvic crest is fine.

Most names, however, are consistent. The ischium is the ischium – there's no need to distinguish it as the ischial tuberosity. But you do need to know that it's the back-most part of an animal's haunch, and always narrower (on the X measurement) than the pelvic crest.

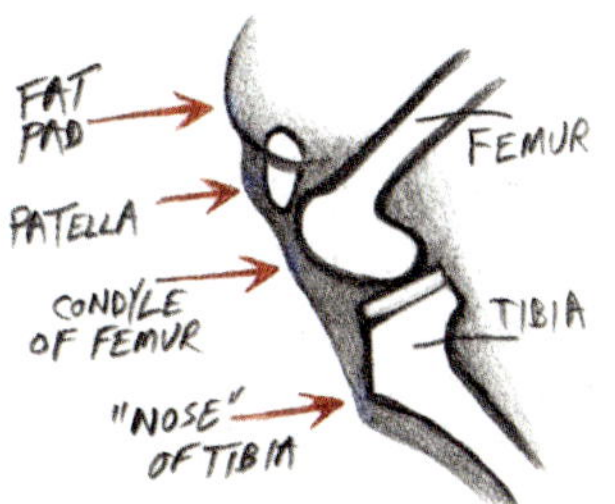

Knee clarity
Knees have several points that alternate for attention. The patella (kneecap) is the most prominent point, but it connects to the nose of the tibia, which is a fixed bump on the lower leg. The outer swell on the femur, and the fat pad that covers the patella when a horse is relaxed, can all seem like the knee.

Sausage legs
Crocodiles don't have kneecaps, so the knee doesn't have the crisp plane-break that we see on a dog or a deer. But they have the same basic bones as other four-legged animals. Since their quadriceps tendons connect directly to the tibia like a belt-strap, they have quick leverage and can move very fast.

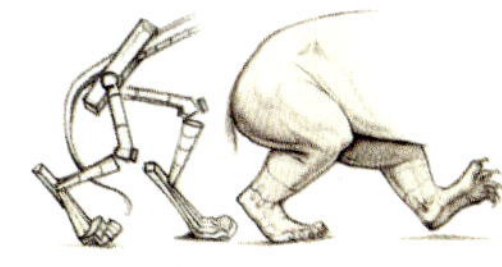

Repositioning
When you get good at visualizing the underlying bones, try repositioning the legs and redrawing them.

4. HIND LEG FORMS

FORMS LET YOU INVENT LEGS THAT DON'T EXIST – UNTIL YOU CREATE THEM...

When we dream, or daydream, we imagine realistic images. The trick is to get those images onto paper. There's no better way to master this than to use wireframe structures based on simple forms. Anatomy is complex – but if you can see the bulk of the upper leg as an egg, the calf as a bowling pin and the foot as a stick and ball, then you simplify your task and turn the leg into something real.

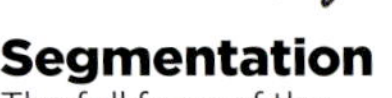

Segmentation

The full form of the body takes shape if you segment it and work on each part as a separate block.

Block it up

Block forms force you into specific choices about plane breaks, and help you chisel the form into crispness. Note also that from behind, you can see the legs facing out at a 30–40 degree angle.

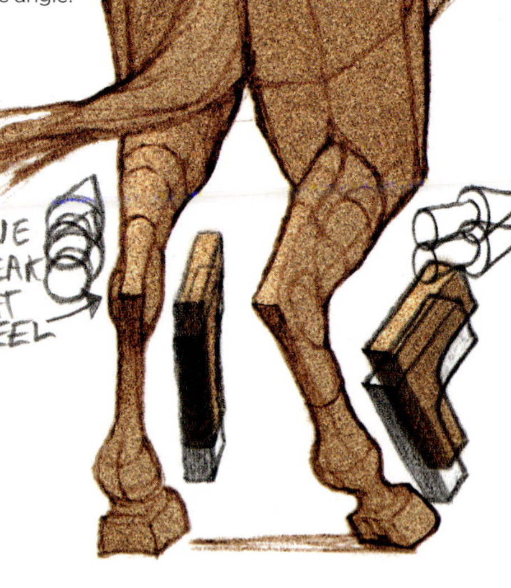

Round it out

Hind legs don't face forward in unison, they splay out. Here's a way to solve it... See how the entire body of the hindquarters fits into a cylinder.

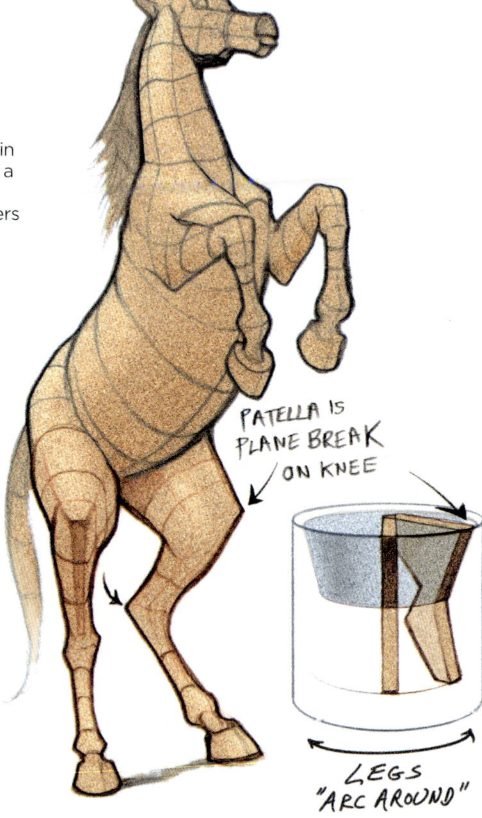

HOMEWORK ASSIGNMENT

Wired forms

Get out those favorite photographs that you used to exercise your X-ray vision. Instead of looking for the bones inside the legs, try to wrap wires around the legs. If you find it tough, treat each part of the leg as a bar or a block, and visualize a rubber band around it. From there, it begins to take on form.

Ron's robot

My student Ron Green invented this contraption. It's strange, but useful for understanding how an animal leaps from its hind legs. Try your own, based on anatomy.

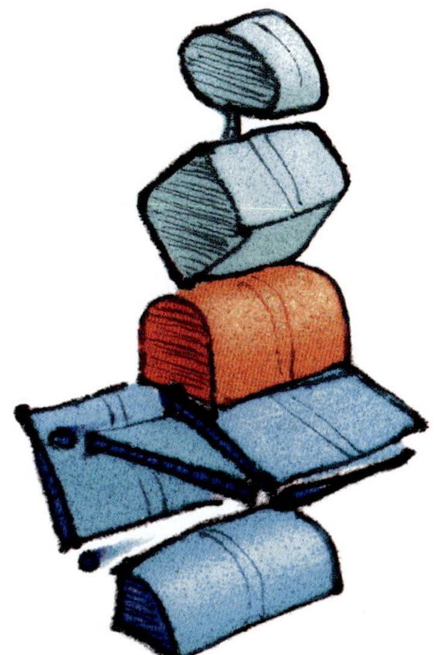

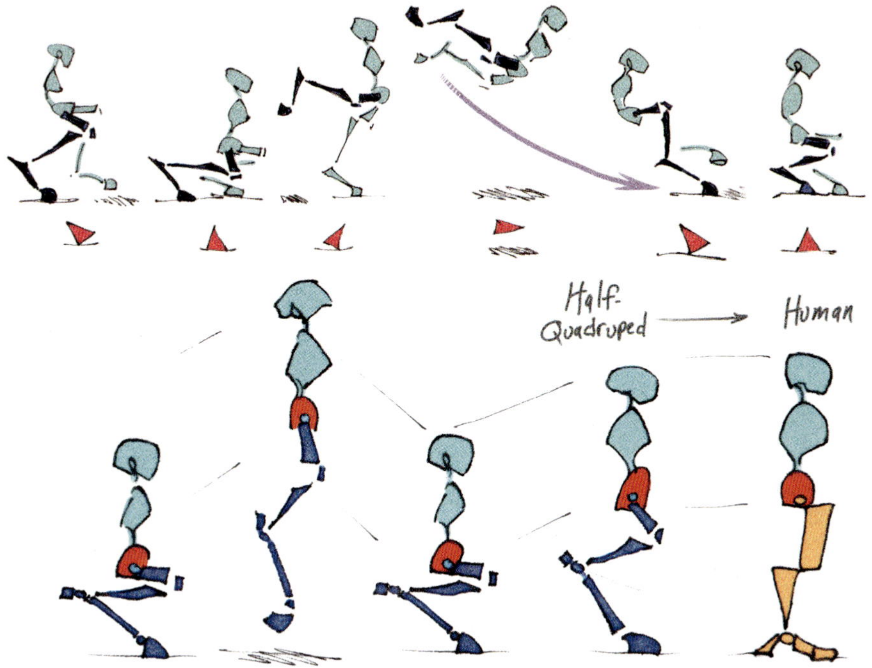

Artists must simplify to understand. Study Ron's drawings and you'll see that he is figuring out two problems: where the joints are, and how this half-quadruped leaps and bounces to get about.

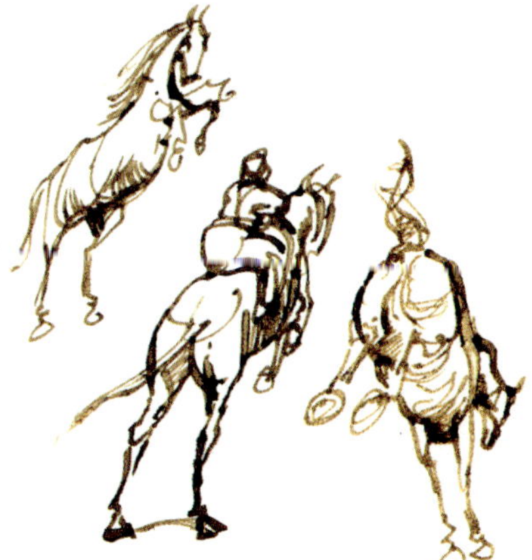

Spontaneous art

The only way to master drawing is to draw, draw, and draw – but not always carefully. Quick, gestural studies with pen and ink don't allow you to get fussy, erase and fix, and they protect you from creating belabored work that looks dead – what Joe Weatherly calls "taxidermy." You'll sharpen your skills by drawing immediately from life, unpredictable and wild as it may be.

Forelimb fandango

We stand on our hind legs and use our arms and hands to perform delicate tasks and manipulate the world. Quadrupeds stand on their arms. The differences between arms and forelimbs are greater than those between legs and hind legs. In the next chapter, we'll study the forelimbs: arms as legs.

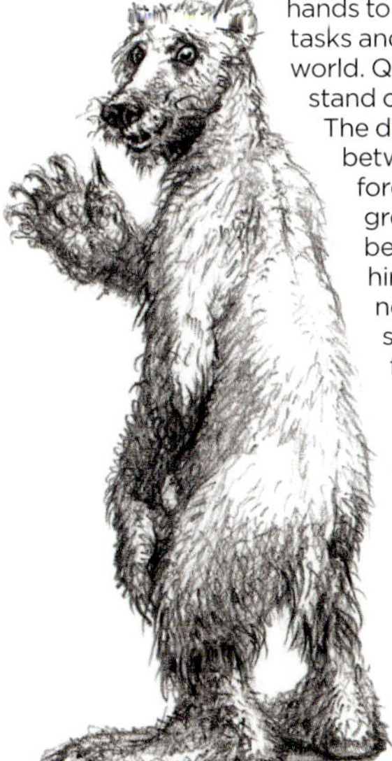

5. THE FUNCTION OF HIND LEGS

THEY JUMP, THEY WALK, THEY RUN, THEY KICK...

Once you know how they're made and how they're shaped, you can go back to the reason legs exist. Legs help support an animal. They get it moving to find food, or to keep it from becoming food. In the blink of an eye they can become a weapon. A lever. A catapult. A spring. Rear wheels. Or a bludgeon. Seeing legs through their functions reminds us why they're worth studying.

THE FORELEGS

Use your knowledge and observation to build the pillars of balance and grip for the animal kingdom

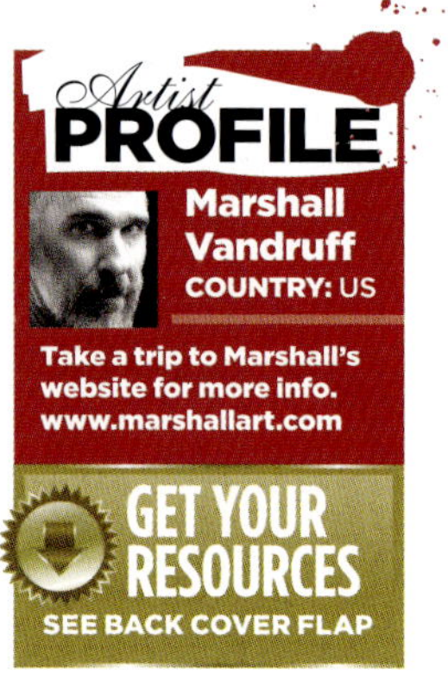

Sometimes you have to take things apart if you want to know how they work. With animals, that gets messy. Beatrix Potter and her brother dissected dead animals together, which served her well as an illustrator. But dissection is not an easy business: you can end up smelly and confused.

There are better ways to study animal anatomy. One is to observe museum skeletons from varying angles to be sure of their forms and connections. But assembled skeletons are often poorly put together and locked into a single position that teaches you next to nothing about how bones move. Another solution is to assemble bones on your own. I've assembled a horse's leg bones with glue and rubber bands. It's full-sized, it's real, and it impresses friends and family, but I could never have done it without at least a reasonable amount of book knowledge.

The lessons that follow will help you understand bones and muscles enough to look at living animals and see their structure, so you can exaggerate proportions, make planes crisp, and invent your own animals – imaginary beasts with real legs to stand on.

Let's have a look at how forelegs are made, and how they work.

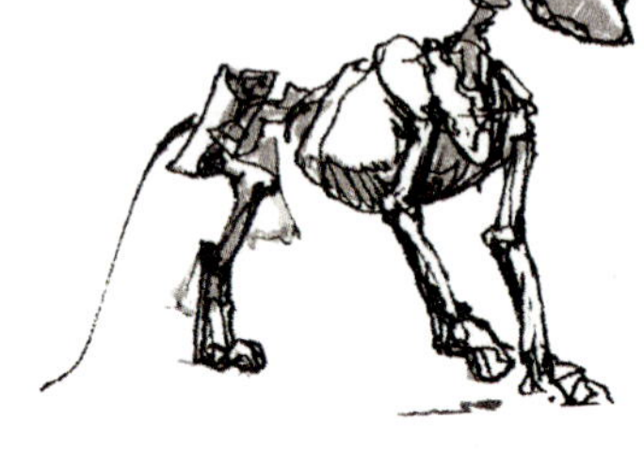

We strip away the surface of an animal to see what makes it work. Artistic anatomy begins with the skeleton. The more familiar you are with the framework, the easier it is to build the body around the bones.

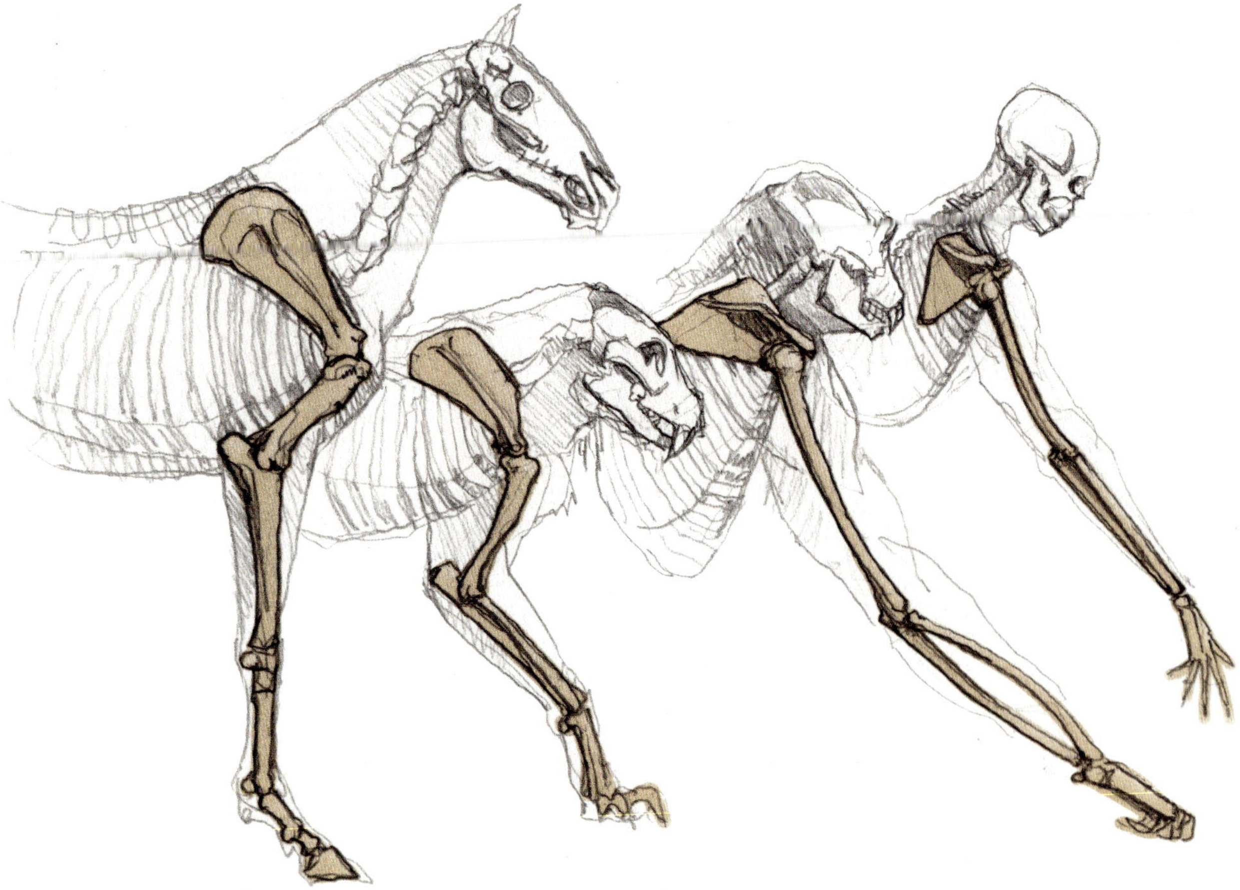

1. FORELEG BONES

ANIMALS HAVE SHOULDERS AND ARMS LIKE US, BUT WITH A DIFFERENCE: THEY WALK ON THEM...

We have shoulder blades on our backs; quadrupeds have them on their sides. The shoulder blade (scapula) connects to the upper arm bone (humerus). This is obvious in a bone diagram, but on a fleshed animal, the upper arm is buried in the side of the body. That means you may mistake the lower arm bones (radius or ulna) for an upper arm unless you can see through the surface.

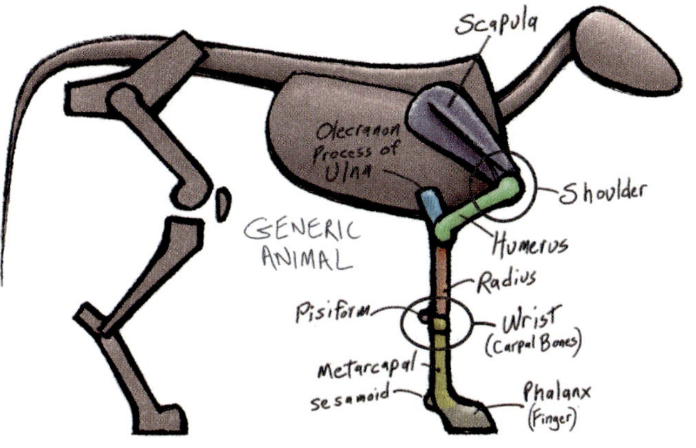

Legs, limbs, and arms

Animal forelegs vary more than hind legs. Primates and the ancient ground sloth below have arms and hands. We'll look at arm mechanics on the next page – but first, notice that there are two bones in the forearm. The ulna is the big bump at the elbow that tapers to a small bump at the little-finger side of the hand. The radius is a small spinning button inside the elbow, which swells to hold the wrist bones at the thumb side of the hand.

Hands usually have 27 bones. Several of them in the wrist make a simple form called the carpal mass.

Hoofed animals have much simpler structures. Their radius and ulna are fused together into a single forearm, but we still distinguish the elbow portion as the ulna and the wrist portion as the radius.

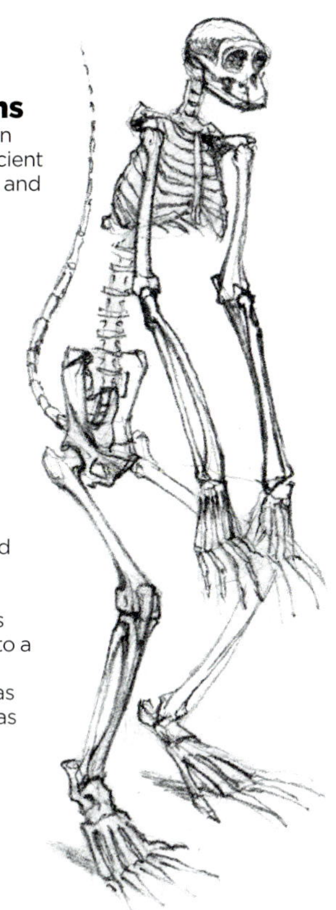

Not all is bone; cartilage happens

Horses and other hoofed animals (ungulates) have cartilage at the top of their shoulder blades. Cartilage wears away, so museum horse skeletons may appear to have the top part of the scapula chopped off. Living horses have larger shoulder blades than their dead relatives.

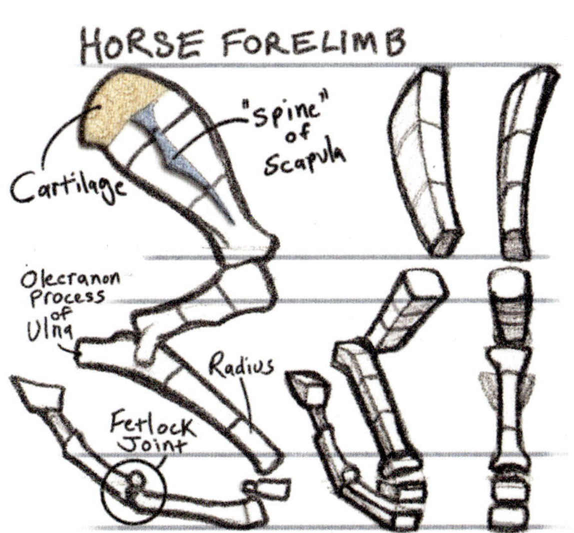

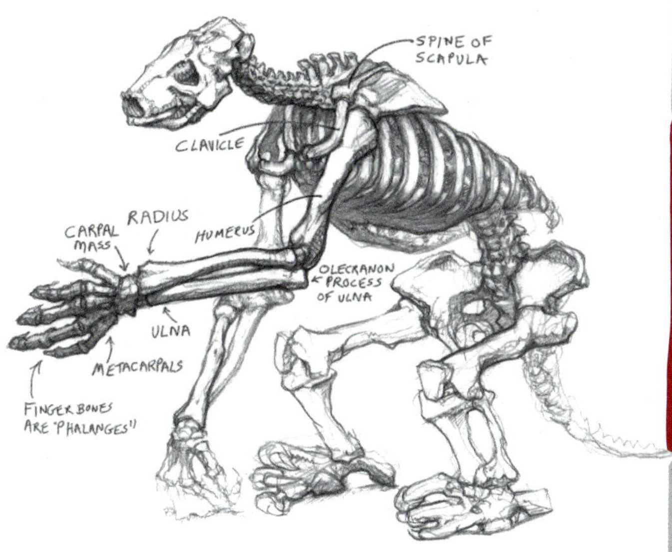

2. BONE MECHANICS

FORELEGS ARE FOR WALKING. IF THEY ALSO HAVE TO SPIN OR GRIP, THEY NEED MORE COMPLEX STRUCTURES...

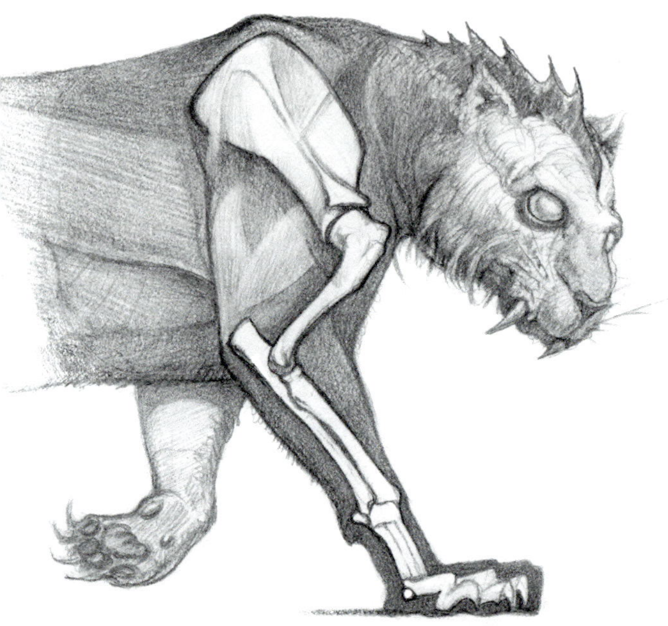

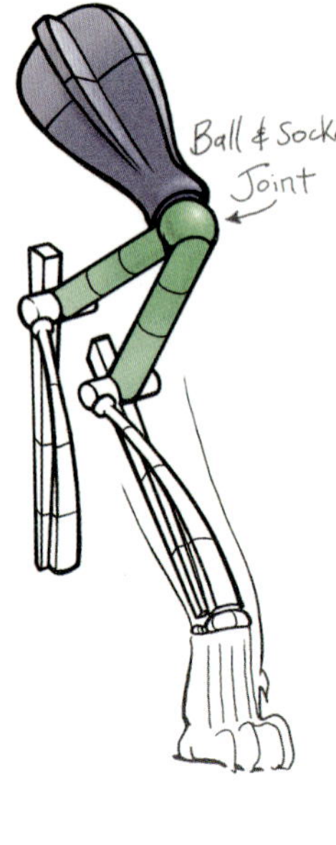

Shoulders and elbows

The ball and socket joint of the shoulder allows some rotation for an arm to spin or reach out to the side, as well as forward and back.

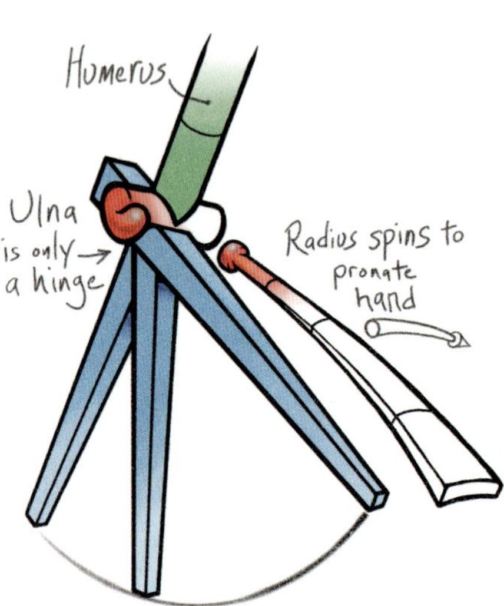

Of the two forearm bones, the ulna is only a hinge. Animals with hands also have a radius that spins

Arm mechanics

Some forearms spin around. Some spin a bit. Some are fixed in a forward position.

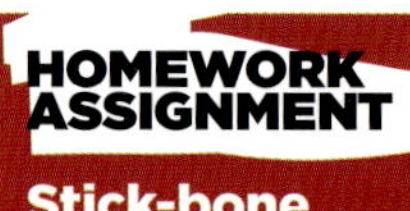

Stick-bone forelegs

Draw a series of arms or forelimbs by constructing them from simple stick-bones. It's usually best to draw the ulna before the radius, because the radius doesn't affect the ulna's position. Keep it simple. Don't try to learn foreleg anatomy by drawing forelegs; rather, learn by drawing their simple components.

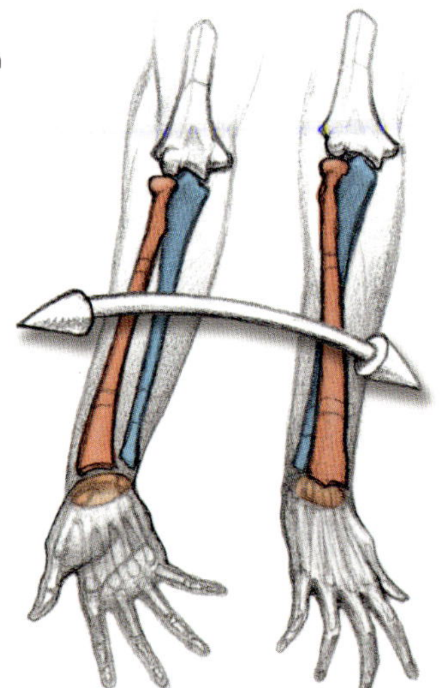

Just as lower legs have two bones, so do lower arms. The difference is that we support ourselves with our legs, but use our arms to grasp and manipulate.

The ulna doesn't spin: all it can do is bend and straighten the arm. The radius is separate and revolves around the ulna to spin the hand. When it's parallel to the ulna, with the thumbs out to the side, it's supine. When the radius crosses over the ulna, carrying the thumb toward the body, it's prone.

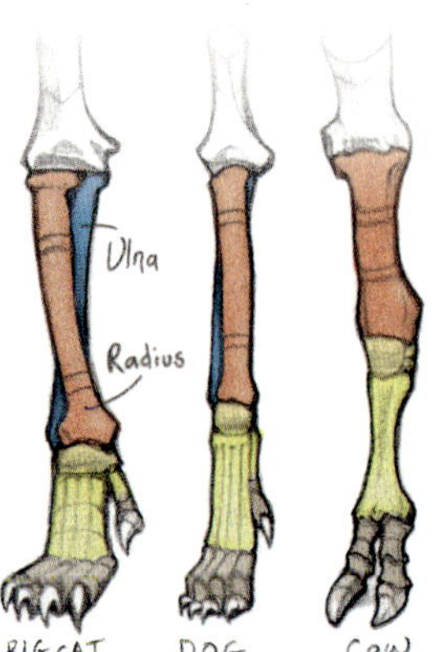

Quadrupeds vary in their ability to spin their hands. Cats do it quite well; dogs not as well. Hoofed animals can't spin their forelegs at all. Their radius bone is fused into the ulna, locked so that they can run but not reach out with an upraised palm.

3. FORELEG MUSCLES

THE MUSCLES IN FORELEGS ARE SIMILAR FOR ALL ANIMALS, BUT THE VARIATIONS ARE MANY...

Human arms and animal forelimbs have many, but not all, muscles in common. Not only do our upper arms extend out from our bodies, but they reach above our heads. It takes a deltoid, anchored to clavicles and scapulae, to lift our arms.

Quadrupeds have smaller and simpler deltoids than humans and apes.

Our lower arms spin partly from the pull of two special muscles called supinators, which make up the ridge of the extensor group.

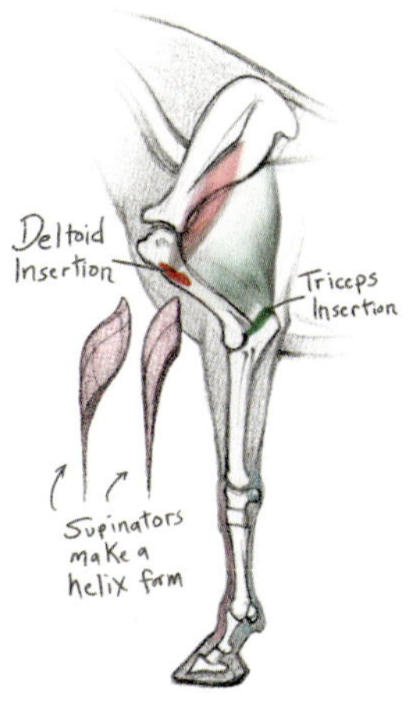

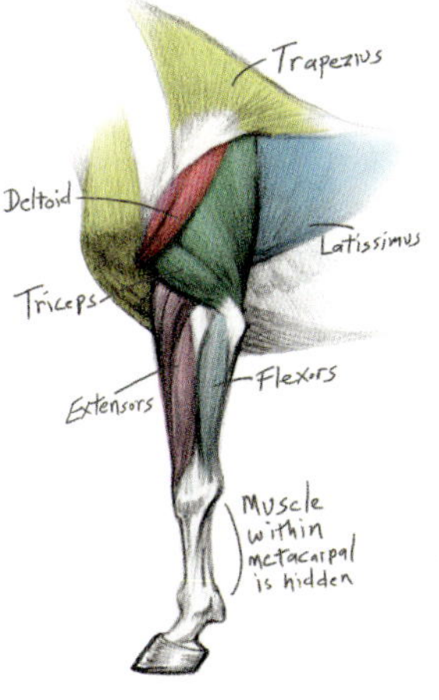

Muscles pull bones. The major muscle forms of a horse's shoulder are the triceps and deltoid. Here we see that they both anchor on the scapula. The deltoid pulls the foreleg away from the body. The triceps extend the foreleg. Even though horses can't spin their arms, they have a slightly helix-shaped group at the ridge like we do

The trapezius and latissimus dorsi appear large on anatomical plates but have little effect on the forms of animals. The trapezius is thin and sits over the top of deeper neck muscles. The latissimus usually disappears as it hugs the torso, but it can show up as a convex sliver on the side.

By the time we get to the metacarpal on an ungulate (analogous to our hand), the muscles are so deep and thin that artists don't study them. The bones, wrapped in ligament and skin, create the form.

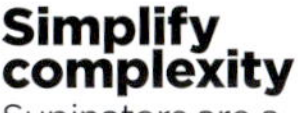

Simplify complexity

Supinators are a group of two muscles. Extensors are a group of three. Flexors can be separated into five or more, but that's too much information. They work as groups, so simplify.

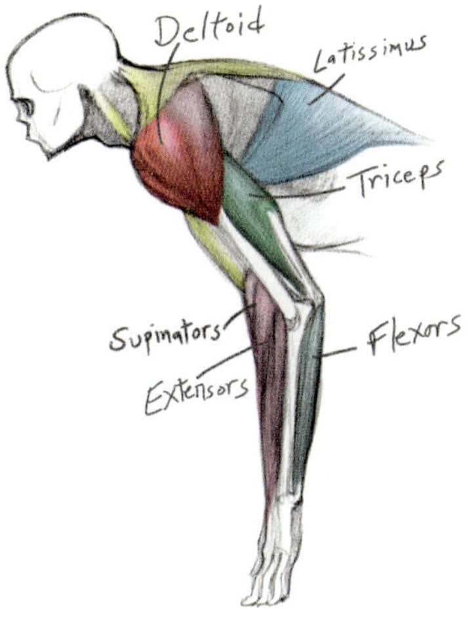

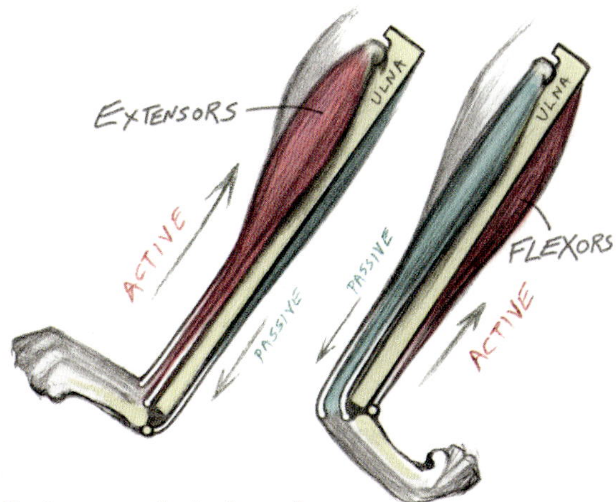

What arms do to hands

Extensors pull on the back side of the hand. Flexors pull on the palm side. Clench your fist, and you'll feel the flexors on your inside forearm harden. On most animals, the flexors are tucked under the inside of their forearms, barely visible on the outside.

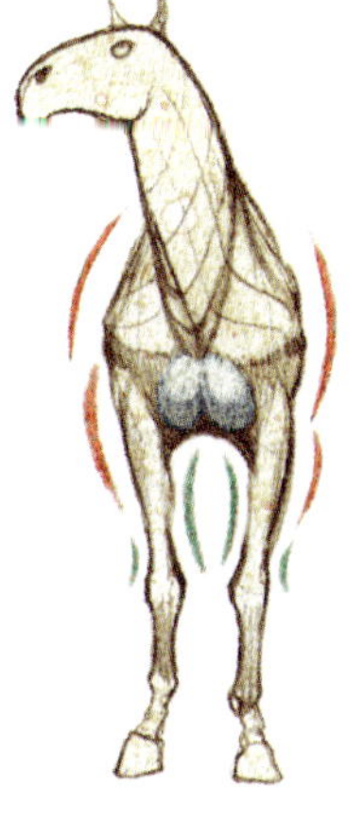

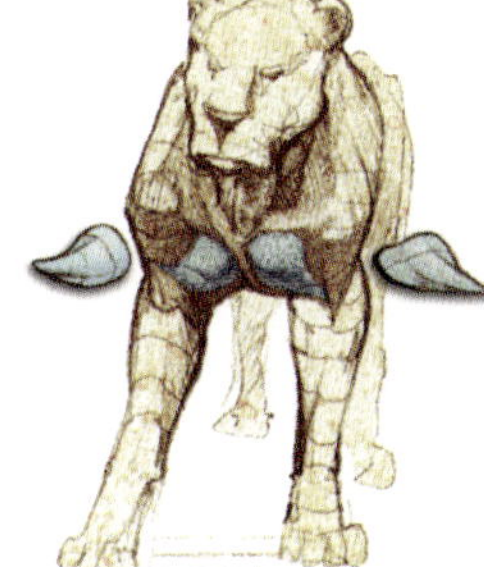

Chest muscle

The pectoralis major anchors on the chest and inserts into the humerus to pull the upper arm down and lift the body. It's the same muscle you use in doing push-ups. It shows on the surface as two varying egg forms on either side of the centerline of the chest. On the horse, notice the rhythm of convex and concave lines. The outer contours tend to be more convex. The inner limbs from the front view have noticeably more concavity.

4. FORELEG FORMS

ANATOMY FOR ARTISTS IS USELESS UNLESS THE ARTIST GIVES IT FORM...

The scapula and humerus create the point of the shoulder. The scapula hugs closely to the centerline at the top and spreads out to the sides as it goes down... but that gets complex. When you construct a horse, it helps to simplify by seeing a wedge form, which is true enough to the anatomy of horse shoulders but simple enough to master from memory.

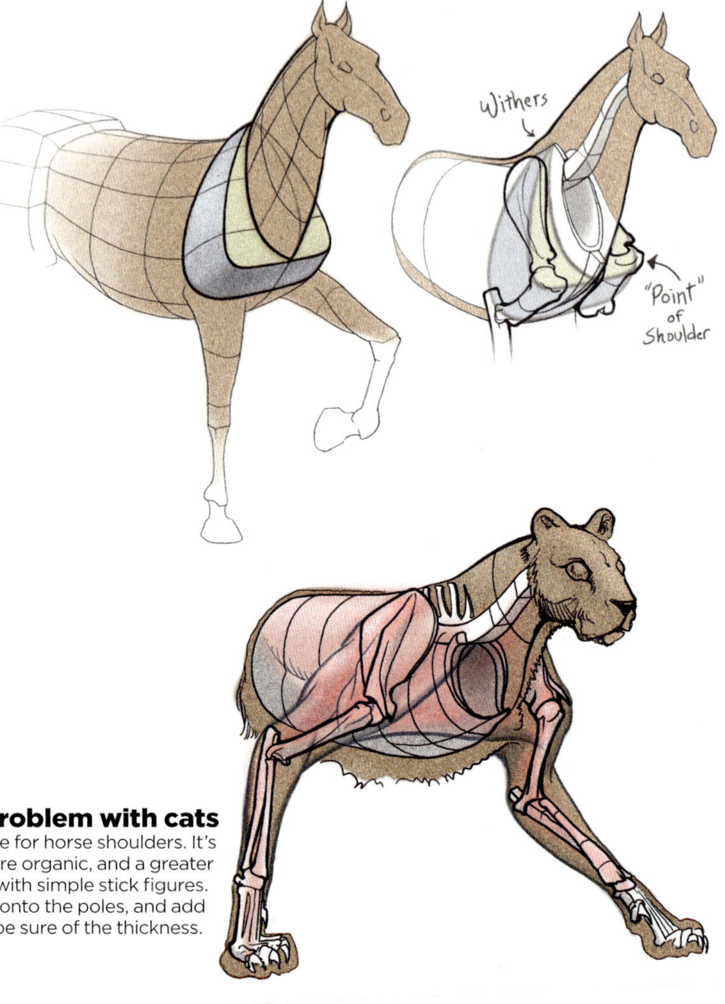

Breaking down knees

Horse knees are very boxy because the carpal bones are assembled in two breakable rows that directly affect the form. Note that the fetlock joints are quite spherical.

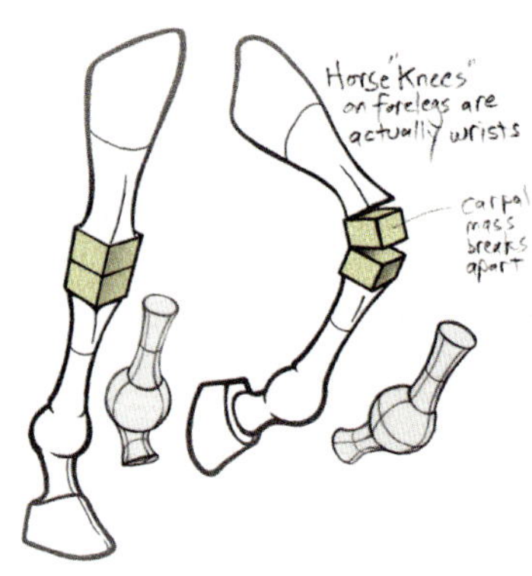

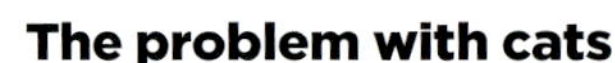

The problem with cats

Cats are so flexible that you can't use the simple wedge form you use for horse shoulders. It's difficult to simplify such fluid animals into box forms – they are more organic, and a greater challenge. You must see through to their bones, but you can do this with simple stick figures. For three-quarter views, turn the sticks into poles, drape some flesh onto the poles, and add cross-contours to be sure of the thickness.

HOMEWORK ASSIGNMENT

Horse legs

Collect a dozen photographs of horses that include their shoulders and forelimbs. The images can be low-resolution – in fact, that's an advantage, as it will keep you from being tempted to copy surfaces. Try to draw the wedge form of the shoulders, the block form of the carpal mass, and the ball-and-shaft fetlock joint. When you can do it successfully, move to the next great challenge – draw the shoulders and forelegs in a new, unseen position. To master forelegs, you master their forms.

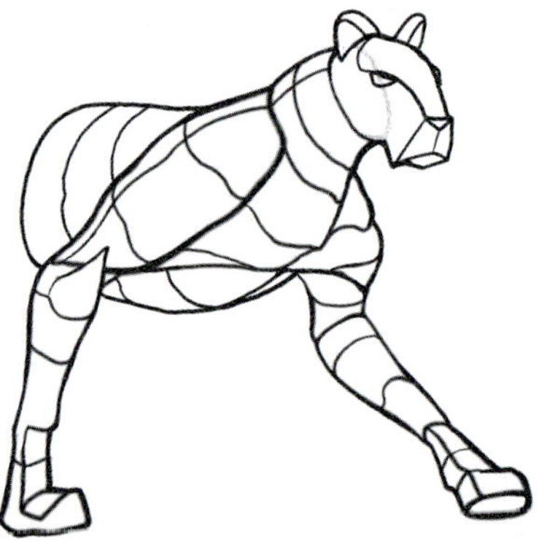

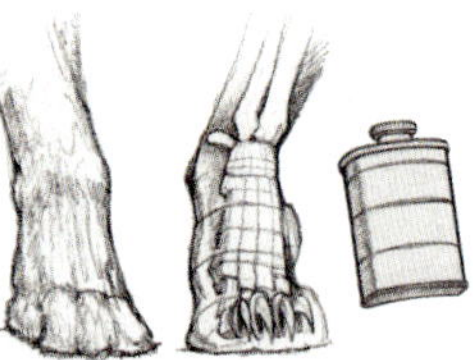

From form to function

A cat's paw has texture and surface that is easy to see, but you must learn to see the form. Anatomy helps, but it may get unnecessarily complex. A paw is a simple block, convex to the front, like a whisky flask. Now you have a comparison that helps you see the form, memorize, and draw it.

The relationship of whisky flasks to a cat's paw ends there: they have very different functions. Cats have claws to survive through violence. Even your housecat, whose only reason for not eating you is that you're too large, can do you serious damage.

For function, it may be better to see a cat's paw as a stapler, switchblade, or mousetrap. Two of those are made to pierce. Two of them are spring-loaded. All three remind us of what a claw does.

5. FORELEG FUNCTIONS

FORELEGS SUPPORT, CUSHION A FALL, WALK, SPRING, SCRATCH, POUND...

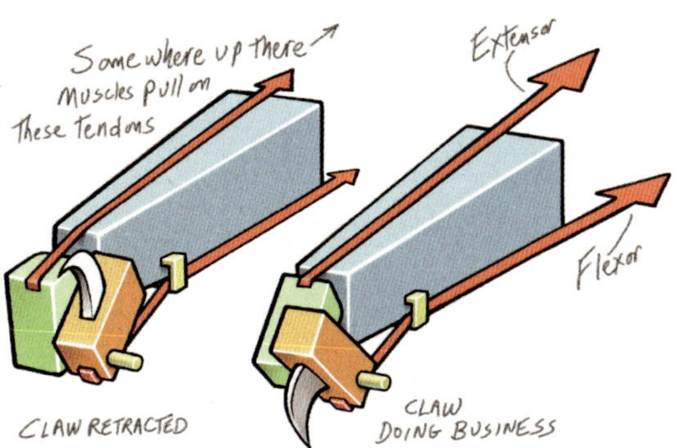

The piercing

Claws spring out of paws to pierce prey. But if muscles can only pull, how can they project a claw out and away from the body? It takes both extensors (to pull back the phalanx, or finger bone) and flexors (to pull down the claw) working together to reach and grip. This diagram shows how it's done.

Once you know how a cat claw works, you can forget it and design as you like. But you mustn't forget the function: a claw is a set of knives to impale, or a spade to dig, or a hook...

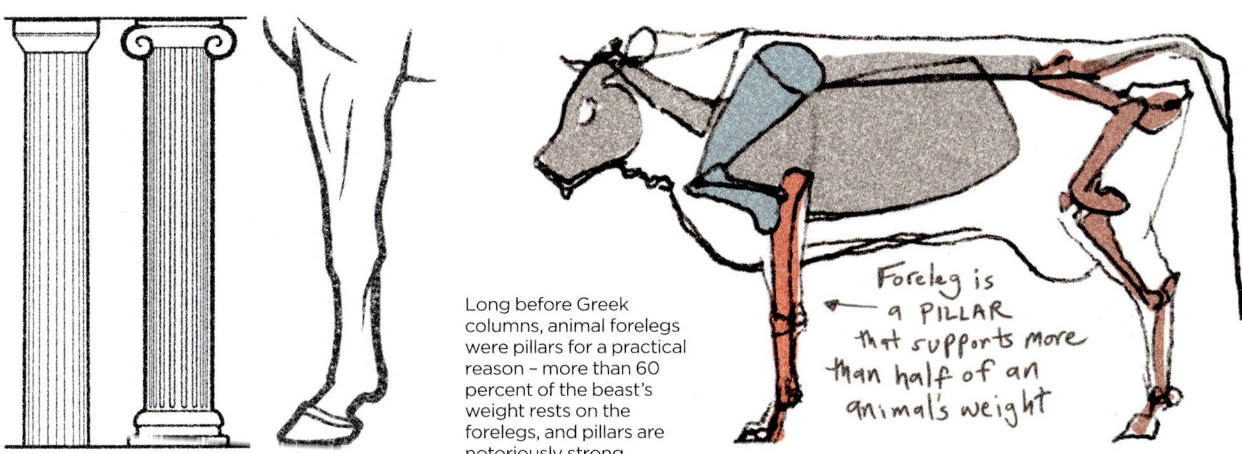

Long before Greek columns, animal forelegs were pillars for a practical reason – more than 60 percent of the beast's weight rests on the forelegs, and pillars are notoriously strong.

A strong support for shoulders

The first Greek columns had no pedestals, they just went straight into the base. As they evolved, they were given feet.

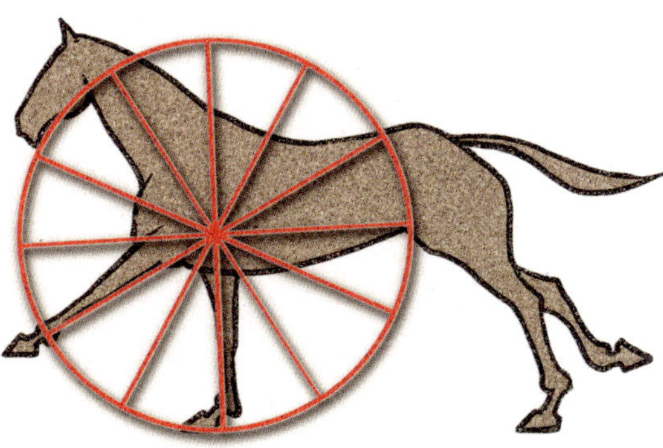

From pillars to spokes

Pillars stay put. Spokes revolve and provide a consistent strong support for a turning wheel – the same as a straight foreleg in an animal galloping at high speed.

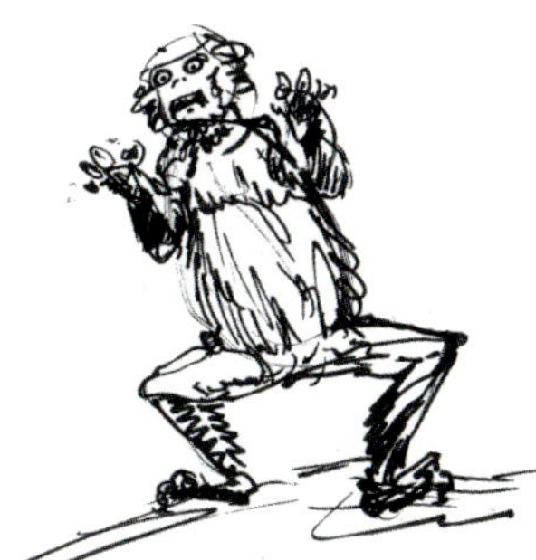

Forelegs have functions: pillars, spokes, hooks, knives, blades, spades, wrenches, pliers, clamps, vices, weapons, shields, paddles, cups, and bowls... Your job is not to copy what you see, but to understand what you see and to use your skills as an artist to create whatever you choose.

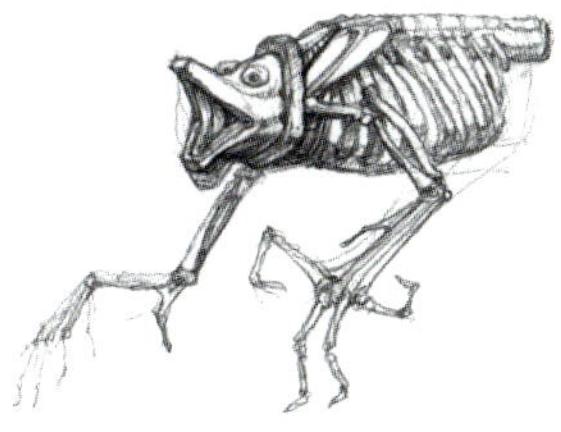

When you see a hoof as a form, you can draw it with spatial credibility. When you see it as a shoe or a cleat or a spike or a sledgehammer, though, you can exaggerate it with meaning.

NECKS AND HEADS

Discover what this part of the animal body tells you about the creature – and the traits all animals share

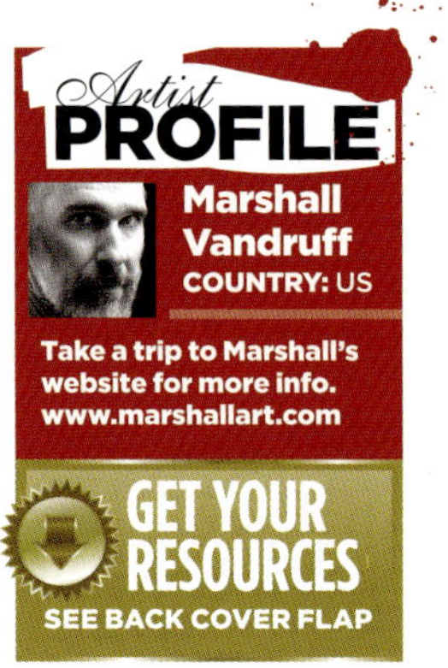

We try to make animal anatomy easier by comparing animals to humans. Unfortunately, many artists barely know human anatomy. Robert Beverly Hale pointed out that an artist who knows human anatomy can learn animals relatively easily. Part of the emphasis should be on "relatively;" it's still something of a task. But the most efficient and fun way is indeed to see creatures as people who run around on all limbs, noses forward, fast and strong.

You can tell a lot about an animal by the position and proportion of its skull. Human heads rest on our necks because we stand upright, and we have large craniums because we rely on our brains. Apes have smaller brains and greater jaws; and because they lean forward on their knuckles, their skulls sit slightly forward from their necks. Quadrupeds are horizontal – their skulls extend from their bodies.

From these basic conditions, skulls vary according to an animal's need to survive and thrive. Cats, for example, have alarming eyes and teeth. Wolves have incredible noses and teeth. But the big differences between animal and human heads are that animals have a snout that leads, and their brains, rather than being on top of their heads, are more toward the back. They hunt and run. They graze. They don't read magazines or draw pictures or concoct fantasy worlds and write them down to enchant others.

In this chapter, you'll study head structure – but we begin with how necks emerge from the torso and hold heads that face the world.

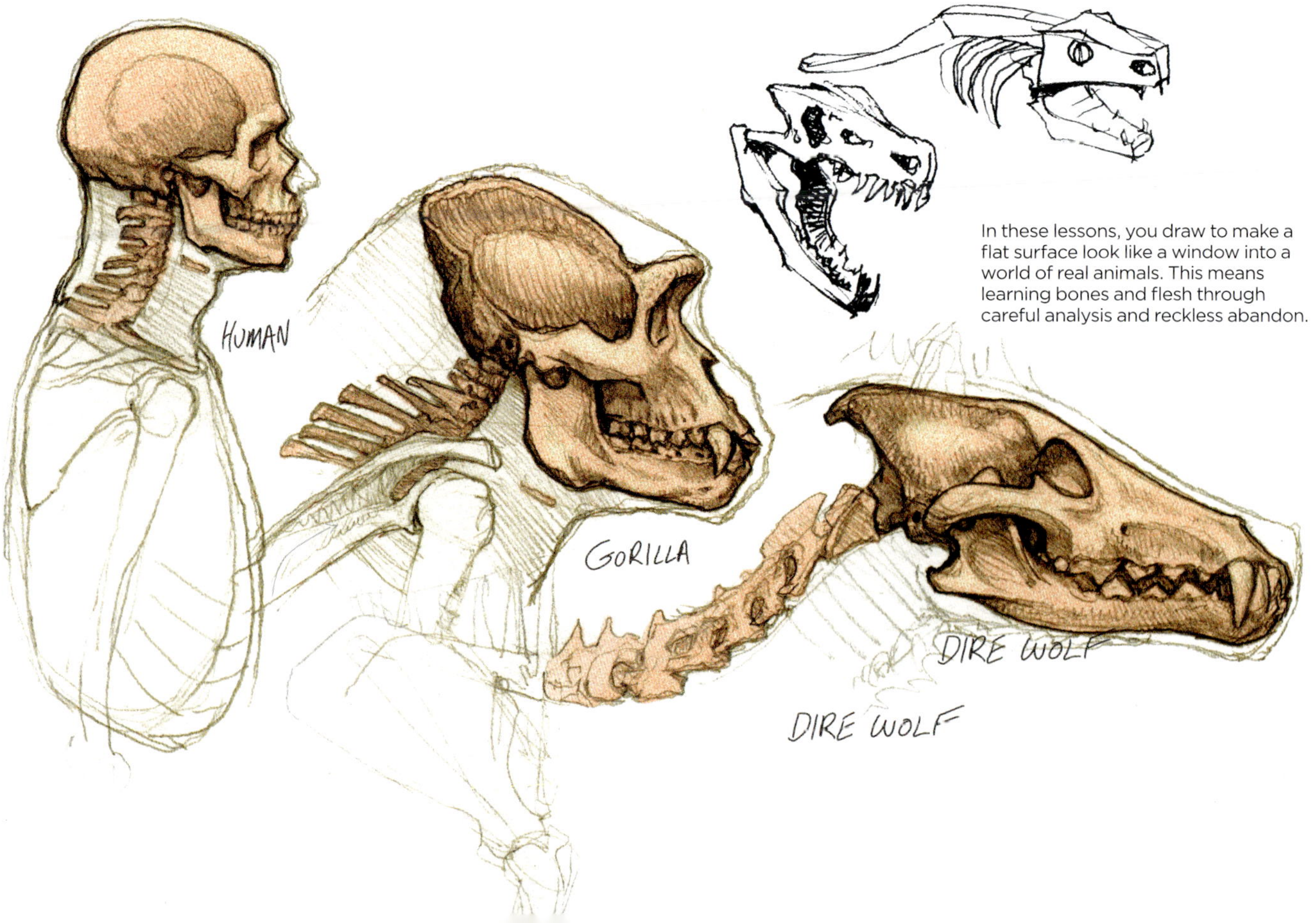

HUMAN

GORILLA

DIRE WOLF

DIRE WOLF

In these lessons, you draw to make a flat surface look like a window into a world of real animals. This means learning bones and flesh through careful analysis and reckless abandon.

1. THE NECK BONES

MOST NECK BONES ARE DEEP AND HIDDEN, BUT THEY AFFECT THE SURFACE WHEN ANIMALS MOVE...

HOMEWORK ASSIGNMENT

Get familiar with the neck

Treat the neck bones as a simple line, beginning low, usually with a bit of an "S" to the curve. When you can see the core of the neck, you know what parts of the flesh squash, and which parts stretch.

Mice have seven neck bones. So do giraffes. So do humans. So do almost all mammals. They're called cervical vertebrae. In a human, the top one (that's C1, for Cervical 1) is so deep it can't be seen, but in many animals it spreads out near the head and can be felt on the side, behind the ears. It's also known as the Atlas bone. It's wide, and may even look like part of the head.

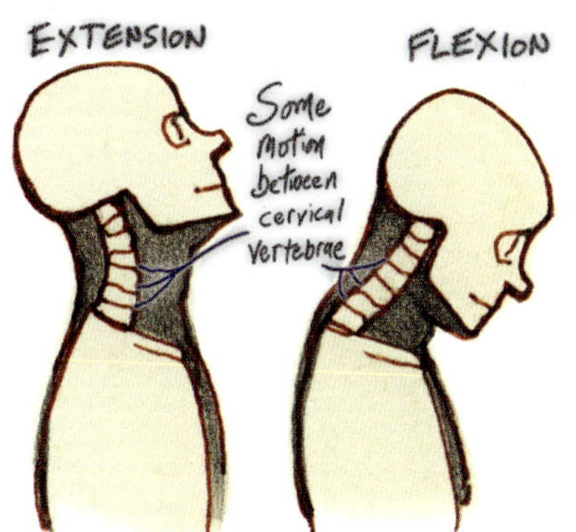

The stretching neck
A little movement between each neck bone adds up to a lot of movement for the whole neck, but rocking motion happens at the Atlas bone.

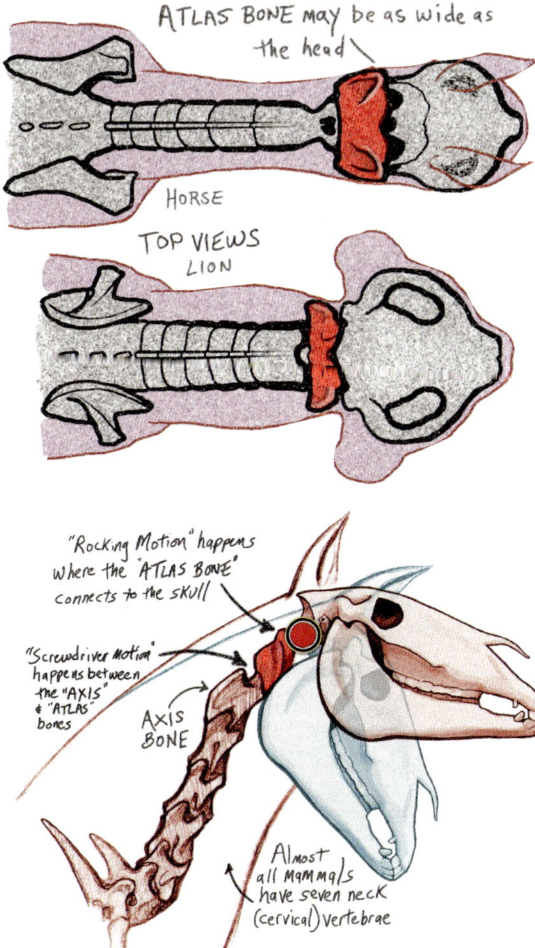

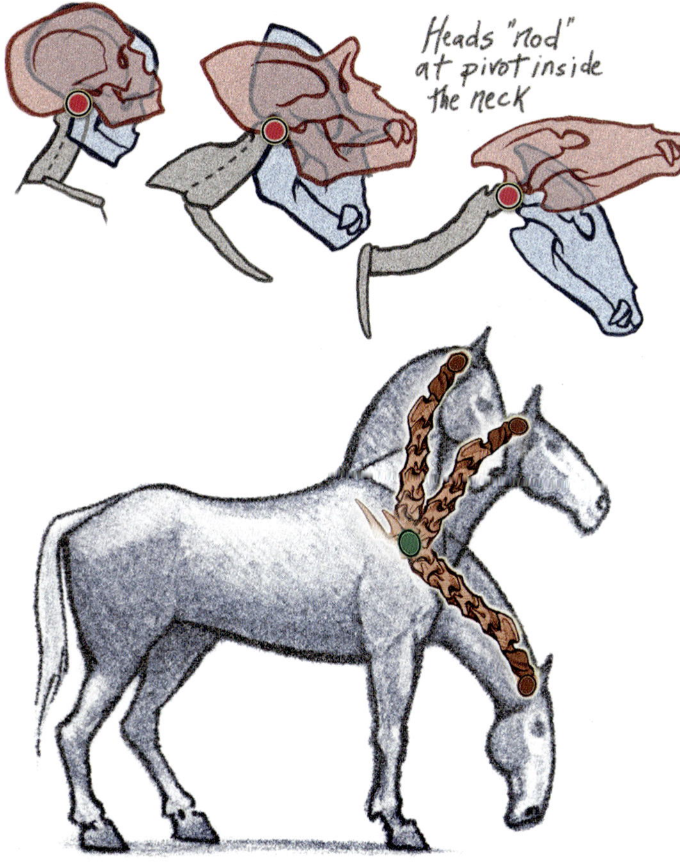

Taking the head to the ground

Grazing animals have necks that reach the ground. An internal ligament goes from the spine into the back of the head like a large, flexible rubber band, enabling tall animals to stretch down to the grass to feed.

Even a flexible neck would never reach the ground on a horse if the vertebrae began at the top. They begin low, almost halfway down the front of the shoulders.

2. ANATOMY AND FORM OF THE NECK

LEAVE COMPLEX NECK ANATOMY TO THE VETERINARIAN – ARTISTS CAN SIMPLIFY NECK FORMS FOR THE INFORMATION THEY NEED…

Neck muscles have inconsistent names because the structures vary. The muscle that goes from your collar bone to the bump behind your ear is the sterno-cleido mastoid. Cleido refers to the part that connects to your clavicle – but most animals don't have clavicles, so that muscle may be called the sterno-mastoid (sternum into mastoid process) or the cephalo humeral (from head to humerus) or other variations.

The names must not bog you down from your concerns. Let's look at what animal necks have in common that artists need to know.

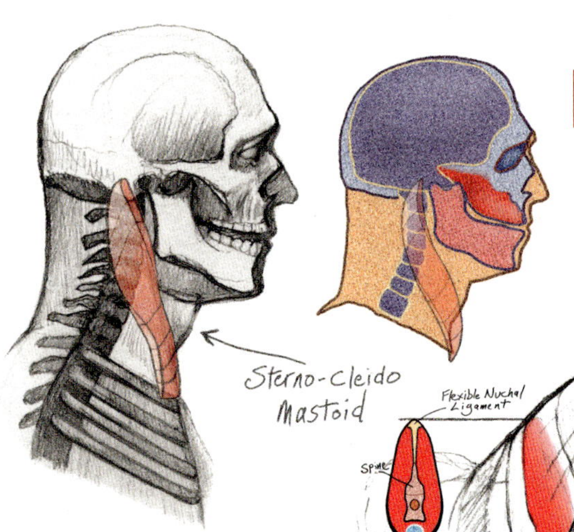

A shoulder base

The torso is the foundation of the neck, which means that it's usually best to begin with the forms of the shoulder to create a neck. Necks are usually a bit thicker toward the base in cross-section; they are mostly tissue (ligament, muscle, and fat), so gravity pulls them into a slightly teardrop-looking shape.

A core of bones

As with all anatomy, don't worry about hidden details unless you're doing research. Seek the simplicity of the neck core. That comes first, then muscles.

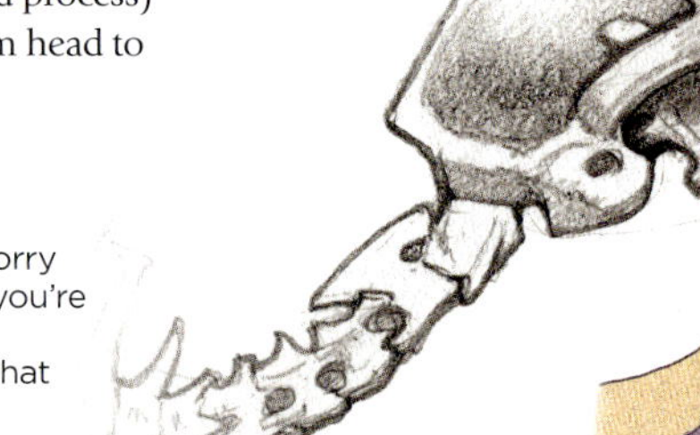

The little gnarls on neck vertebrae are complex… & won't help you draw necks

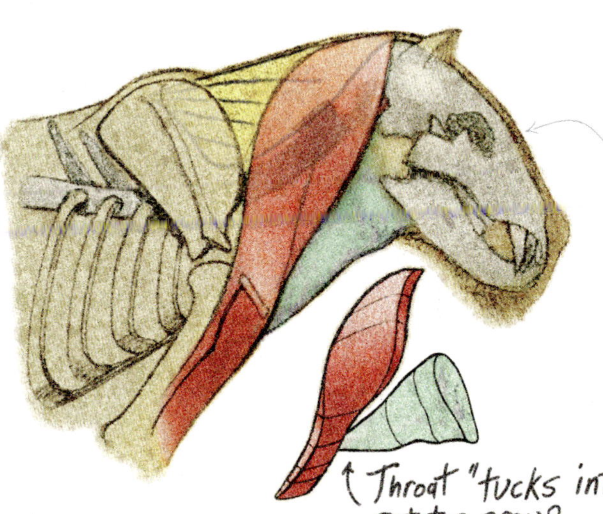

A rotator set and a throat network

There are many neck muscles that overlay each other. The most assertive is the group (with varying names) that spirals from behind the ear into the shoulder point. The throat is made up of muscle, tendon, ligament, cartilage, and even a floating bone, but it's wisest to simplify here. The throat is a passageway, a hose or, better still, a funnel. It inserts between the spiraling neck group.

Squash and stretch

You can see the animator's principle of squash and stretch most obviously at the neck. When a horse turns its head to look behind itself, one set of side muscles contracts while the other side relaxes.

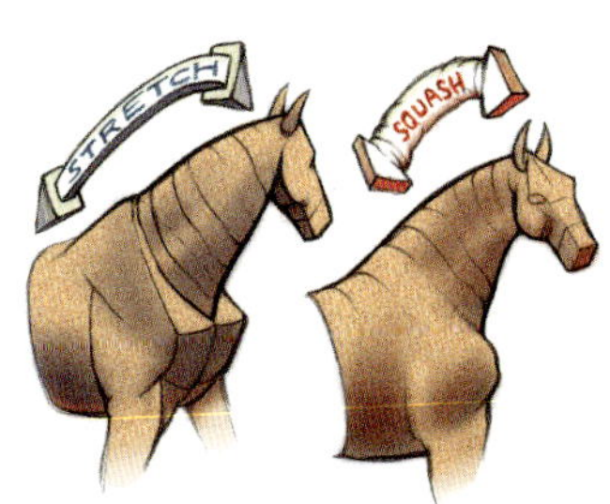

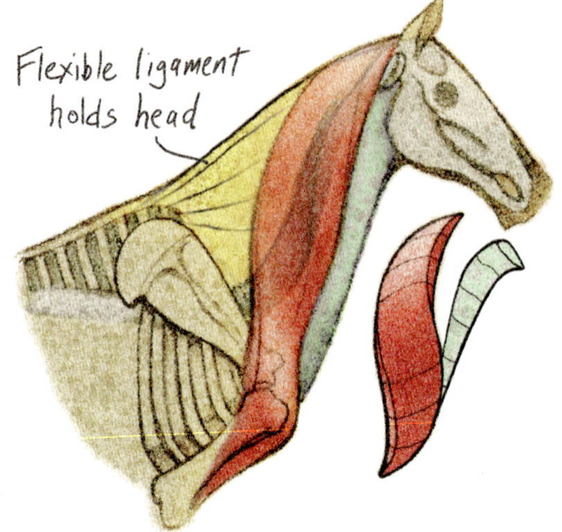

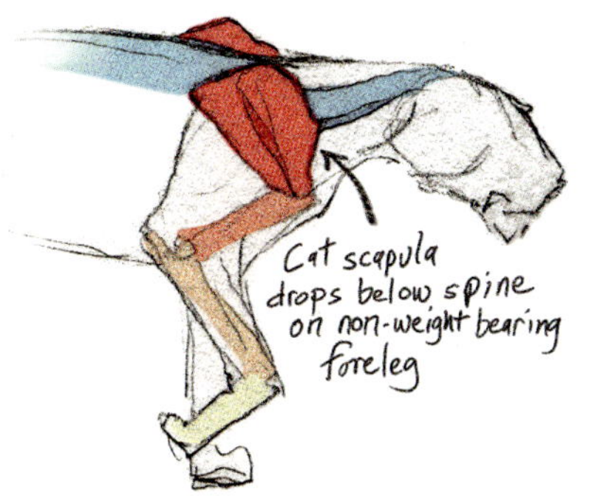

Cat confusion

Cats may appear to have assertive neck vertebrae at the peak where the shoulder and neck meet. Watch it move, though, and you'll see that it's not a neck vertebrae, but a scapula. Cats have shoulder blades that crest higher than their spines.

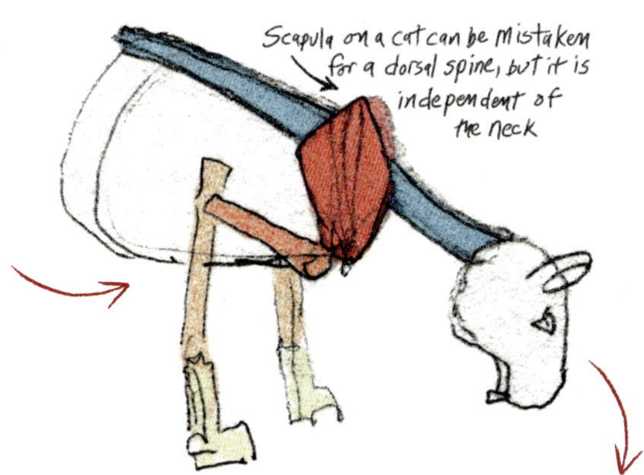

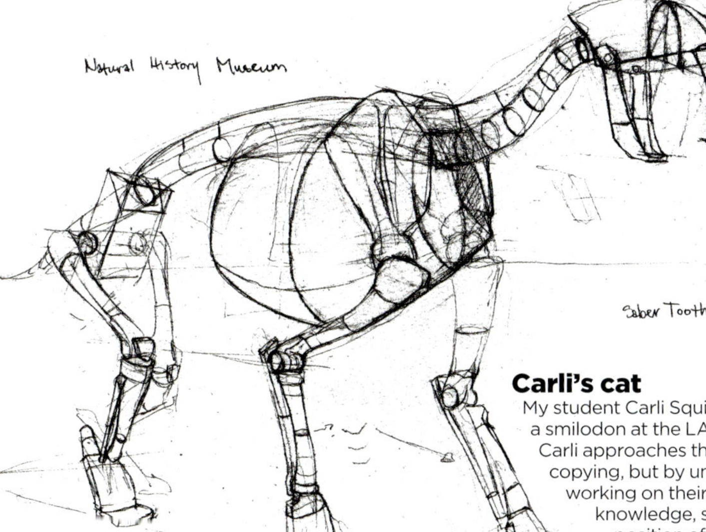

Carli's cat

My student Carli Squitieri did this analysis of a smilodon at the LA Natural History Museum. Carli approaches this complex figure not by copying, but by understanding the forms and working on their connections. With this knowledge, she can change the position of its head without a model.

HOMEWORK ASSIGNMENT

Turn skeletons to architecture

You can almost guess this assignment, as I recommend it all the time: reduce animal skeletons to architecture, like Carli did in the sample on this page. It's the great challenge of draftsmanship, and will help you understand hidden neck anatomy. A twisted pipe is a useful analogy for animals with flexible necks that can look behind themselves.

Twisting necks

If you find it difficult to twist a form, begin by placing two or three box forms. Connect the proper corners, and you'll solve the complexity one step at a time.

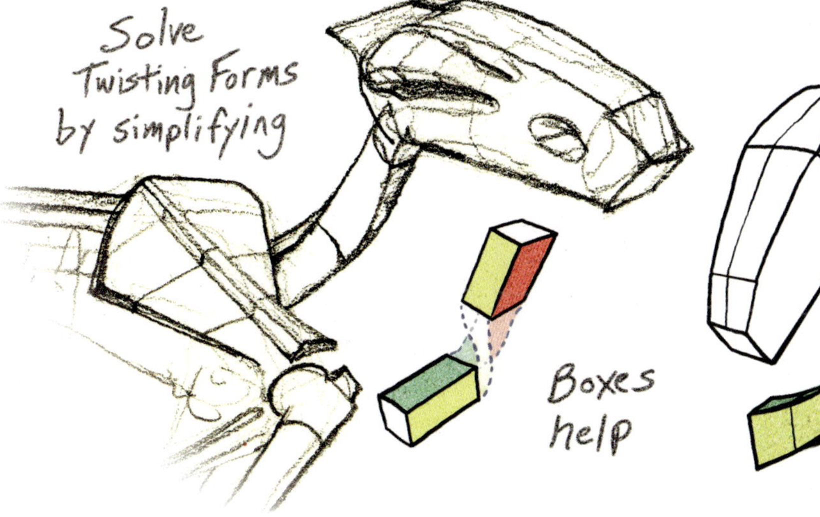

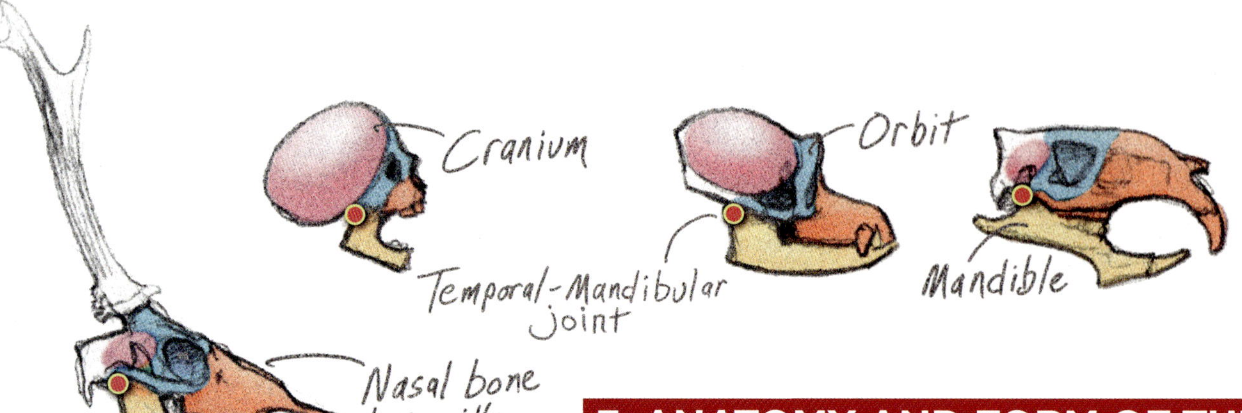

3. ANATOMY AND FORM OF THE HEAD

ANIMAL HEADS HAVE MANY VARIATIONS, A FEW COMMONALITIES – AND THREE DIMENSIONS IN EVERY CASE...

Skulls have many parts, so you must simplify. The cranium is the brain case. It's egg-shaped, which is obvious in human and ape skulls but not in many animals because it can't be seen. It's very small, buried under a cranial ridge, and covered with a large muscle (the temporalis) on the side of the head. The eye sockets (orbits) face forward on most predators, and to the side on most prey animals. The upper jaw is made up of the long protruding nasal bone and the maxilla, which simply holds the teeth. The lower jaw (mandible) is the only moving part on a skull. It has its hinge, the temporal-mandibular joint, just below and in front of the ear.

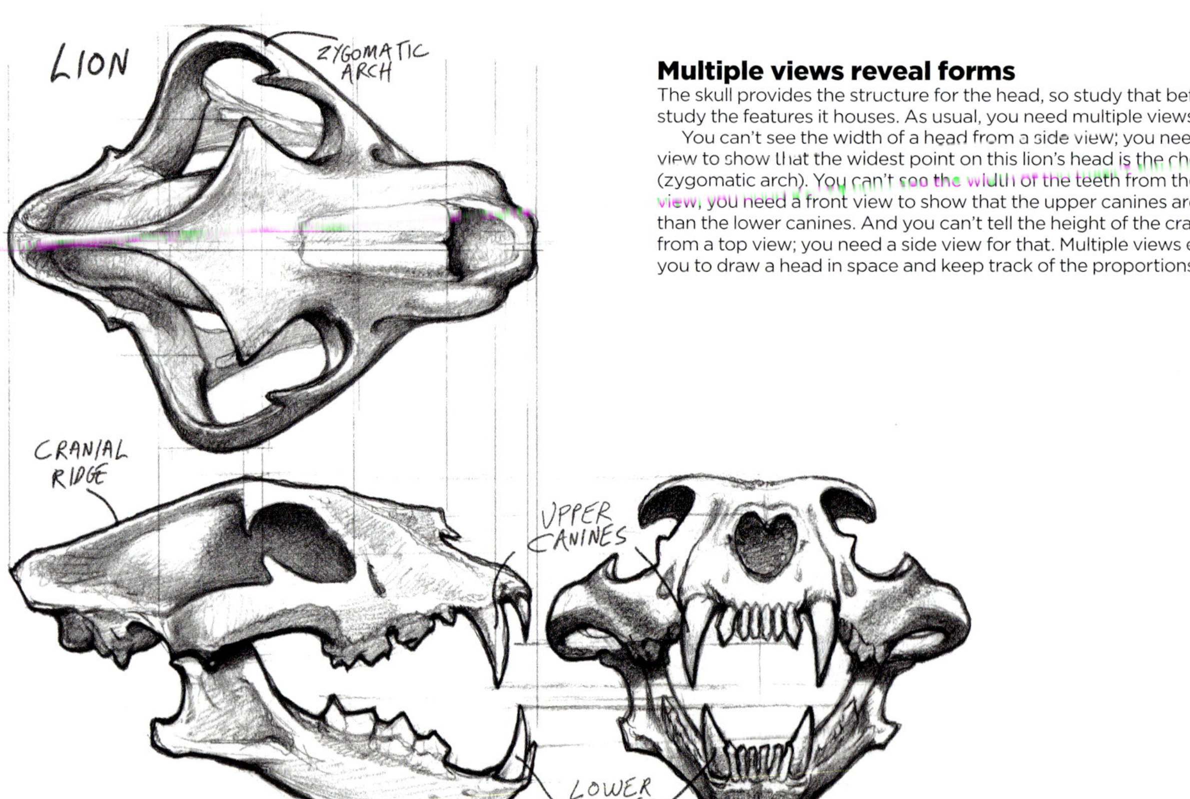

Multiple views reveal forms

The skull provides the structure for the head, so study that before you study the features it houses. As usual, you need multiple views.

You can't see the width of a head from a side view; you need a top view to show that the widest point on this lion's head is the cheekbone (zygomatic arch). You can't see the width of the teeth from the side view; you need a front view to show that the upper canines are wider than the lower canines. And you can't tell the height of the cranial ridge from a top view; you need a side view for that. Multiple views enable you to draw a head in space and keep track of the proportions.

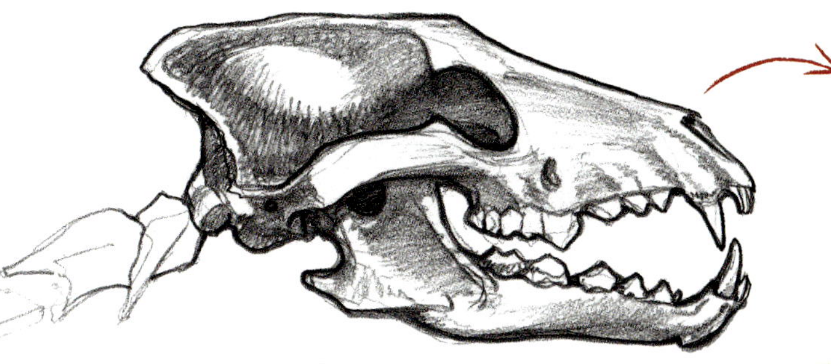

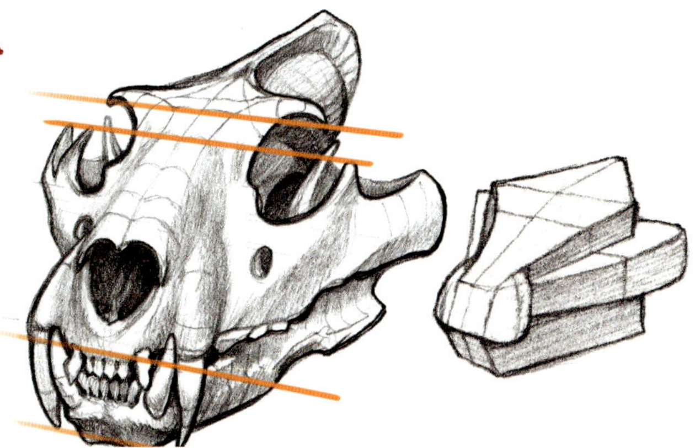

It's tricky to tip

Tipping one of these multiple views in space can get mind-freezingly complex. The solution is to reduce the head to big forms before placing small parts. Get your head around this, and you're well on your way to mastering head movement.

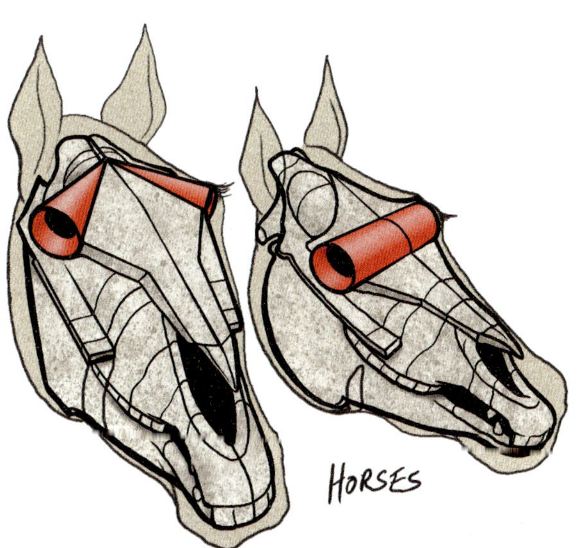

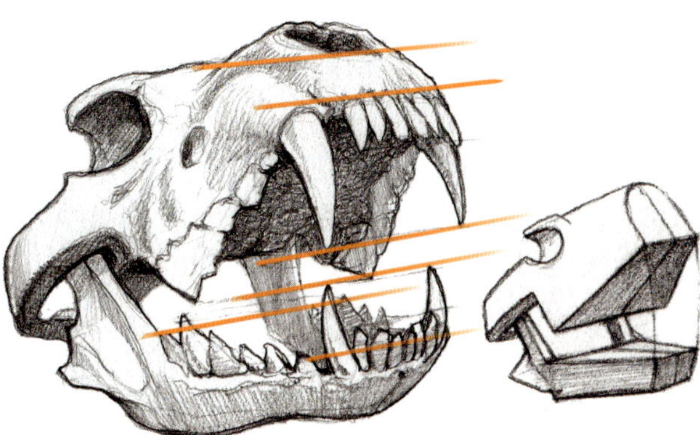

Relying on X

Notice that whether a creature's mouth is open or closed, the X lines (shown here in orange) always stay consistent. That can help you when you're working on a fleshed creature's head and you need to locate the distant canine.

Placing eyes

The eyes on prey animals look out to the side – sort of. If it was that simple, a cylinder across the skull would solve their placement. On most prey animals, the eyes are not completely out to the side, but aimed slightly forward. If you place a center point and create two cones diverging from that center, you have a structure in which to place eyeballs.

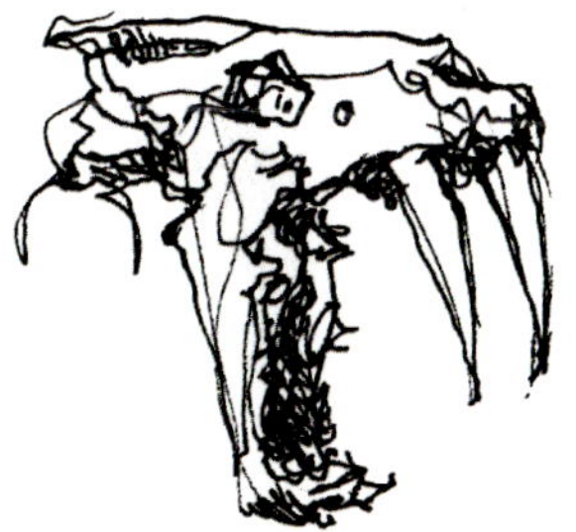

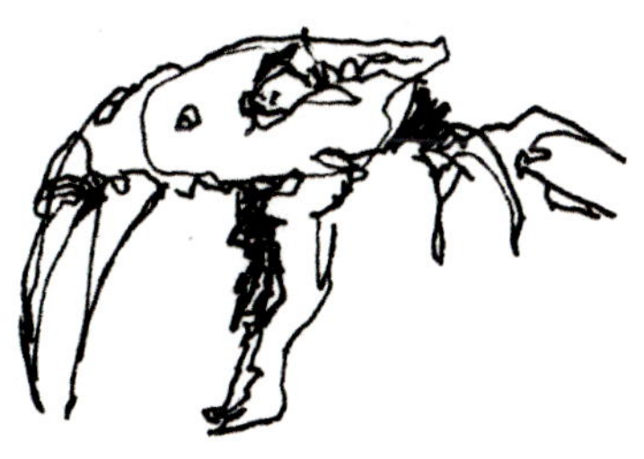

Take the antidote

All this analytical work is necessary for mastery, but it's not the end of it. When you've studied anatomy enough to control the forms you create, don't forget to take the antidote for finickiness. Draw fast; draw recklessly; draw for fun. You may do your best work when you let go of your intellect and follow your impulses.

ANIMAL FACES

Find out what animal faces have in common with human faces, and the crucial ways in which they differ

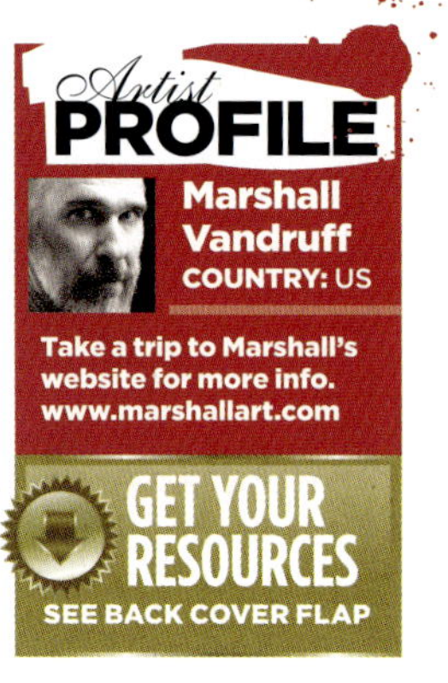

We began this animal workshop with basic forms, then worked from the torso to the hind legs, forelegs, neck, and head. We now finish with the the most emotive and expressive entity in life: the face. When William Blake wrote:

Tyger! Tyger! burning bright
In the forests of the night,
What immortal hand or eye
Dare frame thy fearful symmetry?

...He put into words a mystery that has haunted people ever since we began observing the world – the fact that living phenomena come to us in mirrored halves. Faces are essentially symmetrical. If they were flat, artists would need perspective to represent them in three-quarter views tipped away from us. But they are far from flat; they're made of 3D components, like a puzzle or sculpture.

To draw faces from any position other than head-on, and even to draw them head-on if you want them to look credibly solid, reduce them to simple forms based on anatomy. Then, when you have a solid structure, find expression: glorious, fearful, attractive, or amusing symmetry.

As in previous chapters, we begin here with technical lessons – including how perspective applies to the structure of a skull and how features themselves are made of three-dimensional forms – but we are heading toward a common artistic purpose: to create pictures that channel feeling. Heads display faces, and animals, like humans, are very expressive.

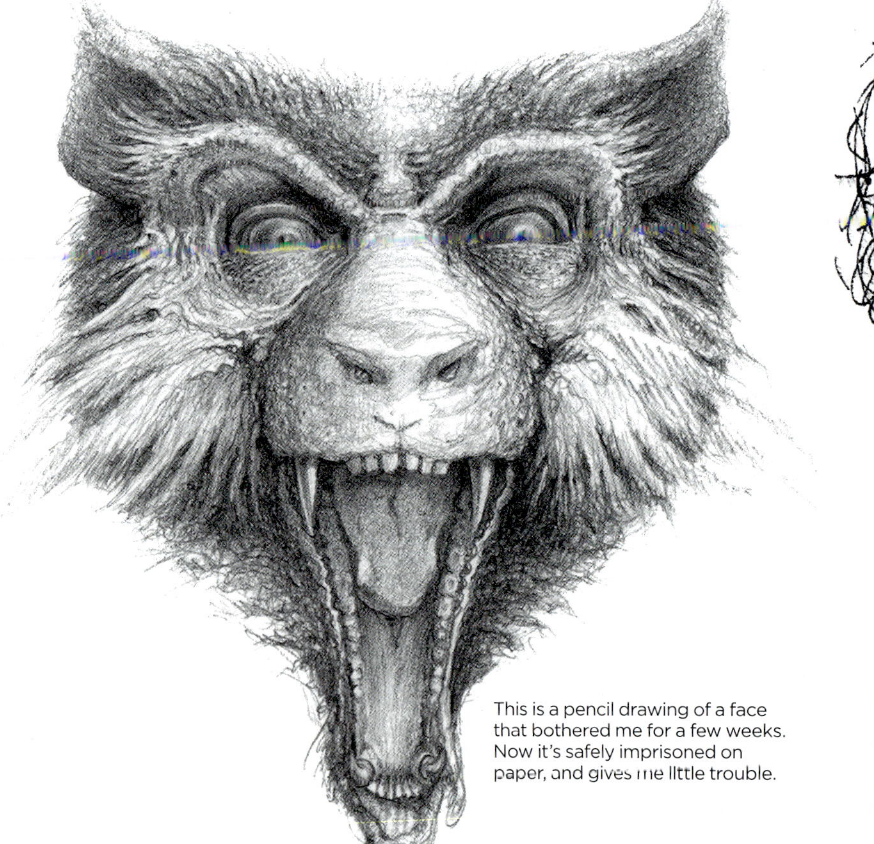

This is a pencil drawing of a face that bothered me for a few weeks. Now it's safely imprisoned on paper, and gives me little trouble.

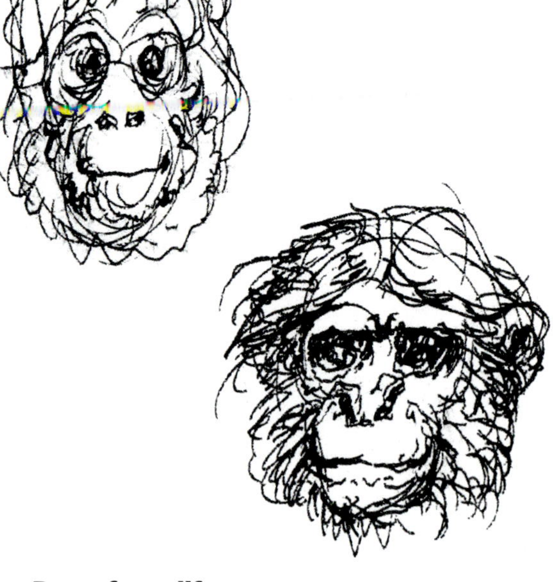

Draw from life

Short of a model or volunteer for a life drawing session? Visit a zoo or wildlife park with your sketchbook, and you'll find plenty of willing subjects. Mix spontaneous scribbles with more in-depth studies.

1. UNDERLYING STRUCTURE

NECKS HOLD HEADS, AND HEADS HOLD FACES. LET'S REVIEW BASIC STRUCTURES...

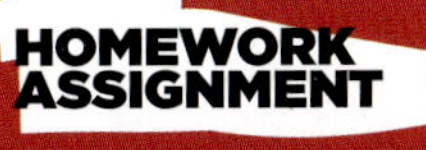

Box clever to carve a head
Choose two views of an animal head. Draw the simplest box into which each will fit. Then try carving out sections to leave the remaining form of the head.

Bones provide the hidden structure of the body – most obviously with the head, where the skull makes most of the form. There are many small and interesting parts on an animal's head, but no matter how perfectly a nose, an eye, or even an expression is drawn, it looks awkward if it doesn't fit onto the skull. So we'll begin with simplifications that enable you to place features where they belong.

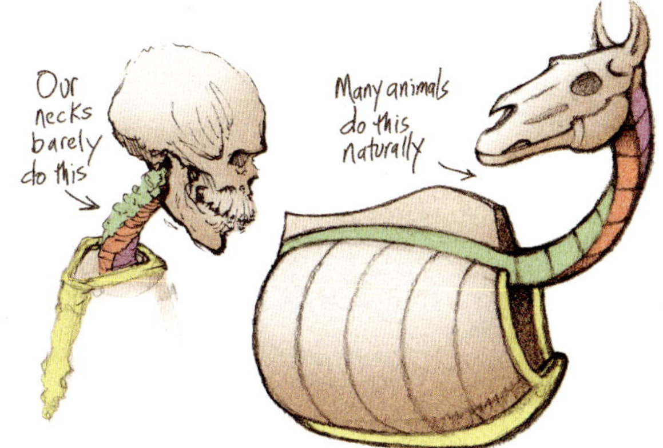

Useful reductions

Here are simplifications of monkey, human, and chimp skulls. Reducing them to their structural foundations enables you to tilt a head into many new positions, where reference is locked into a single position.

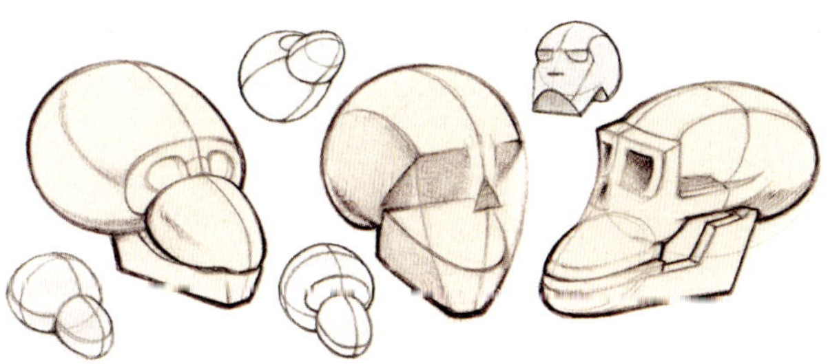

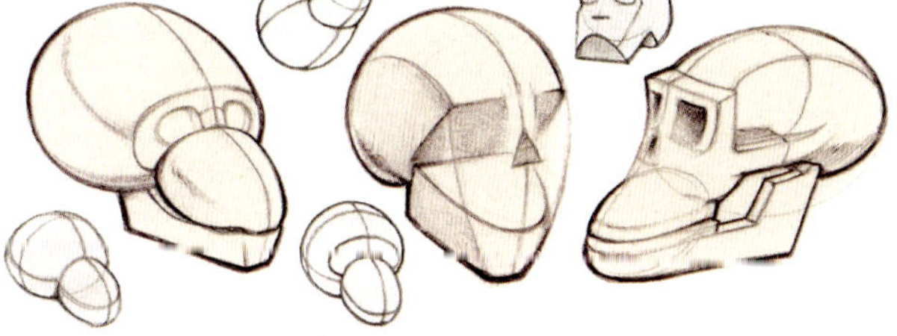

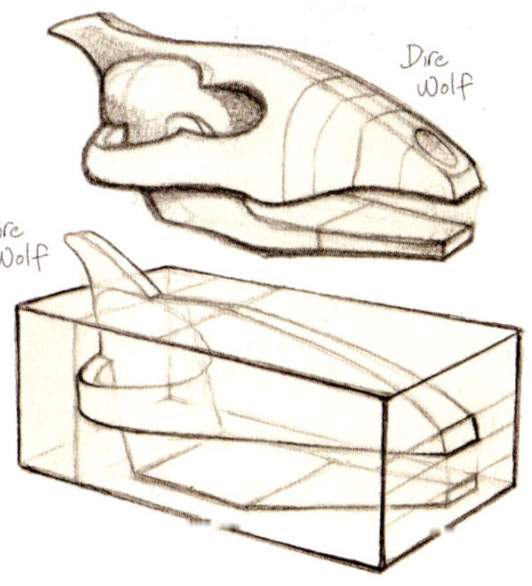

Thinking inside the box

Skulls are complex; boxes are simple. Placing a complex form into a box helps you keep track of width and depth lines. A box is scaffolding for precise construction, and tracking the lines can make your quick sketching more accurate.

HOMEWORK ASSIGNMENT

Eggs, boxes, and cylinders
Using the same heads as above for reference, draw the cranium as an egg, the facial structure as a box or cylinder, and the eye sockets as cylinders or cones. All of this is preparation for features. Always build the house before you start hanging curtains...

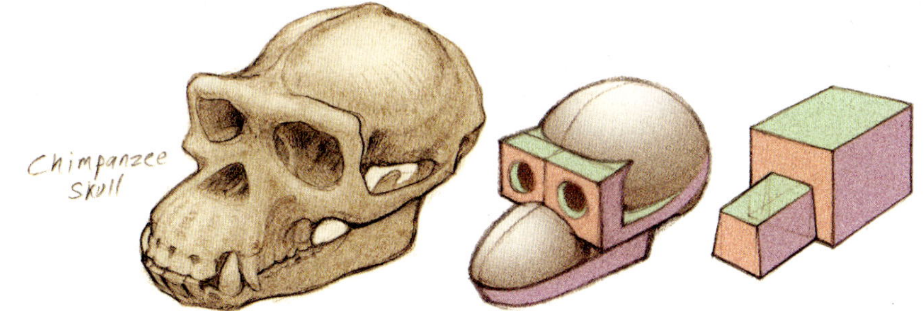

Forms first

Pay all the attention you like to bumps and gnarls and details. It'll mean that your drawings will impress people, but it may distract you from the basic structure that you must master first. If considering a head as a box, a ball, or an egg seems too simple, wait until you try. It's a difficult but rewarding task: difficult because the mastery of basic forms may take months of study; rewarding because the hidden structure of skull forms affects the position of every detail on an animal's head.

2. THE FORM OF FEATURES

EYES, EARS, NOSES, AND MOUTHS HAVE REMARKABLE VARIETY, AND A COMMON SOLIDITY...

Features are not painted on like colors or textures. They have their own shapes and thicknesses. Here are some observations to help you see them not as surfaces, but as smaller forms within bigger forms.

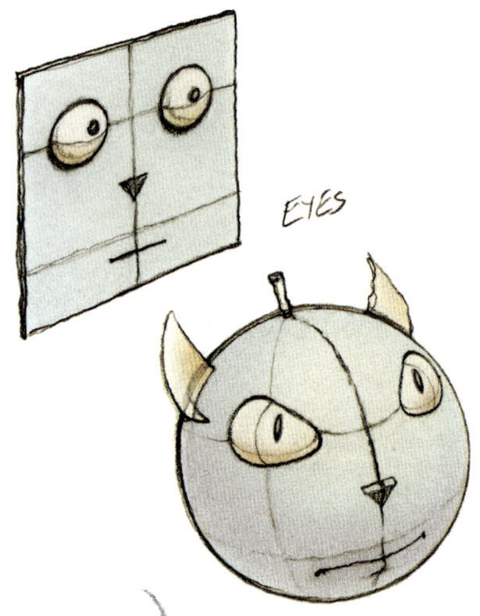

Thick, not flat
When eyes are on a flat plane, as they (almost) are on humans and apes, that simplifies foreshortening. But on animals with round heads, the distant eye wraps around the roundness of the skull.

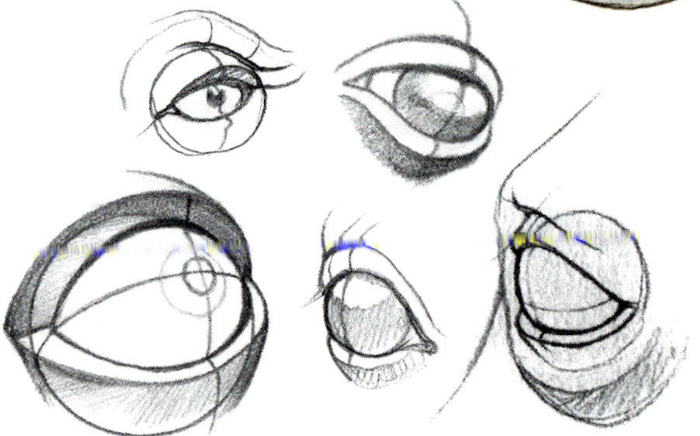

Eye as ball
All eyeballs are spheres. The lid is a sheath, usually rather thick, that wraps around the ball.

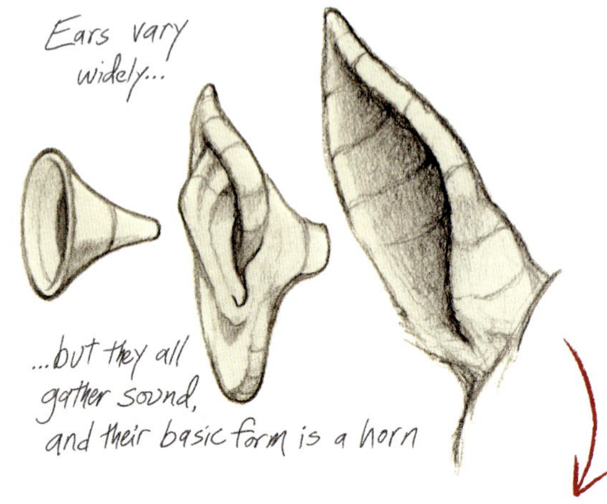

Making sense of ears
Ears are made of varying kinds of skin, cartilage, fat, and (for those ears that move) several muscles. But for artists, an ear is made of one piece - a modified horn that is used to gather sound.

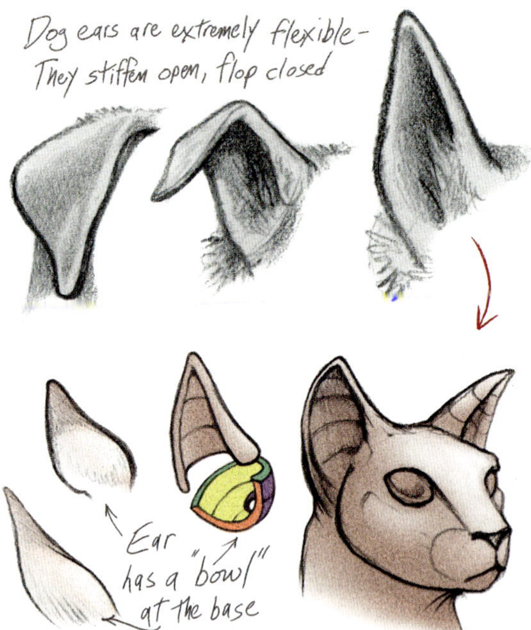

Curved surface
Even though most of the eyeball rests in the socket, the surface is still curved. Get this curve pegged before rendering.

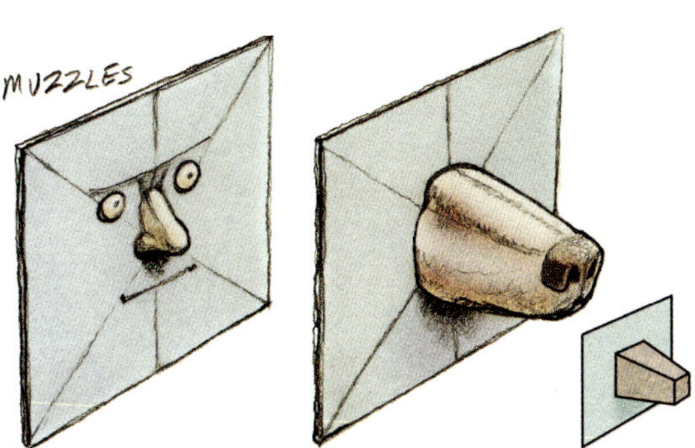

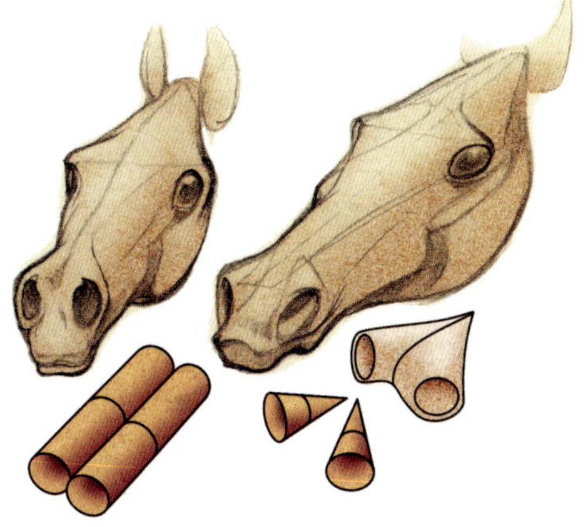

Snouts stick out

Our noses are measly compared to most beasts – the muzzle of an animal's nose and mouth projects forward. It helps to see it as a cylinder or a box. When a muzzle is in a three-quarter position, the planes with details, like jowls or nostrils, will give you a three-dimensional map to help you conform the details to the structure.

When nostrils flare

Horse nostrils, like their eyes, face somewhere between forward and to-the-side. Two cones can help you foreshorten that complex arrangement, but in some extreme conditions when a horse is running, their nostrils may aim forward like shotgun barrels.

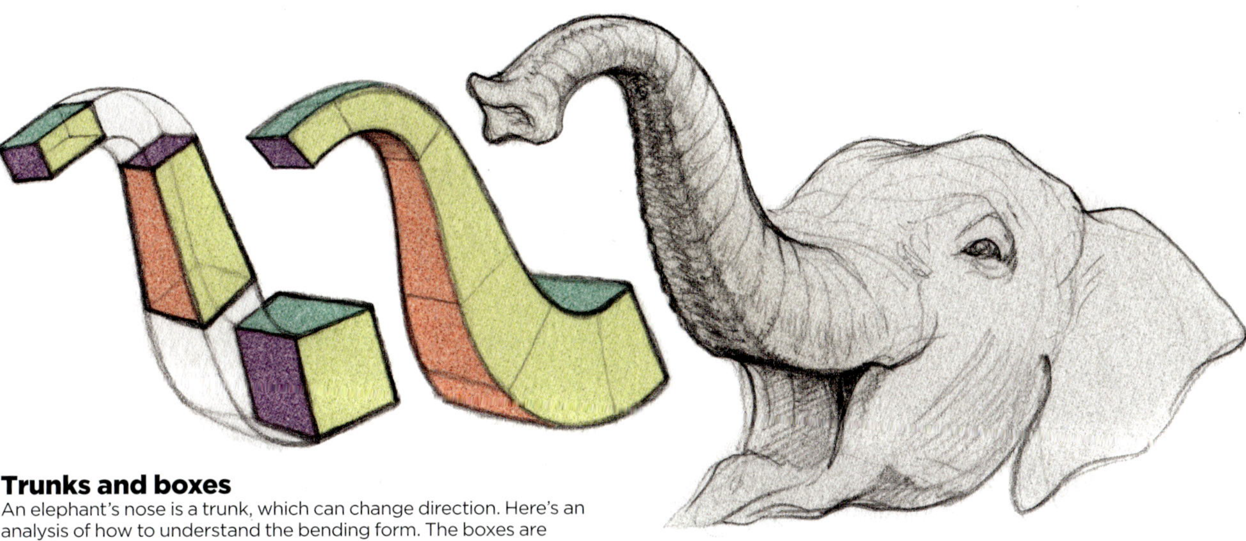

Trunks and boxes

An elephant's nose is a trunk, which can change direction. Here's an analysis of how to understand the bending form. The boxes are color-coded to help you keep track of the disappearing planes. The folds and wrinkles on the fleshy trunk act as cross-contours – perspective lines that define the thickness all along.

Jaws as hinges

Jaws are simple from the side: they're hinge joints. From other angles, they may appear quite triangular – wider at the back and narrow at the front. You must find an area where the side and front of the mouth meet to make a change of planes. In three-quarter views, canines make a convenient break, acting as front corners of the jaw.

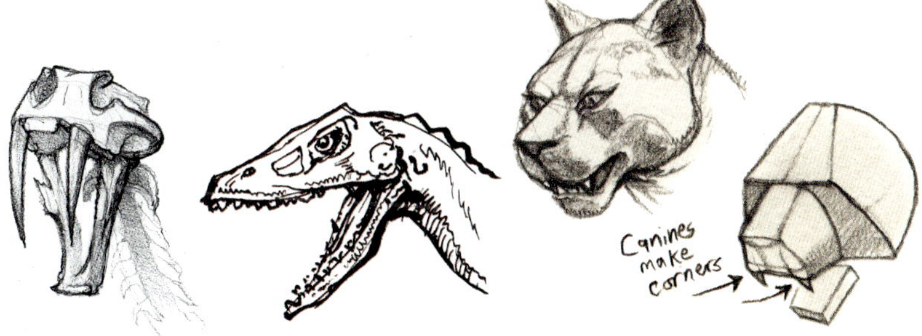

3. ANIMALS AS PEOPLE

HUMANS AND BEASTS HAVE THE SAME PARTS IN VARYING PROPORTIONS. LET'S COMPARE...

Socially, it might not be a good idea to compare your friends and family with animals. Artistically, it's a very good idea if you want to understand facial features. There are so many variations of animal features that it could take a career to learn them all. Comparisons are the most efficient shortcut, and the most fun – as long as they don't end up in hurt feelings or violent responses.

These metamorphoses, courtesy of *www.banedarkart.com*, make the point.

Precious piglet

Sometimes a human face inspires an animal: a monkey, a mouse, a kitten, a cub, a weasel, a chimpanzee. After all, what is a child but a talking animal?

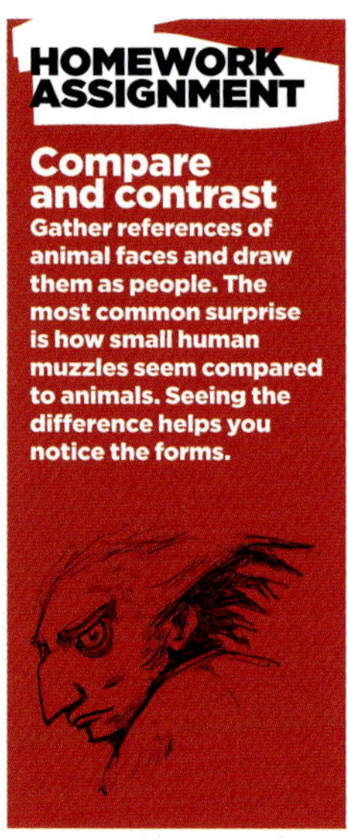

HOMEWORK ASSIGNMENT

Compare and contrast

Gather references of animal faces and draw them as people. The most common surprise is how small human muzzles seem compared to animals. Seeing the difference helps you notice the forms.

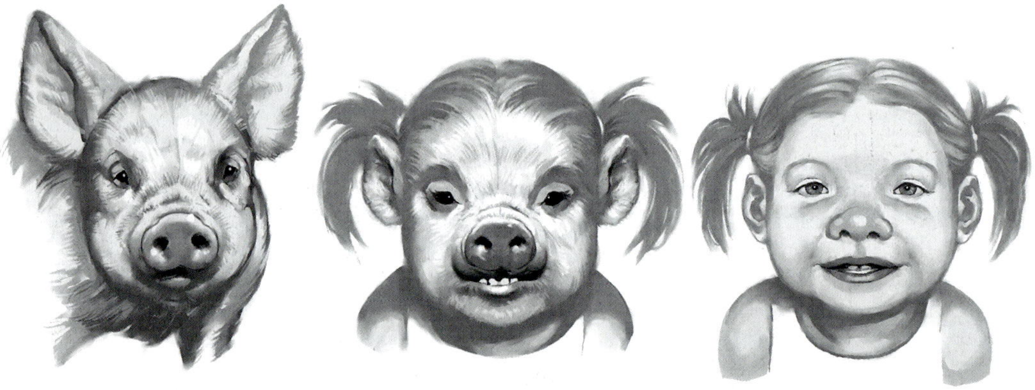

Big bear aspirations

If you lack for ideas when creating characters, or if you find yourself in a rut creating the same human character over and over, try using animal faces for inspiration. They can prompt universal and unique people-types.

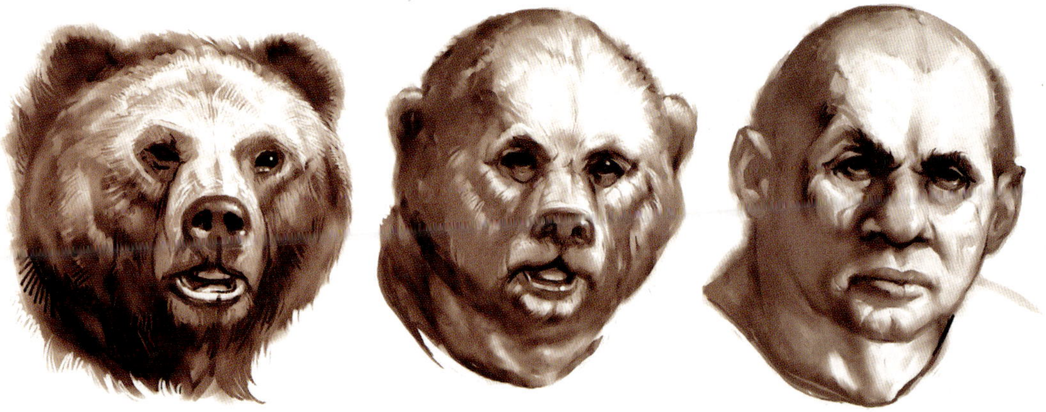

HOMEWORK ASSIGNMENT

Morphing magic

Try painting a morph between an animal and a human face, like Bane has in his studies on this page. The challenge – and the learning – happens during that transition stage in the middle illustration.

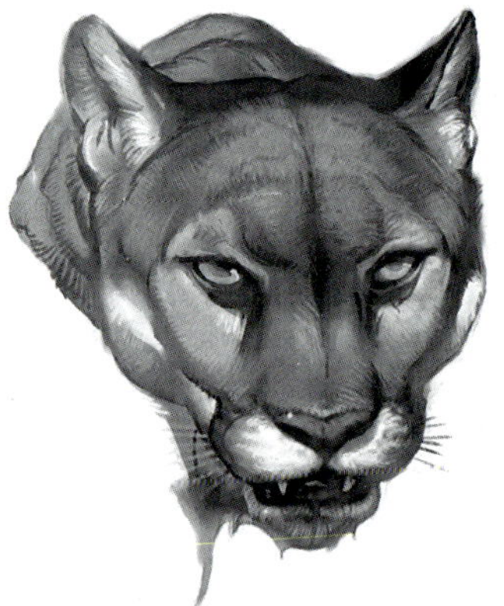

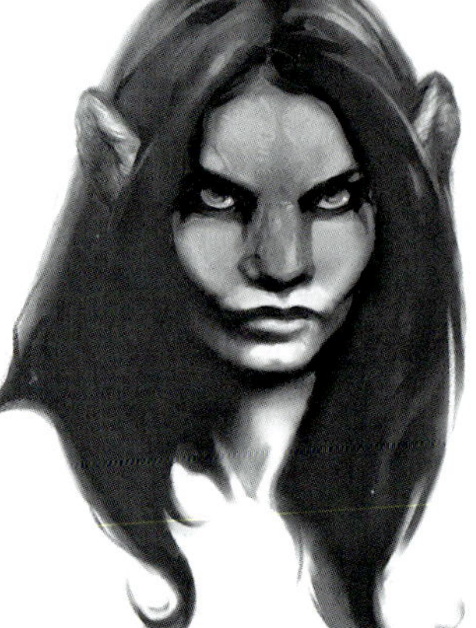

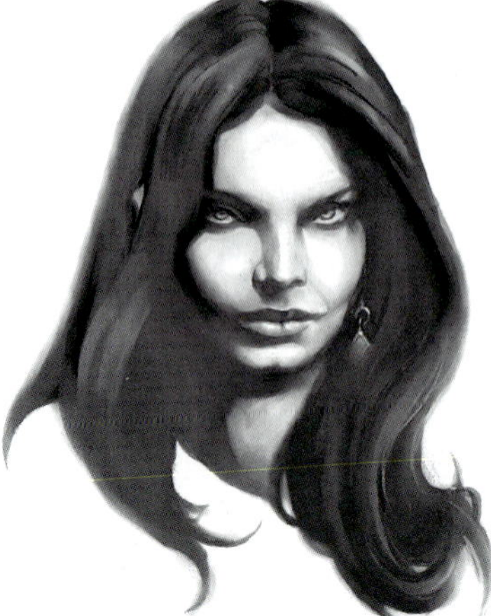

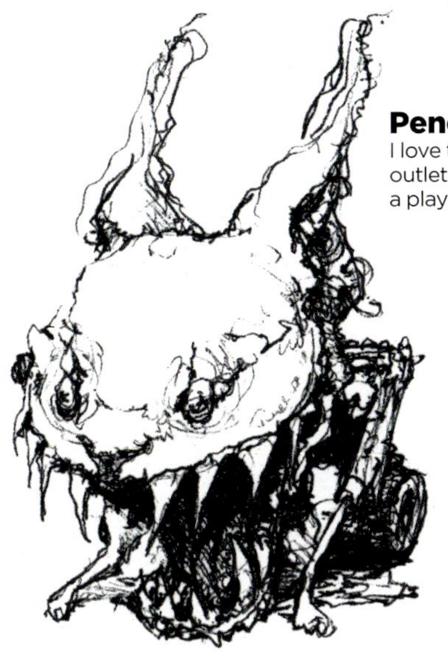

Pencil head
I love to draw. It's an outlet for feelings and a playground for ideas.

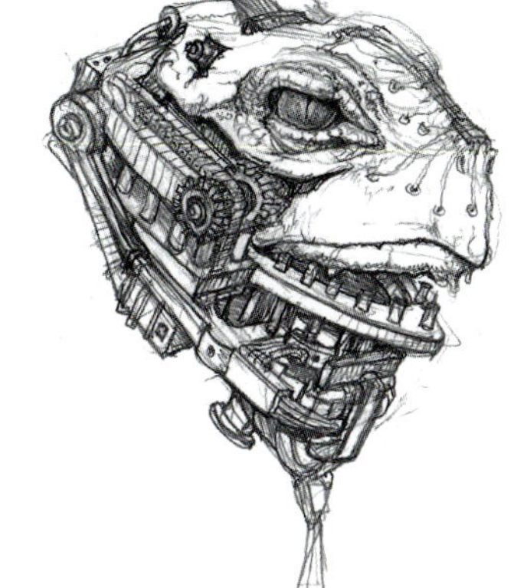

Draw stuff you like
Whatever talent you have, you can only bring it out with practice. The more enjoyable the practice is, the more likely it is that you'll keep at it.

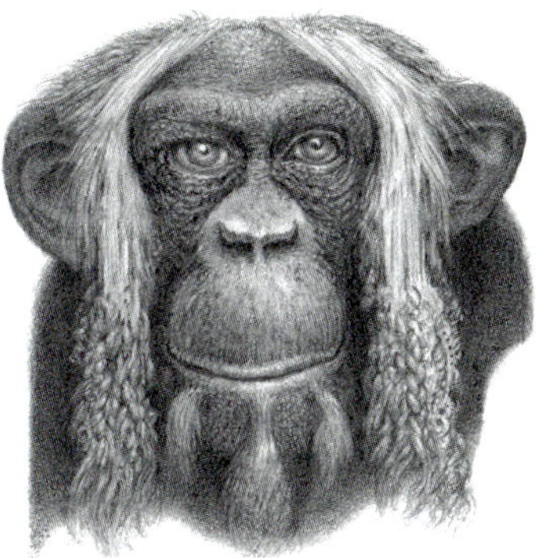

4. EXPRESSION IS THE KEY TO THE FACE

THE FACE IS THE CROWNING COUNTENANCE, SO GETTING THE EXPRESSION RIGHT WILL GIVE YOUR DRAWING LIFE AND MEANING...

It doesn't take a trained artist to draw an animal face. Children do pretty well – not because of their skill, but because of their emotional connections to faces. Most children, however, hope to have the grown-up skills that we've studied in these six workshops.

Technical skill helps you understand anatomy, so that you can keep the bones hard when the flesh stretches. Technical skill helps you understand forms so you can point a snout toward or away from you, or exaggerate a creature into absurdity, yet keep it looking real.

Technical skill is useful for anyone who makes a living at creating animals, but it's only the structure – the heart and arteries. By itself, it's dead. Emotion is the blood.

Animal faces evoke feelings. Their mystery, strangeness, terror, and splendor are more marvelous than we could ever imagine on our own. The more you feed your imagination, the more you can reflect their power in your work.

I hope these pages have helped you to draw animals, and inspired you to give your viewers the best you have to offer!

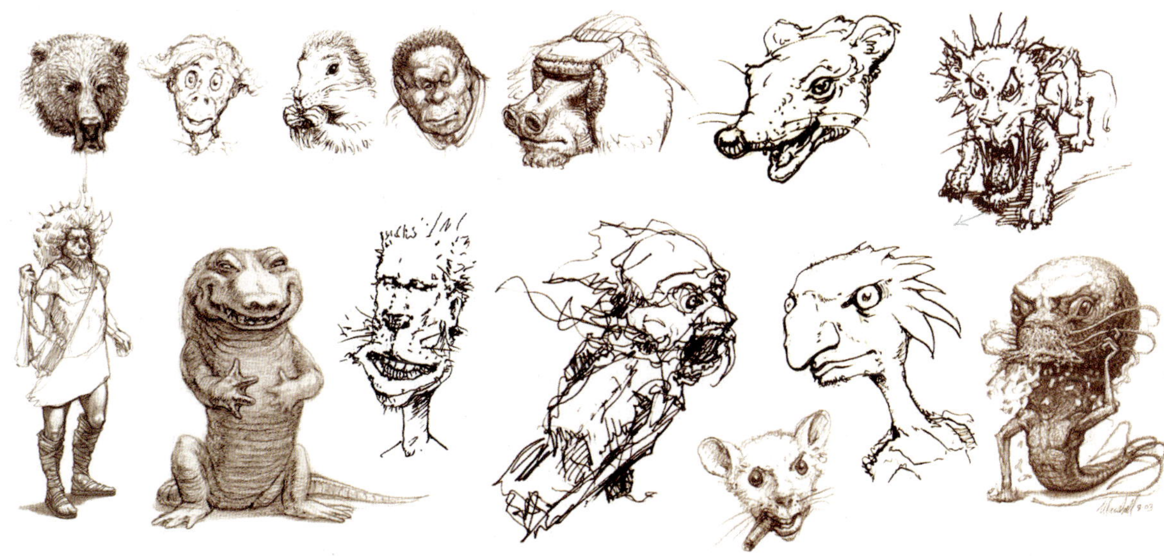

Digital art

Develop your art skills and mix your mediums: move from traditional techniques to digital

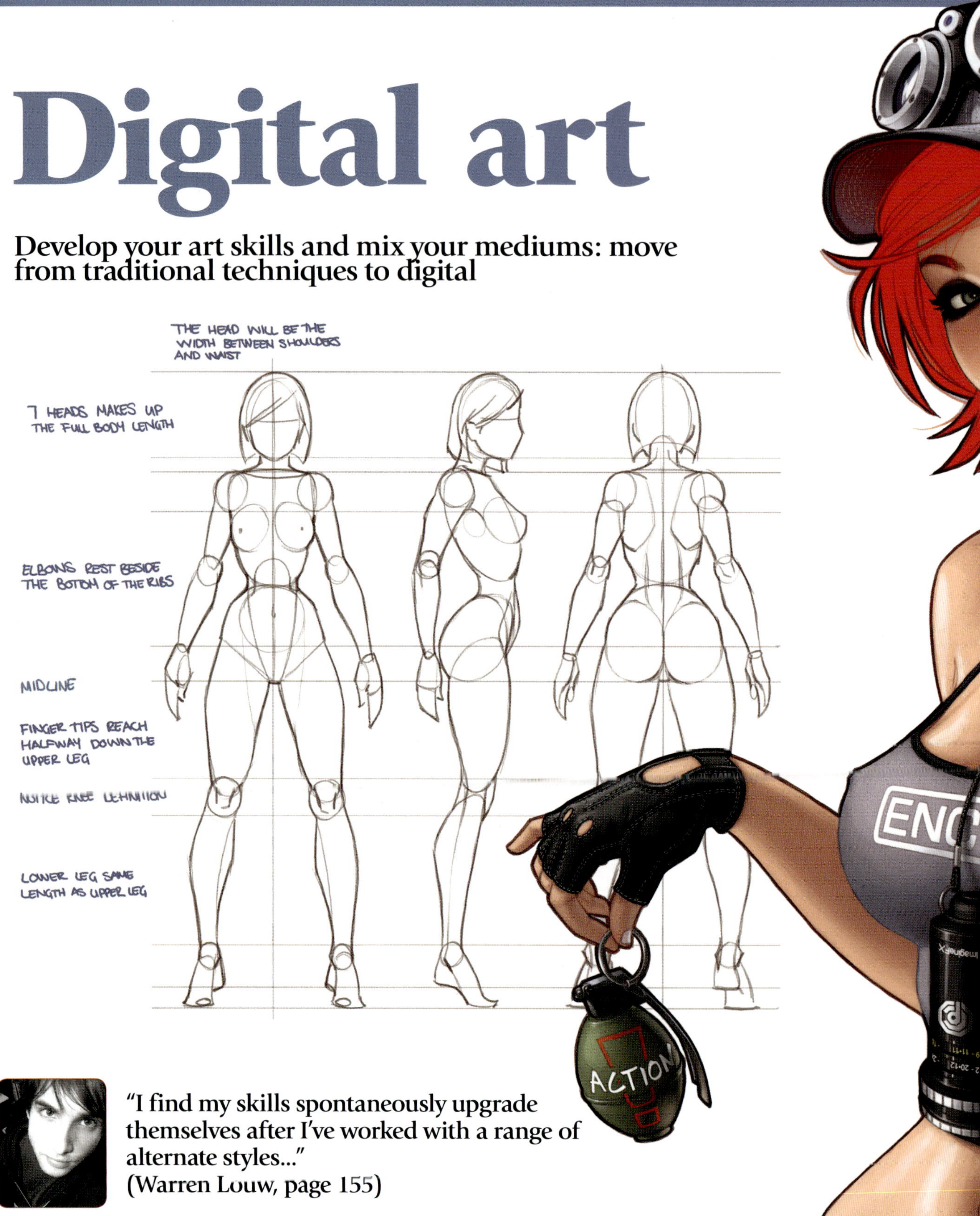

"I find my skills spontaneously upgrade themselves after I've worked with a range of alternate styles..."
(Warren Louw, page 155)

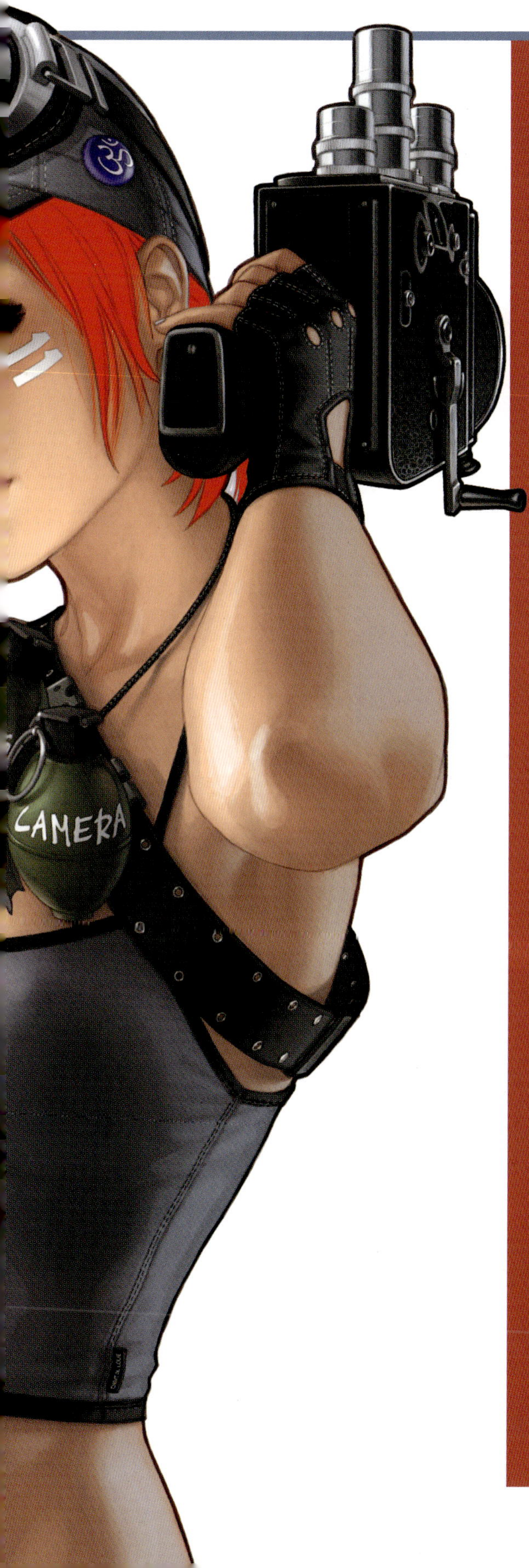

Workshops

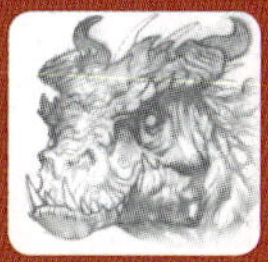

Experiment with digital art techniques

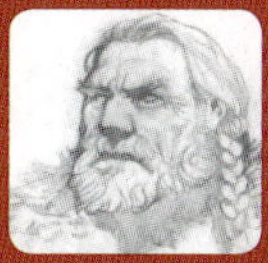

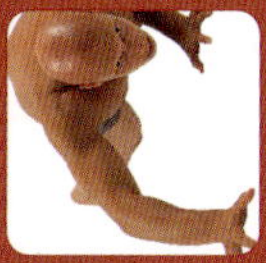

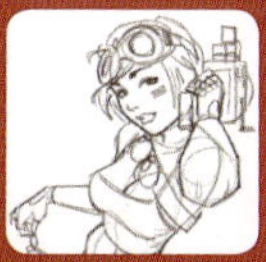

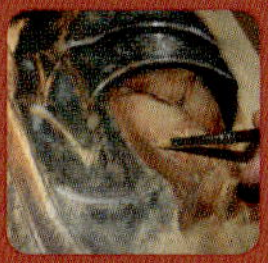

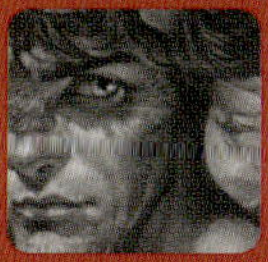

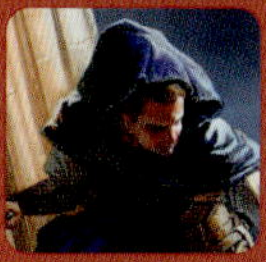

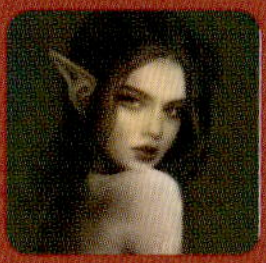

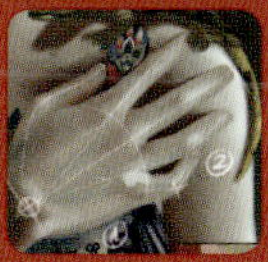

THE ART OF DRAWING: THE THEORY

Neglect your traditional drawing skills at your peril! Master artist **Justin Gerard** reveals how they can improve your art

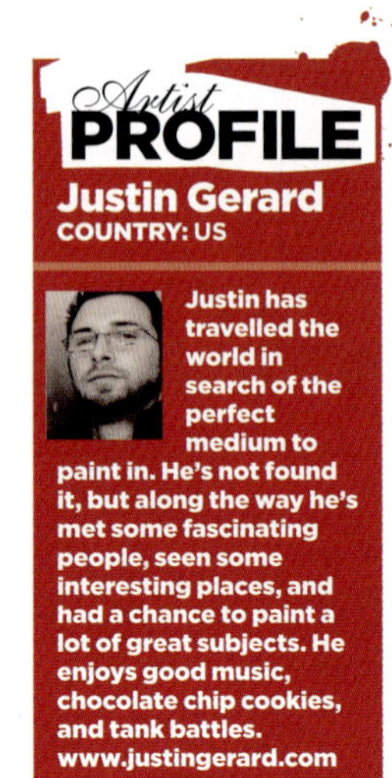

Justin has travelled the world in search of the perfect medium to paint in. He's not found it, but along the way he's met some fascinating people, seen some interesting places, and had a chance to paint a lot of great subjects. He enjoys good music, chocolate chip cookies, and tank battles. www.justingerard.com

There are two sides to art: the emotional and the technical. They are both equally important, but here we're concerning ourselves with the technical aspect of art, which is objective and can be taught with precision to almost anyone. The emotional aspect is less scientific and better left to be discovered rather than taught.

Drawing is the fundamental core of good illustration. Without competent drawing, an illustration may have a lot of heart but no brains. In the development of my particular approach to illustration, I've found the following two books to be of immense value: *Bridgeman's Life Drawing* by George B. Bridgeman and *Drawing Course* by Charles Bargue and Jean-Léon Gérôme.

What should I draw?

What to draw will be determined mostly by what each artist is interested in, but whatever this may be, there are some things that every artist should be extremely familiar with drawing. The most important thing to know how to draw is the human form, and specifically the hands and face. The study of these elements is extremely important if you're planning on communicating with humans; if you're doing art for semi-aquatic reptilians, then it may not be as necessary...

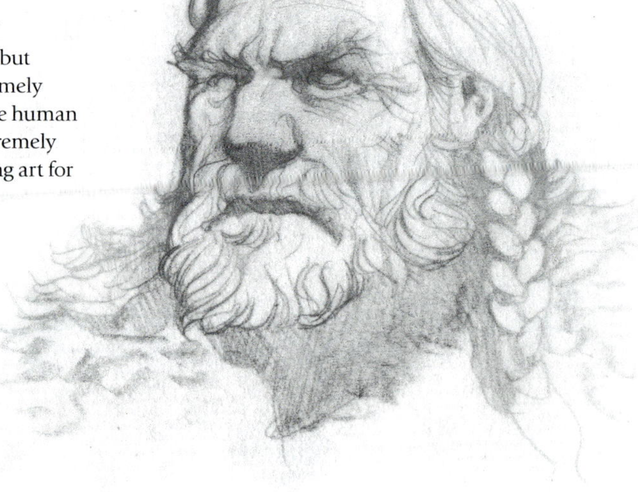

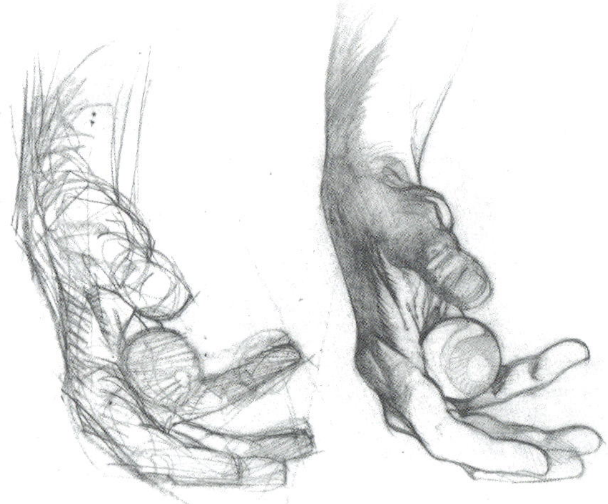

Practice your drawing skills by drawing your free hand, or your face using either a mirror or webcam.

1. Studies from life

Drawing from life is like doing knuckle push-ups for your mind. As well as improving your hand-eye coordination, it also helps build a deeper understanding of how light and shadow fall across a solid form. Communicating the illusion of reality via a thorough understanding of light is essential for an artist.

2. Building a visual vocabulary

When you draw from life you develop your visual vocabulary, made up of all the things you've ever drawn. As you draw a face, your mind remembers the lines and shapes. Later, as you draw from your imagination you'll find that you can recall these lines you've memorized. If you're an artist who enjoys drawing from their imagination, then drawing from life is even more important, to ensure that the ideas you're communicating are grounded in reality.

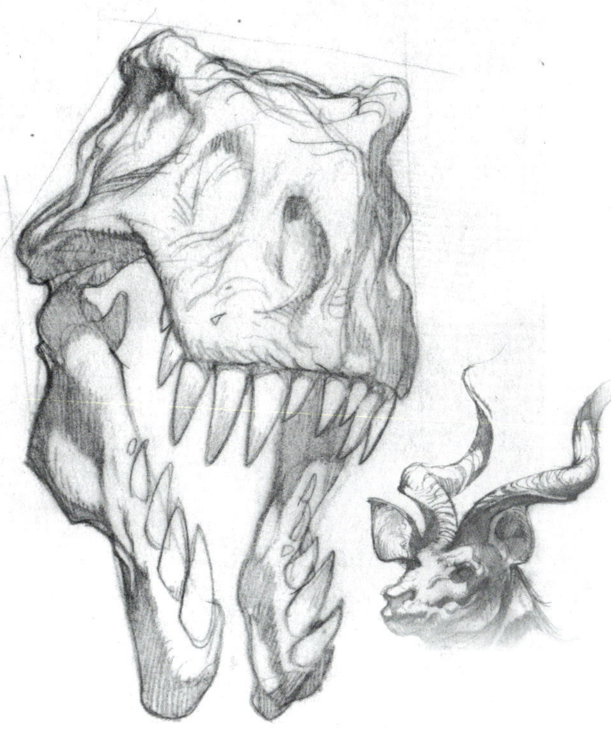

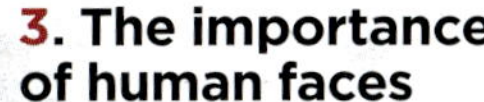

3. The importance of human faces

The human face is the most important study for the artist. The human brain dedicates a considerable amount of energy to recognizing the patterns of muscles on other human faces, to interpret the deeper aspects of what people are saying and to gauge their responses. Because of this inherent study of faces, a face will always be the most interesting aspect of an image and will be the first place that most people look. Therefore, knowing how to draw faces properly is paramount among the tools every artist needs.

5. The importance of animal forms

Humans are all well and good, but sometimes you find yourself drawing things that aren't quite human. In a word, aliens. When doing this, it's still important to ground your work in reality; you want your ideas to be believable, or at least anatomically possible. One of the best ways to do this is to make studies from animals. By memorizing the forms of animals from this planet, you'll be better equipped to draw those from other planets.

4. Mastering the human form

The human form is also an important study for the serious artist. Artists who can render it effectively have always been in demand. Da Vinci made drawings of groups of people he saw to capture their postures and how they related to one another. This attention to the human form is part of what sets a great artist apart from a mediocre one.

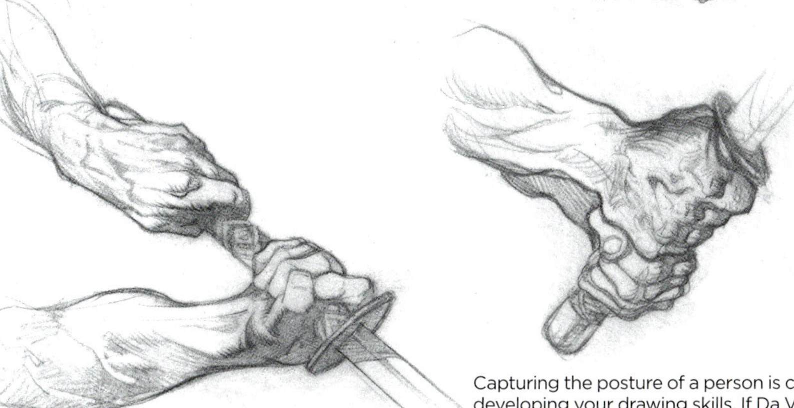

Capturing the posture of a person is crucial to developing your drawing skills. If Da Vinci felt the need to continually draw people, so should you.

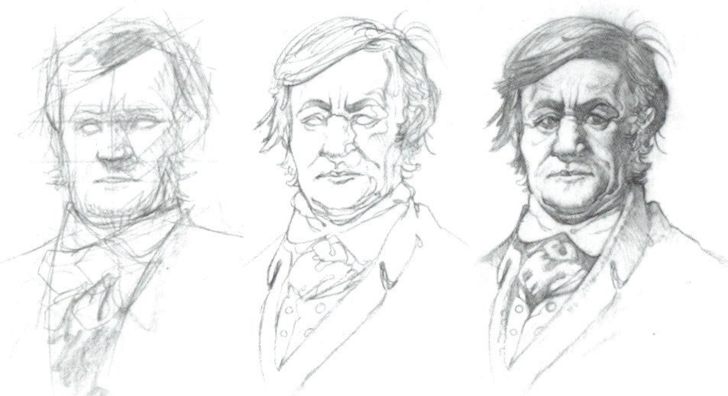

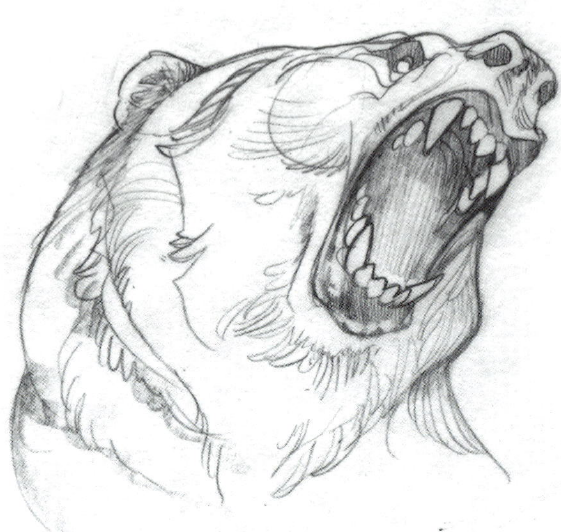

How do I draw?

There's no single correct way to draw. However, certain methods have been tested over time and have proved to be effective at producing good art. These methods aren't mysteries. They're readily available, and all you need is time, dedication, and a few library late fees to master the technical aspects of drawing.

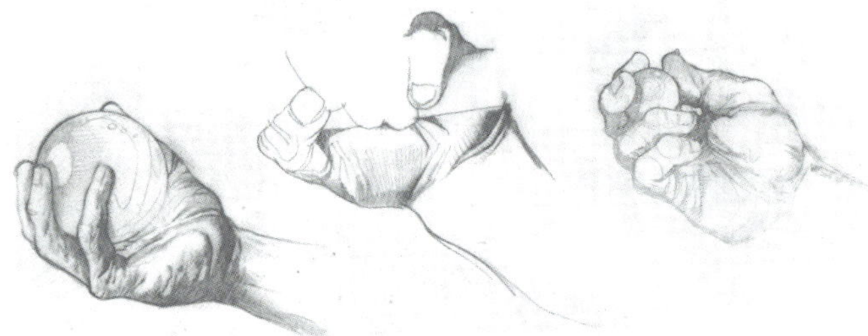

6. Think before you draw

Before you place your first line onto paper, try to see in your mind what the complete image is going to look like. You don't want to just haphazardly throw down lines at random. Then, when you do begin, start with very light lines to establish the shapes.

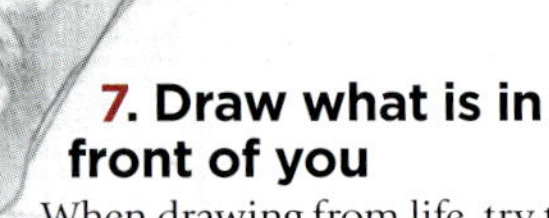

Imagine the lines on the page, study the subject in front of you, and then start drawing. It's that simple.

7. Draw what is in front of you

When drawing from life, try to remain true to what you're actually seeing. Later on you can go wild from your imagination, but your art will always be stronger if you have worked hard to be as faithful as possible to your subject matter in your studies. Remember that you want – and need – to ground your creations in reality

8. Committing to memory

One of the goals of drawing from life is to memorize the details and the general construction of your subjects, which then allows you to recall them later when creating your images. Your drawings don't need to be perfect photographic representations, but they shouldn't be caricatures either. When you're finished, you should come away with a better understanding of the construction of the forms and their details. You will then be able to communicate them with emotion, and not be hampered by a lack of technical skills.

"When drawing from life, try to remain true to what you're actually seeing."

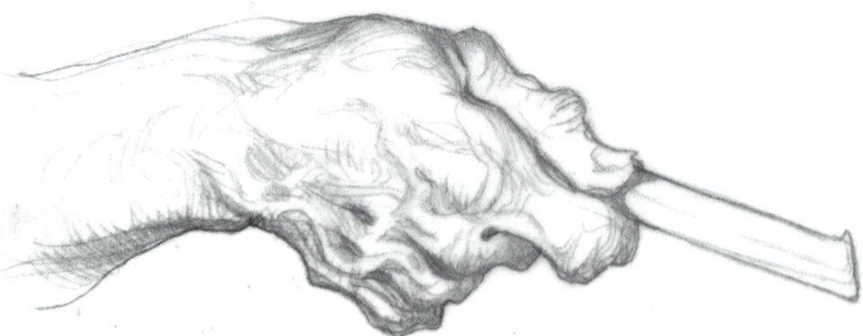

9. Why not just trace photographs?

Some artists trace photographs to achieve these ends. This is usually done in the interest of saving time. If you decide to go this route, then you will derive some understanding of shape and detail. However, I think the final results are less interesting and have less personality than freehand drawings – tracing a photograph is never going to be as helpful in truly understanding the construction of the forms. The drawings where I've had to fight my way through are always the strongest and most visually interesting.

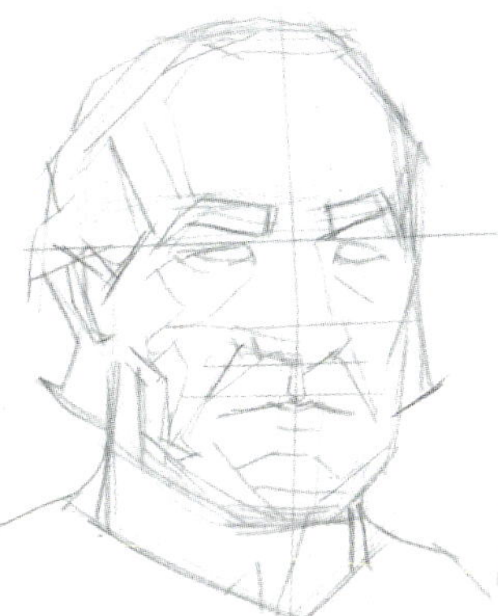

10. Refine an image from a previous study

As you work and rework to solve a difficult problem in an image, you may notice that your drawing becomes quite messy. There are many things artists do to solve this, but I prefer one of two courses of action. If the unnecessary lines are light, erase what's unnecessary and bulk up the lines that are the most important to minimize the stray lines. However, if the unnecessary lines have hopelessly overtaken the drawing, then transfer the drawing – either by vellum, serial graphite, or light table. When retracing an image, simplify the shapes down to what is most essential. The goal is to create fewer, stronger lines as you refine your drawing.

12. Knowing when to stop rendering

It's not necessary to render your entire image as a camera would. The illustrator's purpose in these life studies is not to compete with photography – what would be the point? It's more important to capture the idea of a thing, its shape and form, and the overall sense of its surface and details, rather than recreate a photo.

Drawing an object isn't the same as taking a photograph of it. You're communicating something beyond the subject's mere physical form.

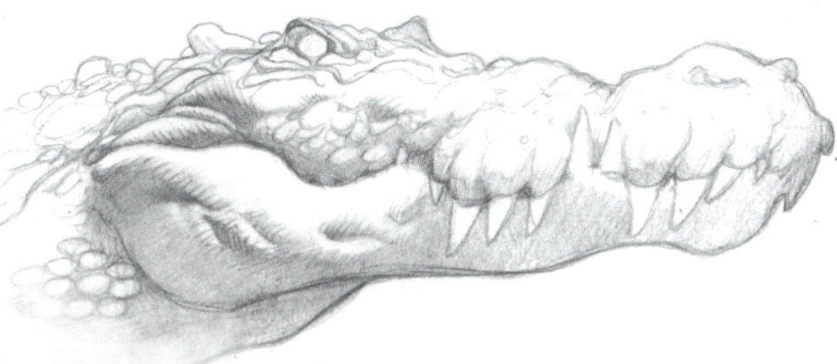

13. Rendering details

If everything is equally detailed, an image becomes flat. The crocodile is covered in scales, but only some of these scales are necessary to communicate the feeling of its scaly hide to the viewer. The sharpest details in your drawing should be reserved for the focal areas; leave the details that are outside these areas as suggestions. The viewer's imagination, using what you've provided them in the detailed areas, will be able to fill in the gaps.

11. Simplifying shapes

Part of the illustration process is knowing what to leave out of your image. We only have so much time available, and choices have to be made on what details we add or leave out. One small shadow may be vitally important, while another may just be visually confusing. Simplifying your shapes will give an image more clarity.

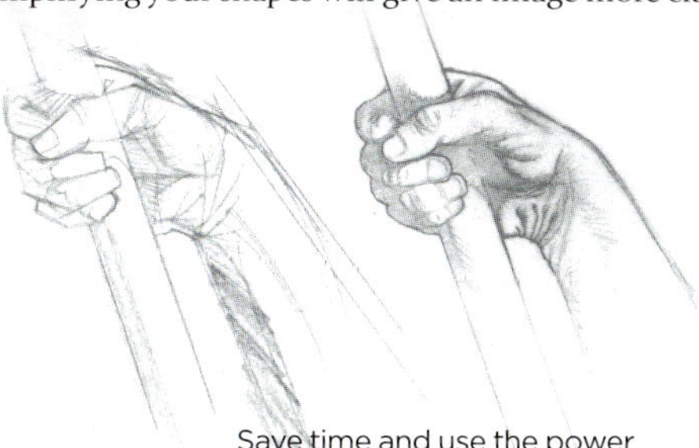

Save time and use the power of artistic suggestion to indicate details in your drawing without having to meticulously draw them.

14. Use shadows to your advantage

The inside of shadows should be vague and transparent, not cluttered and detailed. You'll notice that in a final image, the shadows always support the focal point; they recede so that the focal areas in the light can come forward. Learning to frame your key areas with shadows in this way brings great rewards. If you get this right, then your image's focal areas will stand out.

THE ART OF DRAWING: IN PRACTICE

Justin Gerard reveals how drawing skills and theory can be used on a practical basis in your fantasy art

Artist PROFILE

Justin Gerard
COUNTRY: US

Justin has travelled the world in search of the perfect medium to paint in. He's not found it, but along the way he's met some fascinating people, seen some interesting places, and had a chance to paint a lot of great subjects. He enjoys good music, chocolate chip cookies, and tank battles. www.justingerard.com

Now that we've discussed the theory of drawing in part one, let's talk about the practical side of things. How does drawing work in the grind of a real-life illustration job?

Drawing skills are at the heart of good illustration. Without them, your final illustration will be weak. Drawing provides the intellectual framework of an illustration, and is the primary means by which your ideas will be communicated. It also offers an excellent way of exploring an idea, and slowly refining it down to something truly beautiful, eliminating the errors and weaknesses, and maximizing the impact of its strengths.

Picturing the idea

Before beginning your illustration, you have to know what it is you want to do. If you're working for a client, then this may already be taken care of. Yet often, even if you have been given a brief, how you'll show the idea is still a mystery locked inside your head, and we must find a way to bring it out. What's the mood of the scene? Who or what are its inhabitants? Where is the tension? Wander around in your imagination first. Explore the possibilities mentally.

While technical skill represents the scientific half of art, the idea is part of the emotional half of art – the side that's personal to you. It's this part that can't be taught scientifically. The technical aspects that we've discussed can be learned by anyone, given enough time and dedication. The ideas, though, are your own and they arise out of every experience you have ever had. So think hard on them before you begin.

Quick thumbnails enable you to visualize your ideas.

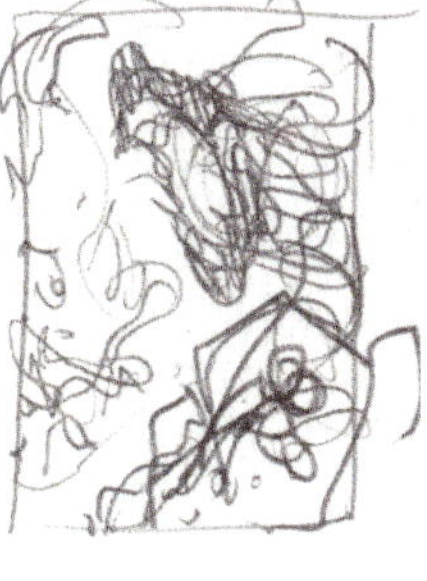

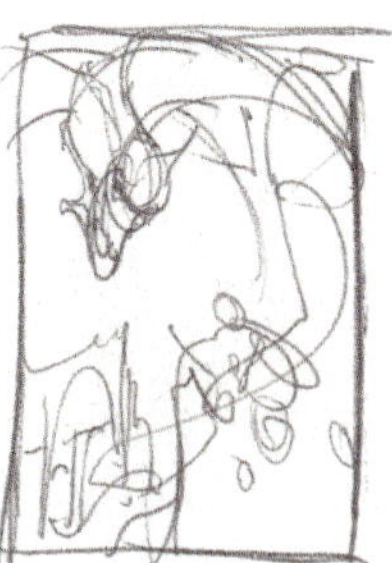

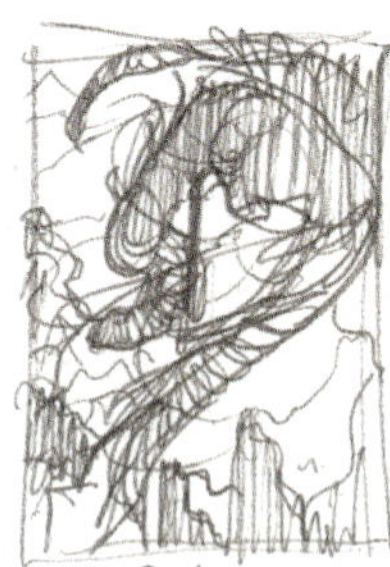

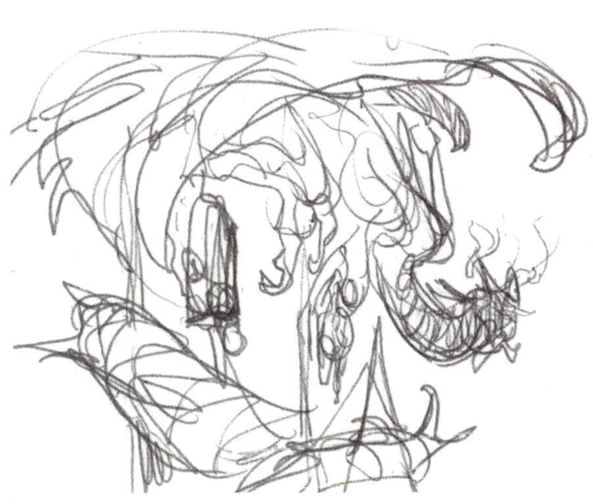

1. Produce thumbnails

Once you have your idea in mind and you have a sense of what you want to accomplish, try to capture it on paper in a thumbnail. Thumbnails enable you to try different approaches and compositions for your idea quickly, without the hassle of redrawing some vast, complicated layout dozens of times. The most important aims of the thumbnail are to nail down the composition and the arrangement of the elements. We must know where things lie in relation to one another before we can leave this stage.

2. Diving for ideas

The aim here isn't necessarily to print out exactly what's in your head. The human mind isn't a desktop printer that can spew out what it sees on the monitor. There are layers of emotion, feeling, and disconnected ideas that must be assembled in a logical format for us to meaningfully express them. The idea is there, and our purpose is to carve down through these layers to find it.

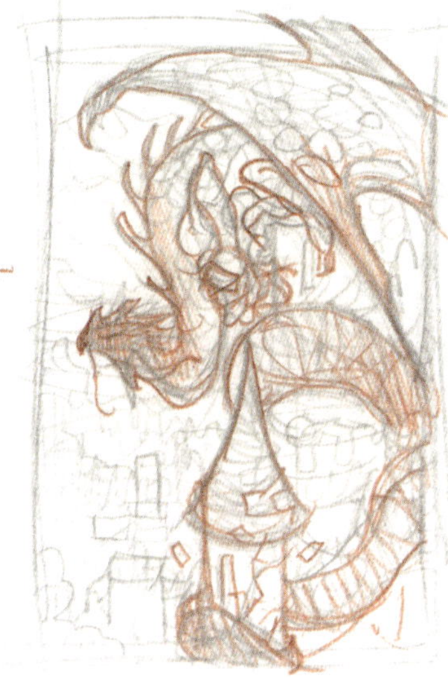

3. Refine thumbnail

After I've drawn a thumbnail that I like, I'll redo it several times, working it slightly differently each time. I'll also begin to explore the expressions of my characters. I want to hone in on the idea's signal in my brain, and to separate what should be there from what shouldn't. I now switch from ink to pencil so I can refine the work. I won't leave this stage until I have a clear representation on paper of what was originally in my mind.

4. First is often best

I never leave the thumbnailing stage until I have a composition that I'm excited about. Often I find that this turns out to be the very first thumbnail that I put down. However, even if you're very excited about your first thumbnail, put down a dozen or so others just to make sure that you have explored all the possibilities.

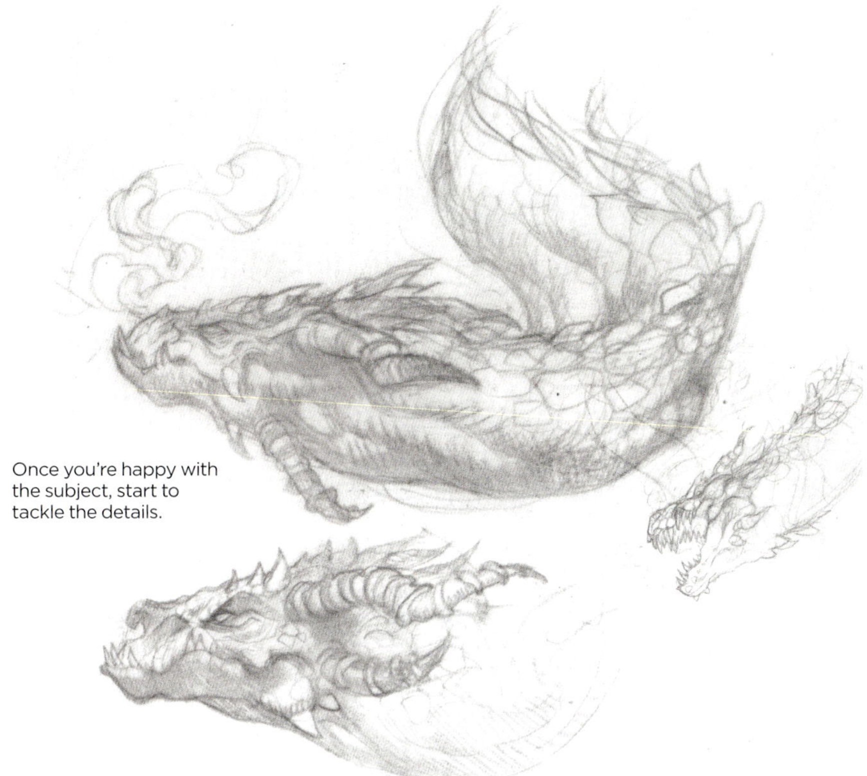

Once you're happy with the subject, start to tackle the details.

6. Sketching the details

After completing my thumbnails, I move on to explorative sketching. In this phase I step away from any broader concerns over composition and arrangement, and instead try out ideas for what things might look like with some details. I'm still working purely from my imagination at this point, with no reference except what's in my head. I try out different positions and expressions to continue to carve down to the core of the idea that's hidden inside my brain.

5. Digital comp

Occasionally, I find it helpful to flesh out the barebones idea contained within the refined thumbnail. This happens mostly in complex scenes involving architecture and perspective. For most projects, I prefer to do this digitally in Photoshop. I'll scan in my thumbnails and sketches, and then paint over them digitally, cutting and moving elements as necessary. I enjoy working digitally because it allows for a great deal of fast experimentation, and I can try out different ideas in far less time than it would take to redraw them several times by hand.

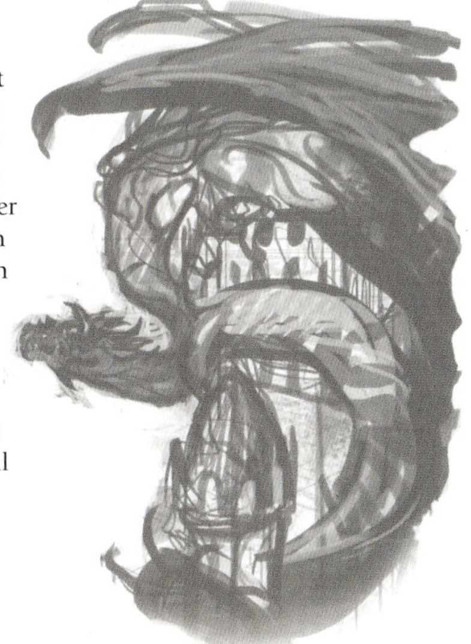

7. Photo reference

I try not to rely too heavily on photo reference. When I do, it begins to look too eerily perfect, and there's a dangerous line that's crossed where an image no longer looks like it's been drawn from imagination, but rather like the product of a camera. However, photo reference is indispensable for good illustration, and it's important that you're familiar in detail with all of the elements you intend to illustrate. To do this, I prefer to draw and memorize the major elements of my reference so that I can recall the construction more naturally later on. Photo reference is at its best when it's serving as an inspiration. I gather a great deal of it for every project, I study, it and then I put it away until the very end, where I'll bring it back out to make sure I haven't made some terrible mistake!

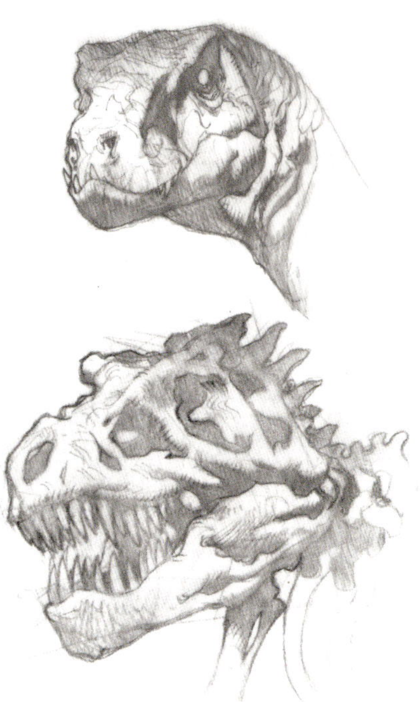

9. Studies from reference and from life

To help memorize forms and yet avoid having our images look too perfect, we do studies from our reference. As we discussed in part one, this helps give us a solid understanding of the construction of the elements we hope to communicate in our illustration. It also enables us to communicate them with a more natural feeling. It makes sense to do studies primarily on detail areas and focal points. Elements such as faces, hands, and objects or designs that'll have to withstand a certain amount of scrutiny are the most important areas to focus on.

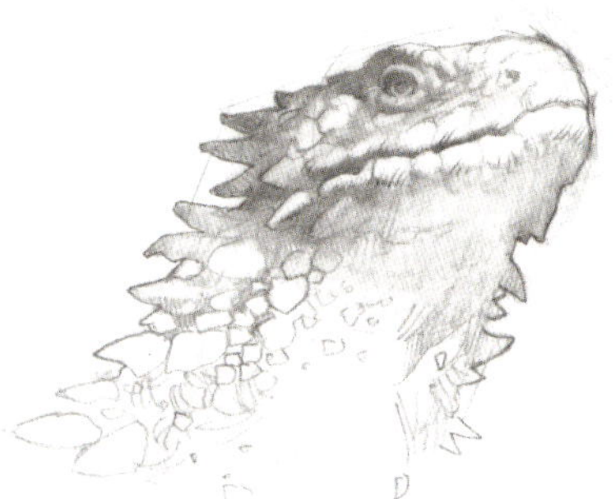

8. A note about dragons

The idea of a dragon exists in everyone's mind, and there are examples in nature that people tend to associate with them. Anyone who's seen a crocodile being fed or watched a snake coiling to strike has a sense of what reptilian cunning in large form might look like. Our job as illustrators is to capture those elements in nature that other people can relate to and communicate them effectively.

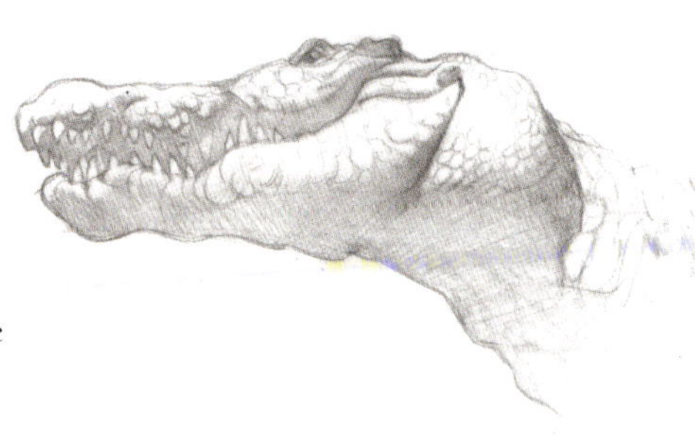

What is a crocodile but a dragon without wings or the ability to breathe fire?

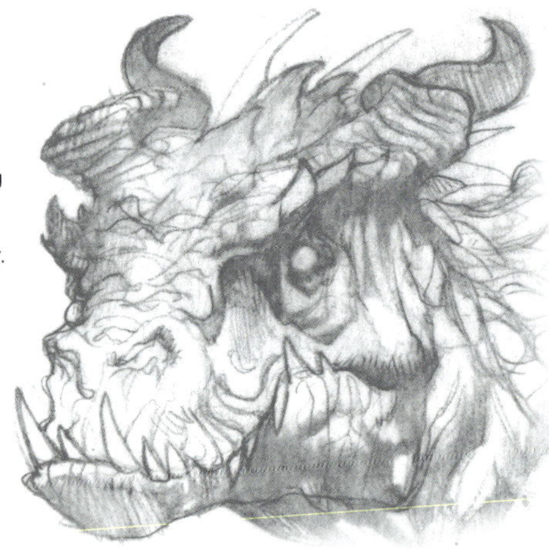

Simply closing the dragon's mouth tells a different story.

"Photo reference is at its best when it's serving as an inspiration."

10. Experimentation

There are a thousand different directions you could take your illustration in, and each subtle change will make it tell a new story. This experimentation can be a source of procrastination – a way of putting off tackling the final drawing – but it's worth it in spite of the danger. It's good to try different ideas at this stage, where you're more engaged in the details and the nuances of expression on your characters. But keep an eye on your original thumbnails; find what it is about that original idea that you found so appealing, and try to play it out in these different ideas.

11. Rough drawing

Now's the time to transfer our composition and all our studies into the rough drawing. We're still carving down to our original idea, so don't spend too much time trying to refine little lines and shadows. Your rough should still look rough. Your main aim here is to nail down proportions and placement and give a suggestion of overall detail. You should finish with a more detailed, cleaner version of your composition, ready to do your final tight drawing. After having finished your rough, you should only be altering small details – there should be no drastic changes after this step...

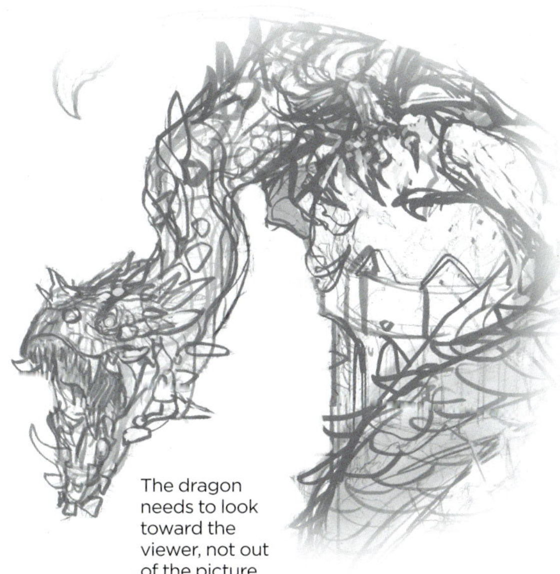

The dragon needs to look toward the viewer, not out of the picture.

12. Drastic changes

...but sometimes disaster strikes! And this is exactly why we do a rough drawing, so that these moments of terrible disaster don't happen in the final painting. The rough reveals the problems in our composition and helps us to correct them. In this case I finished my rough drawing and realized that something was wrong; I had somehow drifted from my original idea. The dragon somehow lacked presence. He was looking off to the side, and for some reason this was pulling me down and out of the composition. After having done my studies, I knew what I would need to do to fix this.

13. Tight drawing

Because the rough drawing is the trial run for the tight drawing, the tight drawing is the trial run for the final painting. By now, you'll be happy with the composition and the character's design. Now you're executing them all together and refining everything. Pay attention to details and to how the light is hitting everything. This tight drawing will be your blueprint for your final painting. When you move on to paint, you'll be able to come back to this illustration and use it to help you solve any problems that you may face.

10 FANTASY ART POSES

Whether you're drawing a hero or a villain, we've got the gestures and silhouettes to help you out

The staff is held ready, giving a sense of impending action.

The face is lifted slightly and looks in the direction of the leading leg.

The leg is straight and powerful, planted firmly on the ground and defining the direction of the character's gaze.

The arm is straight and at a right angle to the line of the eyes, adding stability and strength to the composition.

The stomach muscl are relaxed but sligl twisted to the side.

10 Villain making plans

With sloping shoulders and the head angled slightly down, this pose is closed and still – full of calculating malice. One fist grasps the other, causing the muscles of the arms to bulge, and the feet are planted firmly on the ground.

With the arm muscles tensed, this pose hints at power that's yet to be unleashed.

9 Warrior

This is a beautifully balanced and elegant pose. The extended leg is long and straight, and is at a right angle to the staff, giving the character added balance and strength. The right arm balances the body as it leans forwards, while the slope of the shoulders creates a diagonal almost parallel with the line of the leg. The staff is gripped with a strong hand, giving the pose a focal point.

8 Flying

The leading arm is outstretched, indicating powerful momentum. The other arm is streamlined, held close to the side. Just after the moment of lift-off, the right leg is still bent for balance.

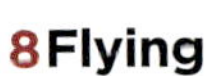

7 slayer

The shoulders are thrust back, the chest pushes forwards, and the slim waist leads to the flare of the hips and a strong balanced stance. Compositionally, the weapon creates a clean line with the back leg, giving the pose a degree of equilibrium.

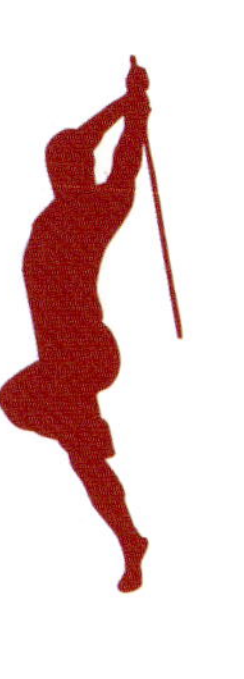

6 Preparing to strike

The extended arms stretch the chest and stomach, and the muscles are clearly defined as a result. The raised leg counterbalances the sword held behind the body. It follows that as the sword falls, the leg will drop down and back in response, feeding more power into the attacking action.

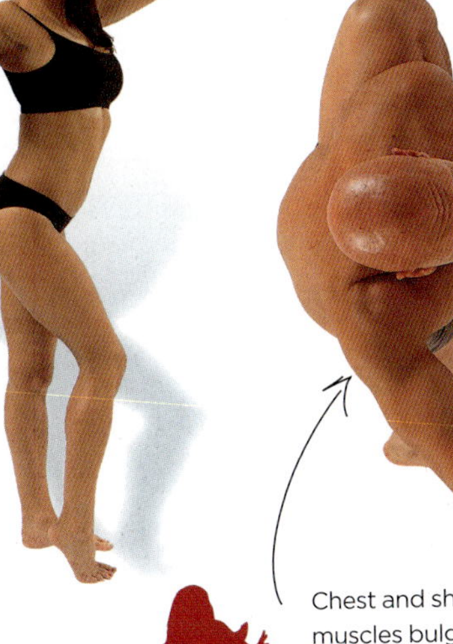

5 Evil sorceress

The arms are raised in twin claws of menace and evil intent, while the face is impassive and coolly confident. This pose suggests an imminent strike.

Fingers are arched and tense as they grip the wall.

Chest and shoulder muscles bulge with the effort of supporting the character's body weight.

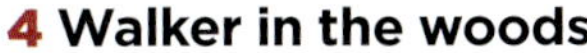

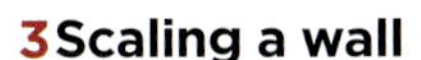

4 Walker in the woods

Both the left arm and the left leg extend forward to suggest stillness (motion is represented by simultaneous movement of opposing arms and legs), creating a diagonal hip line and strong leg shape. The right arm pulls back, causing the shoulders to pull together.

3 Scaling a wall

Viewed from above, we see the gripping hands and arm muscles taut with the strain of clinging to the wall. The raised left leg balances the leading right arm. The upturned face and concentrated stare hint at a sense of purpose and also help create the illusion of height, as the character looks to his destination.

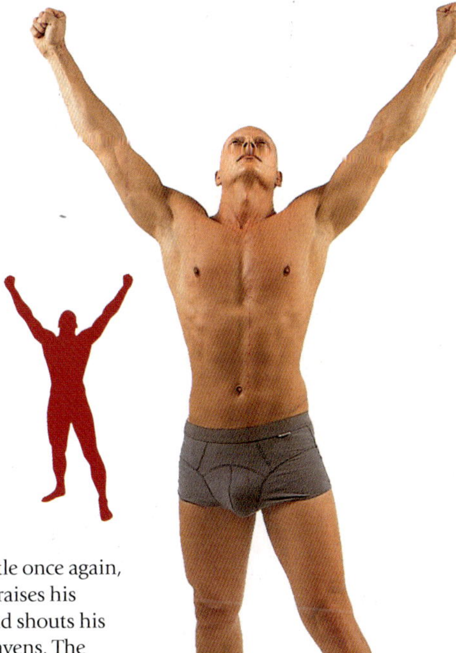

The face is intent and focused, locking a steely gaze upon the victim.

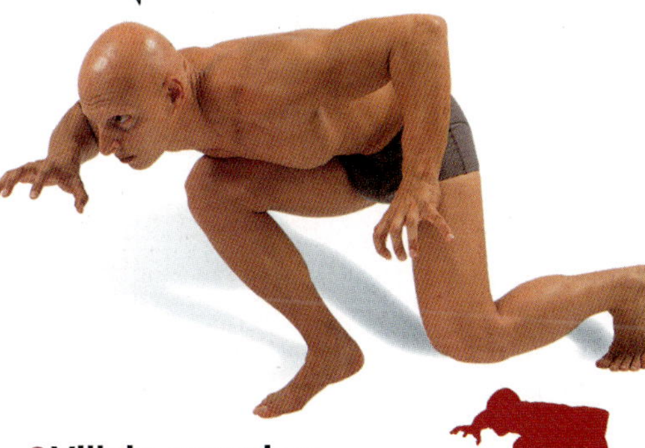

2 Villain creeping

Keeping low, the torso is held parallel to the ground. The arms are ready to lurch forward and grasp the prey.

1 Victory

Successful in battle once again, the mighty hero raises his muscled arms and shouts his victory to the heavens. The straight limbs create an X-shaped silhouette that adds dynamism.

STRIKE A POSE

Warren Louw explains how to fill your characters with energy and dynamism by learning the art of posing

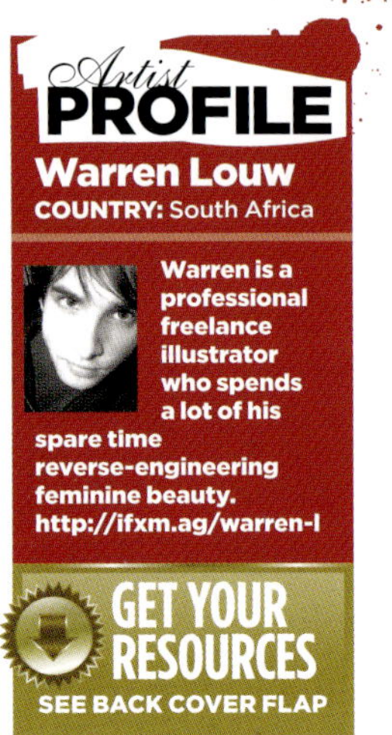

Artist **PROFILE**

Warren Louw

COUNTRY: South Africa

Warren is a professional freelance illustrator who spends a lot of his spare time reverse-engineering feminine beauty. http://ifxm.ag/warren-l

GET YOUR RESOURCES

SEE BACK COVER FLAP

What I'm about to tell you are the crucial basics, the foundations of your characters. If you're not getting this right, don't expect too much else to get better. Posing greatly extends and energizes the personality of your character, giving you the control you need to deepen the relationship that they have with the viewers. This is where you give your characters life and it begins.

Be very specific about what you want and what you like. Study it, understand it, make it a part of you, and expand with it. Nothing is random. Everything has a purpose. Aim high. Aim beyond what's ever been achieved in art. Learn from other artists around you. Art is about self-expression and reaching new undiscovered levels within yourself.

Find your own style. We are all unique expressions of infinite possibilities, so we all have the potential. Make sure that you're loving the experience that art is bringing to your life, and you will only move forward. When you have all the ingredients in place, you can think about your characters in terms of their spatial relationship to the world.

1 State your intention

Before you even pick up a pencil, the most important thing to consider is intention – visualizing and knowing what you want to achieve. You have to be very specific about what you want, you have to believe you can do it, and you must expect it to manifest. Aim the highest you possibly can, higher than anything that's ever been achieved in the history of mankind on Planet Earth. This way you charge the process with positivity, and you'll be sure to get things off to a great start.

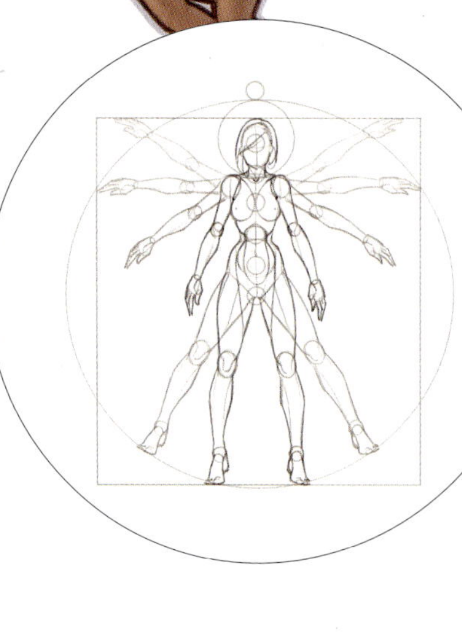

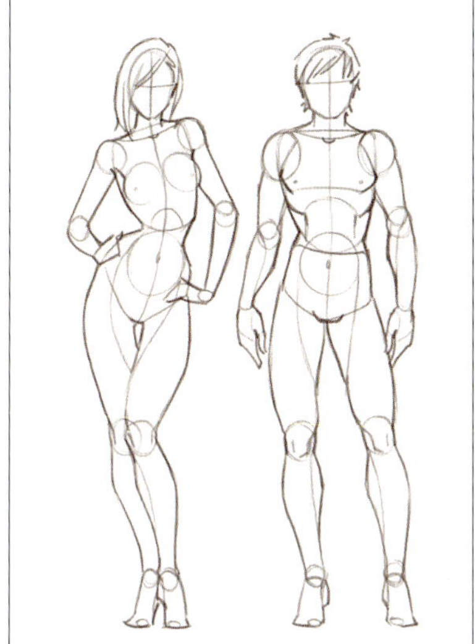

2 Male vs. female

If you can master the feminine, the masculine will be pretty easy. They share many of the same basic characteristics. When dealing with the male, it's just a matter of adjusting a few things here and there. I don't draw males much, but I can do it very effectively because of my work with the female figure. Those who focus primarily on males will have a far greater difficulty achieving feminine beauty and sexiness.

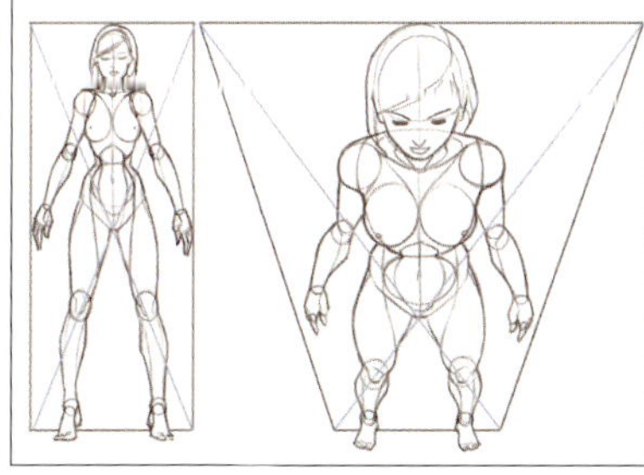

3 Let's rectangle

Foreshortening and perspective can be quite the cow for all of us artists – don't think the pros are excluded from this difficulty. So here's a good starting point. If you know how to give perspective to a box, or even a rectangle, this should help you give perspective to your figures, since both have a front, sides, and a back. Yes, the human form is far more complex than that, with many other things to consider. But if you can keep the proportions within the rectangle guidelines, things will come much easier. Notice the consistency of the center point throughout both boxes.

4 Understanding exactly what you're dealing with

What needs to happen early on is for you to become familiar with the shapes and forms that you'll be working with. You'll need to pay attention to all the curves, joints, and body parts, and understand where they need to be in relation to each other. Finding the hidden lines and patterns where certain points meet and join will be your guide to work from. Just remember: every tiny line you draw has a purpose and is designed to work as one with the rest. You'll notice that if one thing is out, then others will follow.

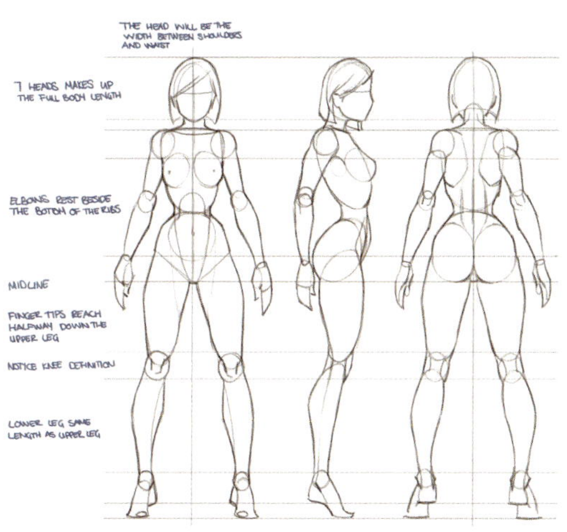

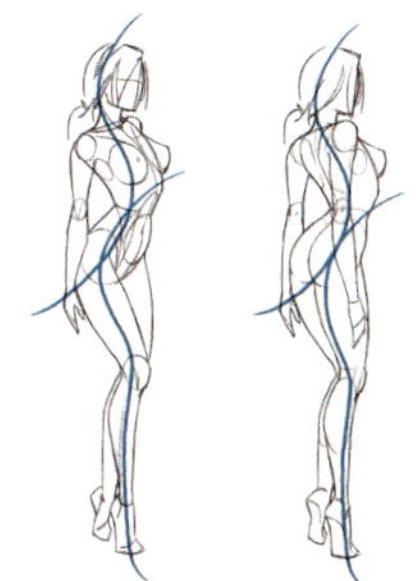

5 Flow

Everything has a flow. With a bit of attention to anatomy and its rhythm, this will soon become clear. The best way to help your poses have flow is to think of an S shape, as this will be the flow leading your eye through the pose, and will even help with your overall composition.

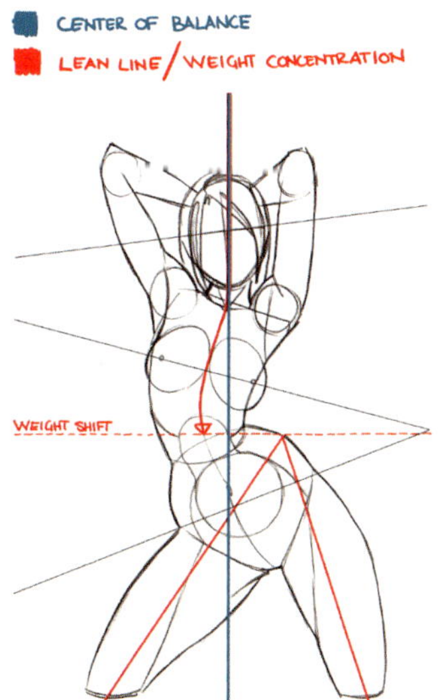

6 The angle effect

When giving your figure an attractive, confident, and sexy pose, you have to adjust the angles of the head, torso, hips, and legs. To draw it, you need to understand it. This pose is achieved by the legs shifting, pushing the channeling of the body's weight to the right side. Now the right hip is confidently exposing itself, and with the legs wider apart, both legs are taking a good portion of her weight.

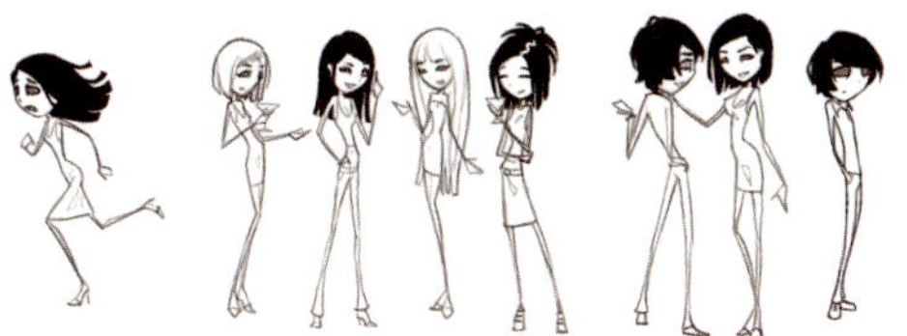

7 Experiment with a different style

Amazingly, you can learn a lot from using a different style. Working from a different perspective on how to approach things can give you a fresh viewpoint. It will only expand your understanding about posing and anatomy in general. I find my skills spontaneously upgrade themselves after I've been working with a range of alternate styles, so this is highly recommended to all.

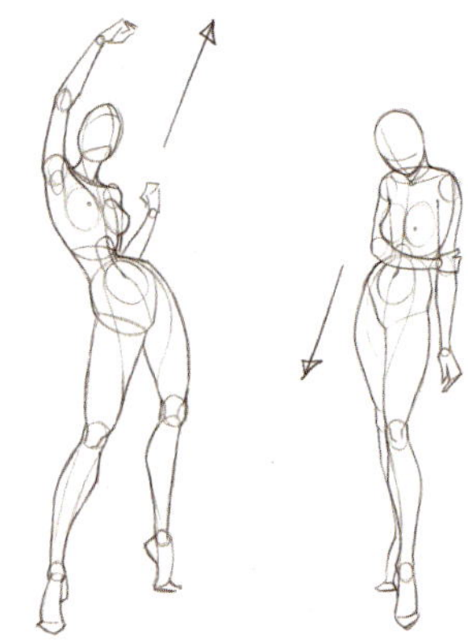

POSITIVE EMOTIONS ARE FULL OF LIFE AND ARE QUITE EXPRESSIONATE. THEIR AMPLIFIED ENERGY ASCENDS THEIR STATE OF BEING. THEIR ESSENCE FLOWS UPWARDS.

NEGATIVE EMOTIONS PULL YOU INTO A DENSE, LOW STATE OF BEING WHERE CLARITY IS LOST AND YOUR ESSENCE BECOMES HEAVY AND IS DRAWN DOWNWARDS.

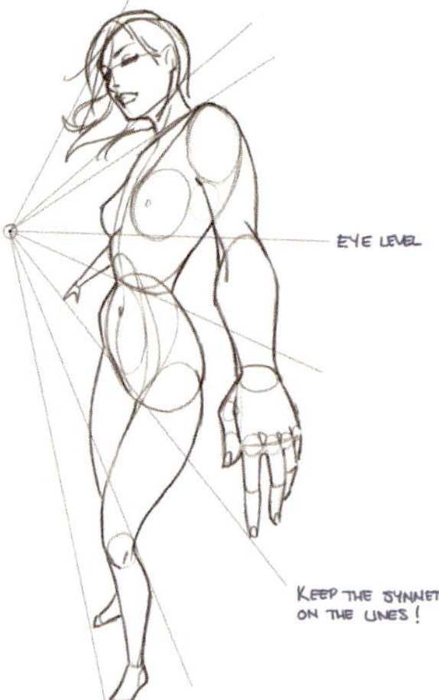

8 Add emotion

Emotion and mood are vital elements when creating a piece of artwork. A pose in itself can convey many emotions without using things like facial expressions. Real emotion is always expressed throughout the rest of your body as well. There are no exceptions: it just depends on intensity. So just be aware of body language.

9 Visualize a vanishing point

You first need to establish the eye level; you'll be looking up at everything above it. Try to keep the symmetry of the body running on the lines. Refer back to the figure's front design to see which areas and elements run parallel with each other.

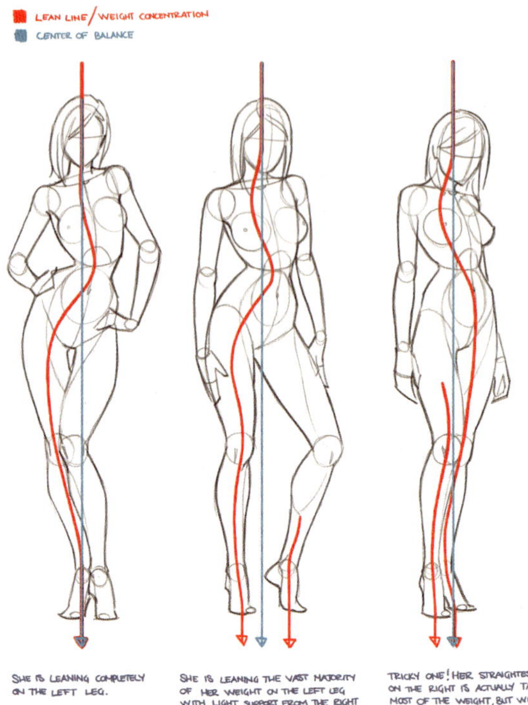

11 Balancing that weight

I'm sure you have been left frustrated sometimes – all you're trying to do is get a simple pose, right? This is normally a result of being oblivious to the physics of balancing and centering weight. The solution is pretty basic: the leg that's the most upright and straightest is the one that takes most of the weight. So keep your footing balanced in relation to your character's center, also keeping in mind where the focus of the weight lies.

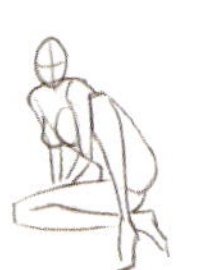
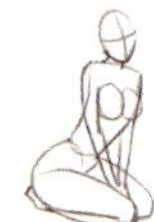
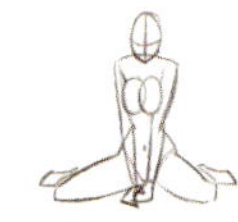

10 The focus you need

Breaking it down to a simpler scale will give you the focus you need to concentrate on the essentials without all the details confusing you. Loosen up your technique and just flow with it. When you think too much, you're acknowledging that you don't already know it all. You know more than you think, so don't let thought obstruct you.

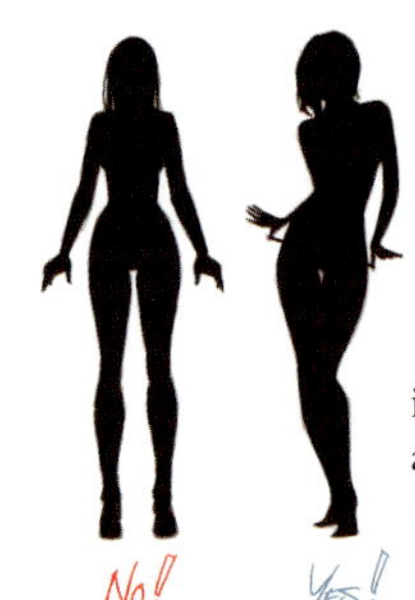

12 Silhouetting

A great way to check if your pose is eye-catching or dynamic is to fill it in with black or a darker color and reduce it to a silhouette. This enables you to see if your pose has flow and impact, and still conveys the same essence that you originally intended. Your focus is being centered on the actual form, with no internal affairs to distract you.

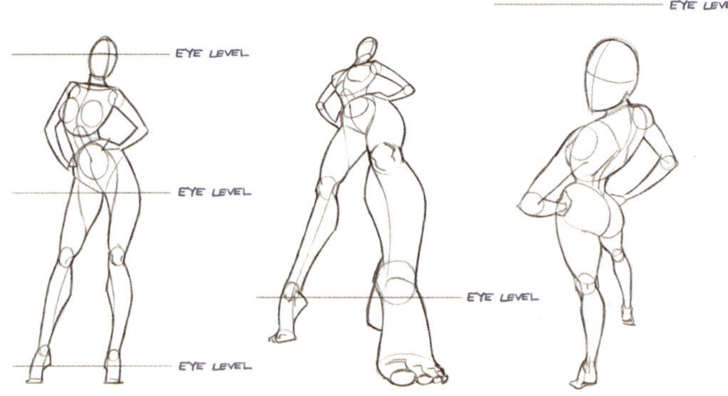

SINCE FROM A DISTANCE EYE LEVEL CAN'T BE IDENTIFIED AT A SINGLE POINT, YOUR PERSPECTIVE WILL BE TOTALLY FLAT.

NOW WE ARE RIGHT BELOW HER WITH THE EYE LEVEL AT ANKLE HEIGHT GIVING HER QUITE A DRAMATIC PRESENCE

NOW LOOKING DOWN ON HER YOU STILL HAVE QUITE A SENSE OF DEPTH ADDING A GOOD ATMOSPHERE TO BREATH IN

13 Level of the eye

Eye level is really important in creating a dynamic pose. Using a low view can make a character seem dominant, heroic, or just plain huge. The point from which you view it plays a critical role in creating a pose, because this is essentially how you want the world to see it. So when deciding on a pose, consider where you want the eye level to be, as this can make even a simple pose appear very dramatic.

MIX DIGITAL AND TRADITIONAL ART

Dave Kendall invites you to join him riding the tide of digital sitting on a raft of used paint tubes and brushes

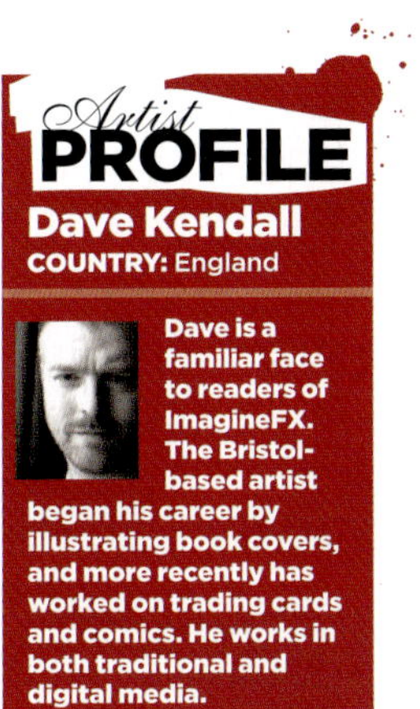

Artist **PROFILE**

Dave Kendall

COUNTRY: England

Dave is a familiar face to readers of ImagineFX. The Bristol-based artist began his career by illustrating book covers, and more recently has worked on trading cards and comics. He works in both traditional and digital media. www.rustybaby.com

Traditional art can be daunting in the age of the digital canvas. It means getting your hands dirty and abandoning the undo key. This absence, however, can be the most liberating and enhancing thing for your art. Before starting a painting with traditional paints, you must know how the color scheme is going to work. Digital can enable you to neglect this, which is not always the best for any artist's development.

You'll find yourself floundering around in the Hue/Saturation swamp before you know it. Although I love working digitally, I started off my art with traditional paints. For speed I mostly work with acrylics, but I will be trying out Artisan Water Mixable Oils for this article.

Setting up a professional digital artist suite can set you back thousands of dollars. To produce pro-standard traditional painting can be a considerably cheaper affair.

Part One: Getting ready

Preparation of a workspace is particularly important where paint is concerned. I will give a few tips to make your workspace, and by extension your work, comfortable and rewarding.

1 Comfortable space

If like me you never liked being told to tidy your room, it's best to find a space which doesn't need to be cleared up after you've finished a painting session. A corner of your room can work, or if blessed with plenty of room a dedicated studio space. It's also essential that the area is well lit. If you can find a north-facing window, that would be ideal. But comfort is essential.

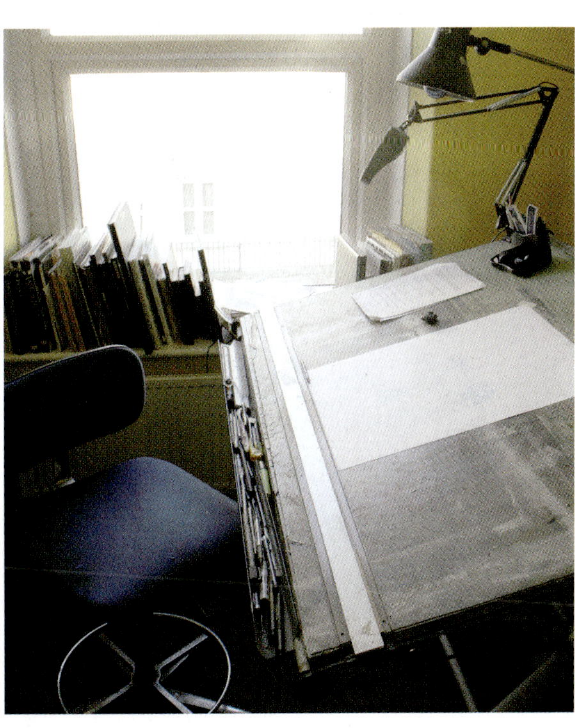

2 Painting place

Artists through the ages have painted on every surface and at all angles. I'll stick within 90 degrees for this introduction. I have an A0 draftsman table, a table easel and a large, free-standing easel for my bigger paintings. You need to be able to see and have access to the whole surface of a painting. While the table and tabletop easel, accommodate smaller illustrations, the large easel can carry paintings up to four or five feet.

TOOLS OF THE TRADE

PENCILS Wooden and mechanical. Staedtler and Pentel.

ERASERS Malleable putty useful for removing graphite from most surfaces.

PENS I love the Faber-Castell art pens for line and wash.

PAPER AND HARD-BACK SKETCHBOOKS Rowney, Winsor & Newton, and Moleskine.

WATERCOLOR PAPER I use Langton satin-smooth hot-pressed for most of my work, although any smooth watercolor paper can be used.

MASONITE Easily purchased and cut to size, available from lumber or hardware stores.

CANVAS Can be bought ready or custom-made from most art stores. With time and experience you will be able to create your own.

MAHL STICK I made mine myself. All that's needed is a firm piece of rounded dowel rod and a soft cushioned end.

ACRYLICS Liquitex and Finity from Winsor and Newton are the makes I use the most.

OILS Wide range from traditional oils to fast drying (Griffin Alkyd) and water mixable (Artisan).

WATERCOLOR They come in tubes and as dry cake versions.

INKS Brilliant color. Useful for glazing if dramatic color is needed.

EASELS There are many types available; your choice should be based on how much room you have you have and how much money you have to spend.

PALETTES Tiles, plates, stay-wet palettes for acrylic from Winsor & Newton and Daler-Rowney, traditional wooden palettes for oils.

BRUSHES Sceptre-gold synthetic/sable mix and Pro Arte for acrylic and oils. Isabey watercolor brushes are my favorite watercolor tools.

VARNISHES Gloss and matte. Liquitex is my favorite for acrylic.

---

3 Bright lights

I use an angle poise for most of my work. It doesn't matter how you get light on your work as long as it's good and strong. I always work with a blue-coated daylight bulb. Try using a normal bulb after using one and you will see how yellow the light is. Not only does it give you accurate color, but it's also less tiring on your eyes. Once again, comfort comes into play.

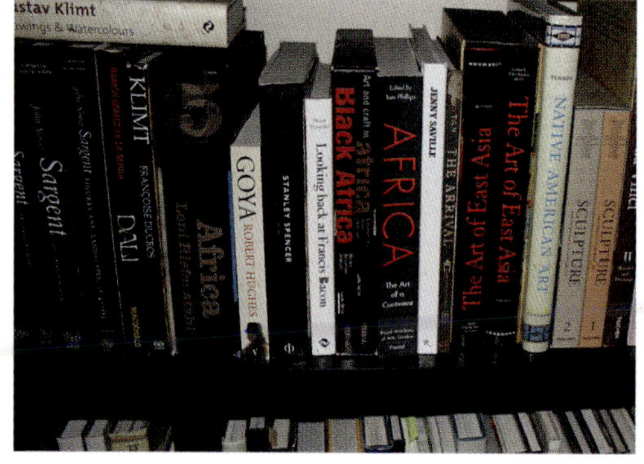

4 Inspiration is key

This comes in the form of books and DVDs. I've been buying books from a very early age, so my collection is pretty large. If I am feeling down or lacking in energy, the images around me have never failed to pull me out of my slump.

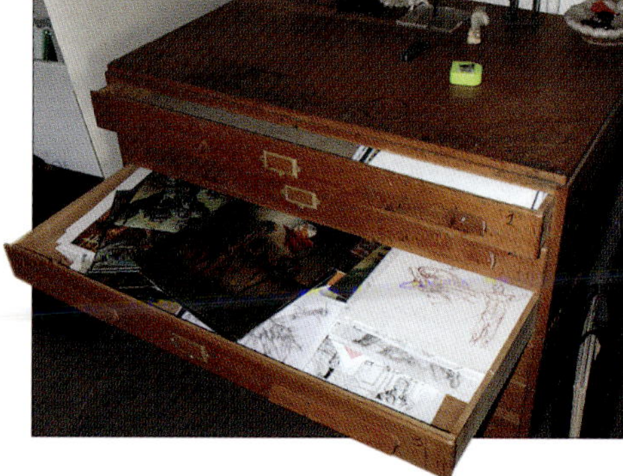

5 Storage

You'll need somewhere to put your raw materials and finished paintings – safer than the floor. If you have room for a planning chest, try to pick one up, though they are sought after, so you may struggle. Make sure you protect your materials any way you can. A sturdy portfolio is always going to be useful, as you'll need to transport the paintings around.

Part Two: Choosing the correct materials

I'll cover what's needed to start you painting. Materials and their uses could fill books, but this is intended as an appetizer.

1 Sketching pencils

Ever since seeing Robert Crumb's beautiful sketchbooks, I decided to try to apply similar values to my own sketching process. I work in hardbound books containing heavy cartridge paper. They will take pretty rough treatment from most media. When they're finished, they get numbered and put on a shelf, which I use often as visual diaries. I have a personal preference for 2B pencils. I use mechanical and good-old-fashioned wooden versions.

2 Canvas and board

This is one area where I apply a do-it-yourself philosophy. I get masonite board cut to size at a local lumber store. Using artist acrylic gesso, I coat the board evenly with an ordinary house brush, allow it to dry, and then apply another coat in an opposite direction. Between coats I use wet and dry paper, which can be bought from any car accessory shop. This can give a very smooth surface to work on. It's very sturdy, forgiving, yet economical.

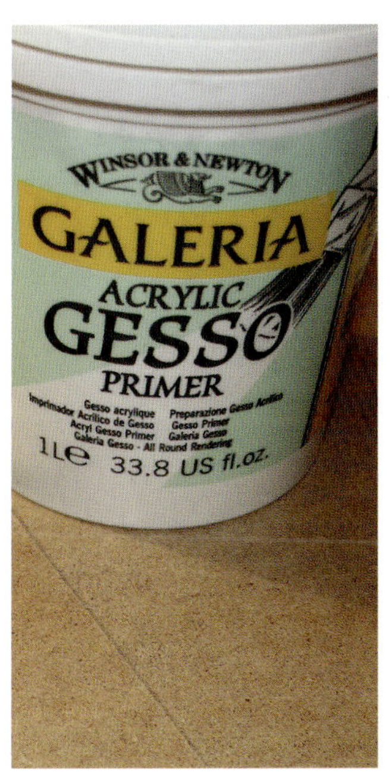

3 Paper

Another surface I use to paint on is hot-pressed watercolor paper. I stretch it by soaking it in a bath of water and then stick it to a sturdy board using gummed sealing tape. Once dry I coat it in a layer of Liquitex matte medium. This seals the paper to prevent the paint soaking into it and becoming dull. Can be used for oils or acrylics.

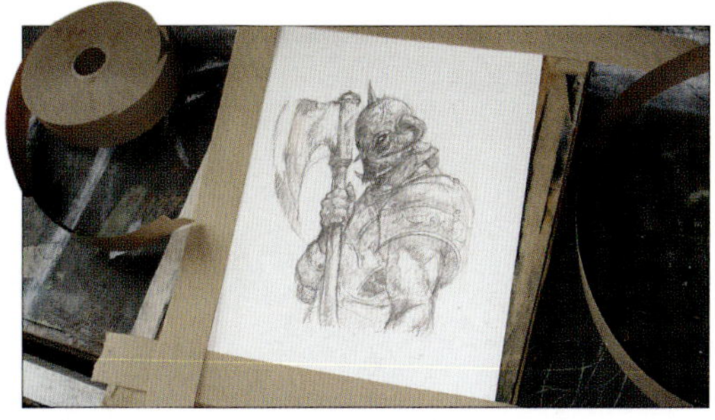

4 Paints and mediums

I like to use good-quality paints, such as Liquitex and Finity acrylics. They have a high pigment yield, and therefore the color is more intense. I find it's a false economy to buy cheap paints. If you are experimenting it doesn't hurt to go for student-quality paints, though.

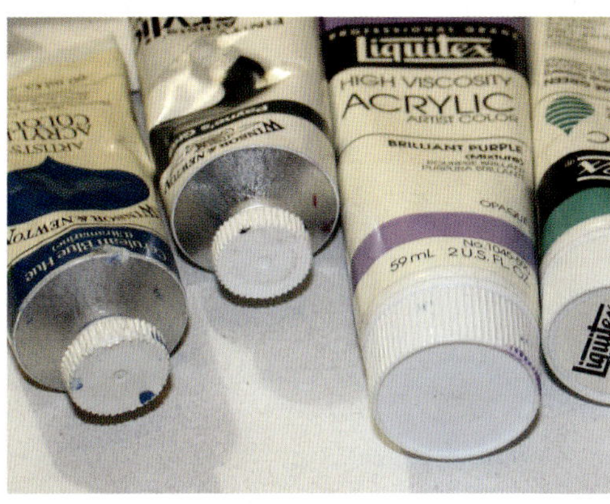

"I find it's a false economy to buy cheap paints, though student-quality paints are okay if you are experimenting."

5 Palettes

Palettes could be any smooth, cleanable surface: plates, glass, the traditional wooden, or the disposable paper versions. For acrylics I do use a stay-wet palette, which keeps the paint workable. Acrylics dry to a plastic film very quickly without it. The paint can be a little liquefied using it, so impasto can be difficult. Oils are different. They remain workable for days without any extra help.

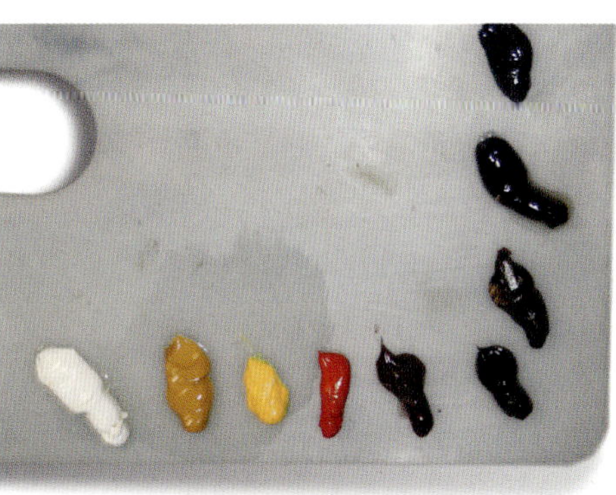

6 Brushes

I always use good-quality brushes. Although expensive, they will serve you and your painting well with a little TLC. They keep their shape and ability to apply paint for longer than cheaper varieties. This is probably the most important purchase you'll make. For a comparison, think of the difference between graphics tablets. I use a selection of synthetic, bristle, and sable. I suggest having different sets of brushes for each medium.

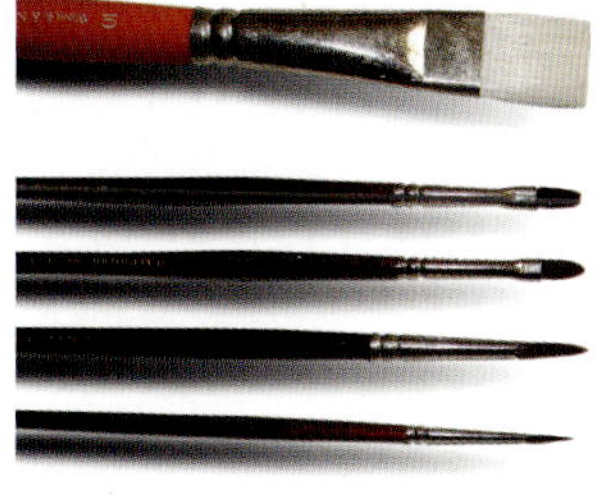

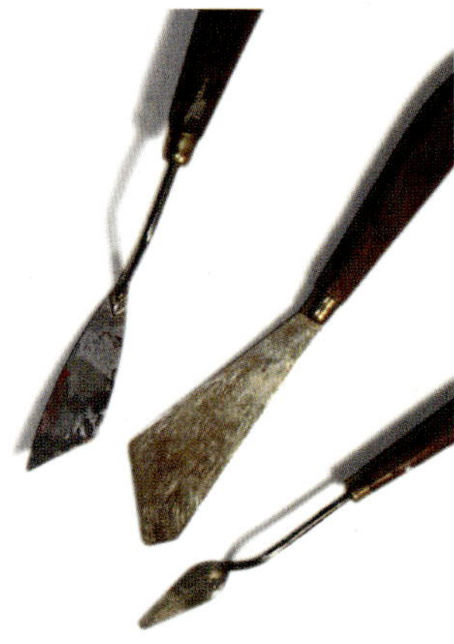

7 Palette knives and color shapers

Other useful mark-making tools are palette knives and rubber-tipped color shapers. These tools apply paint in a totally different way. They enable you to place slabs of color, and to pull grooves and texture your paint. Imagine painting bark and rough surfaces using these devices. Palette knives come into their own with larger paintings on board. You need a sturdy support for this.

8 Cleaning materials

Good-quality brushes and paints should provide you with plenty of good service. However, it's vital that you clean your equipment, especially brushes, if you are using oils and acrylics. Using a normal hardware store brush cleaner should save brushes that have dried dirty. Old and damaged brushes are always useful for rough work such as scumbling.

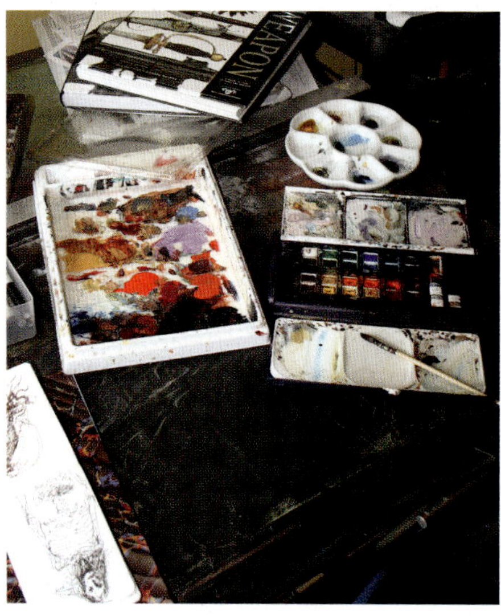

9 Colors

Most makes of paint have a huge range of colors, though over time you will develop a smaller range you'll use more than most. This is down to personal taste to a certain extent. For instance, I particularly like the phthalo blues. As you become more experienced you'll find that you'll be able to get a wide range of mix from just a few core colors.

10 Varnishes and protection

Although not strictly vital, varnishes fulfill an important last stage. When your painting is dry, you'll find that the surface has different textures, such as gloss and matte, and different color intensities because of this. Varnish equalizes and protects the surface. Gloss uniformly intensifies the color, while matte prevents reflections and is useful if you wish to photograph or scan the painting.

Part Three: Hints and tips

Here I'll give you a few pointers and tips when painting. Think of this as an introduction rather than an in-depth treatise. In celebration of Frank Frazetta's 80th birthday, I decided to take the opportunity to produce a Death Dealer sketch. It's quite a simple composition that enables me to experiment with a new media.

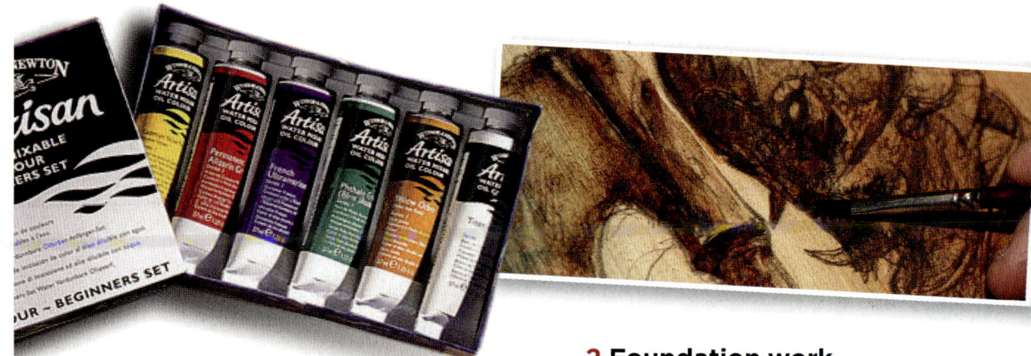

1 General principles

Experimenting with as many different techniques and media as possible is the only way to learn. Mistakes and accidents will happen, but you'll learn lots from them. Working with watercolor will give an entirely different feel to acrylics or oils. Choose your media to suit your subject matter. This is the first time I have used Artisan Water Mixable Oils. I found them to be rather nice to work with, and I'll definitely be experimenting with them further. You have the advantages of oils but without the need for spirits and solvents. They have buttery and smooth consistency, with the extended drying time of oils.

2 Foundation work

I never work from white when using oils or acrylics. Create an underpainting, establishing shadows and values with burnt umber or a mix of burnt sienna and phthalo blues. Acrylics are probably the best paint to use at this stage as they are quick-drying and permanent. You can use almost any media on top of acrylic, but not oils. Work your paint up from thin to thick, especially when using slow-drying paints. It will be impossible to work on top of heavy, wet paint. In the same way, work up to highlights, adding the brightest and usually heavier paint at the end. Keep a roll of paper towel at hand. They're useful to clean brushes and to take excess paint off the surface if a mistake is made.

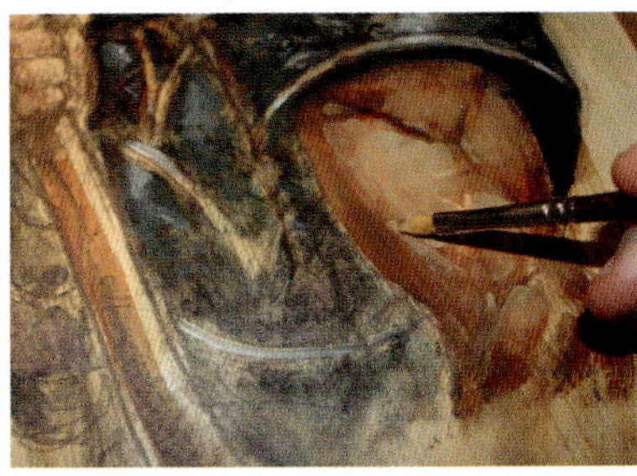

3 Brush types

Brushes come in a number of shapes and with different fiber types. Combinations of these will give very different results. The key is to try all of them as you paint. The most versatile of these are the synthetic/sable mix. These brushes can be used with most of the different paint types. Brushes come in flat and round types, and it pays to have a selection of both. I work with a range of brushes. For most of the early work, I find myself using larger, flatter, and broader brushes. A filbert is a good general brush for blocking in form and paint. It has a dual nature, combining the aspects of flat and round brushes, and so it can cover detail as well as larger areas. I find myself using smaller brushes only at the end of the painting process.

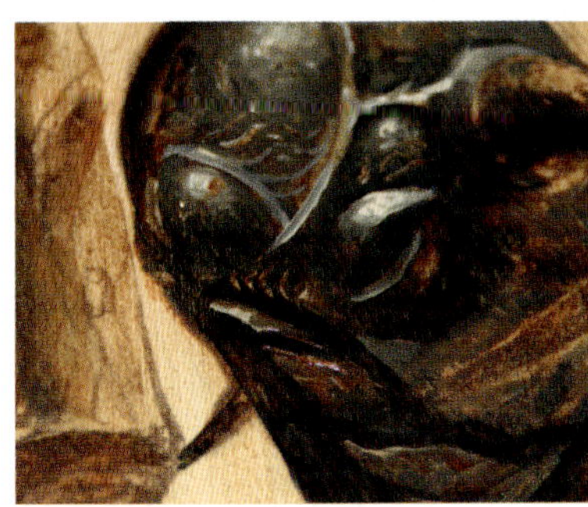

4 Texture

Have a dry, flat brush that you can use to blend and create smooth transitions. I do tend to like lots of texture and like to see brush marks in my own work. Almost anything can be used to add texture to your paint. There are ready-made texture media available, but I have seen items such as egg shell and sand used to add interest to a painting. Use an old toothbrush to spatter your image with paint. This can be remarkably effective at suggesting noise and grain.

5 Dry brush

This is a method of applying color I use that only partially covers a previously dried layer. You should use very little paint on the brush and apply it with very quick, directional strokes. This method tends to work best when applying light paint over dark areas/dried paint and is useful in depicting rock and grass textures.

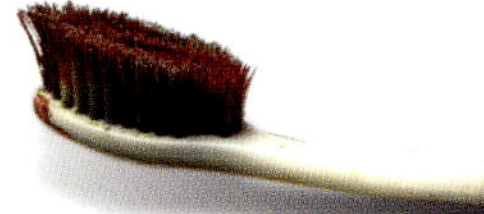

A valuable tool for traditional artists, an old toothbrush is handy for spattering your image with paint.

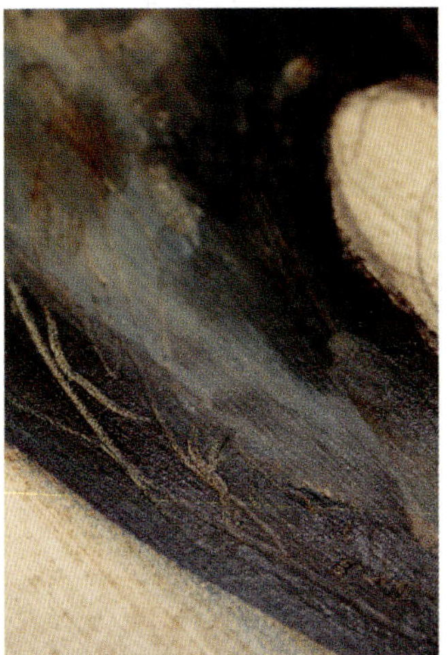

6 Less is more

Removing paint can be as important as applying it. Sgraffito is the term used when you scratch away paint while it's wet to expose the underpainting. It's especially useful when depicting scratches, hair, grasses, and the like. You can use almost any pointed object for this. In the Death Dealer painting, I use rubber shaping tools or the end of a brush to create scratches through wet paint, for battle-worn armor or similar textures.

7 Glazing

Glazing is the process of laying a coat of transparent paint over a dry part of the painting, used for intensifying shadows and modulating color. A light transparent blue over dry yellow will of course create green. Use successive glazes repeatedly.

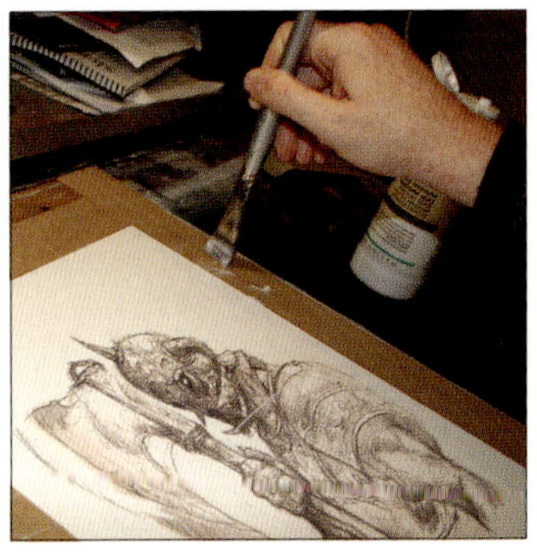

8 Painting Mediums

Mediums are fluids that can be added to paint to modulate their consistency, drying time, and texture. In the case of acrylics, you get different mediums that make the paint matte or gloss. However, my greatest use of matte medium is sealing paper and board so paint doesn't soak into it.

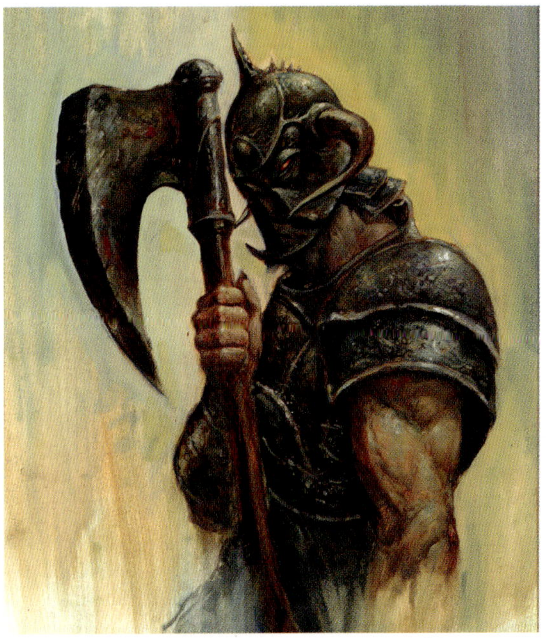

Dave created this Death Dealer image as a tribute to Frank Frazetta to celebrate the artist's 80th birthday. Dave used Artisan Water Mixable Oils.

"A filbert is a good general brush for blocking in form and paint. It has a dual nature and can cover detail as well as larger areas."

Artist PROFILE

Justin Gerard

COUNTRY: US

Justin has travelled the world in search of the perfect medium to paint in. He hasn't found it, but he's met fascinating people, seen interesting places, and painted great things.
www.justingerard.com

GET YOUR RESOURCES
SEE BACK COVER FLAP

PAINT A FAUN USING MIXED MEDIA

Justin Gerard combines oils with Photoshop and produces a compelling and traditional, mythic wood-dweller

I've always enjoyed the idea of fauns. They're creatures that in some mythologies are lighthearted, at one with the countryside, and unsophisticated.

This image was originally commissioned as an erudite, learned faun. I came up with several ideas for what this might look like, and as I was drawing I found myself straying into something that looked too much like a misshapen wizard with horns. It might be a cool idea on its own, but it wasn't what I was after.

So I drew a tiny thumbnail sketch of a classical faun as a kind of anchor-point for myself. It was this sketch that I decided on using for this piece. It was exciting because it gave me a chance to work with natural forms, such as mossy roots, mushrooms, and gnarled horns. It also offered a lot of lighting challenges.

I drew the image at full size, adding details at this stage rather than later on. Doing this ensures that the underpainting stage will hopefully be as painless as possible. Then, in Photoshop, I added some digital magic.

In every piece I create I want to find – and overcome – a new artistic obstacle. This helps me produce a compelling image and teaches me something new along the way as well.

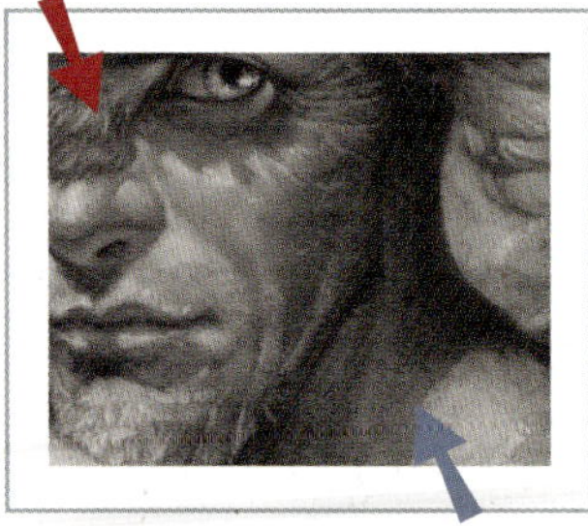

1 Technical lighting

I wanted this scene to have a great deal of light that would bounce around the subject and create warm shadows through diffuse reflection. From the beginning, I established the angle and direction of the sunlight so that the shadows would be consistent (shown by the red arrow). But the direct light isn't the only light source. There's ambient light from all the small patches of sunlight in the forest around this creature too. Furthermore, there's the reflected light (shown by the blue arrow), which will bounce back up from surfaces and project diffuse light. This can all become rather confusing, so keeping a consistent rule is really important when trying to produce a successful image.

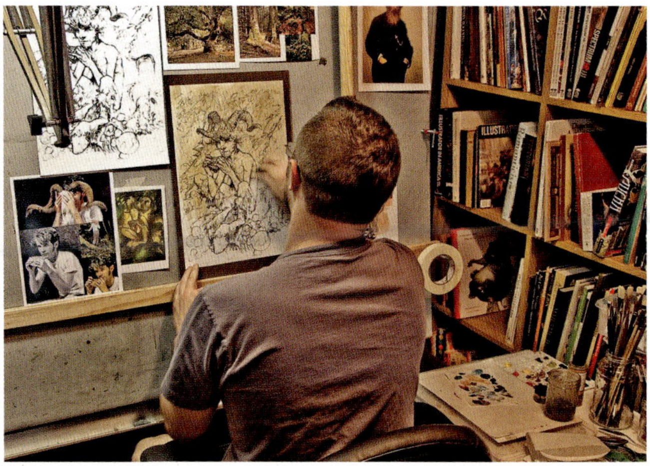

2 Reference material

I collect a great deal of references before starting work. Most are from my photos, which provide details that I might otherwise overlook, and act as place cards for memories. They enable me to journey back to when the photo was taken and immerse myself in the environment. I may not look at the actual references I gather before starting a piece more than once, but the process of collecting it helps. It's nice to know it's there if I need it and that I won't have to break concentration to find something the scene needs.

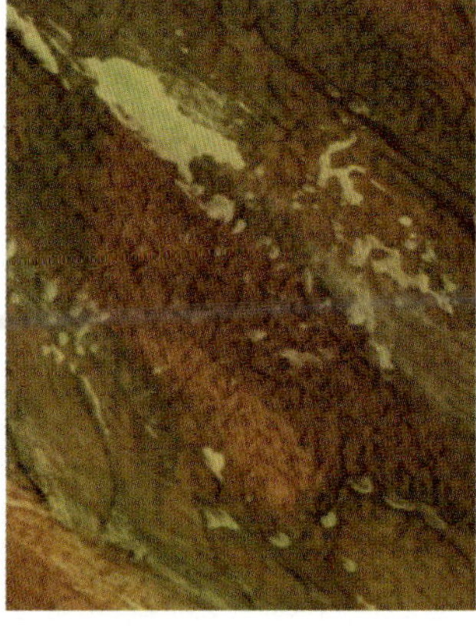

3 Paint textures

The underpainting is in alkyd oil paints, which have a synthetic binder, so they dry very quickly. With alkyds, you can achieve strong textures in your underpainting to help your final image look more natural. When painting digitally over this texture, avoid using too many opaque layers, except in focal areas such as faces. In the background, this texture tells the eye that there are convincing details there, without detracting from the focal points.

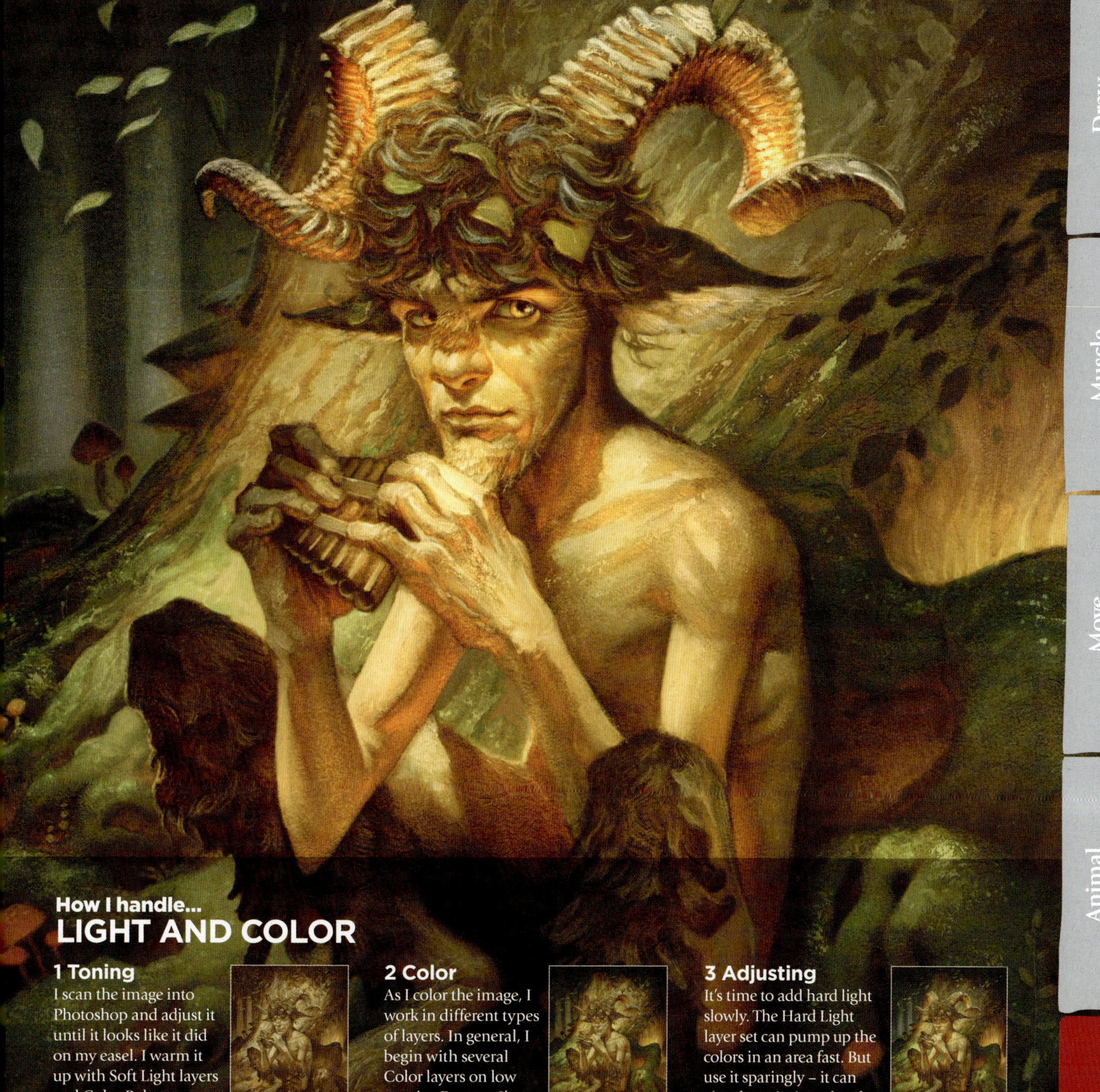

How I handle...

LIGHT AND COLOR

1 Toning

I scan the image into Photoshop and adjust it until it looks like it did on my easel. I warm it up with Soft Light layers and Color Balance adjustment. The scene is in the day, and our figure's spotlit by sunlight coming through the canopy. I ensure I get the atmosphere right at this point – other colors will be affected by it later. Then I intensify some of the pools of light with a Color Dodge layer.

2 Color

As I color the image, I work in different types of layers. In general, I begin with several Color layers on low opacity. Because I've already warmed the piece, I'm more interested in the cooler tones and knocking back areas that shouldn't be so warm. After I have a sense of how warm or cool the colors of the piece will be, I use Multiply layers or Soft Light layers to increase the intensity of the colors.

3 Adjusting

It's time to add hard light slowly. The Hard Light layer set can pump up the colors in an area fast. But use it sparingly – it can give the painting a harsh, nuclear fallout look, and all areas will seem equally intense. This flattens the image and kills atmospheric perspective. I then use Normal layers to refine areas where texture is too strong and to pull back overpowering tones.

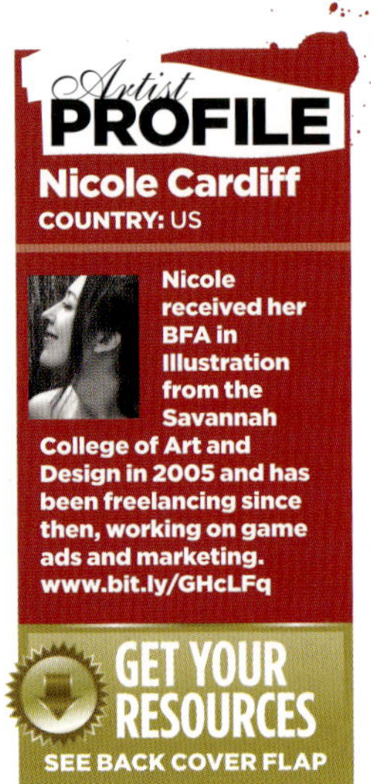

CONVEY THE FEEL OF NATURAL MEDIA

Do you strive to give your fantasy art an illustrative look? Then look no further, as **Nicole Cardiff** uses her traditional skills to paint a cloaked hero

In this workshop I'll describe the painting process that I use for all of my professional projects. I scan in a pencil drawing and import it into Photoshop. I then use a mix of Painter and Photoshop – Photoshop for most of the initial block-in and early work, plus some final tweaks, and Painter for most of the later blending and detailing work. I also shoot photographic references of fabric and the main character's pose.

The process is similar to what I'd do if I were painting traditionally. It starts with a sketch, then I lay in a sepia tone to use as a ground (the base color you tone the canvas with) and then block in my colors. I use Painter IX and Photoshop CS 4, but you could get similar results with most versions of both programs. I recommend using a Wacom tablet for digital painting like this. I have a Graphire from many versions ago, but you can use whatever tablet you have at home.

I also refer to anatomical landmarks, by which I mean the points where you can typically see the skeletal structure under the skin – cheekbones, collarbones, and so on. I also generally recommend that people be somewhat familiar with hard and soft edges as a general concept; typically, I'll have the hardest edges on the forms that are in light, and the softest on forms that are in shadow. This replicates the way that the eye perceives form.

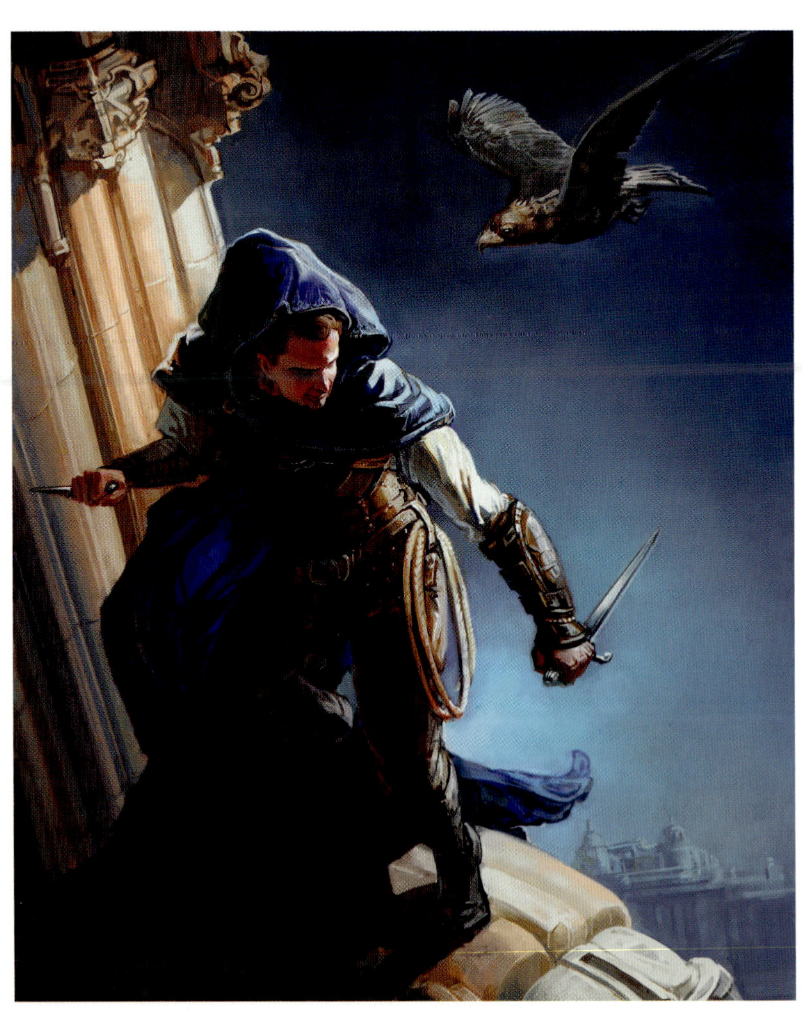

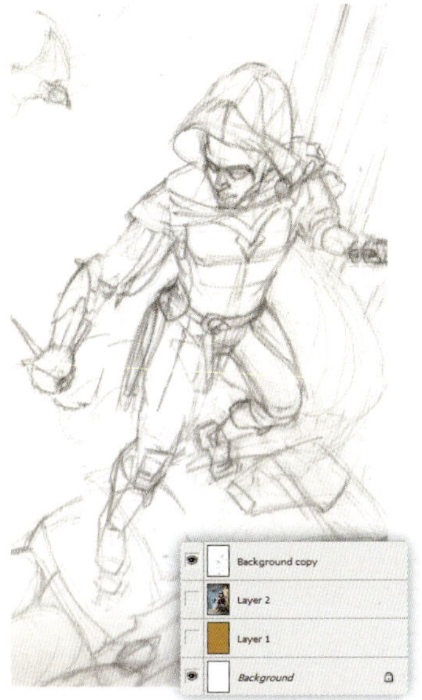

1 Sketch

I sketch a set of thumbnails, clean them up a bit in Painter with the Thick and Thin Pen tool, and then choose one. I do a sketch with an HB pencil and paper and scan it in at 300 DPI. After a bit of Levels tweaking to get the white of the paper looking really white and setting the sketch as a Multiply layer in Photoshop, I'm ready to start painting.

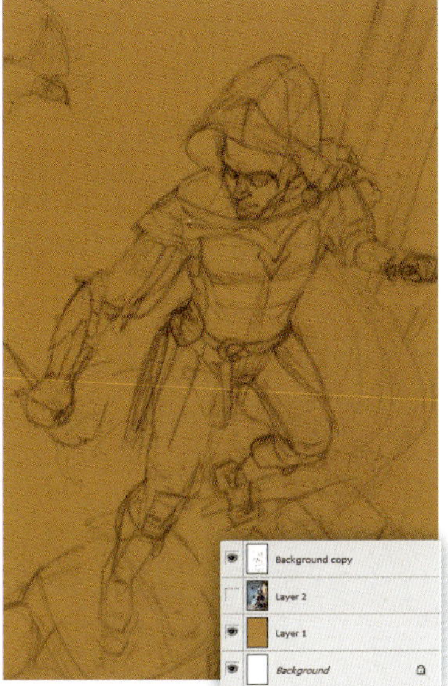

2 Initial painting

I set a brown, sepia tone on a layer beneath my sketch. I find that working on a warm ground with a middle value yields useful results for me. Cool colors look good over it, and it's much easier to maintain good contrasts if you start with something to break up the white. All of my initial block-in is done with a hard round brush in Photoshop. I generally do a few quick color studies for various times of day and lighting situations to find the best solution.

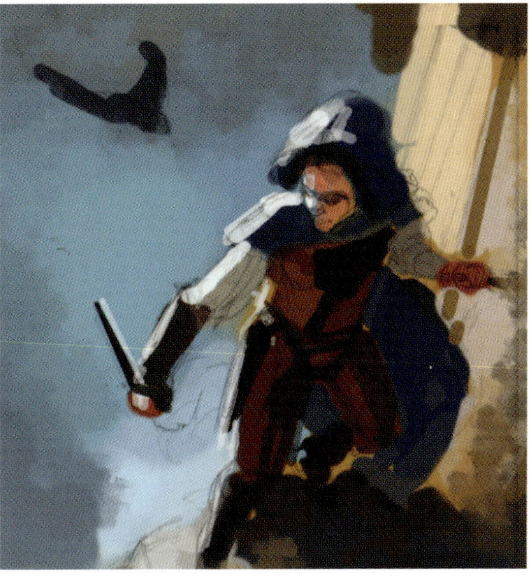

3 Start form rendering

I'm careful while doing this initial block-in to keep a clear value distinction between areas of light and areas of shadow. This will keep the painting from becoming muddy later on as I add detail. I also photograph some references to keep my lighting reasonably accurate to how it wraps around forms. I strongly recommend getting a photo light for doing this, because it's been one of my best artistic investments.

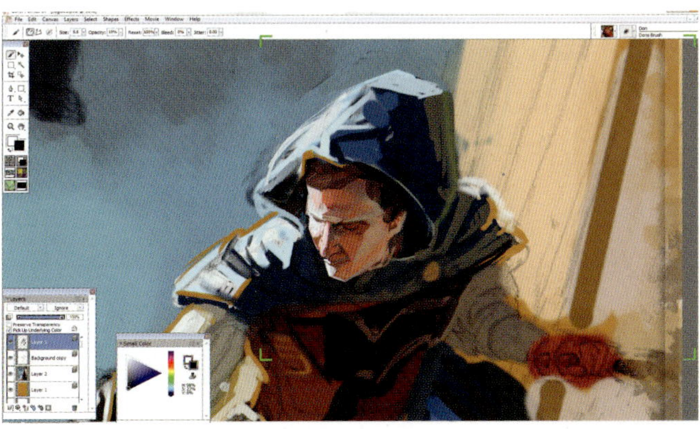

4 Switch to Painter

I'm fond of blocking in at this level with Painter's Marker brush, so I zoom in and start working on the anatomy here. It's important to spend time getting the focal point of the composition right, so I work for a while on getting the anatomy of the figure the way I want it. I also generally lean toward exaggerating the light a bit and using a sketchy touch to mark anatomical landmarks so that the bone structure is in place.

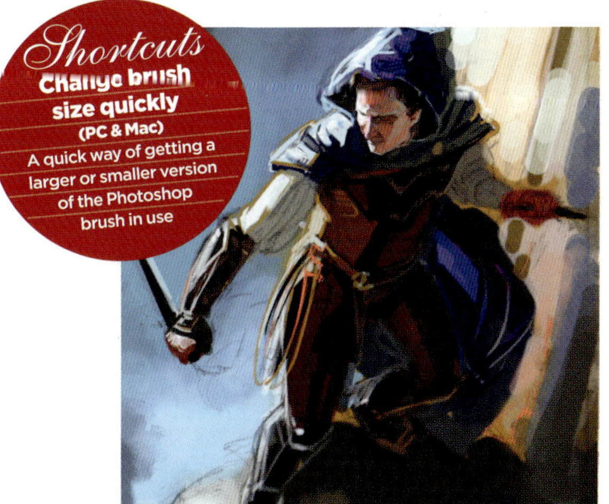

5 Emphasize the shadows

I simplify my values a little bit by moving the midpoint of the Levels in an Adjustment layer to .94. I find that doing this early on tends to keep my shadow areas distinct from the areas in the light. I also add a new layer set to Overlay with a flat medium-blue fill, which introduces a bit more of a mood to the lighting.

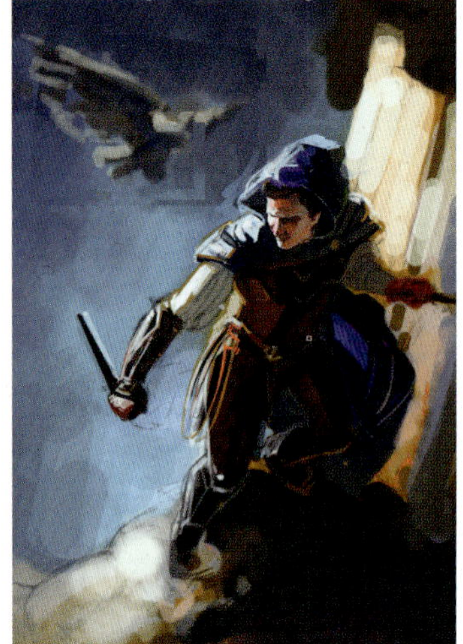

6 Finalize the composition

This is where I make decisions about how the smaller pieces of the composition should fit together. I generally flip the piece horizontally a few times while checking the overall value structure and repositioning pieces, such as the bird. Flipping the piece is an easy way to see it with new eyes.

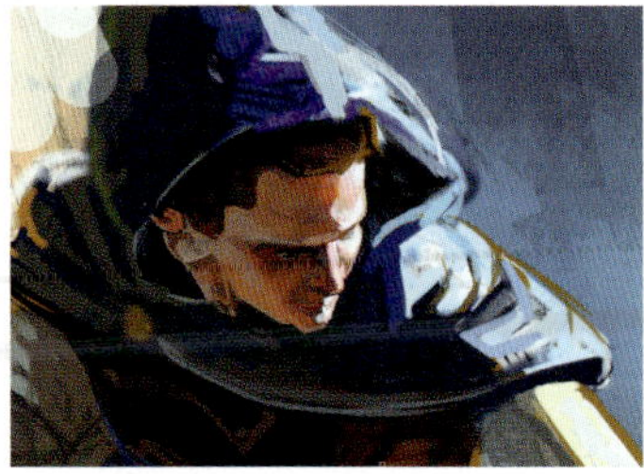

7 Blend in Painter

I blend in Painter with Don Seegmiller's Blender brush – which I got with his book *Digital Character Design and Painting* – and generally soften areas in shadow, areas that are behind other objects and less-important areas. The goal is to get a balance of soft and hard edges, although few of my edges are completely soft, since I paint in a fairly opaque style.

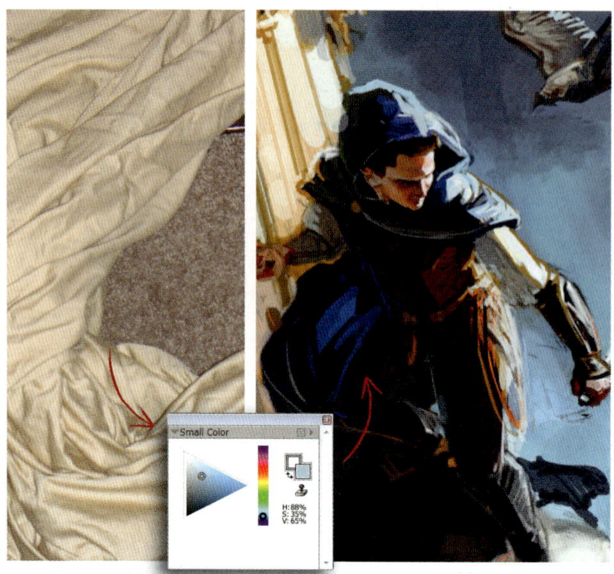

8 Detail the fabric

I usually twist an old sheet into an approximation of what the fabric's doing in any given piece and take some reference photos before I start detailing the fabric too much. This way, I can use the folds of the real fabric (in simplified form) to add authenticity to what I'm painting – in this case, the shadowy cloak. I'm also adding colors other than blue into the fabric, because large areas of similar color and value usually benefit by having little touches of complementary colors added to them.

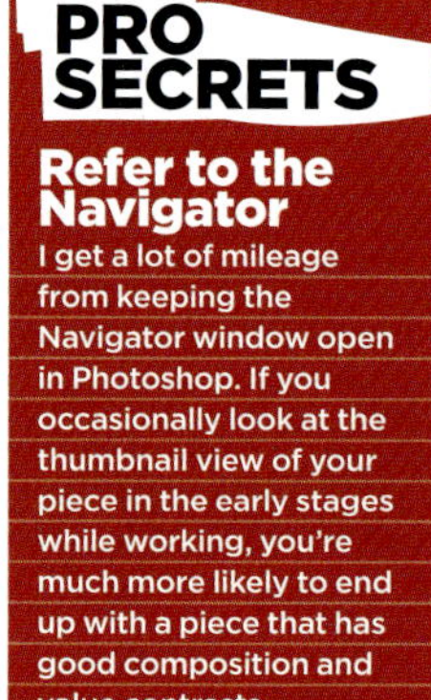

PRO SECRETS

Refer to the Navigator

I get a lot of mileage from keeping the Navigator window open in Photoshop. If you occasionally look at the thumbnail view of your piece in the early stages while working, you're much more likely to end up with a piece that has good composition and value contrasts.

9 Blend and detail

I take the piece back into Painter and blend away any areas that look overly sketchy. In general, I'm aiming to have the most detail in the area just before the core shadow, as the form turns away from the light. I blend and detail areas such as the hands and gauntlet at this stage.

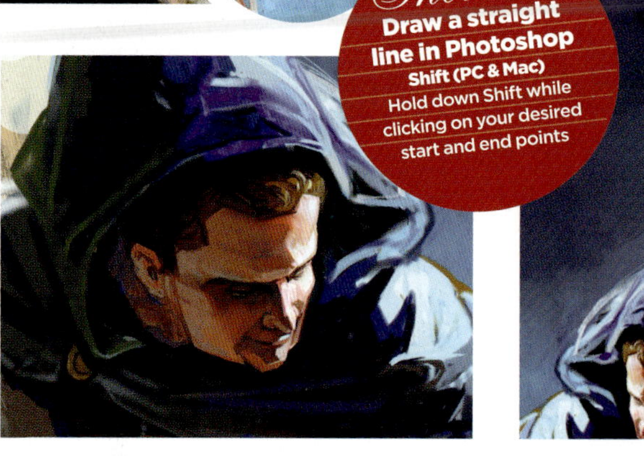

Shortcuts

Draw a straight line in Photoshop

Shift (PC & Mac)

Hold down Shift while clicking on your desired start and end points

10 Anatomy checks

This is the point where I spend a lot of time checking my references and further refining the anatomy. Still working in Painter, I concentrate on my character's face using a mixture of Don's Blender and the Round Camelhair in Oils at 54 percent Opacity, taking several passes to check that the features wrap correctly around the form of the skull.

11 Architecture

I bring the piece back into Photoshop to do the hard architecture detailing. I use the Shift key to make sure I'm getting straight lines, and go to town cleaning up the columns and adding detail. I keep patches of non-local colors with similar values on the background areas of the painting at this stage; they add to the overall traditional effect.

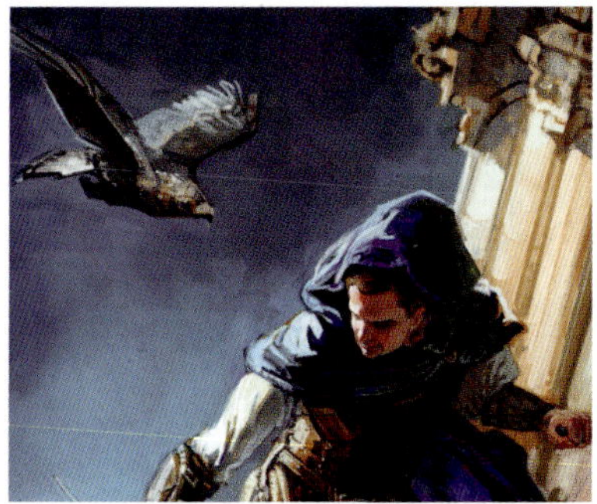

12 Flip and check

I continue flipping the piece horizontally to check the anatomy of my character. I work on the bird in Painter to get it more finalized, refining the feathers and anatomy, and also tweak the architecture in Photoshop. This is the midway point for me – from here, it's pretty much all detailing.

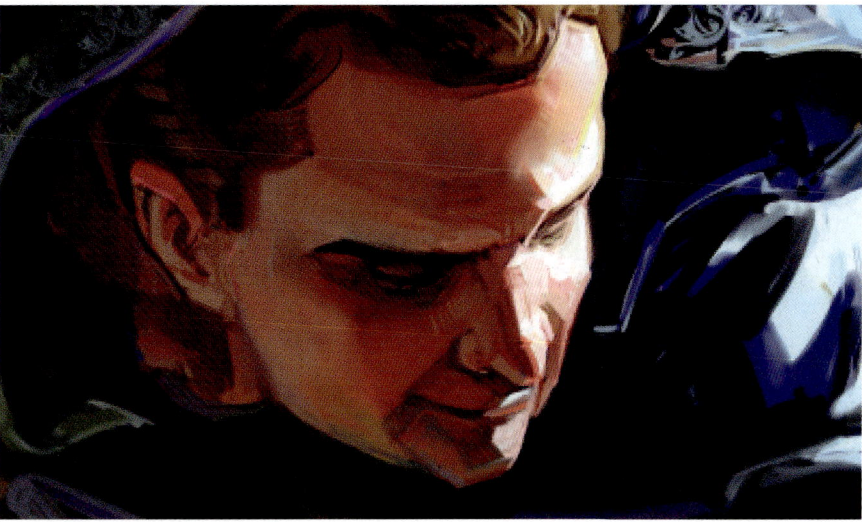

14 More facial work

There still isn't quite enough detail around the character's face, so I add a subtle pattern into the edge of the cloak hood with a custom brush I've made in Photoshop, then painted over it in Painter to integrate the pattern. I also print the piece to check if there are any areas still in need of blending or more detail.

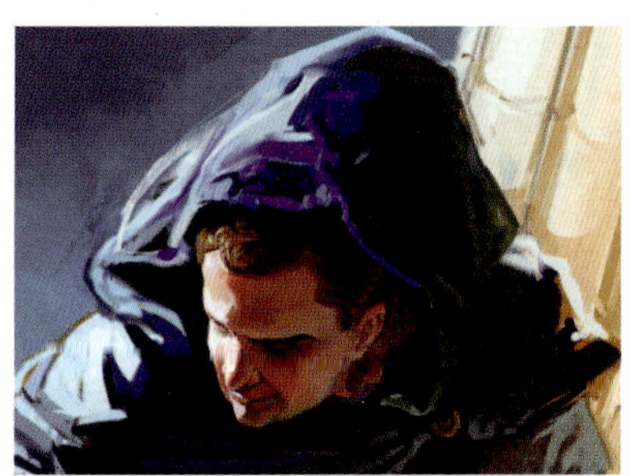

13 Focus on the focal point

Here I add more detail to the character's face, returning to the main focal point at this late stage to ensure that it remains the key element of the piece. I always make sure to touch the focal point at the beginning and at the end of a piece. That way, I can make sure that the rest of the painting is subservient to it.

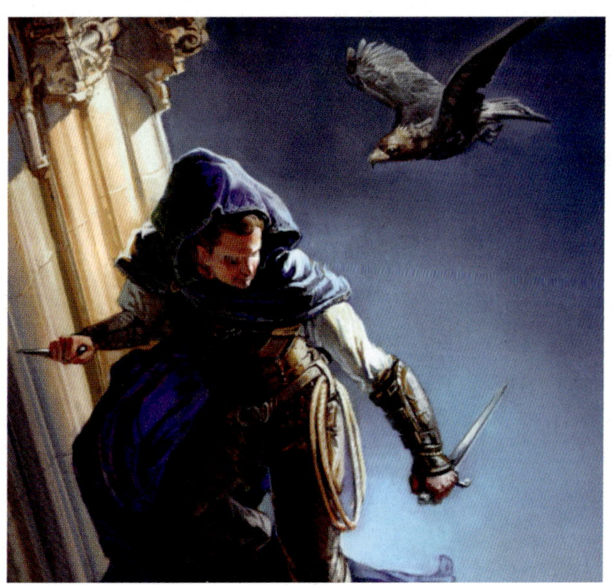

15 Last details

I revisit the bird's anatomy because the front wing looks wrong. Even if I have a reference of something in the pose I've painted, sometimes it'll look odd or incorrect and need adjusting. I detail the last bits of his gauntlet, do the final bits of architecture detailing, and tweak the Levels and up the Saturation slightly in Adjustment layers.

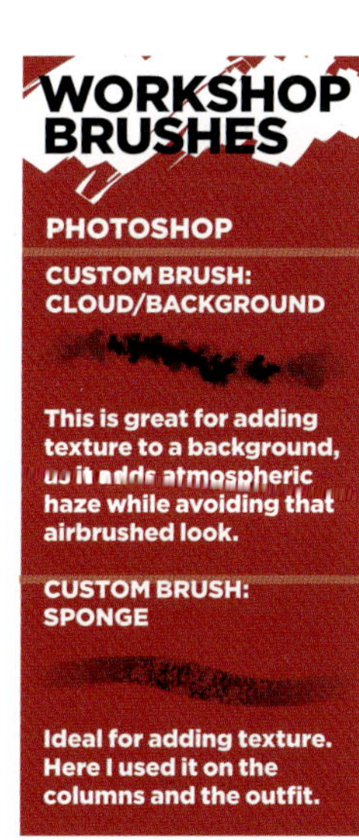

THE SECRET TO PAINTING SKIN

Do your fantasy characters suffer from bad skin? Then it's a good job **Anne Pogoda** is on hand to remedy this unfortunate situation...

With this workshop I'm going to show you my working technique for painting soft skin. All we need are two standard brushes, one texture brush, and one filter from Photoshop – we'll be airbrushing most of the time.

My experience in television has taught me that the good thing about starting in black and white is that you don't become distracted by vibrant or badly placed colors. I also learned that the colors you apply later look much more natural when you add them halfway through your painting and continue working with them. This way you can avoid the metallic shine present in many black and white paintings that are colored in at a late stage. I usually start with a simple sketch on a dark background. Because the eye focuses on bright areas first, this method makes the canvas work for me.

What's important about skin is not so much the texture itself, but the use of colors. Skin can have many different and interesting colors, depending on the surrounding light. I like working with cold and warm contrasts. So, for example, I love to mix yellows and blues together because this makes the skin look more interesting. But usually, before I start mixing the colors, I try out basic color schemes to gain a better idea of what the figure may look like. This also helps me to see if the color scheme I've thought of is, in fact, the best fit for the figure.

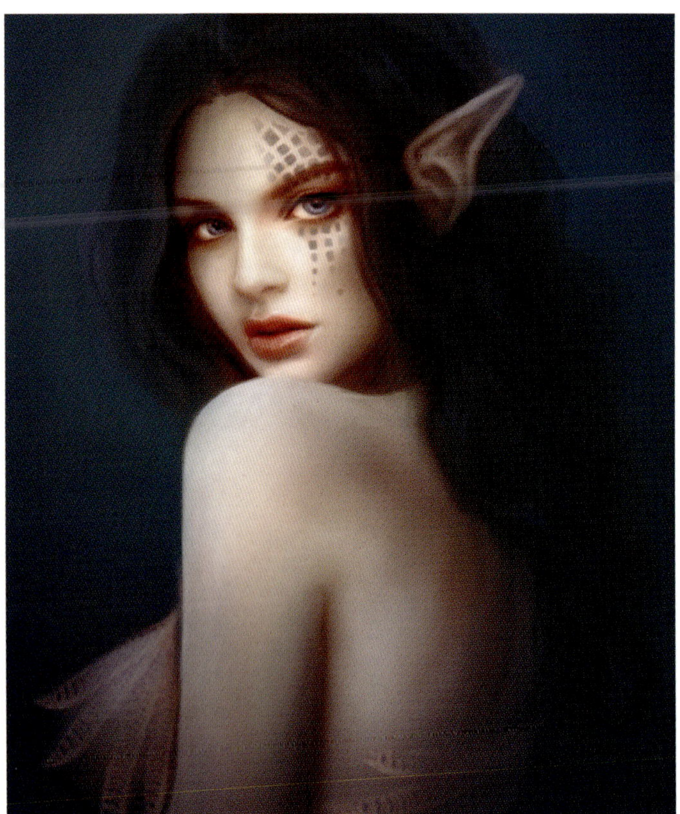

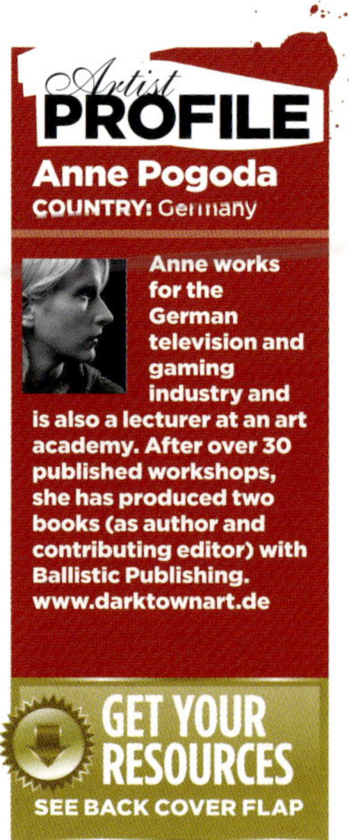

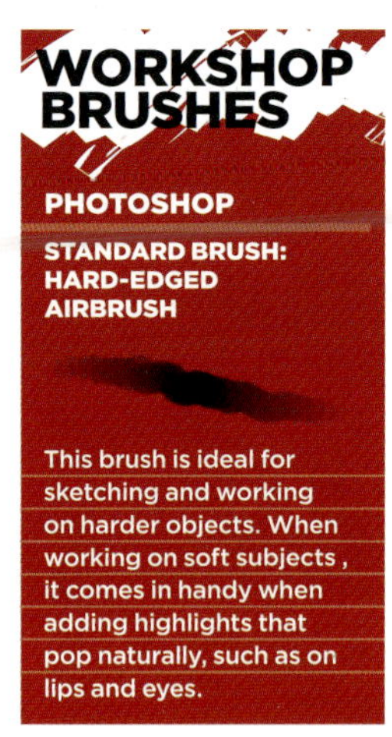

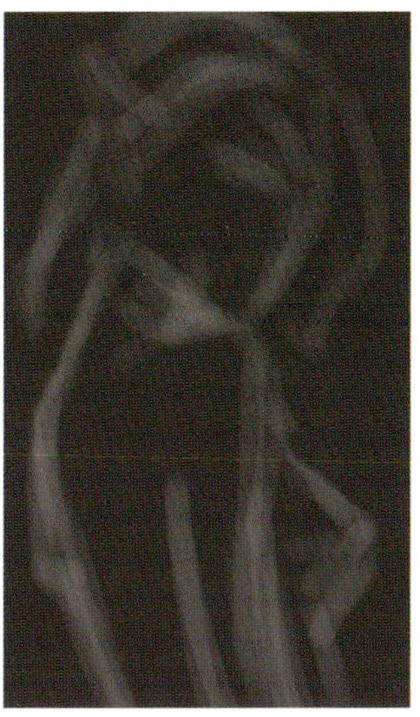

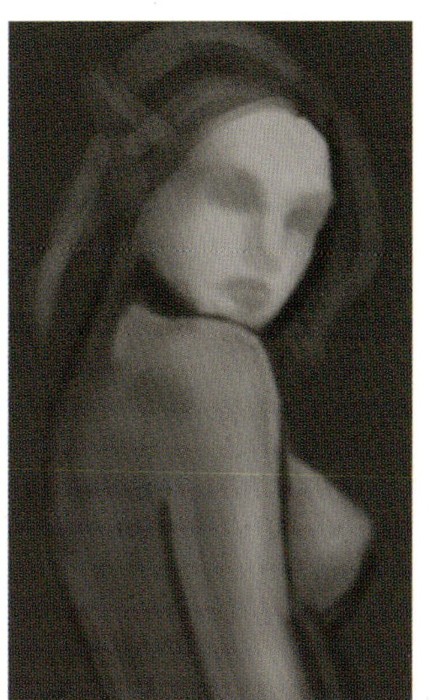

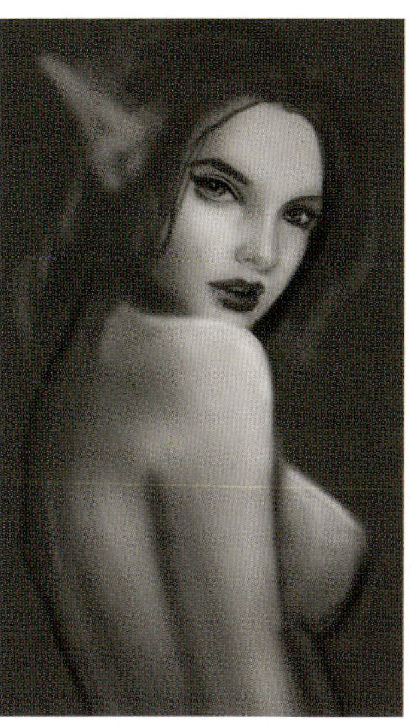

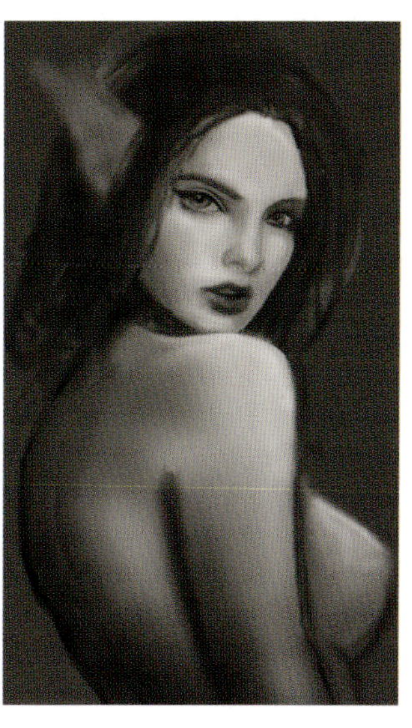

1 Basic sketch
I start off with two layers. One is my dark background layer, while on the second layer I make a rough sketch using one of the standard brushes. Brush number five and number six in Photoshop CS5 are the hard and soft brushes I prefer (in version CS4 and earlier they are called airbrushes). Here I usually work with the second group of airbrushes, using the 19 Rough and 300 Soft.

2 First shapes
I begin by blocking in rough shapes with a soft airbrush at around 30 percent opacity. My dark canvas helps me to see the forms as I work from bright to dark. You can best see this working process on the face: I give it more definition at this stage, using a hard-edged airbrush to make the nose, eyes, and lips more obvious with regards to their shape and position.

3 Define the structure
I define the structure of the shoulder with a large, soft-edged airbrush at around 30 percent opacity. I outline the mouth, eyes, and nose much more now, using a small airbrush at around 80 percent opacity. Then I make a rough sketch of the ear to see if I like its shape and position. At this stage, it doesn't matter that the only brush being used is the soft airbrush.

4 Adjusting the pose
I make the first adjustments to my character's pose by bending her back more. I also become a little clearer about her hair, but don't commit to its length because I'm not sure at this point how much of her bare back should be on display. I also start to correct her face here and there by making the nose smaller and adjusting the position of the eyes.

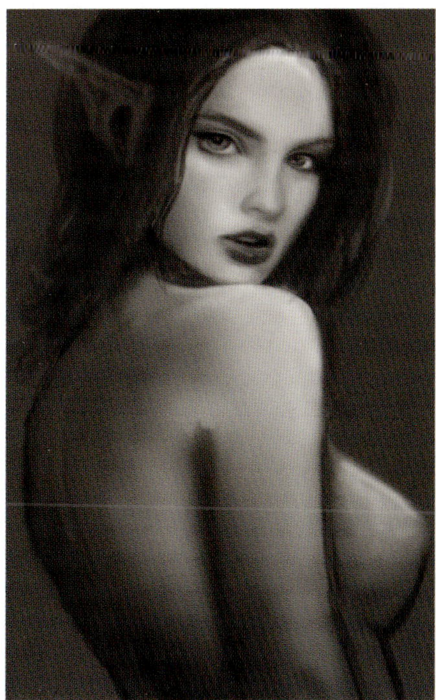

5 Correcting the arm
I now focus on making one more correction to her body. I fix her arm and add more contrast by painting in some dark gray. I usually never work with pure white or pure black, because I think that it makes any painting look too artificial. I then go back to her head and define the shape of her ear. I also make her lips and nose much softer looking by adding some dark gray to them with the soft airbrush.

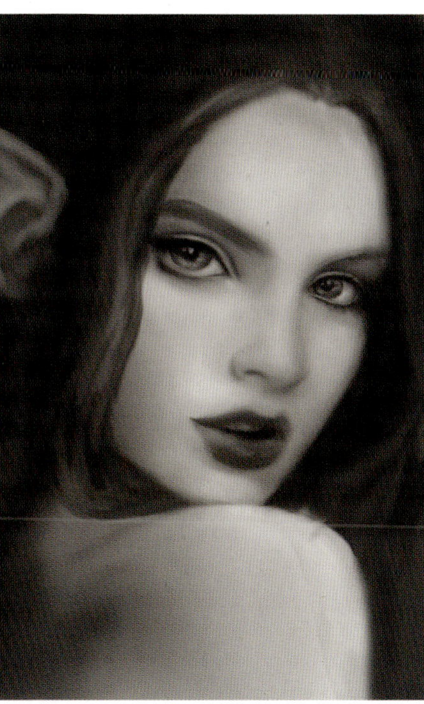

6 Make allowances for the light
The light is coming in from the right, and so her back needs to be much darker, especially around the shoulder blades. I achieve this using a dark gray with a big soft brush, again set to around 30 percent opacity. Using the same airbrush, I define her breast a little more. I then paint in the ear and frame her face better by defining the hair around it a little more.

Shortcuts
Levels
Ctrl+L (PC)
Cmd+L (Mac)
Use Photoshop's Levels tool to adjust your painting's brightness and contrast

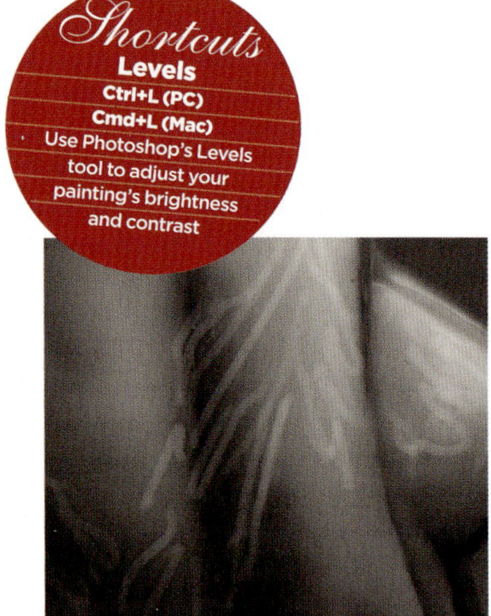

7 What to wear

I'm still unsure how to dress her, so I sketch rough clothing on a new layer and leave it for now. I draw some strands of hair on my dark base; I usually put hair on a new layer so I can push back parts with the Eraser. I continue to define her eyes. I make some minor changes to the face that add a lot to the shape. The lips and nose are softened, the eyebrows are darkened and the skin around her cheekbones is much clearer now. It's brighter around her mouth and on top of the cheek, and darker at its lower end. The face appears to be much rounder this way.

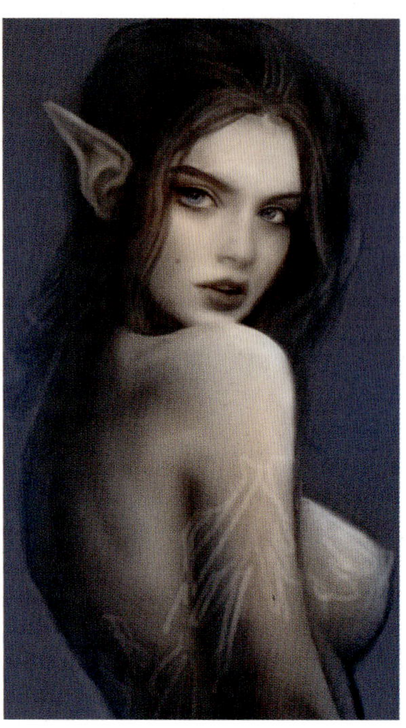

8 A cold color palette...

This is where it becomes interesting. I'm going to experiment with colors, so I make a new layer and set it to Color. I start with a blue background around the figure, because the background light usually influences the figure, I let some of the blue cover her body, too. Her skin seems to be very cold and almost undead now.

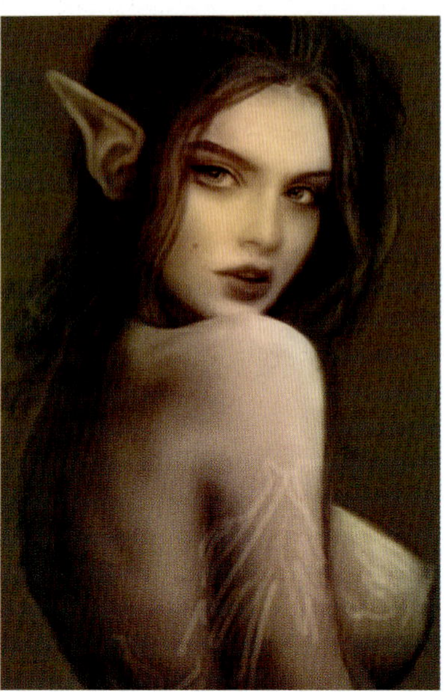

9 ...and a warm color palette

In contrast to the cold color approach is this warm color test, which could be used as part of a conventional faerie theme set in a forest, for example. The green of the background and the soft red of her body are significantly enriched with yellow, which makes the whole theme very warm. Her skin also looks much more appealing now – I've given that cold, zombie look the heave-ho!

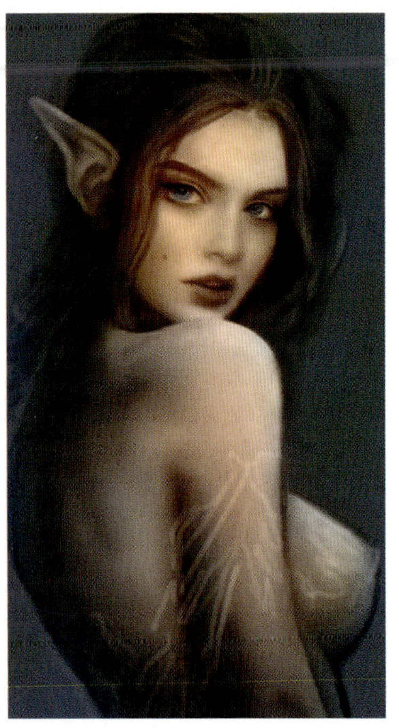

10 Mixing colors

To create an interesting color palette, I decide to mix the two. This isn't much of a problem because each palette is on its own layer. I erase parts of the background and her lower body from the warm color palette, then I set the Eraser to a soft airbrush and use it at an Opacity of 40 percent.

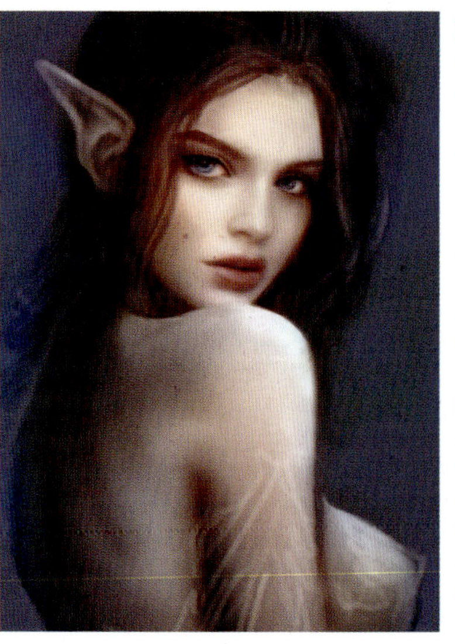

11 Refining the colors

For this step I have to merge the figure that I've already painted on one layer with the background layer, and then save the different versions of the painting as PSDs. The adjustments I make here are done on a duplicate of my merged layer, using the Color Balance and Levels functions. From step 10, the figure still has a lot more of the warm (yellow and red) tones in her face, which I keep to create a definite focal point. The overall image now contains more magenta and stronger contrasts.

PRO SECRETS

Draw from life

It's not really a secret, but many people seem to forget it: practice by drawing from life models. Whether you're a professional artist or a beginner, studying a real human being rather than a photo will make a world of difference. You will notice so many more things about the body when the model is sitting in front of you.

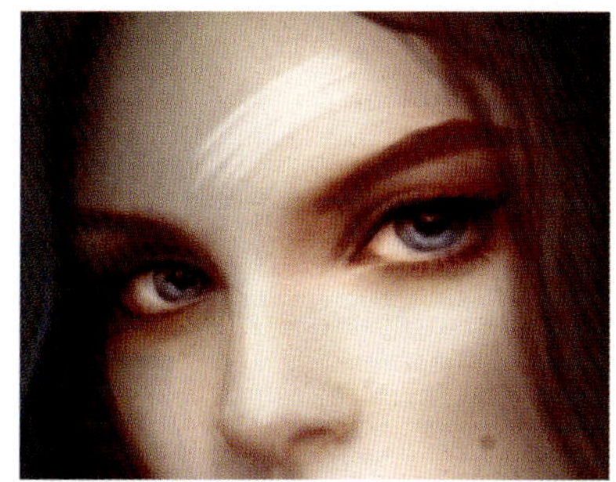

12 The hair

It's time to find a solution for her hair. I make a new layer and roughly paint in a floating structure with a big, soft airbrush, using dark blue. I want the hair to look almost weightless because the dark background could also suggest an underwater scene; a water faerie is something we don't see often. You can download or create a spackled brush to achieve a hand-painted look on your skin. (It's highlighted in white in the picture above.) This brush comes from Linda Bergkvist's brush pack, and is ideal for giving the painting a less clean, traditional look after you've finished airbrushing. You can apply it loosely all over your figure, and it's excellent for painting hair.

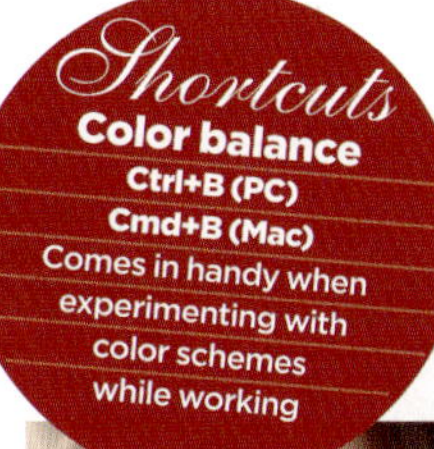

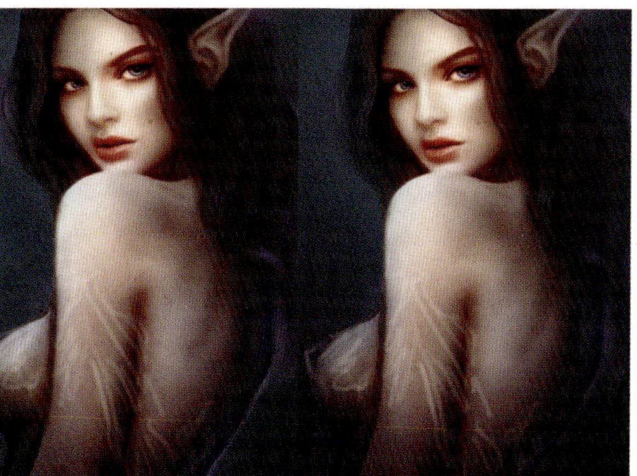

13 Flip the image

Flipping your work – about once every hour, say – lets you see your art in a new light, as well as highlighting errors. In this instance it becomes clearer where the final figure should go. A good trick to neatly merge a figure into the background is to apply color on top on a new layer, using a large, soft airbrush with around 30 percent opacity. Painting with low opacity enables you to mix color directly on your canvas. I also adjust her lips so they're as red as her eye makeup, again to catch the viewer's eye. To use the Noise filter to create some soft skin texture, I make a selection of the skin and copy it onto a new layer. I access the Noise filter and choose how intense I want it to be. The filter might darken the painting a little, but you can readjust the skin with Levels and erase parts you don't like.

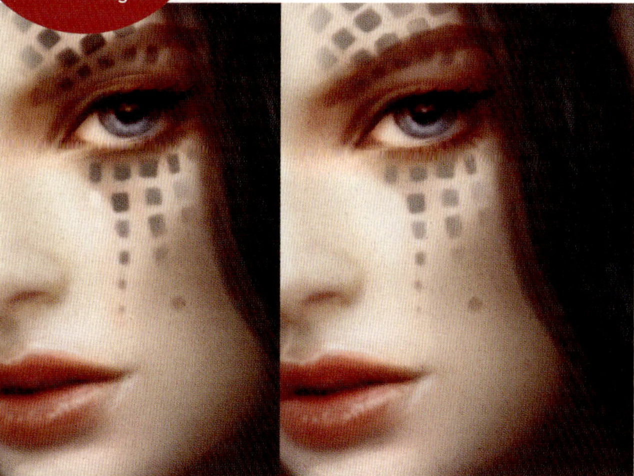

14 Add some interest

I now try to brainstorm on what could look interesting for her skin. A tattoo or interesting makeup would be suitable, so I paint some random shapes over her face using a new layer, and push parts back with the Eraser to ensure the pattern matches the shape of her head. The Eraser can be a big help when painting elements onto a figure, like hair and things that are supposed to rest on the skin's surface. The Eraser method works well as long as all parts of the tattoo that cover darker areas, like the side of the cheek, are pushed back. The areas that cover brighter areas like the top of the cheek are only slightly adjusted. This creates the illusion of the tattoo forming itself along the skin.

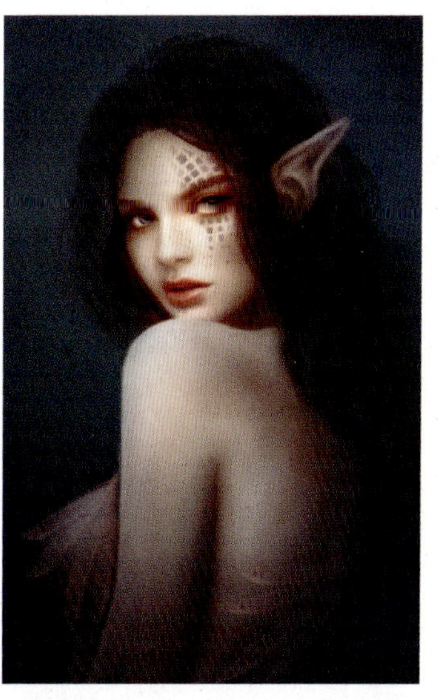

15 Add some final cover-ups

I cover her body with some sort of underwater fantasy leaves and create another layer on the very top of the figure, to which I only add dark violet to fit the leaves better onto her body. This way of painting is a big time-saver and certainly helps to add a soft, tender feeling to the overall figure.

PRO SECRETS

Use a mood board

We often use a mood board for television and advertising projects. It's a collection of images that show the customer what color schemes and styles we're planning to use. The mood board is a time-saver, especially for beginners, because it ensures that you don't slavishly follow a reference image (in case you're working with any). More importantly, it helps you realize if the idea you've already had will work out that way.

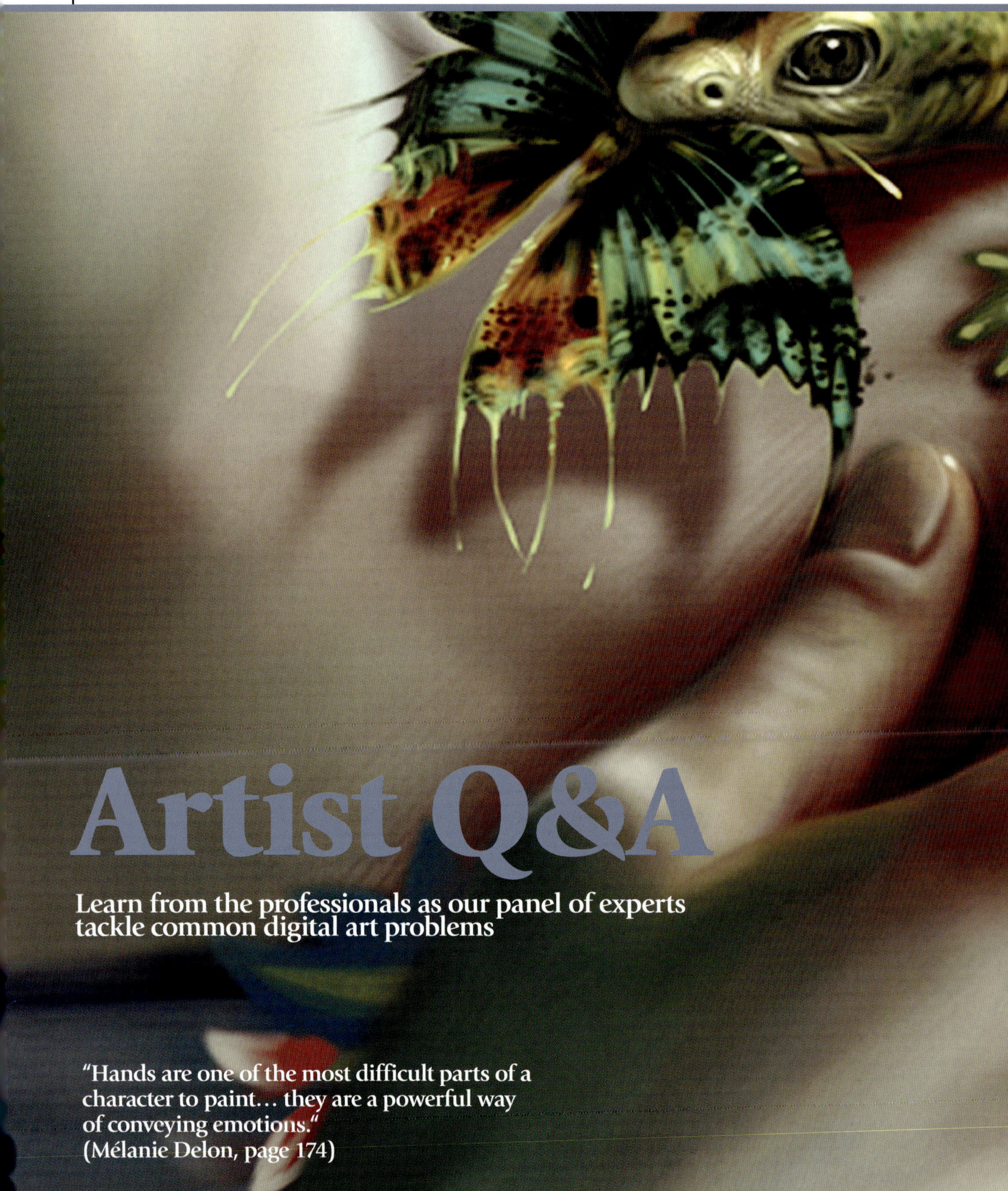

Artist Q&A

Learn from the professionals as our panel of experts tackle common digital art problems

"Hands are one of the most difficult parts of a character to paint… they are a powerful way of conveying emotions."
(Mélanie Delon, page 174)

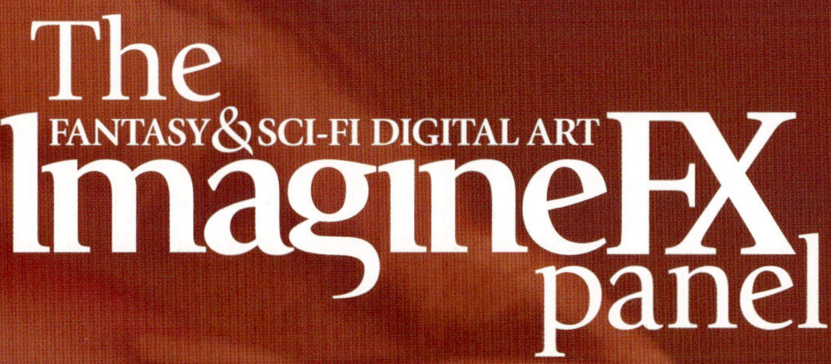

Marek Okon

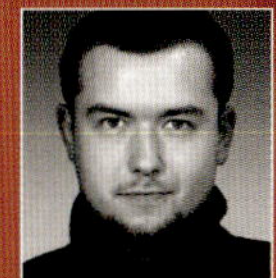

Marek is a sci-fi and fantasy artist, though he started out as a web designer. He's worked with BioWare, Crytek, and Naughty Dog – the latter for *The Last of Us*.

www.okonart.com

Jonny Duddle

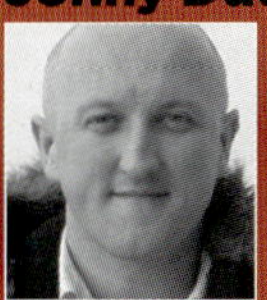

Jonny has worked on the film *The Pirates! In an Adventure with Scientists!*, and has written and illustrated a number of picture books for children.

www.jonnyduddle.blogspot.co.uk

Andy Park

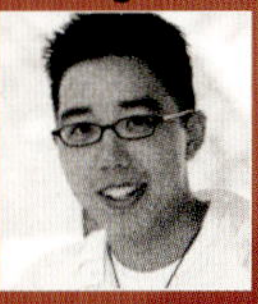

Andy is a talented concept artist who works for Sony. Among the games he has worked on is the popular *God of War* for PlayStation 2.

www.andyparkart.com

Bobby Chiu

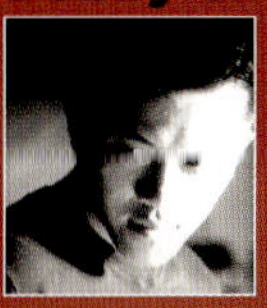

Bobby Chiu is an independent artist from Toronto, Canada. Part of the Imaginism outfit, he's involved primarily in film and TV production.

www.imaginismstudios.com

Jim Pavelec

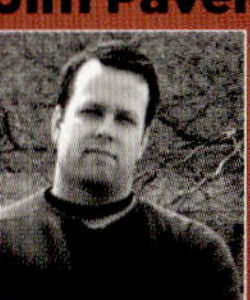

Jim Pavelec lives in a world surrounded by demons, monsters, and devils. He's the author of the how-to monster book *Hell Beasts*.

www.jimpavelec.com

Frazer Irving

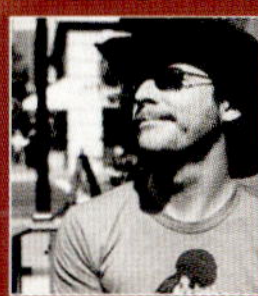

Top comic artist Frazer spends lots of time drawing horrid-looking things on his Wacom Cintiq. He's worked for *2000 AD* and DC Comics.

www.frazerirving.com

Lauren K Cannon

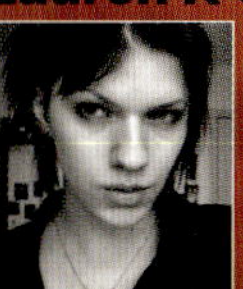

Lauren is a freelance fantasy artist who specializes in the surreal. She lives in a small woodland village in New Jersey.

www.navate.com

Joel Carlo

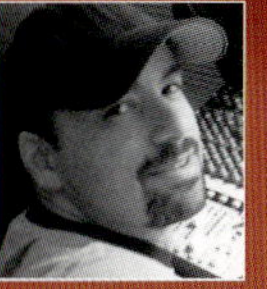

Joel is a multimedia developer by day and a prolific digital artist by night. You may know him from the forums by his alter ego: MechaHateChimp.

www.joelcarlo.net

Marta Dahlig

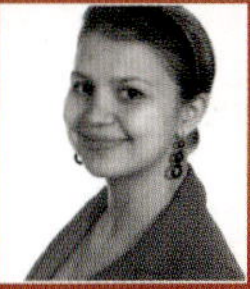

Polish artist Marta has been working with Photoshop and Painter for several years and has become an ImagineFX regular.

www.marta-dahlig.com

Cynthia Sheppard

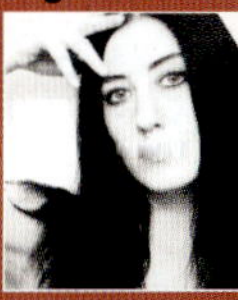

Cynthia is a freelance digital artist. With a trad background, she brings classical techniques to her digital canvas.

www.sheppard-arts.com

Mélanie Delon

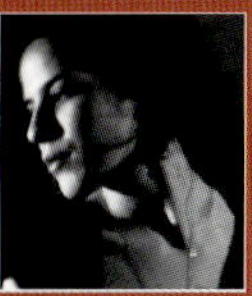

Mélanie is a freelance fantasy illustrator. She works as a cover artist for several publishers, and on her personal artbook series.

www.melaniedelon.com

Jeremy Enecio

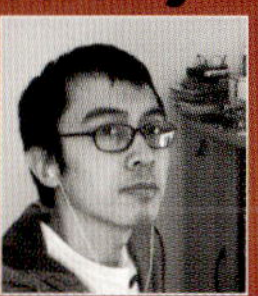

Jeremy is an award-winning, New York-based illustrator. His many clients include Tor Books, Playboy, and Wizards of the Coast.

www.jenecio.com

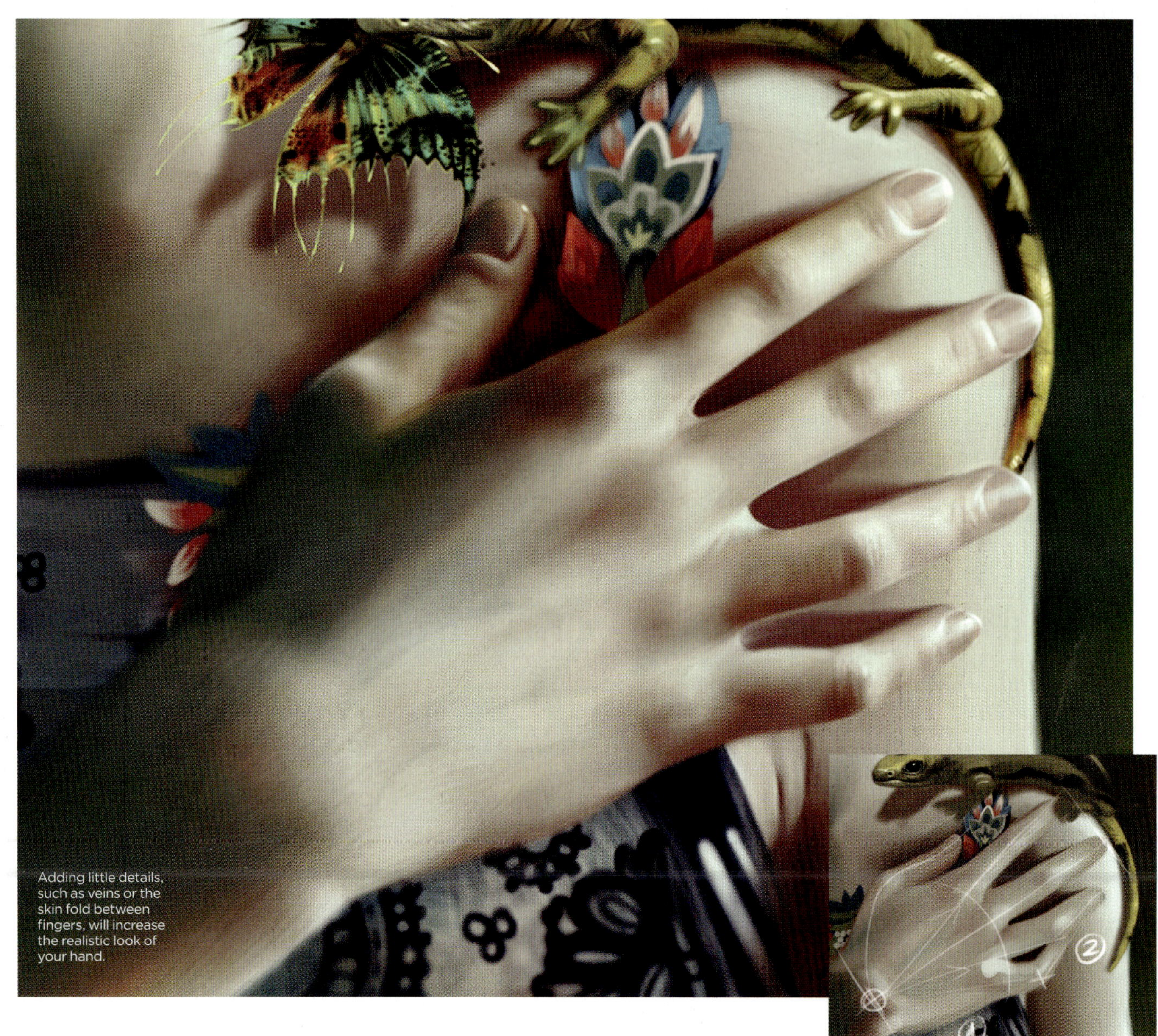

Adding little details, such as veins or the skin fold between fingers, will increase the realistic look of your hand.

The color scheme for a hand is the same as for the character, except for the extremities of the fingers and the joints, which are redder.

QUESTION

How can I make the hands I paint appear more realistic?

ANSWER *Melanie replies*

Hands are one of the most difficult parts of a character to paint. You should bear in mind that they have soft, round edges, and also that they are a powerful way of conveying emotions.

When you begin a hand, think about the construction lines (they all come from the wrist); don't hesitate to use your own hands as a model. In general, fingers are halfway along the hand, and they are more like cylinders than boxes.

When you're satisfied with your sketch, start shading. Try to smooth as best as you can here. Use a basic Hard Round brush tip for the base and a speckled one for the final blending. The light is stronger and redder at the joints, because the skin is thinner there.

The next step is texturing. This stage is the most decisive one. I use a basic Hard Round tip with Hardness set to 70% and Shape Dynamics set to Size Jitter Control set to Pen Pressure. I add a few thin lines and folds on the skin, and some light dots on another layer.

QUESTION

What's the best way to draw a screaming face?

ANSWER

Frazer replies

All the way from Edvard Munch to Jack Kirby, every artist has their own way of depicting screams. The type of scream can vary a great deal depending on the emotion that drives this reaction. As an artist, you need to know the differences between a scream of fear as opposed to a scream of anger, or perhaps of pain. It's not uncommon for a lazy artist to use the wrong expression for an illustration and cause much confusion in the onlooker, especially in comics.

What I'll do here is take you through the process of how I construct an angry scream for a comic, which is all about the scream and the power behind it.

To do this, I employ standard drawing techniques next to graphic elements, in much the same way that Munch used swirls to enhance his Scream painting. Remember, though, that even the most detailed-looking image is really still composed of the most basic elements. The trick is to identify which aspects of the face convey the idea most effectively.

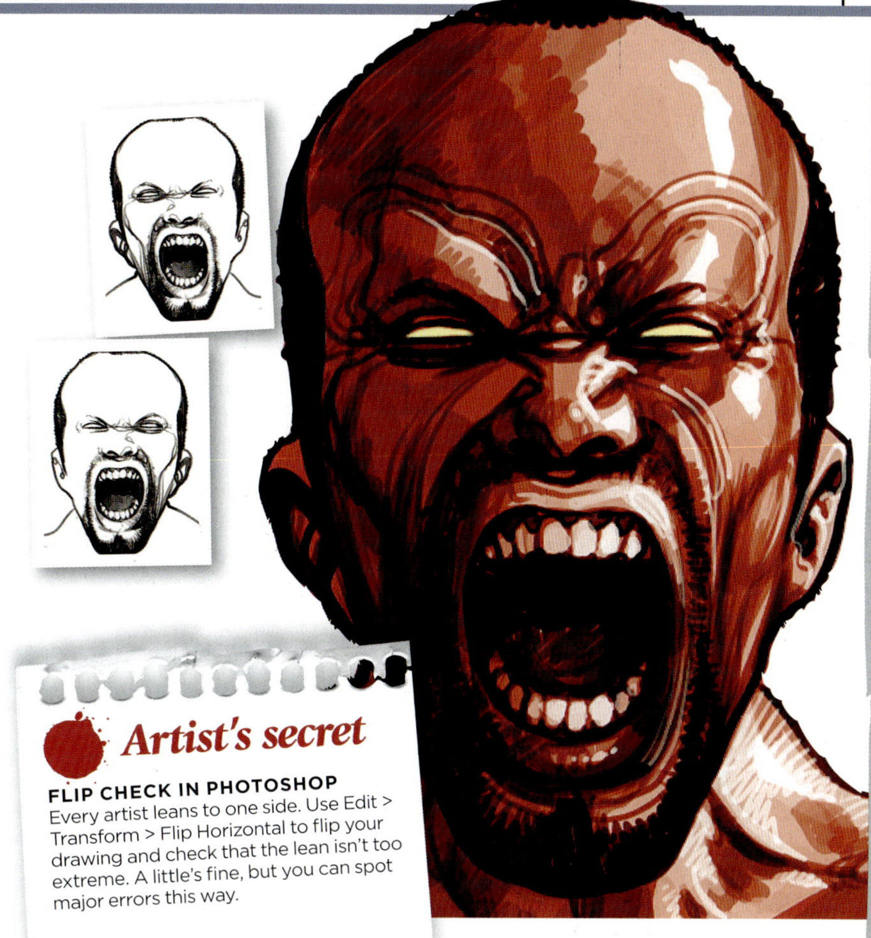

Artist's secret

FLIP CHECK IN PHOTOSHOP

Every artist leans to one side. Use Edit > Transform > Flip Horizontal to flip your drawing and check that the lean isn't too extreme. A little's fine, but you can spot major errors this way.

Step-by-step: The perfect scream

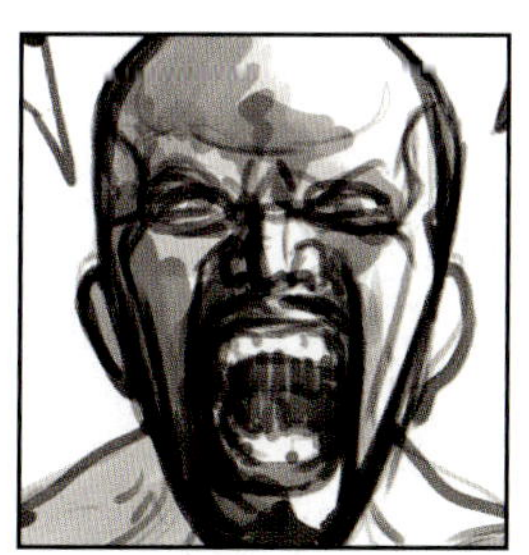

1. I start with a rather basic sketch. This drawing is loose and rough, to effectively capture and reflect the raw energy that's needed to drive the rest of the art. I always find that the initial stage of a drawing – whatever the tone, style, or subject matter – provides the fuel for the final image. You mustn't hold back at all at this point if you want to capture that scream.

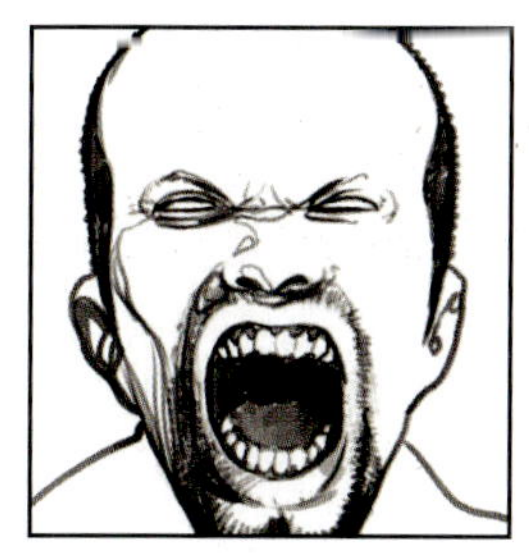

2. Next, I trace over the sketch on a new layer. These lines refine the basic shape and the main features, framing the mouth with a beard and making sure that it reads as simply as possible. A lot of the raw energy from the original sketch is lost at this stage, because of the simplicity of the black line – but this will all return as I progress to the final piece.

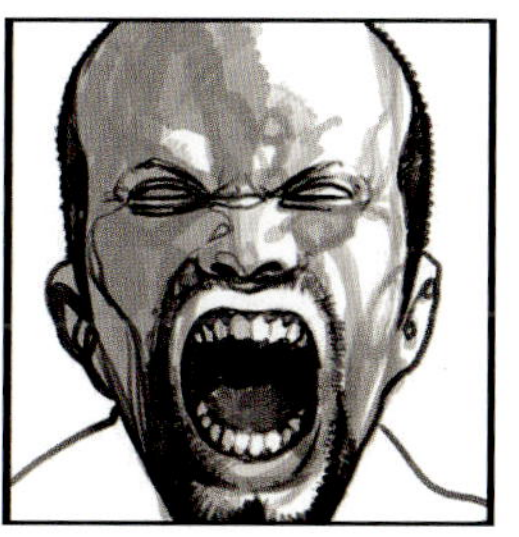

3. The next stage in the process is to block in some shadows on the subject's face. Extreme, dramatic lighting can be an incredibly valuable tool when you're trying to create a particular mood, and is especially useful when defining dramatic lines on the face. Here, I choose to use quite strong side lighting, to imply the conflict of emotion within the character.

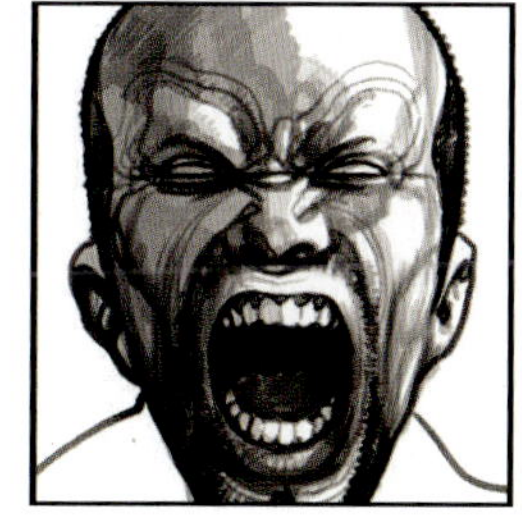

4. The wrinkles stemming out from the eyes are very important in depicting strong expressions. Here I exaggerate the lines on the forehead a little to enhance the anguish, as well as darkening the bridge of the nose to show tension. These features capture the basics of the scream. After this, all you need is the right color palette and a well-chosen background to set it off perfectly.

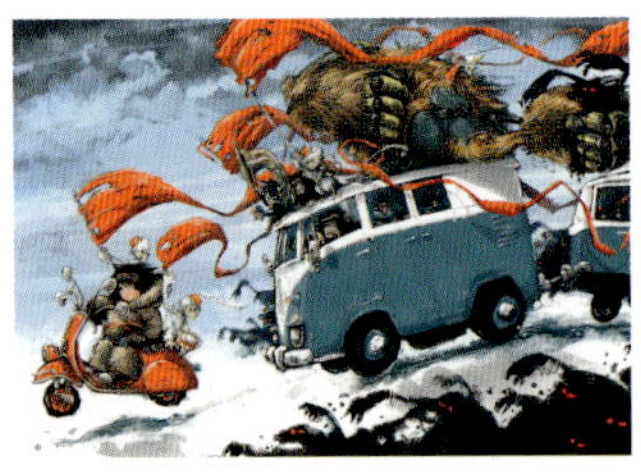

In this painting, I use various tricks to suggest movement, such as adjusting shadows to place vehicles in midair, rough brush marks, and flowing fur and flags.

QUESTION

My figures always look static in my paintings. How can I give them more of a sense of motion and dynamism?

ANSWER *Jonny replies*

It's common to find that the more you work on an image, the more static the end result becomes. I often find myself rendering a successful character sketch, with lots of movement and dynamism, into something dull and lifeless. But there are ways of keeping a character looking dynamic.

The most obvious place to start is the character's pose. To properly convey character, you need to paint figures in poses that suggest their personality and movement. For example, an aggressive character could be hunched over with clenched fists and taut neck muscles.

Sketch the figure, then revise it with a more exaggerated pose. Keep pushing a pose: it will often gain more and more personality. Use layout paper to trace parts of the previous drawing, or sketch digitally and save different versions. You can use Photoshop's Transform tools to stretch, scale, and distort particular parts of a figure's anatomy.

Reference is important. Look at photographs of figures in motion. Analyzing some of the incredible photography online or in magazines can reap benefits when drawing dynamic figures. Skateboarding shots are a good example; they do a great job of showing the human figure in movement and under lots of tension and stress.

Lastly, look at artists and art reference books for tips, tricks, and techniques. There are some wonderful artists, such as Phil Hale and Jon Foster, who are masters of dynamic figure painting. Look closely at how they use composition, perspective, figure drawing, and mark-making to add dynamism to images.

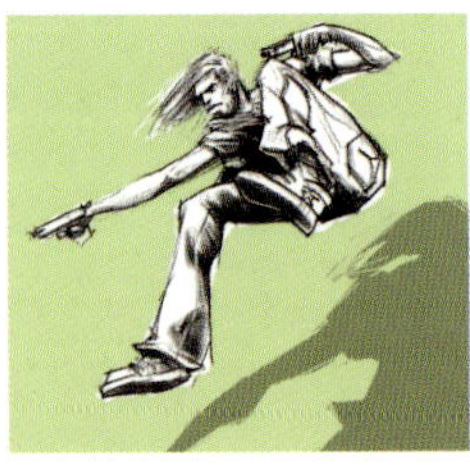

QUESTION

What does the term "heroic proportions" mean in the context of character design?

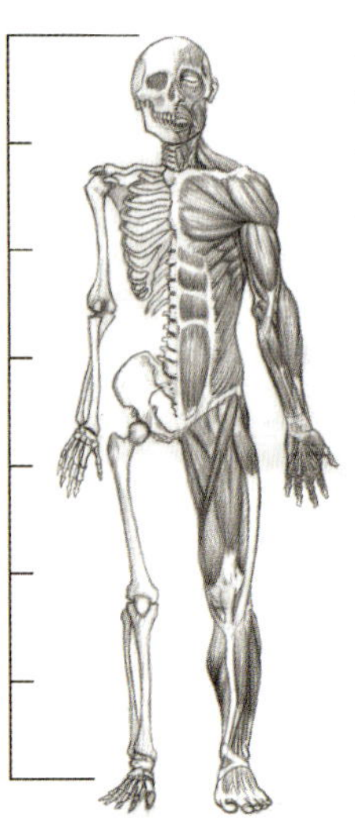

This image shows the proportions of the average human male, and the musculature and skeletal structure beneath the skin.

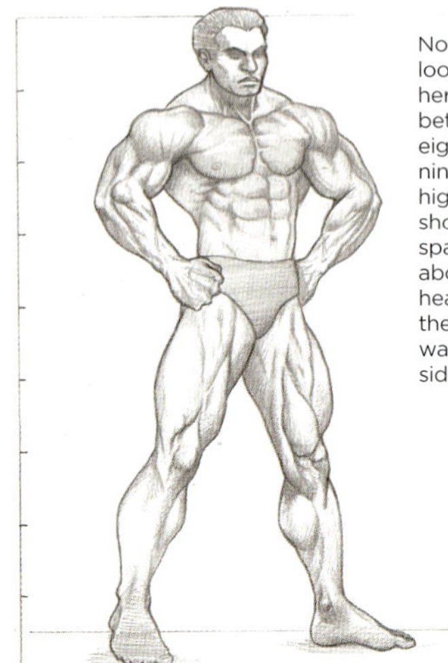

Now take a look at our hero. At between eight and nine heads high and a shoulder span of about four heads, he's the guy you want on your side.

ANSWER *Jim replies*

Heroic proportions are important when working in comic books or fantasy illustration. A common unit of measure when drawing the human body is head height and width. At eye level, the typical human being is roughly six and a half to seven heads tall, and three heads across at the shoulders – the body's widest point. But you don't want your superhero looking average, so design them based on the principle of heroic proportions.

A hero should stand anywhere between eight and nine heads high, with a shoulder width of four heads across. The hero's waist is kept the same as the average person's, to help accentuate the width of their shoulders and the sweep of their crushing thighs.

QUESTION

I've learned how to paint an eye head-on, but there seem to be no workshops on how to paint one from the side. I've tried and failed. What could I be doing wrong?

ANSWER *Andy replies*

The key to drawing or painting an eye is to think of it in three dimensions. Although we instinctively think of eyes as almond-shaped, they're of course spherical, with only about a quarter of the sphere visible. The eyeball is basically a sphere with lids that wrap around it. Keeping these things in mind will help you when you have to illustrate the eye from different angles – even from a direct front-on view.

QUESTION

How do I put realistic mass and weight into my character designs?

ANSWER
Bobby replies

"Weight" is really gravity acting upon a mass. Therefore, the best "weighted" character designs accurately reflect how gravity affects a body. Looking around you, you can gauge this in a couple of different ways: by looking at the body and by looking at how the body affects the environment.

In a soft mass such as a potbelly, where gravity is strong and the forces holding up the fat are weak, the greater the weight is, the lower the soft tissue will droop or hang down.

Also, consider how weight might impact your subject's surroundings. If your character is heavy, it might sink into the mud or cause the bridge or branch that it's standing on to bend noticeably. If it's being lifted (strenuously) off the ground, the vertical forces associated with the action should be tense and taut, to demonstrate how difficult it is to overcome the gravitational forces trying to pull the body back to earth.

In a magical environment, you could guide expectations by making your heavy character appear to be made of stone or something else that's very dense. Your viewer will understand from association that stone is heavy, therefore your character must be very heavy as well.

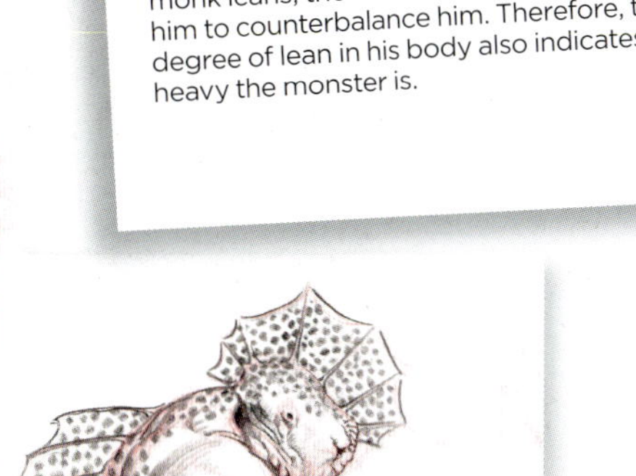

The initial sketch captures the idea and establishes forces. The monk is straining to lift the monster, but the monster does not budge.

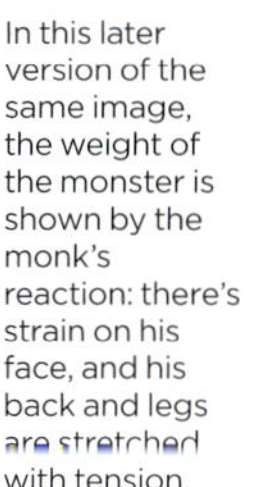

In this later version of the same image, the weight of the monster is shown by the monk's reaction: there's strain on his face, and his back and legs are stretched with tension.

Artist's secret

BALANCE

In the image below, the monk's center of gravity is behind him. If he wasn't trying to lift the monster, he would fall over; the further back the monk leans, the more weight must be in front of him to counterbalance him. Therefore, the degree of lean in his body also indicates how heavy the monster is.

Step-by-step: Painting eyeballs side-on

1. Here's a quick sketch of someone's right eye. As you can see, there is a circle faintly drawn in, which represents the sphere that makes up the eyeball. There are two lids that wrap around the eyeball and, in doing so, cover the majority of it. Take note of the way in which the bottom lid wraps under the top lid on the side.

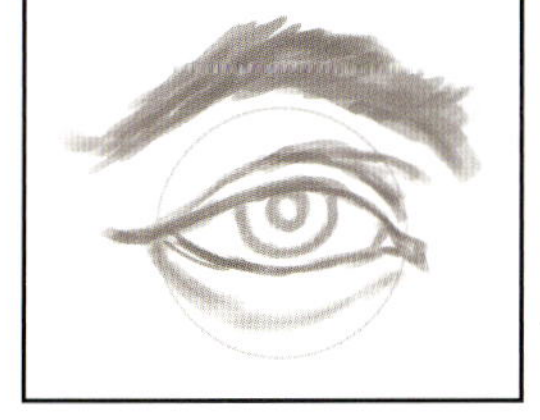

2. This is the same eye, seen from the side instead of the front. I've rendered out the sphere that makes up the eyeball within the eyelids to help to illustrate the three-dimensionality of the form. Again, note how the top lid goes above the bottom lid on the side. It's really important to get the eyes right, or else the picture can distort.

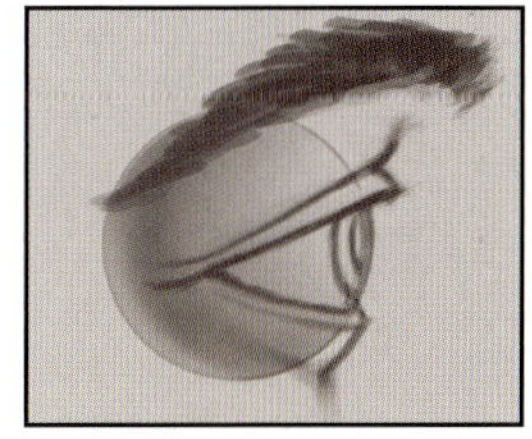

2. Here's the final rendering of the eye. There are a few things that are worth noting here. Because the eye is moist, you need to capture its reflective nature; there's a shadow that the top lid creates on the eyeball; and the whites of the eyes are not solely white – they too need to show elements of form and shadow.

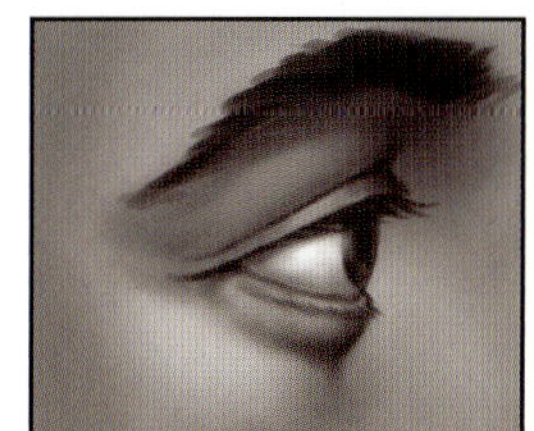

QUESTION

How do I draw facial expressions that convey the right emotion and don't feel stiff or forced?

ANSWER *Jonny replies*

If you're painting figures, drawing cartoons or rendering 3D characters, you need to make them interesting to look at. Whether it's evil, sad, happy or deadpan, their facial expression could be vital in communicating the story or message in your work.

However different people may look, everyone's faces are made up of the same set of bones and muscles. By becoming familiar with the basic anatomy of the face, it can be easier to paint more believable expressions. You don't need to name every muscle or identify every component of the skull, but with practice, you can get to know the main building blocks of the face and how they fit together.

Use reference to practice drawing faces. Reference can be anything from photographs you've taken or in books and magazines, DVD stills or old-master paintings. While drawing, try to identify the main shapes in the face and how they distort and move with different facial expressions. Also try exaggerating the size of particular features to see how subtle modifications can affect the mood. Try big noses, heavy brows or high foreheads. Small changes can make a big difference.

It's also worth bearing in mind that facial expressions work in conjunction with body language, so in most cases you'll need to ensure the face matches the body.

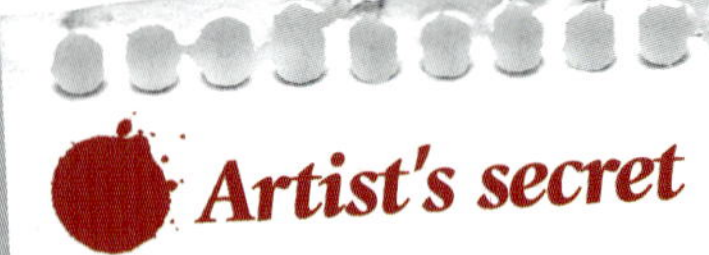

Artist's secret

USE A MIRROR!
This may sound obvious, or even a little embarrassing, but keeping a mirror on your desk can be a great help in painting believable expressions. Take some time out to sketch yourself so you get familiar with the movement of facial muscles while pulling faces, and use these sketches to inform your work.

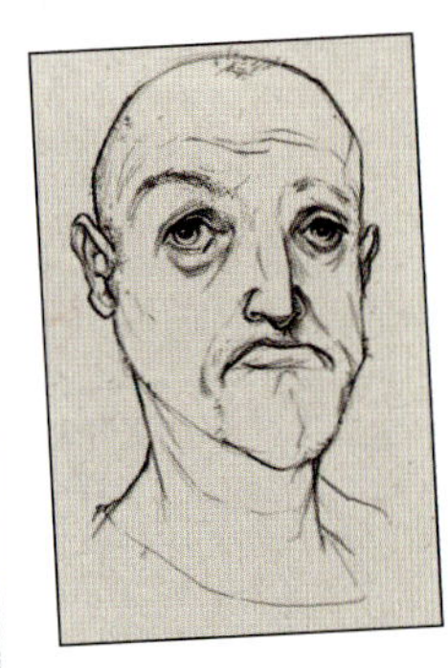

Don't be shy: draw yourself! (If I look a little wonky, that's because I am...)

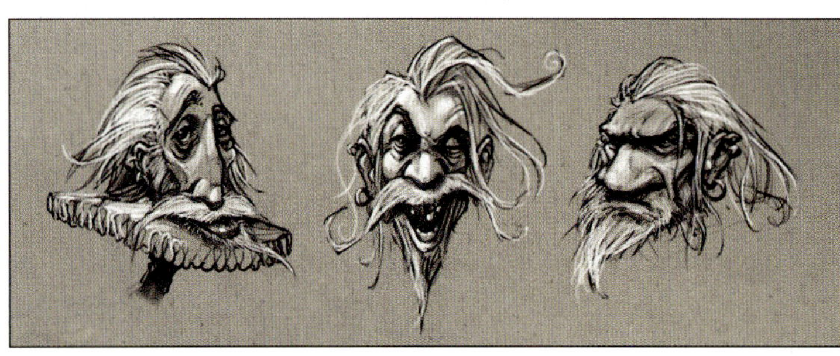

It's a good exercise to draw different facial expressions, whether you try drawing the same character or a variety of different faces from reference.

QUESTION

I have trouble posing figures realistically, particularly when they're in mid-action. How can I make my moving figures better?

ANSWER *Bobby replies*

When you show bodies in motion, you must consider physics and how various forces exert on the figure to push and pull it about. What are the effects of gravity on the pose? What about inertia or momentum? Which way is the body moving? All of these considerations tell you which forces are acting on our figure, and how much strain the body should undergo to do what it wants to do.

Next, consider the restrictions imposed by anatomy. Bodies are limited in the ways that they can bend, twist, stretch and rotate. Artistically speaking, it's acceptable for you to exaggerate these limits, but not to ignore them altogether. Take a leaping figure: when a body is airborne, gravity pulls it down, led by the trunk of the figure. Inertia dictates that the limbs will tend to trail behind the torso as force is applied upward.

With these points in mind, I sketch out my figure accordingly. If I'm unsure about how to position certain parts of the body, I will attempt to recreate that part of the pose myself, looking in a mirror, so that I can see how far back an arm or a leg can extend behind the moving body without it starting to feel too uncomfortable or unreal.

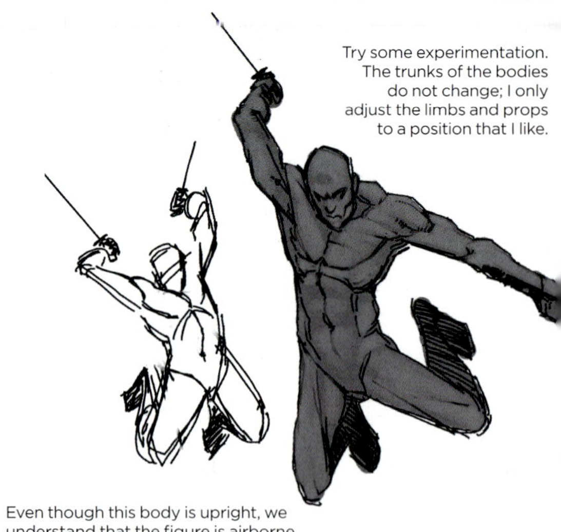

Try some experimentation. The trunks of the bodies do not change; I only adjust the limbs and props to a position that I like.

Even though this body is upright, we understand that the figure is airborne through the posing of the limbs relative to the body.

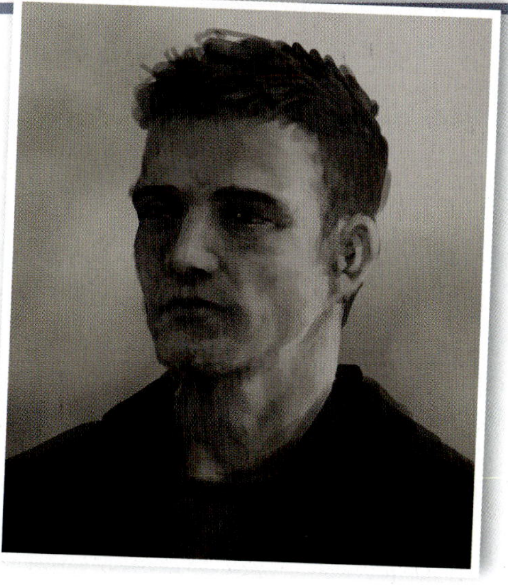

Contrary to initial impression, the human face is an exceedingly complex object, especially when it comes to an accurate portrayal of natural lighting and shadow.

QUESTION

How can I be more true to life when I paint the shading on my character's faces?

ANSWER *Marek replies*

When I was younger, I always wondered why artists practiced light and shadows on such simple objects as spheres, cylinders or boxes instead of on cool robots. Now I know that the simplicity of those objects enable an artist to fully understand how light casts shadow and then to transform this knowledge to more complex shapes.

Let's take the head, for example. It's a complex object with different planes to consider, which can be really tricky to shade properly. But if you break it down into basic shapes like spheres and cubes, it's much easier to grasp it in your mind.

In much the same way, divide complex scenes or objects into familiar shapes, and detail them after basic shading is properly done. This will help you greatly in your efforts to master the art of shading.

Step-by-step: Add shading detail to a plain face

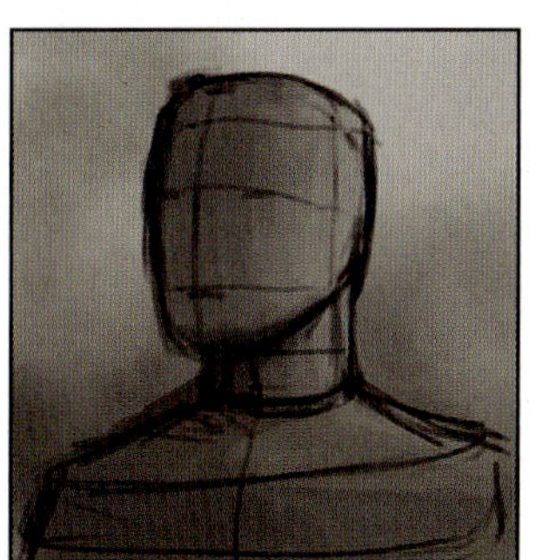

1. Start with some basic shapes for the head, neck and face – ideally a roundish cylinder (the head), attached to another cylinder (the neck) attached to another roundish cylinder (the body). Just to make this easier to understand, let's put a simple grid on our shapes and add some basic shading to them. Quite quickly, our head and face is beginning to take shape.

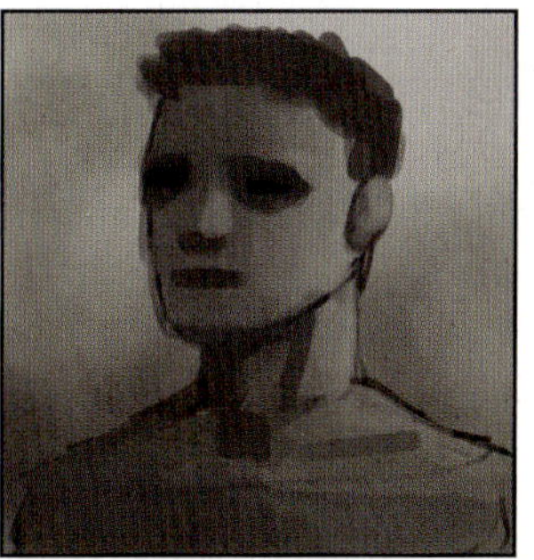

2. Now it's time to begin adding the basic features with some subtle shading. The nose is basically a triangle sticking out in the middle of the face, while the eye sockets are those two symmetrical depressions. The mouth is a simple shaded line. I usually paint these with a simple, single brush stroke to keep everything as basic as possible before starting the next stage.

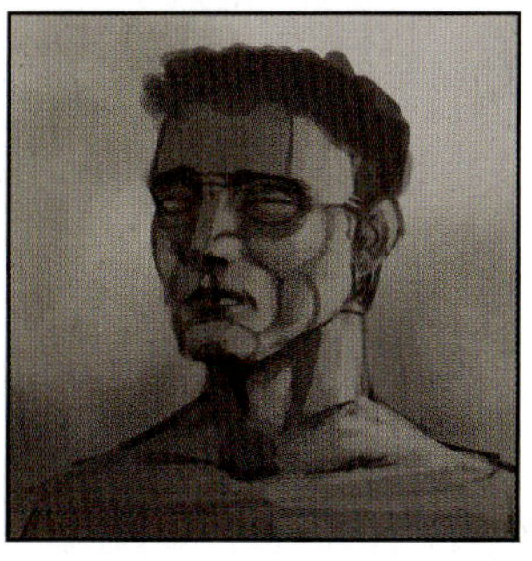

3. Let's shape this face more correctly. Here, I've split the surface of my head into shapes that can be shaded more carefully. All of those features are parts of spheres and cylinders that are fairly easy to shade. Just check out the eye area: it looks like I put another sphere into the middle of my eye socket. With the shapes set, we can move to the next phase and add detail.

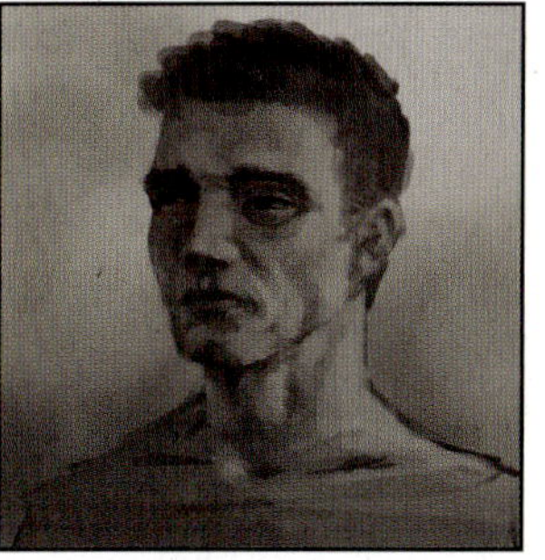

4. The next phase is to blend the borders between these shapes, then add some muscle and skin structure to make the face fuller. Don't forget to stick to the shading you did before; it's a good base for complex detailing. Finally, you add in all the details you need. With good base shading, this head should look pretty convincing by now. Apply the same technique to other body parts.

QUESTION

I understand how to paint light skin but struggle with darker complexions. What are the keys to understanding dark skin tones?

ANSWER

Lauren replies

Dark complexions can often be very challenging to paint because they don't follow the same rules as lighter skin tones.

The basic color components that give life to skin are the same – shadow tones, mid-tones, highlights, and warm tones – but the way they behave are very different.

When painting light skin, the mid-tones have usually desaturated and the highlights are gentle and not much brighter. All of the contrast occurs between the shadows and mid-tone colors. With dark skin we have the opposite situation. It's much more reflective than light skin, so the highlights are much bolder. Therefore, the greatest contrast occurs between the mid-tones and highlights. The mid-tones also are different from lighter skin tones because they tend to be the most saturated colors, rather than the least saturated.

In workshops for light skin, you may have noticed bizarre colors are often used – blues, greens, and purples. This goes for darker complexions too – dark skin is very rich in color, so don't get stuck using only browns!

Also try to always remember that the key to making a deep skin tone look believable is heavily dependant on the treatment of the highlights, and the amount of contrast between the mid-tones and highlights.

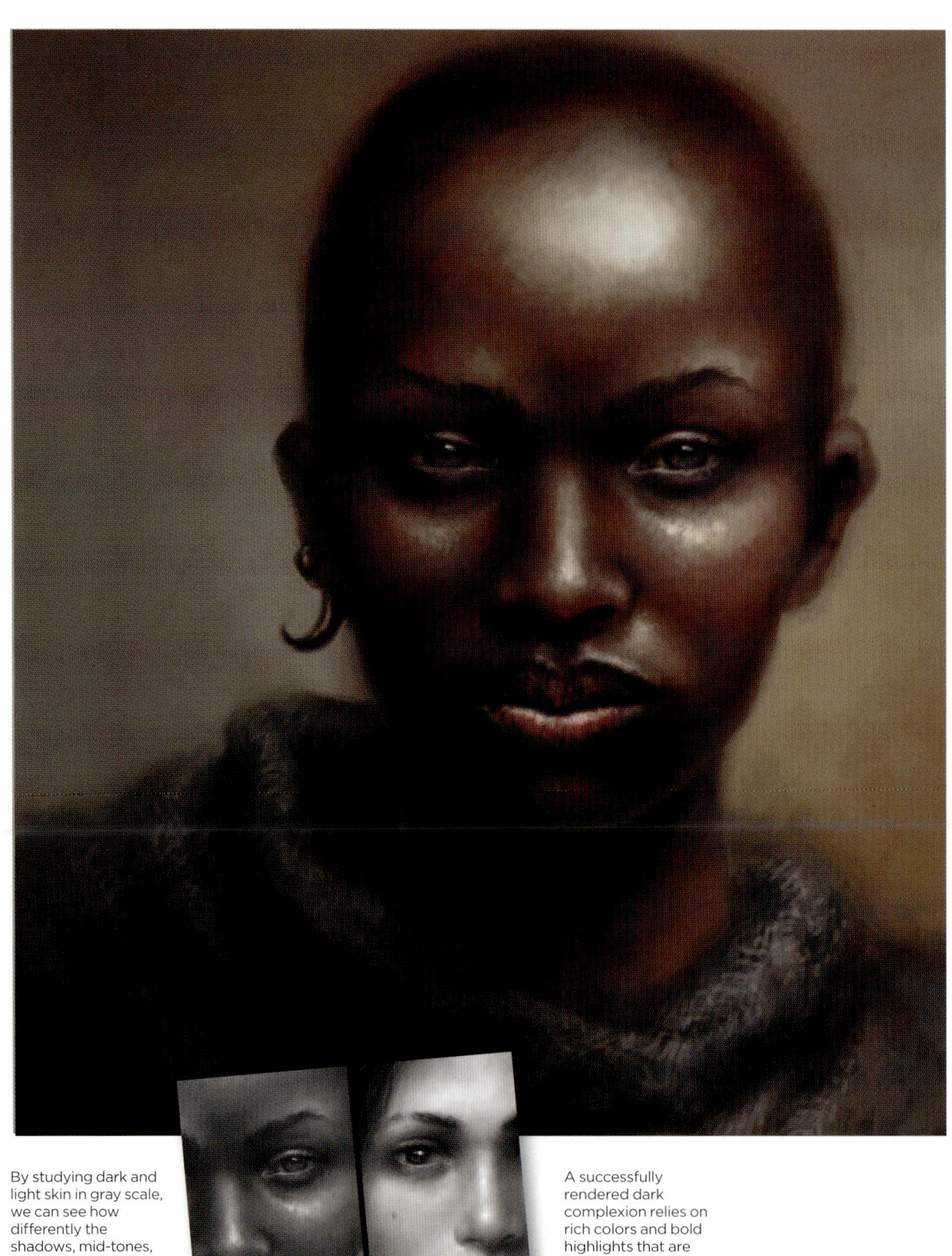

By studying dark and light skin in gray scale, we can see how differently the shadows, mid-tones, and highlights compare in both complexions.

A successfully rendered dark complexion relies on rich colors and bold highlights that are not seen in paler skin tones.

Step-by-step: Painting darker complexions

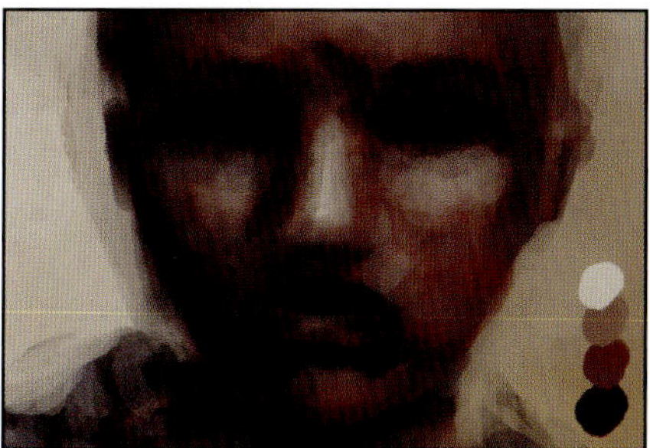

1. Choose your palette and block in the basic shapes. Remember that the colors you use will be dependant on the background – here, I'm using the green and pale gray of the background as a base for my highlights. The mid-tones I choose are a rich reddish-brown, which complement the green very well.

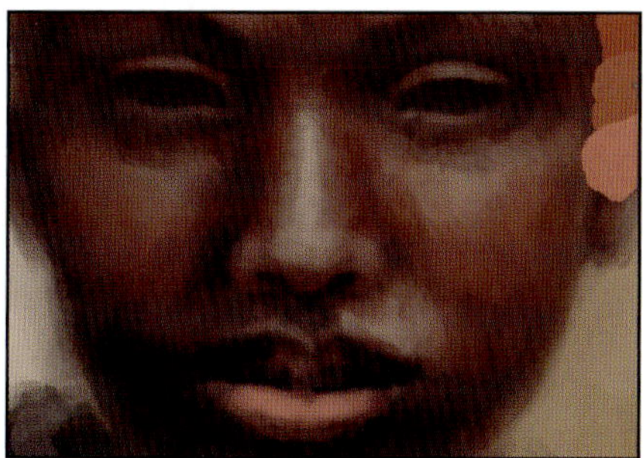

2. Refine your forms before you start adding any strong highlights, and remember that some parts of the body will have different pigments. The most obvious discrepancies are the palms, soles of feet, and the insides of the lips, which will all be lighter and pinker than the rest of the skin. Use warm tones to bring out these areas.

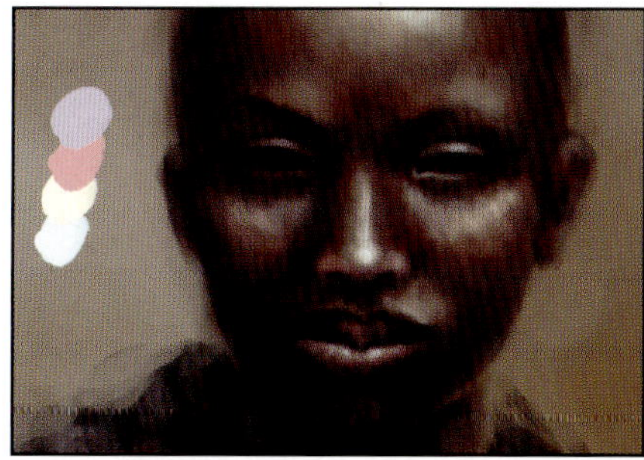

3. Now it's time to add the bold highlights. They don't fall any differently on darker complexions, but they're much brighter than the rest of the skin. Bear in mind that different parts of the face will have different tones, so you need to think about using a variety of light colors to create a realistic look.

QUESTION

My character portraits always look very dull and artificial, just like dolls. How can I make them livelier?

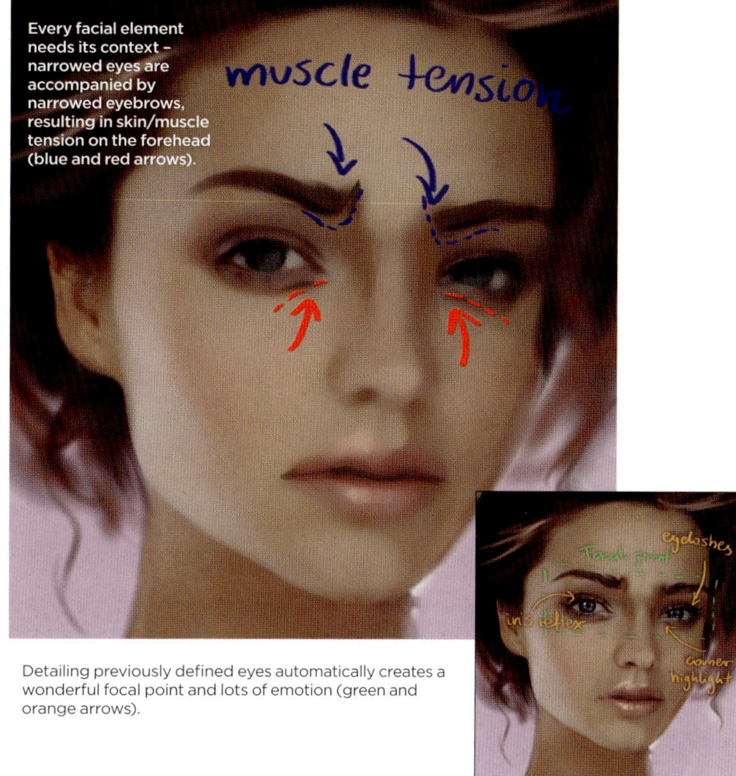

Detailing previously defined eyes automatically creates a wonderful focal point and lots of emotion (green and orange arrows).

ANSWER *Marta replies*

The easiest way to add a spark to any character, whether you're painting a bust portrait or a full body piece, is the correct definition of the face. That's done on two levels – theoretical and technical, of which theory is the most important.

Firstly, you have to decide on your character's facial expression. It doesn't matter whether it's an extreme emotion, like anger, sadness, or happiness, or something more calm, such as regret or apathy – you should always define every face with these elements: eyes with eyebrows, and the interaction of the mouth (not only the lips, but the whole jaw) with the face muscles – for example, gritting the teeth will strengthen the jaw line, opening the mouth will cause the cheeks to change their convexity, and so on.

As far as technical pointers go, there are a few tricks that can really help to bring out that spark in your characters. Firstly, if you're going for a realistic effect, concentrate your efforts on the focal point area (which is usually the eyes). You can do this by adding an eye-catching element (such as vivid makeup), or perhaps by some thorough detailing.

In any case, always use the following tip: when defining the iris, remember to add some color spots on top of it to break the mid-tone color. But most importantly, paint in a small light reflex with the Airbrush tool. This is an incredibly easy task, but can result in amazing effects – be sure to compare the difference.

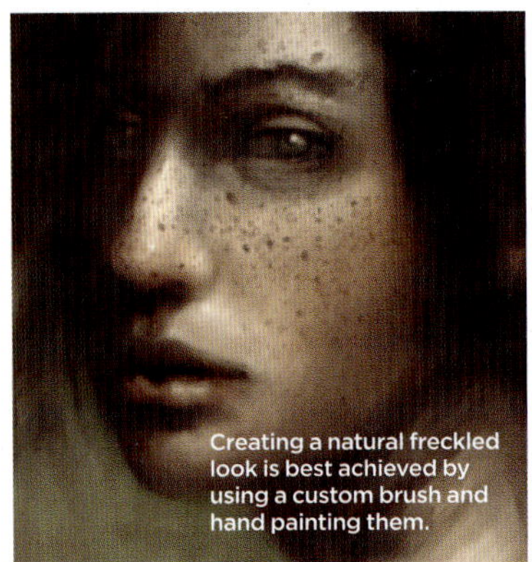

Creating a natural freckled look is best achieved by using a custom brush and hand painting them.

QUESTION

I want to give my character freckles but don't know how. Any tips?

ANSWER *Lauren replies*

Freckles and other marks on the skin help bring a new level of realism to an image regardless of the style. Remembering to add these marks – whether just a few "beauty marks" or a whole face full of freckles – is a simple detail that will add texture to your image and more personality to your character.

Some people have tons of very light freckles; others only have one or two dark freckles. And of course, freckles can appear anywhere, not just the face.

When painting freckles, you can use a combination of hand painting and custom brushes to get any look you need. Hand painting is ideal when you only want a few freckles: just take a small round brush, darken the skin color slightly and use low Opacity. But if you want lots of freckles, this method rapidly becomes tedious. A quick solution is to use a custom Photoshop brush made up of several dots and set it to Scatter. This will instantly give the illusion of many freckles randomly splashed across the skin. However, it may not look convincing up close because the dots will look pasted on to the skin and lack variety. To fix this, go back with your normal Round brush and paint in some variety of your own.

QUESTION

Is there a good way to emphasize movement and speed in my characters?

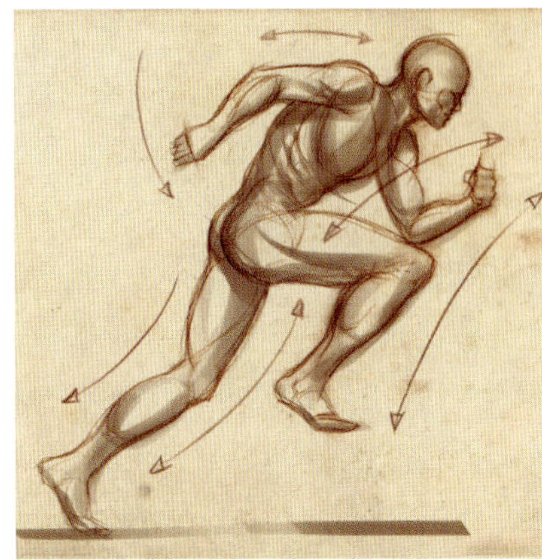

This image clearly conveys a sense of movement. The lines drawn along the contours of the subject's musculature provide a better feel of the rhythm of the character's anatomy in motion.

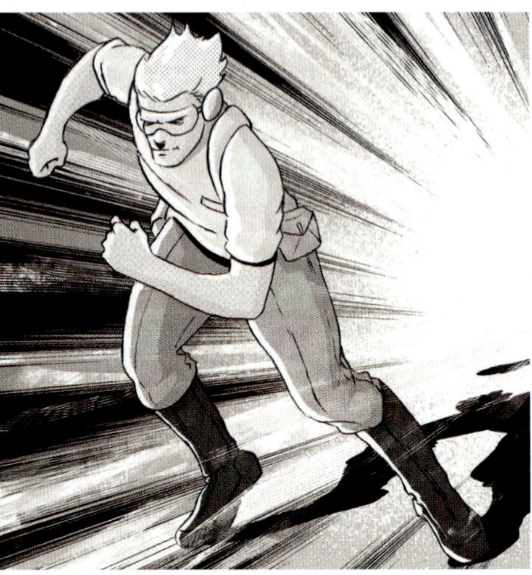

Comic books and manga artwork use action lines not only to emphasize focal points, but also to evoke a sense of speed and movement.

ANSWER *Joel replies*

There are several ways you can convey a character's speed and movement in an illustration. The most common example is gesture – there are specific movements and positions within the subject's musculature and anatomy that leave a viewer with an impression of just how fast or slow that person is moving. A sense of rhythm is also created along the contours of a character's musculature, and being able to exaggerate this rhythm can help emphasize the feel of movement in an image.

Motion blur is another tool you can use to convey speed and movement. It occurs when a camera captures a single image of a moving object over a period of time. The best examples of motion blur can be seen in images when a camera is used with a slow shutter speed and long exposure, which creates a recognizable streaking effect on moving objects.

Action lines are also an effective way of creating a sense of movement, as they tend to draw the viewer's focal point from one area of an image to another. Comic book and manga artists frequently use action lines as a way of exaggerating a sense of speed and movement.

QUESTION

Can you give me the lowdown on foreshortening please?

ANSWER *Cynthia replies*

Foreshortening is a technique that uses perspective to create the illusion of three-dimensional depth in a two-dimensional space. The rules of perspective tell us that objects appear smaller as they recede into space; likewise, long objects start to appear shorter as they're tilted toward or away from the viewer.

You'll notice the effect used a lot in comics when, say, a hero has his fist punching toward the reader and the fist is drawn three times the size of his head. That's because his head is receding in space in relation to the fist, and his arm is now taking up much less space on the page because we're viewing much less of its surface area and mass. But how does our hero arrive at such unseemly proportions?

Many student artists (and not just those interested in fantasy and science fiction!) struggle putting the theory of foreshortening into practice. I've found that the best way to learn how it works is through observation and tons of practice with life drawing, but there are a few quick methods that can help us figure out the distortion using lines...

QUESTION

I know that when painting skin tone highlights it's wise to use a turquoise shade. However, my results look awfully unnatural. What am I doing wrong?

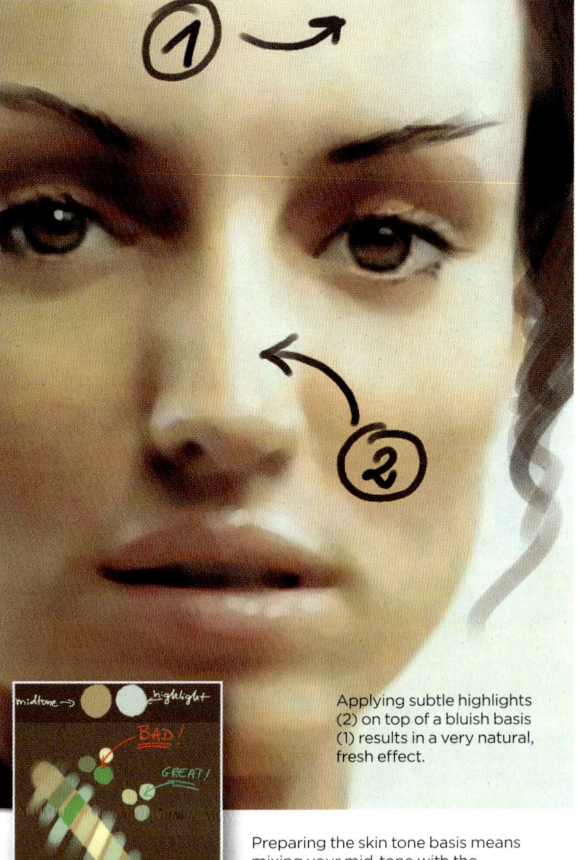

Applying subtle highlights (2) on top of a bluish basis (1) results in a very natural, fresh effect.

Preparing the skin tone basis means mixing your mid-tone with the highlight on different brush modes.

ANSWER *Marta replies*

A common mistake is that the turquoise highlights are too dark or applied with no prepared skin tone basis.

Make your highlight shade lighter and more (bluishly) saturated than your mid-tone. Do *not* pick anything too dark, or it will create a blue light source effect instead of a fresh skin highlight. When you blur highlights and mid-tones together, you'll get a slightly bluer version of your initial skin tone. Apply it on a very low opacity around the areas that you intend to highlight. Only when the basis is ready should you apply the highlight on the most convex areas, starting with lowest transparency and gradually making the brush more opaque as you move on.

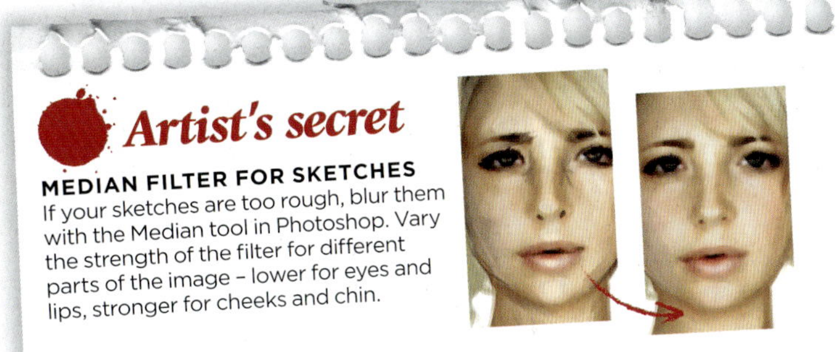

Artist's secret

MEDIAN FILTER FOR SKETCHES
If your sketches are too rough, blur them with the Median tool in Photoshop. Vary the strength of the filter for different parts of the image – lower for eyes and lips, stronger for cheeks and chin.

Step-by-step: Three ways to figure out foreshortening

1. The easiest way to demonstrate how the illusion works is with basic geometric shapes. One of my favorite old examples is what happens when you look at a wheel from the side. In a flat view, the wheel is a perfect circle. But when you walk around it, the shape becomes an oval that becomes slimmer as you keep moving.

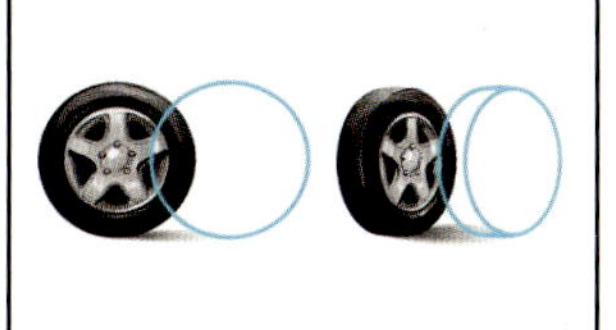

2. So, how much of that arm should we see in the image? Another method uses a plane with a central line drawn through the elbow. When we tilt the plane using the Transform> Perspective tool, this central line recedes and indicates where the elbow joint should be when the arm is foreshortened.

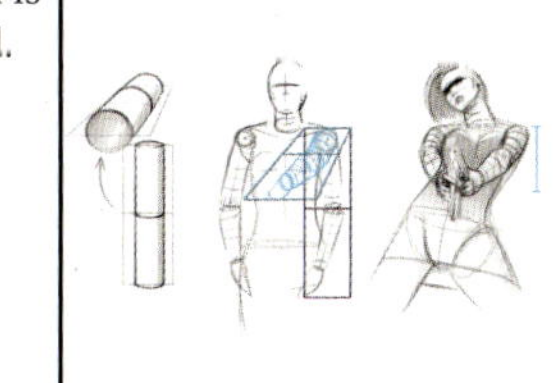

3. There's also a benefit to seeing the effect in reverse. Draw your hand from life. Make a mark at each of the knuckle joints and draw a line between each joint. You should see a vast difference in line lengths – shorter when the finger segment is positioned toward you, and longer when it's parallel to your plane of view.

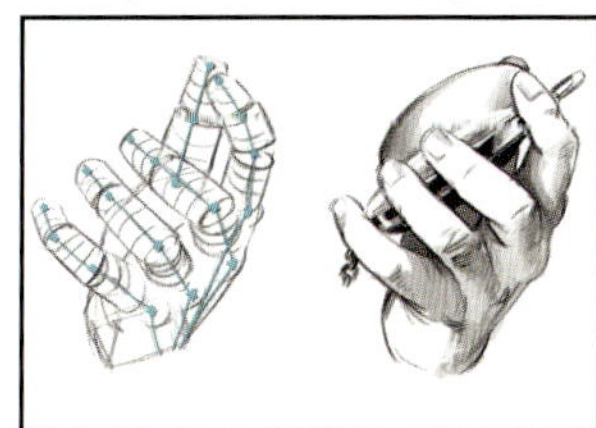

QUESTION

What advice can you give me for painting my character's hair?

ANSWER *Mélanie replies*

The most important thing to do is to think about the general appearance of the hair, which should suit the character's face. I always sketch different haircuts before settling on the right one. You must also consider the nature of the hair: is it curly or straight, thin or heavy?

Once you've decided on the hair type, you can establish the color scheme. I always start with a mid-tone; it's easier to add light and shadows onto one. Don't forget that hair is reflective – it's affected by the environment's light and colors, so don't hesitate to add, say, some touches of blue if the character is outside.

Regarding the details and the texture, I always paint the base with a basic Hard Round Edge set to a large diameter. This helps to achieve the general shape of the hair. Then I switch to a custom Spackled brush to work the strands and primary details. Once I'm happy with it, I focus on specific areas and add details where appropriate. I never overwork and texture the entire head of hair.

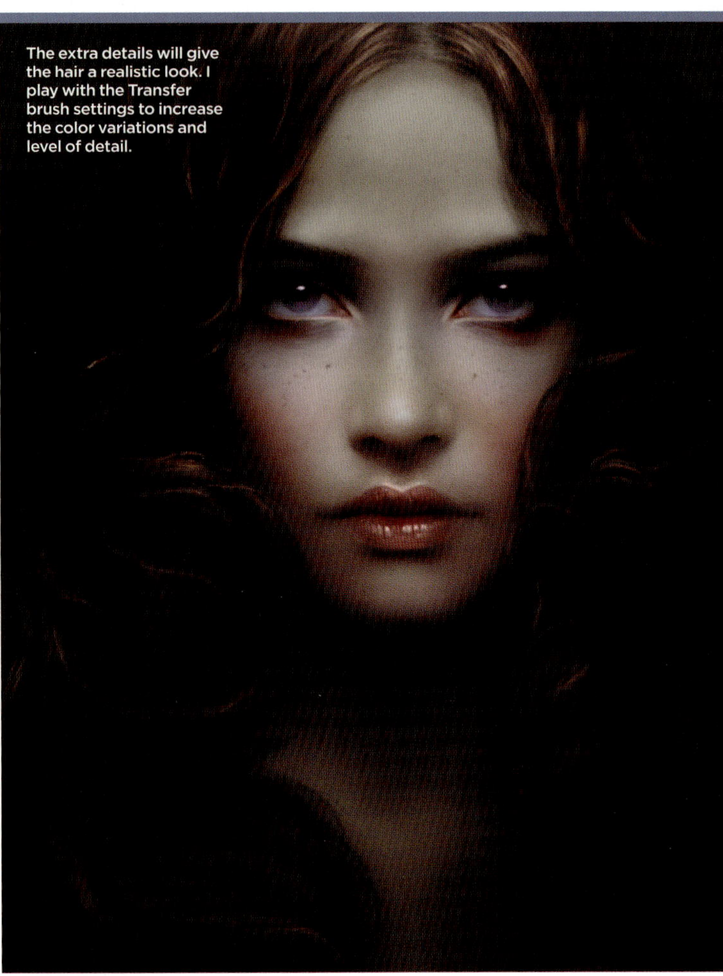

The extra details will give the hair a realistic look. I play with the Transfer brush settings to increase the color variations and level of detail.

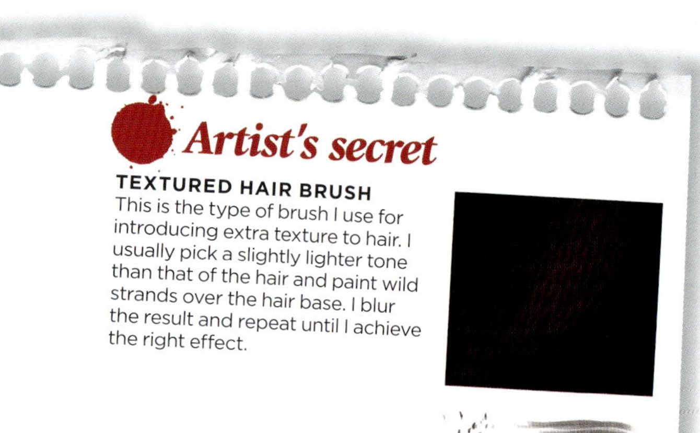

Artist's secret

TEXTURED HAIR BRUSH

This is the type of brush I use for introducing extra texture to hair. I usually pick a slightly lighter tone than that of the hair and paint wild strands over the hair base. I blur the result and repeat until I achieve the right effect.

Step-by-step: Creating a unique hairstyle

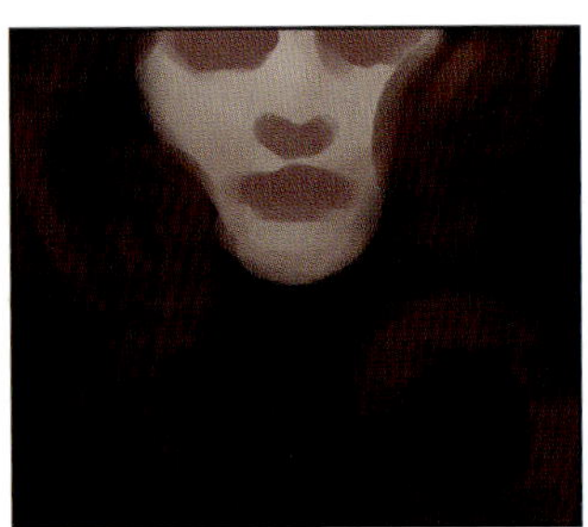

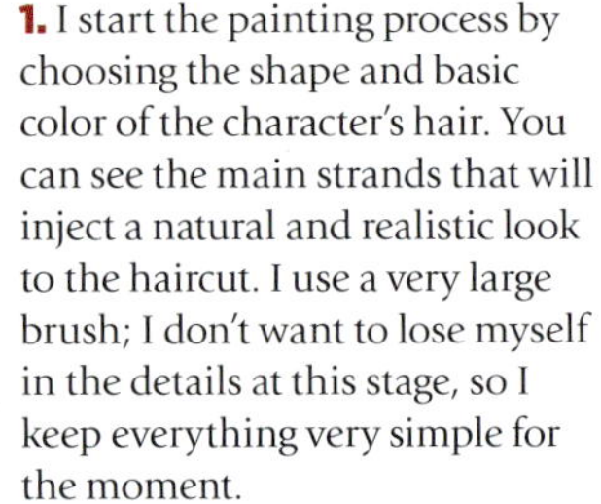

1. I start the painting process by choosing the shape and basic color of the character's hair. You can see the main strands that will inject a natural and realistic look to the haircut. I use a very large brush; I don't want to lose myself in the details at this stage, so I keep everything very simple for the moment.

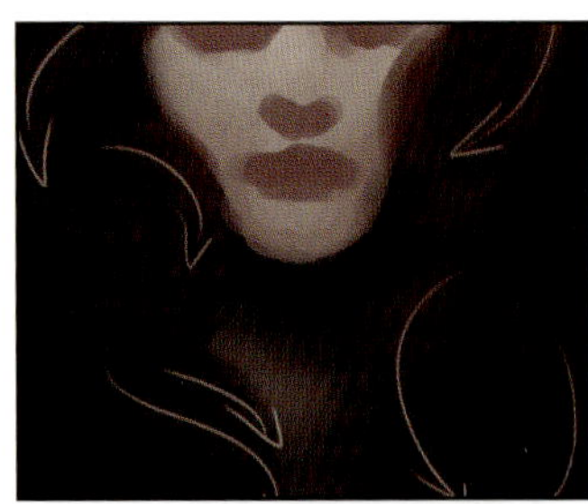

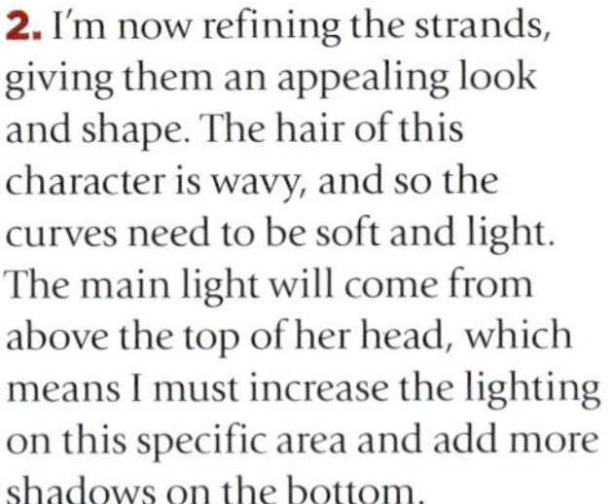

2. I'm now refining the strands, giving them an appealing look and shape. The hair of this character is wavy, and so the curves need to be soft and light. The main light will come from above the top of her head, which means I must increase the lighting on this specific area and add more shadows on the bottom.

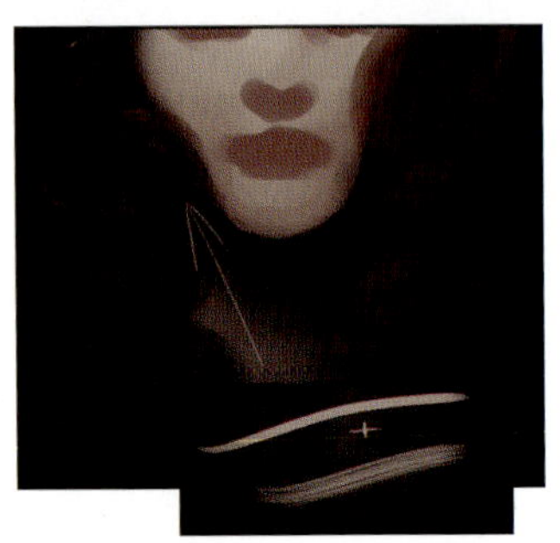

3. It's time to work in the details and the texture of the hair. For this stage I use a Spackled brush and a basic round edge set to Dynamic Shape for the tiny details. I select a strand (ideally one that's near the focal point of the piece, where I want to attract the eye) and carefully paint a few lengths of hair.

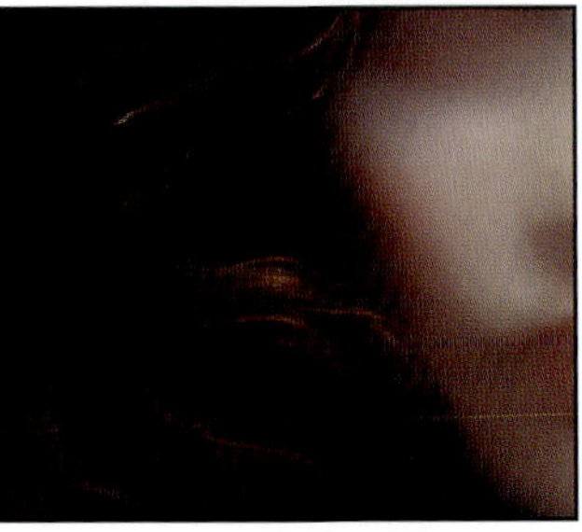

4. I repeat the techniques from the previous step in areas of the character's hair where I want details to be visible, and then add dots of light on those particular strands, to make them stand out that much more. I also apply soft brush strokes with the Spackled brush to add more refinement to the hair.

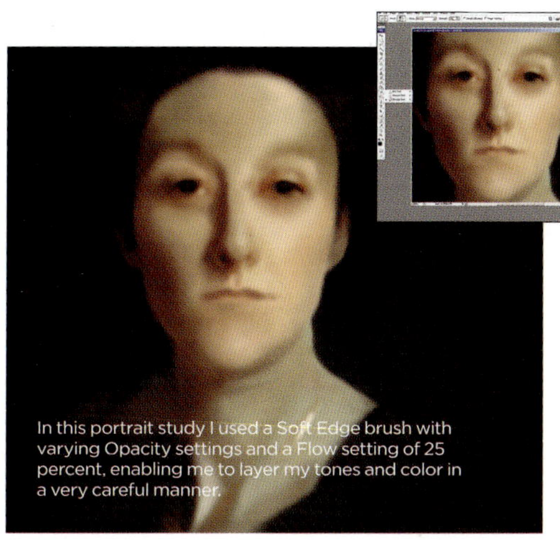

In this portrait study I used a Soft Edge brush with varying Opacity settings and a Flow setting of 25 percent, enabling me to layer my tones and color in a very careful manner.

You can also use the Smudge tool (R on your keyboard) with a strength setting of one percent to help you achieve the subtle transitions more easily.

QUESTION

What exactly is "sfumato," and can you explain how to create it digitally?

ANSWER *Joel replies*

Sfumato – meaning "faded away" in Italian – is a technique that involves layering thin translucent layers of paint in order to create very subtle transitions in tone and color. These transitions are so slight that they create a soft, smokey-edged effect along the contours of a subject.

Sfumato has been practiced extensively throughout art history, and some of the world's best-known paintings, such as Leonardo da Vinci's *Mona Lisa*, were created using this technique.

In order to create the sfumato technique digitally, pay close attention to how you lay down your colors and tones. Since the key to sfumato is creating a very subtle soft edge along the contours of your subject, you should look to tools like the Soft Edge brush tool in Photoshop to help you achieve this effect.

Also, varying the Opacity of your Soft Edge brush, along with the brush's Flow settings, can help you keep control of the amount of paint flow and also assist you in layering your colors in both a careful and subtle manner.

QUESTION

Can you help me make my color shading varied, so it looks realistic?

ANSWER *Cynthia replies*

Whether you begin with a line sketch or value drawing, the key to realistic color shading on any surface is consistent blending. In Photoshop, start with a single color somewhere in the middle value range of the object. On top of that initial color, add a highlight and shadow color, keeping the direction of your light source in mind. To blend between the three shades, toggle your Eyedropper tool (Alt on PC, Option on Mac, while the Brush tool is engaged), and sample from within the area. Using a low flow or opacity, brush over the hard edges of each shade. Once you have the basic three colors blended, add stronger colors and details with finer brushes where necessary. To add extra life to a fabric, for instance, you might use a cross-hatch pattern to suggest a weave, or paint over areas with background colors to suggest sheerness.

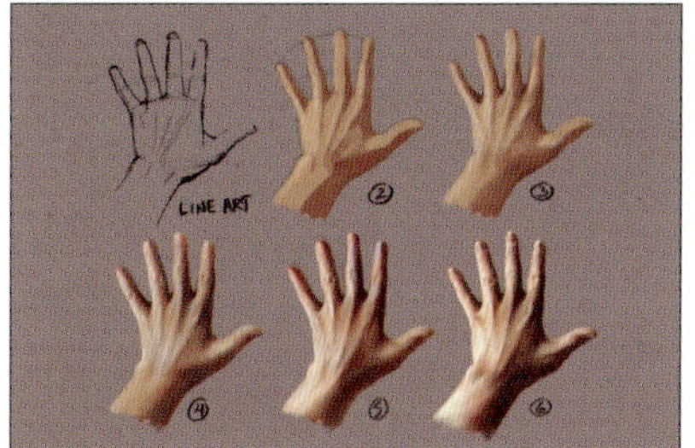

Using the back of my hand, I've created a step-by-step skin-blending demo.

QUESTION

How should I paint skin that looks light and translucent?

ANSWER *Mélanie replies*

The secret here lies in the color scheme. Skin is never only pink or beige, light is never pure white and shadows are never black. To achieve the effect that a bright color has on skin, you have to mix different colors.

The best way to understand this is to study it from real life — you'll notice that skin is composed of myriad colors, such as green, yellow, and even blue for the lights, while violet, gold, brown, or red make up the shadows. The hardest part of the solution is finding the balance between those colors.

Translucent skin is exactly the same; you need to play with saturated colors such as orange, red, or yellow to simulate the thinness of the skin, to achieve the right effect. So don't be afraid to use those tones – just add them on a separate layer to see if they work or not.

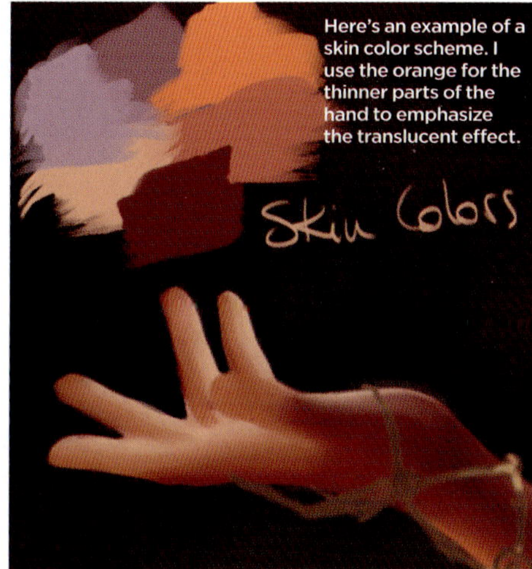

Here's an example of a skin color scheme. I use the orange for the thinner parts of the hand to emphasize the translucent effect.

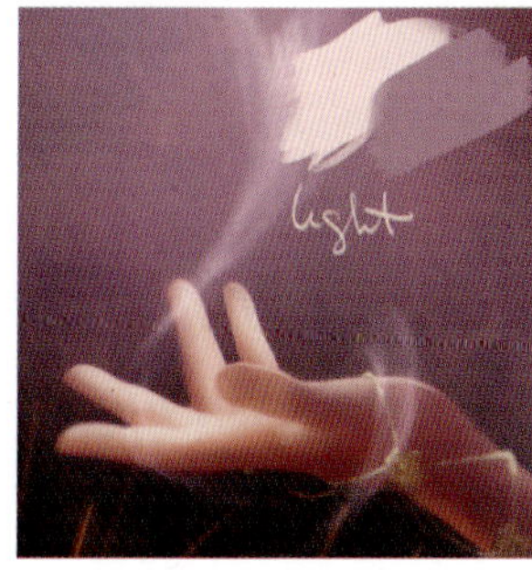

The light isn't pure white here – I choose a very light pink and mix it with a pale mauve to add brightness to the hand.

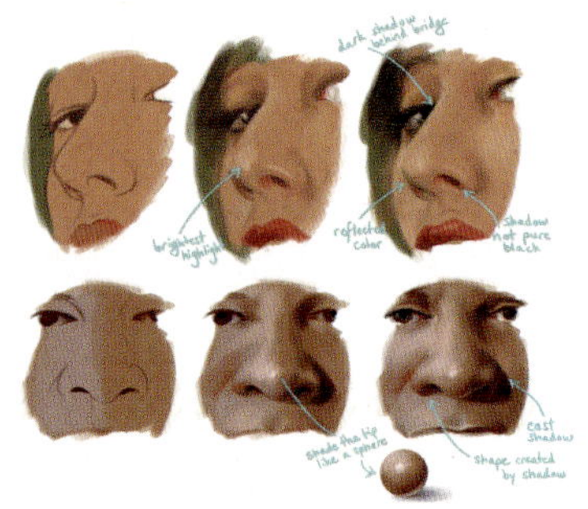

Taking care over positioning shadows and highlights when shading a nose will help you to achieve a higher degree of realism.

QUESTION

How do I paint noses with different angles and shapes?

ANSWER *Cynthia replies*

Start by visualizing the nose as a 3D object that casts shadows. As well as its anatomy, many of the shapes we think of when we imagine a nose are created by shadows that give form to the nose itself.

In its simplest form, the nose is a triangular block that's wide in the back and tapers toward the front. You can use a visual model to determine where the major cast shadows will fall, and see how its bridge would change shape from straight to angled as the head turns. Of course, noses don't have sharp angles, so we have to imagine the tip of the nose as being more like a sphere and the bridge like a cylinder when shading.

When painting the nose, keep these things in mind. Start with a line drawing on a flat skin tone. Bearing in mind the geometric shapes we've already discussed, apply your brushstrokes following the contours. Some noses are shiny, and so they often pick up color from the surrounding environment. Reserve the lightest color on the skin of the face for the highlight on the nose.

Thinking of the nose as a series of geometric shapes can make it easier to visualize at various angles.

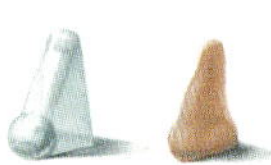

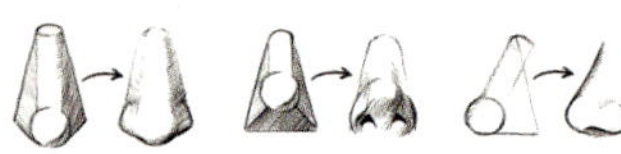

Artist's secret

A NOSE FOR SHADING

Avoid pure black when painting nostrils. The nostril itself is an empty space with very little discernible shape of its own, so what's actually painted is the shadow cast by the surrounding nose. Instead of black, choose a dark color that resembles the other shadows in your painting.

QUESTION

Can you clarify what "chiaroscuro" means?

ANSWER *Joel replies*

Certainly! Chiaroscuro is an Italian term meaning "light" (chiaro) and "dark" (scuro). The technique of chiaroscuro is used as a way to create bold contrast between the lightest and darkest values of an image, and concentrates on the control and rendering of tone.

Leonardo da Vinci has been credited as the first to develop and refine the technique. He understood that in order to recreate the likeness of a subject, it was necessary to duplicate the exact shape of both the light and shadow masses as they appeared on the subject's form.

To do this, he identified two specific types of shadows that are created as light falls across the surface of an object: form shadows (A) and cast shadows (B). To explain further, a form shadow is the shadow mass that you see on the side of a subject that is turned directly away from its light source. A cast shadow, meanwhile, is the shadow mass that occurs when part of a form blocks a light source, resulting in a shadow that is cast on an adjacent surface.

If you'd like to learn about chiaroscuro, visit your local museum. You'll be surprised at how much this technique has been used – including in my image here!

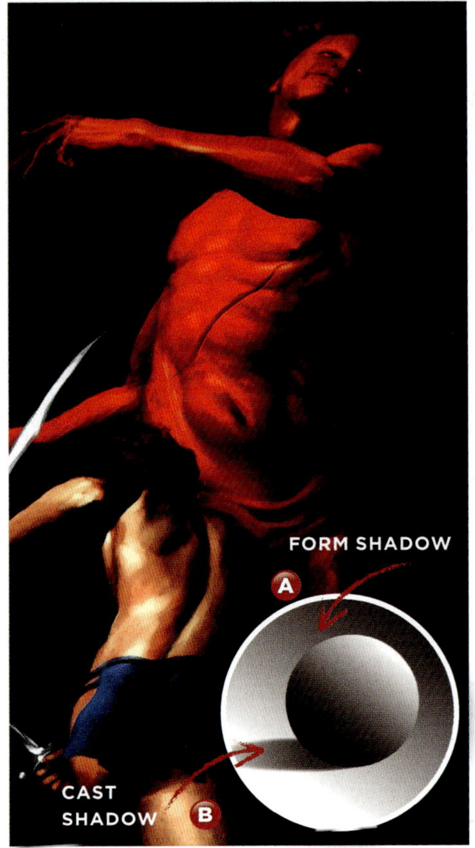

QUESTION

What are the best brushes to doodle with digitally?

ANSWER *Jeremy replies*

Just like sketching with pencil, charcoal, or pen and ink, keeping the materials simple is the key. Most of the time I use just a Hard Round brush with Pressure Sensitivity enabled for Size and Opacity. Lately, however, I've added a bit of texture to the brush too; in the Brush Preset manager, turn on the Dual Brush option. This keeps the shape of the brush the same, but adds a secondary texture as you put less pressure on the stylus. This gives the otherwise smooth digital surface a bit of graininess, which is good if you enjoy sketching with charcoal. If you're a pen-and-ink type, try the Hard Round brush, but uncheck Other Dynamics in the Brush Preset manager. However you work, experiment with the brush options until you get a natural feel.

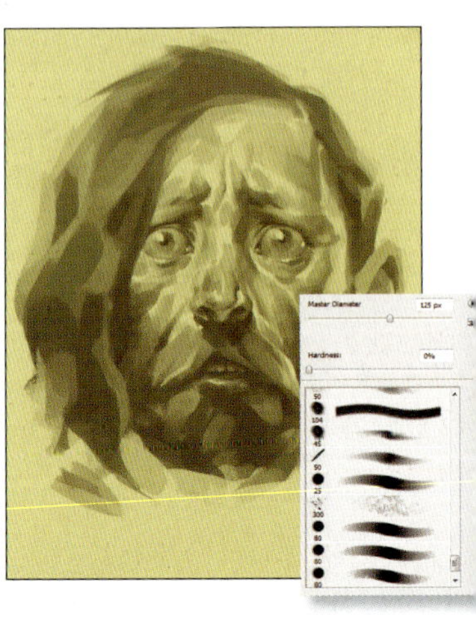

QUESTION

How can I recreate a realistic watercolor effect or style in Photoshop?

ANSWER *Joel replies*

Creating a traditional watercolor in Photoshop is fairly simple. The first thing to consider is the kind of watercolor effect you want to achieve. Water media such as watercolors and gouache can be applied in a very diluted manner or as a dry technique, similar to how you would work with acrylics. It should be noted that there is really no right or wrong way of doing so, as each technique will give a different look and feel to an image. It's simply a matter of preference, but knowing the effect you want to achieve will make things a lot easier.

If I'm using a wet medium in a traditional fashion, I generally like to keep my paints very diluted because of the translucent effect that occurs as the medium dries. Once it's dry, I sometimes opt to work over the image using a dry technique for things like highlights. The key to achieving this effect in Photoshop is to adjust your brush opacity. A lower opacity enables you to lay your color over your image while retaining translucency and nuances of previous brush strokes. A higher opacity lets you work in color in a more opaque manner, which is great for fixing errors or adding highlights.

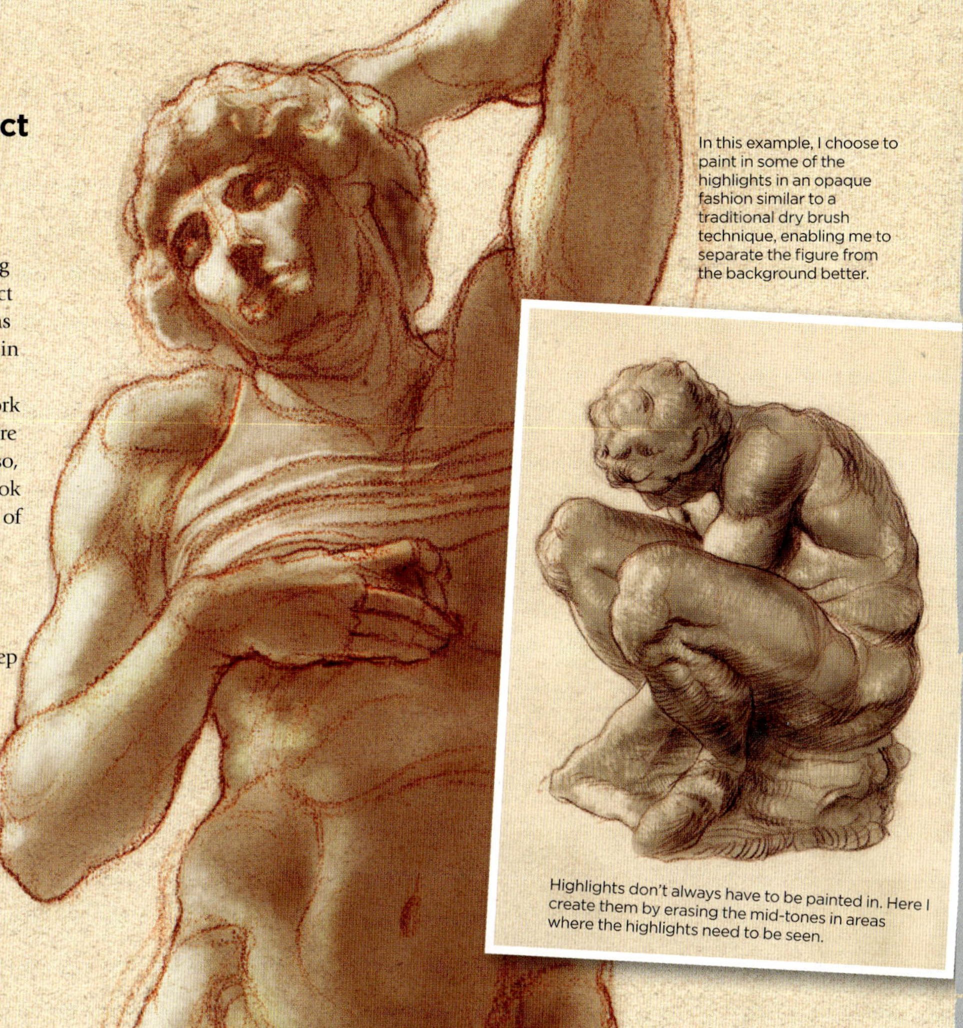

In this example, I choose to paint in some of the highlights in an opaque fashion similar to a traditional dry brush technique, enabling me to separate the figure from the background better.

Highlights don't always have to be painted in. Here I create them by erasing the mid-tones in areas where the highlights need to be seen.

Step-by-step: Getting that watercolor feel

1. I begin by scanning in a torso study created using colored pencil on white paper. I set the blend mode of the sketch layer to Multiply and create a background layer underneath the sketch layer. Here I fill in the background layer with a light beige tone to give the overall image a lovely soft tint.

2. Next, I create a new layer just below the sketch layer and begin to lay in some color in a quick and loose fashion, using a Round Hard-Edged brush. Here it's important to keep the Opacity of your brush at a low setting, anywhere between 30 percent and 50 percent. Any higher than this will obscure your lines.

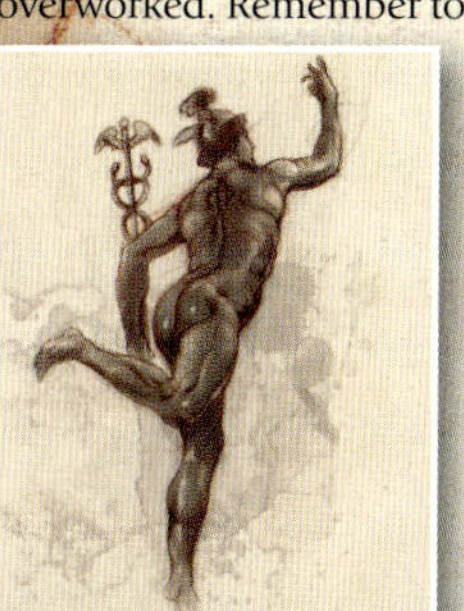

3. Finally, I drop in some watercolor textures using a set of custom brushes. The trick here is not to overdo this effect, as it can tend to make your image look convoluted and overworked. Remember to keep your brushwork light and simple and you should attain the desired effect of a digital watercolor.

QUESTION

How can I paint and convey emotion in eyes? Mine always look dead and flat.

ANSWER *Cynthia replies*

Defining the shape of the eye is the first step in creating emotion. Just by manipulating the way the lids curve and how much of the iris and pupil is showing, you can portray a near-infinite range of expressions. I recommend creating sketches of your own eyes in a mirror, or using friends as live references to really learn how the muscles in the face affect the eyes.

To give several examples of how different emotions in eyes might look in sketch form, I'll start with a neutral, relaxed shape.

For an excited, surprised or startled expression, curve the upper lids into almost a perfect semicircle, leaving some of the white of the eye between the iris and the upper lid. As a general rule, the more white that shows above the iris area, the more wildly intense the look will be.

For a cunning or deceitful glare, bring the upper lid down to around the top of the pupil, and bring the lower lid up to cover part of the iris. This narrow almond shape suggests the eye muscles are being tightened, which could be representative of heavy thought or strain.

For a tired, disappointed, or sad expression, turn both eyes down toward the outside of the face. The downward angle suggests the tightening of the muscles between the eyebrows, which is characteristic of worry and woe.

Then there's the cheerful smile, in which the cheek muscles force the eye's lower lid upward to engulf the lower part of the iris. For a more excited smile, curve the upper lid more dramatically.

Beyond shape, there are a couple of tricks to making eyes capture your viewer's attention. Most people are subconsciously lured in by larger eyes, so one way to grab attention is to enlarge them slightly. Most people don't notice when they're only a tiny bit bigger. In sorrowful scenes you might add some tears pooling up, or some redness in the whites of the eyeball. For intensity, keep the color in the iris very light opposite the highlight, as this can work to add boldness to even very dark eyes

Choosing the shape of the eyes is the first step to determining perceived emotion.

QUESTION

How do I draw face proportions in profile?

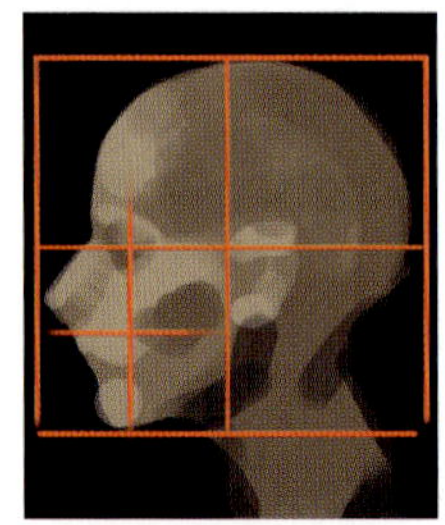

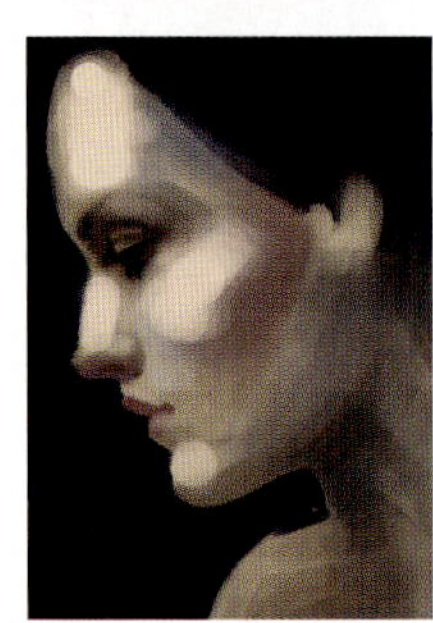

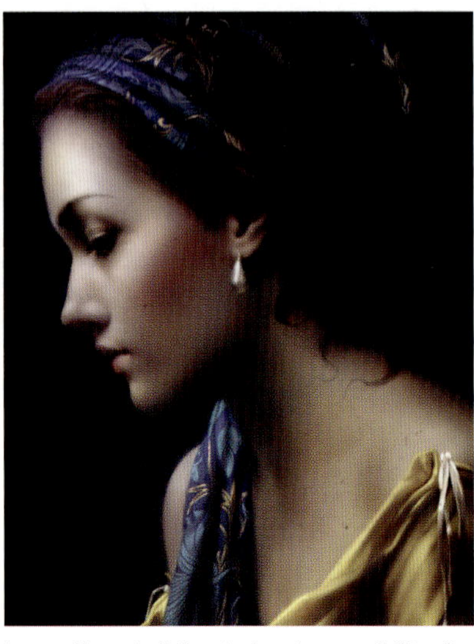

In a profile portrait there's almost no possibility of eye contact, so you must play with the light and details to catch the viewer's attention.

ANSWER *Mélanie replies*

Drawing a face in profile isn't that complicated, but it's quite different than painting a portrait face-on. The proportions are the same; it's just the placement of the features that you must consider.

The first thing to do is to quickly sketch the base of the face. Imagine it as a square: the nose and the back of the head are the left/right extremities and the chin and top of the head are the top/bottom extremities.

Once this is looking okay, almost half the job is done – all you have to do next is place the eye and the mouth. The eye should be on the middle horizontal line, and the mouth placed on the upper part of the bottom square. It might help to draw those lines over your sketch, but don't stick too much to them: they're only meant to be a guide.

The other important factor is the volume. If the light and shadows aren't correctly placed, then the character will look weird, so after thinking about lines, consider the shapes. Here in my sketch the light comes from the top, so I add light on four main areas: the forehead, nose, cheek, and chin, which are the parts of the face that contain the most edges and angles.

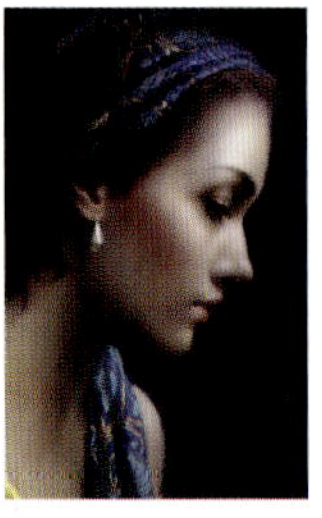

Artist's secret

REFRESH YOUR EYES

Here is a very simple tip that I always follow: I flip my image horizontally and work the illustration in this new position. This way I instantly see the mistakes, especially anatomical ones that you might not notice after working for hours on the same painting.

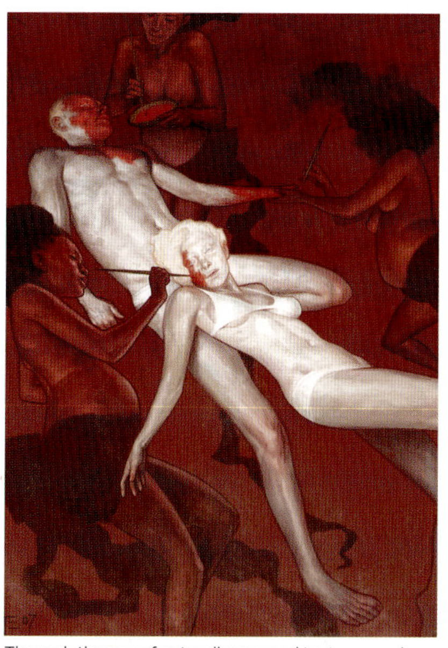
Through the use of naturally sourced textures and overlaid brush strokes, I'm able to tone down any overly digital areas of my art.

QUESTION

How can I introduce a textured, atmospheric effect into my digital art?

ANSWER *Jeremy replies*

There are several ways to add natural-looking textures into your digital work. I approach my textures in two ways: using a range of brushstroke techniques and overlaying scanned textures.

Most of the time, I use a Hard Round brush, with Shape and Opacity dynamics set to Pressure Sensitivity and a little Dual Brush action. I never use blurry brushes to render forms because they always just look too "digital" for me. I layer brush strokes over the top of each other and color pick the overlapped colors as I go using the Eye Dropper tool. This produces a nice gradient while still allowing the brushstrokes to show through.

When it comes to scanned-in textures, you can literally use whatever you want, as long as it fits on your scanner. Mostly I stick with traditional things such as old grainy papers, ink and watercolor splotches, charcoal rubs, messy acrylic brushstrokes, and so on. Once scanned in, you can go to town messing with layer modes and opacities. Even if you've done this a million times, this stage will always be experimental to some degree.

Sometimes, I like to invert the layer and set the layer mode to Screen for some lighter speckling and graininess. This can add a lot of atmosphere to a painting because you can develop pleasing effects that emulate smoke and dust.

Artist's secret

STAYING CONSCIOUS OF YOUR EDGES

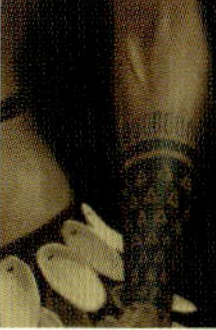

When working digitally, it's easy to have the edges of objects equally sharp throughout. Having softened (not necessarily blurred) and sharpened edges helps with focal points, unifies the image, and produces a painterly look.

Step-by-step: Get more from your textures

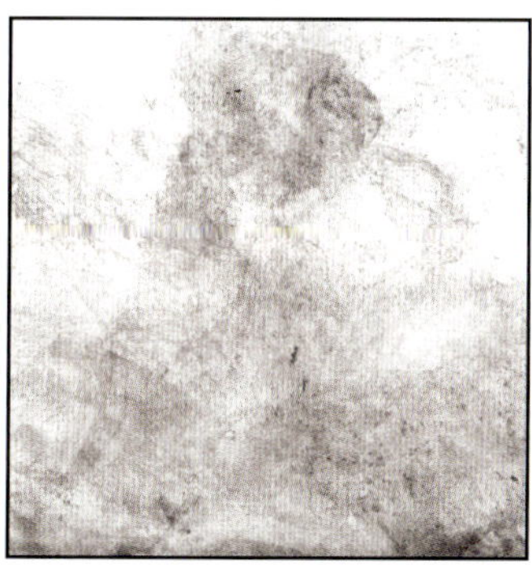

1. When creating textures with natural media, ask yourself whether it's going to lay on top of the image as a faux surface texture, or will it be used as a special effect, like smoke? Play with wet and dry application of ink, use vine and compressed charcoal for different levels of intensity, and go wild with some acrylic paint. Organize them into a collection for use in future pieces.

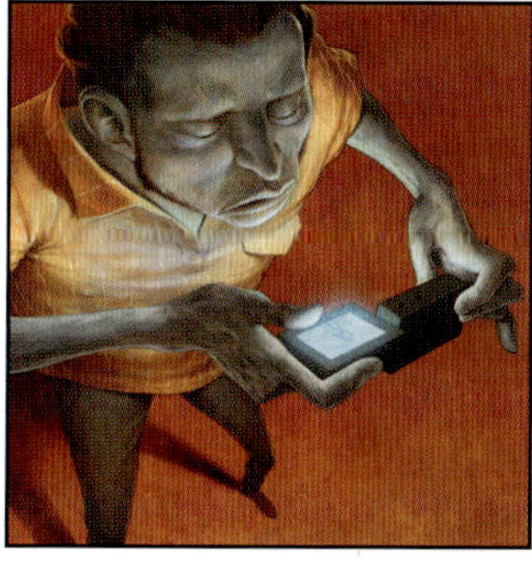

2. Overlaying scanned textures is one of the last stages of a painting for me. Once you've placed the scan over your image, explore all the layer modes to see what looks good. Change the layer's Hue/Saturation so it won't just be black and white, and the layer Opacity to add believability to the texture. I end up with ten or so texture layers, but keep them fairly subtle.

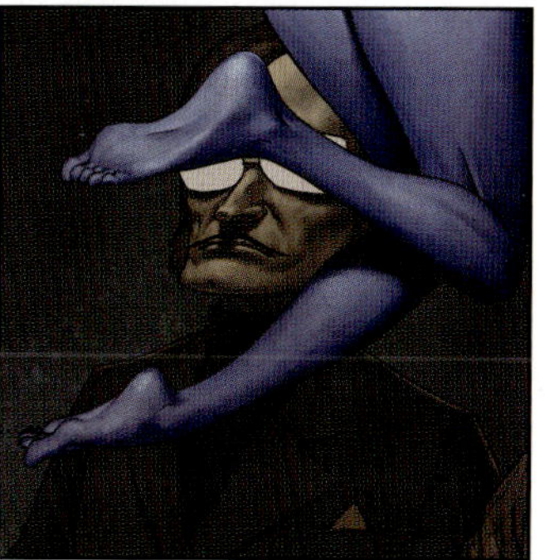

3. If you want to produce an interesting effect in which the texture is lighter than your image, select the texture layer and click Image>Adjustments>Invert. This will turn your scan into a negative. Change the layer mode to Screen or Color/Linear Dodge. Adjust Levels and Opacity to your liking. This can give you an effect of smoke or dust, as well as enhance the faux surface texture.

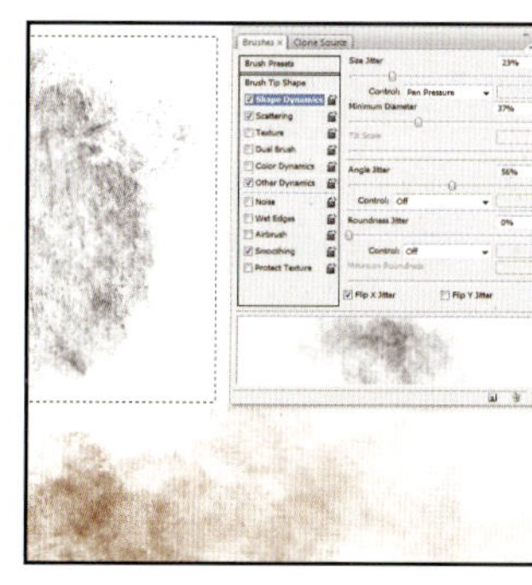

4. You can make your own brushes out of textures. Select a square portion of a scan with the Marquee tool, making sure the texture doesn't touch the edges of the selection box. Go to Edit> Define Brush Preset. This will add your selection to your brush palette. Select the brush and open your Brush Presets to adjust Shape Dynamics, Scattering, and so on.

Index

Index